American Literary Scholarship
1987

American Literary Scholarship

An Annual / 1987

Edited by James Woodress

Essays by Philip F. Gura, Claudia D. Johnson, Benjamin Franklin Fisher IV, Brian Higgins, Vivian R. Pollak, Hamlin Hill, Susan M. Griffin, Reed Way Dasenbrock, M. Thomas Inge, Gerry Brenner, William J. Scheick, David Nordloh, John J. Murphy and Stephen L. Tanner, Virginia Spencer Carr, Jerome Klinkowitz, Melody Zajdel, Richard J. Calhoun, Walter J. Meserve, Michael J. Hoffman, F. Lyra, Marc Chénetier, Rolf Meyn, Massimo Bacigalupo, Keiko Beppu, Jan Nordby Gretlund, Elisabeth Herion Sarafidis, and Hans Skei

Duke University Press Durham North Carolina, 1989

© 1989 Duke University Press. Library of Congress Catalog Card number 65–19450. ISBN 0–8223–0903–3. Printed in the United States of America by Heritage Printers, Inc.

Foreword

With the appearance of *American Literary Scholarship 1987* we complete 25 years of publishing this annual review. I am deeply indebted to Duke University Press for making this project possible, the American Literature Section of the Modern Language Association for sponsoring it, and my long-time coeditor J. Albert Robbins and my recent colleague David Nordloh for helping to carry it out. The current volume is the last one I shall edit, and next year Professor Robbins will conclude his long association with the venture. After the publication of *ALS 1988* the senior editors, who now are professors emeriti, will turn the reins over to the next generation of editors. David Nordloh, who edited *ALS 1986*, will be joined by Louis Owens of the University of New Mexico, and they will alternate editorships beginning with *ALS 1989*. Professor Robbins and I wish them well.

This year we have six essays written by different contributors from last year: Benjamin Franklin Fisher IV replaces Kent Ljungquist in reviewing Poe scholarship, Susan Griffin spells Richard Hocks on James, David Nordloh replaces me on 19th-century authors, Melody Zajdel succeeds Linda Wagner-Martin on early 20th-century poetry, Keiko Beppu continues to alternate with Hiroko Sato on Japanese scholarship, and after the absence of a year we have a triumvirate covering Scandinavia: Jan Nordby Gretlund, Elisabeth Herion Sarafidis, and Hans Skei. For the second year we have had to do without a chapter on black writers, but next year for sure R. Baxter Miller will be on board, and he will cover both 1987 and 1988 in a single essay. We have some coverage of black writers this year in chapters 14, 15, and 18. I welcome the new contributors and thank the old ones for their previous efforts.

As Michael Hoffman notes in chapter 19, the availability of desktop publishing has resulted in a remarkable proliferation of printed materials. Anyone can be a publisher these days, and many have availed themselves of the opportunity. R. R. Bowker, publisher of *Books in Print*, recently assembled figures showing that the number of books published each year has increased dramatically in the last four decades. There were 8,000 new titles in 1949 and 90,000 in 1988. We are truly awash in a sea of print. As a result, it is becoming increasingly difficult for the editors of ALS to keep the book to a manageable size. We are going to have to be more selective in our coverage and insist on brevity from our contributors.

There also is the growing problem of obtaining review copies of books from the burgeoning number of publishers, many of whom apparently print very small editions. If we can't obtain review copies, we can't review. Therefore we urge writers of scholarly books to ask their publishers to send copies to the appropriate reviewers or to send them to Duke University Press or the editor of the next volume (Professor Robbins) for forwarding. In addition, I would urge writers of scholarly articles to send offprints to our contributors, editor, or publisher. There are so many journals now publishing articles on American literature that no library, not even the major ones, can manage to subscribe to them all.

Next year there will be some new names besides Professor Miller. David M. Robinson of Oregon State University, Corvallis, will take over chapter 1; Frederick Newberry of Duquesne University, Pittsburgh, will write chapter 2; and Gary Scharnhorst of the University of New Mexico, Albuquerque, will contribute chapter 14. David Nordloh returns to chapter 12; Stephen Tanner will be the sole author of chapter 13. We will have a new French correspondent in Michel Gresset of Paris VII, and for the first time a Spanish correspondent in José Antonio Gurpegui of the University of Madrid.

On behalf of Professors Robbins and Nordloh I want to thank our retiring contributors: Philip F. Gura, Claudia D. Johnson, John J. Murphy, Virginia Spencer Carr, and Marc Chénetier.

James Woodress

University of California, Davis

Table of Contents

Key to Abbreviations

Festschriften, Essay Collections, and Books
Discussed in More Than One Chapter

American Ambitions / Monroe K. Spears, *American Ambitions: Selected Essays on Literary and Cultural Themes* (Johns Hopkins)

American Fiction / Brian Lee, *American Fiction, 1865–1940* (Longman)

The American Historical Romance / George Dekker, *The American Historical Romance* (Cambridge)

American Letters / J. Gerald Kennedy and Daniel Mark Fogel, eds., *American Letters: Essays in Honor of Louis P. Simpson* (LSU)

American Poetry / Mutlu Konuk Blasing, *American Poetry: The Rhetoric of Its Forms* (Yale)

American Romanticism / David Morse, *American Romanticism*, Vol. I: *From Cooper to Hawthorne—Excessive America* (Barnes and Noble)

The Art of Prophesying / Teresa Toulouse, *The Art of Prophesying: New England Sermons and the Shaping of Belief* (Georgia)

The Brook Farm Book / Joel Myerson, *The Brook Farm Book: A Collection of First-Hand Accounts of the Community* (Garland)

The Cast of Consciousness / Beverly Taylor and Robert Bain, eds., *The Cast of Consciousness: Concepts of the Mind in British and American Romanticism* (Greenwood)

CDLB 5 / *The Concise Dictionary of Literary Biography: The New Consciousness, 1941–1968* (Gale)

Cross-Examinations / Brook Thomas, *Cross-Examinations of Law and Literature: Cooper, Hawthorne,* *Stowe, and Melville* (Cambridge)

Delights of Terror / Terry Heller, *The Delights of Terror: An Aesthetics of the Tale of Terror* (Illinois)

Desire and the Sign / Fred G. See, *Desire and the Sign: Nineteenth-Century American Fiction* (LSU)

Discovering Modernism / Louis Menand, *Discovering Modernism: T. S. Eliot and His Context* (Oxford)

DLB 59 / John W. Rathbun and Monica M. Grecu, eds., *The Dictionary of Literary Biography: American Literary Critics and Scholars, 1800–1850* (Gale)

DLB 64 / ibid., *1850–1880*

Equivocal Spirits / Thomas B. Gilmore, *Equivocal Spirits: Alcoholism And Drinking in Twentieth-Century Literature* (No. Car.)

Essays on English and American Literature / J. Bakker et al., eds., *Essays on English and American Literature and a Sheaf of Poems* (Rodopi)

The Ethics of Reading / J. Hillis Miller, *The Ethics of Reading: Kant, de Man, Eliot, Trollope, James, and Benjamin* (Columbia)

Faulkner: ATNP / Michel Gresset and Kenzaburo Ohashi, eds., *Faulkner: After the Nobel Prize* (Yamaguchi)

Fifty Southern Writers before 1900 / Robert Bain and Joseph M. Flora, eds., *Fifty Southern Writers before 1900: A Bio-bibliographical Sourcebook* (Greenwood)

Fifty Southern Writers after 1900 / Joseph M. Flora and Robert Bain, eds., *Fifty Southern Writers after 1900: A Bio-bibliographical Sourcebook* (Greenwood)

Gender and the Writer's Imagination / Mary S. Schriber, *Gender and the Writer's Imagination: Cooper to Wharton* (Kentucky)

God the Artist / Jan Gorak, *God the Artist: American Novelists in a Post-Realist Age* (Illinois)

Gold Standard / Walter Benn Michaels, *Gold Standard and the Logic of Naturalism: American Literature at the Turn of the Century* (California)

Haunted Presence / S. L. Varnado, *Haunted Presence: The Numinous in Gothic Fiction* (Alabama)

The History of Modern Poetry / David Perkins, *The History of Modern Poetry: Modernism and After* (Harvard)

In Visible Light / Carol Shloss, *In Visible Light: Photography and the American Writer, 1840–1940* (Oxford)

A Literary History of the West / J. Golden Taylor, ed., *A Literary History of the American West* (TCU)

Makers of the New / Julian Symons, *Makers of the New: The Revolution in Literature, 1912–1939* Random House

Models for the Multitudes / Karol L. Kelley, *Models for the Multitudes: Social Values in the American Popular Novel* (Greenwood)

Modernist Poetics / James Longenbach, *Modernist Poetics of History: Pound, Eliot, and the Sense of the Past* (Princeton)

The Modernists / Lawrence B. Gamache and Ian S. MacNiven, eds., *The Modernists: Studies in a Literary Phenomenon* (Fairleigh Dickinson)

Modes of Interpretation / Richard J. Watts and Urs Weidmann, eds., *Modes of Interpretation: Essays Presented to Ernest Leisi* (Narr, 1984)

The New History of Literature / Marcus Cunliffe, ed., *The New History of Literature*, Vol. 8: *American Literature to 1900* (Bedrick)

No Man's Land / Sandra Gilbert and Susan Gubar, *No Man's Land: The Place of the Woman Writer in the Twentieth Century*, Vol. 1: *The War of the Words* (Yale)

Prophetic Woman / Amy Schrager Lang, *Prophetic Woman: Anne Hutchinson and the Problem of Dissent in the Literature of New England* (California)

Pseudo-Science and Society / Arthur Wrobel, *Pseudo-Science and Society in Nineteenth-Century America* (Kentucky)

Psychoanalytic Studies in Biography / George Moraitis and George H. Pollock, eds., *Psychoanalytic Studies in Biography* (International)

Religion and Philosophy / Peter Freese, ed., *Religion and Philosophy in the United States of America: Proceedings of the German-American Conference at Paderborn, 1986* (Die Blaue Eule)

The Representation of the Self / Jeffrey Steele, *The Representation of the Self in the American Renaissance* (No. Car.)

Romantic Foundations / Leon Chai, *Romantic Foundations of the American Renaissance* (Cornell)

Scenes of Nature / Tony Tanner, *Scenes of Nature, Signs of Men* (Cambridge)

Shifting Gears / Cecelia Tichi, *Shifting Gears: Technology, Literature, Culture in Modernist America* (No. Car.)

Short Story Criticism / Laurie Lanzen Harris and Sheila Fitzgerald, eds., *Short Story Criticism*, Vol. 1 (Gale)

Social Criticism / Robert Shulman, *Social Criticism and Nineteenth-Century American Fictions* (Missouri)

The Tall Tale / Carolyn S. Brown, *The Tall Tale in American Folklore and Literature* (Tennessee)

Tropic Crucible / Colin Nicholson and Ranjit Chattergee, eds., *Tropic Crucible: Self and Theory in Language and Literature* (Singapore / Ohio)

Venomous Woman / Margaret Hallissey, *Venomous Woman: Fear of the Female in Literature* (Greenwood)

Visionary Compacts / Donald Pease, *Visionary Compacts: American Writers in Cultural Context* (Wisconsin)

Voices and Visions / Helen Vendler, ed., *Voices and Visions: The Poet in America* (Random House)

Periodicals, Annuals, Series

ABBW / *AB Bookman's Weekly*
ABR / *American Benedictine Review*
AION / *Annali Istituto Universitario Orientale, Napoli*
AL / *American Literature*
ALR / *American Literary Realism, 1870–1910*
ALS / *American Literary Scholarship*
AmBR / *American Book Review*
Amer. Hist. Rev. / *American Historical Review*
AmerP / *American Poetry*
AmerS / *American Studies*
AmerSS / *American Studies in Scandinavia*
Amst / *Amerikastudien*
AN&Q / *American Notes and Queries*
Anglistica
Annales du CRAA / Centre de Recherche sur l'Amerique Anglophone (Université de Grenoble III)
AntigR / *Antigonish Review*
APR / *American Poetry Review*
AQ / *American Quarterly*
Arcadia
ArQ / *Arizona Quarterly*
ASch / *American Scholar*
ASInt / *American Studies International*
ATQ / *American Transcendental Quarterly*
AuLS / *Australian Literary Studies*
BALF / *Black American Literature Forum*
BB / *Bulletin of Bibliography*
BC / *Book Collector*
BHU Journal (Benares Hindu University

Biblio 17
BSUF / *Ball State University Forum*
BSWWS / Boise State University Western Writers Series
BuR / *Bucknell Review*
C&L / *Christianity and Literature*
CCR / *Claflin College Review*
CEA / *CEA Critic*
CentR / *Centennial Review*
ChH / *Church History*
ChLB / *Charles Lamb Bulletin*
Cithara: Essays in the Judaeo-Christian Tradition
CJIS / *Canadian Journal of Irish Studies*
CL / *Comparative Literature*
CLAJ / *College Language Association Journal*
CLAQ / *Children's Literature Association Quarterly*
ClioI / *CLIO: A Journal of Literature, History, and the Philosophy of History*
CLQ / *Colby Library Quarterly*
Clues: A Journal of Detection
CML / *Classical and Modern Literature*
CollL / *College Literature*
Comparatist
CompD / *Comparative Drama*
Confrontation (Long Island University)
ConL / *Contemporary Literature*
CP / *Concerning Poetry*
CR / *Critical Review* (Canberra)
Creative Woman (Governors State University)
CRevAS / *Canadian Review of American Studies*

Crit / Critique: Studies in Modern Fiction
CritI / Critical Inquiry
Criticism: A Quarterly for Literature and the Arts
CritQ / Critical Quarterly
DeltaES / Delta: Revue de Centre d'Etudes et de Recherche sur les Ecrivains du Sud aux Etats-Unis (Montpellier)
DGQ / Dramatist Guild Quarterly
DicS / Dickinson Studies
DLB / Dictionary of Literary Biography
DQ / Denver Quarterly
DQR / Dutch Quarterly Review of Anglo-American Letters
DR / Dalhousie Review
DrS / Dreiser Studies
DSA / Dickens Studies Annual
DUJ / Durham University Journal
EA / Etudes Anglaises
EAL / Early American Literature
EAS / Essays in Arts and Sciences
ECent / The Eighteenth Century: Theory and Interpretation
EigoS / Eigo Seinen (Tokyo)
EIHC / Essex Institute Historical Collections
EiP / Essays in Poetics
EJ / English Journal
ELH [formerly *Journal of English Literary History*]
ELLS / English Literature and Language (Tokyo)
ELN / English Language Notes
ELT / English Literature in Transition (1880–1920)
ELWIU / Essays in Literature (Western Illinois University)
EON / Eugene O'Neill Newsletter
ES / English Studies
ESC / English Studies in Canada
ESQ: A Journal of the American Renaissance
Expl / Explicator
Fabula (Université de Lille)
FForum / Folklore Forum
FicInt / Fiction International
Field: Contemporary Poetry and Poetics
FJ / Faulkner Journal (Ohio Northern University)

Frontiers
FSt / Feminist Studies
FurmS / Furman Studies
GHJ / George Herbert Journal
GPQ / Great Plains Quarterly
GRENA / Groupes d'Etudes et de Recherches Nord-Américaines (Aix-en-Provence: Université de Provence)
HC / Hollins Critic
Helix
HemR / Hemingway Review
HJR / Henry James Review
HLB / Harvard Library Bulletin
HLQ / Huntington Library Quarterly
HudR / Hudson Review
IFR / International Fiction Review
IJLS / Iowa Journal of Literary Studies
Imprint (Stanford University Library)
InR / Indiana Review
IowaR / Iowa Review
JAC / Journal of American Culture
JAmS / Journal of American Studies
JASAT / Journal of the American Studies Association of Texas
JEP / Journal of Evolutionary Psychology
JHI / Journal of the History of Ideas
JMGS / Journal of Modern Greek Studies
JML / Journal of Modern Literature
JMMLA / Journal of the Midwest Modern Language Association
JNT / Journal of Narrative Technique
JPC / Journal of Popular Culture
JPL / Journal of Philosophical Logic
JSSE / Journal of the Short Story in English
KAL / Kyushu American Literature
Kalki: Studies in James Branch Cabell
KanAL / Kansai American Literature
KR / Kenyon Review
LAmer / Letterature d'America: Rivista Trimestrale
L&H / Literature and History
L&M / Literature and Medicine
L&P / Literature and Psychology
Lang&S / Language and Style
LangQ / Language Quarterly (Tampa, Fla.)
LCIB / Library of Congress Information Bulletin

LCrit / Literary Criterion (Mysore, India)
LCUT / Library Chronicle of the University of Texas
Legacy: A Journal of Nineteenth-Century Women Writers
LFQ / Literature-Film Quarterly
LGJ / Lost Generation Journal
LHRev / The Langston Hughes Review
LiLi / Zeitschrift für Literaturwissenschaft und Linguistik
LitR / Literary Review: An International Journal of Contemporary Writing (Madison, N.J.)
McNR / McNeese Review
Manuscripts
MD / Modern Drama
MFS / Modern Fiction Studies
MHLS / Mid-Hudson Language Studies
MHRev / Malahat Review
Midamerica: The Yearbook of the Society for the Study of Midwestern Literature
Midstream: A Quarterly Jewish Review
MissQ / Mississippi Quarterly
MLR / Modern Language Review
MLS / Modern Language Studies
MMisc / Midwestern Miscellany
MOR / Mount Olive Review
Mosaic: A Journal for the Interdisciplinary Study of Literature
MP / Modern Philology
MQ / Midwest Quarterly
MQR / Michigan Quarterly Review
Names: Journal of the American Name Society
N&Q / Notes and Queries
NAR / North American Review
NCF / Nineteenth-Century Literature (formerly Nineteenth-Century Fiction)
NConL / Notes on Contemporary Literature
NDQ / North Dakota Quarterly
Neohelicon: Acta Comparationis Universarum
Neophil / Neophilologus
NEQ / New England Quarterly
NER / New England Review and Bread Loaf Quarterly

NewC / New Criterion
New Republic
New Yorker
NH / Nebraska History
NHR / Nathaniel Hawthorne Review
NMAL / Notes on Modern American Literature
NMHR / New Mexico Historical Review
NMW / Notes on Mississippi Writers
NOR / New Orleans Review
Novel: A Forum on Fiction
NR / Nassau Review
NYQ / New York Quarterly
OhR / Ohio Review
ON / Old Northwest
PAAS / Proceedings of the American Antiquarian Society
P&L / Philosophy and Literature
PAPA /Papers of the Arkansas Philological Association
ParisR / Paris Review
Parnassus: Poetry in Review
PBSA / Papers of the Bibliographical Society of America
PCL / Perspectives on Contemporary Literature
PCP / Pacific Coast Philology
PLL / Papers on Language and Literature
PMHB / Pennsylvania Magazine of History and Biography
PMLA / Publications of the Modern Language Association
PMPA / Publications of the Missouri Philological Association
PNotes / Pynchon Notes
PoeS / Poe Studies
Poetica: Zeitschrift für Sprach- und Literaturwissenschaft (Amsterdam)
Poetics / Poetics Journal
Poetics: International Review for the Theory of Literature
PP / Philologica Pragensis
PQ / Philological Quarterly
Prospects: An Annual Journal of American Cultural Studies
PVR / Platte Valley Review
QJS / Quarterly Journal of Speech
RALS / Resources for American Literary Study
R&L / Religion and Literature

Raritan: A Quarterly Review
Reader: Essays in Reader-Oriented
   Theory, Criticism, and Pedagogy
REAL: The Yearbook of Research in
   English and American Literature
   (Berlin)
RecL / *Recovering Literature: A*
   Journal of Contextualist Criticism
Renascence: Essays on Value in
   Literature
Representations
RFEA / *Revue Française d'Etudes*
   Américaines
RLC / *Revue de Littérature*
   Comparée
RLJ / *Russian Language Journal*
RMR / *Rocky Mountain Review of*
   Language and Literature
SAD / *Studies in American Drama,*
   1945–Present
SAF / *Studies in American Fiction*
Sagetrieb: A Journal Devoted to Poets
   in the Pound-H.D.-Williams
   Tradition
SALit / *Chu-Shikoku Studies in*
   American Literature
Salmagundi
SAQ / *South Atlantic Quarterly*
SAR / *Studies in the American*
   Renaissance
SB / *Studies in Bibliography*
ScLJ / *Scottish Literary Journal*
SCN / *Seventeenth-Century News*
SCR / *South Carolina Review*
SCRev / *South Central Review:*
   Journal of the South Central Mod-
   ern Language Association
SDH / *South Dakota History*
SDR / *South Dakota Review*
SECC / *Studies in Eighteenth-Century*
   Culture
SEL / *Studies in English Literature,*
   1500–1900
SELit / *Studies in English Literature*
   (Tokyo)
Semiotica: Journal of the International
   Association for Semiotic Studies
SFS / *Science-Fiction Studies*
Shenandoah
SJS / *San Jose Studies*
SLJ / *Southern Literary Journal*
SLRJ / *St. Louis University Research*

Journal of the Graduate School of
   Arts and Sciences
SMy / *Studia Mystica*
SN / *Studia Neophilologica: A Journal*
   of Germanic and Romance
   Languages
SNNTS / *Studies in the Novel*
   (North Texas State University)
SoAR / *South Atlantic Review*
SoQ / *Southern Quarterly*
SoR / *Southern Review*
SoSt / *Southern Studies*
Soundings: An Interdisciplinary
   Journal
SovL / *Soviet Literature*
SPELL / *Swiss Papers in English*
   Language and Literature
SR / *Sewanee Review*
SSF / *Studies in Short Fiction*
SSMLN / *Society for the Study of*
   Midwestern Literature Newsletter
StHum / *Studies in the Humanities*
   (Indiana, Pa.)
StQ / *Steinbeck Quarterly*
StTCL / *Studies in Twentieth-*
   Century Literature
Style
TA / *Theatre Annual*
TCL / *Twentieth-Century Literature*
TDR / *The Drama Review*
Theoria: A Journal of Studies in the
   Arts, Humanities and Social
   Sciences (Natal, South Africa)
ThoreauQ / *Thoreau Quarterly*
Three Penny Review
ThS / *Theatre Survey*
Trivium (Dyfed, Wales)
Tropism (Université de Paris X:
   Nanterre)
TSLL / *Texas Studies in Literature*
   and Language
TSWL / *Tulsa Studies in Women's*
   Literature
TUSAS / *Twayne's United States*
   Authors Series
TWA / *Transactions of the Wisconsin*
   Academy of Sciences, Arts, and
   Letters
UDR / *University of Dayton Review*
UFor / *University Forum* (Ft. Hays,
   Kans., State University)
UMSE / *University of Mississippi*
   Studies in English

UWR / *University of Windsor Review*
VC / *Virginia Cavalcade*
VMHB / *Virginia Magazine of History and Biography*
VQR / *Virginia Quarterly Review*
WAL / *Western American Literature*
W&I / *Word and Image: A Journal of Verbal/Visual Enquiry*
WCPMNewsl / *Willa Cather Pioneer Memorial Newsletter*
WCWR / *William Carlos Williams Review*

WMQ / *William and Mary Quarterly*
WVUPP / *West Virginia University Philological Papers*
WS / *Women's Studies*
WStu / *Weber Studies*
WWR / *Walt Whitman Review*
YER / *Yeats Eliot Review*
Yiddish
YR / *Yale Review*
YULG / *Yale University Library Gazette*

Publishers

Aarhus / Aarhus, Denmark: Aarhus University Press
Advent / Chicago: Advent
Alabama / University: University of Alabama Press
Alinéa (Aix-en-Province)
Allen and Unwin (London)
Anchor / Garden City, N.Y.: Anchor Press (imprint of Doubleday)
Apollin-sha (Kyoto)
Atlantic / New York: Atlantic Monthly Press (dis. by Little, Brown)
Arbor / New York: Arbor House
Archon / Hamden, Conn.: Archon Books
Arkansas / Fayetteville: University of Arkansas Press
Arnold / Baltimore: Edward Arnold
Artemis (Munich)
Associated Universities Presses (Cranbury, N.J.)
Banner of Truth (Carlisle, Pa.)
Barnes and Noble (Totowa, N.J.)
Basic Books / New York: Basic Books, Inc. (sub. of Harper and Row)
Bedrick / New York: Peter Bedrick Books
Black Sparrow / Santa Rosa, Calif.: Black Sparrow Press
Black Swan / Redding Ridge, Conn.; Black Swan Press
Blaue Eule (Essen)
Borgo / San Bernardino, Calif.: Borgo Press
Bowling Green / Bowling Green, Ohio: Bowling Green State University Popular Press

Brownstone-Borgo (Madison, Ind.)
Bucknell / Lewisburg, Pa.: Bucknell University Press
California / Berkeley: University of California Press
Cambridge / Cambridge, England, and New York: Cambridge University Press
Carolina / Durham, N.C.: Carolina Academic Press
Chelsea / New York: Chelsea House
Chicago / Chicago: University of Chicago Press
Chronicle / San Francisco: Chronicle Publishing Co.
Columbia / New York: Columbia University Press
Connecticut / Storrs: University of Connecticut Library
Corian / Meitengen, Germany: Verlag Heinrich Wimmer
Cornell / Ithaca, N.Y.: Cornell University Press
Coyote (Salinas, Calif.)
Delaware / Newark: University of Delaware Press
Dialog / Palo Alto, Calif.: Dialog Information Services
Didier / Paris: Didier
Dodd Mead (New York)
Doubleday (Garden City, N.Y.)
Duke / Durham, N.C.: Duke University Press
Ecco / New York: Ecco Press
Enoch Pratt / Baltimore: Enoch Pratt Free Library
Europa / Daphne, Ala.: Europa Media, Inc. (Légèreté)

Fairleigh Dickinson / Madison, N.J.:
Fairleigh Dickinson University
Press

Feedback / Bloomington, Ind.: Feedback Theater Books

Fink / Munich: Wilhelm Fink

Folger / Washington: Folger Shakespeare Library

Franck / Tübingen: A. Franck

Gad / Copenhagen: G.E.C. Gad's Forlag

Gaku / Tokyo: Gaku Shabo Press

Gale / Detroit: Gale Research Co.

Garland / New York: Garland Publishing Co.

Gay Sunshine / San Francisco: Gay Sunshine Press

Georgia / Athens: University of Georgia Press

Gordian / Staten Island, N.Y.: Gordian Press, Inc.

Graywolf / St. Paul: Graywolf Press

Greenwood / Westport, Conn.: Greenwood Press

Grove / New York: Grove Press

Gruner (Amsterdam)

Hall / Boston: G. K. Hall and Co.

Harcourt / New York: Harcourt Brace Jovanovich

Harvard / Cambridge: Harvard University Press

Holy Cow! / Stevens Point, Wis.: Holy Cow! Press

Houghton Mifflin / Boston: Houghton Mifflin Co.

Howard / Washington, D.C.: Howard University Press

Humanities / Atlantic Highlands, N.J.: Humanities Press International

Illinois / Urbana: University of Illinois Press

Indiana / Bloomington: Indiana University Press

International / New York: International Universities Press

Irvington / New York: Irvington Publishers

Kaden-sha (Tokyo)

Kansas / Lawrence: University Press of Kansas

Kenyu-sha (Tokyo)

Kent State / Kent, Ohio: Kent State University Press

Kentucky / Lexington: University Press of Kentucky

Lang (Frankfort)

Liber / Tokyo: Liber Press

Lib. Prof. Pubs. / Hamden, Conn.: Library Professional Publishers (Shoe String Press)

Library of America (New York)

Little, Brown / Boston: Little, Brown and Co.

Longman / White Plains, N.Y.: Longman, Inc.

Loyola / Chicago: Loyola University Press

LSU / Baton Rouge: Louisiana State University

McFarland / Jefferson, N.C.: McFarland and Co.

Macmillan (New York)

Massachusetts / Amherst: University of Massachusetts Press

Meckler / Westport, Conn.: Meckler Publishing Co.

Methuen (London and New York)

Mich. State / East Lansing: Michigan State University Press

Minnesota / Minneapolis: University of Minnesota Press

Mississippi / Jackson: University Press of Mississippi

Missouri / Columbia: University of Missouri Press

Morrow / New York: William Morrow

Nan'undo (Tokyo)

Narr / Tübingen: G. Narr

Nebraska / Lincoln: University of Nebraska Press

New Current / Tokyo: New Current International Co.

New Directions / New York: New Directions Publishing Corp.

New England / Shelburne, Vt.: New England Press, Inc.

New Mexico / Albuquerque: New Mexico University Press

No. Car. / Chapel Hill: University of North Carolina Press

Northeastern / Boston: Northeastern University Press

Ohio / Athens: Ohio University Press

Ohio State / Columbus: Ohio State University Press

Olms / Hildesheim and New York: Georg Olms

Oxford / New York: Oxford University Press

Pandora (Gainesville, Fla.)

Palm / Erlangen: Palm and Enke

Peachtree (Atlanta)

Penn. State / University Park: Pennsylvania State University Press

Pennsylvania / Philadelphia: University of Pennsylvania Press

Penkvill / Greenwood, Fla.: Penkvill Publishing Co.

Peter Lang / New York: Peter Lang Publishing Co.

Pittsburgh / Pittsburgh: University of Pittsburgh Press

Poe Society / Baltimore: Edgar Allan Poe Society

Praeger / New York: Praeger Publishers

Princeton / Princeton, N.J.: Princeton University Press

Prometheus / Buffalo, N.Y.: Prometheus Press

Purdue / West Lafayette, Ind.: Purdue University Press

Putnam's / New York: G. P. Putnam's Sons

Random House (New York)

Rodopi / Amsterdam: Rodopi Editions

St. Martin's / New York: St. Martin's Press

Salamanca / Salamanca: Secretariado de Publicaciones, Universidad de Salamanca

Salzburg / Salzburg: University of Salzburg

Scarecrow / Metuchen, N.J.: Scarecrow Press

Schmidt / Berlin: Erich Schmidt

Schöningh / Paderborn, Germany: Ferdinand Schöningh

Scholars Press (Decatur, Ga.)

Scribner's / New York: Charles Scribner's Sons

Sekai / Kyoto: Sekai Shiso-sha

Shoe String / Hamden, Conn.: Shoe String Press

Singapore / Singapore: Singapore University Press

So. Car. / Columbia: University of South Carolina Press

So. Ill. / Carbondale: Southern Illinois University Press

Solum / Lysaker, Norway: Solum Forlag

Sorbonne / Paris: Presses de l'Université de Paris

Sphere / London: Sphere Books, Ltd.

SUNY / Albany: State University of New York Press

Susquehanna / Selinsgrove, Pa.: Susquehanna University Press

Sydjydsk / Esbjerg, Denmark: Sydjydsk Universitets Forlag

TCG / New York: Theatre Communications Group

TCU / Fort Worth: Texas Christian University Press

Tennessee / Knoxville: University of Tennessee Press

Toronto / Toronto: University of Toronto Press

Trancendental Books (Hartford)

Twayne / Boston: Twayne Publishers

Tyndale / Wheaton, Ill.: Tyndale House Publishers

UMI / Ann Arbor, Mich.: University Microfilms International

UMI Research Press (Ann Arbor, Mich.)

Ungar / New York: Frederick Ungar Publishing Co.

Univ. Press / Lanham, Md.: University Press of America

Utah State / Logan: Utah State University Press

Verso / New York: Methuen (New Left Books)

Viking / New York: Viking Press

Villard / New York: Villard Books (Random House)

Wayne State / Detroit: Wayne State University Press

West. Ill. / Macomb: Western Illinois University

Whitson / Troy, N.Y.: Whitson Publishing Co.

Wilson / Bronx, N.Y.: H. W. Wilson
  Co.
Winter / Heidelburg: Carl Winter
Wisconsin / Madison: University of
  Wisconsin Press
Wright State / Dayton: Wright State
  University

Wyndham / Bristol, Ind.: Wyndham
  Hall Press
Yale / New Haven: Yale University
  Press
Yamaguchi / Kyoto: Yamaguchi
  Publishing House

Part I

1. Emerson, Thoreau, and Transcendentalism

Philip F. Gura

This was not a strong year for studies of individual Transcendentalists (though there were some good essays on Emerson), but this was
more than compensated for by three important general studies of the
American Renaissance, all of which contain provocative chapters on
Emerson, Thoreau, and others. In particular, readers will want to
turn to Leon Chai's *The Romantic Foundations of the American
Renaissance* (Cornell), a wide-ranging study that quite simply is the
best thing we have to assess the connections between European and
American Romanticism. Other high spots were the fourth volume of
the *Letters of Margaret Fuller* (Cornell) and the *Selected Letters of
Lidian Jackson Emerson* (Missouri). Along with Phyllis Cole's work
on Mary Moody Emerson and Charles Capper's work-in-progress on
Fuller, these speak to the too insufficiently studied problem of what
Transcendentalism meant to women. Finally, all readers will want to
refer to Robert A. Gross's work on the Concord public libraries of the
late 18th and early 19th centuries. As I have noted before in these
pages, we too often neglect how much historians—in this case a "historian of the book," as the phrase now goes—can tell us about the
writers whom we think we know so well.

i. Edited Texts, Sources, General Studies

This year saw the appearance of *Representative Men* (1850) in the
Harvard edition of Emerson's works, with the text established from
printer's copy by Douglas Emory Wilson, and the historical introduction and "Informational Notes" provided by Wallace Williams.
As the latter notes, this volume is of particular interest to scholars
because it is based on public lectures only minimally expanded for
publication; hence, it has the "freshness of the spoken word" and the
"daring of the lecture hall" in ways that Emerson's earlier publications

do not. Originally delivered in 1845–46 as a course of lectures at the Boston Lyceum, *Representative Men* also marked a "new efficiency in his compositional methods" as he began a period of extensive lecturing in the Midwest; no longer would his lectures be mined from essays but in fact were the essays themselves, printed with few changes. Certainly one of the most teachable of Emerson's volumes, *Representative Men* now stands before us in definitive shape.

Equally significant is the fourth volume of *The Letters of Margaret Fuller*, ed. Robert Hudspeth, covering the years 1845–47. Early in this period Fuller was a book review editor for Horace Greeley's *New-York Tribune* and published her own *Papers on Literature and Art*; by August 1846 she had left for Europe, to meet such luminaries as Carlyle, Sand, and Wordsworth, and such public figures as Mazzini and Mickiewicz. Over 50 of these letters are to the German businessman James Nathan, with whom she had a love affair; and by the end of the period, Nathan having married someone else, Fuller had found the grand passion of her life in Count d'Ossoli. Assembling over 190 letters, this volume, with its restrained but informative notes, documents one of the most fascinating periods in this remarkable woman's life.

Another treasure trove of correspondence is Dolores Bird Carpenter's *Selected Letters of Lidian Jackson Emerson*. About half of the collection of letters by Emerson's second wife—"Asia" he called her for her great depth of feeling—that are in the Houghton Library are printed here, material dating from 1813, when she was a student at a female academy in Dorchester, through 1885, seven years before her death. Semi-invalid and neurasthenic through many of these years, Lidian Emerson still found much time to devote to such favorite causes as the Anti-Slavery Society, the Women's Suffrage movement, and the Society for the Prevention of Cruelty to Animals. In addition to documenting these interests, the letters show her struggling with her husband's radical religious beliefs, which shook the faith of a woman who always believed in the centrality of Jesus Christ.

In *The Brook Farm Book* Joel Myerson reprints important published notices, descriptions, and recollections of Brook Farm by the press and the community's participants and visitors. Most of these items are from hard-to-locate and obscure periodicals, and thus it is a great convenience to have them all within these covers. Raymond Borst continues his important bibliographical work on Thoreau by offering *Henry David Thoreau: A Reference Guide, 1835–1899* (Hall). This volume lists by year writings about Thoreau, from the first discovered notice of his name in print (in the *Order of Performances for Exhibition* at Harvard on 13 July 1835) to his mention in the letters of Robert Louis Stevenson on the last day of the century. This guide certainly proves that the Concord saunterer in fact was much more noticed in the press in the years immediately following his death than many have thought, even if he had not yet become, as Emerson had, a national institution. Finally, Guy R. Woodall has published some of the fruits of his important research in "The Selected Sermons of Convers Francis (Part One)" (*SAR*, pp. 73–129). Woodall prints only four sermons, but he provides a lengthy description of what scholars can find in the approximately 1,000 extant sermons, covering a 50-year period, that are in Watertown, where Francis ministered most of his life. As Woodall notes, these sermons "form a spiritual autobiography" of this important Unitarian clergyman and provide "a wide range of significant commentary on religious, social, and . . . political activities of his time and place." It is good to know that, like Frederic Henry Hedge (see *ALS 1985*, pp. 23–24), another important secondary figure in the Transcendentalist movement (Francis sided with Ripley and Furness in the "Miracles" controversy) is getting his due.

The most important general study this year is Chai's *The Romantic Foundations of the American Renaissance*, a work of extensive research and erudition that should prove a benchmark for those interested in the relationship of European to American Romanticism. Chai attempts to provide a "history of the assimilation and transformation of the cultural legacy of European Romanticism from roughly 1780 to 1830 by a group of great American authors of the mid-nineteenth-century—above all, Poe, Emerson, Hawthorne, and Melville." He explores this by tracing the development of certain key concepts in Romantic thought—the shift, for example, from allegory to symbolism, the various forms of science in the Romantic age (biological classification, vitalism, the theory of probability), the secularization of religion, the gradual emergence of a historical consciousness and a philosophy of history, pantheism, and a Romantic poetics—and their alteration by these four American writers. Obviously, readers of this chapter of *ALS* will be most interested in what Chai has to say about Emerson and will wonder about the omission of Thoreau. Chai explains that he regards Thoreau (and Whitman) as representative

of a later phase of the American Renaissance, "in which the relationship with Romanticism is mediated through the vision of Emerson."
But scholars of Transcendentalism will delight in Chai's chapters on
Emerson, Fuller, and Alcott and his section on Parker. A far-reaching
and powerful book that ranges widely through English, German, and
French writers and thinkers as well as among the Americans, this is
required reading for all serious students of Transcendentalism.

Another important work, though not with the same range, is Jeffrey Steele's *The Representation of the Self*, in which the author discusses the "psychological mythmaking" of several key American
Romantics. More specifically, his subject is "those privileged figures
and rhetorical strategies through which writers of the American
Renaissance attempted to disseminate their sense of the mind," and
their implicit understanding that psychology is a "self-constituting
myth—mental traits becoming visible once they are named." For
our purposes Steele discusses at length Emerson's "Myth of the Unconscious," as the Concord sage strove to interpret the self from the
depths of the psyche rather than from institutional norms; Thoreau's
"Landscape of Being," in which he argues that this thinker, "rather
than uniting spirit and body through the analysis of human activity
as the predicate of unconscious power," begins "with a consideration
of how decentered physical existence inhibits spiritual expression";
and "Recovering the 'Idea of Woman': *Woman in the Nineteenth
Century* and Its Mythological Background," in which he discusses
Fuller's profound recognition of androgyny as she writes about "fe-
mality." This is a fine study, to be read, say, with Robert D. Richardson's *Myth and Literature in the American Renaissance* (*ALS 1978*,
pp. 3–4) and Martin Bickman's *The Unsounded Centre* (*ALS 1980*,
pp. 13–14), particularly if one wishes to ponder the connections between 19th- and 20th-century concepts of the self. Interested readers
may also want to consult a distillation of some of these ideas in Steele's
"Emerson, Hawthorne, Melville, and the Unconscious" (*UMSE* 5
[1984–87]:39–50).

The third important book-length study was Donald Pease's *Visionary Compacts*. From his observation that writers of the American
Renaissance, because of their concern with such contemporary issues
as the American union, expansionism, and slavery, turned to "visionary compacts"—ways to sanction "terms of agreement from the nation's past" to reunite the citizenry, Pease explores certain writers'
relationships to the "hopes, ideals, and purposes they shared with

their ancestors." His chapter on "self-reliance" as Emerson understood it is particularly strong; he sees Emerson's notion of the concept not as anarchic but rather as directing "the individual as well as the culture to a vision of the innermost principles underlying both." Thus, as memory or reverence for the past is replaced by self-reliance, individuals will begin to recognize that the power that made past deeds great is indeed shared by all. All of Pease's chapters are provocative and should interest students of American Transcendentalism.

Robert A. Gross continued his important social history of Concord in two lengthy essays. In "Much Instruction from 'Little Reading': Books and Libraries in Thoreau's Concord" (*PAAS* 97, pt. 1: 129–88) he explores the extant records of the Concord Social Library and the Concord Charitable Society Library "to gain a larger understanding of the connections that bound Emerson and Thoreau to their contemporaries and simultaneously cut them off." In terms of book purchases from the late 18th century to the mid-19th century he notes a shift from an emphasis on moderate, rationalist religious writers who resisted deism and radical politics in the wake of the French Revolution to writers of histories, biographies, travels, and books of practical science that served an aspiring middle class for whom religion no longer was a primary concern. In a follow-up essay, "Reconstructing Early American Libraries: Concord, Massachusetts, 1795–1850 (*PAAS* 97, pt. 2:331–452), Gross publishes his reconstructions of these same libraries from their extant catalogs. Of the 720 titles listed, he has been able to identify over 95 percent, and he conveniently lists them by both genre and year of acquisition. These two essays are an invaluable contribution to our understanding of Concord's intellectual milieu and as well point out the sort of painstaking work on which the "history of the book" is based.

In "Sculling to the Oversoul: Louis Simpson, American Transcendentalism, and Thomas Eakins's *Max Schmitt in a Single Scull*" (*AQ* 39:410–30), Rob Wilson gives a fascinating deconstructive reading of Simpson's poem "The Champ in Single Sculls" through an analysis of "Eakins's democratized and all-but-transcendental use of sculling as an American 'meditation' promoting unity of body and soul." Wilson believes that Eakins's painting "contains traces of transcendental textuality, especially in its image of self-reliant access to the Over-Soul by the Body Electric of the athlete," and convinces the reader of how the "lingering ideology of Transcendentalism" informs both late-19th-century American painting and 20th-century American poetry, in Kinnell's and Ammons's work as well as in Simpson's. Exploring a different sort of intertexuality, in "Every Man a Scholar: Unitarians, Transcendentalists, and Biblical Criticism" (*Religion and Philosophy* 1:111–24), Gary Collinson speaks to why Transcendentalists ultimately "failed to sustain their interest in historical criticism or to incorporate it into their reformed religion," something he attributes to their emphasis on intutitionism. In *The Renewal of Literature* (Random House) Richard Poirier uses Emerson to center an eloquent and far-ranging discussion of the relation of literature to culture, particularly with an eye to "cultural renovation." Poirier believes that it is unproductive to suggest that literature has a "culturally redemptive power" because writing that is literature tends "to be discernibly on edge about its own rhetorical status." Poirier argues that such notions about literature's putative influence "cannot be sustained by the actual operations of language in literary texts." And finally, admirers of George Hochfield's important introduction to *Selected Writings of the Transcendentalists* (1966) will want to read his "New England Transcendentalism" in *The New History of Literature*, pp. 136–67. I was not able to see John Warren Smith's " 'The Texas Question': Big Burr Under the Transcendentalist Blanket" (*JASAT* 18:24–30).

ii. Emerson

There were no book-length studies of Emerson, but he was well served by many essays and chapters devoted to his life and work. Perhaps the strongest is Mary Kupiec Cayton's "The Making of An American Prophet: Emerson, His Audiences, and the Rise of the Popular Culture Industry in Nineteenth-Century America" (*Amer. Hist. Rev.* 92:597–620). Based in reception theory as well as in Bakhtin's notion of how cultural meanings are generated through dialogic struggle, this essay explores the reception of Emerson's work by different audiences; as she puts it, "Reception theory suggests that Emerson's cultural import may have depended less on what he intended than on what key communities of interpreters made of him." From his early career as an unorthodox clergyman to his emergence in the 1850s as a recognizable national figure, to a large degree Emerson was what his audiences chose to make of him, a fact Cayton brilliantly illustrates in her section on his trip to Cincinnati in the 1850s when he delivered the lectures that became *The Conduct of Life*

(1860). By this time he had tailored his message to a bourgeois mer-
cantile audience, even as he sought to indict such culture for its shortcomings, but newspaper reports of his performances indicate that his
audiences filtered out such critical overtones. A marvelous exploration of how Emerson's notion of self-culture was affected by the increasing consumerism of culture, this essay is well worth any reader's
time, for methodology as well as content.

In *The Art of Prophesying* Teresa Toulouse includes two chapters
on Emerson, to accompany those on John Cotton, Benjamin Colman,
and William Ellery Channing. As a unified work, this book is not
fully convincing, but what she has to say about Emerson's expansion
of Channing's insights into how the "inner Mind" contributes to the
"form" of one's preaching is worth considering, particularly as she
illustrates it in her exploration of four sermons from different phases
of Emerson's career. Not all will agree, however, that "in his attempt
to develop a new sense of the interplay between faith, form, and
audience," Emerson had "unwittingly traveled full circle, back to
assumptions about religious knowledge shared by John Calvin and
John Cotton." Another book that has Emerson as an important con-
stituent is *American Poetry* by Mutlu Konuk Blasing, who argues that
American poetry does not depend, as some would have it, solely on
Emerson as originator but rather is constituted by four separate
traditions, established by Whitman, Dickinson, and Poe, as well as
by Emerson. Blasing argues that the Emersonian poetic strategy rests
primarily in analogy, and she places Frost, Stevens, Moore, Bishop,
and Merrill in this tradition. This book is more for the scholar of
American poetry than for those for whom Transcendentalism is a
main concern.

Anyone interested in Emerson's later, post-"Experience" mode
should refer to Mark Edmundson's "Emerson and the Work of Melancholia" (*Raritan* 6:120–36), in which he focuses on the problem of
loss and how Emerson responded to it through the development of
a "fresh Romantic sublime through what Freud would call 'the work
of melancholia.'" Based in enlightening readings of "Threnody" and
"Fate," this difficult but rewarding essay allows one better to understand to what degree Emerson came to believe that the self is constituted by powers not its own. Less compelling but more playful is
Daniel O'Hara's "Over Emerson's Body" (*CEA* 49:79–88), in which
the author begins with Harold Bloom's ideas about revisionary interpretation. With these in mind, O'Hara reads Emerson's "Literary

Ethics" and demonstrates how, in the case of Emerson's reading of
Schiller and, later, Nietzsche's of Emerson, "cannibalistic revision"
indeed goes on just as Bloom says. Finally, with regard to such speculative essays, *ALS* readers may want to look at Howard Horowitz's
"The Standard Oil Trust as Emersonian Hero" (*Raritan* 6:99–119),
a fascinating exploration of the identification between "Emerson's
logic of the transcendent self and the logic of the trust" as it was
developed in the late 19th century. "The dream of the trust," Horowitz writes, "is to become a powerful person by not being an agent,
or rather by being merely the agent or instrument of transcendent
forces," and thus the common logic between Emerson and the trust
is that "morality of action is justified by the transcendence of personal agency." He concludes that "Emerson's exhortation that the
will uses forms according to its needs theologized a broad ideology
of appropriation that developed with the emergence of a handicraft
and merchant economy," and thus offers a provocative way to consider, in a different way from Cayton's examples (supra), to what
uses Emerson's thought could be put.

In "From the Edwardses to the Emersons" (*CEA* 49:70–78)
Phyllis Cole continues her important work on Mary Moody Emerson's relation to her illustrious nephew. Herein, Cole uses Miss
Emerson to reexamine Perry Miller's famous thesis about the "persistence of a visionary and ecstatic mode in New England religious
history" and argues that there is such a connection, via the twined
history of both families from the Great Awakening to the 1830s.
Earlier generations of the Emerson family were indeed New Lights,
and Mary Moody Emerson was the heir of their beliefs, even as she
deflected these traditions "precisely into the individualism and dissent from patriarchal authority" that gave Waldo's message such
power. This is a nice example of the rewards of sleuthing in family
history. A different sort of exploration is Michael Colacurcio's "The
Corn and the Wine: Emerson and the Example of Herbert" (*NConL*
42:1–28). Like O'Hara's essay, this piece begins with Bloom, for
Colacurcio argues that with Herbert "Emerson finds himself truly
troubled by the example of a writer he much admires, truly uncertain he can go on with his own project, even his own life, unless he
can dispose of another man's literary facts." Colacurcio demonstrates
Emerson's selective use of Herbert's "Man" in *Nature*, nicely explicates Emerson's poem "Grace," and then moves on to a provocative
reading of Herbert's "The Collar" and the Divinity School Address.

Because this last poem is, in Colacurcio's view, "the most powerful poem in English about the (rejected) temptation to apostasize," Colacurcio believes that this work, and through it the example of Herbert's life, haunted Emerson's search for his own private faith. This is a splendid sophisticated example of the fruits of close reading.

Less powerful is Manfred Putz's "Emerson and Kant Once Again: Is Emerson's Thought a Philosophy Before, After, Beside, or Beyond Kant?" (*Religion and Philosophy* 2:621–40), in which he discusses how Emerson, "through a specific reception and application of philosophical nomenclature, fashioned a view of Critical Idealism suited to his own purposes." He concludes that Emerson imperfectly understood Kant and did not build a philosophical system of any rigor that could stand with the master's. In the same collection of essays (1: 267–88) Herwig Friedl speaks to another pairing, "Emerson and Nietzsche, 1862–1874," and argues that from the beginning of his philosophical career in 1862, through the end of his rationally conscious life (1888), Nietzsche "used Emerson's writings as a lens . . . to read the possibilities of his own philosophical future." Based on a study of Nietzsche's notations in a German edition of Emerson's essays, this essay is much more rewarding than O'Hara's (supra). Another study of sources/influences is Jill Fritz-Piggott's "The Law of Adrastia: Emerson's 'Experience' and Plato's *Phaedrus*" (*ATQ* n.s. 1:261–71). She sees Emerson echoing or answering the *Phaedrus* throughout the essay, not just in its last pages when he explicitly refers to Plato's work. In these works, she argues, "Personal empowerment and clear perception" are the goals of both men. Elizabeth I. Dunn in " 'A Deranged Balance': Emerson on Inspiration" (*The Cast of Consciousness*, pp. 141–50) explores how Emerson established "an epistemology that reconciles mysticism and empiricism into a Transcendental theory of knowing: it allows for a mystical experience" but makes it "dependent on information supplied by the senses." These last two essays are useful but not pathbreaking. Finally, with regard to influence studies, readers may wish to refer to Ellen Hunnicutt's "Practical Uses of Emerson: Charles Ives" (*Soundings* 11:189–98), a good discussion of the composer who labeled himself and his music "transcendental."

Fans of the always stimulating work of Philip Young will delight in his "Small World: Emerson, Longfellow, and Melville's Secret Sister" (*NEQ* 60:382–402), a detailed reconstruction of the known facts about Ann Middleton Allen, sired by Melville's father and without doubt the prototype for Isabel in *Pierre*. Young demonstrates, among other things, that she knew Mary Moody Emerson, had an aunt who admired Channing, received a copy of the *Dial* in 1843 from Emerson himself, and had met Longfellow, who lived in the Craigie House in Cambridge that once had belonged to Ann's father-in-law! The essay makes marvelous reading and causes one to ponder the irony of Melville's half-sister as part of Emerson's extended circle of acquaintances. Another strong piece of work on someone who knew Emerson is Nancy Craig Simmons's "Philosophical Biographer: James Elliott Cabot and *A Memoir of Ralph Waldo Emerson*" (*SAR*, pp. 365–92). Simmons discusses at length how Cabot conceived and arrived at his important biography of the man whom he had first met in the 1840s and whose *Complete Works* he eventually was to edit. She concludes that Cabot's biography is so fine because he "simultaneously shared Emerson's relationship to the [Puritan] tradition" that was so important to Emerson and "explores the impact of heredity and culture on the developing individual."

Curtis Fukuchi in "'The Only Firmament': 'Sea-Room' in Emerson's *English Traits*" (*ATQ* n.s. 1:197–209) argues that "sea images provide a loose metaphoric framework for describing the sources of English power" in Emerson's book about our old home; the piece is interesting but not at the level of last year's essays on this important book (see *ALS 1986*, p. 14). And those interested in Emerson's "Terminus" will want to look at John Coakley's "Emerson's 'Terminus'" (*Expl* 45, iii:25–28); he reads it as marking "a partial movement away from the transcendental idealism and romantic conviction" of such essays as "Self-Reliance."

Last year I missed a chapter on Emerson in Richard Forrer's *Theodicies in Conflict* (Greenwood, 1986), in which the author claims that Emerson's refocusing of vision from *Nature* to "Fate" can be understood "in terms of the theological debate about the Puritans and rationalistic theodicies." Finally, I note with pleasure the publication of Maurice Gonnaud's *An Uneasy Solitude: Individual and Society in the Work of Ralph Waldo Emerson* (Princeton), a translation of an important biography that appeared in French in 1964 (see *ALS 1964*, pp. 5–6). This book always has had its admirers among true Emersonians, and it is convenient to have it in English. I note, however, that the notes have not been rewritten, although references to MSS sources have been keyed to now published materials and references to the superseded edition of the journals now cite *The Journals and Miscellaneous Notebooks*.

iii. Thoreau

There were two book-length studies of Thoreau this year. Richard J. Schneider contributed *Henry David Thoreau* (TUSAS 497), seeking to "provide in one volume an evenly balanced introduction to Thoreau as both a person and a writer." Within the constraints of this series this is a good book that touches on many of Thoreau's complexities and ambiguities; it serves as a good introduction for the nonspecialist and will remind the specialist of how many ways Thoreau can be approached. More challenging is Joan Burbick's *Thoreau's Alternative History: Changing Perspectives on Nature, Culture, and Language* (Penn.). Burbick claims that, unlike many of his contemporaries, Thoreau did not view American history in terms of the country's progressive materialist destiny; rather, he saw that it had to be understood and narrated vis-à-vis an attitude toward *nature*. "For civilization to turn from tragic destructiveness," she writes, "the history of the natural world had to be integrated with human history." Thoreau's goal, then, was to integrate the story of civilization into geological time as he attempted "to retain Emersonian idealism in the face of the nineteenth century's emerging sense of natural history." To illustrate her points, Burbick ranges widely through Thoreau's works, including the post-1850 journals, when his frequent descriptions of landscape offered him "an endlessly renewable form of natural history." As with many monographs, this book works its thesis pretty hard, but the author is a sensitive reader of her subject.

To my mind, the strongest piece on Thoreau this year is Leonard Neufeldt's "Thoreau's Enterprise of Self-Culture in a Culture of Enterprise" (*AQ* 39:231–51). In the last few years Neufeldt has demonstrated himself one of the most sophisticated explorers of Thoreau's context, and this essay forwards his reputation along those lines. He focuses on Thoreau's obsession with the question of literary vocation in an age of enterprise, and particularly on his identification of self-culture with a literary career. Toward this end, Neufeldt examines the "spirit of the age of enterprise" at the level "of language and linguistic shifts" and makes us appreciate as never before how such words as *commerce, enterprise, business, profit, industry,* and *corporation* resonate in Thoreau's works as he challenged his contemporaries' general understanding of them. Neufeldt asks us, finally, to recognize that in the early 19th century there arose a "new vernacular of enterprise with its range of semantic differentiation and shifts" and that Thoreau's language offers "the record of a developing alternative to the language and values" of this culture. This is a lovely piece of scholarship.

Another worthy effort is Stephen Fink's "Building America: Henry Thoreau and the American Home" (*Prospects* 11 [1986]:327–65). Like Neufeldt, Fink is interested in context, in this case Thoreau's concern for the "built environment," epitomized by his cabin at Walden, a cut of which graces the title page of the first edition of *Walden.* Recognizing that such construction "expresses fundamental personal, social, and economic values," Thoreau, Fink argues, "saw that Americans in particular needed to build with a deliberation commensurate to the larger endeavor of defining their personal and national identities." Beginning with Thoreau's response to the communitarian dwellings of the Fourierists and other socialists, Fink relates Thoreau's discussions of interior space to the works of Andrew Jackson Downing (particularly on cottage architecture) and finally, through Horatio Greenough's interest in organic style, to the ideas of Louis Sullivan and Frank Lloyd Wright. This is an important "American Studies" essay. Less powerful because much more limited in scope is Paul McCarthy's "Houses in *Walden*: Thoreau as Real-Estate Broker, Social Critic, Idealist" (*MQ* 28:323–39), a survey of the "interesting shelters and occupants" Thoreau discusses in his masterpiece.

James Duban explores another dimension of Thoreau's context in "Conscience and Consciousness: The Liberal Christian Context of Thoreau's Political Ethics" (*NEQ* 60:208–22). Duban focuses on the Unitarian dimension of Thoreau's resistance to civil government, particularly "his dual emphasis on conscience and consciousness." Duban finds in William Ellery Channing, Henry Whitney Bellows, and James Walker, among other Unitarians, the same stress on conscience as an expanded form of consciousness that informs Thoreau's writings on the subject of civil disobedience, and then claims that Transcendental spiritualism was not as important to Thoreau in this matter as we have thought. Not as powerful as Neufeldt's work, this is still a welcome reminder that many of Thoreau's notions have to be understood in light of those of the individuals among whom he most commonly traveled, Boston's and Concord's liberal Christians. Jaques Barzun in "Thoreau the Thorough Impressionist" (*ASch* 56: 250–58) discusses "Civil Disobedience" and its inconsistencies as he goes on to argue, in this occasional essay, that Thoreau's "failure as a writer on politics comes from the same power as made him a matchless depictor of visions." And Bradley P. Dean in "Reconstructions of Thoreau's Early 'Life without Principle' Lectures" (*SAR*, pp. 285–364) painstakingly reassembles from the 91 extant manuscript pages the famous essay that began as Thoreau's lecture "What Shall It Profit?," first delivered in 1854.

There were two solid essays on *A Week*. In " 'A Separate Intention of the Eye': Luminist Eternity in Thoreau's *A Week on the Concord and Merrimack Rivers*" (*CRevAs* 18:41–60), Kevin Radaker sees luminism as playing a significant role in "the most transcendental of Thoreau's works, especially in the development of his thoughts on time and eternity." This, of course, is a topic that has been touched on by others (see, for example, John Conron's work [*ALS 1980*, p. 15], or that of Gayle Smith and Richard Schneider [*ALS 1985*, pp. 11–12, 18]), and Radaker has to shuffle a bit to distinguish what is new in his own conception of the common project of luminist painters and Thoreau in *A Week*. He concludes that Thoreau's "luminist vision of nature informs his thoughts on religion, history, and society," and thus makes the largest claim yet for the importance of luminism to Thoreau. In "Symbolic Landscape in the Greylock Episode of Thoreau's *Week*" (*ATQ* n.s. 1:123–34) Donald Murray focuses on the "curious intensity" in this section of Thoreau's first book, in particular its sequence of portraits of the young woman in dishabille and the surly farmer, Rice. Murray reads this section as a Freudian display of Thoreau's "deep-seated preoccupations . . . with sexuality and self-definition." I will let Murray tell the story: in the Greylock adventure "Thoreau is the son bent on conquest of the mother, replacement of the father. Climbing the mountain is challenging the father; and Rice, the father figure he meets before the ascent, is naturally gruff to the point of hostility." The woman Thoreau meets, Murray notes, has traits in common with Thoreau's mother, Cynthia. We all know what to expect next. He is interested in this woman but doesn't tarry, and "Descent of the mountain brings a depression of spirits like that which occurs after sexual intercourse"! Hmmmm. In "Your Mind Must Not Perspire: Thoreau on Observation, Perception, and the Role of Consciousness" (*The Cast of Consciousness*, pp. 151–59), Lewis Leary comments on how for Thoreau "natural facts were natural facts, and worthy of themselves." No surprises here. And finally, Kenneth Walter Cameron continues his publication of indispensable source material with his *Thoreau's Fact Book, Volume Three* (Transcendental Books).

iv. Other Transcendentalists

Charles Capper gives us a section of his forthcoming study of Margaret Fuller in "Margaret Fuller as Cultural Reformer" (*AQ* 39: 509–28). In this essay he is primarily interested in the extent of Fuller's commitment to the cause of women in 1839 (when she offered her famous "Conversations" in Boston), and he argues persuasively that at this point in her career her primary goal was to extend specifically to women Emerson's and others' notions of self-culture. As a "cultural reformer," then, she wanted to change people's lives by changing their minds about certain things, and not, say, by improving their opportunities in the economic sphere; such commitment came later, in the 1840s, with the emergence of a full-fledged women's rights movement. Capper concludes that Fuller's importance through the "Conversations" was in her understanding of culture as a *social* as well as an individual matter; thus her attitude foreshadowed women's rights groups like those later established by Elizabeth Cady Stanton and others. Laraine Fergensen explores another segment of Fuller's early years in "Margaret Fuller in the Classroom: The Providence Period" (*SAR*, pp. 131–42), with particular emphasis on the extant journals of several young women who attended the Greene Street School with which Fuller was associated. In these sources Fuller is revealed as a sharp and severe teacher who also was able to inspire her charges with a sense of the importance of developing their intellect.

Another good piece on Fuller is Stephen Adams's " 'That Tidiness We Look for in Women': *Summer on the Lakes* and Romantic Aesthetics" (*SAR*, pp. 247–64). Adams argues that this rambling work is more coherent than we think, if we consider it in the genre of the subjective excursion so popular among Romantics. He sees Fuller "defamiliarizing" the expectations of readers by conveying a "complex, unstable, manifold reality," and as well moving constantly from the outer landscape to the inner self, as Wordsworth does in *The*

Prelude and Thoreau in *Walden*. In "*Corinne* and the 'Yankee Corin-
na': Madame de Staël and Margaret Fuller" (*Woman as Mediatrix:
Essays in Nineteenth-Century European Women Writers*, ed. Avriel
Goldberger [Greenwood], pp. 39–46), Paula Blanchard explores the
influence of de Staël's famous novel on Fuller, particularly through
its sympathetic portrait of a woman who has purchased her freedom
at a significant emotional cost. Blanchard suggests that "for both
Fuller and de Staël the strain of having to demonstrate publicly that
women could be as strong and creative as men exaggerated their
need to 'owe fealty' in love until it became a real danger to their
integrity."

In "Amos Bronson Alcott: Natural Resource or 'Consecrated
Crank'" (*ATQ* n.s. 1:49–68) Harry DuPuy tries to revise the common notion that Alcott was a sublime failure at almost all he attempted; the effort is rather strained and adds little to what we know
of this "tedious archangel." A similar and bit stronger effort for another problematic Transcendentalist is Shelly Armitage's "Christopher Pearse Cranch: The Wit as Poet" (*ATQ* n.s. 1:33–47), in which
she argues that wit is "the consistent element in his otherwise various
poems." Armitage regards Emerson's "The Comic," which appeared
in the *Dial* in 1843 but was delivered as a lecture in the late 1830s,
the key to understanding what Cranch was about. This essay succeeds in making us appreciate the craft of Cranch's verse. Another
helpful piece on an often neglected figure is Leonard Neufeldt's assessment of James Freeman Clarke as a literary critic, in *DLB* 59:
80–87.

In "Ellery Channing and Daniel Ricketson: Thoreau's Friends in
Conflict" (*Concord Saunterer* 19, i:22–43) Dan Mortland outlines the
troubled relationship of these two important minor figures, particularly as Ricketson became increasingly disappointed by the other's
eccentricities and moods, and his criticism of Wendell Phillips's position on Frémont's candidacy, which Phillips opposed. Mortland
also contributed "Approaching an Idol: New Light on the Ricketson-
Thoreau Friendship" (*ESQ* 32 [1986]:213–24), in which he uses
newly available manuscript letters from Ricketson to Thoreau for the
period September to December 1855 to assess Ricketson's relationship
to his new acquaintance. Mortland points out that the editors of the
most commonly cited source for the Thoreau-Ricketson friendship,
Daniel Ricketson and His Friends (1902), omitted important materials, so that we are left with "a distorted or, at best, incomplete

view of the emotional or intellectual chemistry between the two friends." One hopes that more such important primary materials will emerge in the next decade to allow us a fuller view of the established pantheon of Concord writers.

In "The True Romance of Anna Hazard Barker and Samuel Gray Ward" (*SAR*, pp. 53–72) Eleanor M. Tilton reconstructs as best as we can expect the relationship of these two figures on the fringes of the Transcendentalist movement. In particular, Tilton wishes us to know that the accounts we have had of these people, based as they have been in the impressions of Emerson and Fuller, have been partly erroneous. Finally, I urge all readers of this chapter to peruse the year's issues of the *Concord Saunterer* and the *Thoreau Society Bulletin*, in which they might find brief articles of some interest to them.

University of North Carolina, Chapel Hill

2. Hawthorne

Claudia D. Johnson

In 1987 post-structuralist criticism of Hawthorne began coming into its own, emerging relatively free of the neologisms that distracted undeconstructed readers earlier. Scholars will find this year a substantial amount of original criticism of Hawthorne. The old canards about having "new light thrown on Hawthorne" or being led to "see his work from a new perspective" are somehow inadequate to the task of describing much of the year's work. These studies *open up* Hawthorne's fiction in extraordinarily creative ways. Their use of biography and history does not provoke us to ask, "So, what?" Their discovery of sources does not leave us to wonder, "What's the point?" We do not nod agreeably over the page as if it were a comfortable old friend who has changed only the color of his shirt. These are challenging scholars who can turn much of what we thought about Hawthorne on its ear. Yet for all their sophistication and complexity, the best of them offer us unforced, lucid arguments.

Instead of the one or two first-rate articles or books on Hawthorne that the scholarly community is accustomed to expect each year, there is a long list in 1987 of exceptionally fine work, most of it on *The Scarlet Letter*, two on *The House of the Seven Gables*. These scholar/critics should be acknowledged at the outset: Louise De-Salvo and Donald E. Pease on Hawthorne's rewriting of history in *The Scarlet Letter*; Agostino Lombardo for his summary article in *The New History of Literature*; Mary Suzanne Schriber and Amy Schrager Lang for their gender studies; Ralph Flores and Allan Lloyd Smith for reevaluations of allegory; Christine Brooke-Rose for a Derridian examination of linguistics in *The Scarlet Letter*; Robert Shulman for his study of the artist's penal subversion; Hugh Dawson for his interpretation of the scaffold scenes as a triptych; and Thomas Brooke and Susan Mizruchi for their legal/social studies of *The House of the Seven Gables*.

Two current trends in criticism in general have lent themselves especially well to Hawthorne criticism in particular. One is the examination of the way in which the author's personal history affects his recasting of the nation's history. The other is an examination of his work in light of the recent rehabilitation of allegory.

i. Primary Materials

In 1987 three collections of primary materials appeared in series volumes already recognized for their exceptionally high quality and utility: the Centenary Hawthorne, the Norton Critical Editions, and the Library of America Classics. The 17th volume of *The Centenary Edition of the Works of Nathaniel Hawthorne* contains *The Letters, 1857–1864*, ed. Thomas Woodson, James A. Rubino, L. Neal Smith, and Norman Holmes Pearson (Ohio State). Scholars will find here the same high quality that they have come to expect in other *Centenary* volumes. The binding, paper, and printing are solid and attractive. The "Abbreviations and Short Titles" section is easy to locate, simplified, and clear. The letters themselves are numbered. Mercifully, notes appear at the end of each letter. One wonders why the tradition of placing "textual notes" in one section at the end persists even when, as brief as they are individually, placing them with the letters to which they refer would be more convenient. The inclusion of the libraries and collections in which individual letters are housed is exceptionally useful. As a general rule, the notes provide background information but not interpretation. The value of this very fine volume could have been increased significantly with a more helpful index. Hawthorne writes in these letters of his experience with farming, on copyrights, about an idea for a mythological dictionary, and on his interest in reforms aboard trading vessels, to name a few topics. None of them can be located in the index. Nor is the material in the notes indexed.

The second handsome volume in The Library of America editions of Hawthorne's work, a printing of the Ohio State Centenary edition of the novels, appeared in 1987; Millicent Bell wrote the notes and chronology which appear at the end of *Nathaniel Hawthorne: Novels*.

Nathaniel Hawthorne's Tales: A Norton Critical Edition, ed. James McIntosh, opens with a brief autobiographical sketch and an explanation of the organization of the edition. A collection of some of the most frequently anthologized tales and a section on "The Author

on His Work" comprise the main portion of part one. The second half
of the edition follows the usual Norton format with one section each
on early and modern criticism. The decision to exclude contemporary
approaches altogether makes the critical section less representative,
less useful, and less interesting, even for advanced undergraduates,
than it would have been otherwise. The edition concludes with a
bibliography and chronology. The one essay which appears for the
first time in this volume will be taken up in a discussion of criticism
of Hawthorne's short works.

ii. General Studies

Two books devoted to Nathaniel Hawthorne's works appeared in
1987, one very unorthodox and one traditional. Louise DeSalvo's
Nathaniel Hawthorne (Humanities) is one in a series of this press's
"Feminist Readings," which makes a somewhat puzzling point of
limiting its studies to standard texts written by men. Even before
opening the book, one suspects that something outside the ordinary is afoot. The cover illustration presents in the foreground a
sensitive, intelligent Dimmesdale in representational style and, in the
background, a grim little stylized caricature of Hester, peeping out
from behind him. DeSalvo aims to explore Hawthorne's and his culture's "ambivalence toward women, which often flares into overt
misogyny," in her first chapter bringing together biographical materials which make Hawthorne's expressed view of woman painfully
evident. Her reading of *The Scarlet Letter* is compelling, provocative,
original. According to DeSalvo, Hawthorne disavows "the facts of
his life" in "The Custom-House" by substituting a fictional and
fatherly Surveyor Pue for the women who in reality made it possible for him to write the romance. Further, Hawthorne disavows
the realities of history (by not having Hester beaten or her child
taken from her) in order to exonerate his ancestors, which is, of
course, his expressed aim in "The Custom-House." In her chapter on
Blithedale DeSalvo speculates that Zenobia may have been dis-
patched by Coverdale, a persuasively argued if radical reading that
has surfaced more than once in the last few years. DeSalvo's decision
to exclude *The Marble Faun* is disappointing, if not astonishing, and
the rationale she offers for the omission is dubious. But although De-
Salvo's work as a whole is spotty and readers may, with justification,

resist some of her conclusions, her daring and original readings, especially of *The Scarlet Letter,* bring a new level of excitement to Hawthorne's work.

Frederick Newberry's *Hawthorne's Divided Loyalties: England and America in His Works* (Fairleigh Dickinson) is as conventional as DeSalvo's is unconventional. The essential ambiguity of Hawthorne's work is seen by Newberry in the writer's affirmation of the democracy won in the rebellion against England and in the somewhat contradictory attempt to recover Our Old Home's "aesthetic and cultural values" that had been lost through the harshness of the early settlers like Endicott. Hawthorne's ambiguity toward the Puritans, which actually intensified in his declining years, is found to be a formative element in his fiction.

The impact of the Puritans on Hawthorne's work, while it is a topic as old as Hawthorne criticism, nevertheless receives the same fresh and insightful treatment in 1987 articles that DeSalvo and Newberry develop in their books. Agostino Lombardo's "Nathaniel Hawthorne" in *The New History of Literature,* pp. 169–95, should be considered a model for scholars who write introductory/summary histories of American literature. The obligatory treatment of Hawthorne's career and broad coverage of frequently anthologized fiction is not accomplished at the expense of a point of view and some original scholarship. Nor does he write down to his audience. The frame of his article is the Puritan legacy, which he expands beyond the customary discussions to trace Hawthorne's debt to the Puritans for his symbolism, which Lombardo illustrates well with the scarlet letter's "ever-changing meaning."

David R. Williams in "Hawthorne, Very, and Dickinson: The Wilderness of the Mind" in *Wilderness Lost: The Religious Origins of the American Mind* (Susquehanna) contends that Hawthorne, being a son of the Puritans, approached the "wilderness" again and again, but, like Young Goodman Brown, refused to surrender, continuing to wander "in the psychological wilderness of despair."

The Puritan preoccupation with witchcraft is the subject of Donald A. Ringe's "Madness in Hawthorne's Fiction" in *The Cast of Consciousness,* pp. 125–40, a volume in honor of distinguished Hawthorne scholar Richard Harter Fogle. Chiefly with the use of treatises on insanity by Dr. Benjamin Rush, whose work was familiar to the Bowdoin faculty, Ringe categorizes types of madness portrayed in Hawthorne's fiction, concluding that in order to explore the connections between the psychological and moral, Hawthorne included an additional category, demonic possession, which was discredited by psychologists of his own day.

In "Nathaniel Hawthorne: Excessive Interpretation," *American Romanticism*, vol. 1: *From Cooper to Hawthorne, Excessive America*, pp. 169–220 (Macmillan), David Morse moves from a discourse on the Puritan system of shifting signs to Hawthorne's fascination with "excessive interpretation" and the "treacherous nature of the puritan experience . . . produced by the instability of the sign."

George Dekker's study of the Waverley tradition in the American Renaissance also turns on Hawthorne's Puritanism. In his chapter "Hawthorne and the Ironies of New England History" in *The American Historical Romance* (Cambridge), pp. 129–85, 220–71, Dekker sees the formative conflict in Hawthorne's thought as between the Puritan past and the Democratic present, a conflict which Hawthorne often shows to the reader with his use of irony. His ambivalence about the past is also revealed in his distrust of the historical romance.

Among works which cover a span in Hawthorne's career, Dekker's is one of several in which the interest is on the effect of Hawthorne's Puritanism on the development of his romanticism. Six chapters of Leon Chai's *Romantic Foundations* are on works by Hawthorne. It is Chai's thesis that Hawthorne's romanticism differs in kind from Emerson's, Hawthorne's symbols showing their relativity as different characters interpret them. His art, subsequently, is less Platonic than organic. His romanticism is also characterized by a "transcendence of historical perspective," by his clear differentiation between love and psychological possession, and by the relationship between immortality and art.

Jeffrey Steele's thesis in "Hawthorne and the Psychology of Oppression" in *The Representation of the Self*, pp. 151–59, is that Hawthorne socializes Transcendentalism in his recognition that "the psyche is shaped as much by external social demands as it is by inner forces." Powerful societies or their representatives, seeking to repress what they suspect is personal weakness, turn on others whom they see as embodying what they hate and fear in themselves, which is usually the feminine, the body, sexuality.

Hawthorne is the subject of a chapter in Maurice J. Bennett's *An American Tradition: Three Studies—Charles Brockden Brown, Nathaniel Hawthorne, and Henry James* (Garland): "Nathaniel Hawthorne's Aesthetic Ambivalence," pp. 116–267, which studies the growth of the artist within whom Puritanism and Romanticism were in conflict. It suffers, as one might suspect, from having once been a 1978 dissertation (Harvard), and the bibliography is decidedly dated.

Hawthorne's view of transcendental idealism comes into play in Carol Shloss's chapter "Nathaniel Hawthorne and Daguerreotype" in her *In Visible Light*, pp. 25–54. Shloss illustrates that Hawthorne's simultaneous distance from and dependence upon the external world contributed to his eventual association of the aesthetic distance he wanted to achieve with photography and his reference to daguerreotypes in his fiction. The eye of the camera, the subject in *The House of the Seven Gables*, becomes the eye of Coverdale in *The Blithedale Romance*.

Two articles which are studies of more than one of Hawthorne's fictions focus on gender. Janis P. Stout maintains in "The Fallen Woman and the Conflicted Author: Hawthorne and Hardy" (*ATQ* 3: 233–46) that in undermining the very stereotypes of the fallen woman that the fictions of Hawthorne and Hardy represent, these two writers display their ambivalence toward the moral codes that shaped their society. Mary Suzanne Schriber probes the ambivalence in greater depth in "Nathaniel Hawthorne: A Pilgrimage to a Dovecote" in *Gender and the Writer's Imagination*, pp. 44–85. Schriber's point is that Hawthorne's imagination was consistently thwarted by the ideology of gender in his own time so that, for example, while at the beginning of *The Scarlet Letter* the narrator appears to challenge his culture's limited view of woman's nature in the person of Hester, he seems to capitulate to the culture's stereotype by the novel's close. In Hawthorne's remaining novels he returns to the gender stereotypes of romance.

iii. Novels

Rarely does one see a year in which *The Scarlet Letter* receives such undivided attention. By comparison and in contrast with earlier years, no essay focuses solely on *The Blithedale Romance* or *The Marble Faun*. Gender and sexuality continue to be the center of superb studies of *The Scarlet Letter*. In her "Introduction" (pp. 1–5) and in a chapter entitled "An American Jezebel: Hawthorne and *The Scarlet Letter*" (pp. 161–92) of *Prophetic Woman*, Amy Schrager

Lang contends that behind Hawthorne's equation of Anne Hutchinson with women novelists is America's ambivalence toward the individualism which it both celebrates and fears and which Hawthorne depicts in the character of Hester Prynne. For Hawthorne, writes Lang, finds the solution to the problem of individualism in gender, correcting what he sees as the error of Hutchinson by having Hester return to the community as an advisor to women alone, to preach a private not a public truth, turning from lawbreaker to lawgiver. Hutchinson is central to another article on *The Scarlet Letter*. Charles Swann in "Hester and the Second Coming: A Note on the Conclusion to *The Scarlet Letter*" (*JAmS* 21:264–68) proposes that an awareness of the millenialism of Hawthorne's day (particularly of the celibate Shakers founded earlier by Mother Ann Lee) strongly suggests that Hester may look forward to God as woman, ushering in the Second Coming as a time when human society will be purged of sexuality.

The argument of Zelda Bronstein's "The Parabolic Ploys of *The Scarlet Letter*" (*AQ* 39:193–210) is that in *The Scarlet Letter*, set up as a form of parable, Hawthorne uses a 17th-century setting as a comment on the 19th century, particularly the society's aversion to literature and Hawthorne's experience in politics. The parable Hawthorne uses is the one referred to in chapter nine of the romance— the story of David, Bathsheba, and the Prophet, Nathan, Hawthorne's namesake. Sexual intolerance in *The Scarlet Letter* reflects on the political intolerance of 19th-century America and of the author himself, contributing to the "indirection" of the work.

The subject of allegory, central to Bronstein's work, arises in several other studies of *The Scarlet Letter*. Ralph Flores's "Ungrounding Allegory: The Dead-Living Letter in Hawthorne's *The Scarlet Letter*" (*Criticism* 29:313–40) is one of the more complex of a number of rewarding deconstructions of *The Scarlet Letter* to appear this year. Flores examines the text as an allegory which undermines its "grounding" in meaning and which challenges the assumption that "meaning" can be discovered at all. Flores finds a union of life and death in the allegorical nature of the characters whose flat personifications are evocative and "whose assertions of life are problematically entangled with death, dying, and deadness."

Allan Lloyd Smith in "The Elaborated Sign of *The Scarlet Letter*" (*ATQ* n.s. 1:69–82) considers the scarlet A as a sign upon which three interrelated thematic concerns rest: that of spoken and unspoken

language, of allegory and typology, and of the preexistent response
which rests on allegory. Unfortunately, the journal's poor proofreading distracts from Smith's illuminating article.

Several critics of *The Scarlet Letter* explore Hawthorne's work
in the context of Puritan theology and history. Reiner Smolinski's
"Covenant Theology and Arthur Dimmesdale's Pelagianism" (*ATQ*
3:211–32) examines the conflict in Dimmesdale's mind between the
Covenants of Grace and Works and his confession. It is Smolinski's
conclusion that Hawthorne does not intend for Dimmesdale to be
damned. Like Louise DeSalvo, Hugh Dawson is interested in Hawthorne's treatment of Hester's sentencing for adultery in light of Puritan legal history. "Hester Prynne, William Hathorne and the Bay
Colony Adultery Laws of 1641–42" (*ESQ* 32:225–31) is on the question of why Hawthorne failed to have the Puritans carry out the 1641
law prescribing death for adultery—a law which William Hathorne
had some part in writing. Although sentence is passed on Hester in
1642, Pearl was born in the spring of 1641, six months before the new
law fixing death as the penalty for adultery. The early scenes associate the women, speaking for the harshest punishment, with Hathorne.
They are in contrast in the novel to the angelic Winthrop who historically opposed Hathorne on the question.

The scaffold scenes are the subject of two of the articles on *The
Scarlet Letter*. Hugh J. Dawson in "The Triptych Design of *The
Scarlet Letter*" (*NHR* 13, i:12–14) asks the reader to consider the
scaffold scenes as the three panels of a tryptych, parodically referring
to (1) the (sinless?) Madonna and child, (2) Jesus on the Cross with
the Madonna and Mary Magdalen below, and (3) the Madonna
holding Jesus' corpse. This fascinating proposition is presented in an
all too brief note, leading students to hope that Professor Dawson has
in mind a more extensive development of the "artistic dimension"
that visual art gave Hawthorne's work. In "Another Look at the Scaffold Scenes in Hawthorne's *The Scarlet Letter*" (*ATQ* 2:135–44)
Michael Clark reads the scaffold scenes as modifications of the romantic faith in intuition as a way of reaching supernal truth.

Two of the year's best articles on *The Scarlet Letter* are studies of
"The Custom-House." In light of recent work on iconicity and spatio-
temporal representation in fiction, Christine Brooke-Rose reads the
Custom-House as an apt metaphor for a threshold between many
oppositions as well as the threshold of the narrative where "custom"
exacts "a toll upon the telling" in "A for But: 'The Custom-House' in

Hawthorne's *The Scarlet Letter*" (*W&I* 3:143–55). Similarly, the style itself is constructed of forked oppositions, the image of which might be illustrated by the lines of the chief symbol of the narrative, the letter A. This Derridian reading lends a freshness to "The Custom-House" that Hawthorne scholars will welcome. Hawthorne's rewriting of his own history in *The Scarlet Letter*, developed by Louise DeSalvo, is the point of Donald E. Pease's "Hawthorne's Discovery of a Pre-Revolutionary Past" and "A Romance with the Public Will" in *Visionary Compacts*, pp. 49–107. Hawthorne, badly bruised by his dismissal from the Custom-House, re-created a Puritan cultural past in *The Scarlet Letter* which could sustain rather than replace him, thus demanding "a collective memory from *our* age to preserve him" (p. 80). Susan Swartzlander's " 'Amid Sunshine and Shadow': Charles Wentworth Upham and Nathaniel Hawthorne" (*SAF* 15:228–33) is one of several explorations of Hawthorne's Salem connections. Swartzlander looks at the influence of Upham's lectures on *The Scarlet Letter*, including "The Custom-House," their feud and Hawthorne's bitterness. However, in her assumption that no previous work has been done on the subject, she misses Helen Ferguson's 1980 monograph on the witchcraft connection between Hawthorne and Upham.

The first of two other studies of *The Scarlet Letter* which deserves special mention is Robert Shulman's "The Artist in the Slammer: Hawthorne, Melville, Poe, and the Prison of Their Times" in *Social Criticism*, pp. 176–96. Using *The Scarlet Letter* as his chief illustration, Shulman shows that the 19th-century writers' symbolism gave them possibilities for indirection and subversion—the techniques of the inmate—to survive in the marketplace society which held the artist prisoner. The second is Xiao-Huang Yin's "*The Scarlet Letter* in China" (*AQ* 39:551–62). *The Scarlet Letter*, which has become the symbol of American literature in China, has been translated three times, each edition having been influenced by the political climate in which it appeared. The first, in 1934, in a Western-world style, emphasizes the merits of Christianity and education. In the 1950s a Soviet-style edition appeared under the title "The Song of the Rustic Poor." The third translation, in 1981, is more independently analytical.

Two extraordinarily fine chapters on *The House of the Seven Gables* appeared in 1987, both in books on Hawthorne and other American authors: Brook Thomas's "*The House of the Seven Gables*:

Hawthorne's Legal Story" and *"The House of the Seven Gables*: Hawthorne's Romance of Art" in *Cross-examinations*, pp. 45–90, and Susan Mizruchi's "From History to Gingerbread: Manufacturing a Republic in *The House of the Seven Gables*" in *The Power of Historical Knowledge: Narrating the Past in Hawthorne, James, and Dreiser* (Princeton), pp. 83–134. After illuminating briefly the history of property law prior to the Civil War, Thomas provides an amazing account of the repercussions of several legal cases involving Salem politics and family histories shortly before and at the time Hawthorne was working in the Custom-House. One Salem murder trial was profoundly complicated by various interpretations of property rights and orchestrated by Salem's favorite son and U.S. Supreme Court Justice, Joseph Story. With an approach that is obviously shaped by more than a nodding acquaintance with deconstructive legal studies and an argument too intricate to be fully summarized here, Thomas lays the groundwork for his conclusion that Judge Pyncheon derives in no small way from Joseph Story (thus, the double meaning in his title) and that the property issues in the real court case are the basis of Hawthorne's fiction. Thomas's work on *The House of the Seven Gables* also appears in *"The House of the Seven Gables*: Hawthorne's Legal Story" (*UMSE* 5:249–71). Susan Mizruchi in her essay sees *The House of the Seven Gables* as an ideological statement in which the characters and narrator cling to the myth of a harmonious, ahistorical society in clear conflict with the socioeconomic reality actually suggested by the fiction's "underground truth" as well as its narrative scheme.

Curtis Dahl finds the distinction between Hawthorne and Melville reflected in what he sees as their architectural style. In "The Architecture of Society and the Architecture of the Soul: Hawthorne's *The House of the Seven Gables* and Melville's *Pierre*" (*UMSE* 5:1–22), Dahl contends that architectural style in Hawthorne's fiction is emblematic of social relationships rather than of the psyche, as it is in Melville's work.

In contrast to earlier years, 1987 yielded very little work on *The Blithedale Romance*. Hawthorne is the subject of one recollection of Brook Farm and is mentioned in several others collected by Joel Myerson in *The Brook Farm Book*. George William Curtis's "Hawthorne, Brook Farm and Transcendentalism" (pp. 92–100) is less on Hawthorne than the titling of the article would imply, as it appeared originally as the "Editor's Easy Chair" column in the January 1869

Harper's Monthly Magazine, shortly after the publication of Hawthorne's notebooks.

iv. Short Works

Two articles in 1987 have as their subjects more than one of Hawthorne's tales. Martin Prochazka in " 'The Sombre Spirit of Our Forefathers': Colonial History and Myth in Hawthorne's Tales and Sketches" (*PP* 20,x:9–17) uses the Max Weber thesis to consider the tales as a means of linking the past to the present and formulating a national consciousness for the future, which would see the rise of the bourgeoisie.

Among articles on short works is one which crosses from the letters to short fiction. Leland S. Person, Jr., in "Hawthorne's Love Letters: Writing and Relationship" (*AL* 59:210–26), writes that Hawthorne's love letters contain his acknowledgment of the gap between writing and feeling, his inability to fix Sophia as a type, and his tendency to surrender his creativity to her.

M. Thomas Inge in "Humor in Hawthorne's *Twice-Told Tales*" (*NHR* 8,ii:1–5) reaches the somewhat uncanny conclusion that "the comic overshadows the tragic by a ratio of two to one." On a different note, Marcia Smith Marzec challenges the view that even one of Hawthorne's less somber tales is lighthearted and optimistic. In " 'My Kinsman, Major Molineux' as Theo-Political Allegory" (*ATQ* 4:273–90) she argues that Robin's journey is a medieval allegory in which he denies Christ (represented by the major) and illustrates that the Democratic ideal can never be realized given the reality of man's innate depravity. In a second essay on the same tale, "Social Change and Divided Selves: 'My Kinsman Major Molineux,' " in Shulman's *Social Criticism,* pp. 114–24, a connection is made between sexuality and American power that Robin experiences on his journey of self-discovery in a landscape made tense by the conflict between aristocracy and democracy.

In 1987 critics turned their attention to several of the other historical tales. Hawthorne's tampering with history to undermine the apparent meaning of "Endicott and the Red Cross" is the main thrust of John Franzosa's "Young Man Hawthorne: Scrutinizing the Discourse of History" in *Self, Sign, and Symbol,* ed. Mark Neuman and Michael Payne (Bucknell), pp. 72–94, a bound issue of the *Bucknell Review* dedicated to former editor, Harry R. Garvin. Since Charles

Upham was critical of Roger Williams, Hawthorne associates himself with the more sympathetically portrayed Williams and connects Upham with the kind of demagoguery he attributes to Endicott, distorting history in the process to present the author as the better man. Franzosa arrives at the conclusion that Hawthorne attempts to "occupy the space between arbitrary signs and luminous symbols."

Thomas Pribek in "Witchcraft in 'Lady Eleanore's Mantle'" (SAF 15:95–100) claims that the severity of Lady Eleanore's punishment is justified in that she has coupled with and borne a fiend, has even before her arrival been the object of gossip as one who has engaged in witchcraft. The epidemic of 1721, to which she falls prey, is compared to witch trials in which inoculation was treated as a form of witchcraft. The tale thus becomes more complex than a simple moral or political allegory.

Writing on one of the least studied of Hawthorne's tales, "A Rill from the Town Pump," Alfred H. Marks in "Hawthorne, G. B. Cheever, and Salem's Pump" (EIHC 123:260–77), uncovers a controversy involving Hawthorne's good friend George B. Cheever, who enraged the community with a satiric tale, "Inquire at Amos Giles' Distillery," and was prosecuted for libel. "A Rill from the Town Pump," which appeared while Cheever's trial was proceeding, is a condemnation of any brand of hotheadedness and fanaticism like that which landed Cheever in jail.

Two scholars in 1987 investigated "Feathertop" as Hawthorne's comment on his own art. Mary E. Rucker in "The Art of Witchcraft in Hawthorne's 'Feathertop: A Moralized Legend'" (SSF 24:31–39) writes that Hawthorne's tale "challenges the critical claim that artists are, for Hawthorne, sinful necromancers" and that "he was ambivalent toward his vocation." John W. Wright contends that the tale is a hieroglyph. He presents an array of source materials designed to allow the reader to determine the extent to which the tale is either a "patchwork" of Hawthorne's earlier materials or a " 'living hieroglyphic' of his art." Wright's article appears in the new Norton critical edition (pp. 439–54) cited earlier.

While some of the lesser-known tales received some attention in 1987, the more popular tales still dominate the criticism. Gregory R. Wegner in "Hawthorne's 'Ethan Brand' and the Structure the Literary Sketch" (JNT 17:57–66) writes that "Ethan Brand" should not be judged by the expectations we have of the short narrative, but should

be recognized as a literary sketch of a type frequently employed by
Hawthorne and highly popular in his day.

In sharp contrast to earlier years when a number of articles were
written on each of Hawthorne's major tales, "Rappaccini's Daughter"
is one of the few tales that is the subject of more than two articles this
year. Lois A. Cuddy in "The Purgatorial Gardens of Hawthorne and
Dante: Irony and Redefinition in 'Rappaccini's Daughter' " (*MLS*
16:39–53) finds that parallels between the tale and Dante's *La Divina
Commedia* clarify the fiction's definitions and concepts, leading the
reader by means of irony to the narrator's bleak philosophical stance.
The argument presented by Beverly Haviland in "The Sin of Synecdoche: Hawthorne's Allegory Against Symbolism in 'Rappaccini's
Daughter' " (*TSLL* 29:278–98) is that "Rappaccini's Daughter" is
Hawthorne's allegorical rejection of the Emersonian view that the real
and the ideal are ultimately united by symbol into an organic whole
and that the ideal is always superior to the real. In showing us that
life and art, flesh and spirit can never be reconciled, the tale invites
a variety of "translations." Only Beatrice senses the duality of her
own nature, which the other characters reject. The final chapter of
Margaret Hallissey's book, *Venomous Woman*, is "Beatrice Rappaccini," pp. 133–41. Her point, not significantly different from other
recent studies, is that Giovanni's poison is his self-protective avoidance of love and sex, that Beatrice's poison is in the eye of the
beholder.

Three articles on "The Minister's Black Veil" appeared in 1987.
Drawing on allusions to the veil of Moses and the veil of the taber-
nacle, Judy McCarthy in " 'The Minister's Black Veil': Concealing
Moses and the Holy of Holies" (*SSF* 24:131–38) bases her interpretation on the identification of Hooper with Moses. So, the veiled
minister in one sense represents the "unremitting inflexibility of Old
Testament Law." More important is the veil's identification with
Christ. The community and even the narrator misunderstand that in
veiling his face Hooper unveils his heart.

The title of Thomas Pribek's "The 'Three Parts of the Visible
Circle' and Hooper's Sin" (*NHR* 13,ii:16–18) refers to the domestic
circle which begins with the child entering adulthood, moves to the
young adult taking on the sacrifices demanded by marriage, and ends
with the responsibilities of the elderly parent. Hooper's sin is his
refusal of his place in the "visible circle."

Lea Bertani Vozar Newman's "One-Hundred-and-Fifty Years of Looking At, Into, Through, Behind, Beyond, and Around 'The Minister's Black Veil' " (*NHR* 13,ii:5–12) is a summary of the major critical moments in the history of "The Minister's Black Veil," ending with a brief bibliography. A similar article by Patricia D. Valenti appears in the same journal issue, "Viewing 'The Prophetic Pictures' During its First One Hundred and Fifty Years" (*NHR* 13,ii:13–15).

"The Birthmark," usually one of the most frequently written upon tales, is the subject of only two essays this year. The thesis of Mary E. Rucker's "Science and Art in Hawthorne's 'The Birthmark' " (*NCL* 41: 445–61) is that Hawthorne questions various tenets of the Neoplatonic vision of the artist, praising the "pursuit of illicit beauty even as he notices the price that nature relentlessly exacts." Thomas Pribek in "Hawthorne's Aminadab: Sources and Significance" (*SAR*, pp. 177–86) rejects speculations that the name Aminadab derives from a biblical source or an anagram. Instead, Pribek contends that the name Aminadab was frequently given to a comic character in the popular fiction and drama of Hawthorne's day.

One of the few source studies is Olga Costopoulos-Almon's "A Previously Unnoted Source for Hawthorne's 'Roger Malvern's Burial' " (*N&Q* 34:40). The new source is Tobias Smollett's novel *Ferdinand Count Fathom* wherein an older warrior must remain behind while a younger one, sent to find help, marries the old man's daughter. Hawthorne had read the novel and visited Smollett's tomb.

v. Biographical Materials

"Hawthorne on the Isles of Shoals" (*NHR* 13,i:4–9) by Rita K. Gollin is an account of Hawthorne's two-week vacation in September following the publication of *The Blithedale Romance*. Robert K. Weis's "To Please and Instruct the Children" (*EIHC* 123:120 and 122) makes two mentions of Hawthorne and his family: "Little Annie's Ramble" as an example of the emergence of a child-directed culture and Rose Hawthorne's letter describing her play with dolls.

vi. Hawthorne and Others

In "Shelley and Hawthorne: Unnoticed Influences" (*PAPA* 13:35–43) Patricia R. Robertson posits that Hawthorne's "style of imagery and his sensibility resemble that of Shelley." Tony Tanner's point in

"James on Hawthorne" in *Scenes of Nature*, pp. 64–78, is that despite James's youthful disdain for Hawthorne's provincialism, Hawthorne is frequently on James's mind as a representative of the American artist. In redefining Hawthorne, James defines himself by speculating on the status of America, the psychology of the American, and the American artist.

Grace Jones, "Literary Kinship: Nathaniel Hawthorne, John Fowles, and Their Scarlet Women" (*SAQ* 86:67–78), maintains that Fowles throws the reader off the track of his profound debts to Hawthorne in order to make his own fiction seem more original than it is. Samuel Coale in "Styron's Choice: Hawthorne's Guilt in Poe's Palaces" (*PLL* 23:514–22) contends that the dark night of the soul experienced by Styron's characters is generally not so unrelievedly hopeless as it is in Hawthorne's fiction, that on balance Styron inherits more from Poe than he does from Hawthorne. In Donald J. Greiner's interview with John Updike, "Updike on Hawthorne" (*NHR* 13,i:1–4), Updike's inscrutable and somewhat peevish commentary is interrupted by the clear declaration that Chillingworth is a "very attractive character."

University of Alabama

3. Poe

Benjamin Franklin Fisher IV

The Poe boom mentioned last year has not abated; it has waxed. Increasing numbers of books or parts of books and articles indicate that Poe studies again are flourishing after a temporary hiatus. Heterogeneity also pervades Poe scholarship, with the old and the new well represented. The new, which often does not build upon the old as carefully as it might, reflects that "indifference toward Poe as a figure in his social milieu," as Kent Ljungquist pointed out last year. To what extent such a stance will vitalize or vitiate the study of Poe, however, we can only conjecture. The year's work in Poe scholarship produced many good essays and one outstanding, indispensable book, Dwight Thomas and David K. Jackson's *The Poe Log: A Documentary Record of the Life of Edgar Allan Poe, 1809–1849* (Hall).

i. Textual, Bibliographic, and Attribution Studies

No new primary texts were published during 1987, although some works on textual concerns may assist in evaluating several texts of recent vintage. Liliane Weissberg's "Editing Adventures: Writing the Text of *Julius Rodman* (*MFS* 33:413–30) shows close reading of that curious work, along with equal attentiveness to the version available in Burton Pollin's *Collected Writings of Edgar Allan Poe* (1981). Weissberg's perception that one may easily confuse editors and authors with Rodman raises intriguing questions about literary creativity. As in *Pym*, mirror concepts increase ambiguities in theme and characterization. In "A Poe Trio" (*MissQ* 39[1986]:111–18) I dealt with pluses and minuses in the Library of America Poe volumes (1984) and in *The Unabridged Poe*, ed. Tam Mossman (1983); see *ALS 1983*, p. 50; *1984*, pp. 50–51. Thomas C. Carlson's "Edgar Allan Poe in Romania, 1963–83" (*BB* 44:75–81) reminds us that Poe has been and is well received in foreign countries other than France. Primary and secondary materials are cited. Romanian critics have been interested both in Poe's artistry and his influence on 20th-century modernism.

In an attribution study, Burton R. Pollin's "Poe as Author of the 'Outis' Letter and 'The Bird of the Dream'" (*PoeS* 20:10–15) argues that Poe is Outis and ascribes to Poe both the poem "The Bird of the Dream" and what he calls the "Whittier fragment," seemingly written by Outis. Pollin's identification rests largely on a manuscript note by Poe, which could refer to his acquaintance with John Neal's *Yankee*, a weekly journal, and which, because Poe bracketed Outis with that periodical as he jotted notes for his projected "Living Writers of America," equates one with the other. Outis's misspelling of "Pinkney" as "Pinckney," a repeated fault of Poe's, also, says Pollin, strengthens Poe's candidacy. The "Whittier fragment" is actually a line from Joseph H. Nichols's "The Falls of the Housatonic," a once popular poem dating from 1829. "The Bird of the Dream" may read like parody and on that count be Poesque, but it may be merely another of those sentimental verses of the period. There are other possibilities for an identification, and I have seen in manuscript a forthcoming study of the Outis question by Kent Ljungquist and Buford Jones, which, among other elements in its investigation, identifies Nichols's poem. Thus the jury on this case, for me at least, is still out.

ii. Biography

Without doubt the outstanding contribution to Poe studies in 1987 is *The Poe Log*. Long in the making, this book marshals factual materials that should dispel notions of Poe as odd man out in American literature. What predominates is a personality at times difficult, often harried, and intermittently unstable. The twitty little creep in black, drinking with his left hand, scribbling jingly verse with his right, all the while watched by a raven as candles gutter in a draft, with debauched women languishing nearby, disappears. An ambitious journalist, one clearly aware of and interested in literary currents, with an eye to markets, steps forth instead. *The Poe Log* assembles conveniently a wealth of documentation hitherto known to few and available to still fewer. The book demonstrates the importance of bibliographical work, of commanding a grasp of a writer's milieu, and of employing resources often not glamorous in themselves but indispensable to genuine literary study. Thumbnail sketches of Poe's acquaintances combine with the detailed index to add value. This magisterial work lays groundwork for a solid narrative critical biography of Poe—one, we hope, not far distant. Generous appreciation of what *The Poe Log* affords in the way of unsnarling tangled skeins in Poe's personal and professional life (and they were there) is tendered by James W. Tuttleton in his essay-review, "The Trials of Edgar Allan Poe" (*NewC* Nov.:17–26).

Two more fine factual-biographical studies are W. T. Bandy's "Dr. Moran and the Poe-Reynolds Myth" and John Ward Ostrom's "Poe's Literary Labors and Rewards" (*Myths and Reality* [The Poe Society], respectively pp. 26–36 and pp. 37–47). Dr. John Moran's unreliability concerning Poe's last days lies in mistakenly substituting —until his final account—"Reynolds" for "Herring" (family members) as persons attending the dying man, which blunder has caused a mare's nest. Ostrom centers on Poe's uncertain, but ultimately meager, financial gains from authorship, a subject he had previously addressed (*PoeS* 15[1982]:1–7). Another study of Poe's mind dividing over artistry and financial gain, Bruce I. Weiner's *The Most Noble of Professions: Poe and the Poverty of Authorship* (Enoch Pratt) reveals how Poe's career in writing for periodicals influenced his attitudes toward the literary marketplace. In "Friend and Enemies: Women in the Life of Edgar Allan Poe," Richard P. Benton draws essential biographical information and literary relevancies on this topic into handy scope (*Myths and Reality*, pp. 1–25), and Francis B. Dedmond's "Poe and the Brownings" (*ATQ* n.s. 1:111–22) examines Poe's efforts to cultivate a friendship (through letters) with Elizabeth Barrett before and after her marriage to Robert Browning in order to promote publication of his work in England. Nothing came of it.

Finally, there are two recent books in the Greenwood Press series, Historical Guide to the World's Periodicals and Newspapers. *American Literary Magazines: The Eighteenth and Nineteenth Centuries*, ed. Edward E. Chielens (1986), and *American Humor Magazines and Comic Periodicals*, ed. David E. E. Sloane, will fill gaps left in Frank Luther Mott's volumes on American magazines. Information about Poe's literary campaigns and wars, artistic strategies (his humor in particular), and images of him created by popular periodicals: all these, and much more of importance about him, may be found here, in both the narrative and bibliographical sections.

iii. General Accounts: Books and Parts of Books

Two books grounded in current critical theory provide general estimates of Poe's work. J. Gerald Kennedy's *Poe, Death, and the Life of Writing* (Yale)—in which Lacan, Barthes, Caws, Derrida, and other recent critical voices mingle with those of recognized students of Poe—gives a better understanding of Poe's blending of the natural with the supernatural than many other books. Analyzing Poe's works in contexts of his and his generation's preoccupation with death, Kennedy offers provocative readings. He also treats the letters as creative works, giving a fresh dimension to Poe's habits and views. Poe's concerns with death, and the pronouncement that the death of a beautiful woman constitutes the greatest poetic theme, are commonplaces, but Kennedy bears newly upon them. However, omission of "The Assignation," Poe's first fictional rendition of this theme, is surprising. In addition, Kennedy seems overly preoccupied with death themes, and he slights considerations of Poe as hoaxer—strangely, in light of some of his own earlier work on Poe. Elsewhere he clouds general issues more than he clarifies them; for example, when he discusses theory and improvisation (p. 186). However, his attention to Poe's revisions, notably in "Loss of Breath," adds interest to this book.

A second survey is Joan Dayan's *Fables of Mind: An Inquiry into Poe's Fiction* (Oxford). She probes Poe's repeated unfoldings of conflicts between the knowable and unknowable, between the material and the mind. She emphasizes "convertibility," i.e., how "facts of matter can be turned into suppositions of mind" (p. 9). Poe is, of course, skeptical toward man's abilities to know, and his style heightens the inherent dilemma because of its convolutions, which intensify an "either/or" situation. *Eureka*, tales about women (excluding, however, "The Assignation"), and some early fiction—"Bon-Bon," "Loss of Breath," and "A Dream"—are discussed. "Eleonora" is given especially close, fresh interpretation as a materialist piece. Dayan argues for Poe's affinities with Jonathan Edwards (some may challenge her on this point) and Locke (no new idea but newly assessed). Dayan's Poe is a materialistic genius. Kennedy and Dayan in the main balance recent critical theory with traditional readings. Kennedy evinces a larger grasp of American literary history; Dayan's comparatist knowledge is a strength in her work; both are worth reading.

Leon Chai's Poe in *The Romantic Foundations* is, as I see it, an attempt to update and supplement F. O. Matthiessen's *American Renaissance*. It will elicit mixed reaction from Poe scholars, just as the older book has. Among Chai's eight "governing concepts"—Allegory and Symbolism, Science, the Secularization of Religion, Historical Consciousness, Pantheism, Subjectivity and Objectivity, Poetics, and "The Question of Representation"—we find Emerson, Hawthorne, Melville, and Poe as chief exemplars. Poe is analyzed mainly under the first, second, and fifth designations. Chai's notion that Poe never attained genuine symbolism, being fettered instead by allegory, is questionable. So is his shaky discussion of "Ligeia": has Poe really no "formal ideal of beauty" (p. 27)? The discussion of Poe and pantheism betrays imperfect command of relevant bibliography on that topic, and Chai contradicts his earlier strictures about Poe's being no symbolist (pp. 368, 374). Much better is Chai's treatment of Poe and science, which sees *Eureka* with its mingling of science and poetry as giving a "unifying theoretical explanation of material phenomena"—p. 105. Chai also rightly sees Poe's admiration for Tennyson and Keats (to me a rather neglected figure in the Poe carpet) as signaling a turn from the Romanticism of Wordsworth and Coleridge toward Shelley's aesthetics, which led into Pre-Raphaelitism.

A slighter and more specialized study is Katrina Bachinger's *The Multi-Man Genre and Poe's Byrons* (Salzburg), which argues overzealously for potential Bryonic elements in "Usher," "William Wilson," and *Politian,* a subject she has previously discussed in articles. According to this book, the two tales resolve dilemmas that left *Politian* fragmentary. To draw close parallels between Byron and Poe, Bachinger overlooks many other sources and backgrounds. Poe's sole venture into drama, *Politian,* for example, reflects as much Poe's interest in Elizabethan and Jacobean plays as it does Byron's poetry. Throughout the book Bachinger ignores crucial scholarship by Richard P. Benton, Patrick Quinn, Darrel Abel, G. R. Thompson, and Craig Howes.

In addition to the books just described, Poe was the subject of two volumes of essays and several chapters in books of various sorts. The introductory and concluding essays by Eric W. Carlson, editor of *Critical Essays on Poe* (Hall), survey outlooks on Poe from his own time to the present. Riding a thesis of Poe as Transcendentalist, Carlson minimizes opinions different from his own, chiefly those presenting a comic-ironic Poe. He thereby weakens his essays, despite some useful historical overview. In "Frames of Reference for Poe's Symbolic Language" (pp. 207–17) Carlson contributes several interesting ideas about Poe's creativity, but he becomes overly polemical in trying to hand down the law, so to speak, as regards Poe criticism. He dismisses those who emphasize Poe's Gothicism and aspects in his writings other than Transcendentalist. The comic Poe, however, is still very much with us. Carlson's marshaling of "mainstream" scholars (p. 215) omits such names as Burton R. Pollin, J. Lasley Dameron, J. Gerald Kennedy, David K. Jackson, Richard P. Benton, and Jay B. Hubbell—and the list could be expanded. Other selections in *Critical Essays*, excepting those by Forclaz and Richard, noted below, are reprints. The second collection of essays, *Edgar Allan Poe: The Design of Order*, ed. A. *Robert Lee* (Barnes and Noble), will be treated where appropriate in subsequent sections of this essay.

Outstanding among the chapters on Poe is Ian M. Walker's essay in the revised edition of *The New History of Literature*. It furnishes a no-nonsense account of the life and works. The criticism, tales (grouped variously), *Pym*, *Eureka*, and the verse are treated from a balanced viewpoint—in all, a model introduction to Poe. A brief, but useful, bibliography of primary and secondary works appears (pp. 364–65). Carlson's essay on Poe in *Fifty Southern Writers Before 1900* is similar in tone and outlook to his essays in *Critical Essays*.

iv. Critical Essays

a. General. Two essays from *Edgar Allan Poe* treat Poe's relation to the South and to southern literature: Richard Gray's " 'I Am a Virginian': Edgar Allan Poe and the South" and James H. Justus's "Poe's Comic Vision and Southwestern Humor." Gray sees Poe as the champion of southern literature, finds his aristocratic tone and manner, his concern with the past combined with suspicion of change, racial fears, and his use of intense family relationships all as southern attributes. *Pym* and "Usher" receive most attention; given its incest motif, the latter adumbrates brother-sister feelings in later southern fiction, notably *Absalom, Absalom!* and *Lie Down in Darkness*. Justus's essay, the best in the collection, treats Poe's comedy as neither aberrant within his canon nor some oddity isolating him from other contemporaneous American writers. Southwest humor posits a frontier vision, Poe's is urban, but both deal in violence and savagery just below surfaces of everyday life. Man-as-animal is another shared trait. A problem that bedevils us as much as it did Poe's contemporaries is that his humor asks "readers to imagine more deeply than they were normally willing to do" (p. 86).

Another long view of Poe's literary endeavors is R. D. Gooder's "Edgar Allan Poe: The Meaning of Style" (*CR* 16:110–23), soon to reapper as part of the American literature section in *The New Pelican Guide to English Literature*, ed. Boris Ford. Poe's geography of interior states substitutes for natural landscape, although his obvious refusal to seek in the latter environs signs of humanity's relationship with higher ideality sets him apart from most of his contemporaries. His narrators wander amid "the chaos of possibility," trying to find signs of order. Gooder's disclaimers of Poe's aligning with surrealism seem more logical than a caveat about Gothicism among influences and paradigms. Irrationality permeates Gothic works more firmly than Gooder admits. He does give credit to Poe's comic side, illustrating from "Valdemar," and stating that trickery in the canon is troublesome to pin down.

Edited by James Barbour and Thomas Quirk, the late Leon Howard's "Artificial Sensitivity and Artful Rationality: Basic Elements in the Creative Imagination of Edgar Allan Poe" (*PoeS* 20:1–9) portrays a writer attuned to popular literary currents. His shrewdness crops up repeatedly, from revising "Tamerlane" with a detachment that takes away from "dreamy" Poe, on through *Eureka*, a work manifesting artful control over a sensitivity to the marketplace. Noting Poe's predilections for sensational subject matter, Howard charts the move from Folio-Club parodies toward more subtle horrors. Sensational and ratiocinative tales complement each other.

Two very different but worthwhile articles are John Dean's "Poe and the Popular Culture of His Day" (*JAC* 10:35–40) and Roger Forclaz's "Psychoanalysis and Edgar Allan Poe: A Critique of the Bonaparte Thesis" (*Critical Essays on Poe*, pp. 187–94). Dean finds Poe a thoroughgoing participant in his cultural milieu. Above all else, Poe's renderings of cities, women, and travel spoke to his audiences. Dean's essay suggests additional popular-culture possibilities for the study of Poe. Forclaz's essay is adapted and translated from his earlier article in French (1970). Forclaz reminds us that Poe the person and Poe the writer were often farther apart than many have admitted.

b. Poe as Critic. Two articles dealt with this topic in 1987. Kenneth Alan Hovey's solidly researched and well-written "Critical Provincialism: Poe's Poetic Principle in Antebellum Context" (*AQ* 39:341–54) terms Poe a poet of "temporal pessimism" and contrasts him with Longfellow, the poet of "temporal optimism." Poe's hits at northeastern poets stemmed from his (and other southerners') preference for Byron to Wordsworth, which attitude distanced him from Bryant and his followers. Hovey sees "The Poetic Principle" as much a social as a poetic document. J. Lasley Dameron and Robert D. Jacobs collaborated to write the Poe entry for the *DLB*: 59. Detailing Poe's life and literary career, they succinctly offer pros and cons of his position as a critic. Not so significant as Emerson or James, Poe was, nevertheless, an important influence upon subsequent theories of aesthetics.

c. Poetry. To evaluate Poe's verse, Mutlu Konuk Blasing's *American Poetry* employs a viewpoint based on Lacan and Derrida but demonstrates insufficient knowledge about 19th-century Anglo-American Romantic poetry and Poe's place in it, scant grasp of Poe criticism (specifically what pertains to "The Raven"), and not much else concerning Poe's poems overall. This book does no favors for Poe. Poe's prefiguring of T. S. Eliot, John Berryman, Sylvia Plath, and Robert Lowell is left vague, though the topic is important. Furthermore, folklore and mythology in "The Raven" (which poem gets the lion's share of the analysis) are not the discoveries they seem to be here. Contrary to Blasing's assumption that Poe's sonorous "o" sounds may be explained by current literary theory, they probably stemmed from Poe's love of language and Tennyson's poetry where they abound. Finally, Blasing's idea that Poe alienated himself from history is doubtful inasmuch as Poe was more in than out of tune with his times.

Claude Richard's "The Heart of Poe and the Rhythmics of the Poems" (*Critical Essays on Poe*, pp. 195–206), in far more positive analyses, offers perspectives on how "hypnotic architectures of language" achieve a poetic state wherein "Being is rhythm." David Murray's "'A Strange Sound, as of a Harp-string Broken': The Poetry of Edgar Allan Poe" (*Edgar Allan Poe*, pp. 135–53) challenges notions of Poe as Symbolist, sensibly links him with his Romantic heritage, and, with like acumen, sets forth his use of symbol, allegory, death, along with a reading of "The Sleeper" as a serious poem. Another, equally sensible, approach for comparison is James Lawler's "Daemons of the Intellect: The Symbolists and Poe" (*CritI* 14:95–110). Lawler deftly distinguishes Symbolist views of Poe thus; for Baudelaire Poe was *poète maudit*, for Mallarmé a prosodist, and for Valéry a theoretician. The French connection is also charted by John Weightman (*Edgar Allan Poe*, pp. 202–19). "Poe in France: A Myth Revisited," outlines Poe's fortunes among Baudelaire and others on into this century. Weightman's findings dovetail well with Lawler's, although the latter's work does not extend so far in time as to take note of short-story writers like Michel Tournier or of latter-day French students like Claude Richard.

d. Pym. Poe's one novel is the subject of three critiques this year. A. Robert Lee's " 'Impudent and Ingenious Fiction': *The Narrative of Arthur Gordon Pym*" (*Edgar Allan Poe*, pp. 112–34) treads the familiar ground of Poe's hoaxing while unfolding the double self of Pym, but Lee's attempts to graft recent critical terminology onto previous hypotheses ultimately produce no fresh reading of Poe's novel. Dennis Pahl's "Poe/Script: The Death of the Author in *The Narrative of Arthur Gordon Pym*" (*NOR* 14,iii:51–60) more deftly employs critical theory terminology, particularly from Foucault on authorship, to analyze *Pym* (especially the conclusion) as Poe's subversion of his own self-presence. If the novel is a journey toward origins, an imaginary voyage that leads to Pym's death, then the postscript implies a wish to save the text and to "establish a sense of authority." Richard Kopley continues his studies of Poe's novel in "The 'Very' Profound Under-Current' of *Arthur Gordon Pym*" (*SAR*, pp. 143–75). He demonstrates convincingly how Poe quarried an account of the loss of a vessel, the *Ariel*, in the *Norfolk American Beacon* and the *Norfolk and Portsmouth Herald* in February 1836. Simultaneously, Poe's interests in biblical lore bubbled up in his imagination. Coalescing, these undercurrents produced an allegorical Christ in the eerie white figure who looms in the conclusion to *Pym*. Kopley's interpretation concludes with a spirited defense of multileveled texture and tighter unity in Poe's novel than many others have perceived.

e. Tales. Harold Beaver's "Doodling America: Poe's 'MS Found in a Bottle'" (*Edgar Allan Poe*, pp. 35–48) stands out among the essays in this volume. Though it is a reprint, it never has been reviewed in *ALS*. Beaver's deconstructionist approach suggests how hoaxer Poe manipulates the narrative to subvert imagination. Al-

though demurrals will occur, this article should stimulate further critical discussion. My own study of "The Assignation," "More Pieces
in the Puzzle of 'The Assignation'" (*Myths and Reality*, pp. 59–88),
takes account of Poe's mining popular magazine fiction—specifically
two stories in *Fraser's* and the *New Monthly* (probably via *Godey's*)
—and other pieces that refer to Byron and to *Romeo and Juliet*. Poe
also infuses vitality and subtlety into the feminine portraiture in the
story.

Feminine portraiture is also the subject of Cynthia Jordan's "Poe's
Re-Vision: The Recovery of the Second Story" (*AL* 59:1–19), which
probes Poe's women-centered tales. "Morella," "Ligeia," "Usher,"
and the Dupin stories are the examples for recovering a "second story"
within, i.e., the story of the victimization of women. Jordan's feminist
reading is compelling, although her use of criticism of "Usher" could
cover more ground. Jordan's article would have benefited if she had
included "The Assignation" and "Eleonora" in her study.

Curtis Fukuchi, whose subject is "Repression and Guilt in Poe's
'Morella'" (*SSF* 24:149–54), thinks that the narrator's warped sexuality brings about the death of his daughter when he projects upon
her the traits of her dead mother. James B. Twitchell enhances studies
of Poe's women characters in *Forbidden Partners: The Incest Taboo
in Modern Culture* (Columbia) with an excellent analysis of "The
Spectacles," a neglected tale. The narrator's marriage to his "sister"
is plausibly stated under Twitchell's incest rubric. He notes (p. 206)
that incest in Poe's writings in all likelihood does not stem from
personal circumstances. Twitchell's terse observations about "Usher"
should be read against those of George R. Uba (*SAQ* 85 [1986]:
20–21); see *ALS 1986*, p. 49.

Another book with a chapter on Poe's tales is Terry Heller's
Delights of Terror, which evinces familiarity with recognized theories
and sophistication in citing them to interpret "Usher" as "terror
fantasy." Live burial, the artistic materials related to Roderick, and
the fear of entrapment are assessed in terms of an implied reader.
"Usher" "entraps the real reader in the role of implied reader by
opening rather than closing" in the conclusion. Terror fantasy takes
center stage in the tale, and the normal response by the reader is to
resist. Heller achieves a provocative reevaluation of this warhorse,
which, along with observations about other tales, "Ligeia" and "The
Black Cat," makes this book essential reading.

A viewpoint for comparison with Heller's may be found in S. L.

Varnado's chapter on Poe in *Haunted Presence*, which elaborates on thoughts originally offered in *The Gothic Imagination: Essays in Dark Romanticism*, ed. G. R. Thompson (1974). Poe's preoccupation with the "numinous," or supernaturalism, often seems bizarre as a result of his lacking an orthodox religious faith. Thus he reiterates moments of *fascinans*, or ecstatic experience. Unfortunately, readers often misunderstand Poe's intents, supposing that his presentations of numinousness—most emphatic in the tales—are little other than horror for sensational effects. Varnado illustrates his ideas with "MS. Found" and "A Descent into the Maelstrom" as texts, and in all he brings quickened thought to the subject of Poe's literary morality and intellectuality.

Mark Kincead-Weekes's "Reflections On, and In, 'The Fall of the House of Usher' " (*Edgar Allan Poe*, pp. 17–34) is an unsuccessful effort to explicate the story. It ignores previous scholarship, misquotes Poe, and makes rather commonplace observations. More interesting is Arnold Goldman's "Poe's Stories of Premature Burial" (*Edgar Allan Poe*, pp. 49–65), but the essay is based on no critical theory in its discussions of "Loss of Breath," *Pym*, "Usher," and "The Premature Burial." Goldman, however, has no trouble in confronting a simultaneously serious and comic Poe.

A fresh approach to Poe marks Daniel Kempton's "The Gold/Goole/Ghoul Bug" (*ESQ* 33:1–19). "The Gold-Bug" exemplifies a self-reflexive investigation of its own language and, to paraphrase Kempton, the "general universe of signs." Sophisticated wordplay functions to make us think of Legrand ultimately as a ghoul or grave robber, who plunders verbal as well as monetary treasure. Old Jupiter's speeches are credited with being far above mere dialect high jinks. With semiotic help, we are led into the verbal intricacies of this tale of ratiocination, with stimulating asides regarding the others. Syndy M. Conger's more traditional, but no less valuable, "Another Secret to the Rue Morgue: Poe's Transformation of the *Geisterseher* Motif" (*SSF* 24:9–14) notes likenesses between Dupin and Schiller's renowned Armenian. Both make comprehensible the seemingly implausible, can penetrate criminal minds, and are awesome, eccentric personages. The era from 1780 into the 1840s demonstrates bonds between early Gothic works and detective fiction. Dupin's powers betray "a special madness very much akin to that of criminals" (p. 14).

Another encounter with the Dupin tales, which perceives the

sleuth's successes as stemming from his peculiarly American quality
of trying the new, is Robert Giddings's "Was the Chevalier Left-
handed? Poe's Dupin Stories," another high point in *Edgar Allan Poe*
(pp. 88–111). Interestingly, Giddings suggests that impacts of print
upon literacy determine effects upon audiences within these tales
and without. The essay reveals knowledge of the secondary bibliography on the ratiocinative tales, and altogether this is, like the
Justus analysis, one not to be missed. E. Kate Stewart's "An Early
Imitative Ape: A Possible Source for 'The Murders in the Rue
Morgue'" (*PoeS* 20:24) posits a jestbook, *The Mirror of Mirth* (1583),
as a plausible origin for Poe's orangutan. Stewart's "The Supreme
Madness: Revenge and the Bells in 'The Cask of Amontillado'"
(*UMSE* 5:51–57) just as convincingly demonstrates affinities that
bracket character, setting, and dramatic method in another tale with
legacies from Elizabethan revenge tragedy. Long ago Killis Campbell
suggested that Poe's debts to Renaissance drama (excluding Shakespeare's plays) were rather slight, but this study may open the way
for rethinking that connection.

Additional worthwhile commentary on "Cask" may be found in
Thomas Pribek's "The Serpent and the Heel" and E. Bruce Kirkham's "Poe's 'Cask of Amontillado' and John Montresor" (*PoeS*
20: respectively 22–23, 23). Pribek argues that Montresor's control
of the situation slips and that he becomes as much victim of revenge,
if an unwitting one—his "Achilles heel" being crushed—as he has
made Fortunato (the titular "Serpent"). Scoundrelly Captain John
Montresor, a British officer during the American Revolution, who
may have figured into the creation of Susanna H. Rowson's Mon-
traville in *Charlotte Temple*, is, according to Kirkham, a prototype
for Poe's fiendish protagonist. Elsewhere, Kirkham shows how "Cask"
features wordplay on the Italian noun "ammontare," meaning sum
or amount. Fortunato's accounts with Montresor are paid as the last
block is placed—"Poe's Amontillado One More Time" (*AN&Q*
24[1986]:144–45).

v. Influences Upon Others

Debts to Poe by later writers constantly rise to the surface. The
concluding essay in Burton R. Pollin's *Insights and Outlooks* (Gordian [1986], pp. 222–34), "Thomas Mann and Poe: Two Houses
Linked," gives us another of those source studies characteristic of its

author (the remaining essays on Poe in this book are reprints.) Showing Mann's undeniable familiarity with Poe's works, Pollin demonstrates bonds between "Usher" and *Buddenbrooks* and between "The Masque of the Red Death" and *Death in Venice*. Several lesser links between Poe's fiction, chiefly "Usher," and several of Mann's shorter stories are noted. Another who returned to Poe more than once for inspiration is studied in Catherine Rainwater's "H. G. Wells's Re-Vision of Poe: *The Undying Fire* and *Mr. Blettsworthy on Rampole Island*" (*ELT* 30:423–36). The "re-vision" is Wells's transformations in his two novels of Poe's cosmological systems— principally that in *Pym*—as well as psychology and symbols into his own literary vision. "MS. Found," "Ligeia," and "Usher" also provide sources for Wells. In Poe, language must be transcended to achieve the ideal, while in Wells language is often the means of freeing and expediting one toward that region. Rainwater extends her previous work on Poe's influence on the Edwardian's early writings (*ELT* 26[1983]:35–51); the Wells novels in her present study date respectively from 1919 and 1928. Another literary descent from Poe, to an American writer of crime fiction, is noted in my *Frederick Irving Anderson (1877–1947): A Biobibliography* (Brownstone/ Borgo). Anderson alluded to Poe and less obtrusively borrowed from him (pp. 3–9, 15, 24, 33, 37, 38). Moving up chronologically, we arrive at Wayne Pounds's "Paul Bowles and Edgar Allan Poe: The Disintegration of the Personality" (*TCL* 32[1986]:424–39). Bowles acknowledged that he owed much to Poe, and Pounds detects that influence most clearly in early Bowles fiction: the novels, *The Sheltering Sky* (1949) and *Let It Come Down* (1952); and two collections of stories, *The Delicate Prey* (1950) and *The Time of Friendship* (1967). No simple paralleling can adequately body forth this relationship, which is sharing of sensibility. *Pym* supplies a sturdy link, as do several of Poe's tales. Disintegrating personalities, harmful family situations, multiple crimes, and distorted sexual impulses are common grounds for these two authors. Finally, Adeline R. Tintner's "Edgar Allan Poe's Influence on Henry James" (*ABBW* 12 Jan.: 105–09) centers on the influence of "Usher" upon "The Jolly Corner" in terms of theme, character, color, and verbal nuances.

University of Mississippi

4. Melville

Brian Higgins

The latest volume of the Northwestern-Newberry edition, volume two of the secondary bibliography, a volume devoted to Melville's sources, a new guide to Melville dissertations, and both a book-length study of *The Confidence-Man* and a concordance to it appeared in 1987. As in 1986, more articles were published on *Moby-Dick* than on any of Melville's other works.

i. Editions

Undoubtedly the most significant event in Melville scholarship in 1987 was the publication of the long-awaited volume 9 of the North-western-Newberry edition, *The Piazza Tales and Other Prose Pieces, 1839–1860,* ed. Harrison Hayford, Alma A. MacDougall, G. Thomas Tanselle, and others. The volume brings together all of Melville's shorter prose pieces from 1839–60 that are known to survive, beginning with *The Piazza Tales* and continuing with the uncollected pieces arranged chronologically, including texts of Melville's unpublished lectures reconstructed by Merton M. Sealts, Jr. A final section prints several pieces that have been attributed with some plausibility to Melville. For *The Piazza Tales* the versions of the stories published in *Putnam's Monthly* served as copy-text; the texts here are thus different in places in wording, spelling, and punctuation from those in *The Piazza Tales* volume of 1856 and 20th-century printings of the stories that are based on it. (See, for example, at pp. 554 and 579 the discussions of Mr. and Mrs. Cutlets, names present in the *Putnam's* text of "Bartleby" but missing from *The Piazza Tales.*) In the "Editorial Appendix" the "Historical Note," by Sealts, gives accounts of the circumstances in which the pieces were composed, their publication arrangements and contemporary reception, and their thematic and stylistic links with Melville's other works. A previously published section of the note on the chronology of the short fiction (*ALS 1980*, p. 65) is updated. The "Notes on Individual Prose Pieces," by the editors, include discussions of possible sources for the pieces in Melville's experience and possible literary sources. The appendix also reproduces leaves from Melville's surviving manuscripts, Elizabeth Melville's lists of Melville's stories published in *Putnam's* and *Harper's* (the "most authoritative contemporary listing"), Melville's notebook of lecture engagements, and chapter 18 of the first edition of Amasa Delano's *A Narrative of Voyages and Travels*, Melville's source for "Benito Cereno."

In addition to the items listed in its title, William D. Richardson's *Melville's 'Benito Cereno': An Interpretation with Annotated Text and Concordance* (Carolina), apparently designed for high school and undergraduate use, reprints the same chapter from Delano's *Narrative* and includes a list of variants between the *Putnam's* and *Piazza Tales* versions of the tale (the text follows the latter, with corrections of obvious errors), and a secondary bibliography.

ii. Bibliographies, Checklists, Concordances

Mary K. Bercaw's *Melville's Sources* (Northwestern) is a major contribution to Melville scholarship. A complementary volume to Sealts's *Melville's Reading* (which lists the books Melville owned and borrowed), Bercaw's lists the sources Melville is known or thought to have actually used in his writing. Her "Checklist of Melville's Sources," which includes all the works (in alphabetical order by author) anyone has claimed Melville used as sources, is cross-referenced to a "List of Scholarship," presented in chronological order "to make readily apparent when Melville's reading of each work was first suggested." An "Index of Scholars" completes the volume. Bercaw's excellent introduction provides an authoritative history of Melville source study, an account of the various ways Melville acquired and used his sources, and suggestions for future research.

The second volume of my own annotated secondary bibliography, *Herman Melville: A Reference Guide, 1931–1960* (Hall), annotates all the known commentary on Melville published in English during the period 1931–60. The introduction surveys the progress of Melville scholarship during those three decades.

Herman Melville: Research Opportunities and Dissertation Ab-

stracts, ed. Tetsumaro Hayashi (McFarland), reprints with minor revisions all the available dissertation abstracts on Melville through 1984 from *Dissertation Abstracts International* and so provides a fuller sense of most dissertations than John Bryant's recent *Melville Dissertations, 1924–1980* (see *ALS 1983*, p. 62). The volume includes an essay by Gary Phillips, "Herman Melville: Research Opportunities" (not always accurate in names and dates), which surveys the topics that the dissertations cover (noting their frequent repetitiveness) and suggests a few potentially rewarding areas of enquiry.

A *Concordance to Herman Melville's* The Confidence-Man: His Masquerade (keyed to the Northwestern-Newberry edition), ed. Larry Edward Wegener (Garland), should prove invaluable for study of certain aspects of *The Confidence-Man*. Like Wegener's concordance to *Pierre*, however (*ALS 1985*, p. 57), the volume would have been better if it had been presented solely as a reference work, without the editor's "Critical Introduction," which attempts to show what the concordance "establishes" about the meaning of the text. According to Wegener, the concordance "demonstrates Melville's satirical criticism of reason in favor of instinct/emotion by proving a strong separation of reason and emotion on the level of image patterns and character identification," yet it clearly shows "the identification or unification of these same elements." Too often Wegener's discussion of those "image patterns" lacks close attention to the context in which particular words and phrases occur. (It also manages to confuse Charlie Noble with the Missouri bachelor.)

iii. Biography

No major contributions to biographical study appeared in 1987, though Merton M. Sealts, Jr.'s "The Melvill Heritage" (*HLB* 34[1986]: 337–61) is potentially valuable to future biographers. It includes a genealogical table of the Melvill family constructed by Jean Melvill and Melville J. Boucher—"the most complete and accurate depiction of five generations of Melvills and Melvilles that has yet been published"—and reproduces Melvill family photographs from an album recently presented, with other memorabilia, to the Houghton Library by descendants of Thomas Melvill, Jr. Sealts's "Thomas Melvill, Jr., in *The History of Pittsfield*" (*HLB* 35:201–17) includes a brief sketch of Thomas Melvill's life by his widow, the full text of Melville's account of Thomas, published in shortened form in J. E. A. Smith's

History of Pittsfield, 1800–1876, and a brief commentary by Sealts on characteristics Melville shared with his uncle.

Howard C. Horsford's aim in "Melville and the London Street Scene" (*EAS* 16:23–35) is to provide part of a "denser context" for Melville's London journal entries of 1849. With the aid of mid-19th-century accounts of the city, Horsford finds that the areas Melville "seems to have sought out were commonly the most desperate, the vilest and most degraded." Horsford speculates that his "searching out of London's lower life had as a more or less vague purpose the development of a background sense for the contemplated *Israel Potter*." Beyond that, Horsford finds "an unstated dimension" to Melville's "persistent wandering about London streets, day and night," about which he reaches only the tentative conclusion that "it may add a further depth to our understanding of the range" of Melville's intellectual concerns and humane sympathies.

Philip Young's "Small World: Emerson, Longfellow, and Melville's Secret Sister" (*NEQ* 60:382–402) provides further details of the life of Ann Middleton Allen, thought to be Allan Melvill's illegitimate daughter (see *ALS 1985*, p. 59), and tells the story of how she crossed paths with both Emerson and Longfellow. Young sheds no light on Melville's knowledge of "A.M.A.," though he speculates that Melville learned of her from his uncle Thomas at Pittsfield in August or the fall of 1838 (mistakenly asserting that Pierre is told of Isabel at the age of 19 by his Aunt Dorothea).

Thomas Pribek's " 'The Man Who Lived Among the Cannibals': Melville in Milwaukee" (*TWA* 74:19–26) tells us something of the nature and expectations of the audience at Melville's lecture on 25 February 1859 at Milwaukee but otherwise adds little to Sealts's account in *Melville As Lecturer*.

iv. General

Richard H. Brodhead's chapter on "Hawthorne, Melville, and the Fiction of Prophecy" in *The School of Hawthorne* (Oxford, 1986, pp. 17–47) makes an important contribution to our understanding of Hawthorne's influence on Melville and the relationship between the two men. Brodhead argues cogently that Melville "seized Hawthorne as a figure of literary possibility": to Melville the older man "incarnated, and so showed the living, present possibility of, literary power prophetically imagined." What structured their relationship, in Brodhead's view, "was the concept of the real possibility of the prophetical artistic career." Hawthorne "drew Melville to him because he seemed seriously to allow what Melville was most ambitious to do. He seemed to license Melville to speak and write as he felt compelled to." Hawthorne's most decisive influence was thus on Melville's "plan of authorship," Brodhead argues, though he goes on to interpret Ahab as a literary descendant of Hawthorne's "self-fracturing or self-fractioning" characters. In the remainder of the chapter Brodhead argues that Melville also "experienced the later abortion of his prophetical career through Hawthorne's eyes" (as his portrayal of Plotinus Plinlimmon in *Pierre* suggests), and then in the stories and *The Confidence-Man* took further guidance from Hawthorne "even in learning how to move away from him." Students of Melville's life may find that Brodhead overstates the case for Hawthorne's influence in places (as when he claims that Melville constructed a *new* plan of authorship on the basis of Hawthorne's example, or when he portrays Melville as in a state of vocational confusion and "anxiety-fraught suspension of purpose" at the time of their meeting). Melville, moreover, undoubtedly brought all kinds of personal needs to bear on Hawthorne, as Brodhead acknowledges; but Brodhead makes a strong case that for Melville the strongest element in Hawthorne's appeal (in his person and his books) lay in the older man's validation of his own literary-prophetic aspirations.

Harrison Hayford's valuable essay on "Melville's German Streak" in *A Conversation in the Life of Leland R. Phelps. America and Germany: Literature, Art, and Music*, ed. Frank L. Borchardt and Marion C. Salinger (Duke Center for International Studies), draws attention to the dearth of scholarship on Melville's whole relation to German culture and specifies in particular the need for "renewed scholarly consideration of Goethe's *Faust* as both a major source and an illuminating analogue" for *Moby-Dick*, illustrating the kind of "grubbing old fashioned research" Hayford has in mind. In the process Hayford refutes part of James McIntosh's "Melville's Copy of Goethe's Autobiography and Travels" (*ALS 1984*, pp. 68–69) and identifies the translation of Eckermann's Goethe conversations Melville used (Margaret Fuller's), a translation that does not contain some of the passages scholars have cited as sources for *Moby-Dick*.

v. Early Works

As in 1986, little was published in 1987 on the works before *Moby-Dick.* In " 'Portentous Somethings': Melville's *Typee* and the Language of Captivity" (*NEQ* 60:549–67) Michael C. Berthold attempts to show that Tommo's discussion of captivity and freedom is "full of contradictions and hesitancies" and that Melville "critiques" many of the presumptions of his desire for freedom as well as his "dependence on fixed and disjunctive categories." The parallels Carol Moses cites in "Typee and Spenser's Bower of Bliss" (*ELN* 25, i:60–65) are not sufficiently close to support her claim that Melville "uses Spenserian allusion to suggest that Tommo has stumbled into a Bower of Bliss, although he is too naive initially to realize the spiritual perils he faces." G. Thomas Tanselle's "A Sample Bibliographical Description with Commentary" (*SB* 40:1–20) presents a bibliographical description of *Redburn,* which Tanselle sees as primarily a sample of descriptive techniques rather than a contribution to Melville studies, though it does include some previously unpublished information.

vi. Moby-Dick

The year's most substantial work on *Moby-Dick* is Leon Howard's *The Unfolding of* Moby-Dick: *Essays in Evidence (a fragment),* ed. James Barbour and Thomas Quirk (The Melville Society), in which Howard pushes further the investigations into the genesis of *Moby-Dick* he began in 1938 and subsequently recorded in his 1940 essay "Melville's Struggle with the Angel," his 1951 biography of Melville, and later essays. As Harrison Hayford observes in the "Historical Note" of the Northwestern-Newberry edition of *Moby-Dick* (forthcoming, 1988), this new and only partly written formulation of the composition of *Moby-Dick,* which accepts James Barbour's theory that the book was written in three major phases and not the two Howard originally proposed (see *ALS 1975,* p. 72), is marred by Howard's speculation that Melville gained access to Coleridge's lecture on *Hamlet* at the Boston Athenaeum on 30 December 1850. (The Augusta Melville papers show that Melville did not visit Boston that December, though his wife and son were there.) The pamphlet is valuable, nonetheless, for its account of Carlyle's influence on *Moby-Dick* and for its sustained investigation into which chapters are derived from Melville's various whaling sources. Not the least of the pamphlet's attractions is Thomas Quirk's engaging memoir of Howard himself.

In a more narrowly focused essay Jack Scherting considers the impact of Melville's reading of *The Oregon Trail* on the composition of *Moby-Dick*, adding to earlier discussions of its influence the plausible suggestion that Parkman's narrative prompted Melville's recurrent sea/prairie imagery. ("Tracking the *Pequod* Along *The Oregon Trail*: The Influence of Parkman's Narrative on Imagery and Characters in *Moby-Dick*," *WAL* 22:3–15.) Less convincingly, he argues that Parkman influenced the central episode in "The Castaway." Melville's use of other works is treated by Kris Lackey in " 'More Spiritual Terrors': The Bible and Gothic Imagination in *Moby-Dick*" (*SoAR* 52:37–50), which examines "the dynamics of biblical-Gothic intertextuality" in *Moby-Dick* "to find out how such a conjunction provided Melville a medium by which he could reinforce the 'spiritual terrors' pervading his narrative." Lackey argues that Melville "fused the popular texts of Gothic romance and holy writ, not only to touch his readers nearer the source of their own (perhaps repressed or vestigial) spiritual fears, but as well to move nearer one another the world of nature and the universe of shifting powers that seem to batter it."

In the wake of Robert K. Wallace's recent examination of J. M. W. Turner's influence on Melville (*ALS 1985*, pp. 59–60), Glen A. Mazis's " 'Modern Depths,' Painting, and the Novel: Turner, Melville, and the Interstices" (*Soundings* 70:121–44) explores the affinities between the two. According to Mazis, Turner in his paintings and Melville in *Moby-Dick* "combined, juxtaposed and sometimes placed in opposition elements, styles, and genres that had been distinct"; taking on in this way "the well constructed worlds of form of their respective media," they "created a rupture, an opening, which allowed a new kind of depth to emerge." "Depth" here is to be understood as "the envelopment of parts by other parts in the creation of a gestalt, whose very oppositions and differences in playing off one another define its unity." Turner and Melville are further linked, in Mazis's view, by their "insistence on the return to the bodily, the sensual, the perceptual, as the primary mode of understanding."

Underlying *Moby-Dick*, in Michael Boughn's view, is Melville's vision of "the usurpation of the world by the anti-erotic, patriarchal imagination," the oppression of the "feminine" by the "masculine"

("Eros and Identity in *Moby-Dick*," *ATQ* n.s. 1:179–96). The book is organized around two modes of being, Boughn claims, "Eros and Anteros, release and constraint," with the "affirmation of Eros" emerging "as an issue in every level of the writing, from diction and tone, to plot, to narrative technique and overall structure." Boughn dismisses too easily the work of scholars who have discovered in the book's discontinuities evidence of its fragmented compositional process, preferring instead to celebrate discontinuity as part of "the fluid, anti-patriarchal structure of the narrative, and the erotic, playful inclusiveness of the novel's overall form," but he writes perceptively in places, particularly on "The Symphony."

There is no hint of the book's playfulness in Wai-chee Dimock's "Melville's Empire" (*Raritan* 7:93–112), which treats, among other things, "authorial sovereignty, both as Melville imagines it and as he enforces it" in *Moby-Dick*—enforces it through the doom he inflicts on Ahab. In Dimock's complex argument, which touches on various facets of antebellum American thought, Ahab shares with Indians a predestined narrative of extinction: like the "doomed savage" in the eyes of antebellum whites, Ahab is his own victim and fate. Melville's strategies of authorial sovereignty, Dimock argues, "replicate exactly the imperialist strategies of Manifest Destiny": the "logic of literary autonomy is ultimately no different from the logic of blaming the victim." It never becomes altogether clear from any of this exactly how Melville does imagine authorial sovereignty.

Thomas F. Berninghausen provides the year's inevitable article on authority in *Moby-Dick*, finding the relationship between writing and authority to be characterized by the legalistic distinction between "Fast Fish" and "Loose Fish" ("Writing on the Body: The Figure of Authority in *Moby-Dick*," *NOR* 14, iii:5–12). In this discussion a waif is referred to as "the primal writing implement in the whaling industry" and a harpoon as an instrument "intended to inscribe the usual relation of Man/Whale"; Moby Dick's dismemberment of Ahab is said to be "one of the two acts of writing which engender Ahab's quest"; Ahab's story is described as "his attempt to invert the arrow [of authority] or pen and to write on those who have written on him" and his attack on Moby Dick as "his ultimate act of penmanship." The value of translating *Moby-Dick* into those terms is not explained.

Another article which, like Boughn's, insists that we simply need to read *Moby-Dick* the right way to explain and justify its incon-

sistencies is Susan VanZanten Gallagher's "The Prophetic Narrator of
Moby-Dick," *C&L* 36, iii:11–25). According to Gallagher, its "nar-
rational mayhem" can be attributed to Ishmael's role as a "prophetic"
narrator: the book "shows Ishmael's education as a prophet and
manifests the result of that education in his narrative"; his "frenzied
tone, occasionally omniscient viewpoint, and oddities of narration are
prophetic traits, not artistic lapses on Melville's part." Manfred Pütz
offers another specialized view of Ishmael in "The Narrator as
Audience: Ishmael as Reader and Critic in *Moby-Dick*" (*SNNTS*
19:160–74), which focuses on Ishmael as a reader of books and
viewer of pictures and sees him as "a personified audience figure"
who functions "as an interpretative model for the reading of the
story he himself narrates" and, in his "predominantly object-oriented
criticism of literature and art," a "writer model."

Treating a broader range of characters than the year's other
articles, Paul McCarthy's "Forms of Insanity and Insane Characters
in *Moby-Dick*" (*CLQ* 23:39–51) discusses examples of "moral insanity" and monomania in *Moby-Dick*, indulging in a good deal of
speculation about what characters did or were like before the action
of the book takes place. As in his related essay on Melville's treatment
of insane characters in the earlier works (*ALS 1984*, p. 71), Mc-
Carthy finds that Melville's knowledge of abnormal psychology,
whatever its sources, "appears to be abreast and in some respects
ahead of scientific knowledge" of his day.

Two essays deal with different aspects of the book's structure.
John G. Blair's "*Multum in parvo: Moby-Dick*, the Swiss Army Knife,
and the Poetics of Infinity" in *The Structure of Texts* (*SPELL* 3), ed.
Udo Fries (Narr), pp. 209–20, finds in Ishmael's cetology a "structural pattern of an openended sequence of alternatives," the alternatives being "the variety of tools ["codes, philosophies, myths, epis-
temic strategies"] wherewith human beings have sought to carve out
useful knowledge, whether about whales or anything else." According to Blair, once Ishmael realizes "there is no point in pursuing
any more tools for knowledge, the Ahab story itself serves as a
means for Ishmael-narrator to escape from infinite regress"; the book
can end "because narrative has provided a refuge from intermina-
bility." Gordon Poole's "The Narrative Structure of 'Moby-Dick'"
(*Anglistica* 27 [1984]:89–103), which attempts to demonstrate the
existence of "a classical narrative pattern" in *Moby-Dick* without
ever defining the term, has an interesting "table of narrative cor-

respondences" involving lowerings for whales and ship meetings.

Students of Melville's prose style will need to consult Gail Coffler's "*Moby Dick*: Classicism in Melville's Style" (*EAS* 16:73–84), which illustrates rhetorical patterns in *Moby-Dick* that show "a clear understanding of classic principles as well as intuitive mastery of those principles." Jeanetta Boswell's "Plant Imagery in *Moby-Dick*: Metaphor for the Unknown" (*UFor* 41:3–8) merely lists the "images of plants and earth scenes" used throughout the book, according to Boswell, as metaphors for the unknown.

vii. Pierre

Only two essays in 1987 were devoted wholly to *Pierre*. James C. Wilson's "The Sentimental Education of Pierre Glendinning: An Exploration of the Causes and Implications of Violence in Melville's *Pierre*" (*ATQ* n.s. 1:167–77) argues that Pierre's violence is the end result of his sentimental education and that Pierre is "a victim of his society and its socially-transmitted illusions of romance and heroism," but the essay offers little more than an extended summary of the book that does not always manage to distinguish correctly between Pierre's thoughts and the narrator's. A more rewarding essay is Philip J. Egan's "Isabel's Story: The Voice of the Dark Woman in Melville's *Pierre*" (*ATQ* n.s. 1:99–110). Egan does not altogether substantiate his grandiose claim that, properly considered, Isabel's story "is nothing less than a manifesto of the Romantic artist-philosopher, complete with an implied philosophy of language," but the essay is welcome for its sustained attention to a part of *Pierre* that has never been fully examined. Curtis Dahl in "The Architecture of Society and the Architecture of the Soul: Hawthorne's *The House of the Seven Gables* and Melville's *Pierre*" (*UMSE* 5:1–22) argues that the primary function of the buildings in *Pierre* and "I and My Chimney" is to represent the characters' inner states or psyches.

viii. Stories and Israel Potter

Among the stories "Bartleby" again attracted the most attention. In "The Empire of Agoraphobia" (*Representations* 20:134–57), the year's most original reading of the story, Gillian Brown draws on 19th-century medical theories and case histories of agoraphobia and sees in Bartleby's "arrested motion" the 19th-century American "iconography of stillness," which features invalidism, woman, and home "as predominant figures of restfulness." After exploring the complex relationship between "Bartleby" and Charlotte Perkins Gilman's "The Yellow Wallpaper," Brown goes on to argue that in his "agoraphobic responses" Bartleby "follows female agoraphobic modes of evading domestic consumerism and repudiating intercourse between private and public realms," ultimately perfecting his agoraphobia in "anorexia," which "secures the agoraphobic division of self from world, home from market."

Maryhelen C. Harmon's "Melville's 'Borrowed Personage': Bartleby and Thomas Chatterton" (*ESQ* 33:35–44) in places strains too hard to establish connections, but cites a number of parallels which suggest that in Bartleby Melville incorporated details from Chatterton's life and character, as depicted by C. B. Wilcox, the editor of the two-volume edition of Chatterton's works he owned and annotated.

Other essays were less rewarding, though William Aarnes's "Qualms: 'Bartleby' and the Death of Scholarly Interpretation" (*FurmS* 32:1–16) expresses sensible reservations about a number of scholarly approaches to "Bartleby" (and other literary works). Carl Schaffer's mainly derivative "Unadmitted Impediments, Unmarriageable Minds: Melville's 'Bartleby' and 'I and My Chimney'" (*SSF* 24:93–101) points out a number of similarities between the two stories, particularly in the narrators and their "doubles." Graham Nicol Forst in "Up Wall Street Towards Broadway: The Narrator's Pilgrimage in Melville's 'Bartleby the Scrivener'" (*SSF* 24:263–70) argues unconvincingly that the role of the narrator is similar to that of Nicodemus in the Gospel of John; according to Forst, the lawyer gradually "begins to die, painfully, to the world" during the story, and the "sequel" confirms "how profound and lasting and morally chastening was Bartleby's effect" on him. Dennis R. Perry's Freudian reading ("'Ah, humanity!': Compulsion Neuroses in Melville's 'Bartleby,'" *SSF* 24:407–15) finds in the tale a structure "based on a continuum of the ego defenses each character erects against its compulsions and obsessions"; according to Perry, the tale documents the way the various characters "ultimately fail to wall out the natural impulses of the id with the artificial social conventions erected by the ego."

Two essays treated groups of similar characters in the stories. Paul McCarthy's pedestrian "Rascally Characters in Melville's Stories" (*NDQ* 53:76–86) identifies economic rascals, religious rascals, "artistic or creatively inclined rascals," and rascals who are adventurers and outcasts from society, illuminating neither the characters nor Melville's concept of rascality. Robert Scott Kellner claims that Melville's stories give "one of the most consistently negative portrayals of women in American literature," women being presented as "either slaves or shrews" ("Slaves and Shrews: Women in Melville's Short Stories," *UMSE* 5:297–310). The "slaves" are the women in "The Tartarus of Maids," Hunilla in "The Encantadas," and Marianna in "The Piazza," all "passive to the extent of being suicidal," while the wife in "I and My Chimney" is "the non-passive woman," the shrew. Kellner does not discuss the women in "The Apple-Tree Table."

Herman Melville's Billy Budd, "Benito Cereno," "Bartleby the Scrivener," and Other Tales, ed. Harold Bloom (Chelsea House) collects previously published essays.

George Dekker's commentaries on *Israel Potter* and "Benito Cereno" in *The American Historical Romance* (Cambridge), pp. 186–208, are mostly routine and shed little light on their relation to the historical romance tradition. Dekker is somewhat more rewarding in his discussion of the narrator of *Billy Budd* (see section x below). Brian Rosenberg in *"Israel Potter:* Melville's Anti-History" (*SAF* 15:175–86) points out interesting similarities and differences between *Israel Potter* and works of historical fiction or "imaginative history" by a number of British authors, including Scott, Carlyle, Ruskin, Dickens, and Thackeray, without managing to demonstrate convincingly that Melville was rebelling against "the confident, largely conservative beliefs of British historical literature" and parodying its traditions.

ix. The Confidence-Man

Holding that Melville's deepest concern during the 1850s was "his relationship to and perceptions of the antislavery movement," Helen P. Trimpi in *Melville's Confidence Men and American Politics in the 1850s* (Archon) sees *The Confidence-Man* as "a pasquinade—a political comedy—analogous to topical stage comedy and to graphic political prints of the period." A satirical commentary on political exploitation of the issue of black slavery, the book satirizes, she claims, "politicians, publicists, and preachers on both sides of the sectional controversy," while the deeper concern Melville addresses is the philosophical question of the trustworthiness of mankind to govern itself in a just manner. Scholars have previously identified, with varying degrees of plausibility, a number of public figures among the passengers aboard the *Fidèle* (see the Northwestern-Newberry edition, pp. 289–92); Trimpi proposes here that Melville was "satirizing more than thirty of his prominent contemporaries." Trimpi is more successful in showing the book's similarities with the traditions of English pantomime and European commedia dell'arte than with American political prints of the period. The links she tries to establish between the book's characters and contemporary political figures generally seem tenuous at best. The kind of difficulty she frequently finds herself in and the kind of solution she too often adopts can be illustrated by her identification of the deaf-mute of chapter 1 with Benjamin Lundy, the Quaker antislavery advocate, and the wooden-legged man of chapter 3 with James Gordon Bennett, the founder and editor of the New York *Herald*. "Although partially and increasingly deaf, Lundy was not mute," Trimpi is forced to concede: "he lectured on his travels. Yet he never enjoyed making speeches. . . . He made his mark through the written word, as the Deaf-Mute does with the writing on his slate." Bennett similarly had no wooden leg, Trimpi is obliged to admit, and so "this deformity" of Melville's character "must be taken as a graphic metaphor for his political liability of foreign birth and his habit of 'stumping' for political causes through editorializing." Trimpi's attempts to link events in the book to particulars in the political careers of the figures she identifies seem for the most part equally arbitrary.

Brook Thomas's *Cross-Examinations* reworks Thomas's earlier essay on "Bartleby," "Benito Cereno," and *Billy Budd* (see *ALS 1984*, pp. 75, 78, 81–82) and adds new essays on *The Confidence-Man* and *Billy Budd*. In "Contracts and Confidence Men" (pp. 183–98) Thomas sees *The Confidence-Man* as one of Melville's "most extensive meditations on the role alloted a writer in the market economy," a work that like "Bartleby" "comments on the craft of writing at the same time that it documents how the legal system was bound to the market economy and how questions of justice are circumscribed by contract ideology." Melville's reflection on his role as artist and the nature of fiction, Thomas argues, "is in part a response to his failure in the marketplace, which in turn is in part the result of his desire to expose the counterfeit claims of America's

republican rhetoric, a rhetoric most obviously exposed in the false
promise of its legal system to provide justice for all." Also concerned
with *The Confidence-Man* and the marketplace, Jean-Christophe
Agnew in *Worlds Apart: The Market and the Theater in Anglo-
American Thought, 1550–1750* (Cambridge, 1986), pp. 195–203,
finds that the book "deploys the ambiguities and contradictions of
market exchange to deconstruct Common Sense, the conventional
novel, and, in the end, Melville's own relation to his reader."

John Bryant in "Citizens of a World to Come: Melville and the
Millenial Cosmopolite" (*AL* 59:20–36) relates the Cosmopolitan to
"various religionists, generally of an anti-Calvinist persuasion" who
up through the 1850s "identified themselves as citizens of the world
or cosmopolites" and in particular to the itinerant preacher Lorenzo
Dow, popularly known as "the eccentric Cosmopolite." Linking Melville's Cosmopolitan with Dow, Bryant argues, are "the notion of the
cosmopolitan as a 'stranger,' the cosmopolitan's resemblance to a
confidence man or, more aptly, a trickster for God," and millenialism.
The extent of Melville's knowledge of Dow remains uncertain, and
the parallels between Dow and the Cosmopolitan are not sufficiently
close to prove indisputable influence; yet Bryant gives grounds
for thinking that Melville probably knew of Dow from his adolescence and that Dow possibly played a part in his formulation of
the Cosmopolitan.

x. Poetry and *Billy Budd, Sailor*

Catherine Georgoudaki's "*Battle-Pieces and Aspects of the War*:
Melville's Poetic Quest for Meaning and Form in a Fallen World"
(*ATQ* n.s. 1:21–32) addresses a potentially rewarding topic: "the
artistic transformation of Melville's travel experiences in *Battle-
Pieces*." As Georgoudaki notes, Melville's "references to historical
figures and landmarks, to various cultural objects, specific geographi-
cal locations, and landscape features enrich the setting, atmosphere,
themes, imagery, and symbols in his poems," but the connections
she cites between the poems and entries in Melville's 1856 journal are
often tenuous. Two better essays appeared on the later poems. Ver-
non Shetley's "Melville's 'Timoleon'" (*ESQ* 33:83–93), which gives
a close reading of the poem and an analysis of its verse form, has
perceptive passages and plausibly relates the work to Melville's state
of mind at the time of its composition. Robert Milder's "Melville's

Late Poetry and *Billy Budd*: From Nostalgia to Transcendence" (*PQ* 66:493–507) comments on *John Marr* and *Timoleon* in rather general terms, yet the essay is worth attention for its attempt to link the two volumes to Melville's "successive intentions" in composing *Billy Budd*, shifts of interest, which in Milder's view, "reflect Melville's inward journey over the last five years of his life." According to Milder, where "the late poetry had lent itself to an allegorized brooding on social and metaphysical injuries, the action of *Billy Budd* gradually lifted Melville out of himself and turned him from the objectification of private trials to an absorbed concern with how tragically doomed individuals might behave."

Two discussions offer opposing views of the narrator in *Billy Budd*. Joseph M. Garrison, Jr., in "*Billy Budd*: A Reconsideration" (*BSUF* 27, i[1986]:30–41) revives Lawrance Thompson's notion that the story is ironic at the expense of the narrator. In Garrison's view, *Billy Budd* does not dramatize Melville's quarrel with God, however; rather it is "a story about perception and about the causes and consequences of extreme literalism," one in which an imperceptive narrator makes "his own intelligence and his own sensibilities the major subject of his discourse," revealing through his assumptions and ways of perceiving his unreliability and "ineffectuality." By contrast, George Dekker in *The American Historical Romance* (pp. 208–19) holds that Melville "takes full responsibility for what the narrator says." According to Dekker, the narrator serves as the dramatic mask of "Melville the historian"; he is simultaneously Melville's "conservative spokesman and a character whose minority reports function thematically" in a novel centrally concerned with "the agonizing difficulty of interpretation and judgment."

Finally, Brook Thomas's wide-ranging chapter "Ragged Edges" in *Cross-Examinations* (pp. 224–50) sees Vere as a representative of Anglo-American legal formalism, the central doctrine of which "is that freedom can be guaranteed only by maintaining the institutions supporting the formal order of the law." Thomas takes issue here with Michael Paul Rogin (*ALS 1983*, pp. 65–66) in arguing that any similarities between the ideas in *Billy Budd* and the thought of Oliver Wendell Holmes, Jr., are reflected not so much in Vere (as Rogin maintains) as in the way Melville questions Vere's orthodox thinking.

University of Illinois at Chicago

5. Whitman and Dickinson

Vivian R. Pollak

Nineteen eighty-seven was a happily eclectic year in which I encountered such diverse topics as photography, France, revolutions, sexual surprises, hypocritical critics, class analysis, the Civil War, the commonly agreed upon, patriarchy, architecture, Egypt, and old age. All that (and more) for Whitman. Dickinson criticism was more homogeneous and there was less of it, with language (including prosody), gender, and religious motifs predominating. There was lots of fuzzy thinking, but I read more good prose this year—the best of it very good indeed.

i. Whitman

a. Bibliography, Editing.   In a special double issue of the *Walt Whitman Quarterly Review* (ii–iii 1986–87) all known photographs of the poet have been brought together for the first time—some 130 in number, ranging from the early 1840s to 1891. The notes by Ed Folsom are informative and touching, employing as they do apt quotations from Whitman, such as "When did I not look old? At twenty-five or twenty-six they used already to remark it," or "My mother's favorite picture of me." Folsom's introductory essay, " 'This Heart's Geography's Map': The Photographs of Walt Whitman" (pp. 1–5), suggests that Whitman preferred photographs to paintings and considered them the more democratic art form. The issue includes a graceful tribute to Henry Saunders, an earlier collector of Whitman photographs, by William White, and "Notes on the Major Whitman Photographers" (pp. 63–72), again by Folsom.

One of the photographers discussed by Folsom is Gabriel Harrison, who is identified with the unconventional 1855 frontispiece portrait of *Leaves of Grass*. But it is the 1856 edition that concerns C.

Once again, I am indebted to Cynthia L. Ragland for able research assistance in the preparation of this chapter.

Carroll Hollis in "Whitman's Sketches for the Spine of the 1856 Edition" (*WWR* 4,ii–iii:75–76). According to Hollis, these sketches reveal Whitman's craftiness and demonstrate conclusively that his use of the famous Emerson letter was thoroughly premeditated, "another of that series of promotional ventures which continue in some form or other for the rest of Whitman's career." Examining Whitman's fortunes and misfortunes later in life, in "Holograph Manuscript of 'Thou Vast Rondure' Comes to Light on Long Island" (*WWR* 5,i:32–36), Joann P. Krieg reports that both British and American magazines bought the poem from Whitman in 1869, but that neither the *Fortnightly Review* nor the *Atlantic Monthly* nor any other journal ever published it separately. In slightly altered form, however, it appeared as section five of the 1871 "Passage to India."

In another issue of the *WWR* William White provides "Two Citations: An Early Whitman Article and an Early Reprinting of 'Death in the School-Room'" (*WWR* 5,i:36–37). The first bibliographic find is an unsigned review-essay from the *Springfield Republican* in 1889, comparing Whittier and Whitman and devoting a long paragraph to Emma Lazarus. And in the spring and summer issues of the *WWR* (4,iv:34–37; 5,i:41–43) White continues to provide valuable bibliographies of recent work, national and international, including reviews, dissertations, and miscellanea, as well as the more standard books and articles.

Holy Cow! Press has reissued *An American Primer: With Facsimiles of the Original Manuscript*, ed. Horace Traubel in 1904, and with a new afterword by Gay Wilson Allen. Traubel calls the material "a mass of more or less disjointed notes . . . never intended" by Whitman for publication. On the back cover C. Carroll Hollis calls them "110 separate notes for a linguistic project never completed," which evinces Whitman's "intense concern with language." For Allen, too, these cullings made by Traubel from Whitman's early notebooks demonstrate "Whitman's infatuation with words." Both Hollis and Allen point out that at one time Whitman thought about using this material for a lecture on language. *An American Primer* (45 pp.) is handsomely turned out and nicely sized. You could possibly slip it in a very large pocket, as Whitman liked to do with his own books.

A very different edition is presented by Charley Shively, who challenges the belief that Whitman was a *suppressed* homosexual. During the Civil War, for example, Whitman is described as actively seeking and discovering opportunities for homosexual intercourse and homosexual fellatio in the hospitals. According to Shively, who has edited and fulsomely commented upon the collection of letters *Calamus Lovers: Walt Whitman's Working Class Camerados* (Gay Sunshine), "Washington provided special opportunities for picking up men because of its unsettled and overpopulated condition during the war. . . . For cruising, this was the perfect milieu." But from his youth and even unto his old age, according to Shively, Whitman was inveterately successful in consummating his sexual desires. The edition is based on the letters written to Whitman by some of the men, especially the young working-class men, who, according to Shively, were his lovers. Shively writes, "This edition may startle scholars but I am only incidentally writing for them." Had the commentary been less startling, I would have had greater confidence in the textual accuracy of this potentially valuable collection.

b. **Biography.** A lean year if this category is narrowly defined, a significantly richer one if biography is conceived as a more or less arbitrary category that subsumes all the rest—including bibliography, editing, criticism, sources, and virtually anything else that bears on a writer's career, psyche, and relation to his or her time. Narrowly conceived, however, there was but one piece of work, an excellent one, as it happens, by Scott Giantvalley, who illuminates " 'Strict, Straight Notions of Literary Propriety': Thomas Wentworth Higginson's Gradual Unbending to Walt Whitman" (*WWR* 4,iv:17–27). The title quote is from Whitman, who ranked Higginson at or near the top of his list of persecutors. This unbending occurred after Whitman's death and may be read as a superb example of Victorian hypocrisy and of Higginson's ability to miss talent. (He also missed Dickinson, as is well known.) Giantvalley isn't headed in this direction, at least not very far, though he does lament that "Whitman could not have looked up from the dirt to which he had bequeathed himself to discover a significant shift in Higginson's stance."

Also concerned with Whitman's reputation is Oreste F. Pucciani in *The Literary Reputation of Walt Whitman in France*, which is part of the reprint series, *Harvard Dissertations in Comparative Literature* (Garland). Despite its age (Pucciani defended his dissertation in 1943), this volume contains information that remains timely, though few readers will care to engage the book as a whole. I found

his extensive summary and analysis of Jean Catel's *Walt Whitman:
La Naissance du Poète* especially pertinent. (Catel's oft-cited psychoanalytic study has never been translated into English.)

c. Criticism: General. In *The Lunar Light of Whitman's Poetry*
(Harvard) M. Wynn Thomas argues that Whitman's poetry was a
complex response to the loss of social and economic power experienced during the post-Jacksonian era by the urban, "artisan" class to
which he is thought to have belonged. Evidently, the approach is
Marxist, but lest that label scare off the nonideologue, let me hasten
to add that this is one of the most beautifully written books I have
encountered in a very long time. From Thomas's second chapter,
"Self-Possession and Possessive Individualism," which concentrates
on "Song of Myself": "By failing nowadays to recognize and react to
Whitman's perfect imitation of the tone of voice characteristic of a
struttingly aggressive individualism, we may also fail to appreciate
how subtly he suggests the limitations of that tone and that voice."
From the introductory chapter, "A Critical Situation," Thomas's deft
comment on "A Song for Occupations": "Two's company, three's a
crowd, and he seems always to be insisting on being just that one
person too many, whose presence is bound to alter the color and tone
of the occasion."

A flexible organization permits Thomas to move chronologically
and thematically through Whitman's career. Throughout, there are
ample citations of Whitman's prose, and his social criticism is genuinely illuminated by this approach. The last three chapters (on Whitman's Civil War) are superb. Nevertheless, there are important areas
of Whitman's sensibility that Thomas has not captured, nor does he
attempt to do so. Gender issues, which Thomas has treated in several
interesting articles, are resolutely excluded. The portrait that emerges
here is of a Whitman who is almost too good to be true. Thus, Thomas
devotes a chapter to "Crossing Brooklyn Ferry" without considering
the personal, passional implications of the wonderful "dark patches"
section, which is described as fulfilling a "fraternal obligation" rather
than as revealing authentic self-distrust or "authentic introspection."
All in all, Thomas treats Whitman as a superbly self-assured but selfless secular saint.

"Walt Whitman and the Vox Populi" in *Visionary Compacts*, pp.
108–57, by Donald Pease is stimulating and frustrating. Pease employs a sometimes illogical, aphoristic style and many short, provoca-

tively titled sections, which to some extent obscure the development of his argument (however interesting they may be in themselves). His critical persona is impatient; Whitman writes for the masses, Pease believes, but he himself doesn't. Whitman is described as having no personal voice, but Pease's staccato voice is highly individualized. His most original insights have to do with Whitman's supposed lack of individual identity, as in his discussion of "Death and Development," in which he observes, "When one has no personal identity to lose, death cannot be experienced as a loss in this world." Pease is unwilling to test his aphoristic conclusions against counterexamples and does not distinguish among Whitman's highly varied styles. Like other New Historicists, he offers next to nothing in the way of close readings—a tendency that I, for one, deplore. Nevertheless, because of the intuitive appeal of many of Pease's propositions and because of the vigor of his style, "Walt Whitman and the Vox Populi" is very much alive—one of the few indispensable essays of the year. Also concerned with the political significance of Whitman's vision is Edward M. Wheat in "Whitman's 'Language Experiment' and the Making of a Therapeutic Political Epic" (*MQ* 28:437–54). But the focus is too broad and much of the article restates the obvious.

"1848 and the Origins of *Leaves of Grass*" (*ATQ* n.s. 1:291–99) by Larry J. Reynolds makes the point that "During 1846 and 1847, when Whitman was serving as editor of the Brooklyn *Daily Eagle*, he anticipated the 1848 upheavals" throughout Europe "and stood ready to applaud and justify them." Moreover, as one of the editors of the New Orleans *Crescent*, Whitman was in charge of the foreign news. Reynolds notes that literary men such as Lamartine were among the leaders of the 1848 French Revolution and that this literary heroism was especially inspiring to Whitman. After his return to Brooklyn, Whitman found in the failure of the 1848 revolutions "a source of inspiration, and his radicalism soon flowed into a poetry of political protest." In a short space Reynolds provides a densely detailed and coherent account of Whitman's response to the 1848 revolutions. He is especially good on Whitman's identification with political martyrs and on the poem "Resurgemus."

"The Coinciding Leaves of Walt Whitman" in *American Poetry*, pp. 119–39, by Mutlu Konuk Blasing is an ambitious but somewhat convoluted approach to Whitman's language theory and practice. Blasing treats *Leaves of Grass* as "a hieroglyph in which the categories of words and things coincide, inscribing the original identity

of 'struck' identities. Thus Whitman's poetic invokes the fully empowered Logos, at once the word and the world." Much of her discussion concentrates on "Song of Myself," which "most closely approaches such an original and apocalyptic language."

According to Harold Aspiz, in "Sexuality and the Language of
Transcendence" (*WWR* 5, ii:1–7), "Sexuality in Whitman's poems
is not usually an end in itself. . . . In fact, most depictions of sexual
arousal in *Leaves of Grass* are structured to culminate in a state of
spiritual and visionary elevation." The article does not prove this
point, which is an interesting one. Equally interesting and equally
debatable is Robyn Weigman's thesis that Whitman's poetry in general and the *Calamus* poems in particular rigorously exclude women.
"Writing the Male Body: Naked Patriarchy and Whitmanian Democracy" (*L&P* 33:16–25) is stimulating, well-written, and committed to demonstrating that Whitman's poetics reinscribes "the
grammar of masculinist culture." His "sexual geography" is described
as "closed" and "decidedly male," but, according to Weigman, the
fault is less Whitman's than that of his culture. Thus "Whitman fails
to embark on a reconceptualization of American democracy that
would challenge its basis in masculine subjectivity."

Though Whitman often succeeds in breaking free of the grammar
of a masculinist culture, a volume that is problematically positioned
in this regard is *On Whitman:The Best from American Literature*, ed.
Edwin H. Cady and Louis J. Budd (Duke). So far as I have been
able to determine, this otherwise excellent collection of 16 of the most
durable articles to have appeared in the journal *American Literature*
from 1932 to 1984 lamentably omits female scholars altogether. This
problem notwithstanding, many of the articles still have a great deal
to teach us, and there is a wonderful biographical period piece from
the 1950s by Emory Holloway, still in quest of Whitman's dark lady.
There is an introduction to the series, but none for the volume itself.

d. **Criticism: Individual Works.** Writing against "the widespread
view that in the 1850s Whitman detached himself from practical
politics in order to advocate a purely spiritual democracy," Herbert
J. Levine, in "Union and Disunion in 'Song of Myself'" (*AL* 59:570–
89), seeks to anchor the poem "in the political discourse of the 1850s."
Citing George B. Hutchinson (see *ALS 1986*, p. 72) and Thomas (*The
Lunar Light*) as his predecessors, Levine identifies figures of inclusion (or union) and figures of exclusion (or disunion) which, in his

reading, unify the poem: "Whitman's poem was intended to show that it was possible to unify a highly stressed self and, by analogy, an increasingly divided country." The idea is a good one, but discussions of "Song of Myself" which purport to demonstrate that all the parts work together to compose a unified whole eventually bump up against Whitman's refusal to commit himself to a stable point of origin. Thus, despite the excellence of its documentation and the clarity of Levine's prose, this article is only partially successful in locating Whitman's multivocal discourse within the politics of his time.

Initially more successful in capturing the open-endedness of "Song of Myself" is Ken Egan, Jr., in "Periodic Structure in 'Song of Myself'" (*WWR* 4, iv:1–8). He argues for "the persona's evolution toward an integrated personality, and the reader's necessary involvement in that process." Yet Egan oversimplifies when he suggests that *sections* of expansion alternate with *sections* of contraction. The *section*, we recall, was not intrinsic to the poem's structure. And few readers will, I think, be persuaded by his summary description of sections 1–7, 17–25, 44–52 as "*sections* of contraction" (*italics mine*). For Jeffrey Steele, "Song of Myself" is "A Field of Potential Being," in *The Representation of the Self*, pp. 67–99. Offering a detailed section-by-section analysis, Steele reads the poem in the context of Emersonian self-reliance, or self-liberation. Whitman is viewed as risking "an unrestrained celebration of the unconscious," but avoiding this danger "first by a ritual exorcism of the self's inflation, and then by the fervent assertion of the poet's transpersonal spiritual and political aims."

"'Catching the Sign': Catalogue Rhetoric in 'The Sleepers'" (*WWR* 5, ii:16–34) by James Perrin Warren is primarily a linguistic analysis of the sort we used to call New Critical, but without the New Critical passion for tensions resolved. This article moves effectively between Whitman's notebooks and the "final" text. "From Anxiety to Power: Grammar and Crisis in 'Crossing Brooklyn Ferry'" by Roger Gilbert (*NCL* 42:339–61) takes off from the very good idea of redefining the poem's genre and psychological range. Gilbert's introduction suggests the possibility of a more accessible "Ferry" for a reader such as myself, and parts of the essay live up to its initial promise. Occasionally, the vocabulary is jargon-ridden, but there is clearly an interesting mind at work here, as in Gilbert's thesis that "Whitman's struggle with death is thus figured in the poem as a struggle with

writing, and more importantly a struggle to cross *out* of writing and
into speech, into a form of language associated with life and power,
not death and absence."

The most fully realized Whitman article of the year was George
B. Hutchinson's "Life Review and the Common World in Whitman's
Specimen Days" (*SoAR* 52, iv:3–23). Appropriately enough, its theme
is Whitman's late maturity. Arguing against the commonly held view
that Whitman was pretty much washed up as a writer after the Civil
War, Hutchinson approaches *Specimen Days* from an Eriksonian perspective, examining the work's utility to Whitman and to anyone
concerned with "negotiating the passage into the final stage of life—
that critical passage which since the late nineteenth century in particular has been fraught with problems in our fragmented and 'agist'
society." The only bad news I have to report about this beautifully
executed essay is that Hutchinson's date is too late, and that the
golden age for the elderly he imagines to have existed in the early
19th century never was. Consider the complaints of Emily Dickinson's
paternal grandmother in the late 1830s. Widowed and impoverished,
she was shunted aside by her children and complained bitterly about
their selfishness, which she likened to "heathenism." Consider, too,
Whitman's utopias of splendid old age, written in the 1850s. Surely
those writings are already responding to a harsher social and biological reality.

e. **Affinities and Influences.** A seemingly inexhaustible topic for
Whitman studies, and this year is no exception. There were no block-
busters, but the cumulative range of the work (including some pieces
I didn't have space to review) was impressive. Many of the essays
concentrated on Whitman as represented by a single poem, as does
Rosemary L. Gates, in "Egyptian Myth and Whitman's 'Lilacs'"
(*WWR* 5, i:21–31). She effectively summarizes the Osiris myth in
the form most likely to have influenced Whitman. Less effectively, she
argues that this Egyptian background is intrinsic to the poem. Emmy
Stark Zitter believes that "despite the poem's pose of independence
from authoritative sources, 'Song of Myself' clearly shows the influence of *Song of Solomon*," which she describes as "the most sensual
work of the Judeo-Christian tradition." Zitter is unpersuasive, but in
an interesting way, in "Songs of the Canon: Song of Solomon and
'Song of Myself'" (*WWR* 5, ii:8–15). Her larger point, that "Whitman's poetry . . . both reflects and rejects conventions and ideas of the

Scriptures," is well taken. Larger in scope is Arthur L. Ford's "The Rose Garden of the World: Near East Imagery in the Poetry of Walt Whitman" (*WWR* 5, i:12–20). Ford offers a useful brief survey of Whitman's often stereotypical references to the Near East, especially Persia and Egypt, explaining that "The poem with the largest number of Near East images . . . is 'Salut au Monde.' "

Examining Whitman mainly in the context of Philip Freneau—the link here is radical politics and the American poet's quarrel with his culture—Robert Pinsky gracefully demonstrates that "With Freneau's battles and trials as a background, the embattled, scornful side of Whitman can seem less merely exuberant, more truly threatened and dark," in "American Poetry and American Life: Freneau, Whitman, Williams" (*Shenandoah* 37, i:3–26). His proof text is "By Blue Ontario's Shore," a poem badly in need of this kind of respectful, intelligent treatment. In "Thinking About Human Extinction (II): Emerson and Whitman" (*Raritan* 6, iii:1–22), George Kateb argues that in Whitman "the democratic political system has [positive] effects upon character other than those provided by the opportunity for actual involvement" in "citizenly participation." Kateb sets up an interesting theoretical context for thinking about the relationship between traditional Christianity, moral identity, and the valuation of the individual by self and by others. But he seems unaware of Whitman's opposition to universal suffrage in 1870 and more generally unaware of Whitman's "New York feeling," that is, residual racial prejudice. Thus statements such as "An essential aspect of Whitman's thought is that equal enfranchisement must be coextensive with the adult population" seem ungrounded in reality. Emerson and Whitman are both seen as striving to transcend the social altogether, so as to liberate the "radical spiritual equality that in certain respects is shared with all natural existence."

Whitman is purported to possess a visual rather than an aural imagination in "Whitman vs. Wordsworth: Visual and Aural Differences Between American and English Poetry" (*JMMLA* 20:76–98) by William E. H. Meyer, Jr. The jingoistic tone, coupled with the paucity of references to contemporary secondary sources not by Meyer, does not inspire confidence. Nor does the highly selective use of quotations. There is a particularly silly one from Dickinson's poem " 'Nature' is what we see," which omits the section beginning "Nature is what we hear." Meyer's explanation of the origins of this purported cultural bias is plausible enough, the idea being that the ear is the

more intellectual and social faculty, and the as yet unproved idea of
national biases in imagery is fascinating.

Despite their national differences, Whitman and Bram Stoker
shared a passionate interest in Lincoln, which is reconstructed by
Robert J. Havlik in "Walt Whitman and Bram Stoker: The Lincoln
Connection" (*WWR* 4, v:9–16). Stoker, too, gave a Lincoln lecture;
the manuscript was recently discovered at Notre Dame and apparently provided the occasion for the article. This is the second article
the *WWR* has published on Whitman and Stoker in two years, but
for those who are not Stoker aficionados, there are some choice biographical tidbits which are retrieved mainly from Stoker's *Personal
Reminiscences of Henry Irving*. There is Whitman concocting a wonderful lie in 1886, for example, a supposedly eyewitness account of
Lincoln's death from the vantage point of one who was "not present
at the time of the assassination" (a nice touch, that), but who "was
close to the theatre" and "one of the first in when the news came." And
Stoker believed him and drew on Whitman's account for his own
lecture.

Playing on another kind of visual image, Lauren S. Weingarden
argues for "A Transcendental Discourse in the Poetics of Technology:
Louis Sullivan's Transportation Building and Walt Whitman's 'Passage to India' " (*W&I* 3:202–20), a subject she also pursued in an interesting article I missed last year, "Naturalized Technology: Louis
H. Sullivan's Whitmanesque Skyscrapers" (*CentR* 30 [1986]:480–95).
The more recent article describes the "allusions to the East" in late
19th-century American culture and is handsomely illustrated. A weakness of Weingarden's presentation is that she argues for "Passage" as
a unique source, whereas there must have been multiple influences
on Sullivan's Transportation Building, which he designed for the
1893 Chicago World's Columbian Exposition. Sullivan's artistic credo—he wanted to affirm America's destiny as " 'Nature's nation' "—
was nevertheless clearly influenced by "his admiration for and emulation of Whitman's transcendentalist poetry and prose," as Weingarden effectively demonstrates. Whitman's influence on the early
Pound is the subject of Bruce Fogelman's "Whitman in Pound's Mirror" (*AL* 59:639–44). This nicely documented article links "On His
Own Face in a Glass" and Section 48 of "Song of Myself," especially
in its critique of Whitman's line, "In the faces of men and women I
see God, and in my own face in the glass." More generally, the fluidity

of states of consciousness in Pound's early work is cogently presented as an extension of Whitman's self-as-kosmos.

ii. Dickinson

a. Editing, Bibliography. No new editions this year, but there was an engaging article on the sexual politics of editing, namely Martha Nell Smith, " 'To Fill a Gap' " (*SJS* 13, iii:3–25). She suggests that the appearance of Dickinson's manuscripts matters more than we had supposed for understanding her major relationships; the line and not the stanza may be her basic poetic unit, an idea that probably originated with the language poet Susan Howe, whom Smith credits. Smith, however, is primarily concerned with the "mutilation" and "censorship" of Dickinson's poems and letters to and about her sister-in-law. Challenging Lillian Faderman's "Emily Dickinson's Letters to Sue Gilbert" (see *ALS 1977*, p. 77), Smith asserts cogently but not definitively that "anxious editing of Dickinson's declarations to Sue persists, even in recent feminist criticism."

A bibliographical bonus is Karen Dandurand's *Dickinson Scholarship: An Annotated Bibliography 1969–1985* (Garland). Picking up where Willis Buckingham left off, Dandurand indexes books, articles and parts of books, and dissertations. Her commentary is succinct and nonjudgmental, but the title is a little misleading; not all the items are annotated and there are some surprising omissions. There are also some surprising typos. The only other bibliographical piece is William White's "Emily Dickinson: A Current Bibliography" (*DicS* 61:8–21), which continues to provide a useful checklist and is especially strong on foreign scholarship.

b. Biography. An important, thoroughly researched, and lucidly written article is by Mary Elizabeth Kromer Bernhard, "Portrait of a Family: Emily Dickinson's Norcross Connection" (*NEQ* 60:361–81). She argues vigorously that the Norcrosses were the economic equals of the Dickinsons and that Emily Dickinson's maternal grandfather was as powerful in his community as was her paternal grandfather in his. Major points of interest along the way: the schooling of the poet's mother, the wealth of her maternal grandfather—he was no simple farmer—and her mother's ample inheritance from her grandfather's estate in the late 1840s. Bernhard writes against Barton Levi

St. Armand's theory, in *Emily Dickinson and Her Culture: The Soul's Society* (see *ALS 1984*, pp. 95–96), that Edward Dickinson embezzled money from the estate of his orphaned nieces in the 1850s. Rather, Bernhard plausibly suggests, Edward Dickinson and his family profited from their Norcross inheritance. It was this inheritance, she concludes, which enabled him to build the Evergreens and to refurbish the Homestead.

c. **Criticism: General.** In *Emily Dickinson: A Poet's Grammar* (Harvard) Cristanne Miller proposes "various explanations for why Dickinson writes as she does." Miller concludes, "She writes antagonistically, that is, in opposition to an existing order that attempts to repress her voice or undermine her seriousness. The disruptions of her style, from this perspective, mark her rejection of the conditions of thought and action in which she has been raised; her language is a nineteenth century anticipation of possibilities for an *écriture féminine*." As these excerpts may suggest, Miller's Dickinson is genuinely in control of her life and style, and this is a book that highlights Dickinson's linguistic control of her medium. Less technical than Brita Lindberg-Seyersted's *The Voice of the Poet: Aspects of Style in the Poetry of Emily Dickinson* (see *ALS 1968*, p. 62), *A Poet's Grammar* is more concerned with linking Dickinson's language to her social values. In certain respects less technical than David Porter's *Dickinson: The Modern Idiom* (see *ALS 1981*, pp. 86–87), Miller's Dickinson is more influenced by her reading, more at home in her world, and less of an extremist.

Miller suggests three primary contexts for understanding the special kinds of difficulty that Dickinson's poetry presents: "her belief in the extraordinary power of language, her responses to the language she reads in mid-nineteenth century America, and her sense of herself as woman and poet." This three-part focus works against critical rigidity; Miller emerges as a critic who is consistently intelligent and evenhanded. *A Poet's Grammar* is excellent at identifying linguistic ambiguities in Dickinson's style and providing consistently plausible close readings of poems. There are no startling new critical departures here. Occasionally, the language is almost banal. And to my taste, *A Poet's Grammar* is a little overinfluenced by Robert Weisbuch's nonrepresentational theory and a little underinfluenced by Dickinson's biography. Much Dickinson criticism is passionately idiosyncratic, whereas Miller's strength lies in making points about Dickinson's language that are indisputably true.

An equally interesting but more overtly passionate book is *Lunacy of Light: Emily Dickinson and the Experience of Metaphor* (So. Ill.) by Wendy Barker. Readings of individual poems are captivating but incomplete, as Barker develops her thesis that the imagination, in Dickinson, generates its own light and dwells with ecstasy rather than with common sense. Thus, Barker finds a "mystical union with a silent and female darkness" empowering many of Dickinson's poems; when "masculine solar power has retreated," "feminine imaginative energy can emerge." Barker associates "customary sunlit constraints" with the patriarchy throughout her book, as when she tells us that "Dickinson drew upon traditional associations with the sun and its force to express her fears of gender constraints," or "Dickinson's metaphoric identification with darkness reveals not only a politics of refusal to engage in a world dominated by a prosaic, patriarchal and prescriptive sun but also a poetics of acceptance, even assertion, of her position as a woman writer." Barker's style is characterized by controlled exuberance, and the book is fun to read. But Dickinson's range is significantly broader than Barker is willing to admit, and I could never quite shake off the suspicion that *Lunacy of Light* is overly polemical. There's a skillful last chapter, which extends her thesis to 20th-century women poets, called "Enacting the Difference: A Whole New Metaphor Beginning Here."

" 'Tender Pioneer': Emily Dickinson's Poems on the Life of Christ" by Dorothy Huff Oberhaus (*AL* 59:341–58) identifies a grouping of some of Dickinson's least original poems, though Oberhaus is obviously very much taken with her material. Dickinson is mistakenly praised as a "devotional" poet (with close links to George Herbert), and we are told that "The salient feature uniting Christian poets in a single identifiable poetic mode is their reverential attention to the life of Jesus Christ and their acceptance of such données as the Trinity, the Incarnation, and the Redemption." Along the way I should have appreciated a more systematic discussion of what constitutes a poem on the life of Christ, as opposed, for example, to a poem that employs Christian imagery to illustrate an event or emotion in the life of the speaker. But it is not clear that Oberhaus recognizes the existence of this latter type, which has been described by Weisbuch and others such as myself as Dickinson's dominant religious mode.

Oberhaus concludes, "By recreating the Gospels, Dickinson makes
them freshly available to modern readers and forcefully affirms their
ongoing relevance." I can only state that after reading " 'Tender
Pioneer' " I did not find either Dickinson or the Gospels more compelling.

An article that puts more muscle behind its conservative religious
politics (one I missed last year) is by Rowena Revis Jones. " 'A Royal
Seal': Emily Dickinson's Rite of Baptism" (*R&L* 18[1986]:29–51)
presents useful historical information about the double baptism informing such classic poems as "I'm ceded—I've stopped being
Theirs." More problematically, Jones contends that "In the poems
that employ baptism as their central image, Dickinson demonstrates
a closer alliance to her religious heritage than she herself probably
would have cared to acknowledge had she consciously recognized
it." Yet, with the instinct for accuracy that characterizes this well-
documented article, Jones acknowledges, "Viewed from an overall
perspective, Dickinson emerges a poet of doubt, critical of the traditional doctrines of Congregational orthodoxy." For Lorrie Smith,
in the deftly titled "Some See God and Live: Dickinson's Later
Mysticism" (*ATQ* n.s. 1:302–09), "A number of Emily Dickinson's
later poems suggest she may have formed a rapproachement [*sic*]
between the Christian doctrines she renounced as a young woman
and the quest for sublime vision she enacted in her writing." Unfortunately, Smith is not equal to the formidable task of showing
that Dickinson's religious attitudes can be periodized, and she mis-
represents Johnson's commentary on the dating of her proof text.
Nevertheless, her discussion of Dickinson's Moses poems should be
considered in the light of Cynthia Griffin Wolff's discussion of a
comparable transformation in the poet's religious values during her
later years (see *ALS 1986*, pp. 77–78). Dorothy Huff Oberhaus, however, in the article discussed above, saw no significant chronological
pattern in Dickinson's Christ poems and observed that Dickinson
wrote such poems continuously, early and late.

"Emily Dickinson's work represents an ironic comment on nineteenth-century poetics, for she plays against each other the rhetorics
that implicitly or explicitly authorize other major nineteenth-century
poets," explains Blasing in "Emily Dickinson's Untitled Discourse,"
in *American Poetry*. The chapter is full of intelligent eloquence, but
for me, at least, Blasing does not effectively place Dickinson in a
tradition or traditions, though she is deeply attentive to the sights

and sounds of Dickinson's language. Taking up one aspect of Dickinson's prosody, her use of iambic pentameter, A. R. C. Finch, in "Dickinson and Patriarchal Meter: A Theory of Metrical Codes" (*PMLA* 102:166–76), draws on "Russian formalist criticism, the work of Roland Barthes, and contemporary feminist criticism." Dickinson, we are sensibly told, "resists the meter, approaches it with tentative ambivalence, and sometimes gains power from it." The article is methodologically sophisticated and intuitively appealing, though some of the examples do not scan to fit the gloss. A case in point is the discussion of "The Soul selects her own Society," which overlooks a second pentameter line at the start of the second stanza. I wish, too, that the author had included a table of the 98 poems on which her study was based and would encourage her to publish such a table elsewhere. But enough of these quibbles. Finch effectively and at times brilliantly points the way to much-needed further studies of Dickinson's meters.

"'Omitted Centers': Dickinson's Metonymic Strategy" by Sherri Williams (*SJS* 13, iii:26–36) considers if there is "a relationship between her preferred rhetorical mode and gender." It is in the nature of such inquiries to answer such questions affirmatively, but never mind. Williams is a very fine close reader, and her theoretical framework is lucid and original, as in her comparison of Whitman and Dickinson, which is organized around the model of sexual difference. Williams suggests that "Dickinson's heterogeneous sexuality, in contrast to the homogeneous masculinity of her American contemporaries, opens up her language and her meaning. In contrast, Walt Whitman's work provides many examples of just such an obliteration of sexual difference." Williams almost avoids making Whitman a scapegoat, as feminist contrasts between the two poets tend to do, while nevertheless arguing that "Whitman seeks to amalgamate sex, age, race, class into one, unitary whole, all the same."

The following three essays are less substantial. In "Emily Dickinson's Word: Presence as Absence, Absence as Presence" (*AmerP* 4: 41–50), Albert Gelpi makes the good point that, in the larger context of American literature, "Dickinson stands at the turning point— Janus-faced, looking backward and forward." The modernist is "the disillusioned romantic." Joyce Carol Oates offers an impressionistic tribute, a stirring encomium to a peerless poet who has "no heirs or heiresses," in "Soul at the White Heat: The Romance of Emily Dickinson's Poetry" (*CritI* 13:806–24). Yet "Like Emerson in his terse,

elliptical poems of 'transcendence' (which Dickinson had read), the
poet refines herself of the close-at-hand, the local, in order to medi-
tate upon the universal." Dickinson identifies with flowers and her
gift of them literally and figuratively becomes "a gift of herself," explains James M. Hughes, in " 'I bring my rose': Emily Dickinson's
Gift of Power" (*DicS* 63:33–42). The idea is promising, but the essay
does not probe deeply.

d. **Criticism: Individual Works.** Not much to report here, with
most of the best work appearing in books or essays on larger topics.
An exception is George Monteiro's "Dickinson's 'Abraham To Kill
Him' " (*Expl* 45, ii:32–33), which shows elegantly and succinctly how
"Dickinson's redaction of Genesis 22 deviates sharply and boldly from
Scripture."

e. **Affinities and Influences.** An unusually full year in this department, though most of the essays I read sacrificed some depth for
breadth, and several of the pieces were extremely superficial. A
middle-order essay is by Walter Hesford, "The Creative Fall of
Bradstreet and Dickinson" (*ELWIU* 14:81–91). Writing against
Emily Stipes Watts (in 'The posy UNITY': Anne Bradstreet's Search
for Order," see *ALS 1979*, p. 81) and David Porter (in *Dickinson:
The Modern Idiom*), Hesford seeks to show that "They are not, as
some have argued, postlapsarian poets, conscious only of absence,
loss, and difference; since they write during, not after, the fall. . . .
Both poets . . . make autumn their season of beginnings, of creativity."
Intuitively, this association of autumn with beginnings does not seem
right for Dickinson, and Hesford is only partially successful in defining its emotional logic. For Dickinson, he explains, "Autumn is
summer's Revelation, an apocalypse that prompts a turn inward."
An important link between Dickinson and Bradstreet is their mutual
interest in Eve.

An essay on a more limited topic that is also more fully in command of its material is by Jane D. Eberwein. After Dickinson heard
the orthodox Congregational clergyman Edwards Amasa Park preach
"a splendid sermon" in Amherst in 1853, she wrote her brother Austin,
"I never heard anything like it, and don't expect to again." According
to Eberwein, in "Emily Dickinson and Edwards Amasa Park: 'The
Loveliest Sermon' " (*ATQ* n.s. 1:311–22), Park's two most popular
sermons, "Peter's Denials of His Lord" and "Judas," were especially

likely to have influenced Dickinson. She argues persuasively that "there are occasional references to Peter in some early poems that gain extra resonance when read in the context of Park's narrative." Park is described as "a verbal artist in his own right, one who applied the dazzling techniques of antebellum American oratory to the service of religion." His great theme was betrayal.

Dickinson is described as a "precursor of the modern existentialist movement" by Toni Ann Culjak in "Dickinson and Kierkegaard: Arrival at Despair" (*ATQ* n.s. 1:145–55). The difficulty with this kind of work is that it seems to call forth an attempt to summarize Dickinson's religious attitudes in ten pages. Less than ten pages, really, so as to summarize some of Kierkegaard as well. The trick, then, must be to delimit a tighter topic, without settling for the merely trivial. At the margin, more careful proofreading would help too. See the description on page 151 of "almost to suffice" as "the *closing* line" (italics mine) of "Deprived of other Banquet," whereas there are four very fine, indeed essential, lines to come.

Despite the absence of any footnotes whatsoever, "Dickinson and Frost: Walking Out One's Grief" (*DicS* 63:16–29) by Mordecai Marcus effectively links "After great pain" and "Acquainted with the Night": "Each poem describes states of grief and alienation whose causes are not stated but only very subtly implied. . . . Frost's poem breathes a sigh of forgiveness for the world and the self. Dickinson's closes down into a resentment too strong to endure any direct contemplation." The essay proceeds by close readings that I found more helpful for Frost than for Dickinson.

For Douglas Leonard, in " 'Chastisement of Beauty': A Mode of the Religious Sublime in Dickinson's Poetry" (*ATQ* n.s. 1:247–56), Dickinson is the poet of unity, who, though in some obscure way "well ahead of her time. . . [, was] also conscious of the long tradition of mystical poetry behind her." The article is highly impressionistic and comparatively innocent of secondary sources. The title quote is taken from an 1855 letter to an unknown recipient in which, as described by Leonard, "Dickinson expanded on the paradoxical character of awe." Except for a too brief discussion of Austin, who knew Longinus, as Dickinson's "closest intellectual companion" before his marriage in 1856, Leonard, who writes gracefully, never settles down to the business of probing his subject deeply.

Also concerned with the sublime is Barton Levi St. Armand, who argues that "The veil in all of its manifestations, whether it be the cloak of nature, the robe of the deity, or the garb of the spiritualist medium, was a basic metaphor for dealing with the problem of the sublime," in "Veiled Ladies: Dickinson, Bettine, and Transcendental Mediumship" (*SAR*, pp. 1–51). The article is a model of careful historical research, in which depth and breadth come together at last. By *transcendental medium* St. Armand refers to Dickinson's "own subtle fusion of nature worship and occult sensitivity." Initially, it appears that Dickinson knew Bettine's writings through Susan Dickinson, who owned an 1842 *Gunderöde* and an 1859 edition of *Goethe's Correspondence with a Child*. One of St. Armand's most telling points is that "These works by Bettine, especially the 1842 *Gunderöde* translated by Margaret Fuller and published by Elizabeth Palmer Peabody, obviously were used as the basis of a 'code' between the young Sue and Emily, just as Dickens and Shakespeare provided scenarios for the poet's later correspondence with such intimate friends as Samuel Bowles and Otis Phillips Lord." Lucidly learned and beautifully written, this extensive article is full of the lively and suggestive surprises we have come to expect of St. Armand. Just one caution. Don't try to read " 'Veiled Ladies' " when you are rushed. It needs to be savored.

University of Washington

6. Mark Twain

Hamlin Hill

It turns out that 1986 *was* simply the eye of the storm for *Huck Finn*, and 1987 saw the return of the deluge, with articles centering on the kid's unreliability, deviousness, and deceit. Huck himself, scrubbed and polished and as unexciting as a chintz lampshade, wrote a letter which *The New Yorker* published in its 26 October 1987 issue; and "what I did last summer" is a wry commentary on what Huck actually did!

i. Biography

Little biographical information saw print in 1987. Sholom Kahn makes a broad-stroke survey of "Mark Twain and Education" in *Scripta Hierosolymitana* (32:229–57), dividing his analysis into "Self-Education," "Apprenticeship," and "High Education." Trained in the first two, Mark Twain strove toward the last in "philosophical and reflective writings." In "Mark Twain and Dickens: Why the Denial?" (*DSA* 16:189–219) Howard G. Baetzhold meticulously catalogs Mark Twain's indebtednesses to Dickens in characters and episodes and then suggests reasons for Mark Twain's 1909 denial of having ever read Dickens: his old age, his desire to seem original, and his "diminished affection" for the English novelist's work. Ronald Wesley Hoag prints five letters from Clemens and one letter to him in "Mark Twain's Correspondence with Two Press Associations . . .," *SLJ* 20, i:3–21, concerned with declining invitations to attend meetings of the National Editorial Association and the Missouri Press Association. One of the letters, from 1888, is interesting for Twain's meditations about humor; the others are much less substantial. Judith Yaross Lee's "Anatomy of a Fascinating Failure" (*American Heritage of Invention & Technology* 3:55–60) describes in detail the history, operation, and ultimate failure of the Paige Typesetter; although Mark

Twain only stands on the sidelines, checkbook in hand, in this article, it is a valuable footnote to his business dealings.

In "Mark Twain and Dan Beard's Clarence: An Anatomy" (*CentR* 31:212–27) Richard Bridgman—as duplicitous as the current interpretations of Huck—announces innocently that his essay is "an attempt to suggest an answer to the question: 'Why did the illustrator, Dan Beard, give Hank Morgan's page the face and figure of Sarah Bernhardt, and then go on to found the Boy Scouts of America?' " In fact Bridgman's essay is as important for Sam Clemens's psychic biography as Leslie Fiedler's "Come Back to the Raft Ag'in, Huck Honey" is to an understanding of the forces at work in *Huck Finn*. Bridgman strings together a series of images which obsessed Clemens for his whole life: the phallic candle in *Tom Sawyer*, "The Burning Shame," and *Letters from the Earth*; the name "Sandy" as the black companion of teenage Sam, Hank Morgan's wife, and "sandy" Mary Jane Wilks; transvestites—Tom, Huck, and Jim, Merlin, Roxy and Tom Driscoll, and 52 young boys at the Battle of the Sand Belt, "as pretty as girls." Bridgman concludes, "Although we do not possess a vocabulary sufficiently precise to enable us to draw together the elements I have been discussing, they do demonstrably repeat themselves and overlap one another: malaise and fear of incapacity in the presence of women; male comfort in one another's company, where sexuality can be joked about; transvestism; and warm sympathy for adolescent boys." Bridgman is entering new and uncharted territory; and, to paraphrase Mark Twain, "I would rather have written this article than slept with General Grant in full uniform."

ii. Editions

In addition to the handful of letters which Hoag prints, there was little editorial activity in 1987. Guy Cardwell added *Innocents Abroad and Roughing It* to the Library of America bookshelf; and I revised the introduction and updated the bibliography for the facsimile first edition of *Huckleberry Finn* (Harper & Row).

A broad spectrum of essays is reprinted in Louis J. Budd and Edwin H. Cady, eds., *On Mark Twain: The Best from* American Literature (Duke). Nineteen essays, all of which originally appeared in *AL* between 1937 and 1985, provide a historical retrospective, beginning with Hyatt H. Waggoner's "Science in the Thought of Mark Twain" and coming up to James Grove's "Mark Twain and the Endangered Family." I miss a few benchmarks, such as Walter Blair's "When Was *Huckleberry Finn* Written?" and Howard G. Baetzhold's "Found: Mark Twain's 'Lost' Sweetheart." In case you're interested, there are two essays on *Innocents Abroad* and two on *Huck*; one each on *Tom Sawyer, Connecticut Yankee, Pudd'nhead Wilson, Joan of Arc*, and "The Man That Corrupted Hadleyburg"; and ten on broader biographical or critical topics.

iii. General Interpretations

Patrick D. Morrow surveys "Bret Harte, Mark Twain, and the San Francisco Circle" in *A Literary History of the West*, pp. 339–58. There are only two extended analyses of Mark Twain in a treatment which emphasizes Harte: one on him as a western local-color protégé of Harte, and the other on *Roughing It* as a foreshadower of contemporary black humor.

Howard G. Baetzhold's essay on Mark Twain in *DLB* (64:34–37) is a broad survey of Clemens as a realist who enjoyed a "strong moral element" in his fiction and was willing to tolerate experimental literature "provided the characterization and action were convincing." Baetzhold discusses Twain's critical methods from the early burlesques to the familiar critical essays. Carolyn S. Brown devotes two chapters of *The Tall Tale* to Twain. She is predominantly descriptive in her discussion of the first 41 chapters of *Roughing It*, in which "the narrator . . ., by taking upon himself the role of tale teller, attempts to create the literary equivalent of a folk group among his readers" and "initiates novices, entertains the group, and delineates, binds, and celebrates the group." More interesting, but underdocumented, is the chapter on the *Autobiography*; in it, "Mark Twain deliberately developed a tall character living a tall life," playing the roles of "both professional liar and professional truth-teller."

James D. Wilson's *A Reader's Guide to the Short Stories of Mark Twain* (Hall) devotes a chapter to each of 65 short stories, sometimes clustered together because of special affinities (like the Mc-Williams trio). Charles Neider's *Complete Short Stories* provided the basic criterion for selection (in spite of Neider's inability to distinguish between short stories, anecdotes, sketches, and essays) with some very early and very late stories added to Neider's list. For each story or cluster, Wilson provides an impeccable five-part commentary: a publication history; an account of composition, sources,

and influences; a commentary on the story's relationship to other
Mark Twain works; a cogent summary of critical analyses of the
story; and a primary and secondary bibliography. I suspect that a
chronological rather than alphabetical arrangement would have been
more illuminating for the development of Mark Twain's skill, but this
is an extremely useful volume for student and scholar alike.

Laura Niesen de Abruña's provocative title, "Green Watermelons
and Loaded Frogs: The Unexpected as Humor in Mark Twain's
Lecture" (*JMMLA* 20:46–56), promises more than it delivers. It explains that Mark Twain was indebted to Artemus Ward and other
Literary Comedians for lecture platform techniques of deflating high
expectations, parodying genteel language, and burlesquing Romantic
travel narratives. Tom Hazuka, "Cooper Was No Architect: Mark
Twain as Literary Craftsman" (*SDR* 25, ii:35–46), also deals with
generalities, amassing snippets from a wide range of sources to
prove Mark Twain's "fascination with, and genuine love of, the
English language, and the craft required to transform . . . linguistic
raw materials into literary art." John Dizikes's "Charles Dickens,
Martin Chuzzlewit, Mark Twain, and the Spirit of American Sports"
(*DSA* 16:247–56) focuses on Dickens, with brief mentions of *The
Gilded Age* and *Connecticut Yankee*, and contrasts British and American notions of gamesmanship. Kingsley Widmer filters Henry Miller
and Nathanael West through *Huck* and the dark humor of Mark
Twain's later writings and stakes out their evolution from their predecessor in "Twisting American Comedy: Henry Miller and Nathanael West, Among Others" (*ArQ* 43:218–30).

More substantial is Bernard Poli's chapter, "Mark Twain's Gods
and Tormentors: The Treasure, The River, The Nigger and the Twin
Brother" in *The New History of Literature*, pp. 297–315. Poli provoc-
atively traces image clusters which surround the basic polarity of the
"double vision of the world seen through the eyes of the god-like
child and the inseparable devilish tormentor": "the treasure and the
beautiful girl, the happy island and the 'good nigger' make up his
private mythical heaven; whereas death, the destructive steamboat
and the 'black' Indian haunt his secret Inferno," according to Poli.

Richard Bridgman's *Traveling in Mark Twain* (Calif.) is a detailed survey of the travel books, with the accent on their underlying
philosophical pessimism. Mark Twain's nervous dissatisfaction and
distrust surfaces relentlessly in "a series of frustrations and humiliat-
ing defeats" in both Europe and the Far West, in his own past, and

in the Far East. Ultimately, according to Bridgman, the dream travels of the late fragments underscore the lesson of factual travel narratives—"the precarious instability of human understanding."

David R. Sewell in *Mark Twain's Languages, Discourse, Dialogue, and Linguistic Variety* (Calif.) uses Mikhail Bakhtin's term *heteroglossia* ("a healthy, indeed essential, conflict of voices that destabilizes language, permitting change and preventing any one form of language from maintaining authority at the expense of others") as his starting point. Sewell charts Mark Twain's various attitudes toward standard and incorrect grammar and toward inflated and honest language. In *The Gilded Age*, characters variously misuse words, tenses, and tones, "creating the illusion of value where none exists"; Mark Twain's comic assaults upon foreign languages presage serious concerns about the ability of words to communicate. In *Huckleberry Finn*, characters speak at five different language levels, each with its correlative moral value. Those languages distill to two in *Pudd'nhead Wilson*, those of power and submission. In his final chapter Sewell traces late Mark Twain's fascination with "linguistic absurdity," when "the basic mechanisms of semiosis . . . create barriers to understanding, and interpretation becomes a guessing game." Sewell's insights are thought-provoking and seminal to a study of Mark Twain's art.

iv. Individual Works Through 1885

Cecil D. Eby resurrects an antecedent to Mark Twain's first comic story in "Dandy Versus Squatter: An Earlier Round" (*SLJ* 20, i:33–36) in Joseph Doddridge's "Dialogue of the Backwoodsman and the Dandy" (1821). Clyde Wade briefly examines "The Jumping Frog," "Grandfather's Old Ram," and "Baker's Blue-Jay Yarn" as examples of psychic farce, in which the irrational provides the basis of humor, in "Twain's Psychic Farce" (*PAPA* 13:59–66). In "Ever Such a Good Time: The Structure of Mark Twain's *Roughing It*" (*DQR* 17:182–99), Bruce Michelson argues that in the beginning chapters "Mark Twain's funseeking passage out to the West" provides the structural principle. Once the narrator becomes disillusioned, "incongruous, half-crazy playfulness is his only hope against a disheveled, intolerable reality." The last 30 chapters, in which the narrator must work rather than play, fall off precisely because "truth and the real world become obligations too intense to be ignored, not only by the traveler but by the writer."

The Gilded Age got more than its usual share of attention in 1987. Thomas C. Caramagno's "Bad Fictions and the Improvident Heart in *The Gilded Age* and *Bleak House*" (*CL* 14:62–75) argues that both novels contrast a traditional work ethic (which succeeds for Charles Dudley Warner's New Englanders) with an imaginative fiction not dependent on Providence (which fails in Mark Twain's western characters). Dickens's view is darker, because evil infects "good and bad alike, as the world sinks back into primeval mind," but the tension is identical in both novels. Tom H. Towers has similar insights. "'The Uniform Operations of Nature': The Unity of *The Gilded Age*" (*JPL* 3:1–21) suggests that each of three major plot lines—the actions of Silas Hawkins, of Laura, and of Philip and Ruth—deals "with cultural and/or generational conflict in which the well defined values and manners of an older, established Eastern civilization are set off against the social and economic disorder" of the frontier in Missouri and of Washington politics. Philip's story provides a corrective to "Laura's vengeful egoism" and to "Sellers's vain destructive fantasies." But this optimistic ending is ambiguous because the uniform operations of nature, upon which Philip depends, are utilitarian, destructive, and cyclical.

Sanford Pinsker filters *The Adventures of Tom Sawyer* through play theory in "*The Adventures of Tom Sawyer*, Play Theory, and the Critic's Job of Work" (*MQ* 27:357–65), arguing that Mark Twain "could only free himself from the worries of 'self-preservation' in the guise of Tom Sawyer, and in the mode of Play."

And then there's *Huck*. Two articles discuss the novel in the classroom context. Vincent J. Cleary reports in "Odysseus, Aeneas and Huckleberry Finn" (*The Augustan Age, Occasional Papers*, 1:45–55) on a class's reaction to the three volumes, in which apparently comparisons and contrasts in the first two were appropriate, but Huckleberry refused to conform. James Gellert surveys the censorship issue in "Shylock, Huckleberry, and Jim: Do They Have a Place in Today's High Schools?" (*CLAQ* 12:40–43). Gellert focuses on the characterization of Jim (but ignores the debate over the word *nigger*) and concludes that the minimum age "to appreciate ideas which involve inferring universal ethical standards is approximately thirteen" but that *Huck* should be reserved for the high school years.

Robert Tracy's "Prisoners of Style: Dickens and Mark Twain, Fiction and Evasion" (*DSA* 16:221–46) examines the relationships between dependence on "fictions" and freedom from that dependence: "Tom and Pip both remain prisoners of fictions," but with the conclusion of his novel, "Huck Finn frees himself from the fiction in which he has been trapped, and from an obsession with that fictional past." Along the same lines, Scott Carpenter's "Demythification in *Adventures of Huckleberry Finn*" (*SAF* 15:211–17) suggests that the "general movement" of the novel, "as the novel and the narrator free themselves from their pasts, sanctions . . . 'demythifying' the world by a constant refusal to interpret or to impute transcendental meaning to the concrete." But, to the extent that this involves "the systematic disintegration of his Romantic illusions," Huck flunks the test in the Evasion chapters.

Then there's the unreliability issue, which is becoming almost as popular as Pudd'nhead Wilson's half-a-dog joke used to be. John Bird in " 'These Leather-Face People': Huck and the Moral Art of Lying" (*SAF* 15:71–80) examines the structure of Huck's lying technique and analyzes the "eight-part" progression of his debate with his conscience in chapter 31; Janet A. Gabler-Hover believes that Huck "is a moral character without moral self-awareness," consistently so characterized by Mark Twain throughout the novel. In "Sympathy Not Empathy: The Intent of Narration in *Huckleberry Finn*" (*JNT* 17:68–75) she proposes that readers who expect too much from Huck, especially in chapter 31, have lost their detachment and hope for more than Huck can deliver. Now fetch up Thomas Pribek, as Huck would say. In "Huckleberry Finn: His Masquerade and His Lessons for Lying" (*ALR* 19,iii:68–79) Pribek argues that Huck's invented guises are faulty except when, "under the mask of Tom Sawyer, Huck finally has a real self"; otherwise, Huck is an incompetent liar. Ring up David Kaufmann, and "Satiric Deceit in the Ending of *Adventures of Huckleberry Finn*" (*SN* 19:66–78) answers the bell. Because Mark Twain had a "confrontational relationship" with his audience, "he intended the evasion to be agonizingly long" in order to deceive his readers. Therefore, Kauffmann says, "the emotional, structural and even *thematic* 'failure' is intentional," so that Mark Twain can "lead the reader away from the central deceit, Huck's unreliability."

Huck and Jim's relationship also heated up in the spotlight. Paulette Wasserstein, "Twain's *Huckleberry Finn*" (*Expl* 46, i:31–33), suggests that Jim is not only a father figure to Huck, but a mother surrogate as well. Jim exhibits "the warmth, the compassion, the strong ethical sense, and the ability to love and to teach about love that characterize the nineteenth-century's view of the ideal woman and mother." Stephen Railton suggests in "Jim and Mark Twain: What Do Dey Stan' For?" (*VQR* 63:393–408) that, because Huck "is not wholly uncontaminated by his society's arbitrary values," he "cannot transcend that society's racist mentality." Jim alternates between sensitive human being and racial caricature—especially during the Evasion, when Mark Twain had to "amuse and reassure the mass audience." Ron Samples sees it another way in "Mark Twain as American Song; The Impact of Culture on *Huckleberry Finn*" (*JASAT* 18:31–39). This time, Huck and Jim are members of two different cultures, Euro- and Afro-American, and Huck cannot bridge the cultural gap. "Culture necessarily restricts freedom, individuality, and imagination." Huck seeks an individualist's freedom; Jim, a collectivist's. Thomas Quirk's " 'Learning a Nigger to Argue': Quitting *Huckleberry Finn*" (*ALR* 20, i:18–33) begins with the intriguing premise that, on the basis of the composition of the novel, chapter 14 with the debate about King Sollermun is actually the conclusion of the novel. He argues that "you can't learn a nigger to argue," and "So I quit," are the true concluding sentences. And the insert "gave to Jim as yet undramatized capacities that at once rounded out his full humanity and deepened his tragedy."

Harold Beaver's *Huckleberry Finn* (Allen & Unwin) is ostensibly a retrospective on a century of debate over the novel; in fact, it is a stunningly brilliant analysis of the paradoxes and polarities in the novel. Beaver bases the meanings of the novel too narrowly in the sociocultural antebellum South rather than in universal unregenerate human nature; and he raises many more critical questions than he can possibly settle in 200 pages. But those insights which flash before us—in historical chapters, cultural chapters, biographical chapters, and critical chapters—should provide Twainians with topics for disagreement and elaboration for a long time to come.

Finally, Louis J. Budd's "The Recomposition of *Adventures of Huckleberry Finn*" (*MOR* 10:113–29) is a sprightly confrontation of the novel which we read these days. Budd proposes five factors that create "new" versions of *Huckleberry Finn*: (1) the Iowa/California critical edition which we will have "in 1986" (*sic transit veritas*); (2) the overlay of movie, television, and Broadway musical versions of the novel; (3) the bannings and bowdlerizings of the novel; (4) the original illustrations "which will become familiar again" (in fact, the paperback facsimile of the first American edition has remained in print for the past 26 years, as its aging editor knows all too well); and (5) the foreign translations of *Huck*. (I wonder how many American academics know that the majority of the world reads *Huck* in a Longmans British edition, in which Tom calls his gang "chaps," and when Huck finds Pap in his bedroom in chapter 4, he exclaims, "Good Heavens, it was father!") Budd continues, contemplating recent criticism, which he says is producing a "thickening dignity" for the novel as a classic for which solemnity is the proper response.

Budd ignores one "new" version of *Huckleberry Finn* which I have encountered reading the scholarship and criticism for 1987— the *Huck* that never was. I have been informed that Sid is Tom Sawyer's brother, that Pap Finn drowned, that Jim Turner and Jake Packard and Bill were rescued from the *Walter Scott*—in addition to discovering that Samuel Clemens was born in Hannibal, that he first used the pseudonym in 1862, and that sumach berries are apples. So far, nobody's said that Huck and Jim didn't really go down the River, but I'm almost prepared for that.

v. Individual Works After 1885

Jane Gardiner's " 'A More Splendid Necromancy': Mark Twain's *Connecticut Yankee* and the Electrical Revolution" (*SN* 19:448–58) proposes that in that novel, "the tension is not, primarily, between pastoral and industrial, primitive and progressive, faith and reason or magic and science, but between two different kinds of nineteenth-century science"—a mechanical one, represented by the bicycle and sewing machine, and a magic, invisible, and lethal one, represented by electricity. Mark L. Sargent traces literary overtones of the Lampton ancestor, Geoffrey Clement, who participated in sentencing Charles I, through *Huck, Connecticut Yankee,* and the autobiographical sketches of Clemens's mother in "A Connecticut Yankee in Jane Lampton's South: Mark Twain and the Regicide" (*MissQ* 40:21–31).

John S. Whitley explores the "anti-detective story" motif in *Pudd'nhead Wilson* ("*Pudd'nhead Wilson*: Mark Twain and the Limits of Detection," *JAmS* 21:55–70). Beneath the traditional formula, there is no restoration of order, no concealment from the reader, and no crime as aberration when an entire society is guilty. Lee

Clark Mitchell's over-long analysis of the polar influences of heredity and environment as the motivating factor in characters' actions (" 'De Nigger in You': Race or Training in *Pudd'nhead Wilson*," *NCF* 42: 295–312) concludes that "neither position allows that behavior might be shaped through intention," and that "the power of the novel lies in its very inability to establish moral priorities." Louis J. Budd's "Mark Twain's Fingerprints in *Pudd'nhead Wilson*" (*EA* 40:385–99) is a finely balanced "retrospective" (à la Beaver, above) of critical positions which the novel has generated and a tantalizing "apologia" for its continued interest to modern readers in spite of its flaws.

James W. Gargano's "Mark Twain and Milton's *Paradise Lost*, Books XI and XII" (*NMAL* 10:item 1) finds parallels in chapter eight of *The Chronicle of Young Satan*—the pageant of human history, the presiding angelic presence, the emphasis on human evil—but Mark Twain, unlike John Milton, allows no redemptive salvation for mankind.

Finally, three articles have the *Autobiography* as their topic. Applying Freudian concepts to boyhood recollections in the *Autobiography*, Minrose C. Gwin, "Repetition and Recollection: The Unconscious Discourse of Mark Twain's *Autobiography*" (*L&P* 33: 120–31), finds the death wish, the impulse for repetition, and the "disruption, horror, guilt, and the [Freudian] uncanny" pervading those sections. Michael J. Kiskis in "Susy Clemens as the Fire for Mark Twain's Autobiography" (*MHLS* 10:43–50) catalogs Susy's influence on the Ulysses Grant segment of the *Autobiography*, on the idea of a dictated mode of composition, and on the tenor of the 1906 dictations. I wish that I could determine the thesis of Louis A. Renza's "Killing Time with Mark Twain's Autobiographies" (*ELH* 54:157–82), but it reminds me of Mark Twain's 1902 reaction to reading Jonathan Edwards's *The Freedom of the Will*. I think Renza is deconstructing the *Autobiography*, arguing that since it is constantly beginning, it is actually about writing an autobiography. I am pretty sure he doesn't like the book. But when I encounter a steady procession of such phrases as "a recuperable psychodramatic topos," "an unalleviated digressive praxis," "a self-referential signifier of a present that reduces such influences to inconsequential or merely epiphenomenal pressures," "latent vocational metaphoricity," "a paradoxically focused and self-conscious mode," and "aggressive or inversely ambitious anti-canonical postures," it gives me the fantods.

For 1988, the first volume of *Mark Twain's Letters, 1853–1866* is in print; John Gerber's TUSAS volume is out; and there are authoritative reports that the Iowa/California *Huckleberry Finn* is actually a printing, a consummation devoutly to be wished!

Texas A&M University

7. Henry James

Susan M. Griffin

The major project of recent James studies continues to be the situating of James's writing, life, and literary identity in their historical, cultural, and economic contexts. (Given this trend, it seems fitting that the best work on James I reviewed is a book on Hawthorne by Richard Brodhead.) The topic of Jamesian epistemology remains of enduring interest; that of theatricality is the focus of new attention. While the previously neglected fiction of the 1880s appears to have come into its own, the finest critical essays this year are on an early James novel, *The American,* and a late one, *The Golden Bowl.*

i. Editions, Letters, Bibliographies, Biographical Studies

Reprinted for the first time since 1908 is the collaborative novel *The Whole Family* (Ungar, 1986), for which James wrote the chapter on "The Married Son." This useful edition includes the original illustrations, a fine introduction by Alfred Bendixen, and brief literary biographies for each of the 12 authors.

In *Henry James: Selected Letters* (Harvard), Leon Edel selects 166 of the thousand-odd letters included in his four-volume edition, adding some two dozen previously unpublished. While several of the new letters will interest Jamesians, and although Edel defends his editorial methods against previous scholarly criticisms, this remains an edition intended for the " 'general reader.' " Other new James letters are uncovered in George Monteiro's "Henry James on the Death of Del Hay: A New Letter" (*ALR* 19, iii:89–90) and Adeline R. Tintner's " 'Dear and Venerable Circe': An Unpublished Henry James Letter" (*Manuscripts* 39:156–61). Monteiro also publishes three letters from Whitelaw Reid in "Henry James and Whitelaw Reid: Some Additional Documents" (*HJR* 8:139–41).

My thanks to Beth Basham for her substantial assistance in the preparation of this chapter.

While Nicola Bradbury makes a good case for the place of a selective, critical overview of recent James criticism in the introduction
to her *An Annotated Critical Bibliography of Henry James* (St.
Martin's), the book itself is a disappointment: too often idiosyncratic,
if not careless, in its selection and occasionally flawed in its documentation.

The Library of Henry James, ed. Leon Edel and Adeline R.
Tintner (UMI), is "an enlarged, corrected version" of the list published previously in the *Henry James Review* (see *ALS 1983*, p. 111);
essays by Edel ("The Two Libraries of Henry James," pp. 1–14) and
Tintner ("The Books in the Books: What Henry James's Characters
Read and Why," pp. 69–96) are also included. Although this inventory of James's books still remains incomplete, the volume is a valuable resource.

New scholarship on the James family continues apace. The major
work in this category is Jane Maher's *Biography of Broken Fortunes:
Wilkie and Bob, Brothers of William, Henry, and Alice James*
(Archon, 1986), an important source of information on Wilkie and
Bob in particular and on the James family in general. Maher's research allows her to correct earlier Jamesian biographers who were
hampered by a lack of data on the lives of the two younger James
brothers. However, her own interpretations of this data lack methodo-
logical sophistication and often remain superficial. Interested readers should consult Carol Holly's review of Maher [*HJR* 8:209–20]
for a fuller discussion of this problem. Holly's own "'Absolutely Acclaimed': The Cure for Depression in James's Final Phase" (*HJR* 8:
126–38) is explicitly informed by psychological theory. Arguing persuasively that James's 1914 recovery from severe depression was the
direct result of the British press's acclaim for *A Small Boy and
Others* and especially *Notes of a Son and Brother*, Holly shows that
James's sense of identity cannot be understood apart from either his
family system or his reading audience. The methodology of biography
is addressed directly in *Psychoanalytic Studies in Biography*, which
contains essays by Leon Edel and Jean Strouse on the writing of
James family biographies, as well as responses to the Edel *Life* by
James E. Miller and Joseph D. Lichtenberg, and Edel's reply. Psy-
chobiographical readings of James's writings are given by Lichtenberg ("The Jolly Corner"), Jerome Kavka ("The Liar"), and Clifton
Rhead (on James's sense of the past). Of these, Strouse's and Rhead's
are the best. Finally, Alfred Habegger's "The Lessons of the Father:

Henry James Sr. on Sexual Difference" (*HJR* 8:1–36) is an informative historical study flawed by an oddly anachronistic tone. Habegger argues that *The Bostonians* should be understood as Henry Jr.'s complex response to his father's "lessons" on women, sexuality, and privacy. Harshly judgmental of Henry Sr.'s views and dismissive of the notion of separate spheres, the essay's stance too often resembles the victim theory that feminist study has moved beyond.

ii. Sources, Parallels, Influences

Nearly half of Richard Brodhead's superlative *The School of Hawthorne* (Oxford, 1986) is devoted to tracing Hawthorne's changing influence on James's literary career. Although Brodhead's topic is not new, his study is fresh and powerful; he consistently goes beyond superficial source-hunting to show how Hawthorne structures James's literary imagination, shapes his literary techniques, and, especially, penetrates both his idea of authorship and his identity as an author. For Brodhead, stories of literary influence are inseparable from the history of literary production and publishing; by so situating his study, he tells us much about James's participation in the professionalization of writing and in the production of the literary canon. Adeline R. Tintner's *The Book World of Henry James: Appropriating the Classics* (UMI), much of which has previously been published in article form (including two 1987 pieces: "Edgar Allan Poe's Influence on Henry James" [*ABBW* 12 Jan.:105–09] and "Henry James's 'Professor Fargo' and *Don Quixote*: American Realism through a Literary Analogy" [*ALR* 19, iii:42–51]), is a more conventional source study. Invaluable as a reference work, this is not a book to be read straight through: its organization makes for much repetition; its inclusiveness, based on an admirable command of Jamesian detail, means that argument and analysis are slighted. If often unsatisfying as to the how and why of Jamesian intertextuality, Tintner's study more than amply documents *what* he "appropriated" from canonical authors from Shakespeare to Balzac. In other new work this year, Tintner's "James Discovers Jan Vermeer of Delft" (*HJR* 8:57–70) argues that in both *The Outcry* and *The Tragic Muse*, James precedes Proust as "the first novelist to introduce Vermeer as a modern taste" (p. 57). "The Art of Rococo Venice in Henry James' Fiction" (*ABBW* 21 Sept.:993–1004) traces James's growing appreciation of 18th-century Venetian art. "Thomas Couture's *Romans of the Decadence* and

Henry James's 'The Siege of London' " (*The Journal of Pre-Rapha-elite and Aesthetic Studies* 1:39–47) contends that Couture's image informs James's tale about an American "barbarian['s]" conquest of a declining English society. In "The Sea of Asof in 'The Turn of the Screw' and Maurice Barrès's *Les Déracinés*" (*ELWIU* 14:139–43), Tintner claims that by associating the lake at Bly with the Sea of Azof, James evokes Barrès's "gruesome" novel. Finally, in "Adventures in Life and Fiction" (*Midstream* 33, vi:55–56) Tintner finds that Philip Roth continues to draw on Jamesian material in *The Counterlife*.

Additional Jamesian sources are detected in notes by W. R. Martin and Warren U. Ober. Their "The Provenience of Henry James's First Tale" (*SSF* 24:57–58) argues that "A Tragedy of Error" is a rewriting of Chaucer's Franklin's Tale, while their "James's 'My Friend Bingham' and Coleridge's 'Ancient Mariner' " (*ELN* 25:44–48) contends that James's story is informed by Coleridge's poem. Gary Scharnhorst in "Henry James and the Reverend William Rounseville Alger" (*HJR* 8:71–75) suggests that a well-known Unitarian minister was the original for *The American*'s Mr. Babcock and *The Europeans*' Mr. Brand. Mary Y. Hallab in "The Governess and the Demon Lover: The Return of a Fairy Tale" (*HJR* 8:104–15) argues that "The Turn of the Screw" makes use of folkloric material found in two fairy tales, "The Adventure of Cherry of Sennor" and "The Fairy Widower," and then goes on to give a Jungian and Neu-mannian reading of James's story. Although some of the parallels among the stories are striking, Hallab gives no evidence that James read either of the two traditional tales and her reading of the story seems finally contrived. More convincing is Ross Posnock's "James, Browning, and the Theatrical Self: *The Wings of the Dove* and *In a Balcony* (*BuR* 30, ii:95–116). Like Brodhead's study, Posnock's essay goes beyond details; he demonstrates that Browning's play permeates James's novel in plot, "characterization, formal strategy, . . . the complicity of author and character," and, most importantly, the subject of theatricality (p. 98).

While Brita Lindberg-Seyersted's slight *Ford Madox Ford and His Relationship to Stephen Crane and Henry James* (Humanities) presents little that is new (apart from printing five previously unpublished James letters to Ford), it does bring scattered information together for the first time. Lindberg-Seyersted's judgments on James's behavior occasionally seem severe, but, given Edel's disdain for

Ford in the *Life*, the book may help to balance our picture of the writers' relationship. Paul Armstrong's *The Challenge of Bewilderment: Understanding and Representation in James, Conrad, and Ford* (Cornell) is a more ambitious interpretative work. Armstrong's contention that these writers "occupy a special, transitional position in the history of representation" (p. x) is not novel, nor is his description of James as the most epistemologically conservative of the three surprising. It is in his careful readings of *The Sacred Fount* and especially *The Ambassadors* that Armstrong is most rewarding, particularly when he shows how James's narrative technique is related to his epistemology.

Carol Shloss's chapter on James and Alvin Langdon Coburn, "The Frame of Prevision," in *In Visible Light*, pp. 55–92, argues that although James regarded photography as the mechanical transcription of nature, rather than a selective, creative art, there is a "fundamental though unacknowledged agreement in aesthetic aims" (p. 67) between him and Coburn. Shloss makes a convincing argument, but her discussion of the Jamesian observer, which focuses on *The Sacred Fount* and *The Princess Casamassima*, covers old territory, and she fails to analyze Coburn's Jamesian photographs themselves in any depth. Lynda S. Boren's thesis in "Undoing the *Mona Lisa*: Henry James's Quarrel with da Vinci and Pater" (*Mosaic* 20, iii:95–111)—that in his fiction James "denounced both the artist who conceived" the *Mona Lisa* and "the esthetic that derived from her overwhelming mystique" (p. 95)—oversimplifies James's ambivalent engagement with the problem of the aesthete/artist. George E. Smith III in "James, Degas, and the Modern View" (*Novel* 21:56–72) complicates the claim that James is an Impressionist by suggesting parallels between his technique in *The Ambassadors* and Degas's non-Impressionist use of formal composition, centers of consciousness, and a "fragmentary, metonymic, psycho-photographic approach to structure" (p. 70). Tony Tanner's "Proust, Ruskin, James and *le Désir de Venise*" (*JAmS* 21:5–29) argues subtly that in locating Venice as the site of desire, of "irresistible presence and intolerable absence" (p. 29), both Proust and James at once revise and repeat Ruskin. Tanner's *Scenes of Nature*, a collection of "essays" not "contributions to scholarship" (p. ix—there are no notes and Tanner pretty much ignores previous criticism), includes two chapters that couple James with other writers. "James on Hawthorne" (pp. 64–78) is a solid, interesting, if not especially original, introduction to

James's *Hawthorne* that gives nuanced attention to the imagery of the biography. That same attention informs "Henry James and Henry Adams" (pp. 94–110), a subtle comparison of the two friends' autobiographical writings. Graham Falconer's "Flaubert, James and The Problem of Undecidability" (*CL* 39:1–18) focuses primarily on Flaubert. Using "The Aspern Papers" as his James example, Falconer distinguishes Flaubertian "undecidability" ("either/or") from Jamesian "ambiguity" ("both/and"). Falconer's argument is based on close analysis of *L'éducation sentimentale* but fails to give the Jamesian story the same careful attention. Heath Moon downplays even Jamesian ambiguity in "Is *The Sacred Fount* A Symbolist Novel?" (*CL* 39:306–26), arguing that the novel owes much to French Symbolist fiction, particularly Gabriele D'Annunzio's *Le Vergini delle Rocce*, but that its Symbolism is modified by the "rational control and discipline" (p. 325) that James inherits from the novels of manners tradition. In "Trollope and James: The 'Germ' Within" (*SEL* 27:647–62) Henry N. Rogers III argues convincingly that the perception of Trollope as a literary "cobbler," fostered by his *Autobiography* and perpetuated by James, is belied by Trollope's practice in "*The Panjandrum*," a short story which describes a distinctly Jamesian creative process. Maurice J. Bennett's, *An American Tradition—Three Studies: Charles Brockden Brown, Nathaniel Hawthorne, and Henry James* (Garland) a revised 1978 dissertation, gives a "symbolic" reading of the international theme as a meditation on art, with extended attention to *The Portrait of a Lady* as an "artist-novel." While the details of Bennett's analyses are sometimes insightful, the usefulness of his study is limited by its dated assumptions about language, genre, and gender. Joan Lescinski's "Heroines Under Fire: Rebels in Austen and James" (*CEA* 49, ii–iv:60–69) is predictable in its examination of changing 19th-century representations of marriage.

Thomas H. Getz's "The Self-Portrait in the Portrait: John Ashbery's 'Self-Portrait in a Convex Mirror' and Henry James's 'The Liar'" (*StHum* 13:42–51) is suggestive, if slight. Edward Recchia, "An Eye for an I: Adapting Henry James's *The Turn of the Screw* to the Screen" (*LFQ* 15:28–35), argues that director Jack Clayton and his cinematographer, Freddie Francis, created Jamesian ambiguity and viewer involvement in *The Innocents* by reducing (rather than, like James, multiplying) the narrative frame. David Adams Leeming's "An Interview with James Baldwin on Henry James" (*HJR* 8:

47–56) reveals unexpected ways in which James served as a model for Baldwin.

Not only James's connections to other writers, but also his treatment by major critics is receiving attention. William E. Cain's excellent "Criticism and Politics: F. O. Matthiessen and the Making of Henry James" (*NEQ* 60:163–86) traces Matthiessen's surprisingly mixed feelings toward James, arguing that this ambivalence testifies "not just to the writer's weaknesses but to the critic's own conflicted attitudes toward the relation between literary criticism and politics" (p. 163). Exploring a related tension, Denis Donoghue judges James more favorably in "Blackmur on Henry James," pp. 21–43, in Edward T. Cone et al., eds., *The Legacy of R. P. Blackmur: Essays, Memoirs, Texts* (Ecco.) Donoghue traces Blackmur's changing opinions of James, focusing on *The Golden Bowl* and analyzing the reasons for Blackmur's final (and, for Donoghue, wrongheaded) judgment that both Maggie and James choose abstraction over life. Veronica A. Makowsky's "Blackmur on the Dove's Wings," pp. 63–72 in the same volume, ties Blackmur's admiration for *The Wings of the Dove* to parallels between his life and those of James's characters. Kent Bales in "Intention and Readers' Responses" (*Neohelicon* 13[1986]:177–94) attempts to uncover the intentions that impel Iser's reading of "The Figure in the Carpet."

iii. Criticism: General

Three books offer general critical introductions to James's fiction. Brian Lee's chapter, "Henry James," in *American Fiction*, pp. 85–107, examines James as an American writer, ably surveying *The Europeans, Washington Square, The Bostonians, The Portrait of a Lady*, and *The Ambassadors*. William R. Macnaughton's *Henry James: The Later Novels* (TUSAS 521) takes the point of view of an intelligent general reader in evaluating James's long fiction from *The Princess Casamassima* on, raising questions of consistency, believability, etc. Macnaughton's "Genesis and text" sections, which give the writing and publishing histories of the novels he discusses, are particularly useful. Completely useless is Benjamin Newman's *Searching for the Figure in the Carpet in the Tales of Henry James: Reflections of an Ordinary Reader* (Peter Lang), a personal quest for the "grand design," the real-life figure, in the work of "poor" misunderstood Henry James (pp. 5, 1).

James W. Gargano is the editor of *Critical Essays on Henry James: The Early Novels* and *Critical Essays on Henry James: The Late Novels* (Hall). Gargano's introductions in both volumes are excellent; his summaries of the critical histories of James's novels are especially well done. The choice of "Reviews and Contemporary Commentary" in both volumes is also fine (although there is some overlap with Gard's *Critical Heritage* [1968]); the selection of recent critical work is solid, but too conservative: feminist, Marxist, and theoretical readings of James are all excluded. Harold Bloom's editorship of *Modern Critical Views: Henry James, Modern Critical Interpretations: Henry James's* Daisy Miller, The Turn of the Screw, *and Other Tales*, and *Modern Critical Interpretations: Henry James's* The Portrait of a Lady is less satisfying (the latter is discussed here, rather than in the section *iv* below, because of the similarity of these volumes). Three of the essays in the first volume are also included in the second, and four of them reappear in the third; all of the contributions are shorn of their footnotes; the *Critical Views* and *Portrait* volumes have the same introduction, half of which is also reprinted in the *Tales* collection; each volume includes its own bibliography of secondary materials, but it is hard to determine what they are bibliographies *of*—the *Portrait* list, for example, contains entries that make no mention of the novel. The essays Bloom collects are both interesting and important. They should have been better served.

In *Metaphors of Mind in Fiction and Psychology* (Kentucky) Michael S. Kearns argues convincingly that James's fiction, along with George Eliot's, completes the historical shift from a metaphor of "mind-as-entity" to that of "sentience-as-life." Kearns contends that these novelists surpass contemporary psychologists by achieving "a new figurative language to give vivid and compact expression to what was literally inexpressible" (p. 180).

Although primarily a reading of Freud, Leo Bersani's *The Freudian Body: Psychoanalysis and Art* (Columbia, 1986) shows briefly how James's fiction stages a confrontation between the narrative self of realism and an unreadable, sexual self, between a general and a psychoanalytic psychology (pp. 81–86).

S. L. Varnado, *Haunted Presence*, employs theologian Rudolf Otto's concept of the numinous to read several of James's ghostly tales, focusing primarily on "The Turn of the Screw." J. Hillis Miller might regard Varnado's reading of James as evidence of what he calls in *The Ethics of Reading* the "almost irresistible temptation to think of the thing, matter, law, or force latent in the text as some kind of religious or metaphysical entity, the 'Absolute' as transcendent spirit," when what we are actually encountering is a law of language (p. 122). Miller himself attempts to trace in James's rereading of his texts in the Prefaces an ethics of writing and reading, to demonstrate the ways in which both are a part of conduct, of doing. Miller's definition of "ethics" finally remains problematic, and his discussion obscures James's use of the term "revision" to mean re-*writing* (as well as to designate the activities that Miller focuses on: re-reading and re-seeing). Nonetheless, his intricately textured argument is responsive to the subtleties of Jamesian "matter" and the texts through which we encounter it. In contrast, Michael Kellogg's evaluation of the late style, "The Squirrel's Heartbeat: Some Thoughts on the Later Style of Henry James" (*HudR* 40:432–36), rests on a crude dichotomy between "thinking" and "doing," and Kathleen Walsh's epistemological study, " 'Things Must Have a Basis': Verification in *The Ambassadors, The Wings of the Dove*, and *The Golden Bowl*" (*SoAR* 52: 51–64), employs key terms like "reality," "facts," and "verification" uncritically.

Robert Weisbuch's *Atlantic Double-Cross: American Literature and British Influence in the Age of Emerson* (Chicago, 1986) maintains that "not until Henry James does the Anglo-American struggle get treated with a fullness that allows it to be authentically left behind" (p. 277). Weisbuch sees in *Portrait* a "treaty of Gardencourt," whereby "the American actualist ideal" is reconciled with "the British appreciation of a reality not all-centered in the self's pleasurable egoism" (p. 291). Weisbuch's consistently interesting analysis is somewhat weakened by his coarse treatment of Osmond and the aestheticism he represents.

John Kimmey's thesis in "James's London Tales of the 1880s" (*HJR* 8:37–46) that these stories reflect "James's increasing disappointment with the London society" (p. 37) is conventional, but he is unconventionally critical of the heroines of both "A London Life" and "The Path of Duty."

Mary Suzanne Schriber's *Gender and the Writer's Imagination* argues that James subverts his culture's idea of woman by dramatizing both female and male consciousnesses. Schriber's study is flawed by her failure to recognize the debt that James's psychological fiction owes to female British novelists, her assumption that the great writer's imagination can wholly detach itself from his or her culture, and her simplistic notions about women's history.

David W. Smit, "The Later Styles of Henry James" (*Style* 21:95–106), charts the varying styles in selected pieces of James's 1899–1900 writing (letters, notebook entries, story, travel sketch, critical essay).

Bruce Bassoff, "Drifting with Henry James" (*Reader* 17:44–57), raises interesting pedagogical issues, but in the end merely re-creates the drift of discussion in a James class centered on *The Sacred Fount*.

iv. Criticism: Individual Novels

New Essays on The American, ed. Martha Banta (Cambridge), is a superb collection of essays by Peter Brooks, John Carlos Rowe, Carolyn Porter, and Mark Seltzer, which continues the recent trend of reading James's fiction in its historical, cultural, and literary contexts. Banta's introduction is itself a solid contribution to *The American* criticism. In the two strongest essays, Brooks investigates the novel's problematic swerve from comedy to melodrama, and Porter, who also treats *The American* as a problem novel, focuses on Claire de Cintré's underdeveloped characterization. Seltzer's analysis of the "relations of bodies, economies, and forms of representation" (p. 132) in the novel is especially interesting in its redefinition of the project of realism, but is marred by a prolix and mannered "theoretical" style. Rowe explores Newman's ignorance of the Bellegardes' political situation; although unconvincing at points, the essay situates James's text admirably. A companion piece is Rowe's excellent "The Politics of the Uncanny: Newman's Fate in *The American* (*HJR* 8: 79–90), which not only uncovers the "strangeness and repression" in Newman's familiar " 'good-nature' " (p. 79), but also freshly rethinks James's international theme. Harry Keyishian's interesting thesis in "Cross-Currents of Revenge in James's *The American*" (*MLS* 17:3–13)—that readers are unsatisfied with the ending of the novel because the logic of revenge that James invokes promotes our "desire for justice" (p. 12)—is given casual treatment. Keyishian draws on neither the historical relationship between revenge and literary forms nor reader-response criticism nor psychological theories of revenge.

Lauren Berlant's "Fancy-Work and Fancy Foot-Work: Motives for Silence in *Washington Square*" (*Criticism* 29:439–58) argues that the novel "painstakingly represents both the public and private conditions of cultural negation within which even the most privileged female subject knew herself and the world in pre-Civil War America" (p. 440). Berlant astutely analyzes the subtle strategies of language (rhetorical as well as bodily) and silence deployed in the text.

John M. Warner, "Renunciation as Enunciation in James's *The Portrait of a Lady* (*Renascence* 39:354–64), claims that the novel is a rewriting of *The American* which documents Isabel's awakening to "society, world, and God" (p. 354). The first two arousals are hardly critical news; Warner's case for the third is unconvincing. Gordon Hutner's "Goodwood's Lie in *The Portrait of a Lady*" (*HJR* 8:142–44) contends briefly that Goodwood lies when he tells Isabel that Ralph has asked him to look after her.

Both Tony Tanner's "*The Bostonians* and the Human Voice," pp. 148–75, in *Scenes of Nature*, and Judith Wilt's "Desperately Seeking Verena: A Resistant Reading of *The Bostonians*" (*FSt* 13:293–316) are fine essays that focus on theatricalization in the novel. Tanner argues that James dramatizes "the complex relationship of the sexual body to language" (p. 154) in and through Verena. Wilt's depiction of Verena as "improvisatrice" is a fascinating feminist " 're-vision,' " informed by literary and cultural history, but the ending beyond the ending that she finally constructs for her heroine seems unlikely.

Joseph Litvak focuses on the female character as a site of authorial anxiety in "Actress, Monster, Novelist: *The Tragic Muse* as a Novel of Theatricality" (*TSLL* 29:141–68). Litvak argues that both Miriam as the Tragic Muse and *The Tragic Muse* itself embody the way "the attempt to set up the theater as a metaphor ends by exposing an intimate complicity between theatricality and metaphor in general and, thus, between theatricality and novelistic discourse" (p. 142).

Peggy McCormack, "Exchange Economy in Henry James's *The Awkward Age*" (*UMSE* 5[1984–87]:182–202), attempts to discredit what she sees as the critical (especially Todorovian) imposition of indeterminacy on James's texts by reading the economic language of the novel; in so doing, McCormack oversimplifies and conflates structuralism and post-structuralism. Mary Y. Hallab, "Love and Death in *The Sacred Fount*" (*PMPA* 11[1986]:27–33), takes off from

Leslie Fiedler's study of the American novel in order to give an archetypal reading of the novel. Her argument that James critiques his narrator's attitudes toward love and death glosses over the novel's interpretative problems.

Janet Gabler-Hover, "Truth and Deception: The Basis for Judgment in *The Wings of the Dove*" (*TSLL* 29:169–86), draws on a mix of 18th-century Common Sense philosophy, Pragmatism, and a quasi-phenomenological view of language to contrive a distinction between Kate's "artistic lie" and Milly's "poetic truth" (p. 179). Lee Clark Mitchell's "The Sustaining Duplicities of *The Wings of the Dove*" (*TSLL* 29:187–214) is a more subtle look at deception and doubling in the novel. Mitchell finds Kate's "embrace of discordancy" (p. 210) both representative of James's technique and a model for the reader. The title of Adeline R. Tintner and Henry D. Janowitz's "Inoperable Cancer: An Alternate Diagnosis for Milly Theale's Illness" (*Jour. of the Hist. of Medicine and Allied Sciences* 42:73–76) makes its claim clear.

Courtney Johnson, Jr., *Henry James and the Evolution of Consciousness: A Study of* The Ambassadors (Mich. State), relies on studies of Transcendental Meditation in his repetitive, lengthy exploration of how Strether evolves toward a "higher consciousness." Symptomatic of the problems with this book is the fact that in order to make his case, Johnson must ignore Maria Gostrey's role in Strether's change while over-valuing that of Gloriani (who, Johnson says, has achieved "universal vision" [p. 59]). Gabrielle Robinson's definition of the nature of patronage in "Patronage in *The Ambassadors*: A False Position or No Position" (*NCL* 42:203–16) is more promising, but her application of it to *The Ambassadors* results in a reading that seems stubbornly at odds with the novel (e.g., Chad and Mrs. Newsome are praised at Strether's expense). David Smit's "The Emperor's Later Clothes—An Experiment in Stylistic Theory and the Writing of Henry James" (*IJLS* 4, ii[1983]:81–90) rewrites sentences from *The Ambassadors* to suggest "alternative ways in which James could have said the same thing while achieving the same effects" (p. 84); most readers will prefer the original. More sensitive to James's text is Leland S. Person, Jr.'s argument in "Strether's 'Penal Form': The Pleasure of Imaginative Surrender" (*PLL* 23:27–40) that Strether's relationships with women aid him in "building punishment into his very experience of imaginative pleasure" (p. 29).

Margery Sabin's "Competition of Intelligence in *The Golden Bowl*," in *The Dialect of the Tribe: Speech and Community in Modern Fiction* (Oxford), pp. 65–105, reads the first half of the novel, which she associates with Charlotte, as establishing "ineradicably in our minds the complex, ambiguous, even vulgar texture of these characters' social experience," while Maggie's (and James's) abstract "method" in Volume Two "transforms and transcends the meanings of Volume One, yet not altogether" (p. 67). Sabin's careful account of the tensions generated by this reading experience is intriguing, but the distinction she draws between the two parts of the novel and of James's career, between ordinary and transcendent language, intelligence, and values, is itself finally too much of a critical abstraction. Martha Nussbaum, in " 'Finely Aware and Richly Responsible': Literature and the Moral Imagination," in *Literature and the Question of Philosophy*, ed. and introduced by Anthony J. Cascardi (Johns Hopkins), pp. 169–91, sets forth the provocative thesis, which is not new for Professor Nussbaum, that "the novel is itself a moral achievement, and the well-lived life is a work of literary art" (p. 169). Nussbaum's important claim is that the moral quality of James's text lies precisely in the images and language that compose it. Unfortunately, she weakens her argument by disregarding the rich ambiguity that literary critics like Yeazell have explored in that language (see Nussbaum's ignoring of James's "might have" and "It could pass, further, for" on pp. 172–74). In contrast, the brilliant analysis of such stylistic details is what supports Meili Steele's contention in "The Drama of Reference in James's *The Golden Bowl*" (*Novel* 21:73–88) that the central drama of the novel is "the designation of an extra-linguistic entity and speculation on the nature of this entity" (p. 73). This powerful essay, informed by current linguistics and philosophy, justifies Steele's large claim that he is opening up "not only a new reading for James's Major Phase but also a new approach for post-structuralist criticism" (p. 88). Also far-reaching are the implications of Lynda Zwinger's finely textured "The Sentimental Gilt of Heterosexuality: James's *The Golden Bowl*" (*Raritan* 7, ii:70–92). Zwinger reads Maggie as a representative "daughter of sentiment," a figure who screens "the story that structures all heterosexual relations of desire," the unarticulated "relation between the impassive desiring father and his acquiescent desirable daughter" (p. 73).

v. Criticism: Individual Tales

A note by W. R. Martin and Warren U. Ober, "Henry James's 'Travelling Companions': Did the Master Nod?" (*N & Q* 34:46-47), points out an error in James's description of Tintoretto's San Cassiano's *Crucifixion*.

Todd K. Bender's *A Concordance to Henry James's Daisy Miller* (Garland), the second volume in a set of projected concordances to James's complete works, is based on the New York Edition version of the tale.

Starting with what has become a standard "deconstructionist" claim—"James plays with and around the notion of authoritative forms and the discourse that enacts them" (p. 91)—George Bishop gives a perspicacious reading of a little-known tale in "Addressing 'A Bundle of Letters': Henry James and the Hazard of Authority" (*HJR* 8:91-103).

Mary P. Freier in "The Story of 'The Author of Beltraffio'" (*SSF* 24:308-09) argues briefly that there is no reliable textual evidence that Beatrice Ambient allows her son to die.

Peg Levine, "Henry James's 'Louisa Pallant' and the Participant-Observer Narrator and Responsibility" (*MHLS* 10:33-41), makes the pedestrian point that James, among others, uses "participant-observers" as narrators in order to suggest that "involvement, not objectivity . . . leads to understanding" (p. 40).

Dorothea Krook's " 'The Aspern Papers': A Counter-Introduction," in *Essays on English and American Literature*, pp. 223-34, argues unconventionally that the narrator is "morally sensitive" and "compassionate" (p. 223). Although much of her close reading of the novella is astute, Krook's argument is finally not persuasive.

Christof Wegelin's note on "Art and Life in James's 'The Middle Years'" (*MFS* 33:639-46) states that the story reflects James's conviction "that although fiction springs from an author's sense of reality the creative process has a core that is not accessible to rational analysis" (p. 640).

Terry Heller in *Delights of Terror* draws on Todorov and Iser to anatomize both the tale of terror and its reader's response. In his chapter on James, "The Master's Trap: James's *The Turn of the Screw*," pp. 147-68, Heller argues (not fully convincingly) that "the tale demands that the implied reader love the governess" (p. 164).

Dale M. Bauer and Andrew Lakritz's suggestive essay, "Language, Class, and Sexuality in Henry James's 'In the Cage'" (*NOR* 14, iii:61–69), situates James's telegraphist in an emerging service economy, showing how her role as interpretant is structured by gender and class.

Donald Gutierrez in "The Self-Devouring Ego: Henry James' *The Beast in the Jungle* As a Parable of Vanity" (*NR* 5, ii[1986]:6–14) offers only a slight variation on standard readings of the story.

Annette Larson Benert's "Dialogical Discourse in 'The Jolly Corner': The Entrepeneur as Language and Image" (*HJR* 8:116–25) attempts in too short a space to bring the theories of Bakhtin, Geertz, and Gilligan, among others, to bear on James's late tale.

vi. Criticism: Specific Nonfictional Works

James L. Machor's *Pastoral Cities: Urban Ideals and the Symbolic Landscape of America* (Wisconsin) argues briefly, but astutely, that in *The American Scene* James recognizes how the American denial of history makes the achievement of urban pastoralism impossible. Also focused on *The American Scene* is Ross Posnock's "Henry James, Veblen, and Adorno: The Crisis of the Modern Self" (*JAmS* 21:31–54), a sophisticated analysis of James's immanent critical engagement with American modernity.

My "James's Revisions in 'The Novel in "The Ring and the Book"'" (*MP* 85:57–64) shows how in converting a commemorative talk to a critical essay, James demonstrates an acute awareness of genre and audience.

University of Louisville

8. Pound and Eliot

Reed Way Dasenbrock

This is probably the first year in a long time in which more was written about Eliot than about Pound. Eliot's centenary—in full swing as this is written; over as it is read—has something to do with this, of course, and it will be interesting to see what balance is struck between Eliot and Pound criticism after the two centenaries are over. But a good deal of interesting work continues to be done on both writers, as I hope the following should show.

i. Pound

a. **Text, Biography, and Bibliography.** The pace of activity in this area of Pound studies picked up substantially this year over last. Somewhat improbably, Pound the dramatist occupies center stage this year. Pound's version of Sophocles' *Electra*, done with Rudd Fleming in 1949, was produced in New York in November, and J. Ellen Gainor provides a report in *Paideuma* 16, iii:127–31; published this year was Pound's *Plays Modelled on the Noh (1916)*, ed. Donald C. Gallup (Univ. of Toledo Library). This interesting little book contains four dramatic sketches written in 1916 at the height of Pound's interest in the Noh. Only one of the four, "Tristan," seems directly modeled on the Noh in the way Yeats's *At the Hawk's Well* is. The others seem modeled more on Synge's plays, showing that Pound as well as Yeats saw the Noh through Irish eyes. Pound was no dramatist, in my opinion, and we don't need to regret that these are unfinished sketches, but it is fascinating to watch Pound attempting to master yet another artistic form.

Pound/Zukovsky, ed. Barry Ahearn, is a beautifully edited addition to the New Directions series of Pound's correspondence with his peers. The real interest of this volume is Zukovsky's letters more than Pound's. Pound tended to give "Zuk" avuncular advice, but Zukovsky reacted against that advice. Politics occasioned their

fiercest disputes, and as Pound's other friends tended to turn a
deaf ear to Pound's politics, the resulting interplay is fascinating.
Sanehide Kodama's well-edited and handsome *Ezra Pound and Japan: Letters & Essays* (Black Swan) covers Pound's contacts with
Japan from 1911 to 1968 and is valuable for helping to correct the
common conception that the sustaining source of Pound's Orientalism
was China alone—not Japan. The volume could almost be called
"Pound/Kitasono," for it finds its focus in Pound's correspondence
with the Japanese poet Kitue Kitasono. Kitasono—like Zukovsky—
wrote Pound about poetry and received letters about politics in return, but even he must have enjoyed Pound's wonderfully wacky
proposal to head off World War II by trading Guam to the Japanese
in return for a complete set of recordings of the Noh plays!

Other published correspondence includes "A Letter from Ezra
Pound to Etienne Gilson," ed. David Brooks (*Helix* 19[1984]:29–33),
a 1932 letter responding to Gilson's review of Pound's *Cavalcanti*,
and Ann Massa's "Ezra Pound to Harriet Monroe: Two Unpublished
Letters" (*Paideuma* 16, i–ii:33–47), in which the letters unfortunately
are quoted from—not given whole—and are swamped by commentary. Mohammed Shaheen's "Pound and Itrat-Husain" (*Paideuma*
16, iii:81–88), an account of Pound's limited acquaintance with a
Pakistani educator, suffers from the same fault, as well as from con-
fusing exposition. Editors of letters ought not to be simultaneously
writing articles, and this mixed genre apparently encouraged at
Paideuma doesn't serve anyone very well.

A new biography appeared this year, John Tytell's *Ezra Pound:
The Solitary Volcano* (Anchor). The ideal biographer of Ezra Pound
would need three qualities: first, the ability to tell a good story in
order to construct a coherent narrative of Pound's life; second, an
ability to see Pound steadily and see him whole, to write neither
apology nor diatribe; and third, a thorough mastery of Pound's
oeuvre, his literary and intellectual contexts, and the contexts needed
to understand his work. Tytell has the first two but not the third,
which means that he has produced a readable, balanced, and relatively compact biography of Pound. Pound scholars, however, will
notice many mistakes and oversimplifications in Tytell's account,
particularly when he deals with the intellectual contexts of Pound's
work. The definitive biography has yet to be written, and it will require a massive, multivolume work of the kind Tytell deplores in his
introduction.

While we are waiting for that definitive biography, however, biographical portraits of Pound continue to be written. The most substantial of these this year is James Laughlin's *Ez as Wuz: Essays and Lectures on Ezra Pound* (Graywolf), which collects the biographical and critical pieces Laughlin has written on Pound in recent years in one handsome and useful volume. Thomas Cole offers an interesting account of "Ezra Pound and *Imagi*" (*Paideuma* 16, iii:53–66), *Imagi* being a little magazine edited by Cole with Pound's encouragement from St. Elizabeths. Jaime Garcia Terres in "Clock of Athens" (*Paideuma* 16, i–ii:75–77) offers a brief memoir of an encounter with Pound in the 1960s.

Two bibliographical aids for the Pound scholar were published this year: Volker Bischoff and Eric Homberger provide "A Checklist of Creative Responses to Ezra Pound" (*BB* 44, i:35–37), a list of parodies of and homages to Pound from the 1910s to the present; and Joseph Brogunier has compiled "An Annotated Bibliography of Works about Ezra Pound: 1980–1984" (*Paideuma* 16, i–ii:93–257), concrete evidence of just how much work is being done on Pound.

b. General Studies. Two good books by James Longenbach and Kathryne V. Lindberg open up new ground in Pound studies this year. Lindberg's central thesis in *Reading Pound Reading: Modernism after Nietzsche* (Oxford) is that Pound's method of reading, found particularly in his prose works, is Nietzschean in its move away from objectivity toward a kind of will to textual power, what today we might call strong reading. Lindberg relates this to Pound's attempt to upset established orthodoxies, particularly the critical orthodoxy being established by T. S. Eliot in the 1930s. All of this makes good sense, though Lindberg is less sensitive than she might be to Pound's desire to create his own new orthodoxy in turn. My major reservation about the book, however, is that mingled with her discussion of how Pound parallels Nietzsche is a more traditional source study that tries to show Nietzsche's influence on Pound; the source study just doesn't deliver what it should, and she would have been better off just arguing for an interesting parallel.

James Longenbach's excellent *Modernist Poetics* is a more traditional study, offering less of a challenge to our received image of Pound, but—for my taste—it strikes a more satisfactory balance between traditional scholarship and interpretive criticism. It also relates Pound to Continental thought, but to a rather different tradition, to the "existential historicism" of Dilthey, Croce, and others. For this tradition the key value of history is not in itself, but in how it has helped create the present, and Longenbach's line of inquiry provides a richer context than we have had before for Eliot's notion of tradition and Pound's poem containing history. But Longenbach portrays Pound turning away from this tradition in *The Cantos* toward a more positivist conception of history in a discussion that sheds a valuable and critical light on Pound's use of documents in the poem.

Three other books contain brief discussions of Pound as part of larger studies. Julian Symons's *Makers of the New* is an unpretentious and clear narrative of Anglo-American modernism. Hugh Kenner's *The Mechanic Muse* (Oxford) is a delightful book focusing on the relation between major modernist writers and technology, though I found the chapter on "Pound Typing" less suggestive than others, particularly the one on Eliot. In contrast, Mutlu Konuk Blasing's *American Poetry* is a bizarre study that plots 12 American poets on a chart according to the four master tropes: Pound is a poet of synecdoche along with Whitman and O'Hara; Eliot a poet of metonymy along with Poe and Plath; and so on. The useful part of her book is her critique of Bloom's notion that American poetry has a father in Emerson and one tradition of Emersonian verse, but the map of four discrete traditions she puts in its place is unpersuasive and just as unsatisfactory. Bloom himself contributes to Pound studies with his collection of criticism on Pound, *Ezra Pound* (Chelsea House). This is simply a terrible book: Bloom's introduction says nothing illuminating at all; his choice of essays slights crucial early essays in favor of a mishmash of generally good but necessarily less seminal recent Pound criticism; and, finally, all of the notes to the essays have been excised, so that one has to return to the essays' original publication to find them in a usable form.

The two discussions of Pound's politics in *Paideuma* (16, iii) this year unfortunately suggest that the journal's ambition is to become the center of Pound apologetics rather than Pound studies. William Mcnaughton's "New Light on the *Pisan Cantos* and *Rock Drill*: Milton Friedman and Herman Kahn" (pp. 23–51) says nothing at all about the *Pisan Cantos* or *Rock Drill* and very little about Herman Kahn or Milton Friedman. For Mcnaughton, Pound was right about everything, and he tries to show this by anecdotes about money he has made in the markets and by quotations he can't quite remember from books he doesn't have at hand. *Paideuma* simply has to do better than this. Marjorie Perloff's "Fascism, Anti-Semitism, Isolationism: Contextualizing the 'Case of EP' " (pp. 7–21) is better, of course, as she has a number of smart and witty points about how the orthodox American left in the late 1930s was isolationist and anti-Semitic in ways that remind one of Pound's stances in the same years. But this doesn't quite add up to a defense of Pound, as she seems to think, as much as an attack on some of those who have attacked him in turn.

Three articles in *Critical Inquiry* (14) provide another look at the "case of Ezra Pound." A trial judge, Conrad L. Rushing, looks in " 'Mere Words': The Trial of Ezra Pound" (pp. 111–33) at some of the legal issues and precedents surrounding Pound's incarceration without trial. Rushing argues that had Pound's case come to trial in the 1940s, he probably would have received a shorter stay in prison than he actually received by avoiding trial. William M. Chace in "Ezra Pound: 'Insanity,' 'Treason,' and Care" (pp. 134–41) makes a parallel—if less concrete—argument that those who helped Pound avoid trial were not the friends they seemed, as putting him in St. Elizabeths "extracted from him the dignity as a man" he should have had. Both articles are Monday-morning quarterbacking and ignore the charged climate of the time; Pound's friends were trying to keep him alive, an understandably higher priority on their part than legal probabilities or Pound's subsequent dignity. (Though it must be said that Ronald Duncan criticized the insanity defense and urged precisely Rushing's strategy in correspondence in 1948.) The best of the three *CritI* articles is Richard Sieburth's "In Pound We Trust: The Economy of Poetry/The Poetry of Economics" (pp. 142–72), a comparison of Pound's aesthetics and economics that makes good use of the recent theoretical and Lacanian work done on Pound.

Pound's politics continue to attract a good deal of commentary elsewhere. M. L. Rosenthal's "The 'Actaeon-Principle': Political Aesthetic of Joyce and the Poets" (*SR* 23:541–56) and Bob Perelman's "Good & Bad/Good & Evil: Pound, Céline, and Fascism" (*Poetics* 6[1986]:6–25) provide two good examples, respectively, of the traditional and the emerging approaches to this issue. The traditional approach explains away rather than explains the politics. Rosenthal has some perceptive remarks about the lyricization of epic form in Pound, but he has considerably more to say about aesthetics than politics and tries unsuccessfully to explain Pound's politics as "the inevitable blundering into violation of the forbidden that attends the free, exploring imagination." In contrast, Perelman's generally good essay errs—as much of the new work on Pound's politics does—on the side of giving Pound a harder time than he deserves, and I find Perelman's use of Céline to criticize Pound more than a little disturbing given Céline's political record, considerably more reprehensible than Pound's. Peter Viereck is one of the few critics who has been giving Pound a hard time for the last 40 years. He continues in "Pound, Williams and the Road Not Taken" (*Parnassus* 13, ii[1986]:125–39), an article that complains about the course taken by modernist poetry, about Pound's anti-Semitism, and about the bad reviews his own poetry has received, according to Viereck, because of his attacks on Pound. Viereck, in short, is more cranky than interesting.

Three articles in the *Journal of Evolutionary Psychology* (8, iii) on Pound focus on his anti-Semitism, and the results of three psychologists analyzing Pound are pretty dismal. None of them is well enough informed about Pound to keep from making lots of mistakes; his remarks about Freud give them fits; and the reductiveness of their explanations tends to supply new evidence for Pound's views on psychology. If you believe "all strong feelings of racial prejudice have their origin in the relative irresolution of infantile inner conflict," then Arnold Maddaloni's "Ezra Pound: A Study in Contradiction" (pp. 171–78) is just for you. Betsy Kufta's "Ezra Pound and Anti-Semitism: Confronting the Pisan Cantos" (pp. 179–86) is even less substantial, being mostly a familiar summary of Pound's life. Paul Neumarkt's "The Ezra Pound Issue: A Psychological Assessment" (pp. 187–90) labels Pound "a schizophrenic with a strong current of paranoia" as well as having "an immature, infantilistic proclivity in his psyche."

Other general studies include Cordell D. K. Yee's "Discourse on Ideogrammic Method" (*AL* 59:242–56), which usefully relates Pound's poetry to empiricism, though it argues less persuasively that Pound's method never changes, an argument that trips over itself in trying to account for the overt didacticism of the Middle Cantos. Mary de Rachewiltz doesn't say much about her ostensible subject in "Translating the Cantos" (*MQR* 26:524–34), which is mostly a general introduction to *The Cantos* with a few specific remarks about the Adams Cantos. K. K. Ruthven's "Ezra's Appropriations" (*TLS* 20–26 Nov.:1248, 1300–01) is a slanted account of Pound's transformation of *The New Freewoman* into *The Egoist*; a much more interesting study from the same writer is "The Disclosures of Inscription: Ezra (Loomis) (Weston) Pound" (*Jour. of the Aus-*

tralasian Universities Lang. and Lit. Assn. 66[1986]:159–78), which plays around with Pound's various names and interest in playing with names, both of which Ruthven finds significant for Pound's career. Finally, *Voices & Visions*, a book of essays designed to accompany the PBS series on American poetry of the same title, has an essay by Hugh Kenner on "Ezra Pound" (pp. 205–41), an excellent brief general introduction to the poetry.

c. **Relation to Other Writers.** Pound's relation to other American poets and writers is the central focus of work belonging to this section this year, and most of the work turns on quarrels with Pound, either quarrels of the writers themselves or quarrels brought to the subject by the critics. Maud Ellmann's *The Poetics of Impersonality: T. S. Eliot and Ezra Pound* (Harvard) is more about Eliot than it is about Pound, but places Pound's views on impersonality under the same rubric as Eliot's and attacks both. Carolyn Burke's "Getting Spliced: Modernism and Sexual Difference" (*AQ* 39:98–121) is a rather confused article about Pound's relation to Stein, Marianne Moore, and Mina Loy: she wants to criticize Pound for his "phallogocentrism" and to praise Stein for arriving at a modernist aesthetic before Pound, but the story she tells also reveals that it was the "phallogocentric" Pound, not Stein, who promoted the work of Loy and Moore. The line that Pound and others buried an alternative feminist modernism doesn't quite square with Pound's promoting of so many of these feminist modernists. Jay Rogoff's "Pound-Foolishness in *Paterson*" (*JML* 14, i:35–44) explores how Williams progressively exorcizes Pound's voice from *Paterson*. A pair of good articles in *American Poetry* (4, i) explore the Olson-Pound relationship. George F. Butterick's "Ezra Pound and the 'Truculent Ummugrunt'" (pp. 22–37) offers a careful look at Olson's disagreement with Pound over the issues of race and ethnicity; Michael F. Harper's "The Sins of the Fathers: Charles Olson and Ezra Pound" (pp. 38–53) focuses on Olson's early poem "Thomas Granger," showing how it appropriates Pound's documentary techniques yet quarrels with Pound's ideas. Perhaps the most interesting of these articles is Michael Davidson's "'From the Latin *Speculum*': The Modern Poet as Philologist" (*ConL* 28:187–205), which focuses on the "lexical insert," the momentary turn to the dictionary to gloss a word or phrase and inclusion of that gloss in a poem. Davidson finds such "lexical inserts" in the poetry of Duncan, Snyder, Whalen, and Olson as well as

Pound, but he finds the role of the lexical inserts changing in the turn
from a modernist to a postmodernist aesthetic.

d. **The Shorter Poems and Translations.** Not a great deal was published on Pound's shorter poems this year. John R. Clark briefly
explores the theme of *"Nada* in Pound's *'Portrait d'une Femme'"*
(*NConL* 17, ii:2–3). A pair of articles by Bruce Fogelman in *Paideuma* (16, i–ii) find models for *The Cantos* among the earlier poems.
In "Pound's 'Cathay': A Structural Model for *The Cantos*" (pp. 49–
60) Fogelman argues that *Cathay's* organization into a sequence anticipates the construction of *The Cantos*; I am partial to arguments
for the centrality of *Cathay*, but Fogelman seems to me to be reaching a bit. That is clearly the case in "Beddoes in the Sea Surge, or a
Glimpse of *The Cantos* in 1908," (pp. 89–91), in which Fogelman
finds a model for Canto I in the 1908 poem "Beddoesesque." If a
critic feels compelled to conclude, "This may seem to be loading too
much onto the little poem," he probably is.

Paying needed attention to one of Pound's neglected works is
Edith Sarra in "Whistling in the Bughouse: Notes on the Process of
Pound's Confucian Odes" (*Paideuma* 16, i–ii:7–31), whose study—
informed by work with the manuscripts—focuses on Pound's knowledge of and attempts to imitate Chinese sonority.

e. **The Cantos.** Specific commentary on *The Cantos* seems to have
slowed somewhat in comparison with recent years. Barry Ahearn
provides "An Early Schema for *The Cantos*" (*Paideuma* 16, i–ii:79–
81), with some interesting speculations about Pound's 1922 reshap-
ing of *The Cantos* based on some of Pound's rather sketchy notes.
Another good article on the opening of the poem is Robert Mc-
Mahon's "Homer/Pound's Odysseus and Virgil/Ovid/Dante's Ulysses: Pound's First Canto and the *Commedia*" (*Paideuma* 16, iii:67–
75), which has some new and interesting things to say on the reading
of Dante in Canto 1 and about why the material from the Homeric
Hymns is in that Canto. Robert McNamara also has new things to
say about a familiar topic, arguing in "Pound's Malatesta: An Alternative to the Martial Ideal" (*PCP* 20[1985]:57–64) that Pound's interest in Malatesta was as a Nietzschean artistic hero to be opposed to
the martial ideal Pound found enshrined around him. Walter Sut-
ton has a related theme in *"Trilogy* and *The Pisan Cantos*: The Shock
of War" (*Sagetrieb* 6, i:41–52), which compares H.D.'s and Pound's

responses to World War II in terms of their revision of the "heroic code." Margaret M. Dunn briefly explores "Eine Kleine Wortmusik: The Marriage of Poetry and Music in the *Pisan Cantos*" (*PCL* 13: 101–09). Michael Coyle's "The Implications of Inclusion: Historical Narrative in Pound's Canto LXXXVIII" (*ELH* 54:215–30) reads closely a chunk taken from Thomas Hart Benton in Canto 88; the close reading is interesting, the general conclusions less so, as his general point about the "subordination of syntactical-grammatical relations to visual-perceptual ones" is surely well understood by now.

Omar Pound in "Canto 77: 'Rebel Rose'" (*Paideuma* 16, i–ii:83–85) offers a brief explication of the passage about Margaret Cravens's grandmother in Canto 77. Massimo Bacigalupo finds in "A Quotation from Whittier in Ezra Pound's Canto 90" (*N&Q* 232:58–59) that the quotation attributed to John Randolph in that canto actually comes from Whittier's "Randolph of Roanoke." And Thomas Willard's "John Heydon's Visions: 'Pretty' or 'Polluted'" (*Paideuma* 16, i–ii:61–72) is informative about the strange figure John Heydon in Cantos 87 and 91.

ii. Eliot

The *Yeats Eliot Review* has found a new home at the University of Arkansas at Little Rock and began appearing quarterly at the end of 1987.

a. **Text and Biography.** As usual, a much smaller part of Eliot studies than of Pound studies. Michael Tilby publishes and comments on "T. S. Eliot's Unpublished *Marginalia* on Gide's Translation of 'Little Gidding'" (*RLC* 60[1986]:219–24). Most of Eliot's comments, dissents from the translation, are interesting pointers to Eliot's sense of his own work. William Baker describes "Some T. S. Eliot Inscribed Copies" in *BC* (36:124–27); the only item of interest here is Eliot quoting Dante in an inscribed copy to Emily Hale.

Donald E. Stanford's "The First Mrs. Eliot" (*LCUT* 40:88–111) is a portrait of Vivienne Eliot based on what can be gleaned about her from her unpublished letters and those of Ottoline Morrell, Bertrand Russell, and others in the collections of the University of Texas. Ignatius G. Mattingly's "Mr. Eliot Visits the Elizabethan Club" (*YULG* 62:19–22) purports to be a verbatim transcription of remarks Eliot made at Yale 40 years ago. And Tjebbe Westendorp's "How

Pleasant to Meet Mr. Eliot! An Account of a Forgotten Interview"
(*Essays on English and American Literature*, pp. 173–76) is an account of an untranslated 1948 interview with Eliot by a Dutchman,
Michel van der Plas. Lawrence Durrell's "Letters to T. S. Eliot" were
included in the first of two issues of *Twentieth Century Literature*
(33:348–58) devoted to the younger writer's 75th birthday; these
letters mostly treat publishing matters, adding to our knowledge of
Eliot's role as mentor to several generations of younger British poets.

b. **General Studies.** One of the best books on Eliot this year is Cleo
Kearns's *T. S. Eliot and Indic Traditions* (Cambridge), a good,
original book on a subject that one would have thought didn't afford
the material for a new book. Kearns is particularly good on Eliot's
interest in Buddhism, which has been largely neglected in favor of
an emphasis on Hinduism. And she isn't committed to a debilitating
either/or, Western or Eastern, model of influence, which causes so
many exaggerated claims in studies of this kind. Without overstating
her case, she persuasively finds Indic elements in many more places
in Eliot's work than the allusions we all recognize; in particular, the
themes of memory and desire in *The Waste Land* look rather different after her treatment.

Two British introductions to Eliot are offered this year, Angus
Calder's *T. S. Eliot* (Humanities) and F. B. Pinion's *A T. S. Eliot
Companion: Life and Works* (Macmillan and Barnes & Noble). Of
the two, Calder's has a more unusual approach, as it tries to sidestep
the existing mass of work on Eliot by ostensibly offering a fresh
reading of the poems' surface. This approach is often supplanted,
however, by Calder's generally Marxist attempt to place Eliot's work
as right-wing, which necessarily involves a move beyond surfaces
toward contexts, and this rather contradictory combination of approaches doesn't really deliver any particularly new insights. Pinion
seems less at odds with the kind of book he is writing, so his *Companion* does a fairly good job of the difficult task of introducing all
of Eliot's life and work in brief compass. Both books, however, help
to indicate why Eliot criticism is so much livelier in America than in
Britain. Both have some rather bizarre notions about how Eliot's
American background shaped his work, and generally speaking
Eliot's American critics seem much more conversant with the British
contexts of his later life than the British critics are with the earlier
American contexts. Given the Marxist bent of so much British criti-

cism these days, Eliot's politics also gives the British critics fits, posing less the interesting challenge that has led to good British work on Pound than a vague irritant that sets the critics' teeth on edge. Frank Kermode's general survey, "T. S. Eliot," in *Voices and Visions*, pp. 277–311, also seems to fuss unduly about the poet's nationality in an otherwise good introduction to his life and work.

This general characterization of British Eliot criticism makes me welcome all the more Robert Crawford's *The Savage and the City in the Work of T. S. Eliot* (Oxford). Crawford's study, finding its focus in Eliot's application of ideas from anthropology and comparative religion, is a perceptive and well-researched look at the images of the savage and the city in Eliot's work and at how these apparent opposites sometimes interpenetrate. It is particularly good on Eliot's childhood and his poetry from "Prufrock" to *The Hollow Men*; though Crawford admits finally that the "city/savage confrontation" trails off into "gentle pastoral," he traces it quite a bit further into Eliot's later Christian thinking than I think tenable, and this is part of a general tendency to push his points farther than they will really go. I'm also a little disturbed at Crawford's overly comfortable acceptance of the term savage; it is true that he is following the general usage of Eliot's day, but in so doing he sometimes seems more condescending toward "the savage" than he should be or than Eliot ever was. But this is an important contribution to Eliot studies.

More general treatments of modernism this year that include discussions of Eliot are Julian Symons's *Makers of the New* (New York), a good general treatment of modernism that discusses Eliot at length, and Hugh Kenner's *The Mechanic Muse* (Oxford). Kenner's chapter on Eliot, "Eliot Observing," is one of the best general studies on Eliot I know, relating a wide range of Eliot's works to aspects of modern life such as commuting and telephones. This is Kenner at his most suggestive.

Eliot is a poet who crosses cultural boundaries easily and widely, and some good articles from Asian scholars on Eliot this year testify to this. Victor P. H. Li's "Narcissism and the Limits of the Lyric Self" (in *Tropic Crucible: Self and Theory in Language and Literature*, eds. Ranjit Chatterjee and Colin Nicholson [Singapore and Ohio, 1984], pp. 3–23) argues suggestively—if too briefly—that narcissism is the inevitable concomitant of lyric poetry and that Eliot's (and Pound's and Williams's) critique of narcissism is related to their turn away from lyric. Considerably more substantial are a pair of long articles by Shunichi Takayanagi, S.J., published in *ELLS*, "T. S. Eliot: Christianity, Politics and Criticism" (22[1985]:43–87) and "'The Years of *L'Entre Deux Guerres*': Politics of the Nineteen-Thirties and T. S. Eliot's Political Philosophy" (23[1986]:91–142). These are long, careful, and sympathetic expositions of Eliot's search for a satisfactory Christian political position, less original research than synthesis of existing work. And Midori Matsui's "The Submerged Self: The Displacement and Return of the Lyric Subject in T. S. Eliot's Early Poems" (*SELit* 64:61–77) traces the contradiction between Eliot's desire to move away from subjectivism and his continuing to hold onto a unifying "lyric subject" or point of view in his early poetry. This covers some of the same material covered by Maud Ellmann's *Poetics of Impersonality* but more satisfactorily because less dogmatically. Less interesting is Ranajay Karlekar's "T. E. Hulme and T. S. Eliot: Crisis and Tradition" (in *The Romantic Tradition*, ed. Visvanath Chatterjee [Jadavpur Univ., 1984], pp. 130–45), which goes over familiar material about Hulme and Eliot and their critique of romanticism.

Other general studies include Paul Oppenheim's "Eliot as Revolutionary" (*AmBR* 9, iii:1, 12), which makes a rather dubious argument that Eliot is the only true revolutionary in 20th-century poetry, and two essays by Laura Niesen de Abruña. Her "Lengthened Shadow of a Myth: The Herakles Motif in T. S. Eliot's Work" (*SoAR* 52, ii:65–84) is a study of Eliot's use of Herakles that pushes its case way too far, finding Herakles and anti-herculean figures everywhere in Eliot's work, whereas "Pattern in T. S. Eliot's Poetry" (*MHLS* 10: 51–61) is more interesting though more general, contrasting the generally cyclical pattern of his early poetry to the ascending patterns of the poetry written after his conversion. Two essays in *The Modernists* discuss Eliot: Richard D. Lehan's "Cities of the Living/Cities of the Dead: Joyce, Eliot, and the Origins of Myth in Modernism" (pp. 61–74) wanders from Sumerian myth through Joyce and Eliot to Pynchon without finding a focus; E. L. Epstein's considerably more interesting "Purgation by Form in the Poetry of T. S. Eliot" (pp. 192–201) discusses "the appearance of regularity in the middle of irregularity" in Eliot's versification.

If I were to recommend any one general study of Eliot published in 1987, it would be Wyndham Lewis's delightfully irreverent look at "T. S. Eliot—The Pseudo Believer" in his 1934 *Men Without Art,*

reprinted this year by Black Sparrow in a beautiful edition edited by
Seamus Cooney. That Eliot's close friendship with Lewis survived
this attack is perhaps the best testimony we have to Eliot's tolerance,
as not much is left of Eliot's notions of objectivity after Lewis has
his fun with them.

c. Relation to Other Writers. This continues to be the liveliest area
of Eliot studies. I have already praised James Longenbach's *Modernist Poetics*, which is as good on Eliot's sense of history as it is on
Pound's, though Pound is given more space. Maud Ellmann's *The
Poetics of Impersonality: T. S. Eliot and Ezra Pound* (Harvard) is
considerably less compelling. The central thesis of her book seems
to be that both writers worked with and advocated a rather confused theory of impersonality in poetry. But the confusion is more
Ellmann's than Eliot's or Pound's: in a familiar deconstructive move,
she fails to find a coherent theory and therefore proclaims their theory
to be an incoherent failure, but she never establishes that they were
trying to develop such a coherent theory in the first place. What is
perceptive in the book is mostly taken from Wyndham Lewis's critique of Eliot and Pound on precisely this point, and Lewis on these
matters remains considerably more cogent, entertaining, and concise.

But Longenbach and Ellmann share a fairly traditional sense of
Pound and Eliot as close partners, a sense that comes under challenge
from two books published by Oxford: Stanley Sultan's *Eliot, Joyce
and Company* and Louis Menand's *Discovering Modernism*. Men-
and's primary concern is to distinguish Eliot from Pound and the
aesthetic of Imagism, and he focuses on how Pound's Imagism is still
caught up in the poetry of sincerity and with establishing the profession of literature. Eliot inherits this problematic but doesn't get
caught up in it, according to Menand, because he somehow deploys
Imagist strategies but maintains a critical distance from them. Men-
and's reading does a good job of specifying the relationship between
Eliot's early work and Imagism; my reservation is that I wonder if
any poet was ever as conscious, deliberate, and ingenious in position-
ing his work as the young T. S. Eliot Menand describes. Sultan's
book is harder to summarize: its curiously elusive thesis seems to be
that Eliot and Joyce are closer to each other than they are to the
other modernists. There are some obvious respects in which this is
true, but I don't really see how Sultan has advanced the argument
particularly. The central section of the book for readers of Eliot is

the chapter, "*Ulysses* and *The Waste Land*," which retraces the evidence in the manuscript and the argument concerning the order of composition again; some interesting points are also made about the role of the Notes to the poem.

Sultan's portrait of Eliot and Joyce as close working partners in modernism is clearly more satisfactory than Perry Meisel's attempt in *The Myth of the Modern* (Yale) to present them as polar opposites. Meisel has three chapters on Eliot, largely devoted to a party-line Bloomian reading of Eliot's relation to Pater and Arnold: Eliot as a victim of the "anxiety of influence" must repress his own latent Romanticism. This has all been said before, and Meisel's restating of it departs as far from any perceptible empirical record as Bloom's own incompetent discussions of modernist writers; what is new in Meisel's study is his bizarre choice of the writers of the Bloomsbury group as somehow representing a successful splitting of the difference between Eliot's Arnoldianism and Joyce's Paterianism. Another overly derivative study is Michael Beehler's *T. S. Eliot, Wallace Stevens, and the Discourses of Difference* (LSU). Post-structuralist criticism at its most automatic or formulaic, this contributes little to our understanding of Eliot or Stevens, who are in any case a rather odd pair to examine together. But the absolute bottom for irrelevant comparisons and irrelevant theoretical baggage is reached in Blasing's *American Poetry*, which presents Eliot as part of a tradition of metonymy in American verse descending from Poe through Eliot to Sylvia Plath.

Another strange pairing is to be found in Melvin Wilk's *Jewish Presence in T. S. Eliot and Franz Kafka* (Scholars Press). I wasn't sure before or after reading Wilk's study what Eliot had to do with Kafka, but there is a generally good study of Eliot's anti-Semitism here, an aspect of his work most critics have preferred to ignore. Wilk is particularly informative on the American roots of Eliot's anti-Semitism.

Other comparative work divides as usual between interesting analogies and lines of influence. Edward Mozejko's interesting "Two Versions of Classicism: O. Mandelstam and T. S. Eliot" (*RLJ* 40[no. 136–37] [1986]:111–21) sketches the affinities he finds between the two poets, primarily their classicizing modernism and great interest in Dante. In influence studies, two essays treat Eliot's debt to previous poet-critics. David Macaree gives us "T. S. Eliot and John Dryden: A Study in Relationship" (*ESC* 13:35–48), a generally good study though Macaree wastes some time criticizing previous Eliot critics for ignoring his subject. David Perkins traces a familiar line of influence in "Johnson and Modern Poetry" (*HLB* 33[1985]:303–12), which focuses on Eliot. Two essays also treat Eliot's debt to French poetry: W. H. Bizley in "The Decadent Metropolis as Frontier: Eliot, Laforgue and Baudelaire" (*Theoria* 68[1986]:25–35) and Michele Hannoush in "Metaphysicality and Belief: Eliot on Laforgue" (*CL* 39:340–51). Of these studies, only Hannoush opens up new ground, adroitly using material from Eliot's unpublished Clark and Turnbull Lectures to argue that Eliot saw Laforgue in the context of metaphysical poetry and therefore as raising moral—not simply formal—issues in his poetry. Two notes in *Notes and Queries* (235) find Eliot echoing less commonly pointed to sources: in "T. S. Eliot and Fenimore Cooper" (pp. 506–07) Robert Crawford finds echoes of *The Pioneers* in "Prufrock" and "Marina"; Jocelyn Harris in "T. S. Eliot and Locke" (pp. 508–09) finds a source for Eliot's dissociation of sensibility in Locke. Finally, in "T. S. Eliot and Evelyn Underhill: An Early Mystical Influence" (*DUJ* 80:83–98) Donald J. Childs studies the wide-ranging influence of Underhill's *Mysticism* on Eliot; Childs is particularly good on the place of Dante in Underhill's work and how that may have shaped Eliot's interest in Dante.

Eliot's considerable influence on others is studied in a number of essays. Barry J. Scherr gives us an extended account of "Leavis' Revolt Against Eliot: The Lawrence Connection" (*RecL* 15:37–104), which I would recommend only for those who share the author's belief that Leavis was the greatest critic of the century. More interesting is Robert Crawford's "A Drunk Man Looks at *The Waste Land*" (*ScLJ* 14, ii:62–78), a good study of Eliot's influence on Hugh MacDiarmid. Also interesting—though considerably less weighty—is Gene Bluestein's account, in "Prufrock-Shmufrock" (*Yiddish* 7, i:53–56), of a Yiddish parody of "Prufrock" written by Isaac Rosenfeld. Vincent Sherry argues in "George Orwell and T. S. Eliot: The Sense of the Past" (*CollL* 14, ii:85–100) that Orwell grew less antagonistic to Eliot later in life as he came to share Eliot's stress on tradition. A less convincing study is Mary Jane Dickerson's "*As I Lay Dying* and *The Waste Land*" (in *William Faulkner's* As I Lay Dying: *A Critical Casebook*, ed. Dianne L. Cox [Garland, 1985], pp. 189–97), which sees the novel as indebted to the poem's Frazerian interest in vegetation myths. George Thaniel's "Seferis and England" (*JMGS* 5:85–109) focuses on Seferis's interest in Eliot. Prabhat K. Pandeya takes us into less familiar territory in "T. S. Eliot's Influence on Modern

Hindi Poetry" (*BHU Journal* 29, i[1983]:1–13). William E. Mc-
Carron gives us a very brief account of Pynchon's debt to Eliot in "A
Pynchon 'Waste Land' Scene in *Gravity's Rainbow*" (*NConL* 17, iv:
5). Finally, Joan F. Adkins's "The Dove Descending: Poetics of Tradition in Eliot and Stravinsky" (*Renascence* 39:470–83) deals with
both influence and affinity in this discussion of the poet and musician,
offering an interesting account of Stravinky's setting in *Anthem* of
part of "Little Gidding."

d. The Poems and Plays. Unfortunately, the high quality of the
work done on Eliot's place in literary history isn't matched by most
of the explications of individual works published this year. Only *The
Waste Land* and "Prufrock" are attracting a good deal of attention,
but little of this work challenges or deepens our received sense of
these poems. Max Nanny's "Michelangelo and T. S. Eliot's 'The Love
Song of J. Alfred Prufrock' " (in *Modes of Interpretation*, pp. 169–75),
argues unpersuasively that the reference to Michelangelo in the poem
is a reference to his love poetry. No better is Joseph E. Riehl's
"Procter, Lamb and Eliot: Mermaids Calling Each to Each" (*ChLB*
58:47–54), which finds a source for the mermaid imagery in "Prufrock" in Lamb's *Essays to Elia*. Two pieces on "Prufrock" in *The Explicator* are unconvincing: Kathleen A. Sherfick's "Eliot's 'The Love
Song of J. Alfred Prufrock,' 83 I" (46, i:43) finds a reference to Amos
7:14 in line 83; in "T. S. Eliot and Stephen Foster" (45, iii:44–45)
George Montiero finds an allusion to "Jeanie with the light brown
hair" in the reference to "light brown hair." J. K. Keogh's "Mr. Prufrock's Big City Blues" (*AntigR* 66–67[1986]:75–79) expands on a
piece by McLuhan in the same journal a decade previously, relating
the music of "Prufrock" to blues and nonsense verse. In "Richard
Lovelace and Eliot's 'Whispers of Immortality' " (*Trivium* 22:103–12)
Richard Bradford finds that elements of Lovelace's "La Bella Bona-
Roba" "migrate compulsively through Eliot's text." Analogously and
suggestively but no more conclusively, Sidney Gottleib sees a connection between "Eliot's 'The death of Saint Narcissus' and Herbert's
'Affliction' " (*GHJ* 9, ii[1986]:54–56). The best essay on the early
poetry this year is Edward A. Geary's "T. S. Eliot and the *fin de siècle*"
(*RMR* 40, i–ii[1986]:21–33), which sees "La Figlia che piange" as a
critique of Laforgue and Paterian aestheticism that marks Eliot's turn
away from fin de siècle attitudes.
    The one new book on *The Waste Land* this year, John Xiros

Cooper's *T.S. Eliot and the Politics of Voice: The Argument of* The Waste Land (UMI), is rather irritating. In the worst tradition of Marxist criticism it argues that the poem is really about the politics and class division that shaped its context. No one between 1922 and Professor Cooper has understood the *argument* of *The Waste Land* because we haven't put the poem "back in the socio-verbal environment" in which it was composed. But despite all of the dismissive remarks about Eliot himself and Eliot criticism, what this reading then delivers isn't anything especially original. It is not particularly news that Eliot criticizes "the liberal-romantic hegemony of thought and experience" from a conservative "collocation of lyric consciousness, myth and Indo-Christian spirituality." Harold Bloom's *T. S. Eliot's* The Waste Land: *Modern Critical Interpretations* (Chelsea House, 1986) is a rather distressing volume, containing a terrible introduction by Bloom claiming that the poem is mostly about Whitman, and a mishmash of essays shorn of their notes and hence of their utility for scholarly readers. It's sad to see a critic of Bloom's stature and intelligence waste his time and ours (and library funds) on what an *ALS* colleague last year called the "gratuitous piece of bookmaking" represented by this Chelsea House series.

Many of the baker's dozen articles on *The Waste Land* aren't much better. In "Legends of Lil: The Repressed Thematic Center of *The Waste Land*" (*WS* 13[1986]:87–102) Eileen Wiznitzer is as ideological and tendentious as Cooper, arguing that because Lil is the only fertile figure, she is the most important person in the poem, whose unique significance has been repressed, presumably again by all of us reactionary Eliot critics. In "Eliot's Personality in *The Waste Land*" (*KAL* 27[1986]:13–20) Hirofumi Iwamatsu has a more traditional candidate for the most important figure in the poem, arguing on slender evidence that Tiresias is Eliot's persona in the poem. George Montiero suggests unpersuasively that the role of "Ophelia in *The Waste Land*" (*NMAL* 10[1986]: item 4) is to suggest the theme of abortion. S. A. Cowan fails to convince me that there is "An Allusion to Thomas Hood's 'Mermaid of Margate' in T. S. Eliot's *Waste Land*" (*AN&Q* 24[1986]:75–77). And Charles Chappell also fails to convince me that there is any relationship between "*The Waste Land* and an Ozark Version of 'Red Wing'" (*PAPA* 13:1–6). In "T. S. Eliot and the Original 'Waste Land'" (*UWR* 19, ii[1986]: 61–64) Robert Ian Scott finds a model for the poem in Madison Cawein's mawkish "Waste Land," published in *Poetry* in January

1913, by which time Scott thinks—in defiance of all chronology—that Pound may have sent "Prufrock" to the same journal. Equally defiant of chronology or our reading experience is Julie Hall Knowles's "London Bridge and the Hanged Man of *The Waste Land*" (*Renascence* 39:374–82), which presents the poem as a straightforward Christian allegory of salvation.

A good deal better than these is Philip Cohen's "*The Waste Land*, 1921: Some Developments of the Manuscript's Verse" (*JMMLA* 19, i[1986]:12–20), which argues correctly that the development of the poem is away from narrative and satire toward "a literary equivalent of Cubist collage." Arguing along similar lines is Clare R. Kinney, who in "Fragmentary Excess, Copious Dearth: *The Waste Land* as Anti-Narrative" (*JNT* 17:273–85) discusses how movement toward narrative coherence in the poem keeps being undercut. Maxine Rance briefly but persuasively finds in lines 379–82 an echo of "*Dracula* in *The Waste Land*" (*N&Q* 235:508–09). One source study I find it difficult to make my mind up on is Peter Know-Shaw's "Another Explorer in *The Waste Land*?" (*N&Q* 232:57–58), which finds a source in H. M. Stanley in the passage on lines 62–66 about the tide of people flowing over London Bridge. More substantial than these are two essays on classical sources, J. G. Keogh's "O City, City: Oedipus in *The Waste Land*" (*AntigR* 69–70:89–112) and Gareth Reeves's "*The Waste Land* and the *Aeneid*" (*MLR* 82:555–72). Keogh's wide-ranging study looks at the influence of Sophocles on Eliot and argues for a parallel between the Thebes of the plays and the London of the poem. In the best essay this year on *The Waste Land*, Reeves argues persuasively for the importance of the *Aeneid* in the poem but also against reading Eliot's later Christian reading of Virgil anachronistically back into the poem.

Stephen G. McLeod finds in Frazer's *Golden Bough* "A Possible Source of the 'Broken Jaw' Image in T. S. Eliot's *The Hollow Men*" (*YER* 9, i:31–33). Arnold P. Hinchliffe's The Waste Land *and* Ash Wednesday: *An Introduction to the Variety of Criticism* (Humanities) is a rather pedestrian survey of the criticism of these two poems; it is part of a series designed to introduce students to the diversity of critical opinion about the texts they read, but I can't quite see the utility of having students read such a rehash of the criticism as opposed to the text or the criticism.

Doris Wight's "Metaphysics through Paradox in Eliot's *Four Quartets*" (*CCR*[Spring 1986]:3–11) and "How the Serious Play of

Words Opens Minds to the Mystical in Eliot's *Four Quartets* (*ABR* 38, ii:139–58) are typical of the kind of bad criticism that this poem often receives, meandering around among metaphysics and St. Augustine in a way that contributes neither to criticism of the poem nor to metaphysics. A more useful exploration of the religious aspect of the poem is Susan McCaslin's "Vision and Revision in *Four Quartets*: T. S. Eliot and Julian of Norwich" (*Mystics Quarterly* 12, iv[1986]: 171–78), which is informative on the 14th-century mystic Eliot quotes in "Little Gidding." Ole Bay-Petersen's "T. S. Eliot and Einstein: The Fourth Dimension in the *Four Quartets*" (*ES* 66[1985]:143–55) finds Einsteinian sources for aspects of the poem that clearly derive from Eastern thought. Considerably better but not wholly persuasive is William M. Burke's "Style and Consciousness in T. S. Eliot's *Four Quartets*" (*SMy* 10, iii:3–19), which doggedly argues that the essential stylistic device of the poem is synecdoche.

No one is summoning up too much enthusiasm for Eliot's plays these days, and the work that is done on them seems to miss what is interesting about them. The only article on Eliot's drama this year is Kurt Tetzeli von Rosador's "Christian Historical Drama: The Exemplariness of *Murder in the Cathedral*" (*MD* 29[1986]:516–53), a rather formulaic study of how the play exemplifies and dramatizes Christian conceptions of history. The only full-length work on the plays this year is S. S. Deo's execreble and almost illiterate *T. S. Eliot, Philosophical Themes in Drama* (Advent), which is of no use to anyone.

e. **The Criticism.** The interest in Eliot's criticism continues to increase. The one full-length book that falls into this category, Charles Warren's *T. S. Eliot on Shakespeare* (UMI), is a thorough tracing of everything Eliot ever said about Shakespeare. The problem with the project is that Eliot's discussions of Shakespeare were nearly always part of a larger context, so there is a tug-of-war between Warren's overly narrow focus and Eliot's broader concerns. A book on Eliot's relation to the Renaissance including Shakespeare would have been far more valuable. Robert P. Tantingco's "An Evaluation of Eliot's Shakespearean Criticisms" (*SLRJ* 17, i[1986]:84–108) is considerably less interesting, a comparison of Eliot's positions to the main lines of Shakespearean scholarship that inevitably finds Eliot's to be eccentric.

A. H. Tak's *Coleridge and Modern Criticism* (B.R. Pub. [India],

1985) has a chapter dedicated to arguing the uninteresting proposition that "Eliot is a true Coleridgean." Another Indian study of
Eliot's criticism, Sumany Satpathy's "Eliot's Early Criticism and the
TLS" (*LCrit* 22, iii:33–40), is essentially an expansion of a remark
by Kenner to the effect that Eliot's early criticism in the *TLS* often
parodies the style of other *TLS* essays. The best work on Eliot's
criticism this year is Richard Shusterman's "T. S. Eliot on Reading:
Pleasure, Games and Wisdom" (*P&L* 11:1–20), a careful and adroit
reading of Eliot's aesthetic, which makes good sense of Eliot's remarks about poetry being an amusement and being like a game.

New Mexico State University

9. Faulkner

M. Thomas Inge

The flow of Faulkner scholarship continues unabated. A dozen books and 70 articles are discussed in this essay, and while no major new trends are discernible on the basis of this year's sampling, a few distinguished books appeared and many of the articles build intelligently on the work of the past. Despite the variety of critical methodology, the consensus of Faulkner's importance as a major world writer remains certain.

i. Bibliography, Editions, and Manuscripts

While William Boozer's valuable quarterly checklists of new books and articles continue to appear in issues of *The Faulkner Newsletter*, we will soon have to do without the other major source of bibliographic information. Dianne C. Luce's "Faulkner 1986: A Survey of Research and Criticism" (*MissQ* 40:413–31) is the tenth and last to appear in the special Faulkner issue of *MissQ*, since James B. Meriwether has retired as editor after 24 such issues and Luce has decided not to continue the survey as well. This valuable critical guide will be greatly missed. Philip Cohen provides a sensible overview of several 1985 and 1986 publications in "Some Recent Titles in Faulkner Studies" (*RALS* 15:31–47), and Thomas E. Dasher briefly but usefully surveys the biography, major themes, and the criticism in his entry on Faulkner for *Fifty Southern Writers After 1900*, pp. 158–76. Glen E. Lich surveys the efforts of recent critics to come to terms with Faulkner's parabolic circularity as a structural device in his novels in "Faulkner's Formula" (*NOR* 14, iv:9–14). Of limited use to students are the excerpts from over 20 critics published between 1931 and 1985 on selected short stories in the first volume of *Short Story Criticism*.

Catalina Montes has gathered more data than has ever been available before about translations and criticism in her impressive "The

Reception of William Faulkner in Spain" (*NMW* 19:41–61), in which she much improves on information gathered by the present author and published in 1971 (see *ALS 1971*, p. 105). The reception and translation of Faulkner after 1950 in Japan and France are briefly outlined by editors Kenzaburo Ohashi and Michel Gresset in the introductions to their *Faulkner: ATNP*, pp. 3–12 and 13–25, while the Japanese novelist most heavily influenced by Faulkner, Kenji Nakagami, pays an obscure tribute to him in an afterword, "Faulkner: The Luxuriating South" (pp. 326–36).

The first Faulkner novel to appear in a Norton critical edition designed for students is *The Sound and the Fury*, ed. David Minter. A model of its kind, Minter's edition includes the Noel Polk text based primarily on the original carbon typescript, textual annotations, background documents, 15 reprinted critical essays, and a selected bibliography. Now one can teach this most difficult novel with greater ease than ever before. Louis Daniel Brodsky's "William Faulkner's 'Impressions' of 'Danzas Venezuela': The Original Manuscript" (*SB* 40:326–36) publishes Faulkner's notes on his impressions of a dance performance seen in Venezuela in 1961.

ii. Biography

Stephen B. Oates's *William Faulkner: The Man and the Artist* (Harper) advances no new biographical evidence or critical territory. It is a summary of the existing body of biographical material interlaced with plot summaries of the fiction (not always accurate) and occasionally relating the two but in simplistic terms. Oates assumes to enter Faulkner's thoughts and emotions, a daring tack which proves more presumptuous than telling, and many events are overdramatized. Little of the complexity or power of either the man or the work is captured here. The biography is no substitute for either Joseph Blotner's or David Minter's efforts, lacking both the detail of the former and the acumen of the latter. (Strangely, Oates recommends in the notes Beatrice Rick's error-ridden bibliography of 1981 rather than the earlier authoritative ones by John E. Bassett and Thomas L. McHaney.)

"William Faulkner, Poet to Novelist: An Imposter Becomes an Artist" by Judith L. Sensibar, in *Psychoanalytic Studies in Biography*, pp. 305–35, is another version of chapter four of her excellent 1984 study *The Origins of Faulkner's Art*, but it appears with "A Discussion of Dr. Sensibar's Paper" by Harvey S. Strauss, M.D. (pp. 337–46), in which a psychoanalyst expands upon the idea of Faulkner as imposter to locate the source of his need to pretend to be a wounded war hero and a poet. The result is intriguing but offers nothing new. Using Faulkner's ambivalence in his attitude toward the South as his starting point, in "William Faulkner: Tell About the South" (*Confrontation* 35–36:110–28), Melvin Backman has provided a biographical reading of the fiction which is balanced and reasonable but which provides little that is new in interpretation. John A. Howland's "Sunday Tea with an Old Soldier" (*Confrontations* 35–36:129–30) is a pleasant memoir of two visits with Faulkner in 1943 when the author invited to his home some soldiers temporarily stationed in Oxford for "Sunday tea and conversation." In *The Faulkner Newsletter* William Boozer continues to provide useful biographical details and cultural tidbits.

iii. Criticism: General

One of the most original general studies to appear this year is *Faulkner's Fictive Architecture: The Meaning of Place in the Yoknapatawpha Novels* (UMI Research Press) by William T. Ruzicka, in which the author applies the phenomenological study of architectural space and place to Faulkner's fiction with truly rewarding results. He finds that "Yoknapatawpha barns, cabins and homes, and Jefferson's town square and civic buildings are objects as meaningful as any symbolic or metaphorical phenomenon in the fictive county's inventory," and his analysis of *The Unvanquished, Sartoris, Absalom, Absalom!, Requiem for a Nun,* the Snopes Trilogy, and *Go Down, Moses* demonstrates the extent to which the mansions, homes, and natural settings through which the characters move are remarkably congruent with the larger thematic and plot patterns. This is an approach which could be applied with profit to other southern and regional writers.

Another original work is James G. Watson's *William Faulkner: Letters and Fictions* (Texas), after a reading of which one is never likely to write or read a personal letter in the same way again. Watson convincingly demonstrates that "Faulkner's private and public letters show that he was acutely aware of epistolary strategies and conventions that give letters their uniqueness as written texts, and that his understanding was important to his creative work into which he almost immediately began inserting fictional letters." Watson's study contributes to an understanding of both the author and the work, and his strategy too could be applied to other writers with profit. Michel Gresset uses a similar approach in "A Public Man's Private Voice: Faulkner's Letters to Else Jonsson" (*Faulkner: ATNP*, pp. 61–73), in which one set of letters is seen to provide a striking self-portrait of the author.

Warwick Wadlington's *Reading Faulknerian Tragedy* (Cornell) is an exercise in reader-response criticism intended to provide an adequate description of Faulkner's practice as a tragedian and discuss the importance of performing Faulkner's prose, that is, readers assuming roles in the completion of the text they are reading. True believers will welcome his analyses of *The Sound and the Fury, As I Lay Dying, Light in August,* and *Absalom, Absalom!,* but the unconverted will hesitate in the face of the special vocabulary. In any case, Wadlington's implications are provocative.

Cleanth Brooks, still Faulkner's most lucid and precise commentator, has brought together 12 essays published or delivered on special occasions between 1971 and 1985 in a volume entitled *On the Prejudices, Predilictions, and Firm Beliefs of William Faulkner* (LSU). Like the rest of his work, they are indispensable reading. Harold Bloom's anthology, *William Faulkner* (Chelsea), is one in a 200-volume set called "Modern Critical Views." Since presumably one man cannot be reading the vast body of criticism available on 200 major authors, someone else must be performing that task with Bloom approving the final choice and writing the introductions. The 16 essays here are drawn entirely from books published between 1963 and 1984, nearly all readily available on the shelves of most libraries, for which one assumes the book is primarily intended.

In "Faulkner's Dispossessed" (*ArQ* 43:141–50) Robert A. Martin reexamines the old contention that Faulkner was a literary Naturalist and predictably finds that nature does exercise a powerful influence on his characters, but there is no philosophic determinism working in the fiction. Marilyn R. Chandler's "The Space Makers: Passive Power in Faulkner's Novels" (*CollL* 14:120–27) is a brief but intriguing overview of how "The law of physics stating that nature abhors a vacuum provides a governing principle of action, characterization, and narrative strategy in five of Faulkner's major novels." This may sound more unlikely than it proves to be. Daniel Hoffman's "History as Myth, Myth as History, in Faulkner's Fiction" (*Ameri-*

can Letters, pp. 237–54) is a brief but suggestive overview of the functions of history and folklore in the novels, especially *A Fable, Light in August*, and *Go Down, Moses*.

iv. Criticism: Special Studies

The most informative book on Faulkner's influences and intellectual background to appear this year is Lothar Hönnighausen's *William Faulkner: The Art of Stylization in His Early Graphic and Literary Work* (Cambridge), a carefully researched and balanced consideration of the influence such figures as Swinburne and Beardsley had on his drawings and first poetic efforts. By placing Faulkner in the full cultural and artistic contexts of his time, Hönnighausen sharply illuminates the making of the young author's artistic sensibility. This book will remain a standard work on his early career. In a related article, "William Faulkner: The Symbolist Connection" (*AL* 59: 389–401), Alexander Marshall III demonstrates convincingly just how much the young Faulkner learned stylistically from Verlaine, Laforgue, Mallarmé, and the other French writers of their school and how Symbolist techniques were employed throughout the writing of his major fiction. In another influence study, "Faulkner's Use of 'Quo Vadis'" (*MissQ* 40:393–400), Margaret J. Yonce effectively nails down his adoption of language and images from the Henryk Sienkiewicz novel.

George Dekker's *The American Historical Romance* places several of Faulkner's novels, especially *Absalom, Absalom!* and *Go Down, Moses*, in that mainstream literary tradition and finds that he participates as strongly in that genre as do most major American writers. The intersection between reality, history, myth, and fiction are fully explored in this welcome full-scale study of the subject. There are two studies of Faulkner's influence on other writers. Harley D. Oberhelman's "William Faulkner and Gabriel García Márquez: Two Nobel Laureates," in *Critical Essays on Gabriel García Márquez*, ed. George R. McMurray (Hall), pp. 67–79, is a fairly mechanical recitation of parallels in plots and themes. Masao Shimura's "Pynchon and Faulkner" (*Faulkner: ATNP*, pp. 282–303) notes several tenuous similarities between the fiction of the two writers without proving influence.

Two essays address the topic of Faulkner and race. John C. Inscoe's "Faulkner, Race, and Appalachia" (*SAQ* 86:244–53) examines historically the initial encounters between 19th-century white mountaineers and blacks and Faulkner's use of such material in the story "Mountain Victory" and *Absalom, Absalom!* The traumatic consequences are found to have parallels in works Faulkner probably read by Emmett Gowen, Grace Lumpkin, and George Washington Harris. (The psychological and historic subtleties of the story are sensitively explored in an explication by M. E. Bradford, "A Late Encounter: Faulkner's 'Mountain Victory'" [*MissQ* 40:373–81], but he does not see its central concern as a matter of race.) "Faulkner and Miscegenation" (*ArQ* 43:151–64) by Gene Bluestein attributes too many attitudes and opinions of a racist nature to Faulkner on the basis of debatable readings of the fiction. There is nearly always a distance between what Faulkner's characters say and what the author believed.

The entire Spring 1987 issue of the *FJ* (2, ii) is devoted to papers read at a symposium on "William Faulkner and the Military" held at West Point in July 1986 on the anniversary of Faulkner's appearance there in 1962. The introductory lecture by Joseph Blotner (pp. 4–11) traces the changes in Faulkner's attitudes about warfare and the military from a youthful romanticism to humanistic hope. Lothar Hönnighausen in "The Military as Metaphor" (pp. 12–22) deftly and sensitively interprets the uses of military metaphors from "Crevasse" to *A Fable* in appreciation of Faulkner's ability to use them with symbolic and psychological import. Noel Polk's "Response to 'The Military as Metaphor'" (pp. 23–28) voices agreement with Hönnighausen and proceeds to find legitimate artistic grounds on which to base an appreciation of and admiration for *A Fable*. "Colonel Falkner—Prototype and Influence" (pp. 28–34) by Donald P. Duclos is one more, but a slightly more detailed, account of the parallels between Faulkner's great-grandfather and the fictional John Sartoris. "An Episode of War in *The Unvanquished*" (pp. 35–44) by Thomas L. McHaney turns up interesting new turf by examining Civil War records that document parallels between actual events and "Retreat," chapter two of the novel. A new figure of likely influence is also brought into the picture—Robert G. Ingersoll, Federal officer and popular orator of the 19th century. A response (pp. 45–46) by Edmund L. Volpe approves of both the Duclos and McHaney papers.

In "Fictional Facts and Factual Fiction: William Faulkner and World War I" (pp. 47–54) Duane J. MacMillan sensibly examines

Faulkner's treatment of the First World War in the fiction, especially
Soldiers' Pay and nine short stories, with special attention to the
distinction the author drew between "truth" and "fact," a useful perspective. Louis Daniel Brodsky's "Faulkner's Wounded Art: The
Aftermath of Hollywood and World War II" (pp. 55–66), with characteristic thoroughness and scruple, demonstrates how Faulkner's desire
to become involved in that war was sublimated and invested in various writing projects, such as his scriptwriting, the "Appendix" to *The
Sound and the Fury,* and *The Reivers.* " 'I Ain't a Soldier Now':
Faulkner's World War II Veterans" (pp. 67–74) by James B. Ca-
rothers helpfully compares his treatment of veterans of the Civil War
and World War I as physically or psychically wounded with World
War II veterans, who are found to be endowed with hope, determination, and lust, a reflection of sentiment about the war itself and
changes in Faulkner's attitudes. Joseph L. Fant records some anecdotes and vignettes in "Faulkner at West Point Remembered" (pp.
75–78), as does Jack L. Capps in his "Editor's Preface" (pp. 2–3) to
the special issue.

Seven of the essays in *Faulkner: ATNP* discuss Faulkner's attitudes, beliefs, and public pronouncements during the last 12 years
of his life. Kenzaburo Ohashi's "Behind the 'Trinity of Conscience':
Individuality, 'Regimentation,' and Nature in Between" (pp. 30–44)
rephrases many of Faulkner's statements on what he saw as the opposition between individual freedom and conformity in modern society, and André Bleikesten's "A Private Man's Public Voice" (pp.
45–60) laments Faulkner's tendency to preach and become involved
with political issues which he feels hurt the fiction. In the process
Bleikesten makes some interesting comments about Gavin Stevens
as spokesman for his creator. In "William Faulkner and the American
Dream: A Furious Affirmation" (pp. 74–87), François L. Pitavy intelligently traces Faulkner's vision of the meaning of America, beginning with *The Wild Palms* in 1939, and concludes that the prose
statements in the latter years of the *political* dream are basically a
metaphor of "the only dream ultimately worth the anguish, the *poetic*
dream."

"William Faulkner's Late Career: Repetition, Variation, Renewal"
(pp. 247–59) by Hans Skei views the post-Nobel work as a series of
repetitions and extensions of earlier writings and thus makes out a
good case for seeing Faulkner's entire oeuvre as of a piece and thematically unified. Mick Gidley's "Explanation as Composition: Faulk-

ner's Public Comments on His Fiction" (pp. 260–81) is a lucid analysis of the ontological suppositions underlying Faulkner's creative assumptions about writing fiction, which Gidley finds parallel many of the beliefs of Gertrude Stein. Cleanth Brooks clearly and sensibly describes the book that Faulkner failed to complete on the basis of the two finished chapters in "Faulkner's *The American Dream: What Happened to It?*" (pp. 307–25), an essay which also appears in his book mentioned above.

v. Individual Works to 1929

John S. Williams applies the insights of depth psychology to Bayard Sartoris of *Flags in the Dust* to affirm that the character is *both* reckless and suicidal in "Ambivalence, Rivalry, and Loss: Bayard Sartoris and the Ghosts of the Past" (*ArQ* 43:178–92). The result reads like a psychoanalytic case study, interesting but perhaps reductive in its conclusions. In a comparison of Bayard with Quentin Compson of *The Sound and the Fury*, Janet St. Clair's "The Refuge of Death: Silencing the Struggles of a Hungry Heart" (*ArQ* 43:101–18) argues that both characters' lives were destroyed because they were unable either to give or receive love. She too uses psychology, but her approach yields richer results. Philip Cohen compares Horace Benbow of *Flags in the Dust* with earlier passive, disillusioned idealists in the unfinished *Elmer* and *Mayday* in "Horace Benbow and Faulkner's Other Early Failed Idealists" (*SCR* 18[1986]:78–92) and not only clarifies Benbow but also sheds light on Quentin Compson, Faulkner's most complex ineffective idealist.

Qui-Phiet Tran is also concerned with self-destruction on the part of Quentin Compson in "The Question of Suicide in *The Sound and the Fury*" (*NOR* 14, iv:52–57). Aware of the impossibility of a definitive analysis of motive, Tran applies with tact the theories of Bergson and Freud to useful purpose. "Checking in on Time in *The Sound and the Fury*" (*ArQ* 43:133–46) by John C. Hampsey once more reviews Faulkner's aesthetic intent to note that Jean-Paul Sartre and other critics have not fully understood his use of time, which is more creative than consistently theoretical. Karen Kaivola proposes a revealing feminist reading in "Becoming Woman: Identification and Desire in *The Sound and the Fury*" (*Reader* 17:29–43), with particular attention to the way women readers respond to Caddy through male-mediated narrators. The argument and conclusions are convincing. In an exercise in literalism Sara McLaughlin demonstrates that Benjy is not scientifically an idiot but rather shows all the symptoms of autism in "Faulkner's Faux Pas: Referring to Banjamin Compson as an Idiot" (*L&P* 33:34–40), even though she admits that Faulkner could not have known about the condition which would not be recognized until 1943.

Cheryl Lester makes some excellent and well-documented points in "To Market, to Market: *The Portable Faulkner*" (*Criticism* 29: 371–92) about the extent to which the "Appendix" should *not* be read as a gloss on or an introduction to *The Sound and the Fury*, because of its inclusion of contradictory and new material, but rather should be viewed in the larger context out of which it came—negotiations with Malcolm Cowley over the shape and content of *The Portable Faulkner*. Tom Bowden explicates the importance of two typographical corrections in the 1984 edition of *The Sound and the Fury* in "Functions of Leftness and 'Dam' in William Faulkner's *The Sound and the Fury*" (*NMW* 19:81–83), and K. J. Phillips locates another source for the allusions to pigs in the novel in the New Testament in "Persephone and the Pigs in William Faulkner's *The Sound and the Fury*" (*IFR* 14, i:14–17). Lewis Layman's "The Influence of the Cyclops Episode of *Ulysses* on the Jason Section of *The Sound and the Fury*" (*CJIS* 13:61–74) is a detailed effort to prove that Joyce's episode was a primary source for Faulkner.

vi. Individual Works, 1930–39

All three of the essays on *As I Lay Dying* deal with the importance of language. "Characterization and Language: A Case-Grammar Study of *As I Lay Dying*" (*Lang&S* 20:73–87) by Mary Jane Hurst applies the concepts of case grammar, "the universal, interlanguage patterns of a deep structure based on semantics" rather than syntax, to monologues by six of the major characters. She demonstrates that each has a distinct, definable voice suitable to his/her personality or behavior. This is highly technical proof of something we already know. Less mechanical and more informative is Judith Lockyer's "Language and the Process of Narration in Faulkner's *As I Lay Dying*" (*ArQ* 43:165–77), which applies Mikhail Bakhtin's theory that "the novel is the ultimate recognition of language as always contingent upon context and thus never absolute" to statements by Addie and other narrators.

"'The Man Who Suffers and the Mind Which Creates': Problems of Poetics in William Faulkner's *As I Lay Dying*" (*SLJ* 20, i:61–73) by Martin J. Jacobi takes as its point of departure the opposition between acts and words which provide dramatic tension in the novel and applies the theories of Kenneth Burke on artistic creation in a convincing reading of the text as an allegory on the limits of talent. John B. Sherrill attempts a definition of "*Sanctuary* as Tragedy" (*ArQ* 43:119–32) by focusing on Popeye as the "apotheosis of alienated twentieth-century man who possesses an unbending set of values" that lend him dignity. The application of classic and Shakespearean concepts of tragedy are provocative, but the conclusions are not entirely convincing.

Light in August garnered the largest number of essays this year, led off by Michael Millgate's distinguished collection of *New Essays on* Light in August (Cambridge). After a concise and accurate account of the composition, publication, and critical response to the novel in the introduction (pp. 1–29), Millgate goes on to assert its aesthetic and technical brilliance in "'A Novel: Not an Anecdote': Faulkner's *Light in August*" (pp. 31–53). Millgate reads the novel as one in which Faulkner took the most risks and made the most self-conscious artistic investment and successfully makes out a case for it as a major 20th-century text. Martin Kreiswirth turns to "Plots and Counterplots: The Structure of *Light in August*" (pp. 55–79) and identifies "juxtaposition, parallelism, montage, and counterpoint" as bases for the novel's structural coherence. He finds the work a brilliant example of Bakhtin's "polyphonic" structure.

André Bleikasten takes a probing and broad-gauged look at the influence of society's values and assumptions on the characters, especially in matters of race and sex, in "*Light in August*: The Closed Society and Its Subjects" (pp. 81–102), and clearly identifies the inflexible nature of Puritan ideology as the source of tragedy in Faulkner's fictional community, itself a reflection of the real community in which he lived as a southerner. Judith Bryant Wittenberg takes one more look at "The Women of *Light in August*" (pp. 103–22). While noting the ambiguities in the text on attitudes toward women, she takes a fresh look at the minor female characters and finds a clear understanding on Faulkner's part of the restrictive contexts in which they had to struggle and survive, which is counted to his credit. Wittenberg's insights are new and engaging. In the final essay, "On the Difference between Prevailing and Enduring" (pp. 123–47), Alexander Welsh outlines Erik H. Erikson's definitions of the two types of heroes—the active or combative, and the passive or self-sacrificial—and places Christmas in the first category and Hightower in the second. The discussion raises more questions than it answers, perhaps the appropriate conclusion to an anthology about a most provocative book. *New Essays* on Light in August eschews specialized vocabulary and will, therefore, be useful to undergraduate readers as well as advanced scholars. It may stand as a major statement on the novel.

Calling into question the interpretations of Cleanth Brooks and Thadious M. Davis, among others, of the importance of community in the novel, John N. Duvall's "Murder and the Community: Ideology In and Around *Light in August*" (*Novel* 20:101–22) reassesses the topic, but his own political assumptions and semiotic techniques do not resolve problems as much as they raise new ones. The essay deserves a hearing, in any case. Noting that her character has been too often misunderstood by the critics, Susan Hayes Tully's "Joanna Burden: 'It's the dead folks that do him the damage'" (*MissQ* 40: 355–71) fully explores her central importance to the narrative and finds that she suffers from the same forces that destroy Christmas and Hightower, even though she is a woman. Tully's argument is clear and persuasive. In three influence studies, Martin Bidney examines "Faulkner's Kinship with Schopenhauer" (*Neophil* 71:447–59), Donald P. Duclos notes "A Plank in Faulkner's 'Lumber Room': *The Emperor Jones* and *Light in August*" (*EON* 11, ii:8–13), and Joan Wylie Hall finds a source of names in *Pilgrim's Progress* in "Burdens, Bunyan, and *Light in August*" (*AN&Q* 24:48–50). All three may be matters of striking coincidence rather than direct influence, but the points are well taken.

The one essay on *Pylon*, "The Killer in *Pylon*" (*MissQ* 40:401–12) by Susan Paul Johnson, goes against the traditional interpretation of the reporter as benevolent to define him as a selfish, willful, amoral killer. Johnson finds plenty of evidence in the text to substantiate her claim.

David Paul Ragan's *William Faulkner's* Absalom, Absalom!: *A Critical Study* (UMI Research Press) is a carefully considered, thorough, and helpful analysis of the narrators in the novel, the stories they tell, and the links between this novel and the earlier *The Sound and the Fury*. Patterns of imagery and continuing themes suggest that a knowledge of the first enhances the reader's understanding of the second. Ragan establishes a chronology for the action covering

over 100 years and includes an extensive annotated bibliography.
Students can use this study to good advantage.

According to an introduction (*NOR* 14, iv:5–8) by editor Dennis
Patrick Slattery, four essays in a special section of the *New Orleans
Review* devoted to *Absalom, Absalom!* were the product of a summer
seminar on Faulkner and modern critical theory. "Ogre and Pigmies:
Sutpen's Stature in *Absalom, Absalom!*" (pp. 15–23) by Terrell Tebbets attempts to define the source of Sutpen's drive and vitality (to
create a pattern of order in the face of meaninglessness and raise
himself above the level of the beast) and redefines the outcome of his
effort as a success rather than a failure. The argument and evidence
are forcefully marshaled by Tebbets. James D. Gray in "Shreve's Lesson of Love: Power of the Unsaid in *Absalom, Absalom!*" (pp. 24–35)
sees the failure of discourse, in speaking and hearing, as central to
the novel's concerns, and using semiotic theory finds new and complex layers of meaning. Larry Allums provides a phenomenological
reading in "Overpassing to Love: Dialogue and Play in *Absalom,
Absalom!*" (pp. 36–41). Quentin, his father, and Shreve McCannon
represent variations on how to read the text of Sutpen's story and
reveal things not only about Sutpen but the act of reading as well.
Allums applies theories of Richard E. Palmer and Hans-Georg Gadamer in reaching his conclusions. Slattery's contribution, "And Who to
Know: Monuments, Text, and the Trope of Time in *Absalom, Absalom!*" (pp. 42–51), builds on Allums's approach to describe the
interplay of monuments and memory in the narrative. Primarily those
with a deep interest in the contemporary trends in criticism will find
these last three essays of interest.

"Desire and Reciprocal Violence in *Absalom, Absalom!*" (*ESC* 13:
420–37) by Evelyn Cobley is an analysis of character behavior in
accordance with the French theorists René Girard, Jacques Lacan,
and Alexandre Kojève, who maintain that "the human subject becomes aware of itself only through identifications with others." A
prior familiarity with their ideas would be helpful in reading this
difficult essay. Karen McPherson's "*Absalom, Absalom!*: Telling
Scratches" (*MFS* 33:431–50) is another reader-response exercise in
narrative theory which suggests that the text cannot be definitively
read. Unlike others, she argues with a playful sense of humor. Neither
of these two essays can be effectively summarized here in a sentence.
Shreve McCannon is given his due as a narrator by Pierre Michel in
"Shreve McCannon: The Outside Voice in *Absalom, Absalom!*"

(*DQR* 17:214–25). Linda E. McDaniel discovers noteworthy parallels with Emily Bronte's Novel in "Designs in *Wuthering Heights* and *Absalom, Absalom!*" (*NMW* 19:73–80). Harold Bloom's *Modern Critical Interpretations: William Faulkner's* Absalom, Absalom! (Chelsea) collects seven essays previously published as parts of books between 1975 and 1986 and therefore already available in most libraries. Bloom's brief introduction does double duty since it also serves as the introduction to the anthology mentioned above, except here three pages have been added on the novel. The book jacket reproduces an 1879 genre painting of black life by Thomas Pollock Anshutz of Kentucky oddly irrelevant to the novel, its plot, or the Mississippi setting. Perhaps the designer thought anything vaguely southern would do.

John H. Hafner's "Southern Places in Adolescent Fiction: William Faulkner and Julia Coley Duncan" (*CLAQ* 12:61–63) compares *The Unvanquished* with Duncan's *Halfway Home* (1979) as adolescent novels, but the comparison sheds no new light on Faulkner. "Faulkner's 'Old Man' and the American Humor Tradition" by W. Craig Turner (*UMSE* 5:149–57) compares the story of the Tall Convict in *The Wild Palms* with the humor of the Old Southwest, Down East, and the Literary Comedians and finds comparable devices and techniques. Turner rightly suggests that writing this was probably an effective exercise that enabled Faulkner to complete his comic novel *The Hamlet*.

vii. Individual Works, 1940–1949

In "The Panzaic Principle in *The Hamlet*" (*RecL* 15:1–17) Gerald Butler applies a concept drawn from *Don Quixote*, which sees Sancho Panza as a force that undercuts the ideal with the real. It is a concept that works in a novel so heavily concerned with the erosion of human principles and ideals. Philip Cohen's "French Peasants and Southern Snopeses: Balzac's *Les Paysans* and Faulkner's *The Hamlet*" (*MissQ* 40:384–91) finds extensive parallels between the two works and persuasively argues for direct influence.

In another influence study, "Isaac McCaslin and the Burden of Influence" (*UMSE* 5:172–81), Paul J. Lindholdt looks to *A Portrait of the Artist as a Young Man* by James Joyce as a source of inspiration for "The Bear" and argues that the work can be viewed as a misreading of Stephen Dedalus. Lindholdt uses the poetic influence theories of Harold Bloom in a stimulating but not entirely convincing argument. Dorothy C. Whitely summarizes some of the classical and Christian myths that underlie "The Bear" in "The Rites of Initiation in Faulkner's *The Bear*" (*MOR* 1:11–27).

viii. Individual Works, 1950–62

The complex relationship between the narrator, the audience, and the reader in the part-novel, part-play *Requiem for a Nun* are keenly explored by Charles F. Dameron, Jr., in "The Audience's Hypothetical Role in *Requiem for a Nun*" (*NOR* 14, iv:58–61). He finds that Faulkner offers the reader a singular opportunity to become a part of the narrative context.

Two excellent studies of *A Fable* are offered by Doreen Fowler, "'In Another Country': Faulkner's *A Fable*" (*SAF* 15:43–54), and John E. Bassett, "*A Fable*: Faulkner's Revision of Filial Conflict" (*Renascence* 39:15–29). Fowler thoroughly explicates a repeated line taken from Christopher Marlowe to support her thesis that "Faulkner's work involves a reading in which distinctions between time and place coalesce, and, thus blurred, time and place cannot be invoked . . . to contain human iniquity." Bassett gives a careful reading of themes and ideas in *A Fable* within the context of Faulkner's previous work and his psychological state at the time of writing. Both essays are models of lucid criticism.

Four essays in *Faulkner: ATNP* predictably focus on *A Fable*. "The Critical Difference: Faulkner's Case in *A Fable*" (pp. 91–109) by Fumiyo Hayashi argues that looking at character, and the relations between characters, is a way to clarify theme and structure and draws some interesting parallels with Melville's *Billy Budd*. Noel Polk, in "Enduring *A Fable* and Prevailing" (pp. 110–26), selects an image in which man's ability to endure is likened to a Gothic cathedral and finds it close to the center of the novel's various themes. Polk thoroughly examines the various modes and meanings of "endurance" in the text. "The Indestructible Voice of the British Battalion Runner in *A Fable*" (pp. 127–46) by Ikuko Fujihira analyzes the significance of one character as a key to the novel, and Lothar Hönnighausen discusses "The Imagery in Faulkner's *A Fable*" (pp. 147–71), especially typological imagery and the way it functions structurally and stylistically. The Polk and Hönnighausen essays are especially significant.

The remaining essays in *Faulkner: ATNP* not discussed so far consider the Snopes Trilogy and *The Reivers*. Kiyoyuki Ono argues that the trilogy is really a chronicle of the town, its history and inhabitants, rather than a chronicle of the Snopeses, and is best read that way, in "The Invisible Principle of the Southern Spirit in the Snopes Trilogy" (pp. 172–96). Michiko Yoshida finds "Faulkner's Comedy of Motion: *The Reivers*" (pp. 197–210) to be mainly impelled by forward action via automobile, train, and racehorse; Judith Bryant Wittenberg examines the politics of the novel in *"The Reivers*: A Conservative Fable?"* (pp. 211–26) and finds that Faulkner took a reactionary turn toward the last in the direction of Russell Kirk; and Toshio Koyama demonstrates how the first two words of the novel, "Grandfather said," define the narrative strategy for the remainder of the story in "Faulkner's Final Narrative Vision in *The Reivers*: Remembering and Knowing" (pp. 227–43). The amount of attention given to Faulkner's latter years in *Faulkner: ATNP* should contribute to rectifying the arguably wrong impression that he failed after 1950 to live up to the promise and power of his early career.

Randolph-Macon College

10. Fitzgerald and Hemingway

Gerry Brenner

The Fitzgerald fishery continues to fall off, as this year's small catch shows. With the exception of four showpieces—bibliographic, biographic, deconstructive, and thematic—fewer and fewer scholars and critics are taking their best gear to work Fitzgerald's waters. In contrast, Hemingway scholars are riding full tides to port with their harvests. Along with a major biography, a new collection of Hemingway's stories, and two collections of criticism, one flotilla of scholars took their nets to Hemingway's *The Garden of Eden* while another took theirs to Hemingway's Spanish Civil War period. The year's writing landed a few trophies—among them an essay on *The Sun Also Rises* by a pair of deconstructionists. But Hemingway scholars still show little venturesomeness, reluctant to ply currents with the tackle of recent critical theories. Unlike last year's scholars, who clustered to fish the channel of *The Sun Also Rises*, this year's fanned out, landed more small fry than large, and, for several, found themselves lured by the siren call of the newest sea-creature in Hemingway's depths, Androgyny.

i. Text, Biography, and Bibliography

Just in time for Christmas giving, Scribner released *The Complete Short Stories of Ernest Hemingway*, a hefty, three-part volume of 70 stories in readably reset texts. But once again the House of Scribner displayed objectionable editorial practices. Part I includes the standard 49 stories first gathered in 1938. But left intact are the altered text of "A Clean Well-Lighted Place" (without so much as a footnote to indicate the rearranged dialogue) and the foul copy of "The Short Happy Life of Francis Macomber" (without some text and the many meticulous changes Hemingway made in the *Cosmopolitan* version of September 1936.) More objectionable are the principles behind the selections in Part II, "Short Stories Published in Books or

Magazines *Subsequent* to 'The First Forty-nine,' " (my italics). Now
a dozen of the 14 stories draw no quarrel: the five Spanish Civil War
stories (1938–39), the two fables (1951), the two *Atlantic* stories
(1957), "Summer People" and "The Last Good Country" from *The
Nick Adams Stories* (1972), and "An African Story," plucked from
The Garden of Eden (1986). But the first two stories in this section,
"One Trip Across" and "The Tradesman's Return," formed the first
two parts of *To Have and Have Not* (1937) and were published in
Cosmopolitan in 1934 and 1936, respectively. And omitted from this
section are a good handful of stories that have seen print in books,
juvenilia like "Sepi Jingan," "A Matter of Colour," and "Judgment of
Manitou," gathered in Matthew J. Bruccoli's *Ernest Hemingway's
Apprenticeship* (1971); and the five "Chicago-period" stories in Peter
Griffin's biography, *Along With Youth* (1985). Of the seven stories
in Part III, "Previously Unpublished Fiction," the two best, "A Train
Trip" and "The Porter," are from Hemingway's unfinished, mid-
1920s novel *Jimmy Breen* and need his revisions to properly glaciate
them into icebergs. The others include two mediocre, slightly fic-
tionalized war experiences, a pair of autobiographical miniatures that
do little to veil Hemingway's vindictiveness toward youngest son
Gregory, and "The Strange Country," the tediously long follow-up
segment cut from the "Bimini" section of *Islands in the Stream*. But
why these five, rather than better unpublished stories like "A Lack of
Passion" and the untitled battle fantasia of the British soldier Orpen,
Item 445 in the Kennedy Library? Despite frequent typographical
errors, the collection corrects one egregious error: the nickname,
"Stut," replaces the slur, "slut," in "Summer People." Too bad it failed
to correct the other problem, referred to in Charles Scribner, Jr.'s
opening sentence to his "Publisher's Preface": "There has long been
a need for a complete and up-to-date edition of the short stories of
Ernest Hemingway."

The biggest event for Hemingway scholars in 1987 was the publication of Kenneth S. Lynn's provocative, penetrating, briskly styled,
and revisionist biography, *Hemingway* (Simon and Schuster). Bringing psychoanalytic insight, historical research, and a nose keen for
androgynous scents to the findings of prior biographers and memoir-
ists, Lynn assembles a strong, thesis-driven account of Hemingway's
life, arguing the dominating influence of his mother Grace on his attitudes, problems, and works. Some scholars will object to Lynn's

sustained attention to Hemingway's childhood years. But no other biographer has gathered the varied strands of that period and woven them into a fabric that exhibits Hemingway psychologically clothed in Grace's mixed gender signals, sexual confusions, and obsession with twinness—all contributing elements in Hemingway's hair-fetished, androgynous personality. Thesis in hand, Lynn freshly examines some overlooked fiction ("Up in Michigan" and the battle fantasia of Orpen, mentioned above), reconsiders the gender and sexual oddities that recur in Hemingway's novels (from *The Sun Also Rises* and *A Farewell to Arms* to, most fully, *The Garden of Eden*), and attends to Hemingway's curious heterosexual relationships with mistresses and wives, remarking Pauline's and Mary's lesbian or androgynous tendencies. Lynn occasionally gets mired down in minor arm-wrestlings (disproving other views of Hemingway's World War I wounding) and in labored investigations (linking Jake Barnes's name to Natalie Barney, whose Paris address was 20 rue Jacob, and to lesbian Djuna Barnes, who lived in the Hotel Jacob). And he lapses into melodrama, remarking young Ernest's "sexual rage" at being called "Dutch dolly" by his mother. And he indulges himself in snide characterizations, delightedly flailing Malcolm Cowley's credulousness as Hemingway's first biographer. And he succumbs to wild editorializing, claiming that to Doctor Hemingway Grace's dressing and raising Ernest and his year-and-a-half older sister as twins "was among the first and deepest humiliations he suffered during their marriage."

Offsetting these zits are the biography's strong features: Lynn's thesis, his succinct political analysis of the Spanish Civil War, his cogent dismantling of accepted "facts" (such as the alleged episode of Hemingway's checking Fitzgerald's penis size for "A Matter of Measurements"), his bold mockery of Hemingway's claims as knowledgeable Spanish Civil War correspondent and efforts to establish his credentials with the left, and his excellent cameos of the legions of people, big and little, who populated Hemingway's life: Pound, Stein, Dos Passos, Ford, Robert McAlmon, Van Wyck Brooks, Dorothy Parker, Chard Powers Smith, Horace Liveright, Jane Mason, Lady Duff Twysden, Djuna Barnes, and other Paris lesbians. Irreverent toward the conventional Hemingway myths, Lynn nevertheless maintains a regard for Hemingway's troubled genius and significant achievements, minimized though they were by his compulsion for self-publicity, the wide shadow of his unflagging war with Grace, and the "long, eventually horrifying decline into illness" that began, writes Lynn, as early as 1937.

One sizable blemish in Lynn's biography is the disporportionate space he lavishes on the years between Decembers 1921 and 1929 (over one-third of his book's 600 pages). But the greater blotch is his literary criticism, although superior to Jeffrey Meyers's, whose *Hemingway: A Biography* (1985) Lynn betters in most respects. Reading everything through a biographical lens, he twists stories like "Fifty Grand" into an anti-Semitic analogue on Horace Liveright and other Jews, "The Mother of a Queen" into a reflection of Hemingway's financial squabbles with mother Grace, and "Indian Camp" into a biographical parallel to Hemingway's getting the telegram of his father's suicide. Lynn also likes to joust with elder critics. In his discussion of "The Big Two-Hearted River" he puts them down for their commentaries on the story's psychological ramifications, pronouncing that "Proof of Nick's state of mind was not to be found in the story," then contradictorily declares that the story deals with "the murky depths of [Nick's] troubled inner life." Lynn's penchant for sparring with elder critics reveals also that he is outdated on matters of criticism. He champions Margot Macomber as though he were the first astute reader of "The Short Happy Life," ignoring the critical centurions who have pitched their tents before the story. Neglectful of his homework, he also fails to argue his thesis against work that stole a long march on him—to other psychoanalytic conclusions—my *Concealments in Hemingway's Works* (1983).

This year's other biography is Denis Brian's *The True Gen: An Intimate Portrait of Hemingway by Those Who Knew Him* (Grove). In this lively, entertaining, and occasionally informative patchwork "biography" Brian assembles his interviews with and observations from over 70 people who knew, studied, or were eyewitnesses to Hemingway's myth-making life. The volume reads like a marathon gossip column, Brian allowing space not only to wives, siblings, and sons, but as well to high school acquaintances and war chums, to fellow correspondents and writers, to psychiatrists and lackeys, to biographers and critics, to sweethearts and rivals—literary and sexual. Brian welcomes comment on many of the controversial areas of Hemingway's life: the romance with Agnes von Kurowsky, the Jew-baiting of Harold Loeb, the recriminations against rival writers, the clashes with Martha Gellhorn, the World War II heroics, the ambiguities of his Catholicism and communistic leanings, and the troubles with fourth-wife Mary. The opinions and perspectives of such a welter of interviewees stir rather than resolve the controversies, Brian's intent, of course. His gossip columnist's instincts show clear in the last third of the volume. He brings on stage various Hemingway biographers and critics—the Hemingway Hunters, he cutely terms them—to comment on the various versions of Hemingway's life and character; naturally some sprightly disparagements, insults, and self-defenses result. The book also includes second-guessings on the Mayo Clinic's shock treatments, FBI files, varied reappraisals, the transcript of General Patton's inspector general's interrogation of Hemingway on his war correspondent activity, a glossary on the interviewees, and Brian's attempt to spoon-feed two psychiatrists his evidence for concurrence that "To all but a few, manic depression was a hidden fact of Hemingway's life."

Two additional items contribute to specific biographical areas of Hemingway's life. In "The Ernest Hemingway/Carlos Baker Correspondence" (*Imprint* 8, i:13–19) Robert E. Gajdusek quotes liberally from that 1951–54 correspondence, a portion of Stanford University's Charles D. Field Collection of Ernest Hemingway, which "includes first editions, galley proofs of Hemingway's fiction, articles, scripts, poems, translations of his work into thirteen different languages, photographs, and letters Hemingway wrote to and received from nearly forty correspondents." Gajdusek finds that because of Baker's "delicacy of introduction and evident code of values" when he was preparing the first edition of *Hemingway: The Writer as Artist* (1952), Hemingway's letters to him quickly became confidential, confessional, candid, and vulnerable. Topics in the letters include Hemingway's dedication to his art, "the pain of betrayal by critics," the writing he is doing, and his recognition of "the distance between his own awareness of his art and the general critical unreceptiveness." In "'Only kind thing is silence': Ernest Hemingway vs. Sinclair Lewis" (*HemR* 6, ii:46–53) Robert L. McLaughlin carefully documents the two men's three meetings and references to each other, corrects biographers' errors, and explains that in person Hemingway usually treated Lewis with the courtesy due a fellow author, but at a distance Lewis became a literary rival, fair game for the open season of Hemingway's denigrations.

Of this year's two bibliographic items, the major one is Matthew J. Bruccoli's *F. Scott Fitzgerald: A Descriptive Bibliography*, rev. ed.

(Pittsburgh). An expanded, corrected, and updated version of his earlier bibliography (1972) and supplement (1980), it chronologically lists by editions and printings all of Fitzgerald's books and pamphlets, all collections in which his work first appeared, all of his writing first published in magazines and newspapers, and his interviews and film scripts. Included as well are facsimiles of title pages and dust jackets of first editions, itemized keepsakes, and a complete bibliography of Zelda Fitzgerald's publications. The minor but valuable second item is William White's "Hemingway: A Current Bibliography" (*HemR* 6, ii:58–60).

ii. Influences, Sources, and Parallels

The Lawrences, D. H. and T. E., dominated this year's influences. The D. H. Lawrence–F. S. Fitzgerald connection got looked at again, this time in Robert Wexelblatt's "F. Scott Fitzgerald and D. H. Lawrence: Bicycles and Incest" (*AL* 59:378–88), which connects images and ideas from Lawrence's *Fantasia of the Unconscious* to Fitzgerald's *Tender Is the Night*. Lawrence's bicycle metaphor of the soul-rider atop the body-bicycle may explain several bicycling episodes in the novel, notably the race that passes by the café in which Tommy Barban and Dick and Nicolle Diver are discussing divorce, a race Wexelblatt allegorically translates. The novel's incest motif, which he briefly develops, may also have its provenance in Lawrence's book, and Dick's "fatal pleasingness" Wexelblatt argues, is more than a "trivial tragic flaw, a personal weakness," for as a representative trait it reflects Lawrence's diagnosis of the "disease of niceness" that besets modern love. In "*Meaulnes, Gatsby* and the Possibilities of Romance" (*EiP* 12, i:15–40) John Coyle elaborately compares the tensions between romantic illusions and realistic forces in *Gatsby* and Alain-Fournier's *Le Grand Meaulnes*, published 15 years before Fitzgerald's novel. Of interest are parallels in narrators, imagery, and events, particularly Gatsby's parties and the carnival of *la fête étrange, Gatsby's* wasteland and *Meaulnes's* landscapes of *le domain perdu*. John Skinner's "The Oral and the Written" (*JNT* 17:131–40) contrasts *Gatsby* and Conrad's *Heart of Darkness* in terms of narrative poetics. Borrowing terminology from Gérard Genette, Walter J. Ong, and Dorrit Cohn, Skinner reviews the "fragmentation of the linear narrative" to find that *Gatsby*—"a self-conscious (and sophisticated) rupture of the linearity privileged by chirographic culture"—"makes subtle use of analepsis, self-consciously subverting the linear norm of the written mode." In "The *Jazz History of the World* in *The Great Gatsby*" (*ELN* 25, ii:57–62) Darrel Mansell identifies the allusion in the novel's bizarre orchestral episode to Richard Strauss's *Also Sprach Zarathustra*. Fitzgerald's penchant for citing music and songs in his novels, the period's pleasure in hearing the classics "jazzified," Strauss's performance of *Zarathustra* before a Metropolitan Opera House audience, and the novel's earlier manuscript, in which Nick Carraway attempts in three paragraphs to describe the sounds and themes of *Jazz History of the World*—these lead Mansell to conclude that Fitzgerald transmogrified Strauss's music to fit *Gatsby*'s theme of "America's brash, energetic and meretricious vulgarization of European culture."

Two parallels between Hemingway's work and predecessors found print this year. William Adair sketchily argues in "Hemingway's Debt to *Seven Pillars of Wisdom* in *For Whom the Bell Tolls*" (*NConL* 17, iii:11–12) that several parallels between T. E. Lawrence's autobiographical account of his guerrilla exploits and events in Hemingway's Spanish Civil War novel show the latter's indebtedness to the former. Besides the train- and bridge-blowing episodes common to both works, Adair perfunctorily notes resemblances between Lawrence and Robert Jordan. In "Jake Barnes, Chaucer's Pardoner and the Restaurant Scene in *The Sun Also Rises*" (*Cithara* 26, ii:48–55) Wolfgang E. H. Rudat peers into the novel's closing scene and discovers that Jake and Brett's "gluttony-as-surrogate-sex scene at Botin's" contains not only Brett's strategies of psychological castration and Jake's parody of homosexual diction but erudite allusions as well to the exchange and resolution at the end of "The Pardoner's Tale" between the Host and the Pardoner.

iii. Criticism

a. **Full-Length Studies.** Neither of the two books on Hemingway is particularly impressive. Kenneth G. Johnston's *The Tip of the Iceberg: Hemingway and the Short Story* (Penkevill) is a choppy, uneven volume, each of whose 22 chapters briefly analyzes a story. Its sequence is erratically chronological, starting with "Up in Michigan" and "The Big Two-Hearted River" (in one of Johnston's better chapters, on Hemingway's attempt to imitate Cézanne) and ending with chapters on "The Denunciation" and the two fables of 1951. Sixteen of the chapters have seen previous publication, dating as far back as 1971, and while Johnston claims that he "revised, edited, and retitled" some of them for this volume, there is little evidence that he updated the research on many of them. Indeed, many of his chapters are curiously deficient in acknowledging visits from a host of critics before Johnston. Lacking index, bibliography, and citations to scarcely any criticism since the early 1970s, the study is a dull and rusty tool for any reader eager to get up to snuff on a story. More, despite Johnston's subtitle, his collection lacks connective bridges between chapters and any rationale for selecting the stories he analyzes, revealing that no thesis unifies his assembled materials. Nevertheless, he has a small handful of fine chapters—on "The Denunciation," "Out of Season," "The Revolutionist," "Fathers and Sons," and "Wine of Wyoming." And he includes at the end of each chapter a page or two of sometimes useful, sometimes interesting, sometimes odd splinters that he calls "background": "information on publication, revisions, alternate titles, as well as quotations" from Hemingway's writings.

The Politics of Ernest Hemingway (UMI Research Press) by Stephen Cooper, Jr., is a journeyman trek through Hemingway's political terrain. It covers his copy as a foreign correspondent linked to three wars, his Depression-years' expositions, his varied fictions, and his irrepressible utterances, involvements, and correspondence. Cooper reports little new about Hemingway's political views: at the time of Farewell they were pragmatic and isolationist, they altered during the 1930s, but they remained a "mix of strongly held attitudes . . . acquired from his upbringing and experience." Finding that Hemingway's "opposition to Fascism and censorship was liberal, whereas his dislike of the New Deal and increasingly centralized government was conservative," Cooper concludes that a better label for him would be libertarian. Cooper examines Hemingway's overtly political work: The Fifth Column, Farewell, To Have and Have Not, For Whom the Bell Tolls, and such stories as "The Revolutionist," "Che Ti Dice La Patria?" "Under the Ridge," "The Denunciation," and "Nobody Ever Dies." Most of these readings rework standard views and review the early critical reception. But two segments of the book are valuable. One is a chapter on the Spanish Civil War, Cooper explaining the complex, contradictory, and nonideological reasons Hemingway went to Spain and supported the Loyalist cause. The other is a section in his penultimate chapter, Cooper ably disputing claims that Hemingway fervently supported Castro's revolutionary overthrow of Batista.

b. **Collections.** I continue to see that the Harold Bloom–Chelsea House industry keeps rolling out its boilerplate collections of previously published criticism, but I cannot seem to wheedle a copy of either of this year's volumes on *The Sun Also Rises* or *A Farewell to Arms* from the publisher. No cause for sorrow, thanks to two collections by Linda W. Wagner-Martin. In *New Essays on* The Sun Also Rises (Cambridge) she gathers five essays plus her introduction to surround the novel with a good variety of viewpoints. Her "Introduction" (pp. 1–18) discusses background information, recapitulates some of the recent scholarship on the manuscript versions of the novel, and reprints and remarks on Fitzgerald's criticism of the novel's beginning chapters. She also includes several examples of Hemingway's revisions, and she comments on materials in the Kennedy Library's Hemingway Collection that date from the period Hemingway worked on *The Sun Also Rises*. Scott Donaldson's "Humor in *The Sun Also Rises*" (pp. 19–41) surveys the novel's ludic qualities. After discussing Hemingway's early forays into humorous writing—parodic verse, Lardneresque imitation, irreverent journalistic copy, and the satiric *The Torrents of Spring*—Donaldson takes up with the novel's different kinds of humor: inside jokes (the lost generation epigraph and some new manuscript material on it), witty dialogue (as between Count Mippipopolous and Lady Brett), narrative sarcasm (Jake's recurrent innuendoes), and self-deprecating banter (Mike Campbell's barbs). But Donaldson centers on Bill Gorton's "crazy humor" and discusses him as the model whose conduct deserves emulation. Michael S. Reynolds, in "The *Sun* in Its Time: Recovering the Historical Context" (pp. 43–64), briskly overviews the 1920s and its central moral issues, quoting selectively from the *American Mercury*, the Paris *Tribune*, and other publications, to provide information, like that on the 1925 Lourdes mania, to explain now-obscure allusions, especially in the Jake Barnes–Bill Gorton episodes. Steeped as Reynolds is in the old historicism, he insists that it is "hopelessly romantic" to interpret the novel without good knowledge of its historical context. Reynolds argues that *Sun*, a "fable of ideological bankruptcy," reflects "accurately the failings of an age," "just how schizophrenic American moral behavior became in the twenties." Historical background may well inform these conclusions. But the text informs Reynolds's other conclusions: that Jake is the novel's "moral barometer" and that the novel is "about the corruption of Jake Barnes, whose hopeless love for Brett leads him to pimp away his membership in Montoya's secret club of *aficion*," leads him to destroy "one of the last values left him in an already impoverished world." Wendy Martin's feminist-inspired, intelligent essay, "Brett Ashley as New Woman in *The Sun Also Rises*" (pp. 65–82), is one of the year's better pieces, even though it is misleadingly titled: her balanced essay attends as well to Jake Barnes as to Brett, finding them representatives of the shift in gender roles during the 20s. Indeed, although Martin includes useful information on the gender gains made by feminists in the 19th century and consolidated in the 1920s, she finds Brett no New Woman. Instead, Martin focuses upon Brett's vacillations between self-abnegation and self-indulgence; notes that her relationships with men "are filled with ambivalence, anxiety, and frequently alienation"; remarks her flip-flopping from being "insouciant, careless, a femme fatale" to being the "redemptive woman" who uses sexuality to save men; and finds her "caught between two modes of gender representation." Martin regards Jake in a similar state of imbalance and astutely considers his sexual affliction a cultural signifier that registers man's "loss of masculine power and authority and the axiomatic right to exercise social control." Because he relinquishes the wish to control Brett, writes Martin, he becomes "nurturing and *reponsive*," able "to accept the discomfort and uncertainty that come with his loss of authority."

In "Decoding the Hemingway Hero in *The Sun Also Rises*" (pp. 83–107) Arnold E. and Cathy N. Davidson bring deconstructive theory and semiotic skills to the novel in the best critical essay on Hemingway this year. They correctly call *Sun* a *writerly* text (one that permits competing and contradictory interpretations to coexist) rather than regard it, as do the essays immediately above, a *readerly* text (one that expects readers to reach like interpretations that the author intended and that informed readers will agree upon). The Davidsons examine six brief passages from the novel to show the subtlety and contradictory signs that resist unequivocal meaning. They shrewdly analyze Jake's accounts of Brett's entrance into the novel with her homosexual escorts and of his admission into the fraternity of aficionados. In all the passages the Davidsons unravel sexual sublimations and repressions knitted into the novel's fabric, repeatedly thwarting any basis for a "code of heroic solitary selfhood" at work in the novel. They thus undercut icons—Brett, Romero, bullfights, idyllic retreat—that interpreters have attempted to erect, and they dismantle attempts at "establishing any concluding finality or promis[e of] a different future beyond the text, [for] Jake's last words readily devolve into an endless series of counterstatements that continue the same discourse . . . ." After two such fine essays Wagner-Martin's collection ends with a fizzle, John W. Aldridge's "Afterthoughts on the Twenties of *The Sun Also Rises*" (pp. 109–29), an essay whose first part saw print in *Commentary* in 1973, much of whose second part saw print in *Sewanee Review* last year. Nevertheless, Aldridge discusses Hemingway's contemporaries, his "powerful responsiveness to experience," and his "tight minimalist style."

Linda W. Wagner-Martin also edited *Ernest Hemingway: Six Decades of Criticism* (Michigan State), a gathering of 28 essays, none duplicating any in her 1974 *Five Decades of Criticism*. Of these essays three are previously unpublished, 13 are from the 1980s, six from the 1970s, and two or three each from the 1920s, 1930s, 1950s, and 1960s. The essays appropriately range from biographical matters to stylistic considerations to readings of individual works and discussions of thematic issues. And the essayists include vintage figures (Dorothy Parker and Malcolm Cowley), established scholars (Michael Reynolds, Larzer Ziff, Max Westbrook, and Scott Donaldson), recent voices (James Hinkle and James Nagel), and well-known writers (John Wain, Nelson Algren, and E. L. Doctorow). But the essays make an unsatisfying collection for several reasons. The historical principle underlying the collection is feeble, oddly ignoring the 1940s, including only nine essays from the 20s through the 60s, and overweighting the 1980s. The decision to include no excerpts from books omits some work quite superior to a number of the essays here. The rationale to use essays "taken from journal sources that might be difficult for the general reader to obtain" is rationalization in all but a few cases. The disproportionate number of essays from this decade (16) argues for a separate collection. And the three previously unpublished essays, all on *A Farewell to Arms* are weak. In the first of these, "Catherine Barkley and Retrospective Narration in *A Farewell to Arms*" (pp. 171–85), James Nagel scrutinizes the differences between time of narration and time of action so as to find it indisputable that narration occurs ten years after action and that Frederic Henry's motive for narration is to come to terms emotionally with his relationship to Catherine. Nagel cites the text's allusion to Babe Ruth to prove that the narration followed the novel's events by ten years, naively assuming the allusion's referent to be Ruth's feat of 60 home runs in 1927, not his early years on the mound for the Red Sox— winning 23 games and leading the league with an earned-run average of 1.75 for Boston in 1916, winning 24 and leading the league with 35 complete games in 1917—nor his bleacher-rattling early years for the Yankees with 54 homers in 1920 and 59 in 1921. Nagel tendentiously studies the many indications of two time frames to conclude optimistically that Frederic's confessional narrative marks his preparation "to resume living once again, to seek new relationships and new commitments, and to end his fixation on loss and pain, a process that has taken him a decade." In "A Téssara for Frederic Henry: Imagery and Recurrence in *A Farewell to Arms*" (pp. 187–93) Gwen L. Nagel re-explores the novel's pervasive identity theme. Briefly commenting on a passage Hemingway cut from the manuscript, she then sorts out the many appellations assigned to Frederic, the scenes in which others misidentify him, the confusions caused by his clothing, and the imagery and pronouns that contribute to the novel's "iconography of identity." Robert A. Martin in "Hemingway and the Ambulance Drivers in *A Farewell to Arms*" (pp. 195–204) argues that the etymology of the names of the novel's two groups of ambulance drivers comments significantly upon Frederic's progress in his commitment to Catherine. As mirrors to his "indifferent and impersonal relationship and attitude toward Catherine before he is wounded," three of the ambulance drivers in the first group of four— Manera ("farmer or worker of the land"), Gavuzzi ("common man"), and Passini ("sufferer")—represent abstractions without political or social convictions. As mirrors to Frederic's "altered beliefs and attitudes toward love and life" after his wounding, the second group of ambulance drivers assigned him have names that "reflect moral and spiritual qualities" to match the priest's definition of love and to "parallel Frederic's transformation from lust to love": Aymo ("I love"), Bonello ("good," "kind"), and Piani ("soft," "gentle").

c. **General Essays.** Of three items on Fitzgerald, the important one is Thomas B. Gilmore's "The Winding Road to Pat Hobby: Fitzgerald Confronts Alcoholism" in his *Equivocal Spirits*, pp. 96–118. By tracing the effects of Fitzgerald's alcoholism on his writing, Gilmore differentiates among a number of effective and ineffective works. Fitzgerald's denials, delays, or evasions in presenting a character's alcoholism become Gilmore's yardstick for determining a fiction's merit. He contrasts the "powerfully authentic portrayal of alcoholic decline and fall" in Anthony Patch of *The Beautiful and the Damned* to *Tender Is the Night*, flawed partly because Fitzgerald fails to dramatize Dick Diver's alcoholism. Gilmore discusses a number of stories—"One Trip Abroad," "Family in the Wind," "The Lost Decade," "An Alcoholic Case," "A New Leaf," "Babylon Revisited," "Her Last Case," and "Crazy Sunday"—and "The Crack-Up," to show that while Fitzgerald occasionally confronts the alcoholism and alcoholic behavior that accounts for a story's weakness, more frequently he sentimentally sidesteps it. Especially good are Gilmore's analysis of "Babylon Revisited" and "Crazy Sunday," the latter "Fitzgerald's most desperate and least satisfying attempt to distance himself from his alcoholic reality." But Gilmore also redeems the Pat Hobby stories from being regarded as hackwork, explaining how they effectively sublimate Fitzgerald's alcoholic traits. Julie M. Irwin sips from the same topic in "F. Scott Fitzgerald's Little Drinking Problem" (*ASch* 56:415–27). After identifying the traits that accompany the three stages of alcoholism, she mechanically discusses *Tender* and seven of the stories covered also by Gilmore, explaining how each reflects one of the stages and, collectively, how they reveal Fitzgerald to have been "the victim of a disease, not a self-destructive drunk bent on wasting the talent he was given." In "Fitzgerald's Climatology" (*LGJ* 8:9–11, 23) Robert A. Martin remarks Fitzgerald's descriptions of weather in several stories and novels, concluding that they function as emotional barometers of characters' states of being: hot weather signifies being emotionally and physically drained, rain conflict, mist confusion, and snow solitude and loneliness.

Among the important essays on Hemingway is Charles Molesworths' "Hemingway's Code: The Spanish Civil War and World Power" (*Salmagundi* 76–77:84–100), a wide-ranging, perceptive study that, well-versed in historical matters, examines the writing of Hemingway's Spanish Civil War period. Starting from his version of Hemingway's code—"the hero must not be afraid to die or to kill, but he must never delight in killing or mistake it for anything but what it is"—Molesworth discusses several works, observing the different mediations in Hemingway's moral vision and the "emotional pressures entailed in accepting such a vision." More important, he takes on Hemingway's political detractors—Kazin, Trilling, Bessie,

and Bergum—to argue the political poise Hemingway achieved in
Bell Tolls, finding it "as a reflection of the political forces at work
a fairly compelling statement," and finding in Robert Jordan an
achieved balance, "a reasoned position based on his anarchist impulses and his generally cynical reading of other people's political
struggles and complexities." To Molesworth, Hemingway's devotion
to the Republican cause issued from cultural identification with the
Spanish people rather than from a political ideology. But he credits
Hemingway with the perception to see "the extent and consequences
of Russia's involvement and ulterior motives" and to realize that the
war resembled a family quarrel. An essay of equal, but failed, am-
bitiousness is Hubert Zapf's "Reflection vs. Daydream: Two Types
of the Implied Reader in Hemingway's Fiction" (*CollL* 14:101–19).
Zapf attempts to account for the "strange emotional intensity" in
Hemingway's fiction by differentiating two kinds of readers who,
responding to two kinds of "appelative structure" in the fiction, have
dissimilar experiences. Drawing largely upon Wolfgang Iser's reception theory and Freud's psychodynamic theories, Zapf erects opposing reader responses: reflection (a vertical, cognitive, deep-struc-
ture, negative, and constitutive act) and daydream (a horizontal,
emotive, temporal, positive, and "processual" act). Examining *The
Sun Also Rises* as an instance of reflection response, Zapf contends
that Jake's "disillusioned subjectivity" neutralizes both any hope of
change or development in the novel and any "psychodynamic potential of the temporal-horizontal position [that change] would create." It also leaves only "a reflective, vertical tension between different levels of meaning and reality that are interrelated in a sort of
negative coexistence." After briefly discussing "Big Two-Hearted
River" as a variation of the same kind of reader appeal, Zapf turns to
"Short Happy Life" as his daydream example, remarking the reader's
emotional participation in the "dynamic process of experience inscribed into the text." Zapf's Germanic dichotomy views readers as
binary decoders, able only to toggle on their reflection or daydream
modes one at a time, never together. Worse, he categorizes some of
Hemingway's fictions as primarily accessible by one mode, some by
the other. His view of Jake's narrative, for example, regards it lacking
suspense elements and forbidding emotional participation from readers who may find Jake, for all of his subjectivity and sarcasm and
self-pity, emotionally engaging.

    Two commendable essays take up with the large issues of Hemingway's relationship to nature and to Catholicism. Troubled by long-standing and recurrent references to Hemingway's "primitivism," Glen A. Love reexamines the concept in "Hemingway's Indian Virtues: An Ecological Reconsideration" (*WAL* 22:201–15). He finds it inapplicable primarily because of Hemingway's tendency "to exploit the natural world for its self-aggrandizing properties" and his "aggressive and isolated individualism which wars against those natural manifestations he claims to love." Instead of registering humility when fronted by nature's powers, Hemingway regarded them as hostile agents he must control and manage. Love acknowledges that Hemingway's attempt at a primitive character, *The Old Man and the Sea*'s Santiago, is often praised as his "final testament of acceptance, his coming to peaceful terms with the natural world." But the novel's tragic ingredient of Santiago's spirit in lethal conflict with natural laws shows nature unequal to Santiago's pride and subdued but strident self-exaltation. Further, Love sees anthropocentrism in Hemingway's treatment of the novel's creatures, judging them as either friends or enemies, rather than as equals of value and nobility. Nevertheless, Love cites statements and actions during Hemingway's last decade (oddly ignoring his mid-decade safari to Africa) which suggest "that Santiago's inner struggle between feelings of wrongdoing and necessity may be related to his creator's own questioning of long-held beliefs as he approached the end of his career." In "The Lord of Heroes: Hemingway and the Crucified Christ" (*R&L* 19, i: 21–41) Kathleen Verduin quotes countless quips about and allusions to Christ in Hemingway's letters and fiction, providing a veritable christological concordance to Hemingway's canon. She links them not only to Hemingway's creation of fictional heroes, whose deaths manfully replicate Christ's death on the cross, but also to the characterizations of Christ from the many Lives of Christ (over 600 in English alone between 1874 and 1920), which repeatedly replaced the notion of His "feminine feebleness" with that of His manly virility and solitary courage. Inasmuch as the author of one of these lives, *Jesus of Nazareth* (1903) was none other than "Rev. Willeam Eleazer Barton, minister of the First Congregational Church in Oak Park during the Hemingway family's attendance there from 1916 on," Verduin implies that Hemingway's unflagging respect for men who cope with the agonies of their analogous crucifixions derives from the valorized portrayal of Christ's behavior, in which Hemingway had to have been well inculcated.

The other five general essays deal with an assortment of issues. In one of his two essays Paul Smith, "Hemingway's Luck" (*HemR* 7, i:38–42), discusses several instances of Hemingway seeing the good and bad faces of Lady Luck. Contesting the notion of Hemingway the conscientious craftsman, Smith notes that her face shone on several of his deletions between manuscript and publication. One was the lopping off of the epilogue to "Big Two-Hearted River," which resulted from a publisher's delayed response and then Gertrude Stein's dismissal of it as "a little story of meditation," scolding Hemingway that "remarks are not literature." Similarly, Fitzgerald's reading of the typescript of *The Sun Also Rises* in late May or early June 1926— rather than in August, as planned—resulted in the excision of the novel's first chapter and a half. Lady Luck glowered on Hemingway, Smith finds, when it came to editorial decisions made in the House of Scribner, as in the instances of the gaffe in "Summer People" (slut for Stut), a significant cut in "The Last Good Country," and the "corrected" dialogue in "A Clean Well-Lighted Place." In his other essay, "Impressions of Ernest Hemingway" (*HemR* 6, ii:2–10), Smith comments on some of Hemingway's unpublished letters and manuscripts, discusses an unpublished Hemingway prose-poem, remarks on Hemingway's attempts at getting Cézanne-like dimensions in his fiction, and argues the importance of three women in *A Moveable Feast*: Gertrude Stein, Hadley Richardson, and the anonymous, rain-freshened woman who stops briefly in the good café on the Place St. Michel where young Hemingway is writing—a muse.

In "Hemingway as *Auteur*" (*SAQ* 86:151–58) Peter L. Hays reviews the many critical evaluations of Hemingway's early style to argue its cinematic techniques—deferred-subject constructions, paratactic syntax, definite articles, repetitions, short and simple or compound sentences, and lack of abstract terms. Because these all contribute to the effect of "pictorial presentation devoid of authorial commentary," they compel readers, as do good films their audiences, to engage with Hemingway's fiction and "to make connections, judgments, evaluations." In a word, Hemingway's cinematic techniques make reader-response criticism obligatory. In another of his articles on Hemingway's writers-as-characters, Robert E. Fleming in "Portrait of the Artist as a Bad Man: Hemingway's Career at the Crossroads" (*NDQ* 55:66–71) reconsiders Richard Gordon of *To Have and Have Not*. Hemingway partly attacks him as a writer "who cashes in on timely trends" but also uses him to reflect upon the uncertainty of his own artistic direction halfway through the 1930s. Comparing Gordon to Harry of "The Snows of Kilimanjaro" and to other writers in Hemingway's fictions, Fleming sees Hemingway harboring misgivings about himself and all writers whose need to gather material and experiences for their art could become perverse, could "risk violating the dignity of the human soul." And from typescripts, manuscripts, letters, initial publication in magazines, and Carlos Baker's biography Kenneth G. Johnston enumerates discarded titles for a number of Hemingway's stories in "Hemingway's Search for Story Titles," (*HemR* 6, ii:34–37). Sample: "One More for the Nazarene" and "The Seed of the Church" became "Today Is Friday." Johnston also corrects Carlos Baker's errors "in listing 'A Budding Friendship' as a provisional title for 'The Snows of Kilimanjaro' and 'The Happy Ending' as a tentative title for 'The Short Happy Life of Francis Macomber.'" Switch the tentative titles to get it right.

d. **Essays on Specific Works: Fitzgerald.** The year's best essay on Fitzgerald was Neill R. Joy's "*The Last Tycoon* and Max Eastman: Fitzgerald's Complete Political Primer" (*Prospects* 12:365–92), a superb discussion both of Fitzgerald's astute creation of political resonances in his last novel and of his use of the character and career of Max Eastman for the novel's Marxist adversary, Brimmer. Working from the novel's drafts and notes, Joy reconstructs its thoroughgoing political dimensions, finding in Monroe Stahr and Brimmer "the conflict between two hostile and competing ideals of economic ego, founding but antiquated laissez-faire opposing presumptive Marxist correction." More, Joy finds Fitzgerald's sympathies shrewdly neutral and the novel "a sadly ironic and elegiac political estimation" in which Fitzgerald "works out remorsefully the parody of manifest destiny." Joy also traces Eastman's representative career as a disenchanted Marxist—one whose work and person Fitzgerald knew—to document his resemblances to Brimmer and to explain Fitzgerald's treatment of him in the novel. Although not in the same league as Joy's scholarly essay, Ernest Lockridge's deconstructive reconsideration, "F. Scott Fitzgerald's *Tromp l'Oeil* and *The Great Gatsby*'s Buried Plot" (*JNT* 17:163–83) was a worthy competitor. Lockridge argues that Fitzgerald created Nick Carraway as an unreliable narrator who not only misperceives or ignores many events in the novel, but is blind to the novel's two "buried plots"—both based on circumstantial evidence and both overingeniously manufactured, many

readers will conclude. The first is that Daisy, jealous of Tom's adul-
teress, learned of Myrtle Wilson's identity through Ferdie, the butler-
chauffeur. Recognizing her as the woman dashing out to Gatsby's car,
Daisy was "smart enough to integrate coincidence and purpose," to
seize the opportunity of running down her rival and eliminating her
from Tom's life. The second plot pegs Wolfsheim's protégés as Gatsby's and Wilson's assassins. The new servants who came to Gatsby's
house after Daisy and Gatsby's first meeting were not hired to keep
Daisy and Gatsby's adultery hushed up, as Gatsby thought. They were
there to keep in line Gatsby, whom Wolfsheim had "made" and whose
affair with another man's wife violated the reason Wolfsheim valued
him, his integrity that "would never so much as look at a friend's
wife." Because Gatsby and Daisy's affair jeopardizes Wolfsheim's
business "gonnections," Lockridge argues, Wolfsheim's protégé-ser-
vants eliminate Gatsby and, in a windfall parallel to Myrtle's timely
appearance on the road before Daisy, eliminate as well the crazed
George Wilson, making him the fall guy for Gatsby's death.

A thin quartet focused on individual Fitzgerald short stories this
year. George Monteiro's "Fitzgerald vs. Fitzgerald: 'An Alcoholic
Case'" (L&M 6:110–16) discusses Fitzgerald's refusal to own up to
his alcoholism and tuberculosis, and commends his artistry in divulg-
ing them in the story's anonymous alcoholic cartoonist and its center
of consciousness, an equally anonymous nurse whose sympathy for
her patient violates the detachment her professionalism requires.
Sanford Pinsker comes away from "Fitzgerald's 'The Baby Party'"
(Expl 45, ii:52–55) impressed by this "death-haunted" story because
John Andros's pugilistic defense of his daughter exudes "intimations
of mortality" that universalize the story, providing a fine instance of
Fitzgerald's "special genius," his "ability to arrange the Romantic
Dream and a foreboding sense of doom about that Dream into an
equipoise . . . by incorporating both aspects within himself." In "Fitzgerald's 'Babylon Revisited'" (LGJ 8:16–19) David Cowart discusses the story's royalty, hearth, and ghost imagery and allusions to
reveal Charlie Wales as a ghost-haunted and royal exile, a tragic
character of limited recognition, unable as he is to "recognize the
radical incompatibility of his money and the home he seeks." And
Helge Normann Nilsen conventionally reads "The Rich Boy" as a
telling indictment of the American rich, their spiritual laziness, self-
indulgence, superficiality, and "frequently inflated image of them-

selves as the leaders of their nation" in "A Failure to Love: A Note on
F. Scott Fitzgerald's 'The Rich Boy'" (*IFR* 14:40–43).

e. Essays on Specific Works: Hemingway. *The Garden of Eden*
drew a half-dozen writers this year, among them Tom Jenks, whose
"Editing Hemingway: *The Garden of Eden*" (*HemR* 7, i:30–33) divulges nearly nothing of his methods, problems, or process in editing
the manuscripts of the novel. Claiming at the 1986 MLA Hemingway
session, during which he read his essay, that "There's no one here
who doesn't know more about Hemingway and his work than I do,"
Jenks nevertheless acknowledges both that he made no changes
"When there was any chance that a change might injure the author
or the work" and that while "Hemingway's risks are evident in the
published book," he himself "cut risks only when they failed," hoping
to do right by what he saw as the manuscript's "strongest, clearest
impulse," "Hemingway's desire to take on his own myth without,
however, destroying or relinquishing it." In "Where's Papa?" (*New
Republic* 9 March:30–33) Barbara Probst Solomon succinctly and
scathingly derides "the thin and disjointed novel that Scribner's published" as *The Garden of Eden*. Measuring the published novel
against the manuscripts, she crisply describes the differences in plot,
tone, theme, and ending, declaring "that Hemingway's publisher has
committed a literary crime." Solomon discusses the novel's aesthetic
focus and isolates several passages from the manuscripts to buttress
her lament at the violation done to this "summa of Hemingway's
aesthetics."

Among the quartet of academicians to cut swaths into Hemingway's *Garden*, the least of them is Robert B. Jones, whose "Mimesis
and Metafiction in Hemingway's *The Garden of Eden*" (*HemR* 7, i:
2–13) discovers two novels, a complex realistic fiction of David
Bourne's "evolution of authentic selfhood" and a novel that conforms
to the criteria of metafiction—texts that simultaneously construct and
deconstruct a fictional illusion. On *Garden* as mimetic novel Jones
views Catherine Bourne a "willful and sympathetic character," despite her "neurotic oscillations," for her moments of lucidity and self-
awareness alternate with her efforts to destroy David as man and
writer by collapsing his sexual identity and by driving him to write
the story of their honeymoon. David, gradually realizing Catherine's
"emasculating influence," reclaims his identity as man and author by

writing the elephant story, which achievement marks "the authentic selfhood requisite for creative experience and creative language." On the novel as metafiction Jones labors with the jargon of contemporary literary theory to elevate the novel about a writer into a self-reflexive, deconstructive text. In another double reading Frank Scafella mulches "Clippings from *The Garden of Eden*" (*HemR* 7, i:20–29) with ample quotations and passages from the holograph versions of the novel's "complete" manuscript to argue not only that David Bourne both writes and exists in his narrative but also that only while writing it can he recognize the "spiritual entailments" of his life with Catherine. The "spiritual entailments" include "the origin and nature of Catherine's gamble for David's soul," her hostility toward his writing, and David's "deep sorrow" and "unbearable sense of loss" as she descends down "the via dolorosa of lesbianism." During her Ovidian metamorphosis and fascination with evil, David realizes that he can do little to help her "metaphysical plight." Assigning no complicity to David in Catherine's decline, Scafella links the sorrow that young David feels at the death of the huge elephant to the sorrow the older David feels for Catherine and his wish to revivify and make whole again both the beast and the woman. Because Marita understands the "*mystère*" of David's work as a writer, a creator, she becomes the soulmate who enables him to write "from beyond personal feelings and even from beyond knowledge, out of an inner core of being" or soul.

A virtually free-associational, allusively oblique essay is Robert Gajdusek's "Elephant Hunt in Eden: A Study of New and Old Myths and Other Strange Beasts in Hemingway's Garden" (*HemR* 7, i:14–19). Gajdusek finds *Garden* related to Hemingway's major novels in its focus on the need for men to relinquish their power and to achieve a balance of masculine darkness and feminine lightness. But unlike his other works, in Catherine Bourne Hemingway studies the contemporary woman's dissatisfactions with her role as excluded accessory and thus her self-compensating grab for unilateral power and her retaliatory manipulations to be as creative in the dynamics of a living relationship as David is in his fictional constructs. From David's story of the elephant, Gajdusek extracts three implications: a confession of David's double guilt (his "betrayal of the killer and the killed, of both the elephant *and* his father"); an analogue to "the story of Catherine's envy of David's art," an "abstract exemplification of her acted-upon desires"; and an allegory of the penalty every artist must pay for both satisfying the voracious "public avidity for the artist's art," and betraying "his moonlight vision of the double-sided equally greatly right-and-left tusked mystery elephant."

The most ambitious, insightful, and accomplished essay on *Garden* is Mark Spilka's "Hemingway's Barbershop Quintet: *The Garden of Eden* Manuscript" (*Novel* 21:29–55), marred by occasionally strained connections, as between the launching of the novel in 1946 and the "lesbian lark" and the barbershop showdown in the late sequences of Fitzgerald's *Tender Is the Night*. Spilka draws strongly from biographical resemblances among Hemingway's wives and mistresses both to establish their latent or manifest androgyny—or lesbianism in Pauline's case—and to claim that in the novel Hemingway confronted and overcame "the hazards of androgyny that Fitzgerald . . . had only dimly understood." Like Scafella, Spilka draws heavily upon unpublished manuscript materials, deploring much of what Tom Jenks excised for violating "the novel's narrative status as an expansive account of an inner journey, a 'sea change' as seen from inside the iceberg and therefore not an ordinary novel at all." Taking his cue from the Rodin statue that David and Catherine saw together of two lovemaking lesbians, "The Metamorphosis of Ovid" (from a group occasionally called "The Damned Women," pictured), Spilka argues its "edenic invitation to forbidden mysteries and disturbing sexual ambiguities." Spilka regrets the deletion of the Nick and Barbara Sheldon subplot, for it omits Barbara and Catherine Bourne's direct lesbian link and obscures the idea that David Bourne had earlier been wed to a woman resembling Barbara Sheldon, whom Catherine urged him to betray so as to marry herself. The novel's African story is indebted to Kipling's *Jungle Books*, Spilka reasons. But the story, which emphasizes the "breakdown in trust" between male friends, improves upon Kipling and identifies David's oscillation between his two narratives, his novel of "failed sexual relations" and his tale of "stoic male endurance." With excellent discussion of Catherine's complexity, of the "expansive conversation" in the "dialogic manuscript," and of alternate endings of the novel, Spilka esteems the manuscript for "Hemingway's bravery as he saw it in the daily struggle to transcend his own terrible dependencies and passivities."

Before I turn to a handful of articles on Hemingway's short fiction, five minor articles ask for brief mention. William Adair's "Hemingway's *The Sun Also Rises*" (*Expl* 45, iii:48–49) asserts that Jake Barnes borders on xenophobia, at least slightly prejudiced against

most of the characters in his novel and certainly against women, finding favor in nary a one. In "Catherine Barkley: Hemingway's Scottish
Heroine" (*HemR* 7, i:43–44) Charles J. Nolan, Jr., disabuses readers
for mistakenly identifying Catherine as English rather than Scottish
and suggests that inasmuch as both the Barclay (Berkley) and Ferguson families hail from Ayrshire, Scotland, it is likely that Catherine
and fellow-nurse Fergy have had a long friendship that predates
their nursing in Milan. That probability explains Fergy's anger at
Frederic's impregnation of Catherine, her self-pity at being left alone
at Stresa, and Catherine's assurances to Fergy that she will stay with
her, should she wish her to. Erroneously proclaiming that except for
Carlos Baker it is "all but impossible to find any reader who does
more than politely dismiss" Hemingway's African book, A. Carl Bre-
dahl sets out to right this "powerful juggernaut of dismissal" in "The
Body as Matrix: Narrative Pattern in *Green Hills of Africa*"(*MQ* 28:
455–72). He argues the return to health of Hemingway's narrator
during the hunting episodes: because "consumption and transformation are the dominant images in the book and motivating urges in the
narrator himself," they reveal his process of getting "into life rather
than perceiv[ing] it from a distance." Differentiated from the characters Kandisky, Garrick, and Karl, the narrator seeks "art and a life
expressive of each other," and he purges competitive jealousies and
"old ideas, stultifying sentiments, and complicated patterns of life,
making possible renewal and growth." And so while 12 chapters of
the book record his drive to unify his powers, the last chapter's failed
sable hunt aptly makes him acknowledge his weaknesses and accept
his responsibilities for them, the final stages in restoring him to health
and articulateness.

Raymond Conlon, in "*The Fifth Column*: A Political Morality
Play" (*HemR* 6, ii:11–16), characterizes Hemingway's polemical play
as his "only truly ideological work," for readers must judge its action
and characters' behavior from a political viewpoint. Conlon belabors
Philip Rawlings's dilemma, noting on the one hand his sense of duty
to the Republican cause, on the other his passion for the bourgeois
beauty of Dorothy Bradley and his moral uneasiness over the torture
and execution of interrogated fascists. Analyzing the play's schematic
characters who tug on Rawlings's allegiance—Max and Anita and
the hotel manager vying against the self-indulgent and parasitic
Dorothy—Conlon concludes that Rawlings undergoes political development and resembles Everyman. Robert A. Martin, "Heming-

way's *For Whom the Bell Tolls:* Fact into Fiction" (*SAF* 15:219–25), has pored over several histories of the Spanish Civil War and over biographies of several of its figures to succinctly connect characters and events in the novel to their historical counterparts. In addition to identifying, among others, the originals for Jordan, Maria, Golz, and Karkov, Martin also identifies the historic events of the bridge-blowing, the failed offensive, the persecution of the fascists by Pablo's band, and the plot to assassinate several Republican leaders.

While a majority of the articles on Hemingway's short fiction dealt with usually neglected items, neither they nor the others made significant inroads into this well-traveled terrain. Five articles focused on *In Our Time* or one of its stories. James Nagel boldly begins "Literary Impressionism in *In Our Time*" (*HemR* 6, ii:17–26) with the claim that the volume is "one of the most important documents in the history of Literary Impressionism in America." By article's end he back-pedals, admitting that "none of the stories in *In Our Time* is a perfect work of Impressionism, but all of them reveal Impressionistic tendencies in both technique and theme." Between the claim and the backpedal Nagel traces the history of Impressionist painting and literature, noting similarities between a few of Hemingway's prose-poem efforts and Imagistic conventions. When he turns to the vignettes and stories of *In Our Time*, he fudges. The criteria for an Impressionistic work become too inclusive to sharply rule some work in and some work out; more, they let Nagel focus upon visual details and sensations, downplaying, for instance, the preponderant (and non-Impressionistic) dialogue in "Indian Camp." Impressed with "Big Two-Hearted River" as a complex instance of Hemingway's literary Impressionism, Nagel ignores the discrepancy between what he cites as Impressionism's focus "on an intense, abbreviated moment of experience, a Vistazo" and the story's lengthy attention to Nick Adams's slow trek and methodical activities and freeze on any rush of emotion. In "Hemingway's 'On the Quai at Smyrna' and the Universe of *In Our Time*" (*SSF* 24:159–62) Peter A. Smith segments the story into seven episodes, each isolating a pedagogical principle or didactic message about the "senselessly brutal universe" of the volume as a whole. Nakajima Kenji's "Literary Bravery in Hemingway's 'Chapter III' and 'Chapter IV' of *In Our Time*" (*KAL* [1986] 27:47–56) argues that the narrative voice in the two vignettes issues from a brave, not an ironically callous, soldier. In "Chapter III" the narrator's language reflects the faithful callousness of a survivor who sees the reality of war and its emotional void; the hyperbolic modifiers in "Chapter IV" express the psychology of a soldier "trying to cover up his anxiety." Albert E. Wilhelm worries "Dick Boulton's Name in 'The Doctor and the Doctor's Wife'" (*Names* 34:423–25), discovering that since "bolt" meant "an arrow with a thick, blunt head," Boulton's name may have "originally identified a maker of crossbows," hinting at his being "an invader from the Indian camp who attacks the Doctor on his own ground and destroys all peace and security in and around the Adams cottage." Other bolts: lightning (that the Doctor has assured Nick would not strike a beech tree but does strike him on the "beach" encounter), shotgun (that the Doctor ejects shells with), and gate (that Boulton leaves open when he departs). In "The Far Shore: Gender Complexities in Hemingway's 'Indian Camp'" (*DR* [1986] 66:181–87) J. Andrew Wainwright, without so much as a nod in the direction of an earlier critic, belabors the story both for its implied criticism of the attitudes and limitations of its male figures and for its implied affirmation "of essential female life-qualities."

Ann Putnam traveled from Wyoming to the Alps in two separate articles. In "'Wine of Wyoming' and Hemingway's Hidden West" (*WAL* 22:17–32) she rehashes the story and comments on others with western scenes before identifying the story's motif of betrayal—the narrator's failure to honor his promise to return on the last night to share wine with the Fontans. She links that motif to Hemingway's paradoxical habit of valuing good country and desiring to remain in it but always succumbing to the desire to abandon it for another country. In "Dissemblings and Disclosure in Hemingway's 'An Alpine Idyll'" (*HemR* 6, ii:27–33) Putnam teases readers to believe she will connect the story's two stories, will reveal how "the peasant's story provides the images or visual signs through which the story of the skier-narrator is implied." Yet aside from her conclusion (that the story ends with a quiet reflection on the "inexplicability of why we do the things we do") and her moralistic reading of the story's ethic of pleasure (don't indulge any pleasure too long), she merely questions both the "bundle of letters" that have accumulated in the narrator's absence and the narrator's attentiveness during the tale about the peasant: might these suggest "some lapse, some estrangement or omission in the narrator's own life for which the peasant's story acts as a kind of reminder of perhaps other, more subtle kinds of blindness?"

Yamomoto Shoh, in "Hemingway's Macomber Story: Its Structure and Meaning" (*Poetica* [1986] 23:98–115), elaborately charts out the story's 1,207 lines into parts and scenes (all 37 of the latter!) to show that it "resembles an ellipse with two centers," one center poised over Francis Macomber's traditional coming-of-age story, the other over Robert Wilson's coming-of-understanding story, his appreciation of Francis, exemplar of "a new type of manliness."

Perhaps the place to end is with the upbeat or offbeat, Donald Junkins's "Hemingway's Bullfighter Poems" (*HemR* 6, ii:38–45). Justly disdaining Hemingway's four poems in *88 Poems* that mention bullfighting, Junkins plucks nine paragraphs from *Death in the Afternoon* and "re-lines" each to resemble a poem, what he incoherently defines as "the creation with words of an effect which simultaneously makes a circular statement following itself outside of its own circularity." Justifying his liberties in rearranging Hemingway's paragraphs, Junkins draws upon Ezra Pound's iconoclastic but sensible dispute with purists who wished to differentiate poetry from prose—"The thing that counts is 'good writing.' And 'good writing' is perfect control." But Junkins neglects to explain that the re-lined paragraphs display "perfect control." Instead, his introductions to each of the nine "poems" pedagogically list his personal criteria of specific things that must occur at the beginning and end of a poem. Despite the arbitrariness of Junkins's selections, re-linings, and commentary, the selected "poems" highlight some fine passages in Hemingway's bullfighting treatise that otherwise get forgotten or swamped by the book's lengthy exposition. (For corrections to the formatting of two of the poems, see *HemR* 7, i:62–63.)

University of Montana

Part II

11. Literature to 1800

William J. Scheick

This year we celebrated the bicentennial of the American Constitution, and appropriately the outstanding contributions in colonial American literary studies during 1987 concerned the writings of Revolutionary authors. This year also saw the appearance of the *Columbia Literary History of the United States,** but the revisionism sought after in this valuable work was not very evident in early American studies this year. The genuine exception is Norman S. Grabo's "Ideology and the Early American Frontier" (*EAL* 22:274–90), which reviews in pithy observations Puritan and non-Puritan responses to the New World in order to suggest that these reactions (e.g., the impulse toward insularity) are less the product of religious ideology than an ethnically and nationally attitudinal response to the frontier as a psychological barrier. Whereas French and Spanish colonists absorbed the New World through their cultural and literary traditions, Grabo contends, the Puritans were less attentive to environment or tradition and tended to perceive a place defined by their imagination.

i. Puritan Poetry

Anthony Burgess, insensitive to "Contemplations," has said that "the homage due to [Anne] Bradstreet . . . has little to do with literary merit," and now Edward Taylor too gets a swift kick from John Mc-Williams in "Writing Literary History: The Limits of Nationalism" (*RALS* 13[1983]:127–33), which calls for comparatist studies of early American literature rather than more close readings of weak authors like Taylor, whose "numbing" *Preparatory Meditations* lacks even one successful poem. As if this devaluation were not bad enough,

---

* Although advance copies of this work were available in 1987, it carries a 1988 copyright date and will be reviewed in *ALS* next year—Ed.

what are we to make of the paucity of interest in or of imaginative work on colonial American poets this year?

In "The Creative Fall of Bradstreet and Dickinson" (*ELWIU* 14: 81–92) Walter Hesford has nothing new to say about Bradstreet's use of poetic language as a vehicle to articulate her joys and sorrows, in contrast to her silent resignation to religion, and as a means of listening to herself in her "fallen" roles as wife, mother, and grandmother. Not the poet as her or his own audience, but all members of the Puritan community are emphasized in J. Daniel Patterson's pedestrian "*Gods Determinations*: The Occasion, the Audience, and Taylor's Hope for New England" (*EAL* 22:63–81), which argues that this poem is not directed only at halfway members; the poem differentiates between the elect of the first rank and the elect of the second and third ranks, who take longer in their evolution of salvation and who must look toward full members as models.

ii. Puritan Prose

David Laurence, who would have benefitted from a glance at an essay by Ursula Brumm (see *ALS 1977*, p. 190), argues in "William Bradford's American Sublime" (*PMLA* 102:55–65) that the scene of the Pilgrims coming ashore at Cape Cod anticipates Kant's idea of the dynamical sublime as well as a trait of 19th-century American literature; Bradford, in a characteristic American gesture, withdraws from empirical fact and retreats into literature for satisfactory meanings. A different sort of literary retreat from the Pilgrims themselves is made by a Bradford contemporary, whose book was nearly printed at least twice in England but was finally suppressed there. This curious case is discussed in Paul R. Sternberg's "The Publication of Thomas Morton's *New English Canaan* Reconsidered" (*PBSA* 80 [1986]:364–74). The sources, importance, and nature of the writings of a member of another group antagonistic to the Puritans are detailed in *William Penn's Published Writings, 1660–1726: An Interpretative Bibliography*, ed. Edwin B. Bronner and David Fraser (Penn., 1986).

Trouble for the Puritans did not come only from outside agitators like Morton and the Quakers. An internal troublemaker is the subject of Amy Schrager Lang's well-written *Prophetic Woman*, which focuses on Anne Hutchinson and the special relevance of the rise of antinomianism to a sense of female empowerment in defiance of the colonial fathers. Lang manages her discussion of the interaction of these women and John Cotton, who had reservations about the nature of the female sex, better than did Ann Kibbey (see *ALS 1986*, p. 186), even when the two critics touch on similar topics; for example, Lang points out Charles Chauncy's fear of the language of antinomianism as an expression of the repudiation of visible signs. Histories like Edward Johnson's *Wonder-Working Providence*, Lang argues, generalize Hutchinson into an image of the typical dissenter figuring in a plot consisting of a conflict between masculine reason (embodied in father, minister, ruler) and female enthusiasm. A conflict between two apparently contradictory strains of Puritanism, influencing Johnson's portrait of Hutchinson, is noted by David R. Williams, whose *Wilderness Lost: The Religious Origins of the American Mind* (Susquehanna) studies the tension between an Arminian communal pessimism (emphasizing the wilderness of human depravity) and an antinomian individualistic optimism (emphasizing the transformed wilderness of human salvation). Another characteristic of Johnson's history is exposed in "Autobiographical Role-Playing in Edward Johnson's *Wonder-Working Providence*" (*EAL* 22:291–305), in which Dennis R. Perry describes the textual instructions and roles Johnson includes in his book to involve his readers directly in the drama of the New England past and thereby to make them ideal readers, like himself. Because he felt Puritanism was declining, Johnson tries out various personae, particularly the ideal military leader and the omniscient prophet, to encourage his readers to reconstruct the colony's sense of unity and purpose.

Similar to Johnson, John Cotton pondered the enigma of Hutchinson and the rhetorical management of his audience. In *The Art of Prophesying* Teresa Toulouse discloses how Cotton transformed the interpretative method (text, doctrine, reasons, uses) of William Perkins by fragmenting his hearers' apprehension of its continuity and by denying their desire for conceptual satisfaction. While providing possible connections and analogies, Cotton also stresses logical and metaphorical inconsistencies, thereby preventing the sure correspondences which would allow for the resolution of argument. This procedure results in a form of suspension of mental processes that invites the listener to complete the discourse and that, as a result, might have encouraged antinomianism. If Toulouse sees a possible origin of antinomianism in the fragmentation of Perkins's method, Ross J. Pudaloff in "Sign and Subject: Antinomianism in Massachusetts Bay" (*Semiotica* 54[1985], 147–63) discerns a rupture between opposing *epis-*

temes of the language of Puritan belief as a possible source of the antinomian controversy, a time of reaction to the dominance of classical contractualism (emphasizing separation, division, human agency) over Renaissance organicism (emphasizing dependence, nurture, human passivity).

Rupture also characterizes, in Toulouse's opinion, Benjamin Colman's expansion of the Perkins model nearly to the breaking point. Colman imparted to his works an unrelieved tension between older appeals to doctrine and new appeals to feeling (especially self-interest), and between religious and secular claims, so that affective passages attractive to the emotions of his hearers are often framed by passages requiring reason. Narrative tension also interests Kathryn Zabelle Derounian, whose "Puritan Orthodoxy and the 'Survivor Syndrome' in Mary Rowlandson's Indian Captivity Narrative" (*EAL* 22:82–93) describes, first, a split between empirical narration told from the participant's point of view and rhetorical narration told from an interpreter's point of view, and, second, a split between the narrator's experience of psychological trauma (the survivor syndrome) in confronting the unknown and the narrator's knowledge of Puritan dogma that displaces the unknown with the conventional. And an inventive tension, combining memory of a conventional concept (appealing to a loving subjection to authority) and perception of new frontier conditions, is highlighted in Edmund S. Morgan's "John Winthrop's 'Modell of Christian Charity' in a Wider Context" (*HLQ* 50:145–51).

Just as Winthrop tried to manage the image of settler submission to authority in a land potentially subversive to this ideal order, so too Cotton Mather made use of the example of pirates to encourage sanctity. But as Daniel E. Williams remarks in "Puritans and Pirates: A Confrontation between Cotton Mather and William Fly in 1726" (*EAL* 22:233–51), in spite of Mather's attempts to reduce Fly's insolent resistance to salvation into a negative example, in effect his description presents his audience with a new sort of character, the nonrepentant criminal. If Fly frustrated Mather, so did his wife, Lydia Lee (George), whom he thought was insane. Virginia Bernhard's "Cotton Mather's 'Most Unhappy Wife': Reflections of the Uses of Historical Evidence" (*NEQ* 60:341–62), however, emphasizes that all we have is Mather's perception of his wife, that her insanity has not been substantiated, and that in all likelihood she was only subject to mercurial moods and the need to vent her anger. Mather must certainly not have been easy to live with, particularly if he evinced the "pushy insecurity" attributed to him by Monroe K. Spears in *American Ambitions*, pp. 3–9. Spears reads Mather as a self-assertive, self-deprecating elitist who believed in the hierarchy of the pious.

Mather's sense of other kinds of hierarchies in the natural world informs two predictable essays by Winton U. Solberg. In "Cotton Mather, *The Christian Philosopher*, and the Classics" (*PAAS* 96:323–66) Solberg observes Mather's sophisticated use of the Platonic-Augustinian tradition defining the whole world as an orderly architectonic with no gaps in the hierarchical scale bridging the natural and the supernatural. In "Science and Religion in Early America: Cotton Mather's *Christian Philosopher*" (*ChH* 56:73–92) Solberg identifies Mather's sources as John Ray, William Derham, John Harris, George Cheyneand, and Nehemiah Grew. Popularizing the new science, Mather interweaves the laws of nature and the decrees of God to reveal a design in nature in harmony with scripturally informed beliefs.

A concern with providential design also informs Mather's writings on the death of children, explains Howard A. Mayer, whose predictable "Puritan Triumph: The Joyful Death Books of Cotton Mather and James Janeway" (*Triumphs of the Spirit in Children's Literature*, ed. Francelia Butler and Richard Rotert [Lib. Prof. Pub., 1986], pp. 209–20) focuses on the didactic message for youth and adults in Mather's portraits of children overcoming their sinful nature. Mather's portraits of Puritan divines figure in Sacvan Bercovitch's "The Modernity of American Puritan Rhetoric" (*American Letters*, pp. 42–66), which claims that Puritan symbols derived from a scriptual pretext for their sense of American promise persist today and provide a cultural continuity which absorbs change through an ongoing dialectic between imaginative response and cultural reflex.

A Boston minster who participated in Cotton Mather's ordination is the subject of "Samuel Willard and the Spectres of God's Wrathful Lions" (*NEQ* 60:596–603), in which Stephen L. Robbins argues that in 1692 Willard advocated reason and moderation in lieu of a trust in spectral evidence. A particular trust in the senses of sight and hearing characterizes at least one Puritan diary, according to Bruce Tucker's "Joseph Sewall's Diary and the Rhythm of Puritan Spirituality" (*EAL* 22:3–18). Sewall tried to detect God's intention for him through the natural world, with the result that he experienced cycles of rap-

ture and melancholy, certitude and doubt. The diary of Joseph Sewall's father provides the basis for a series of poems in *Samuel Sewall
Sails for Home* (Coyote, 1986) by Robert Chute.

iii. The South

In *The Diary, and Life, of William Byrd II of Virginia, 1674–1744*
(No. Car.) Kenneth A. Lockridge successfully undertakes an inner
life of Byrd, who in isolation turned to books at an early age, who exposed himself to fears of rejection in trying to achieve his father's
ambitions for him, who became withdrawn and unable to accept his
place as a colonial until late in his life, and who after his father's
death returned to Virginia, where he eventually turned to his diary
for reassurance and recorded there the mastery of his emotions and
his colonial social status. In his diary, Lockridge explains, Byrd presents his actions in a practiced order expressed in similar language as
if in a ritual at once indicative of confidence and of a fearful warding
off of death. His *The History of the Dividing Line* demarcates Byrd's
personal sense of a need for a line of social order in a cultural wilderness, as he poses as Steddy, the calm, cheerful gentleman responsive
to the needs of a young civilization.

A review of Byrd's writings, with attention to their contribution
to the myths of the South, is provided by M. Thomas Inge in "William Byrd of Westover: The First Southern Gentleman and Author"
(*VC* 37:4–15); and an account of Byrd's futile effort to entice Swiss
emigrants to his land is reported by Michael L. Nicholls in "Searching for Eden: William Bryd, the Switzers, and the Disaster of 1739"
(VC 36[1986]:88–95). Letters from naturalist James Petiver to Byrd
appear in Edmund Berkeley and Dorothy Smith Berkeley's "The
Most Common Rush or Vilest Weed" (*VMHB* 95:481–95). And an
extraordinarily comprehensive bibliography of writings by and about
Bryd on the subject of music is provided by Richard Turbet in *William Byrd: A Guide to Research* (Garland).

The happy, tranquil summer vacation of another Virginian poet
in 1786 is detailed in "A Virginian Abroad: St. George Tucker Goes to
New York" (*VC* 36:100–111) by Bettina Manzo. In the writings of
a Maryland minister, explain Donald K. Enholm, David Curtis
Skaggs, and W. Jeffrey Welsh in "Origins of the Southern Mind:
The Parochial Sermons of Thomas Cradock of Maryland, 1744–1770"
(*QJS* 73:200–18), exists an ideational sense of the South well before

the Revolutionary War; this view includes a notion of a caste system of an elite upper class directing a disciplined lower class, a belief in a chivalric moderation and disregard for wealth, and a regard for an orthodox religious doctrine that appreciates a certain inscrutability concerning the mystery of existence. Also in Maryland, according to Robert Micklus's "The Secret Fall of Freemasonry in Dr. Alexander Hamilton's *The History of the Tuesday Club*" (*Deism, Masonry, and The Enlightenment*, ed. J. A. Leo Lemay [Delaware], pp. 127–36), a learned physician covertly defended Freemasonry as a club by playing on misconceptions of it without worrying about its public image.

More serious humor by the Virginian brother-in-law of Byrd is scrutinized by Lemay, whose "The Amerindian in the Early American Enlightenment: Deistic Satire in Robert Beverley's *History of Virginia* (1705)" (*Deism*, pp. 79–92) analyzes Beverley's description of a Native American religious ritual, pinpoints its probable source in an engraving by Theodore DeBry, and remarks its use as Enlightenment propaganda to satirize philosophically all religion as imposture. The use of this same work by American revolutionaries, who might have learned from it and similar early sources by New World colonists as much as they learned from English opposition writers, is the convincing thesis of Lemay's "Robert Beverley's *History and Present State of Virginia* and the Emerging Political Ideology" (*American Letters*, pp. 67–111).

Lemay has also authored more of an abstract than an essay in "Captain John Smith: American(?)" (*UMSE* 5:288–96), which claims that Smith combined facts with visionary ideals in his identification with America and thought the New World provided an individual with an opportunity to create himself. Peter Hulme's *Colonial Encounters: Europe and the Native Caribbean, 1492–1797* (Methuen, 1986), pp. 137–73, focuses on the omission in Smith's *A True Relation* of any information about his "rescue" by Pocahontas, in contrast to the inclusion of this episode 16 year's later in his *The General History*. Hulme concludes that unwittingly Smith ignored the Pocahontas story in his earlier book because in 1608 neither he nor other colonists could comprehend it; it did not fit their predisposed ideas about Native Americans as an inferior culture. But by 1624, after costly warfare with them, Smith had a context for including the account, for he now could portray in the noble Native American princess how the Algonquians could have, like her, recognized the superior values of European culture, accepted them, and lived in harmony with the settlers. Now her act served him as a justification of the colonists' pursuit of any course in resistance to unregenerate savagery in the American wilderness.

iv. Edwards and the Great Awakening

Whereas Cotton Mather abandoned the older Puritan psychological meaning of the wilderness by stressing the world of fact, Jonathan Edwards (according to David R. Williams in *Wilderness Lost*) recovered it by emphasizing the realm of the mind. For Edwards the perception of the beauty and excellence of the deity comes after entering the wilderness of affliction, crossing the subconscious wilderness of confusion, and annihilating the prideful self's illusions. The transformation of nature into symbol also interests Clyde A. Holbrook, whose *Jonathan Edwards, The Valley of Nature: An Interpretative Essay* (Bucknell) proceeds along a familiar path and observes Edwards's response to nature as sensately manifest, typologically instructive, and metaphysically real. Arguing that nature often provides a controlling structural feature in Edwards's thought, Holbrook discusses how the minister first found in the landscape of the Connecticut Valley a concrete condition of valley-like confinement that encouraged his narrow, insulated idea of religion (albeit not a limitation of the range of his ideas), and then found in nature a repository of images for spiritual truths (e.g., beauty as proportion, symmetry, agreement) that ultimately lessened the value of the transient, perishable natural world for Edwards. Holbrook's Edwards struggles to construct a language which will join nature and idealism.

There is also not much new in *Jonathan Edwards: A New Biography* (Banner of Truth), in which Iain H. Murray asserts that Edwards was not absent-minded, aloof, or remote and touches on Edwards's contact with and influence on Scottish evangelicals, a subject in need of careful study. A rather small step toward this big topic is made by Harold P. Simonson, whose "Jonathan Edwards and His Scottish Connections" (*JAmS* 21:353–76) reviews Edwards's questions concerning religious experience and his personal trials. One episode of Edwards's life is the subject of "Jonathan Edwards' 'Personal Narrative' and the Northampton Controversy" (*Cithara* 26, ii: 31–47), in which Parker H. Johnson concludes from the presence of the words "appears" and "seems" that the minister believed in the ability of language to refer to the spiritually real even if the professor experiences doubt about the adequacy of language. Edwards, according to Johnson, was convinced that since appearances are a means of the perception of reality, a visible profession of piety is sufficient evidence for his congregation, in Christian charity, to judge a professor.

If Johnson discerns an Edwardsean use of language that bridges phenomenological perception and spiritual reality, David Jacobson interestingly suggests that the Edwardsean concept of the spiritual experience did not pit emotion against reason. In "Jonathan Edwards and the 'American Difference': Pragmatic Reflections on the 'Sense of the Heart' " (*JAmS* 21:377–85) Jacobson stresses Edwards's fusion of reason and will in a theory of the affections which anticipates the logical terms of the pragmatic method of Charles Sanders Peirce. A subject guide to other main areas of Edwards's thought is provided by John H. Gerstner, whose *Jonathan Edwards: A Mini-Theology* (Tyndale) rightly focuses on Edwards's orthodoxy but unfortunately overlooks the subtleties and complexities of the theologian's beliefs.

A negative judgment on the adequacy of Edwards's evangelical and doctrinal style was made by Samuel Smith, the subject of A. Owen Aldridge's "An Early American Adaptation of French Pulpit Oratory" (*ECent* 28:235–47). Smith preferred the sentimental earnestness of the style, not the thought, of Roman Catholic Jean-Baptiste Massillon. And another person who disapproved of Edwards's writings and who was concerned about Yale students and their curriculum is the subject of "Ezra Stiles and the Yale Graduates" (*YULG* 61:105–15) by the late Cora E. Lutz.

v. Franklin, Jefferson, and the Revolutionary Period

Interest in Franklin dominated early American studies this year. Besides the appearance of *Papers of Benjamin Franklin*, Vol. 25: *October 1, 1777, through February 28, 1778*, ed. William B. Willcox (Yale, 1986), the publication of J. A. Leo Lemay's edition of *Benjamin Franklin: Writings* (Library of America) provides the best single-volume collection of Franklin's work we have ever had. Lemay's editing is scrupulous, his selection rich, his notes valuable—in short, an exemplary performance.

Lemay has also authored "The American Aesthetic of Franklin's Visual Creations" (*PMHB* 111:465–99), which demonstrates very well how Franklin, who was inventive in the visual arts, Americanized his easily understood, rhetorically symbolic devices by adapting traditional designs to reflect egalitarian, nationalistic concerns. Were Franklin's drawings in some way influenced by George Berkeley? In "George Berkeley's Visual Language and the New England Portrait Tradition" (*CentR* 31:122–45) Ann Gibson and Lucia Palmer argue that Berkeley's assertion that "Esse est Percipi" affected 18th-century artistic style in which isolated, precise perception (the primary creative act) re-creates the world and thereby is close to the deity, whose perception keeps creation in existence.

Managing the perception of his readers is certainly an issue in "Authorial Discourse and Pseudo-Dialogue in Franklin's *Autobiography*" (*EAL* 22:94–107), Malini Schueller's discussion of Franklin's artistic intention to write a didactic treatise related by an authoritative narrator who also gives the impression that he is receptive to different ideologies. The *Autobiography* is dialogic, in Mikhail Bakhtin's sense, enabling the paternalistic narrator to privilege arguments for utilitarian ethics. A similar attempt to control audience awareness is described by Michael Warner, whose "Franklin and the Letters of the Republic" (*Representations* 16[1986]:110–30) argues that Franklin saw an equivalency between shaping a life and designing a piece of writing, and in his career exploited the homology between printed discourse and representative polity; thus when Franklin speaks in print with the full authority of representative legitimacy he holds in suspension the American tension between embodying proper power as a statesman and the republican task of removing this power from individuals. Perhaps management of perception is also involved in Dennis Barone's claim in "A Note on Benjamin Franklin's 'English Grammar'" (*ELN* 23, iv[1986]:31–33) that the recollection in the *Autobiography* of what grammar Franklin used is mistaken, probably intentionally. Appearance matters as well in "Ideology and the Framing of the Constitution" (*EAL* 22:157–65), in which Robert A. Ferguson detects Franklin's and James Madison's use of framing (as a visual aid implying congruity) to convert a necessarily ambiguous text into an effective tool of ideological conformity within a divided world.

Current perceptions of Franklin are also under challenge in two interesting essays. In " 'He that best understands the World, least likes it': The Dark Side of Benjamin Franklin" (*PMHB* 111:525–54)

Ronald A. Bosco observes that Franklin appreciated the advantages of a philosophy of deliberate optimism, but he actually acknowledged (particularly in his letters to John Fothergill and Joseph Priestley) the reality of pessimism, the contemptibleness of human pride, and the discouragements of human nature. This reading is reinforced in Elizabeth E. Dunn's "From a Bold Youth to a Reflective Sage: A Reevaluation of Benjamin Franklin's Religion" (*PMHB* 111:501–24), which differentiates between Franklin's later private skeptical pessimism and his public, seemingly optimistic deistic beliefs conforming to his public image. A similar differentiation is made by Donald H. Meyer, whose "Franklin's Religion" (*Critical Essays on Benjamin Franklin*, ed. Melvin H. Buxbaum [Hall], pp. 147–67) discerns a discrepancy between Franklin's public image as religiously affirmative and tolerant, and his private experience of occasional religious doubt and hostility toward any institutionalized and socially dominant sect. Whatever ambiguities or inconsistencies occur in his thought about religion, Meyer concludes, Franklin urged a commonsense approach joining the world of fact and humanity's moral need for virtue.

That Franklin's influence is akin to that of a religion is the focus of Ormond Seavey's "Benjamin Franklin and D. H. Lawrence as Conflicting Modes of Consciousness" (*Critical Essays*, pp. 60–80), which discusses Lawrence's sense of Franklin as a rival in the shaping of modern sensibilities, a rival as powerful and deceptive as past proponents of religious doctrine. The charge of dogmatic narrowness emerges as well in "Franklin's Last Years in England: The Making of a Rebel" (*Critical Essays*, pp. 96–110), William B. Willcox's assessment of Franklin's political thought (in contrast to his scientific ideas) as inflexible, provincial, and contentious. What Willcox sees as a grudge against England, Edmond Wright defines as ambivalence toward liberal social views in London ("'The Fine and Noble China Vase, the British Empire': Benjamin Franklin's 'Love-Hate' View of England" [*PMHB* 111:435–64]). Whatever his ambivalence toward British thinking, Tracy Mott and George W. Zinke's "Benjamin Franklin's Economic Thought: A Twentieth-Century Appraisal" (*Critical Essays*, pp. 111–27) finds correspondences between the economic vision of Adam Smith, David Hume, and Franklin.

Franklin's use of the English model of writing exemplified by Addison and Steele as a means of achieving a greater sense of confidence in ingratiating himself with the common reader is a topic in

Albert Furtwangler's readable *American Silhouettes: Rhetorical Identities of the Founders* (Yale). Several of Franklin's peers also turned in times of stress to a literary identity as a means of resolving crisis: in the guise of Novanglus the lawyer and patriot, John Adams debated a Loyalist; and posturing his membership in the learned society of Francis Bacon, Isaac Newton, and John Locke, Thomas Jefferson debated Alexander Hamilton.

Furtwangler specifically kicks at what he perceives as Jefferson's overestimated abilities and overvalued cultural presence, but happily this ill-considered peculiarity does not characterize other work on Jefferson this year. In "Telling Off the King: Jefferson's *Summary View* as American Fantasy" (*EAL* 22:166–74) William L. Hedges discerns how *Summary View* transforms itself from the resolution of an official paper to an epistolary dramatic monologue emphasizing an imagined ideal possibility. Another kind of transformation, the metaphoric application of images of natural order to ideas of social and political order, interests Christopher Looby, whose "The Constitution of Nature: Taxonomy as Politics in Jefferson, Peale, and Bartram" (*EAL* 22:252–73) observes that Jefferson and others saw in the invariability of nature a promise of social harmony and stability that disguised an anxiety over political dissonance. Similarly, in "Education and the Constitution: Instituting American Culture" (*Laws of Our Fathers: Popular Culture and the U.S. Constitution*, ed. Ray B. Browne and Glenn J. Browne [Bowling Green], pp. 23–41), Ross J. Pudaloff probes into Jefferson's desire in *Notes on the State of Virginia* to create, through education, a uniform culture as a basis for an emergent national identity and stability, a desire bridging the conflict between his egalitarianism and his sense of human "rubbish."

A egalitarian view of Jesus emerges in Jefferson's abridgments of the New Testament, the topic of Susan Bryan's convincing "Reauthorizing the Text: Jefferson's Scissor Edit of the Gospels" (*EAL* 22:19–42). In transforming Jesus into a humanized subversive skeptical of his culture's social texts, Jefferson finds an image of himself challenging not only all claims for a providential reading of Jesus' teachings but also the alleged authority of all printed texts. Concerning his own texts, there is a review of literature on Jefferson as a man of letters in *Thomas Jefferson: A Reference Guide*, ed. Merrill D. Peterson (Scribner's, 1986), and there is a review of his optimistic and rationalist beliefs as a man of politics in *In Pursuit of Reason: The Life of Thomas Jefferson* (LSU) by Noble E. Cunningham, Jr., who provides a readable synthesis of our current sense of Jefferson's ideas.

The man with whom Jefferson exchanged sympathetic letters about the French Revolution figures in "Thomas Paine's Apostles: Radical Émigrés and the Triumph of Jeffersonian Republicanism" (*WMQ* 44:661–88), Michael Durey's study of the political emigrants from Britain and Ireland in the 1790s as carriers of a radical Painite message supporting the dominance of the Jeffersonian republican image of America's future as an egalitarian blend of agriculture, commerce, and industry. Not everyone accepted Paine's message, observes Richard H. Popkin, whose "*The Age of Reason* versus *The Age of Revelation*: Two Critics of Tom Paine: David Levi and Elias Boudinot" (*Deism*, pp. 58–70) indicates that the French Revolution struck some as a sign of the close of providential history. The plot of certain Painite works, explains Martin Roth in "Tom Paine and American Loneliness" (*EAL* 22:175–82), shows how provincial false bondings are transformed into an ideal self-determined America of enlarged views; but within this plot exists a melodrama of human isolation presenting humanity as lost in space and the present moment beyond the solace of an ideal American brotherhood.

The fear that the new American republic would not live up to its ideal because of a decline of religion led John Adams to call for days of humiliation in 1798 and 1799, which Charles Ellis Dickson ("Jeremiads in the New American Republic: The Case of National Fasts in the John Adams Administration" [*NEQ* 60:187–207]) thinks probably cost Adams reelection. That other fears specifically about the rise of Freemasonry were satirically dismissed by some as ill-founded is the topic of David S. Shields's "Clio Mocks the Masons: Joseph Green's Anti-Masonic Satires" (*Deism*, pp. 109–26). Fear of conflicting motives in the rising republic, as described by Daniel W. Howe in "The Political Psychology of *The Federalist*" (*WMQ* 44: 485–509), were answered by Publius's rhetorical application of faculty psychology to encourage the subordination of parts to the whole, the maintenance of balances, and the establishment of order through a rational hierarchy. The specific fear of mob oppression, tyranny, and self-aggrandizing agendas, among other topics, is evident in *John Leacock's The First Book of the American Chronicles of the Times, 1774–1775* (Delaware), a parody of the Bible designed to encourage an elite social and political ideology that has been superbly edited and annotated by Carla Mulford.

The life-and-times biography of a man who had to fear for his life and who wrote a fine example of Augustan satire during the Revolution is treated in Cynthia Dubin Edelberg's *Jonathan Odell: Loyalist Poet of the American Revolution* (Duke), detailing the themes and moods of his poems. Apparently Odell, who had to flee to Nova Scotia, never deviated from the central core of his Loyalist ideology.

vi. The Early National Period

Someone who did deviate in his views figures in "Brackenridge, *Modern Chivalry*, and American Humor" (*EAL* 22:43–62), in which John Engell traces a development from the early to the later volumes of *Modern Chivalry*. Whereas Brackenridge's narrator at first speaks ironically and satirically, his indirect didacticism later becomes nonironic, direct pronouncement. Another change in viewpoint is featured in "Agrarianism in Hugh Henry Brackenridge's Articles for *The Pittsburgh Gazette*" (*EAL* 22:306–19), James Sanderson's assessment of Brackenridge's early belief in an agrarian ideal (later abandoned) as a means for deriving a wholesome community where the yeoman farmer would legislate democracy and farming would provide economic stability.

Agrarian views are remarked too in Gay Wilson Allen and Roger Asselineau's *St. John de Crèvecoeur: The Life of an American Farmer* (Viking), which emphasizes their subject's French background (including his role in the French Colonial Army in Canada) and tries to solve some of the mysteries and contradictions in his adventurous life. A consideration of the original manuscript of *Letters from an American Farmer* and related essays appears in "Library of Congress Acquires Crèvecoeur Manuscripts Through Gift of the Cafritz Foundation" (*LCIB* 46, iv:41, 44). The image of slavery in Letter IX is not only literal, contends Doreen Alvarez Saar in "Crèvecoeur's 'Thoughts on Slavery': *Letters from an American Farmer*" (*EAL* 22: 192–203). Possibly informing this image is the relationship between Britain and America, and this Whiggish tenor might explain the narrator's eventual shift from political neutrality to his rejection of monarchy in Letter XII.

A poet who hardly cherished the idea of monarchy receives attention in Carla Mulford's "Radicalism in Joel Barlow's *The Conspiracy of Kings*" (*Deism*, pp. 137–57), focusing on the poet's seerlike defense of the French Revolution and his renunciation of conservative policies as an incentive for anarchy. A fellow poet antagonistic to monarchies interests Judith R. Hiltner, whose *The Newspaper Verse of Philip Freneau: An Edition and Bibliographical Survey* (Whitston, 1986) tries to determine the accurate version of many of Freneau's poems, and Robert Pinsky, whose "American Poetry and American Life: Freneau, Whitman, Williams" (*Shenandoah* 37, i:3–26) reports that Freneau did not know how to write a poem situated in relation to American life.

The biography of a man who seemed to some to aspire to kingship is scrutinized in Christopher Harris's uninspired "Mason Locke Weems' *Life of Washington*: The Making of a Bestseller" (*SLJ* 19, ii:92–101), which suggests that to please his readers Weems made such revisions as the addition of dramatic scenes as well as anecdotes of friendship, intimacy, and social harmony. Revisions, whether the author's or her editor's, figure too in "The Methodist Connection: New Variants of Some Phillis Wheatley Poems" (*EAL* 22:108–13), Mukhtar Ali Isani's report on some alterations in Wheatley's verse printed in the abolitionist *Arminian Magazine*. Revising the political views of his audience was the aim of a fervent Jeffersonian Republican, who aspired to be an ethical and responsible newspaper columnist, and who is described by Louise Chipley in "William Bentley, Journalist of the Early Republic" (*EIHC* 123:331–47). And a revision of our attribution of Quaker influence on an early Republic naturalist is urged by Bruce Silver's "Clarke on the Quaker Background of William Bartram's Approach to Nature" (*JHI* 47[1986]:507–10).

The background of early Republic humor is documented by Robert K. Dodge, whose anthology *Early American Almanac Humor* (Bowling Green) prints typical comic treatments, written between 1776–1800, of American heroes, stereotyped professionals, Yankees, ethnic and racial issues, marriage and sex, and tall tales. Revising one of these stereotypes, according to Henry Louis Gates Jr.'s revealing "James Gronniosaw and the Trope of the Talking Book" (*SoR* 22[1986]:252–72), led black authors to refashion themselves as speaking subjects so that they could alter their status as objects; some of them seized upon the trope of the talking book, an image fusing the white tradition of the written literate text and the black tradition of vernacular speech, a paradoxical image which finally highlights the very tension these authors sought to end.

vii. Brown and Contemporaries

In "The Republican Wife: Virtue and Seduction in the Early Republic" (*WMQ* 44:689–721) Jan Lewis reviews novels, essays, and short stories to discern an emphasis on the need for both males and females to become representatives of republican ideology. The republican wife is an Eve figure who can be seduced by Satanic characters, who are really enemies of society; but ideally she should seduce men to virtue and use marriage as a paradise regained where the individual is subordinated for the greater good of the familial/communal whole. The ideal of republican marriage symbolizes the ideal of republican government, a conclusion supported as well by Shirley Samuels's "Infidelity and Contagion: The Rhetoric of Revolution" (*EAL* 22:183–91), which focuses on the family as the cornerstone of early Republic national identity. Sexual infidelity, representing a great threat to the family, served as an image expressing the greatest menace to the young nation, especially after the French Revolution when women tended to represent mob democratic rule and liberty tended to be characterized as a whore.

Samuels mentions Brown in her discussion, and the role of women is also featured in Kathleen Nolan Monahan's "Brown's *Arthur Mervyn* and *Ormond*" (*Expl* 45, iii:18–21), which claims that Brown is particularly interested in the problem of women alone, who are plagued by severed familial connections and by loneliness, and who must choose between dependence and independence. Discomfort in the new Republic is at issue as well in "Charles Brockden Brown's *Edgar Huntly*: The Picturesque Traveller as Sleepwalker" (*SAF* 15:25–42) by Beth L. Lueck, who discusses Brown's use of a bewildered, lost narrator engaged in a parody of the English daytime tour of an American wilderness which is beautiful in accord with the expectation of picturesque tradition but which is also nonpicturesquely dangerous in the wildness of its beauty.

If Lueck discerns in Brown's romance that American nature remains beyond control, in the same work Peter J. Bellis notices that human nature is out of control. In "Narrative Compulsion and Control in Charles Brockden Brown's *Edgar Huntly*" (*SoAR* 52:43–57) Bellis

argues that Huntly cannot close with the past through managed
retrospection, but only through a compulsive narration divided
against itself as an ambivalent expression of its insecure protagonist's
need to relive events and to defend against them, to tell and forget,
to identify and fail to recognize. The deceptiveness of appearances
probably figures as well in Marietta Stafford Patrick's "The Doppel-
ganger Motif in *Arthur Mervyn*" (*JEP* 7 [1986]:91–101), which I
have not seen; and it certainly informs Robert D. Arner's clever suggestion, in the "Historical Essay" of a new and very good edition of
Alcuin and *Memoirs of Stephen Calvert* (Kent State), that Alcuin's
naiveté and innocent enthusiasm are ploys in the attempted seduction of Mrs. Carter. Arner also reviews the variant versions of these
texts, the scholarship on them, and the effects on them of the popular
reaction to the excesses of the French Revolution.

The popular response to the theme of seduction in another romance is reported in "Ideology and Genre: The Rise of the Novel in
America" (*PAAS* 96:295–321), in which Cathy N. Davidson repeats
the findings of her book of last year. Seduction is also considered by
Frank Shuffelton, whose "Mrs. Foster's *Coquette* and the Decline of
the Brotherly Watch" (*SECC* 16[1986]:211–24) discusses the di-
minishment of congregational authority and church discipline under
pressure from the more fashionable forces of the decriminalization of
sin and the rise of personal independence in the early Republic.
Useful is Edward J. Piacentino's "Susanna Haswell Rowson: A Bibliography of the First Edition of Primary Works and Secondary
Sources" (*BB* 43[1986]:13–16). And in the limp "Mercy Warren and
'Freedom's Genius'" (*UMSE* 5:215–30) Cheryl Z. Oreovicz detects
in Warren's plays and poems an antipathy to deism, a blend of Calvin-
ism and republican thought, and an eventual encounter with uncertainty, even disillusionment.

In contrast to Jacobin attacks in Britain on socioeconomic class
distinctions, at least one picaresque, epistolary novel reflects an American Jacobin assault on the East (Philadelphia), explains John Seelye
in "Jacobin Mode in Early American Fiction: Gilbert Imlay's *The
Emigrants*" (*EAL* 22:204–12). Imlay depicts the Ohio Valley as a
zone of racial transformation, and his book emphasizes the salutary
influence of western landscape (Pittsburgh) as an agent of change on
eastern manners. Landscape is important as well in "Beyond the
Shining Mountains: The Lewis and Clark Expedition as an Enlight-

enment Epic" (*VQR* 63:36–53), in which Seelye defines the tension between Lewis and Clark's actual experience of the wilderness and their desire for order and symmetry in what was for them an American psychogeography.

viii. Miscellaneous Studies

In *Puritan Legacies: Paradise Lost and the New England Tradition, 1630–1890* (Cornell) Keith W. F. Stavely uses Milton's poem as a paradigm and analogue for the broad course of the development of American Puritan sensibility and ideology. The characters in the poem share two contradictions experienced by Puritan settlers: the tension between hierarchy and equality evident in the fall of Adam and Eve, and the tension between acceptable materialism and spiritual idealism evident in the fall of Satan. Stavely's fascinating book particularly scrutinizes the diary of Ebenezer Parkman, an 18th-century minister, to detect the profound ambiguities of the New England Puritan heritage.

How the heritage of New World experience can inform certain created words (not found in the *OED*) and expand the limits of conventional colonial vocabulary is explained by Paul J. Lindholdt in "John Josselyn's New England Neologisms" (*SCN* 45:45–46). And the more recent heritage of contemporary investigations of New England society is intimated in Larry L. Carey's *Colonial and Revolutionary American Literature: Recent Scholarship since 1975* (Irvington), while the heritage *informing* these contemporary investigations is the subject of David D. Hall's "On Common Ground: The Coherence of American Puritan Studies" (*WMQ* 44:193–229). Hall points out that current work, however multiple its voices, shares a belief in the role of language as essentially symbolic, as providing an order signifying cultural meanings.

Informing this *ALS* chapter too is an implied confidence in the capacity of language to signify the underlying meaning of the scholarly pursuit of colonial American literature through critical discourse. However, this signification can remain elusive, especially in a year of *generally* gelid scholarship capped by icy scorn for the achievement of Edward Taylor and Thomas Jefferson. As I completed the first draft of this chapter at the end of a particularly frigid January, I recalled an experience in Cotton Mather's life (recorded in a letter to John Winthrop in January 1720) that seemed apropos: " 'Tis dreadful cold. My ink-glass in my standish is froze and split, in my very stove. My ink in my very pen suffers a congelation, but my wit much more. For it serves only to tell you that ... you may (if we live) hear further from me."

University of Texas at Austin

12. 19th-Century Literature

David J. Nordloh

The study of 19th-century literature continues to be energized by ongoing efforts to redefine the canon, to reconceive the deeper relationships of literature and culture, and to reexamine even the traditional list in more subtle and sophisticated ways. The effect of these initiatives on the contours of critical production in 1987 meant a greater number of broader theoretical studies and of work on women writers, a continuing solidity of work on the major fiction writers, and less attention to the lesser male writers, particularly the poets.

i. General Studies

A muscular traditional perspective rather than theoretical innovation shapes George Dekker's *The American Historical Romance*. Dekker's introductory "Prospectus" emphasizes his interest in explicating all three of the terms in his title, though his "American" must often step aside for Walter Scott. Dekker is concerned "with both the history *of* historical romance and the history *in* historical romances. How did the genre rise, redomesticate itself in America, and retain an identity while also changing in response to the changing circumstances of American social, political, and intellectual life? What shape did our romancers see American history taking, and what settings did they favor for disclosing the emergence of the shape?" The book is selective rather than exhaustive, with Cooper's *The Wept of Wish-ton-Wish*, *Satanstoe*, and *The Prairie* most emphasized. The entire discussion is solidly informed by previous scholarship but also bright with its own discoveries, unhindered by programmatic theory, and worth both admiring and arguing with.

In *Cross-Examinations* Brook Thomas examines the uses of legal ideology in the work of imaginative writers, with the notion of moving beyond literary analysis to an understanding of the dynamic of culture. The first chapter, "*The Pioneers*, or the Sources of American Legal History: A Critical Tale," is a reworking of an essay on Cooper first published in 1984 (see *ALS 1984*, p. 218). The fifth, "A Sentimental Journey: Escape from Bondage in *Uncle Tom's Cabin*," partly continues Thomas's discussion from an earlier chapter to understand the ambiguities of Melville's portrayal of a slave rebellion in "Benito Cereno," but also discusses Stowe's antislavery attitude as organic to her "entire social vision," identifies the legal cases which Stowe employed in both *Uncle Tom's Cabin* and *Dred*, and concludes that the feminine values at work in the novel are incapable of reforming slavery and serve rather as an alternative to it. The argument is dense and wide-ranging; the book works better when it is explicating texts rather than encompassing national values.

Walter Benn Michaels adopts in *Gold Standard* many of the perspectives and argumentative strategies for examining consumer culture advanced by T. J. Jackson Lears and Alan Trachtenberg. But he differs significantly from them in conceiving consumer culture not as fundamentally opposed by literary culture but as essential in materials, language, and ideology to its creation. In advancing his highly theoretical discussion of the influence of the emerging marketplace on the writer's conception of the materials of identity, Michaels emphasizes Hawthorne and Dreiser, but also discusses Charlotte Perkins Gilman's "The Yellow Wallpaper," Harriet Beecher Stowe's *Uncle Tom's Cabin* and *Key to Uncle Tom's Cabin*, and Frank Norris's *McTeague*, *Vandover and the Brute*, and *The Octopus*.

Stowe, Rebecca Harding Davis, and W. D. Howells receive extended treatment in Fred G. See's equally engaging *Desire and the Sign*. Drawing on Barthes, Saussure, and others, See is generally interested in "the changing status of literary signs . . . in American fiction, roughly in the second half of the nineteenth century, when romanticism gave way to the realist endeavor," and specifically concerned with the various literary signs associated with desire, a subject which of its nature requires signs emphasizing doubleness and internal contention. "Harriet Beecher Stowe and the Structure of Desire" (pp. 37–65) explores Stowe's subtle use of theology as a basis for literary convention, for example in *The Minister's Wooing*, where desire as a passionate erotic relationship is made "chaste and inviolate" through association with theological "icons of maternity." "Howells and the Failure of Desire" (pp. 95–121) contrasts Davis's "commitment to the incarnate meaning of an apparently enigmatic and squalid reality" with Howells's notion of realism as a level of perception "increasingly isolated from a corresponding system of essences." Explicating *A Modern Instance*, See also sets out a contrast, this time with Stowe, finding the novel "informed by Howells' sense of a failed theological structure, for which his motif is the institution of marriage." The general issue of the book is a productive one, and the discussion exciting, though marred by an overenthusiasm which clothes both fresh insights and stale ones in an aggressive language of discovery. Howells and Cooper are among the five writers discussed in Mary Suzanne Schriber's *Gender and the Writer's Imagination*. Schriber's topic is "the impact of received ideas about woman on the literary imagination." In Schriber's view, Cooper faced in fiction the conflict between the conventional definition of the lady and the spontaneity appropriate to the American woman, a conflict resolved most successfully in Eve Effingham. In Howells, on the other hand, the conflict, though more subtly expressed, is not resolved but heightened: he is sensitive to the plight of the modern woman who wastes away in affluence and has no extra-domestic outlet for her talents, but he also fails to explore the sources of her unease, instead ascribing to her a vapidity which he would identify as woman's nature.

Michael Denning's *Mechanic Accents: Dime Novels and Working-Class Culture in America* (Verso) has Marxist ideology as its basis. The book offers ambitious and wonderfully readable answers to Denning's two principal questions: "what can be learned *about* these popular narratives, their production and consumption, and their place and function within working class cultures; and what can be learned *from* them, as symbolic actions, about working class culture and ideology." The book discusses the conventional understanding of the function of the dime novel, traces the evolution of its production by "one of the United States' first cultural industries," discusses the relation between the reading and its readers, and describes the attempts on the part of the "higher cultures" to reshape that literature as they also attempted to reshape its audience to better fit their notion of America's cultural and economic needs. The doctrinal underpinning is especially telling in Denning's description of the interplay of text and audience: "If historical struggles do take place in borrowed costumes and assumed accents, if social and economic divisions appear in disguise, then the source for these disguises and the manifestation of these roles lie in the conventional characters of a society, played out in its popular narratives." This is the Marxist "ruse of representation," involving the "rhetorical and metaphorical aspects of class ideologies."

A *Literary History of the West* applies a traditional perspective toward a broad construction of its topic. The coverage is exhaustive enough to include chapters and accompanying bibliographical commentary on Hamlin Garland and on Midwest farm fiction (both by Roy W. Meyer), on western American Indian writers (by LaVonne Brown Ruoff), and on Frank Norris (by Don Graham).

Brian Lee's *American Fiction* is a well-paced and sufficiently thorough introductory survey which says the usual things well in chapters on realism and naturalism, the regional novelists, and "Impossible Future and Impossible Pasts" in the work of Bellamy, Howells, Ignatius Donnelly, Jack London, and Harold Frederic. Edited by Arthur Power Dudden, *American Humor* (Oxford) is a collection of eight new essays resaying the usual things. The volume is mostly focused on the 20th century but with Artemus Ward, Jack Downing, and Finley Peter Dunne in the background, particularly in Dudden's own contribution, "The Record of Political Humor" (pp. 50–75) and Joseph Boskin and Joseph Dorinson's "Ethnic Humor: Subversion and Survival" (pp. 97–117). Gale's new series on critics and scholars (*DLB* 59) includes John Neal, Irving, Simms, George Ticknor, Edward Everett, Rufus Wilmot Griswold, Longfellow, and Nathaniel Parker Willis among the 43 figures given the usual wonderfully illustrated *DLB* treatment (Irving for the *fourth* time—he's also treated in volumes 3, 11, and 30). As with all contributed volumes, the quality in this one varies; but it's a resource we've needed. A book we certainly don't need is Karol L. Kelley's *Models for the Multitudes*, a tedious, jargonological, passive-tensed, quasiscientific survey of the treatment of success, fraught with sentences like "Most protagonists do experience both emotions because 90 percent are usually loving and another 90 percent are friendly."

From which it is a pleasure to turn to a skillful essay like Terence J. Martin's "Telling the World Over Again: The Radical Dimension of American Fiction" (*American Letters*, pp. 158–76), as the title suggests a broad exploration of a fundamental cultural and narrative issue. Cooper is one of the three major authors whose works Martin finds "heightened in implication by the accoutrements of genesis or by the grandeur of elemental forces." Daniel Aaron's "The Unholy City: A Sketch" (*American Letters*, pp. 177–90) describes the slowness of the evolution of American literature away from antiurban bias, and includes references to Richard Henry Dana, Howells, Robert Herrick, Henry Blake Fuller, Hamlin Garland, Frank Norris, and Stephen Crane. Joan Burbick's " 'Intervals of Tranquility': The Language of Health in Antebellum America" (*Prospects* 12:175–99) concentrates on the writings of three prestigious superintendents of early mental asylums as prime examples of the national concern to find sources of ease in natural environment and behavior; Burbick includes references to the wider enactment of that concern in such writers as Harriet Beecher Stowe and Louisa May Alcott. And in an essay I missed two years ago, Leland S. Person, Jr., pursues the direction of Annette Kolodny's *The Land Before Her* (1984) to identify the differing male and female attitudes toward the frontier experience. More specifically, Person's "The American Eve: Miscegenation and a Feminist Frontier Fiction" (*AQ* 37[1985]:668–85) contrasts the perspectives of James Everett Seaver's *Narrative of the Life of Mrs. Mary Jemison*, Catharine Sedgwick's *Hope Leslie*, Harriet V. Cheney's *A Peep at the Pilgrims*, and Lydia Maria Child's *Hobomok* with those of works by Cooper, James McHenry, Simms, and Robert Montgomery Bird, seeing in the treatment of miscegenation in the works by and about women not threat and abasement, as the male writers typically characterized it, but "a preferable alternative to the traditional status of a wife in a patriarchal and authoritarian society."

Several essays on Chicago round out this survey of general studies. William J. Kenny's " 'Creative Defiance': An Overview of Chicago Literature," appearing in a special issue of *Midwestern Miscellany* (14[1986]:7–24), is necessarily broader than it is deep, but does acknowledge among its generalizations radical and ethnic literature, as well as depictions of—though not by—Chicago women. In the same issue Roger J. Bresnahan's "Mr. Dooley and Slats Grobnik: Chicago Commentators on the World Around Them" (pp. 34–46) compares the personalities and views of the fictive spokesmen of Finley Peter Dunne and contemporary newspaper columnist Mike Royko. Finally, Guy Szuberla surveys versions of the melting-pot myth in Edward Payson Roe's *Barriers Burned Away* and Henry Blake Fuller's *The Cliff-Dwellers*, as well as William T. Stead's sociological tract on miscegenation, *If Christ Came to Chicago!* (1894), and Sigmund Krausz's collection of photographs, *Street Types of Chicago* (1892). His "Reborn in Babel: Immigrant Characters and Types in Early Chicago

Fiction" (*MidAmerica* 13[1986]:31–48) discovers in all four works a magnification of the immigrant into both "a symbol of the future and a sign of the city's present corruption and decay."

ii. Irving, Cooper, Simms, and Contemporaries

The year saw two major and two minor essays on Irving. In "A Crisis of Identity: *The Sketch Book* and Nineteenth-Century American Culture" (*Prospects* 12:255–91), Jeffrey Rubin-Dorsky offers a toughly speculative, if somewhat too long and too general, reading of the whole of Irving's most important single work. He sees its popularity not in its "patina of romanticism" but in its subliminal betrayal of Irving's "profound sense of homelessness and his acute longing for stability," feelings his American audience must obviously have shared. Albert J. von Frank's "The Man That Corrupted Sleepy Hollow" (*SAF* 15:129–43) is an effort to understand what kind of figure, sympathetic or ridiculous, Ichabod Crane is, and what kind of story he inhabits. Von Frank concludes that Ichabod is an aggressive Yankee lecher whose expulsion constitutes a defense of the tranquility of the Dutch community, but that, consistent with "Legend's" being a version of the "Mysterious Stranger" story, the saved community is also changed, displaced at last by Yankee New York as the old narrator Knickerbocker is displaced by Geoffrey Crayon. The minor essays are George Hendrick's "Washington Irving and Homoeopathy" (*Pseudo-Science and Society*, pp. 166–79), exploring the author's conversion to this form of medical practice and the controversies associated with the decision, and Ralph M. Aderman's "Irving's Income as a Diplomat" (*UMSE* 5[1984–87]:140–71), collecting information from government records and Irving's own account books to demonstrate the extent of financial security his extra-literary posts provided.

Cooper was served by a provocative variety of materials. Scholarly editions of his major works continue to appear regularly from "The Writings of James Fenimore Cooper" centered at Clark University. The most recent title is *The Deerslayer* (SUNY), with introduction and explanatory notes by James Franklin Beard, general editor of the series, and text established by Lance Schachterle, Kent Ljungquist, and James Kilby. Beard's essay is a mine of biographical and historical information as well as a defense of the novel's artistic coherence, and the usual comprehensive apparatus is bulkier than usual,

since the copy-text in this instance is a corrected holograph manuscript. (*The Deerslayer* and *The Prairie* were also released in photo-
facsimile reprints from the SUNY text in Penguin paperback; the
exactness of reproduction apparently doesn't extend to title and copyright pages, however, and *The Prairie* has lost its subtitle, "A Tale.")
The edition is now sufficiently advanced that it is the subject of comprehensive reviews: see Robert Sattelmeyer, "The Writings of James
Fenimore Cooper" (*PBSA* 81:245–60), and Hershel Parker, "The
Writings of James Fenimore Cooper: An Essay Review" (*UMSE*
5[1984–87]:110–19).

Warren Motley's *The American Abraham: James Fenimore
Cooper and the Frontier Patriarch* (Cambridge) concentrates on
Cooper's strong interest in tales of "patriarchal settlement," tales
which "offer insights into the relationship between Cooper's art and
his evolving position in family and society." The book, which is lucid,
reflective, and free of theoretical smokescreens, combines readings
particularly of *The Wept of Wish-ton-Wish*, *The Prairie*, and *Satanstoe* with biographical speculation and stylistic analysis. It doesn't
address, however, the larger cultural question of the American preference for myths of Adam over those of Abraham. A more modest
variation on a similar theme is Michael Clark's "Biblical Allusions
and William Cooper in James Fenimore Cooper's *The Pioneers*"
(*UDR* 18:105–11), examining Cooper's association of Judge Temple
with his own father and with warnings about "the declension of
values in early American society." Mitchell Eugene Summerlin's *A
Dictionary to the Novels of James Fenimore Cooper* (Penkevill) is
well intentioned, with a sensible modesty about eschewing interpretation for description in entries. The master list, on people, is supple-
mented by another on animals and other nonhuman characters and
yet another on ships, and by an index arranged by works.

James Fenimore Cooper: His Country and His Art, ed. George A.
Test (SUNY College at Oneonta), recapitulates the 1986 conference
on Cooper at the State University of New York at Oneonta and
Cooperstown. The papers, running a modest gamut of current
scholarly concerns, are Kay House, "Cooper as Historian" (pp. 1–13);
Susan Shillinglaw, "Cooper's Father and Daughters: The Dialectic
of Paternity" (pp. 14–21) and "Pictorial Space as Identity in *The
Deerslayer*" (pp. 54–66); Abby H. P. Werlock, "Courageous Young
Women in Cooper's Leatherstocking Tales: Heroines and Victims"
(pp. 22–40); Donald A. Ringe, "*The Last of the Mohicans* as a Gothic

Novel" (pp. 41–53); Leland S. Person, Jr., "The Leatherstocking Tradition in American Fiction: Or, The Sources of *Tom Sawyer*: A Descriptive Essay" (pp. 67–77); James D. Wallace, " 'The Paradise of Women': The Domestic Sphere in *Notions of the Americans*" (pp. 78–93); and Jeffrey Walker, "Fenimore Cooper's *Wyandotte* and the Cyclic Course of Empire" (pp. 94–104). Two other, more ambitious essays explore issues of response. In "The Reception of Cooper's Work and the Image of America" (*ESQ* 32[1986]:183–200) Renata R. Mautner Wasserman surveys the correlation of authorial aims and audience reaction, particularly in the reception accorded *Notions of the Americans*, which set out political and economic novelties less easily assimilated than the notions of origin and prelapsarianism driving the popularity of the Leatherstocking Tales. And in "Wish Fulfillment in the Wilderness: D. H. Lawrence and the Leatherstocking Tales" (*AQ* 39:563–85) Allan M. Axelrad questions the authority of Lawrence's reading, reviewing his errors of fact and basic interpretation and the history of his "engagement" with Cooper and his works on the way to concluding that Lawrence and those who approve his readings are advancing their own agendas rather than representing the original cultural content of the romances.

There were only two items on Simms, the more important of them also highlighting Cooper. Louis D. Rubin, Jr., in "The Romance of the Colonial Frontier: Simms, Cooper, the Indians, and the Wilderness" (*American Letters*, pp. 112–36), reads *The Yemassee* and *The Last of the Mohicans* as diametrically opposed visions, the former offering "the dream of natural freedom in the wilderness, the mythic escape from history and society into the pathless forest," the latter the dream of "fulfillment *in* society and history." James Everett Kibler, Jr., "The First Simms Letters: 'Letters from the West' (1826)" (*SLJ* 19, ii:81–91), reprints with minimal annotation a four-part series to a Charleston weekly newspaper written when Simms was only 19.

Two of the lesser lights of the age receive some illumination. Christopher Harris notes the importance of anecdote to the cause in "Mason Locke Weems's Life of Washington: The Making of a Bestseller" (*SLJ* 19, ii:92–101), though without convincingly establishing that commercial success was Weems's motive. David S. Reynolds assembles *George Lippard, Prophet of Protest: Writings of an American Radical* (Peter Lang), an anthology, with introduction and secondary bibliography; Reynolds prefers Lippard the prophetic reformer to the hack sensationalist of *The Quaker City; or The Monks of Monk Hall* (1845), though he prints a good deal of the hackery.

iii. Popular Writers of Midcentury: Poetry and Prose, Women and Men

The year saw only the most modest efforts on behalf of the Fireside Poets and their male contemporaries. For example, Longfellow was represented by Philip Young's exercise in scholarly persistence and statistical coincidence, "Small World: Emerson, Longfellow and Melville's Secret Sister" (*NEQ* 60:382–402), and by Kenneth Hovey's "'A Psalm of Life' Reconsidered: The Dialogue of Western Literature and the Monologue of Young America" (*ATQ* n.s. 1:3–19), a reading of the poem as double in form and ambivalent in intent in its rendering of the contrast of America's youth with the Old World's age. Whittier was the subject of a biography and a library catalog. Roland H. Woodwell's *John Greenleaf Whittier: A Biography* (published under the auspices of the John Greenleaf Whittier Homestead, 1985) is "old-fashioned . . . without 'interpretation' or 'themes,'" massive, and apparently exhaustively researched; Woodwell went to the original sources and does not even cite John B. Pickard's three-volume edition of the letters (1975). Pickard himself prepared *A Descriptive Catalogue of the John Greenleaf Whittier Collection* of the Parkman Dexter Howe Library, University of Florida (Rare Books and Manuscripts, University of Florida Libraries), which lists 114 manuscripts, most of them letters but at least ten manuscripts or autograph copies of poems and essays, among 900 items gathered by Howe. Norton was the other half of a double bill in John Lewis Bradley and Ian Ousby's edition of *The Correspondence of John Ruskin and Charles Eliot Norton* (Cambridge). The editorial policy sets exact reproduction as it's goal, and so differs from the editions prepared by Norton himself and by Sara Norton and M. A. DeWolfe Howe, which sometimes tidied and sometimes censored. Ruskin's illustrations are reproduced within the text, and the whole is packaged with good survey introductions and annotation that is thorough and vital without becoming obtrusive. In another edition of correspondence, Edward L. Tucker prepared "James Russell Lowell and Robert Carter: The *Pioneer* and Fifty Letters from Lowell to Carter" (*SAR*, pp. 187–246); none of Carter's letters to Lowell are known to have survived. Oliver Wendell Holmes received the most modest attention. Walter

H. Eitner's "Samuel Latham Mitchell's Elegy on a Chambered Nauti-
lus" (AN&Q 24[1985]:10–12) offers circumstantial evidence that
Holmes could have known and been influenced by another's work
on a transcendental shell. The Danas fared a bit better. Doreen M.
Hunter's *Richard Henry Dana, Sr.* (TUSAS 511) is a competent
critical biography, in the pattern of the series, of the intriguing
figure—today identifiable primarily as his son's father—whose various transformations saw him a romantic critic and poet, nihilist,
orthodox Christian, Christian romantic poet, and conservative cultural critic. Conrad Bryce's essay on the son's most famous work,
"Richard Henry Dana, Jr. and *Two Years Before the Mast*: Strategies
for Objectifying the Subjective Self" (*Criticism* 29:291–311), plays
on "eye" and "I" to explore the detached perspective which allowed
Dana "to gain some epistemological certainty regarding the existential questions raised by his experience."

By contrast to this modest attention paid the men, the popular
female writers got spotlights and curtain calls. A general survey of
the best known of them, though not entirely successful, nonetheless
indicates the solidity of this state of things. Ann R. Shapiro's *Unlikely
Heroines: Nineteenth-Century American Women Writers and the
Woman Question* (Greenwood) devotes a chapter each to six major
writers—Stowe, Elizabeth Stuart Phelps, Alcott, Jewett, Freeman,
and Chopin—and a major work, and reaches in every instance the
now standard conclusion about rejection of the ideal of true womanhood "in favor of greater freedom and equality for women."

In *New Essays on* Uncle Tom's Cabin (Cambridge, 1986) Eric J.
Sundquist has edited five new essays on Harriet Beecher Stowe's
novel and supplied an introduction (pp. 1–44) identifying the general
contours of critical discussion and the novel's imaginative and ideo-
logical dimensions. The essays, all strong but somehow inclined to
peripheral rather than central concerns, are Richard Yarborough,
"Strategies of Black Characterization in *Uncle Tom's Cabin* and the
Early Afro-American Novel" (pp. 45–84); Jean Fagan Yellin, "Doing
It Herself: *Uncle Tom's Cabin* and Woman's Role in the Slavery
Crisis" (pp. 85–105); Karen Halttunen, "Gothic Imagination and
Social Reform: The Haunted Houses of Lyman Beecher, Henry Ward
Beecher, and Harriet Beecher Stowe" (pp. 107–34); Robert B. Stepto,
"Sharing the Thunder: The Literary Exchanges of Harriet Beecher
Stowe, Henry Bibb, and Frederick Douglass" (pp. 135–53); and
Elizabeth Ammons, "Stowe's Dream of the Mother-Savior: *Uncle*

Tom's Cabin and American Women Writers Before the 1920s" (pp. 155–95). The novel is also the subject of Kathleen Margaret Lant's "The Unsung Hero of *Uncle Tom's Cabin*" (*AmerS* 28:47–71), which proposes that Cassy is Stowe's solution to her "writer's nightmare," the creation of a "system of belief in which love conquers all" confronting a real human dilemma—slavery—which is "obviously impervious to the powers of love." The essay is powerful but odd, with boxed inset discussions of relevant general issues interrupting its course. In "'As John Bunyan Says': Bunyan's Influence on *Uncle Tom's Cabin*" (*ATQ* n.s. 1:157–62) Gayle Edward Wilson identifies Stowe's allusions and uses, demonstrating once again—though without making the point—that Bunyan served as a crucial Victorian source for biblical ideas. Susan Wolstenholme's "Voice of the Voiceless: Harriet Beecher Stowe and the Byron Controversy" (*ALR* 19, ii:48–65) employs elements of the theory of biography to discuss the strategies of critical reaction to the issue and Stowe's alignment of Lady Byron with silence and her husband, the villain, with writing. Somehow, however, Stowe's essay and the book she made from it are still no better than her 19th-century readers thought them.

Work on Louisa May Alcott covered a narrower range. *The Selected Letters of Louisa May Alcott,* ed. Joel Myerson and Daniel Shealy (Little, Brown), with assistance from Madeleine B. Stern, who also wrote the introduction, provides texts of 271 of 649 known letters by Alcott, 138 of them printed for the first time. There are no letters to Emerson, Hawthorne, or Thoreau, many to Mary Mapes Dodge, Laura Hosmer, and Alfred Whitman. Myerson and Shealy also edited "Louisa May Alcott on Vacation: Four Uncollected Letters" (*RALS* 14[1984]:113–41), sketches printed in the Boston *Commonwealth* in 1863; and Myerson added "Louisa May Alcott on Concord: A New 'Tribulation Periwinkle' Letter" (*Concord Saunterer* 17[1984]:41–43). Two critical essays took vastly different tacks. In "The Artist at Home: The Domestication of Louisa May Alcott" (*SAF* 15:187–97), Veronica Bassil uses *Little Women*, the short story "Psyche's Art," and the Gothic romances to establish that "Alcott's fiction . . . reflects profound tension between dependency and independency, between the domestic ideal and the need for artistic freedom, between love within the family and the romantic love that lies outside it." Janet S. Zehr's "The Response of Nineteenth-Century Audiences to Louisa May Alcott's Fiction" (*ATQ* n.s. 1:323–42) is as concerned with Alcott's response to her readers' demands as it is with their response to her and raises questions on the way about the "integrity" of an art that constantly strives to meet external expectations.

Susan Warner was the subject of three essays. In "Pleasure, Duty, Redemption Then and Now: Susan Warner's *Diana*" (*AL* 59:422–29), part of a forthcoming collection on women writers, Joyce Carol Oates speculates on the differences between 19th- and 20th-century conceptions of the romance. Mary P. Hiatt's "Susan Warner's Subtext: The Other Side of Piety" (*JEP* 8:250–61) contrasts the independence of Ellen Montgomery of *The Wide, Wide World* with the novel's official message. By way of biography, John A. Calabro's "Susan Warner and Her Bible Classes" (*Legacy* 4, ii:45–52) provides information from a cadet's diaries on Warner's activities at West Point during the late 1870s.

Others of the most popular women writers received more limited attention. Sandra A. Zagarell's "Expanding 'America': Lydia Sigourney's *Sketch of Connecticut*, Catharine Sedgwick's *Hope Leslie*" (*TSWL* 6:225–45) examines the directions women writers could take "in creating revisionary views of the nation," proposing by the way that the official masculine definition of America (she refers particularly to Cooper's fiction) has "handicapped the American national character." Mary G. De Jong's "Her Fair Fame: The Reputation of Frances Sargent Osgood, Woman Poet" (*SAR*, pp. 265–83) suggests that conventional critical and cultural reaction to Osgood as poet and as friend of both Poe and Griswold constitutes a case study of role bias in literary history. Susan K. Harris's "The House That Hagar Built: Houses and Heroines in E. D. E. N. Southworth's *The Deserted Wife*" (*Legacy* 4, ii:17–29) reads the novel as an unconventional subversion of the conventional narrative issues of desertion and reconciliation and the conventional imagery of houses as feminine: the woman is happily married to a man who is her inferior. Celia Thaxter as poet is both explicated and defended for her feminine psychological boldness by Pauline Woodward ("Celia Thaxter's Love Poems" [*CLQ* 23:144–53]). Elizabeth Stuart Phelps Ward is the subject of Frances M. Malpezzi's pedestrian "*The Silent Partner*: A Feminist Sermon on the Social Gospel" (*StHum* 13[1986]:103–10), exploring the effects of the movement on the novel. Donald R. Makosky prints the manuscript of "Rose Terry Cooke's *Matred and Tamar, A Drama*" (*RALS* 14[1984]:1–84. Rita K. Gollin supplies a "Legacy Profile: Annie Adams Fields, 1834–1915" (*Legacy* 4, ii:27–36), and

Cathy Giffuni "A Bibliography of Anna Katharine Green" (*Clues* 8: 113–33), author of the pioneer detective-formula novel *The Leavenworth Case* (1878).

The only essay of significance on Horatio Alger—and a relentless example of humorless culture criticism—is "'The Gentle Boy from the Dangerous Classes': Pederasty, Domesticity, and Capitalism in Horatio Alger" (*Representations* 19:87–110). Michael Moon proposes that the rags-to-riches myth expanded from Alger's notions of "modest philanthropy toward younger needy boys" by means of the conscious or unconscious male pederastic impulse linking capitalism to sexuality. Moon's crucial premise is that American capitalism is homoerotic, men of power and success looking for "deserving" and "attractive" boys on whom to bestow their gifts.

iv. Humorists and Southern Writers

Work on the humorists proceeds with energy if not consistency. Carolyn S. Brown's survey, *The Tall Tale*, announces its interest in the tale as performance, but nonetheless deals extensively with content. Thomas Bangs Thorpe, William Trotter Porter, A. B. Longstreet, George Washington Harris, and the Crockett almanacs receive substantial treatment. Performance is also the focus of John Wenke's "*Sut Lovingood's Yarns* and the Politics of Performance" (*SAF* 15: 199–210), which concludes that the purpose of Harris's collection was "to offer the disenfranchised the therapy of laughter." David C. Estes's "Sut Lovingood at the Camp Meeting: A Practical Joker Among the Backwoods Believers" (*SoQ* 25, ii:53–65) applies the theoretical terms of Roger Caillois's *Men, Play, and Games* (1958) to sketch a Sut who emerges "as the sole admirable resident of this backwoods community because only he acknowledges the unavoidable chaos that destroys all hopes for a civilized life." In "Thomas Bangs Thorpe's Backwoods Hunters: Culture Heroes and Humorous Failures" (*UMSE* 5[1984–87]:158–71), Estes provides a good introductory discussion of Thorpe's *The Mysteries of the Backwoods* (1846). James H. Justus supplies introduction and annotation to a facsimile reproduction of Joseph G. Baldwin's *Flush Times of Alabama and Mississippi* (LSU); the introduction emphasizes Baldwin's artistry in translating the raw stuff of southwestern humor into a literary self appropriate to the confrontations of a changing culture. Michael A. Lofaro provides introduction, bibliographical notes, and comparative tables of contents to an "enlarged facsimile edition" of *The Tall Tales of Davy Crockett: The Second Nashville Series of Crockett Almanacs, 1839–1841* (Tenn.). Raymond C. Craig's *The Humor of H. E. Taliaferro* (Tenn.) is an anthology of selections prefaced by biographical and critical introductions. Ronald M. Grosh's "Civil War Politics in the Novels of David Ross Locke" (*MidAmerica* 13[1986]:19–30) points to the "remarkable degree of concrete objectivity" in Locke's use of Civil War politics as a backdrop for his narratives. The war figures as well in William E. Lenz's "The Failure of Conventional Form: The Civil War, Southwest Humor, and Kittrell Warren's *Army Straggler*" (*UMSE* 5[1984–87]:120–30), which argues that the ambivalences of characterization, structure, and attitude in Warren's 1865 work mirror the "predictable chaos of national conflict."

Several items highlight the creator of Uncle Remus. *Joel Chandler Harris* (Georgia), though a reprint of the 1978 TUSAS volume by Bruce R. Bickley, Jr., is valuable for its updating of the annotated secondary bibliography. Jefferson Humphries discusses Harris in *The Puritan and the Cynic: Moralists and Theorists in French and American Letters* (Oxford); his "Aphorism and Fable: La Fontaine and Joel Chandler Harris" (pp. 75–90) proposes that the "myth of the Old South depended above all else on the figure of the black man." Eric L. Montenyohl in "The Origins of Uncle Remus" (*FForum* 18, ii[1986]:36–67) identifies Sam Small's "Old Si" sketches in the Atlanta *Constitution* as Harris's model and his early competition. Doris Lanier's "James Whitcomb Riley's Georgia Connection" (*ON* 11[1985–86]:173–93) traces the sectionalism-defying friendship of Riley and Harris and makes claims for Riley's influence on the Georgia regionalist.

Studies of George Washington Cable include Alice Hall Petry's *A Genius in His Way: The Art of Cable's Old Creole Days* (Fairleigh Dickinson). Petry emphasizes the artistry of each of the eight stories and is especially interested in Cable's "dense, organic, highly evocative language." Her readings are exhaustive if somewhat mechanical, and she makes little effort to see the collection whole. Robert O. Stephens's "Cable's Grandissime Saga" (*ALR* 20, i:3–17) places Cable in a cultural context, reading *The Grandissimes* from the perspective of his earlier work rather than his later and seeing him "seized by history and capable of condensing history into the saga of a family."

In another essay on the same work and with a similar interest, "*The Grandissimes*: A Story-Shaped World" (*L&H* 13:257–77), Charles Swann sees Cable's narrative myths as informed by the classic theme of the 19th-century historical novel—the rise of the middle class— and as enacting the tensions of past and present. More pedestrian studies are Elaine Ware's "George W. Cable's *The Cavalier*: An American Best Seller and Theatrical Attraction" (*SLJ* 19, ii:70–80), which argues that Cable yielded to commercial concerns and thus missed his true artistic potential, and an edition of the manuscript of "*Triomphe de Villandry*" (*UMSE* 5[1984–87]:272–87) prepared by Benjamin Franklin Fisher IV and Michael P. Dean.

Interest in Kate Chopin revived with a vengeance. In a volume with her name as title (Chelsea House) Harold Bloom reprints ten essays, several of them retitled, and offers his own tantalizing introductory proposition that Walt Whitman is the source of the "autoerotic vision" of *The Awakening*. That novel was also the topic of six other essays. Suzanne W. Jones's "Place, Perception, and Identity in *The Awakening*" (*SoQ* 25, ii:108–20) argues the function of geographically specific place for indicating forms of behavior. Merritt Moseley's "Chopin and Mysticism" (*SoSt* 25[1986]:267–74) describes the evolution of Edna Pontellier's consciousness through mystical rather than logical experience. Joseph R. Urgo's "A Prologue to Rebellion: *The Awakening* and the Habit of Self-Expression" (*SLJ* 20, i: 22–32) insists that the essence of the story is "Edna's inherent need to speak" and that she dies because she "would rather extinguish her life than edit her tale." A more provocative examination of the essential issue of expression is Patricia S. Yaeger's "'A Language Which Nobody Understood': Emancipatory Strategies in *The Awakening*" (*Novel* 20:197–219), which begins as a response to the basic paradigm of Tony Tanner's *Adultery in the Novel* (1979) but proceeds to draw upon linguistic and extralinguistic theory to argue that Chopin succeeds "in inventing a novelistic structure in which the heroine's very absence of speech works productively" to define desires antithetical to those held and articulated by men. In "*The Awakening* and *The House of Mirth*: Studies of Arrested Development" (*ALR* 19, iii:27– 41) C. J. Wershoven describes rather than explains the failure of Wharton's and Chopin's characters to develop a "new self." Richard Ruland's "Kate Chopin and *The Awakening*" (*Essays on English and American Literature*, pp. 119–30) is both a critical-biographical introduction to Chopin and a reading of her novel as a philosophical tragedy in which pursuit of the divinity of self is confused with selfishness.

Two Chopin stories received more modest readings in Kristin B. Valentine and Janet Larsen Palmer's "The Rhetoric of Nineteenth-Century Feminism in Kate Chopin's 'A Pair of Silk Stockings' " (*WStu* 4:59–67) and Martin Simpson's "Chopin's 'A Shameful Affair' " (*Expl* 45, i[1986]:59–60). Chopin in her own world, and particularly in her St. Louis houses and neighborhoods, is the topic of Bonnie Stepenoff's "Freedom and Regret: The Dilemma of Kate Chopin" (*MHR* 81:447–66). Finally, Per Seyersted adds modest biographical information with "Kate Chopin's Wound: Two New Letters" (*ALR* 20, i:71–75).

Only a few items dealt with other southern writers. Jan Bakker's "Overlooked Progenitors: Independent Women and Southern Renaissance in Augusta Jane Evans Wilson's *Macaria; or, Altars of Sacrifice*" (*SoQ* 25, ii:131–42) notes the parallels between political and personal alternatives in Wilson's 1863–64 romance. In "The Novelist as Soldier: Cooke and De Forest" (*ALR* 19, iii:80–88) Eric Solomon offers an introductory comparison of the writers' uses of war experience in fiction. Clara Juncker's "Grace King: Woman-as-Artist" (*SLJ* 20, i:37–44) is a jargony examination of King's feminist concerns, drawing especially on the story "Mardriléne; Or, The Festival of the Dead."

v. The Howells Generation; Nonfiction

There was a surprising flurry of interest in Helen Hunt Jackson, though with not very exceptional results. The better of two critical biographies is Rosemary Whitaker's *Helen Hunt Jackson* (BSWWS 78), which stresses Jackson's concern with official treatment of the Indians. Antoinette May's *Helen Hunt Jackson: A Lonely Voice of Conscience* (Chronicle) touts Jackson as literary and political pioneer. Valerie Sherer Mathes's "Helen Hunt Jackson and the Campaign for Ponca Restitution, 1880–1881" (*SDH* 17:23–41) reviews Jackson's support for the Indian cause, which culminated in *A Century of Dishonor* (1880).

Work on Sarah Orne Jewett was less plentiful but more engaged. In "Local Color and a Mythologized Past: The Rituals of Memory in *Country of the Pointed Firs*" (*CLQ* 23:16–25) Philip G. Terrie identifies Jewett as exploring the fundamental implications of the local-color genre, particularly the process of nostalgia. Michael E. Holstein's "Art and Archetype: Jewett's *Pointed Firs* and the Dunnet Landing Stories" (*NCF* 42:188–202) forsakes the regional perspective to read the book as a "metafictional narrative" by which Jewett struggles with strategies for creating general human relevance. In another close analysis of the same work, Cynthia T. Goheen proposes that "the seafarer's orientation toward life, the seafarer's wisdom," is resurrected in other characters in the community and finally in the narrator ("Rebirth of the Seafarer: Sarah Orne Jewett's *The Country of the Pointed Firs*" [*CLQ* 23:154–64]).

Mary E. Wilkins Freeman was the subject of two comparative essays, a survey of criticism, and an introductory critical-biographical essay. In "A Community of Women: Surviving Marriage in the Wilderness" (*Rendezvous* 21, ii[in error for 22, ii] [1986]:3–11) Victoria Aarons argues that the consequences of independent action in Susan Glaspell's "A Jury of Her Peers" are not nearly so "benign and regenerative" as they are in Freeman's "The Revolt of Mother." And in " 'Love-Cracked': Spinsters as Subversives in 'Anna Malann,' 'Christmas Jenny,' and 'An Object of Love' " (*CLQ* 23:4–15) Barbara A. Johns identifies the "stereotypically eccentric, amusing old maid" character in one story by Annie Trumbull Slosson and two by Freeman as really a "heroic subversive" whose career undermines the patriarchal system that confines her. The survey is Mary R. Reichardt's "Mary Wilkins Freeman: One Hundred Years of Criticism" (*Legacy* 4, ii:31–44), and the introductory essay Leah Blatt Glasser's "Legacy Profile: Mary E. Wilkins Freeman, 1852–1930" (*Legacy* 4, i:37–45).

John W. Crowley weighed in with two effective overviews of the realistic period and a survey of Howells criticism. His "Polymorphously Perverse? Childhood Sexuality in the American Boy Book" (*ALR* 19, ii:2–15) argues that the ideas of childhood development implicit in such works as Howells's *The Flight of Pony Baker* (1902) are closer to the Freudian notion of the "repression of sexual spontaneity" than they are to the ideas of American theorists of the same period. Crowley's "The Whole Famdamnily" (*NEQ* 60:106–13), an essay-review of Alfred Bendixen's 1986 reprint edition of *The Whole Family: A Novel by Twelve Authors*, demonstrates how a simple "collaborative" fiction became a complex of twisting plots and strategies devised to foil other authors' strategies. Part I of his two-part "Howells in the Eighties: A Review of Criticism" (*ESQ* 32[1986]:

253–77; 33:45–65) discusses research tools and recent general criticism, part II criticism of individual works.

The only Howells book of the year centered not on William Dean but on his wife, Elinor. *If Not Literature: Letters of Elinor Mead Howells*, ed. Ginette de B. Merrill and George Arms (pub. for Miami Univ. by Ohio State), prints roughly 130 letters by her, 20 letters to her, passages from her Venetian diary of the 1860s, and selections from her artistic and architectural scketches. The volume does more than fit the pattern of the volumes of her husband's selected letters: it brings vividly before us the energetic (possibly even clinically hysterical), perceptive woman living her own life and her husband's career. In "*A Hazard of New Fortunes*: The Crosscurrents of Cultural Hegemony" (*Social Criticism*, pp. 241–67) Robert Shulman, concerned with the interrelationship of writers and a market society, supplies a provocative reading of the novel as an effective mirror of the "dominant-class hegemony" Howells both opposed and accommodated. John Updike's "A Critic at Large: Howells as Anti-Novelist" (*New Yorker* 13 July: 78–88), honoring the 150th anniversary of Howells's birth, is an elegant explication of the American realism which Howells defined and Updike upholds. Three essays examine individual Howells works. John E. Bassett's "*Their Wedding Journey*: In Search of a New Fiction" (*SNNTS* 19:175–86) is more effective at asserting than proving Howells's search for fictional strategies based on the significance of ordinary middle-class experience. Jane Marston's "The Law of Nature and the Design of History: *The Landlord at Lion's Head*" (*NCF* 42:171–87) sees Howells in the novel describing "evolution in a way new for him: as the dynamism of a vitalistic principle in nature" rather than as a wholly natural force. Edward J. Piacentino's "Arms in Love and War in Howells' 'Editha' " (*SSF* 24:425–32) emphasizes the coherence of imagery in the story. Two other essays treat Howells and contemporaries. David Rife's "Hamilton Wright Mabie and William Dean Howells: A Literary Friendship" (*ALR* 19, ii:30–47) traces Mabie's conversion from disdain of Howells's cold scientific pessimism to appreciation of his larger motives. Marysa Demoor's "Andrew Lang versus W. D. Howells: A Late Victorian Literary Duel" (*JAmS* 21:416–22) defines aesthetic and sometimes sharply personal differences which throw light on both the British-American and the romantic-realistic disputes of the period.

Only one item, but that a book, dealt with Henry Blake Fuller. In

A *Varied Harvest: The Life and Works of Henry Blake Fuller* (Pittsburgh), Kenneth Scambray offers a skillful critical biography, both thorough and nonjudgmental—the latter quality important because Scambray must discuss Fuller's homosexuality. Lucien L. Agosta's *Howard Pyle* (TUSAS 514) conforms to the pattern of that series while successfully meeting the special critical demands imposed by the popular and influential author-illustrator. Agosta is especially good on the interaction of story and picture in Pyle's books for young people.

All three essays on Harold Frederic dealt with his best-known novel. Sydney J. Krause's "Harold Frederic and the Failure Motif" (*SAF* 15:55–69) reads *The Damnation of Theron Ware* not just as the failure of good intentions but as an emblem of the closing of "an assumedly boundless personal frontier" more crucial than the physical one. Elmer Suderman's "Modernization as Damnation in 'The Damnation of Theron Ware' " (*BSUF* 27, i[1986]:12–19) sees "modernization" as only the newest of the alternatives through which Theron can't cope with a rapidly changing world. And George C. Carrington, Jr.'s "Harold Frederic's Clear Farcical Vision: *The Damnation of Theron Ware*" (*ALR* 19, iii:3–26) tests the book against the characteristics of farce as genre, in terms derived from Henri Bergson and from Jessica M. Davis's *Farce* (1978).

As usual, criticism of Henry Adams was as toughly intellectual as the work discussed. In "Henry Adams and History" (*JHI* 48:467–82) Keith R. Burich explores Adams's basing the theory of history enunciated in *A Letter to American Teachers of History* (1910) on the Second Law of Thermodynamics. Burich proposes that Adams took that position precisely because the Second Law was being undercut by more contemporary theory; thus he was also ironically undercutting the willingness of his fellow historians to acquiesce in the "stifling conformity required by modern society." In "The Limits of Contradiction: Irony and History in Hegel and Henry Adams" (*ClioI* 15[1986]:391–410) Joseph G. Kronick offers an extensive discussion of irony as intellectual process and attitude. He finds in *The Education* an explicit rendering of what in Hegel "remains the implicit ironization of dialectics," but neatly avoids any consideration of direct influence. Less imposing essays are David Partenheimer's "Henry Adams and Goethe: *Dichter und Denker*" (*ATQ* n.s. 1:83–93), a survey of Goethe's influence on Adams's life and work that's short on methodology; David Cody's "Henry Adams and the City of Brass"

(*NEQ* 60:89–92), which locates the source of an unflattering allusion in *The Education* in the *Book of the Thousand Nights and a Night*; and George A. Kennedy's "*Fin-de-Siècle* Classicism: Henry Adams and Thorstein Veblen, Lew Wallace and W. D. Howells" (*CML* 8: 15–22), a cursory evaluation of attitudes toward classical literature and learning.

Some of the letters printed in *William James: Selected Unpublished Correspondence, 1885–1910*, ed. Frederick J. Down Scott (Ohio State), are of literary interest, but the volume itself is not well executed, with a perfunctory biographical-critical introduction, minimal notes, awkward arrangement, an eccentric index, and incomplete manuscript-location information. James is also the topic of Alfred Habegger's highly speculative "New Light on William James and Minny Temple" (*NEQ* 60:28–53). Habegger suggests that Minny's influence on William's 1869–70 breakdown arose from her willingness to directly confront her own suffering; in doing so "she bequeathed to William an image of heroic independence that only aggravated his already incurable self-loathing."

Single essays treated other nonfiction writers. In "John Muir on Mount Ritter: A New Wilderness Aesthetic" (*Pacific Historian* 31: 35–44) Philip G. Terrie offers a shaky conception of Romanticism in asserting that Muir added a further imaginative dimension to wilderness aesthetic by incorporating "the further perception and appreciation of nature's processes." Diane Lichtenstein's "Word and Worlds: Emma Lazarus's Conflicting Citizenships" (*TWSL* 6:247–64) sees Lazarus as combining American and Jewish ideas of womanhood and thus reconciling her multiple citizenships. Timothy Miller offers an interesting look at the interplay of literature and religious culture in *Following* In His Steps: *A Biography of Charles M. Sheldon* (Tenn.), a study of the author of the most astonishing success in the "Social Gospel" genre.

vi. Crane, Norris, and Bierce

Stephen Crane was the subject of three essay-anthology volumes. *New Essays on* The Red Badge of Courage, ed. Lee Clark Mitchell (Cambridge), is the most successful, both interesting and consistent, and with the text of the work itself an issue throughout. Mitchell's introduction (pp. 1–23) surveys biography, reputation, critical reception, and textual problems. The essays are Hershel Parker, "Getting Used to the 'Original Form' of *The Red Badge of Courage*" (pp. 25–47), advancing Parker's attack on Ripley Hitchcock as censor; Andrew Delbanco, "The American Stephen Crane: The Context of *The Red Badge of Courage*" (pp. 49–76); Amy Kaplan, "The Spectacle of War in Crane's Revision of History" (pp. 77–108); Howard C. Horsford, " 'He Was a Man' " (pp. 109–27); and Christine Brooke-Rose, "Ill Logics of Irony" (pp. 129–46), on ironic deconstruction and free indirect discourse. Harold Bloom edited two volumes, *Stephen Crane* and *Stephen Crane's* The Red Badge of Courage (both Chelsea House), reprinting essays and sections of books, often under new titles. The newest major Crane work, also represented by the reprinting of the same selection from it in both Bloom volumes, is Michael Fried's *Realism, Writing, Disfiguration: On Thomas Eakins and Stephen Crane* (Chicago). Fried's concern is the "thematics of writing," and especially "a problematic of the *materiality* of writing as that materiality enters into Eakins's paintings and Crane's prose." The images and narrative issues in Crane's major writings, Fried proposes, involve analogies to the writing process—upturned faces are blank pages, for example, and Henry Johnson's scarred face is the blank page violently disfigured by words. Too often Fried's imaginative method, and not Crane, makes the meaning.

Britta Lindberg-Seyersted serves up a stale rehash of slight evidence in *Ford Madox Ford and His Relationship to Stephen Crane and Henry James* (Humanities). By contrast, Michael Schneider's "Monomyth Structure in *The Red Badge of Courage*" (*ALR* 20, i:45–55) is tightly argued and illuminating, addressing the novel's meaning in light of Joseph Campbell's "hero monomyth" and Northrop Frye's "quest-romance." Schneider concludes that the supposed ambiguity of *Red Badge* is rather an indictment of our irrational impulses which also identifies them as "the source of our richest, most meaningful experience." Kirk M. Reynolds's "*The Red Badge of Courage*: Private Henry's Mind as Sole Point of View" (*SoAR* 52, i:59–69) lays out a somewhat fuzzy case for the novel as indebted to Bierce's "An Occurrence at Owl Creek Bridge," creating the illusion of an external observer-narrator when the voice and perspective of the novel are those of Henry Fleming alone. Daniel K. Muhlestein explicates the cigar as symbol in "Crane's 'The Open Boat' " (*Expl* 45, ii:42–43).

Work on Frank Norris was modest. The more provocative of two substantial essays is Hugh J. Dawson's "McTeague as Ethnic Stereotype" (*ALR* 20, i:34–44), seeing in Norris's treatment of the "social-climbing Irish outsider" a strong nativist bias of which anti-Celtic prejudice was a component. Joseph R. McElrath, Jr., identifies a sensitive and knowledgeable depth in Norris's use of musical allusion in "Frank Norris's *The Pit*: Musical Elements as Biographical Evidence" (*PLL* 23:161–74). McElrath also contributed to bibliographical discussion with "Frank Norris at Del Monte: Two New *Wave* Essays from 1895" (*ALR* 20, i:56–70), which reprints the items, though its real point is to establish that earlier attribution of them to Norris is correct. Issues of the newly launched *Frank Norris Studies* contain other bibliographical items by McElrath, including supplements to *Frank Norris: A Reference Guide*, as well as minor biographical materials and notes.

One of the two essays on Ambrose Bierce was a kind of sidelight. Don Kunz's "Arthur Barron & Bitter Bierce" (*LFQ* 15:64–68) examines Barron's imaginative rather than literal rendering of "Parker Adderson, Philosopher" as a television film. A useful close look at Bierce's own technique is provided by Clifford R. Ames. His "Do I Wake or Sleep? Technique as Content in Ambrose Bierce's Short Story, 'An Occurrence at Owl Creek Bridge'" (*ALR* 19, iii:52–67) discusses the strategy by which Bierce hides delusion and the distortions of time and space behind a sympathetic alignment of reader and victim which seems to establish omniscience.

Indiana University

13. Fiction: 1900 to the 1930s

John J. Murphy and
Stephen L. Tanner

Clearly, Cather, Wharton, Dreiser, and Stein are the major writers of this period. Centennial celebrations and seminars are no longer the lifeblood of interest in them. If they take place it is because interest necessitates rather than depends on them. How long these pages can continue to accommodate these writers adequately in the present format is a concern. What this chapter has become is the only alternative—a survey of a few important writers with lesser ones crowded into the background.

Since this is a shared project, it is helpful, we think, to indicate authorship. Sections i, ii, and iv are by Murphy, and iii and v are by Tanner; vi is a collaboration.

i. Willa Cather

Foremost among this year's Cather studies are James Woodress's *Willa Cather: A Literary Life* (Nebraska) and Sharon O'Brien's *Willa Cather: The Emerging Voice* (Oxford). The value of the Woodress book is its comprehensiveness; it tells the known facts of Cather's own story and times in prose that is clear and jargon-free. O'Brien's book, while thesis-ridden, extremely padded, and overwritten, is a breakthrough speculation on Cather's development as lesbian and artist. Cather's Virginia background and genealogy, early Nebraska life, Pittsburgh and *McClure's* years, and European and southwestern travels are handled more fully by Woodress than by any previous biographer or critic, as are the later phases of her life in New York and frequent sojourns in New Hampshire and New Brunswick. O'Brien concentrates on the first half of the life (until Cather found her own voice and stopped imitating Henry James).

Woodress's conclusion, while recording Cather's years at the University of Nebraska and mannish phase there, that it is "arguable"

whether her affair with Louise Pound "should be considered a serious love affair or a short-lived freshman's 'crush' on a senior" will be
debated by those who, like O'Brien, use the Cather-Pound correspondence at Duke University to assert Cather's lesbianism and
awareness of the deviance associated with women whose erotic-
emotional ties are primarily with other women. Woodress's handling
of Cather's intimate friendship with Isabelle McClung will be a problem for the same critics, in that he refuses to accept as fact what cannot be supported by fact about Cather's sexual orientation: "Was [the
McClung] friendship a physical lesbian relationship? Some critics
believe it was, but there is no external evidence to support it. . . . in
all the hundreds of [Cather's] letters that have survived."

Perhaps it is unfair to dwell on this sexual issue in reviewing
Woodress's book, since it is not his emphasis. However, it is definitely
the emphasis or presumption in the growing body of criticism on
Cather. The full picture, then, for some critics will involve the kind
of psychological speculating Woodress refuses to do. But he paints
another kind of full picture, one which presents the development of
the artist and her work from multiple, factually based perspectives:
the raw materials she made into art, her career as journalist and editor and its effect on her work, her developing philosophy and disillusionment with the 20th century, her professional relationships,
the importance of family and the traumatic loss of her parents, her
comfort in Nebraska friends like the Pavelkas (prototypes of *My
Ántonia's* Cuzaks and the family in "Neighbour Rosicky") and Carrie Miner Sherwood, and the cosmopolitan Menuhin family in New
York.

Woodress devotes a chapter to each major work after launching
Cather into her delayed novel-writing career. Each of these chapters
is a testimony to this biographer's long experience with and appreciation of the novel under consideration, recording its genesis and
sources while interweaving plot summary with commentary on narrative techniques, imagery and symbolism, motifs, characterization,
and so on. Each chapter also surveys a selection of criticism generated
by the work, sometimes leaning heavily on Susan Rosowski's 1986
study of Cather's fiction, *The Voyage Perilous: Willa Cather's Romanticism.* The argument shared by Woodress for Cather as a romantic need not exclude classifying her a realist as well, however,
even in the Howellsian sense—despite the disparaging remarks she
made about Howells early in her career. Although Woodress seems

to prefer the romantic label, he tempers his view through the perceptive statement that "Perhaps at the highest levels of art realism and romance begin to merge." Cather is at that high level.

Using studies by Nancy Chodorow and other feminist theorists to explain Cather's difficulty in establishing autonomy from her mother, O'Brien explores various strategies Cather used in her fiction to satisfy her need for her mother without endangering her own autonomy or revealing "deviant" eroticism. Foremost among these was the use of male characters as masks to explore love for other women. While O'Brien insists that in a story like "A Burglar's Christmas" the son-mother relationship is a simple cover for the mother-daughter relationship, she concedes that such simple substitution is not characteristic of the mature fiction and suggests the "need to develop interpretive strategies for determining when a male character is a 'mask' rather than an opposite-sex character whom Cather created by drawing, in part, on herself . . . . I suggest that only if textual clues contradict or question the male character's assigned gender can we proclaim him a 'mask' or 'cover.' . . . Since at times she was writing two stories at once, a heterosexual and a homosexual one . . . we are frequently faced with indeterminate meaning rather than with a clearly encoded subtext that constitutes the 'real' message of the text." The problem with such a thesis is that, while it titillates for a time, it threatens to reduce the fiction to narcissistic psychoallegory. It is beneficial to read Woodress and O'Brien back to back, but in essence their works are like different sides of a coin that make 1987 a banner year for Cather studies.

Other general and biographical considerations include John J. Murphy's extensive chapter on Cather (pp. 686–715) in *A Literary History of the West*, which concludes that "Cather's career 'came together' in *Death Comes for the Archbishop*, a work which approached perfection. It is her most western and historically embracing novel, and its importance is that it increases the dimensions of [American] western literature by introducing alternatives to heroic traditions." Murphy divides Cather's career into three phases in concentrating on the major western novels: "Epic Heroines," "Lesser Men," and "A Great Western Hero." In *My Ántonia* Cather created the "maternal counterpart" of the spouseless protagonists of *O Pioneers!* and *The Song of the Lark*, thereby completing a tryptic of female achievement intimately associated with the land, and in Jim Burden, her narrator, her first significant portrait in a series of self-defeating western men, including Niel Herbert in *A Lost Lady* and Claude Wheeler in *One of Ours*. *The Professor's House* becomes strategic in detailing male careers previous to and after the Great War, which seemed to provide escape from but then contributed to social decline in America. Finally, in turning to history, Cather found in celibate Archbishop Lamy of Santa Fe the inspiration for a western hero who was an effective civilizer without marital problems and capable of viewing the landscape of the West as symbolic of eternal truths and mysteries. Gleaning her information from Cather's interviewers, critics, acquaintances, and casual friends (among them Burton Rascoe, Fanny Butcher, Fanny Hurst, Mary Ellen Chase, and Truman Capote), Marilyn Arnold in "The Other Side of Willa Cather" (*NH* 68:74–82) tries to balance the image of the testy reclusive novelist with that of a more generous, outgoing nature—a bit masculine to some but very feminine to others, staccato in conversation yet given to paragraph-long replies, forthright and laughing yet shy and kind.

The year's collection of new work includes seven essays in the "Special Literary Issue" of the *Willa Cather Pioneer Memorial Newsletter* (31:11–42). Stephen Tatum's "Word Music in 'The Ancient People,' Part IV of *The Song of the Lark*" (pp. 25–31) is a careful analysis of key passages in the novel's shortest book tracing Cather's movement from visual to aural energies in order to release characters and readers from temporal selfhood for epiphanal immersion in the "restitutive beat of the world's continuity." Lance Larsen in "The Howlett Basis of Vaillant and Latour's Friendship" (pp. 18–25) provides a supplement to Edward and Lillian Bloom's 1955 treatment of Cather's use of Rev. William Joseph Howlett's *The Life of the Right Reverend Joseph P. Machebeuf* (Pueblo, Colo., 1908) as a source for *Death Comes for the Archbishop* by indicating Cather's altering of the biography to make her priests complementary opposites rather than similarly constituted friends and her embroidering of the white mule episode for purposes of characterization. Larsen suggests sources in both Howlett and the Bible for the crown imagery in the climactic blessing scene between the two priests. In " 'The Colour of an Adventure': Pictorial Dimensions in Cather's *Archbishop*" (pp. 11–15) Kevin A. Synnott considers as another way of telling the vigorous visual qualities of the novel, comparing the prologue to the opening of the first book to define and illustrate Cather's approximation of the monumental style of French painter Puvis de

Chavannes, which reflects the fine aesthetic sensibility of her priest protagonist. In "Con-Quest or In-Quest? Cather's Mythic Impulse in *Death Comes for the Archbishop*" (pp. 15–18) Marilee Lindemann sees the novel as a revisioning of American romance from appropriation to accommodation as Latour is saved by Mexican and Indian associates from the ideology of "spiritual imperialism" by one of "genuine pluralism." Joseph C. Murphy gives a trendy air to the collection in "*Shadows on the Rock* and *To the Lighthouse*—a Bakhtinian Perspective" (pp. 31–37) by using Mikhail Bakhtin's dialogic and monologic discourse definitions to show that the dialogic, associated with the feminist world in Woolf, can be applied to the best aspects of the patriarchal world of Cather's Quebec. The collection is rounded out by considerations of two short stories. Mellanee Kvasnicka in " 'Paul's Case' in the High School Classroom" (pp. 37–39) tells of her experiences teaching this and other Cather stories in a blue-collar area of Omaha, detailing student responses to Paul's dilemma and to the upsetting "reality" of his suicide. In "Cather's 'Two Friends' as a Western 'Out of the Cradle' " (pp. 39–41) John J. Murphy parallels the Cather story and the popular Whitman poem as reminiscences of childhood framed by adult perspectives and containing parallel moonlit settings in which love relationships are disrupted. Where the Whitman poem ends with insight into death and love, Cather's story merely reflects on the permanent scar of unnecessary loss of security. Harold Bloom gives *My Ántonia* Chelsea House's Modern Critical Interpretations treatment in reprinting eleven essays on the novel, from David Daiches's 1951 introduction to Deborah G. Lambert's 1982 lesbian reading. Bloom dusts off his introduction from the Modern Critical Views *Willa Cather* (1985) to introduce these essays.

My Ántonia continues to motivate ongoing critical response. In "Sunsets and City Life: Place in *My Ántonia* and *Sister Carrie*" (*McNR* 31 [1984–86]:23–32) Nancy H. and James L. Davis see both novels as demonstrating the influence of place on the American psyche, and Carrie Meeber and Jim Burden as comparably unfulfilled in leaving the land to pursue happiness in the city, yet different due to Jim's recognition of the importance of the land connection in resuming active friendship with Ántonia. George Dekker in "The hero and heroine of historical romance" chapter in his *The American Historical Romance*, pp. 220–71, speculates that "Cather may well be the preeminent American historical romancer-novelist of our cen-

tury" and then applies Schiller's concept of "Sentimental" (nature-
estranged) and "Naive" (nature-connected) characters to the Jim-
Ántonia relationship. Along the way, Dekker comments perceptively
about the function of the wolf episode, Cather's rare gift of "negative capability," her balancing of matriarch Ántonia with patriarch
Grandfather Burden, mythic associations (Lena as Aphrodite, etc.),
and plasticity of gender roles in this novel. He pinpoints Jim's problem as failure to discover a "mature and independent masculine
identity," parallels the hired girls with Hawthorne's dark heroines,
and sees the society they challenge as the descendants of his Puritans. Judith Fetterley overlooks the existence of Ántonia's son Rudolph, who is six foot two and has a blacksmith's chest and a deep
baritone voice, to affirm that "daughters, not sons, stand tall" in this
novel in her contribution, "My Ántonia, Jim Burden and the Dilemma
of the Lesbian Writer," to Judith Spector's Gender Studies: New
Directions in Feminist Criticism (Bowling Green, 1986), pp. 43–59.
Also, she reveals a simplistic sexist attitude toward males in making
Jim's uneasiness in the snake and rape scenes prove that Cather used
him to masquerade writing about one woman's lesbian love for another. Fetterley's thesis, while not new, might have validity if her
methods didn't distort.

Cather's other major novels keep pace with My Ántonia in critical interest. Besides the three essays on Archbishop in the WCPM
Newsl, two other essays on this novel merit commentary. James C.
Work considers Archbishop as a morality play of unconnected anecdotes involving personified abstractions of the seven deadly sins and
opposite virtues and Latour as a recurring figure dramatizing "attributes of sainthood" struggling with sin in "Willa Cather's Archbishop
and the Seven Deadly Sins" (PVR 14[1986]:93–103). Though Work
lapses at times into the conversational and makes no references to
other work on this topic, notably D. H. Stewart's 1966 Queen's Quarterly essay, he points in a direction in need of definitive treatment.
Christina Murphy in "Mythopoeic Consciousness and the Structure
of Willa Cather's Death Comes for the Archbishop" (NDQ 55, ii:99–
105) overwhelms the novel with theories by Edmund Husserl, Inder
Kher, Lévi-Strauss, and others to establish that Cather structures her
work around the development of Latour's mythopoeic consciousness
"to capture the essence of . . . phenomenological thought as it re-
creates a transcendental awareness of reality and meaning." In Old
Southwest, New Southwest, Essays on a Region and Its Literature,

ed. Judy N. Lensink (Tuscon Library), David Lavender's "The Tyranny of Facts" (pp. 62–73) accuses Cather of slander in her portrait of Padre Antonio José Martinez of Taos but mostly of glossing over history for dramatic effects in *Archbishop*. Alice Hall Petry continues her series of essays on Cather with "In the Name of the Self: Cather's *The Professor's House*" (*CLQ* 23:26–31), claiming that the novel's final paragraph announces the spiritual serenity that will follow the professor's letting go of his previous self during the epiphanic integration of his professional and primitive selves, and seeing Tom Outland's similar epiphany "on the mesa" after his troubles with the Smithsonian and Roddy Blake as anticipating the professor's in the near-asphyxiation scene. Merrill M. Skaggs pits Tom Outland against seamstress Augusta as "ideas . . . appropriate for specific life stages" in "A Glance Into *The Professor's House*: Inward and Outward Bound" (*Renascence* 39:422–28). She sees the crisis of St. Peter's midnight as the relinquishing of the romantic youth Outland represents for the outward-bound realism of Augusta, "which endures from day to day." In " 'We Contacted Smithsonian': The Wetherills at Mesa Verde" (*NMHR* 62:229–48) David Harrell examines correspondence between B. K. Wetherill (father of pioneer archaeologists Richard and his brothers) and the Smithsonian—specifically secretary Samuel Pierpont and staff archaeologist William Henry Holmes—to discover the source of the bad press Cather gave the Institution in *The Professor's House* regarding its neglect of the Wetherills' findings at Mesa Verde. Harrell establishes the Smithsonian's concern and the Wetherills' mercenary interests as realities either unknown or ignored by Cather.

A Lost Lady is the subject of two essays previously unreviewed in these pages. In "From Region to the World: Two Allusions in *A Lost Lady*" (*Midamerica* 13 [1986]:61–68) Bruce Baker explores references in the novel to hyacinths and narcissus and explicates Shakespeare's Sonnet 94 for ways Cather transcends provinciality through floral imagery. In "Cutting and Planting"—Cather's *A Lost Lady*" (*PVR* 13[1985]:35–41) the late Brent Bohlke connects Cather's campaign to save Nebraska's cottonwoods to her views on the decline of pioneer values in the drama of Captain Forrester, the pioneer planter; his rootless wife Marian, for whom the "cutting of plants was . . . orgasmic," and villainous Ivy Peters, who cut down the willows in the Forrester marsh. *The Song of the Lark* is Shirley Foster's topic in "The Open Cage: Freedom, Marriage and the heroine—Early

Twentieth-Century American Women's Novels," her contribution to
Women's Writing: A Challenge to Theory, ed. Moira Monteith (St.
Martin's, 1986), pp. 154–74. Foster clusters Cather's novel, Wharton's
The House of Mirth, and Kate Chopin's The Awakening as a progression in viewing women in society: in Wharton's novel Lily Bart is
compared to a bird caged by conditions restricting her to marriage;
Chopin's doomed Edna Pontellier identifies with a free but injured
bird, while Thea Kronborg soars like an eagle to achievement outside marriage. In "Willa Cather and Football: A Strange Duality"
(PVR 14[1986]:7–19) Virgil Albertini examines two of Cather's college essays, the ghost story "The Fear that Walks by Noonday,"
and the football sequence in One of Ours to establish Cather's fundamental understanding of the game and awareness of its changes
and modifications between the 90s and the teens. He speculates
convincingly that Nebraska football great Guy Chamberlain, whom
Cather saw play against Notre Dame in 1915 and who was lured
away from Nebraska Wesleyan by the Cornhuskers, might be a prototype for football-playing Claude Wheeler. Cather's last novel is
Marilyn Arnold's subject in "'Of Human Bondage': Cather's Sub-
narrative in Sapphira and the Slave Girl" (MissQ 40:323–38). Arnold
makes Cather like Wharton in this antebellum southern novel (although she doesn't make the connection) in reflecting through language and architecture (the opening sentence as well as the facade
of Sapphira's house, for example) a society based on privilege and
appearances while exploring the effects of such a system on characters: the slave Till, Rachel Blake, Henry Colbert, and Sapphira
herself.

Cather short stories are the subject of Virgil Albertini's "Willa
Cather and the Bicycle" (PVR 15:12–22), a somewhat rambling
speculation on Cather's prowess as a cyclist, on her athletic friend
Louse Pound as the prototype of the title character in "Tommy, the
Unsentimental," and on the role of and allusions to bicycles in this
story, "A Death in the Desert," "Ardessa," and "Before Breakfast."
In "Why Willa Cather Revised 'Paul's Case': The Work in Art and
Those Sunday Afternoons" (AL 59:590–608) David A. Carpenter
says Cather revisioned Frank Norris's brand of naturalism in her
editing of this story from The Troll Garden (1905) for inclusion in
Youth and the Bright Medusa (1920), emphasizing environment
("life-destroying" American business values) over heredity as the
destructive force within Paul. The points the article makes are valid

if obvious, although Carpenter's complaints about criticism failing
to do justice to the story are weakened by his failure to consider
significant work of the last dozen or so years. Ada L. Van Gastel
calls attention in "An Unpublished Poem by Willa Cather" (*RALS*
14[1984]:153–59) to "Sunday on the Seine" in the Library of Pennsylvania State University, a poem omitted by Bernice Slote in her
"Checklist" of Cather poems in the 1962 reissue of *April Twilights*
(1903). Van Gastel notes that motifs of Nebraska, France, and hero
worship, and the description of Rouen connect the poem to other
Cather works, dates the manuscript as 1920 rather than 1902, as is
penciled in, and includes the 71 lines of free verse with a list of
textual emendations.

There are some interesting general considerations of Cather from
a variety of perspectives. Judith Fryer's "Desert, Rock, Shelter, Legend: Willa Cather's Novels of the Southwest" in *Desert Is No Lady:*
Southwestern Landscapes in Women's Writing, ed. Vera Norwood
and Janice Monk (Yale), pp. 27–46, is much more focused than her
book-length study of space in Wharton and Cather (*Felicitous Space*,
1986) and interesting for suggesting comparisons between Georgia
O'Keefe's multisensory memory approach to the southwestern landscape and Cather's approach in *The Song of the Lark, The Professor's*
House, and *Death Comes for the Archbishop* to "A place that can
be both sensed and touched, one that concentrates being within
limits that protect" and "one that frees the imagination." In the first
and last of these novels two complementary and integrating responses
to space are treated: the first, Thea Kronborg's, is tactile, physical, erotic"; the second, Bishop Latour's, is "spiritual, meditative, mystical."
Between these, in *The Professor's House*, Godfrey St. Peter's and
Tom Outland's are "mere mental operation[s]," "dividing mind and
body and celebrating in this division the supremacy of the rational."
Susan Rosowski's contribution to *The Rural Vision: France and*
America in the Nineteenth Century, ed. Hollister Sturges (Joslyn
Museum), "Willa Cather and the French Rural Tradition of Breton
and Millet: *O Pioneers!, The Song of the Lark*, and *My Ántonia* (pp.
53–61), relates *O Pioneers!* and *My Ántonia* to paintings of both
artists: the pastoral peacefulness of Alexandra Bergson in the first
novel reflects Breton, while a vigorous rendering of landscape and
sky reflects Millet; in *My Ántonia* tension exists between Jim Burden's Breton-like tendency toward pastoral and Ántonia's refusal to
be so typed. Rosowski claims that *The Song of the Lark*, titled from

Breton's painting, weakens where art substitutes for nature as artistic inspiration, or as Breton's example substitutes for Millet's. Rosowski tackles another connection in her contribution to *Geography and Literature: A Meeting of the Disciplines*, ed. William E. Mallory and Paul Simpson-Housley (Syracuse), "Willa Cather and the Fatality of Place; *O Pioneers!, My Ántonia*, and *A Lost Lady*" (pp. 80–94), which tries to mold these novels into a "trilogy of place." In the first Cather revised the fairy tale "Beauty and the Beast" to show in Alexandra Bergson a creative female interacting with land which then manifests its beauty. Ántonia Shimerda in the second novel is seen as the nature child of this female-land union, and in the third novel status, class, and power emerge with control of the land by petty men who sacrifice it to materialism. Finally, in *Cather's Kitchens: Foodways in Literature and life* (Nebraska) Roger L. and Linda K. Welsch provide a valuable fun book, which, besides including prairie recipes in chapters ranging from "Meat" to "Sweets and Treats," shows the importance of food as a literary device in *My Ántonia, O Pioneers!, One of Ours*, and "Neighbour Rosicky." "Foods in Cather's works are never employed casually or superficially," they conclude. In her perceptive foreword to this volume (ix–xv) Susan Rosowski notes that food quality and service decline in relation to life itself in Cather's darker fiction before *Death Comes for the Archbishop*, which then "offers a vast array of foods and meats." Some wonderful photos are included, one depicting a middle-aged Cather at a golf course picnic and another of an elderly Anna Pavelka (prototype of Ántonia) carrying a birthday cake.

ii. Edith Wharton

Wharton approaches Cather in getting the lion's share of attention from critics, confirming her status as a major American novelist of this century. *College Literature* devoted an entire issue to Wharton's fiction (14:iii:193–309), making available the papers given at the June 1987 Edith Wharton Society conference, "Edith Wharton at the Mount." Katherine Joslin surveys Wharton's reputation at the hands of an unsympathetic critical establishment from Percy Lubbock to Alfred Kazin in "Edith Wharton at 125" (pp. 193–206). These critics successfully consigned her to the marginal in American literature for reasons of genre (the novel of manners) as well as gender until feminist critics like Cynthia Wolff and Elizabeth Ammons rescued her as a major writer. Ammons's contribution, "New Literary History: Edith Wharton and Jessie Redman Fauset" (pp. 207–18), draws some parallels between Wharton's life and that of the Harlem Renaissance author and between Fauset's *Comedy, American Style* (1933) and *The Custom of the Country*, and Fauset's *Plum Bun* (1929) and *The House of Mirth* to conclude with a challenge to white feminists and male critics that what they conceive of as universal often amounts to "race-bound paradigms." In "Muzzled Women" (pp. 219–29) Marilyn French questions why women writers like Wharton, Cather, and the "Georges" (Sand and Eliot) failed to create women characters as independent and extraordinary as they themselves were, choosing instead to depict restricted and drab women's lives. She feels sexual prejudice inadequate to explain the disparity between these novelists and male counterparts whose "work does not as nearly universally focus on constrictions." Cynthia Griffin Wolff admonishes us in "Cool Ethan and 'Hot Ethan'" (pp. 230–45) against forcing parallels between authors' lives and works and then proceeds to draw them between Wharton's marriage to Teddy and affair with Morton Fullerton and the situation of her title character in *Ethan Frome*, who fails to escape marriage to an invalid in another relationship, and Charity Royall's failure with Lucius Harney in *Summer*. The sobering lesson Wharton learned from life is echoed in these Berkshire novels: "Freedom can never be complete, and insofar as joy can be sustained, it must be accomodated to the demands of the real world." Margaret B. McDowell's "Edith Wharton's *The Old Maid*: Novella/Play/Film" (pp. 246–62) is a detailed comparison of the original Wharton story with Zoë Akins's 1935 play and Warner Brothers' 1939 film, which makes the point that the success of these subsequent dramatic forms (in which Wharton's attention to social milieu, "inutility of sacrifice" theme, and the conflict between passion and orderliness were either distorted or obscured) depended as much on departure from the Wharton original as on faithfulness to her basic story line and dialogue. In "Lilies That Fester: Sentimentality in *The House of Mirth*" (pp. 263–75) Robin Beaty sees the novel's "tension between the popular sentimental form and the ironic art of unfolding" as breaking down in the last two chapters, in which sentimentality overwhelms both Lily Bart's complexity as a character and the distance between the reader and Lawrence Selden's feelings. In "Ward McAllister: Beau Nash of *The Age of Innocence*" (pp. 276–84) Rhoda Nathan identifies McAllister as the prototype of Sillerton

Jackson and Lawrence Lefferts, the social "authorities" in Wharton's novel, and McAllister's book *Society As I Have Found It* as one of Wharton's sources. A recently unearthed copy with notations by Mc-Allister himself establishes his intimacy with Wharton's family (the Joneses) and identifies several personages she later used as characters. Moira Maynard contrasts Sophy Viner and Anna Leath in "Moral Integrity in *The Reef*: Justice to Anna Leath" (pp. 285–95), favoring the latter as "the thinking person's heroine" over the former, a more popular character who follows her feelings rather than, like Anna, disciplining herself to discover the disturbing truth and her responsibility to others. Finally, Annette Zilversmit analyzes "The Pomegranate Seed" (1931) and "All Souls'" (1937) as representing the suppressed feelings of defeated women about other women in "Edith Wharton's Last Ghosts" (pp. 296–305). The earlier story expresses the heroine's fears that she is neither sexually desirable nor deserving, and "Souls'," the last story Wharton completed, expresses its heroine's denial of guilty passions.

In a perceptive general chapter, "Edith Wharton: The Female Imagination and the Territory Within" in her study *Gender and the Writer's Imagination* (pp. 157–82), Mary Suzanne Schriber makes Wharton revolutionary in using a major rather than a lesser genre to "imagine more fully and deeply than her male counterparts [Howells and James] the consequences of the culture's ideology of women." Wharton was able to dramatize the effects of issues like unformalized sexual partnership in *The Gods Arrive*, female intellectual superiority in *Twilight Sleep* and *Hudson River Bracketed*, and sexual prohibitions for women in *The Reef* and *The Custom of the Country*. Schriber concludes that while Wharton did not deny the distinct nature of each sex, she argued that American women suffered from being kept in kindergarten, excluded from extra-domestic concerns. In another general article, "Edith Wharton's Erotic Other-World" (*L&P* 23, i: 12–29), Virginia L. Blum sees the "recurrence of a certain pattern" involving male "fascination" with dead women in three ghost stories ("Miss Mary Pask," "Pomegranate Seed," and "Bewitched") as reflecting Freudian bisection of the feminine into angel-whore and complicated in Wharton's major works where male attitudes make dead women "safer (because less demanding)" than living women but vampire women as the whore carried to her logical extreme, the "fulfillment of the male dread of sexual depletion." According to Blum, Lily Bart in *The House of Mirth* and Mattie Silver in *Ethan*

Frome sense that their men require them dead, and the marriages of Charity Royall in *Summer* and May Welland in *The Age of Innocence* are equated with death of the senses.

The *House of Mirth* continues to emerge as Wharton's most analyzed novel, generating eight significant articles. In "Divided Selves and the Market Society: Politics and Psychology in *The House of Mirth*" (*PCL* 11[1985]:10–19) Robert Shulman sees the novel as an exploration of the effects of American capitalism, the collapse of social relations into market relations, and Lily Bart's failure as stemming from a conflict involving self-alienation. While Lawrence Selden counters Lily's mother's advice on preserving and peddling her beauty for profit with his ideas on the "republic of the spirit," his alternative encourages her alienation from sexuality and contributes to self-disgust. A curious example of contemporary textual re-creation and association, Walter Benn Michaels's comments on this novel in *Gold Standard*, pp. 217–44, relates accident to what is artistic in photography, economic speculation, gambling, ethics. Selden's accident-free "republic of the spirit" (I have always interpreted accident here as the opposite of essence and not the result of chance!) trivializes human efforts by making them mechanical. Writing itself becomes "a paradigm for an exciting loss of self-control" (a complete reversal from late Victorian psychology), and Lily's appearance as Reynolds's "Mrs. Lloyd" in the act of writing represents Wharton herself taking "the risk [in this world of accidents] that produces the power of dramatic interest." Frances L. Restuccia essentially bases the novel on "two feminisms" in "The Name of the Lily: Edith Wharton's Feminism(s)" (*ConL* 28:223–38). It is at once an indictment against society's creating and then crushing women as ornaments and, more significantly, an exploration of male attempts to define the illusive feminine. Restuccia applies Roland Barthes's theories on works and texts to Selden's emphasis on fate and tendency to harden Lily into a work while she puts faith in luck and acts paradoxically: "Wharton invites us to view Lily as an analogue of art, but we must take care in constructing the parallel, avoiding the legalistic [male] tendency to . . . wash away . . . ambiguity, . . . to read Lily as art *object* . . . as a work rather than a text." In spite of some overly authoritative statements on Wharton's beliefs and theories on fiction and society, Roslyn Dixon in "Reflecting Vision in *The House of Mirth*" (*TCL* 33:211–22) argues convincingly that Wharton's overriding concern in this novel is morality and that she was modern in substituting for a moral center conflicting points of view on what society really values. Lily tries to measure up to the ideals Selden mouths but fails to live and to the Christian principles which would give meaning to her sacrifice but no longer function as the basis of society. Rosedale is considered crucial for showing Lily how to survive in the new power context. In "'Natural Magic': Irony as Unifying Strategy in *The House of Mirth*" (*SCRev* 4:82–91) Carol Miller sees Wharton's major achievement in the use of irony as a bonding mechanism with the "intended effect of overcoming the intrinsic separation of writer and reader." Applying this mechanism to Lily Bart's painful growth and final alienation becomes ironic in itself and enables Wharton to juxtapose "superficially contending elements of romance, realism, and naturalism." Miller analyzes the scene between Lily and Selden at Bellomont as an instance in which naturalism and romantic images merge to create tensions among freedom, isolation, and Lily's immediate obligations. In "*The Awakening* and *The House of Mirth*: Studies of Arrested Development" (*ALR* 19, iii:27–41) C. J. Wershoven distinguishes the Chopin and Wharton novels as unique in posing questions about failed female struggles for self-development rather than offering "paragons of uplift," heroines who emerge as mythic or strong enough to achieve intellectual or emotional independence: "Both Lily and Edna move, albeit unsteadily, through the steps— dissatisfaction, rebellion, renunciation and isolation—toward a new identity. . . . [but] are doubly trapped; they have developed an embryonic new identity, but this new self is too weak to struggle alone." Sea imagery, opposing states of awareness, and symbols of childbirth encapsulating this aborted identity crown the significant parallels Wershoven discovers. Robert A. Gates's second chapter, "The Polarized City: Edith Wharton's *The House of Mirth* and Stephen Crane's *Maggie*," in his *The New York Vision: Interpretations of New York City in the American Novel* (Univ. Press), pp. 29–61, is valuable for background on what was unique in the city, the extreme disparity between the wealthy and the poor, and how that provided both novelists with subjects. The determinism of the economic disparity theme is treated in both novels with considered attention to the rootlessness, ignorance, confusion, isolation, and moral paralysis caused by the system. Although Wharton is given full credit as historian of wealthy New York, it is perhaps presumptuous to make Crane her counterpart, in light of his somewhat minuscule output, as historian of New York's poor. Finally, in "*Vanity Fair* in America: *The House*

of Mirth and *Gone with the Wind*" (*AL* 59:37–57) Paul Pickrel backs
into a speculation on Wharton's debt to Thackeray in her masterpiece
before gauging Margaret Mitchell's debt to the Englishman in hers.
Comparing titles, characters (Lily Bart to Becky Sharp, Lawrence
Selden to Rawdon Crawley, and Gus Trenor to Lord Steyne), the
heroines' involvement in entertainments and gambling, the importance of written material, and noting a cluster of structural parallels,
Pickrel concludes that what Wharton owed to Thackeray in her portrait of a fragile and tragic social insider was merely a "vehicle to
express attitudes more or less the opposite of his."

Foremost among the work on other novels is James W. Gargano's
"Tableau of Renunciation: Wharton's Use of the *Shaughran* in *The
Age of Innocence*" (*SAF* 14:1–11), a much-needed analysis of Wharton's employment of Dion Boucicault's Irish comedy to balance her
use of Gounod's opera *Faust* and reflect the theme of restraint and
renunciation as opposed to freedom and self-gratification. Gargano
shows how the farewell episode in the play's second act as staged for
the 1874 New York production influenced seven scenes in the novel:
when Archer advises Ellen against divorce, during and after the enactment of the play itself, the end of the first book, on the Newport
Beach, the Boston boat, May's carriage scene, and the conclusion.
Using feminist theories of Shoshana Felmen and Luce Irigaray, Lin-
ette Davis associates patriarchal society, including male sexual and
economic power, with linguistic cover-up and skillfully controlled
innocence in "Vulgarity and Red Blood in *The Age of Innocence*"
(*JMMLA* 20, ii:1–8). Since Ellen Olenska's "vulgar" habit of speaking
straight threatens Newland Archer and his society, he remains with
May, who preserves the facade of innocence while being "the only
one to whom we can ascribe a knowledge at least as comprehensive
as our own." In "Mocking Fate: Romantic Idealism in Edith Wharton's *The Reef*" (*SNNTS* 19:459–74) James W. Tuttleton examines
the 1912 novel within the context of Wharton's sexual awakening and
disillusionment during and after her affair with Morton Fullerton and
sees the "Jamesian geometry" of its structure as controlling potentially
explosive material. While many modern feminists favor the sexually
liberated Sophy Viner, it is Anna Leath who reflects the author and
approaches an independent, uncompromising heroine, he argues.
The novel becomes "problematic for feminists who wish to assert a
conception of sexual freedom . . . which seems suspiciously like the
promiscuity for which men have usually been condemned." Whar-

ton's four novellas on Old New York occupy two critics. In "The Narrative Structure of *Old New York*: Text and Pictures in Edith Wharton's Quartet of Linked Short Stories" (*JNT* 17:76–82) Adeline R. Tintner tries to establish with limited success that these 1924 works intentionally combine and develop several techniques Wharton found in her models: Balzac's "La Comédie humaine," James's *The Finer Grain*, F. Marion Crawford's 1894–95 New York novels, and Proust's *Swann's Way*. Such techniques include arranging stories according to decades and separate social sins, vivid openings, a recurrent narrator and recurrent characters and family names, concealment and gradual revelation of crucial factors, accumulation of ironies, and indexical icons. Wharton's collaboration with her illustrator recalls James's partnership with photographer Alvin Langdon for the New York Edition. Leslie Fishbein discusses the final work in this volume as a commentary on fluctuating moral standards during the sexually tolerant 1920s in "Prostitution, Morality, and Paradox: Moral Relativism in Edith Wharton's *Old New York: New Year's Day* (The 'Seventies')" (*SSF* 24:399–406). Because Freudian doctrines were being popularized and conveniently distorted, and drama, fiction, and films were blurring distinctions between "good" and "bad" women, the sympathy given adultress Lizzie Hazeldean is not a shocking "anomaly" but a reflection of the "moral ambiguities" of the author herself in the decade when she wrote the novella.

Four articles appeared on Wharton's short stories. In *Poe and Our Times: Influences and Affinities*, ed. Benjamin Franklin Fisher IV (Poe Society, 1986) Eleanor Dwight's "Edith Wharton and 'The Cask of Amontillado' " (pp. 49–57) establishes that "The Duchess at Prayer" owes its dialogue and setting to the Poe story and its plot to Balzac's "La grande Bretèche." Although Poe's and Wharton's techniques are opposite (hers depending on gaining readers' confidence before luring them into fantasy), Dwight sees other Wharton stories as probably indebted to Poe ("The Eyes" to "The Tell-Tale Heart," "Kerfol" to "The Black Cat"). Jean Frantz Blackall confines her discussion to short stories in "Edith Wharton's Art of Ellipsis" (*JNT* 17: 145–62), illustrating Wharton's calculated use of ellipses to "entice the reader into imaginative collaboration with the writer," represent the inexpressible, suggest colloquial speech, emulate thought rhythms, indicate mental realignment, and so on. In "Framing in Two Opposite Modes: Ford and Wharton" (*Comparatist* 10 [1986]: 114–20) Mary Ann Caws uses "The Other Two" to illustrate the ironic effects of a shifting framing narration in contrast to the tragic effects of the stable frame used by Ford Madox Ford in *The Good Soldier*. In "A Twist of Crimson Silk: Edith Wharton's 'Roman Fever' " (*SSF* 24:263–67) Alice Hall Petry analyzes knitting as both shielding Grace Ansley and then exposing her sensuality to the previously domineering Alida Slade, who after her defeat hides behind the knitting Grace has relinquished. Through knitting we "perceive the ladies as stereotypical matrons; and the story will be devoted to obliterating this stereotype . . . ."

Foremost among miscellaneous items is Mary Suzanne Schriber's "Edith Wharton and Travel Writing as Self-Discovery" (*AL* 59: 257–67), which speculates on the reasons for Wharton's expatriation in 1910 and sees *A Motor-Flight Through France* (1908) as anticipating her decision. Associating travel writing with self-discovery, Schriber ingeniously views it as a quest for the Grail, analyzing Wharton's shaping of materials into a struggle for salvation with the art and history of Europe substituting for the Savior. Using America as an inferior point of reference for a superior European culture, "Wharton could no longer resist the desire to immerse herself continually in the history and culture that energized her." Shari Benstock re-creates in two chapters of her book *Women of the Left Bank: Paris, 1900–1940* (Texas, 1986), p. 37–98, Wharton's introduction to life in Paris's Faubourg St. Germain, emphasizing the traditional conservatism of the salon society she frequented, one outside of and denigrated as sterile and stuffy in sexually liberated Parisian intellectual circles. Wharton is grouped with Colette, Stein, and Natalie Barney, women for whom "writing was a remedy for a life . . . too rigidly controlled by tradition" but out of sympathy with the "radical otherness" of lesbianism. What emerges is the portrait of a writer on the edge of modernism calling for liberated women so they could be stimulated by male intellects. Finally, Marlene Springer and Joan Gilson in "Edith Wharton: A Reference Guide Updated" (*RALS* 14 [1984]:85–111) supplement the Wharton material in Springer's 1976 *Edith Wharton and Kate Chopin: A Reference Guide* with secondary sources published between 1973 and 1984. Each entry receives a brief and informative annotation adequate for articles but not for book-length studies. The listing seems comprehensive enough, and I am indebted to the bibliographers for calling my attention to Leon Edel's biographical analysis of "All Souls' " in his 1982 *Stuff of Sleep and Dreams* (pp. 36–41); however, the omission of R. W. B. Lewis's groundbreaking *Edith Wharton: A Biography* among the 1975 entries is somewhat baffling. The 166 entries this update contains indicate decidedly growing interest in Wharton and her fiction.

iii. Theodore Dreiser and Jack London

No books were devoted exclusively to Dreiser this year, but continuing strong interest in this author was manifested by the appearance of about 20 articles and chapters. Most of these fall within three main categories of interest or approach: (1) treatments of Dreiser's leftist political-social-economic opinions and the way they are reflected in his fiction; (2) examinations of Dreiser's knowledge and use of Freudian concepts and applications of such concepts to Dreiser and his fiction; and (3) presentations of hitherto unpublished or unrecognized writing by Dreiser and considerations of the interpretive implications of evolving versions of Dreiser texts.

Boris Gilenson provides in "Dreiser and the Soviet Union" (*SovL* 5:142–48) a Soviet perspective on Dreiser's communist sympathies. Providing little new information, Gilenson summarizes Dreiser's 70-day visit to the Soviet Union in 1927–28 and notes his knowledge of and admiration for Russian authors. Emphasizing Dreiser's move to the left after that visit, he disagrees with American critics who see Dreiser's last 20 years as a decline and asserts that his topical writing and public activism patterned after the Soviet Union moved him beyond mere creative writing into the political forum of the left. Philip Gerber's informative and authoritative biographical essay "Dreiser: The Great Sloth of the Thirties" (*ON* 11[1985]:7–23) gives a very different view of the significance of Dreiser's political activism in the 1930s. Gerber addresses the question of why Dreiser's fortunes and reputation declined during that decade when they were at their zenith at the end of the 20s. His answer is that changing literary fashions combined with personal troubles to frustrate his attempts at writing and undermine his health. At the same time that he was drawn into leftist activism and social causes, he was unsuccessfully trying to finish his trilogy with *The Stoic*, a work that went against the grain of leftist fashion. Moreover, despite his strong political views, he resisted the notion that fiction could be written out of ideology. It wasn't until the 1940s in Hollywood that he recovered his fortunes with movie rights and eventually completed *The Stoic* and *The Bulwark*. Joseph Griffin provides a sidelight to Dreiser's communist sympathies in "Howard Fast, James T. Farrell, and *The Best Short Stories of Theodore Dreiser*" (*IFR* 14:79–83). World Publishing Company commissioned Howard Fast, a communist, to select and introduce a collection of Dreiser stories in 1947. When World reissued the collection in 1956, they followed the temper of the times and employed James T. Farrell to do an introduction without emphasis on Dreiser's communism.

The recent interest in a historicism that views literature in relation to socioeconomic circumstances, particularly those emphasized by Marx, is reflected in Stanley Corkin's "*Sister Carrie* and Industrial Life: Objects and the New American Self" (*MFS* 33:605–19) and Carol A. Schwartz's "*Jennie Gerhardt*: Fairy Tale as Social Criticism" (*ALR* 19, ii:16–29). Noting that *Sister Carrie* appeared in the midst of a fundamental economic and social upheaval caused by industrialization and urbanization, Corkin suggests that the novel was poorly received partly because its impact depends on the reader's comprehension of "the world of commodities." The public at that time was only beginning to understand Marx's notion of the alienating and objectifying effects of industrial labor and consequently failed to recognize the industrial workplace as the key metaphor for all human relationships in the novel. Schwartz argues that emphasis on Dreiser's naturalism and determinism misleadingly prevents us from appreciating his social-political concern with economics and class distinctions. Emphasizing "the primacy of class consciousness in the human psyche," she asserts that even the fairy-tale elements in *Jennie Gerhardt* lead toward rather than away from class conflict because "the economic and social bases of the fairy tale anticipate the overt commodification of sex and human values under industrial capitalism." Similar concerns are displayed in Walter Benn Michaels's *Gold Standard*. This volume in a series titled "The New Historicism: Studies in Cultural Poetics" includes two previously published essays on *Sister Carrie* and *The Financier*. Carol Shloss's chapter "Theodore Dreiser, Alfred Stieglitz, and Jacob Riis: Envisioning 'The Other Half'" in her *In Visible Light*, pp. 93–139, also focuses on Dreiser's treatment of the working class. The contrasting views of Stieglitz and Riis (the former interested in the picturesque aspects of the poor, the latter with liberal reform) helped Dreiser assess his own relation to poverty and how to treat it in fiction. Dreiser could see the virtues of both perspectives but eventually went beyond Stieglitz's detached artistic approach to a commitment to social justice. Shloss interprets

The "Genius" as demonstrating the two modes of seeing represented by Stieglitz and Riis and the dilemma of the artist outgrowing the photographic picturesque of the first and assuming the obligations of the second.

Among the category of articles concerned with psychoanalytic concepts, the most ambitious is Stephen C. Brennan's "Theodore Dreiser's *An Amateur Laborer*: A Myth in the Making" (*ALR* 19, ii: 66–84). Drawing upon Freud, Lacan, Lévi-Strauss, Girard, Frye, and others, Brennan provides an ingenious psychoanalytic-mythic interpretation of the unfinished autobiographical piece (published 1983) that tells of Dreiser's nervous breakdown in 1902–03. The essay is overly ingenious, and the interpretive concepts seem too pliable and accommodating. There is something Procrustean in its selecting of concepts from fashionable theorists and then delineating parallels in Dreiser's work. Terry Whalen displays a more modest approach in "Dreiser's Tragic Sense: The Mind as 'Poor Ego' " (*ON* 11[1985]:61–80). Without pressing the point too hard, Whalen argues that Dreiser was influenced by Freud. The characters in *Sister Carrie* and *An American Tragedy* are not shaped solely by rigid deterministic forces but are in an embattled position similar to that in Freud's description of the ego, and Dreiser's tragic sense displays an affinity with Freud's. George H. Douglas reacts against Vera Dreiser's essentially Freudian treatment of Dreiser's mother in her *My Uncle Theodore* (1976), which he sees perpetuated in Richard Lingeman's 1986 biography. In "The Revisionist Views of Sarah Schanab Dreiser" (*DrS* 18, 1: 22–30) he finds the psychoanalytically founded indictments of the mother unconvincing and ultimately irrelevant to explaining Dreiser and his work. Implicit psychoanalytic assumptions underlie Joseph Church's observation in "Minnie's Dreams in *Sister Carrie*" (*CL* 14: 183–87) that Minnie's dreams not only foreshadow Carrie's future but also reveal disturbances in Minnie's own psyche. Through an examination of the textual history of Dreiser's play *The Hand of the Potter*, which contains a reference to Freud, Frederic E. Rusch in "Dreiser's Introduction to Freudianism" (*DrS* 18, ii:34–37) attempts to clarify exactly when Dreiser was introduced to Freud's writings and by whom.

In the category of articles introducing unknown or unavailable Dreiser texts are Thomas P. Riggio's "Dreiser: Autobiographical Fragment, 1911" (*DrS* 18, i:12–21) and T. D. Nostwich's "Dreiser's 'Poet of Potter's Field' " (*DrS* 18, ii:2–20). The former introduces and annotates a printed version of a 22-page holograph fragment in which Dreiser assesses his merits as a novelist, considers his role as a realist, and provides a glimpse of his state of mind in 1911. The latter is a reprint of and commentary on an 1893 feature story in the *St. Louis Republican*, which Nostwich identifies by internal and external evidence as Dreiser's. Three articles analyze and interpret the history of particular Dreiser texts. In comparing the 1981 Pennsylvania edition of *Sister Carrie* with the 1900 edition in "Robert Ames Restored: The Third Man in the Unexpurgated *Sister Carrie*" (*PMPA* 11[1986]:34–40), Charles C. Nash concludes that the revised Ames (1900 edition) is a more consistent character but less satisfying because aloof and detached. A misplaced quotation mark in a key scene of *Jennie Gerhardt* (Jennie's final interview with Lester Kane) is James L. W. West III's focus in "Double Quotes and Double Meanings in *Jennie Gerhardt*" (*DrS* 18, i:1–11). In "The Composition and Publication of 'Another American Tragedy': Dreiser's 'Typhoon' " (*PBSA* 81:25–35) James M. Hutchinson reconstructs the compositional history of the short story "Typhoon," annotating the variations, delineating the revisions made by editors, and concluding that the prepublication versions are richer and more characteristic of Dreiser.

Among the books on Jack London this year, James Lundquist's contribution to Ungar's Life and Literature series, *Jack London: Adventures, Ideas, and Fiction*, is the most significant. This competent critical biography, which includes a useful chronology and selected bibliography, is unified by the thesis that London's reading and devotion to ideas shaped his writing just as much as did his adventures: "In few other writers can we find such a successfully complex intermingling of experience and ideas." Lundquist tends to be suspicious of biographical information coming only from London and questions the commonplace that London lived a greater story than he wrote. For better or worse, London put every action and decision to the test of an idea or theory. Also focusing on London's reading is David Mike Hamilton's *"The Tools of My Trade": The Annotated Books in Jack London's Library* (Washington, 1986), the purpose of which is to explore, through an introductory essay and annotated bibliography, London's use of books and pamphlets as source material for his fiction and reference material for his general education. Hamilton's introduction corroborates Lundquist's thesis in noting that expression was easier than invention for London, who relied heavily on what he read for material to supplement his own experience. Hamilton's 47-page introduction is primarily an extensive listing of the books London read during different stages of his career. Also of interest is a reprint of *Jack London on the Road: The Tramp Diary and Other Hobo Writings*, ed. Richard W. Etulian (Utah State). First published in 1979, this was the first complete printing of the tramp diary and also includes all of London's fiction, essays, and other writings (except *The Road*) dealing with his tramp experience.

Most of the articles and chapters on London this year were biographical. In a 1984 interview London's daughter Becky, who was in her second year of high school when her father died, describes her childhood memories of London's appearance and behavior (Tony Williams, "Memories of Jack: An Interview with Becky London," *JLN* 19[1986]:1–10). On the assumption that few people—even among London enthusiasts—realize the extent to which London was an orator, Mark E. Zamen in "London" (*JLN* 18[1985]:36–46) describes the author's career as a lecturer, from his high school graduation speech to a dinner speech just months before his death. Miriam Shillingsburg examines and contributes to what is known about London's five months in Australia recuperating from various illnesses acquired during his cruise of the South Pacific on the *Snark*. In "Jack London, Socialist, in Sydney" (*AuLS* 13:223–36) she adds information from recently uncovered newspaper articles, one of which from a socialist paper she reprints as an appendix. Earle Labor provides a brief overview of London's life and career with an emphasis on the stories and books dealing with California in his contribution to *A Literary History of the West*, pp. 381–97.

Feminist criticism is represented in the articles treating London's fiction by Joseph A. Boone's "Male Independence and the American Quest Genre: Hidden Sexual Politics in the All-Male Worlds of Melville, Twain and London" in *Gender Studies: New Directions in Feminist Criticism*, ed., Judith Spector (Bowling Green, 1986), pp. 187–217. Diverging, on the one hand, from the view of male questing in classic American fiction as arrested adolescence and, on the other, from the view of feminist critics who dismiss the genre as exclusively patriarchal, Boone claims that beneath the surface of such works is "an ambivalent exploration of sexual politics, including a potentially radical critique of the patriarchal norms, restrictive roles, and sexual inequality characterizing nineteenth-century American familial and social life." He fits *The Sea-Wolf* into this thesis.

Film criticism is represented in two articles by Tony Williams: "From London's *The Unexpected* to Kuleshov's *By the Law*" (*JLN* 19[1986]:55–68) and "History and Interpretation in the 1941 Version of Jack London's *The Sea-Wolf*" (*JLN* 19[1986]:78–88). The former begins with a concept from recent film theory stipulating that a film has "a specific textual system" differing from its literary source and argues that *By the Law*, a film adaptation of London's *The Unexpected* done by Lev Kuleshov, an early and important talent in the development of Soviet cinema, is a successful reworking of the source in the context of Marxist ideology and a new school of cinematic techniques. The latter article likewise focuses on the political ideology behind the film in question and explains that the 1941 version of *The Sea-Wolf* was an antifascist allegory made by a director, producer, scenarist, and actors who were all of leftist-liberal sympathies and attuned to the film's contemporary relevance. Tony Williams, the dominant voice of *JLN*, demonstrates the same social-political concerns in "*The Mutiny of the Elsinore*—A Re-evaluation" (*JLN* 19 [1986]:13–41), an attempt by an enthusiast to stimulate interest in a neglected and devalued London work. He wishes to persuade us that the racism and glorification of the ruling class conveyed in the novel are not expressions of London's own beliefs.

iv. Gertrude Stein and Sherwood Anderson

The more dense of the year's 16 entries on Stein concern theoretical questions. Stein's invitation to lecture at Cambridge and Oxford in 1926 and the translation of some of her writing into French between 1926 and 1928 motivated her to develop theories about the work she had been doing, according to Ulla Dydo in "Landscape Is Not Grammar: Gertrude Stein in 1928" (*Raritan* 7, i:97–113). Dydo examines her juxtaposition of landscape and grammar in "Arthur A. Grammar" (1928), a "show-and-tell book of Stein grammar," and in *A Bouquet. Their Wills.* (1928) a six-act "Baltimore opera." Stein "came to perceive, in areas other than language, the stifling nature of 'grammars'— structured forms and closed systems. It was a dark vision." Dinnah Pladott's "The Semiotics of Post-Modern Theatre: Gertrude Stein" in *Approaches of the Opera: Proceedings of the IASPA Seminar*

(Didier, 1986), pp. 302–14, relates the central concerns of Stein's postmodern operas and plays to the central topics in current theoretical and critical debate (Derrida's rejection of the primacy of the work, Bakhtin's insights about "heteroglossia," Kristeva's notions about intertextuality, and so on) while tracing them back to the revolutionary ideas of Richard Wagner—the use of music to achieve a "waking dream" rather than rational and conscious coherence in theater. In "Postmodernist Portraits" (*Art Jour.* 46:173–77) Wendy Steiner sees the very paradoxes and shortcomings of the portrait genre as challenges to a modernist writer like Stein, whose own portraiture includes repetition, tension between arrested time and sequence, conflict between type and individual, ambiguity between individuality and public image, and the threat of self-reference—elements applicable to postmodernist portraits by Andy Warhol, Robert Rauschenberg, Chuck Close, and David Hockney. Elizabeth Winston in "Making History in *The Mother of Us All*" (*Mosaic* 20, iv:117–29) affirms that in her libretto Stein used characters as alter egos, played with names, and manipulated biography and history to convey her central theme of women's relationship to the patriarchal tradition. In the character of Indiana Elliot, whose name alludes to Stein's literary foremothers ("Georges" Eliot and Sand and Charlotte Brontë), Stein traced her development from male-identified artist to one acknowledging kinship with the sisterhood. Cynthia Merrill's "Mirrored Image: Gertrude Stein and Autobiography" (*PCP* 20:11–17) is a complex exploration of the problem of identity in Stein as similar to Jacques Lacan's concept of the role of the visual (mirror) image of the self in establishing identity and to conventional narrative structure in its dependence on chronology, circumstance, and memory. Thus identity, like narrative, is relational and, for Stein, interfered with creativity, as she indicated in telling about Picasso's portrait of her. To satisfy both the audience's desire for narrative and her own artistic principles, Stein flaunted rather than concealed gaps between the writing subject and narrator in *The Autobiography of Alice B. Toklas* by writing as Alice and creating a fiction to reveal a fiction. Nancy Blake's "'An Exact Precession': Leonardo, Gertrude, and Guy Davenport's *Da Vinci's Bicycle*" in *Critical Angles: European Views of Contemporary American Literature*, ed. Marc Chénetier (So. Ill., 1986), pp. 145–52, also concerns Steinian concepts of identity and the other. When Stein questioned "the use of being born a little boy if you were going to grow up to be a man . . . . She was simply saying that when we look at our own life, we might as well be schizophrenic, because we are looking at the history of another. This is the refrain of the whole of *Da Vinci's Bicycle*."

Three articles focus exclusively on poetry. Catharine R. Stimpson's "Gertrude Stein and the Transposition of Gender" in *The Poetics of Gender*, ed. Nancy K. Miller (Columbia, 1986), pp. 1–18, examines and illustrates three poetic strategies Stein used to "juxtapose a reconstitution of patriarchal ideas about gender with their repudiation": preference for reconstitution over repudiation, balance of reconstitution and repudiation, and preference for repudiation over reconstitution. As a lesbian who both parodied and rebelled against heterosexuality, Stein was *the* encyclopedia of the poetics of gender among modern women poets. Doris T. Wight in "Hidden Feminism in Gertrude Stein's Roses and Rooms" (*Creative Woman* 8, ii:5–9) examines *Tender Buttons* as a Divine Comedy in which Alice, like Virgil and Beatrice, leads Gertrude through a hell of "Objects" and a purgatory of "Food" to a paradise of "Rooms" where Gertrude is free of domination by her brother and can accept herself of woman, lesbian, and writer. In "Woman as Eros-Rose—Gertrude Stein's *Tender Buttons* and Contemporaneous Portraits (*TWA* 4[1986]:34–40) Wight offers an analysis of "A Petticoat," relating it to other poems in the 1913 work ("In Between," "Red Roses," "Colored Hats," and "A Little Called Pauline") and to the portraits "Susie Asado," "Preciosilla," and "A Sweet Tail (Gypsies)," to argue that behind the dualism of Stein's Sibyllic (intellectual) and Sapphic (passionate) stances toward objects lurks the presence of Alice Toklas, the heroine who saves Gertrude through loving support in many of the portraits.

Stein's life seems to be of perennial interest. In "Visiting Gertrude and Alice" (*NYRB* 33, xvii:[1986]:36–38) Maurice Grosser, scenarist for *Four Saints in Three Acts*, recalls his dealings with Gertrude and Alice and the wreckage in friendship caused by the latter's jealousy and the former's perversity, claiming that the *Autobiography* presents "word for word" stories he heard Alice tell and is "entirely Alice's work." Alan R. Knight in "Explaining Composition: Gertrude Stein and the Problem of Representation" (*ESC* 13:406–19) expounds on Stein's frustration in interesting large commercial publishing houses in her work and uses her 1926 lecture at Oxford and Cambridge, "Composition as Explanation," to explore the method of reading her writing demands, differentiating between discourses of readerly and writerly texts. In her lectures and tours Stein tried to

create a market for the writerly text. In "Altered Patterns and New
Endings: Reflections of Change in Stein's *Three Lives* and H.D.'s
Palimpsest" (*Frontiers* 9, ii:54–59) Margaret M. Dunn compares
Stein's and Doolittle's lives and the styles and structures of their
novels, concluding that Stein altered the conventional patterns of
women's fiction by removing marriage as the pivotal point of success
and by making relationships with women more satisfying than those
with men. In *Women of the Left Bank* Shari Benstock devotes a long
chapter to Stein and Toklas (pp. 143–93), noting that Paris provided
Stein the freedom to establish a domestic homosexual relationship,
even though she remained separated from the city's literary community. Benstock praises Stein's ability to submit her will to language
and to cross-dress linguistically by using heterosexual grammar to
celebrate lesbian eroticism. *Three Penny Review* (31:3–5) makes
available a 1987 Elizabeth Hardwick lecture on Stein. Hardwick reviews the life and achievements with affection and candor, contributing a few gems in comparing the lifelike dialogue in "Melanctha" to
the "pre-fab" speech in Crane's *Maggie*, Stein's gift for epigram to
Oscar Wilde's, and Gertrude and Alice to a "diptych . . . . incono-
graphic in the Byzantine style." Erlene Hubly's "Gertrude Stein:
'When this you see, remember me. . . .'" (*NAR* 271, iii[1986]:65–74)
is a beautifully written account of a literary pilgrimage to Stein's
France by a group including the author and Stein scholar Robert
Haas. Hubly describes the house and gardens at Billignin, where
Stein and Toklas summered from 1929 to 1943, and the house at
Culoz where they hid from the Nazis during World War II. During
her visit Hubly grapples with the question of Stein's importance, noting her experiments with time, her capturing of ongoing change and
daily life in these French locales, and the bond her presence has
established between Frenchmen and Americans. Finally, in "Picasso's
Time of Decisive Encounters" (*ART News* 86, iv:136–41) Pierre Daix
comments on the role played by Leo and especially Gertrude Stein in
helping the painter move beyond his circle of Spaniards in Mont-
martre toward friendship with important young French painters of
his time, including Henri Matisse. Picasso may have seen in Gertrude,
whose portrait he began soon after their meeting in 1905, a prototype
for his massive female figures.

    In *Sherwood Anderson* (Houghton Mifflin), a new biography,
Kim Townsend tells the story of a man who never really fit, whether
in his Ohio small town, his Chicago advertising firm, among the

literati of Chicago and New York (he was the middle-aged member
in a group of young contemporaries), or as the political activist of
the 30s (Granville Hicks said *Beyond Desire* failed to go far enough
as a revolutionary statement). "Even in a cemetery," says Townsend
referring to Anderson's grave-stone on Round Hill, Marion, Virginia,
"it seems that Anderson doesn't quite belong." Perhaps it is that very
quality of not belonging that made him so American and compelled
him to be constantly moving on. His youthful ambition to succeed
materially where his ne'er-do-well father failed is somewhat representative, as are his ongoing struggle for sexual maturity and identity,
his suspicion of his feminine nature, his three failed marriages, and
his constant need to be loved yet free of women—a paradigm summed
up in his comment on wife number three: "Poor E[lizabeth Norman
Prall] is very very nice, much nicer than I will ever be—and I do
not want her any more." His long period of burnout, beginning soon
after the acceptance of *Winesburg*, increasingly challenged his relationships, including those with Hemingway and Faulkner. Eleanor
Copenhaver, his fourth wife, managed to keep their marriage alive
through Anderson's declining years, and hers; Marietta (Bab) Finley's and Gertrude Stein's were his most successful female friendships. Perhaps Stein's was the most ideal: "To him she was another
mother figure, but one who did not distract him with her sexuality."
It becomes clear that Anderson's boyhood, which he never really
outgrew, was the climax of his life and the source of his best work to
the point of tedium. Townsend has written a very readable yet sufficiently scholarly biography, using the fiction, the *Memoirs*, and letters to illustrate and evaluate Anderson's view of his life and times.
Also of biographical interest is Walter B. Rideout's "Sherwood Anderson's Political Pilgrimage" (*LAmer* 5[Autumn 1984]:181–99), a review of Anderson's life as representatively American, his 1912 breakdown providing a myth for other writers to reject business for art,
and his pilgrimage from socialism and communism to New Dealism
providing insight into the political naiveté of the 30s. Anderson's relationship with Chicago is explored in David D. Anderson's "The
Chicago Short Fiction of Sherwood Anderson and Saul Bellow"
(*SSMLN* 17, i:12–24); for both writers the city was "where they
tested the reality of their early work." Although Anderson used Chicago again and again (in "The Rabbit-pen," "The Triumph of a
Modern," "A Chicago Hamlet," "Milk Bottles," "The Sad Horn Blow-
ers," "A Man's Story," and *Dark Laughter*), his relationship with the

city, unlike Bellows's ongoing if ambivalent one, ended in bitterness.
The Sherwood Anderson Diaries, 1936–1941 (Georgia), superbly
edited by Hilbert H. Campbell, makes available the daily record
Anderson began to keep in small bound desk diary volumes during
the third year of his marriage to Eleanor Copenhaver. The entries
begin on New Year's Day 1936 and continue to 28 February 1941,
eight days before Anderson's death en route to South America. In
a brief but informative introduction Campbell cites Anderson's love
for and dependence on Eleanor as the "most constant thread running
through this record." The diaries also reveal the restless wanderings
of the writer's last years, his bouts with ill health, his last visits to his
boyhood home of Clyde, Ohio. In a preface on the editing Campbell
notes his concern with reproducing a readable text and consequently
his altering of spelling and punctuation for purposes of clarity; where
baffled by poor handwriting, he introduces question marks in brackets. To save living persons from embarrassment 146 words in total
have been omitted but are located for readers wishing to peruse the
manuscript in the Newberry Library. Campbell provides almost 40
pages of notes identifying persons and providing background to make
entries intelligible; an index locates references to persons and works.
In "Sherwood Anderson, Diarist" (*SSMLN* 17, iii:23–27) David D.
Anderson comments on the importance of these diaries and on the
three-month daily record Anderson kept in 1921 during a trip to
France and England (*France and Sherwood Anderson: Paris Notebook, 1921,* ed. Michael Fanning [1976]), which anticipated them.
He distinguishes the later diaries as "a model for the genre."

Winesburg, Ohio generated most of the comments on the fiction.
In "The Implied Community of *Winesburg, Ohio*" (*ON* 11[1985]:
51–60) Stephen C. Enniss accents the positive qualities of Anderson's
created town, the beautiful qualities of many of its inhabitants, the
opportunities for happiness the place offers, instances of true love,
the energy and order in Winesburg life. All these attest to Anderson's
ambivalent tenderness toward the place as a representative rather
than unique community. Margaret Nims's "Sherwood Anderson's Use
of Setting and Sexual Symbolism in 'The Mother' " (*JEP* 8:219–22)
explores the relationship of the Willards within the entrapment of
the hotel. Their abortive communication of the potentially incestuous
relationship between George and his mother, and his father's hints at
the possibility of George's homosexuality lead to George's escape

from the hotel and illustrate Anderson's belief that the tragedy of life is man's inability to communicate thoughts and feelings. In "'Tandy': At the Core of *Winesburg*" (*SSF* 24:66–70) Judith Arcana sees this briefest, central story in Anderson's masterpiece as a variation on his theme of the grotesque and as reflecting his concept of woman as love object and feeder. Rather than discovering her own truth like other grotesques, Tandy becomes the too fragile vessel of the drunkard's addiction to search fruitlessly for his love object, "a vessel into which he can pour his desire, and out of which he may drink to sustain himself." Ray Lewis White in "Socrates in *Winesburg*" (*NMAL* 10 [1986]: item 2) sees Wing Biddlebaum in "Hands" as based on Plato and Socrates: "From the legend of Plato, Anderson retrieves the idea of handsome youths in a pastoral setting learning from a wise elder how to think [Wing's "dream"]; and, from the legend of Socrates, Anderson recalls the sentence of death for misleading youths who ought indeed to question the voices about them and learn to dare to dream their own dreams." Finally, Thomas E. Kennedy's "Fiction as Its Own Subject" (*KR* 9, iii:59–70) perceptively discusses "Death in the Woods" as similar to contemporary experiments in "Metafiction" or "self-reflexive fiction," where "the fiction-making process is used as a metaphor for the self-creation of human identity." Through the process of time, which enables him to supplement the old woman's story with his own experiences, the narrator "progresses from recorder to creator." The "real story" concerns "how the artist's imagination can perceive the likeness of scattered elements" and shape them into meaning.

v. Sinclair Lewis and H. L. Mencken

If we are to credit Harold Bloom in his brief introduction to *Sinclair Lewis*, another in the Chelsea House Modern Critical Views series, "Lewis is of very nearly no interest whatsoever to American literary critics of my own generation and younger, so that it seems likely his decline in renown will continue." This attitude is reflected in the fact that the most recent piece in this collection is from 1975. The large body of essays generated by the 1985 centennial are ignored, perhaps because they were not readily available when Bloom made his selections. Bloom describes Lewis as essentially a satirist with a camera eye, "a master neither of narrative nor of characterization," and asserts that even his satire "has no edge in the contemporary United States," opinions which may more accurately reveal Bloom's critical taste than Lewis's critical reputation.

In any case, Lewis's contradictory and tormented personality continues to fascinate and provoke contrasting responses. Ruel E. Foster in "Lewis's Irony—A Paralysis of the Heart" (*WVUPP* 33: 31–40) finds the hospital ledger notation that Lewis died from "paralysis of the heart" an apt metaphor for "the strange coldness that lay beneath his everlasting garrulity," a coldness that informs the irony in his fiction and accounts for his inability to found a home, his indifference to his sons, and his alienation of wives and friends. John Hersey provides a contrasting view in "First Job" (*YR* 76:184–97), a recollection of his four months working for Lewis in 1937. At age 22 and fresh out of Yale, Hersey was unaware of Lewis's drinking problem and saw a surface that was "gentle, kindly, boyish, and vividly entertaining." Robert L. McLaughlin describes and analyzes Lewis's association with Hemingway in " 'Only Kind Thing Is Silence': Ernest Hemingway vs. Sinclair Lewis" (*HemR* 6, ii:46–53) and concludes that the relationship was mixed: congenial personal encounters conjoined with derogatory comments in print, with Hemingway more inclined to criticize and Lewis to praise.

Main Street continues to receive attention from those interested in the nature of small-town life. Without providing new insights into the novel, Ellen Andrews Knodt in "Understanding *Main Street*: The Interdependence of Fiction and Sociology in the Study of American Communities" (*JASAT* 17[1986]:31–37) makes the obvious point that fiction can complement sociology in the study of small American communities because it provides emotions and value judgments as well as factual observation. John E. Miller's "The Distance Between Gopher Prairie and Lake Wobegon: Sinclair Lewis and Garrison Keillor on the Small Town Experience" (*CentR* 31:432–36) provides one more comparison of Gopher Prairie and Lake Wobegon (two appeared last year). Miller favors Keillor's more balanced and gentle view: "If Lewis is obsessed by a desire to smash the idols of tradition, complacency, prejudice, and provinciality, Keillor, living in the postmodern era, is searching for serviceable values and places of repose for people traumatized by culture in which all fixed principles and values are rendered problematical."

Glen A. Love's perceptive contribution to *A Literary History of the West*, "The Western Writings of Sinclair Lewis" (pp. 754–63), demonstrates that Lewis was concerned with more than smashing idols. Love points out that behind the satire was an ideal for a maturing America, an ideal linked with the pioneering spirit of the West. This western theme emerges strongly in two of the early novels and remains evident in varying degrees in those that follow, but Lewis failed to engage fully the concept of new pioneering that so much fascinated him and was "the victim of an idea which compelled him even as its formulation resisted his efforts to bring it to fictional life." Another essay that treats in some measure Lewis's concern with the cultural ambiguities of the movement west is William Holtz's "Sinclair Lewis, Rose Wilder Lane, and the Midwestern Short Novel" (*SSF* 24:41–48). Rose Wilder Lane, daughter of Laura Ingalls Wilder, was a friend of Lewis's wife Dorothy Thompson. Lewis admired her stories of the Midwest, which treat some of the same pioneering themes that intrigued him.

Despite Harold Bloom's announcement of Lewis's current irrelevance, he was not ignored completely this year by theory-oriented critics. Caren J. Town's "A Dream More Romantic: *Babbitt* and Narrative Discontinuity" (*WVUPP* 33:41–49) draws upon theoretical concepts of Bakhtin, Lacan, and Derrida to answer why Babbitt is both an object of satire and of sympathy. She concludes that the multiple perspectives are the successful result of Lewis's use of "the art of suspended compromise," her version of what Bakhtin calls "dialogism," in which the reader is not allowed to choose between Babbitt as hero and clown but must keep the two views in suspension.

The growing body of Mencken scholarship was expanded this year by two significant books. *Mencken and Sara: A Life in Letters*, ed. Marion Elizabeth Rodgers (McGraw-Hill), makes generally available for the first time the 12 years of correspondence—during courtship and marriage—between Mencken and the woman he married. The letters provide new and sometimes surprising insights into Mencken's private life, thoughts, and feelings, and the introduction supplies a good deal more information about Sara than previous biographies of Mencken have done. The letters are thoroughly annotated to provide narrative continuity and clarify every possibly obscure allusion to people and events for today's general reader. *Critical Essays on H. L. Mencken* (Hall) contains, in addition to editor Douglas C. Stenerson's introduction, two new essays. The introduction is a useful and authoritative bibliographical essay that furnishes a chronological survey of material dealing with Mencken, an appraisal of the present state of Mencken scholarship, and suggestions for further study. Fred Hobson's "'This Hellawful South': Mencken and the Late Confederacy" (pp. 174–86), one of the new essays, examines the effects of Mencken's attacks on the South as epitomized in the 1920 piece "The Sahara of the Bozart," which provoked and stimulated southern writers and journalists and won him disciples in the South. Among those disciples, incidentally, was Sara Haardt. "The Sahara of the Bozart" plays an important role in the other essay written specifically for Stenerson's collection, "H. L. Mencken and James Weldon Johnson: Two Men Who Helped Shape a Renaissance" by Charles Scruggs (pp. 186–203). Scruggs first describes Mencken's encouragement of black writers and his influence on the Harlem Renaissance and then focuses on his relationship with Johnson, which was mutually influential. Johnson influenced the final version of "The Sahara of the Bozart," and Mencken's *The American Language* helped Johnson formulate his own theory of language for the Negro poet.

This year's numbers of *Menckeniana* include a continuing bibliographic checklist that appears thorough and comprehensive, including the kind of newspaper articles and minor references often overlooked in such bibliographies.

vi. Western and Southern Writers

Owen Wister received more attention than usual this year. Robert Murray Davis brings together from a variety of sources a miscellaneous collection of Wister's nonfiction treatment of the West in *Owen Wister's West: Selected Articles* (New Mexico). His introduction emphasizes Wister's impulse to place the region and society historically, his mythic vision of the West as a place of physical and spiritual renewal, and his realistic portrayal of the land and people. His comments on the individual selections, while often informative, are marked by a condescending preoccupation with what he sees as Wister's racism and elitism and display less than an insider's appreciation of hunting and western attitudes. Wister is treated in conjunction with other western writers in Merchant Vorpahl's "Roosevelt, Wister, Turner, Remington," a chapter of *A Literary History of the West* (pp. 277–302), and in the chapter "The Western Formula and the Disappearing Frontier" in Christine Bold's *Selling the Wild West: Popular Western Fiction, 1860–1960* (Indiana). Vorpahl's main point is that the individual investigations of the West done by the writers he treats "had a large collective effect on the course of American cultural history." Together they produced a complex consciousness of the West in American thought. Bold focuses on Wister's concern with providing a record of a West that was already disappearing and his preoccupation with reconciling eastern and western values. The similarities and differences between North American and South American views toward nature and the frontier are examined by John Donahue in "Nature in *Don Segundo Sombra* and *The Virginian*" (*GPQ* 7:166–77). Donahue concludes from his comparison of *The Virginian* with a novel by the Argentine Ricardo Guiraldes that the similarities are environmental (humans adapt to similar environments in similar ways) and the differences are cultural (Latin Americans tend to view nature as an enemy, debasing, uncivilized). Frank Scafella informs us about Wister's friendship and correspondence with Hemingway in "*The Sun Also Rises*: Owen Wister's 'Garbage Pail,' Hemingway's Passage of the 'Human Soul'" (*HemR* 6,i[1986]:101–11). The information about the correspondence and the excerpts from it are combined rather tangentially with an idiosyncratic interpretation of Hemingway's novel. The most important treatment of Wister is Lee Clark Mitchell's "'When You Call Me That...': Tall Talk and Male Hegemony in *The Virginian*" (*PMLA* 102:66–77). This perceptive and forcefully argued essay claims that while the novel is considered the prototypical western it really doesn't satisfy formula expectations. Wordplay is more important that gunplay; language more important that physical action. The novel celebrates the rhetorical triumph of the Virginian over the schoolmarm and the silencing of her feminism in favor of the "logic" of patriarchy.

The western novel is a prime candidate for feminist criticism, of course, and Fritz H. Oehlsschlaeger addresses feminist concerns to the fiction of two writers of westerns in his contribution to *Gender Studies*, "Civilization as Emasculation: The Threatening Role of Women in the Frontier Fiction of Harold Bell Wright and Zane Grey," pp. 177–87. Considerably less penetrating than Mitchell's treatment of *The Virginian*, this essay settles for the psychoanalytic chestnut that women in westerns, representing the forces of civilization, threaten the primitive hero with emasculation. The recurring pattern in such novels, says Oehlsschlaeger, involves the triumph of the primitive hero over the threatening, civilized woman, who must accept complete subservience in return for sexual gratification and

chivalric adoration. Zane Grey is also treated in the third chapter of
Selling the Wild West, pp. 79–91. According to Bold, Grey's desires
to achieve artistry by transcending the western formula were thwarted
by his magazine and book publishers, but he did try to develop con-
sequentiality within the bounds of formula by adding social discussion and altering narrative technique.

Interest in other than cowboy literature of the West is evident
in the year's work on Ole Rölvaag and Mary Hunter Austin. Harold
P. Simonson's monograph on Rölvaag's masterwork, *Prairies Within:
The Tragic Trilogy of Ole Rölvaag* (Washington), portrays the
Norwegian-American author as a somber figure with an expansive
vision, identifying more with Beret Holm, the heroine of all three
novels (*Giants in the Earth, Peder Victorious,* and *Their Fathers'
God*), than with her husband Per Hansa, who dies in the first. Simonson intriguingly relates the Beret-Per Hansa conflict to that between
"Christian faith rooted in historical events" and "Romantic celebration of the expanding and ultimately non-historical self." In *A Literary
History of the West* (pp. 716–38) Arthur R. Huseboe cogently surveys Rölvaag's career and works with those of Herbert Krause, often
labeled Rölvaag's successor, and argues for Rölvaag's place in American literature: "As Rölvaag himself argued, two chapters in American
history stand out above the rest, the Westward Movement and Immigration. He was fully a part of both. Moreover, in large measure
the two are inseparable and can be defined only in terms of one another." Ann Moseley's pamphlet *Ole Edvart Rölvaag* (*BSWWS* 80)
offers an excellent introduction to this author, surveying his career
and works and including intelligent plot summaries. Moseley stresses
Rölvaag's combining myth with psychological realism.

Jacqueline D. Hall's brief chapter on Mary Hunter Austin for *A
Literary History of the West* (pp. 359–69) makes a study of the
growth of Austin's ideas by comparing *The Land of Little Rain*
(1903), her first book, and her later *The Land of Journeys Ending*
(1924). The first, a California desert nature book, provided a model
for humans to learn from and emulate the natural world; the other
grew out of travels in the arid plateaus between the Colorado and
Rio Grande and admiration for pueblo culture, especially its spiritual
responses to nature. Between these phases of her career, Austin spent
many years in New York and became involved in social issues, years
which are the subject of Karen S. Langlois's "Mary Austin and Lincoln Steffens" (*HLQ* 49[1986]:357–83), a fascinating examination

of Austin's presumably fantasized affair with the famous journalist. Langlois uses a collection of letters dated 1910–11 from Austin to Steffens at Columbia University to tell the story of what began as a literary friendship and developed, on Austin's part, into hysterical outrage and charges of abandonment. Whether the relationship ever got physical cannot be determined, but it did influence Austin's conservative opposition to free love, and she vicariously killed off her two-timing "lover" in her novel *No. 26 Jayne Street* (1920). In an extensive introduction to *Stories from the Country of "Lost Borders"* (Rutgers), pp. vii–xxxviii, editor Marjorie Pryse places Austin among literary regionalists like Stowe, Freeman, and Jewett as well as among nature writers like Thoreau and Muir and notes her acquaintance with feminist activists like Margaret Sanger, Emma Goldman, and Ida Tarbell. Pryse groups *Lost Borders* (1909) with *The Land of Little Rain* for its "intensity of connection between natural landscape and human life" and surveys portraits of betrayed and deprived women, concluding that Walking Woman holds the key to healing in the desert.

Interest in writers from the South during this period has continued to decline. The latest issue of *Kalki* (33) delays oblivion for James Branch Cabell with some 1976 comments by his widow in Geoffrey Morley-Mower's "An Interview with Margaret Freeman Cabell" (pp. 3–10), which contains information on the author's finances and his being linked to the murder of John Scott in 1901. In "The James Branch Cabell Library" (pp. 11–14) Dorys C. Grover and Katherine H. Bachman record the naming of the Virginia Commonwealth University library for the author and describe the contents of the Cabell collection there. Paul Spencer in *"The Certain Hour* as Mini-Biography" (pp. 15–18) sees the 1916 work as containing the various forms, styles, and viewpoints Cabell employed throughout his multivolume sequence, the Biography of the Life of Manuel, and as the "Biography in miniature" of that project. In "Affinity and Diversity: Cabell and Arthur Machen" (pp. 19–27) Harlan L. Umansky evaluates the career of this minor writer whose novel *The House of Souls* (1906) influenced Cabell's Life of Manuel. Desmond Tarrant uses Erich Neumann's theories of depth psychology to evalute Cabell's achievement in "Cabell: Master Myth-Maker" (pp. 28–30), concluding that his life contained all the stages of human development and "provides the catharsis which can heal [modern] fragmentation, helping to make us spiritually whole again." Paul

Spencer's contribution, "Cabell: Fantasist of Reality," to *Exploring Fantasy Worlds*, ed. Darrell Schweitzer (Brownstone-Borgo, 1985), pp. 97–106, concludes "that those who are led to Cabell by a love of fantasy will find his books so interwoven that it would be pointlessly arbitrary to segregate them into fantasy and non-fantasy."

Cabell's friend Ellen Glasgow, who deserves much more attention than she gets, is the subject of two short pieces. In "Ellen Glasgow's Allegory of Love and Death: 'The Greatest Good'" (*RALS* 14[1984]: 161–66) Linda Pannill retrieves an undated piece of juvenilia from the University of Virginia library, important, she insists, because it introduces "one of the author's persistent myths, the gifted woman's fatal choice between love and ambition." Fritz H. Oehlsschlaeger includes several Glasgow letters from 1925 in "Ellen Glasgow and Stuart Pratt Sherman: The Record of a Literary Friendship" (*RALS* 14:143–51). Now among the Sherman papers at the University of Illinois, these provide insight into Glasgow's purposes in *Barren Ground* and *The Romantic Comedians*, reveal her thoughts on other writers, and provide information about her relationship with the critic. Linda Tate's "Against the Chaos of the World: Language and Consciousness in Elizabeth Madox Roberts's *The Time of Man*" (*MissQ* 40:95–111) analyzes heroine Ellen Chesser's "innate ear for sounds and rhythms, her receptivity to the power of remembered phrases, and her sensitivity to the voices of those around her," demonstrating that "while she is not very literate, she is using language to achieve a sense of herself as a growing and separate identity unique from all others." Finally in *The American Historical Romance* (pp. 281–95) George Dekker puts Roberts's *The Great Meadow* in the tradition of Scott and Cooper, noting that despite its weakness in characterization it is a minor classic of its kind, "richer in substance, and finer in execution" than *Gone with the Wind*. Dekker makes similar claims for Glasgow's *The Battle-Ground*, which although partly sentimental fiction, seriously questions the wisdom and worth of male ascendancy in the Old South and if the punishment of the Civil War was in excess of society's sins.

Brigham Young University

14. Fiction: The 1930s to the 1960s

Virginia Spencer Carr

Adherents of all genres of critical thought are producing quality works in the area of American fiction, but, as has often been the case in recent years, some of the most challenging and innovative scholarship is offered by feminist critics. The field of southern studies continues to grow with O'Connor and Wolfe receiving the lion's share of the attention in 1987. The relatively scant scholarship on detective fiction has necessitated the elimination of that category. The newly created "Jewish-American Experience" category should prove illuminating as well as utilitarian.

i. "Art for Humanity's Sake"—Proletarians

a. Edmund Wilson, Richard Wright, and Others.   An excellent article focusing on the personal life of Edmund Wilson is Monroe Engel's "An Exemplary Edmund Wilson" (YR 76:323–33). Engel, who was a close friend and neighbor of Wilson's in the early 60s, relates several incidents that provide revealing glimpses into the critic's personality. Engel's brief but close association with Wilson enables him to present a rich character sketch. Engel's Wilson is proud, brilliant, determined, and certainly intriguing. Isaiah Berlin provides another intimate look at Wilson in "Edmund Wilson at Oxford" (YR 76:139–51). Berlin's article chiefly details a visit Wilson made to Oxford in 1954. A crotchety Wilson "in a splendidly Anglophobic mood" spent most of his stay railing against academia, English literary life, and Britain in general. Berlin identifies Wilson as a man more aligned with the hale and hearty Edwardians in his literary personality than with the delicate British literati of the 1950s. As Berlin writes, "It was the aestheticism, the prissiness, the superciliousness, the cliquishness, the thin, piping voices, the bloodlessness, the preoccupation with one's own emotions both in life and in literature . . . that irritated him." Berlin describes Wilson as a critic who believed in the importance of socal, historical,

and cultural contexts in examining literature, and he saw little purpose in "purely literary scholarship." Berlin's portrait of Edmund
Wilson is candid but affectionate and shows his great admiration for
the critic as well as a clear perception of his character.

Another personal portrait of a public man is provided by Robert
Brustein's "Lionel Trilling: Memories of a Mentor" (YR 76:162–68).
Brustein, who was a student and later a colleague of Trilling's at
Columbia, presents candid recollections of his fervent admiration for
the critic. Although Trilling was not enthusiastic about Brustein's interest in drama, he was supportive of and important to Brustein's
career. Trilling's standing has diminished recently, but Brustein
cogently insists that his idol still has much to teach us: "Trilling
penetrated deeper into life and literature than any American critic
before or since, and I believe a less ideological day is near when
readers will once again regard with astonishment the exemplary
qualities of his mind."

In *How I Grew* (Harcourt) Mary McCarthy presents in her inimi-
table fashion her life as she remembers it, much in the manner of
Memories of a Catholic Girlhood. Relating events as diverse as her
study of Latin at Vassar and the loss of her virginity, McCarthy is consistently entertaining. Readers of McCarthy's novels and her other
works will appreciate, too, Carol Gelderman's new biography, *Mary
McCarthy: A Life* (St. Martin's), to be reviewed in next year's annual.

Michael Atkinson's "Richard Wright's 'Big Boy Leaves Home' and
a Tale from Ovid: A Metamorphosis Transformed" (SSF 24:251–61)
is an important contribution to Wright scholarship. The article is a
creative and careful comparison/contrast of Wright's "Big Boy Leaves
Home" and the classical myth of Actaeon and Diana, as told by Ovid
in *Metamorphoses*. Among the many parallels that Atkinson points
out is that between the carefree and playful outing of Big Boy and
his friends and Actaeon's lively hunting party—both of which end in
bloodshed. Atkinson also points to the similar woundings of the two
heroes and their shared muteness. Most striking is Atkinson's comparison of Bobo's destruction and Actaeon's dismemberment and the
discussion of their similarly painful and dehumanizing transformations. Divergences in the works are equally revealing, and Atkinson
suggests several. As he writes, "The parallels—and the divergences—
between the myth and the story play off one another, creating a denser
texture of emotional response and a suppler philosophical grasp as
we read and reflect."

The *Paris Review*'s printing of excerpted interviews from the "James Jones: Reveille to Taps" documentary makes fascinating reading. The excellent documentary, originally broadcast on PBS in 1985, included memories of Jones shared by friends, teachers, and family. Portions from many of the most illuminating interviews are included in "Glimpses: James Jones 1921–1977" (*ParisR* 103:205–36). The excerpts are effectively arranged to create a chronological recollection, beginning with the memories of school friends.

Sarah Toombs's *James Thurber, An Annotated Bibliography of Criticism* (Garland) is the first extensive bibliography of the still relatively small body of Thurber criticism. In addition to the excellently annotated entries, Toombs provides a substantial introduction that serves as a history of critical thought concerning Thurber and of his reception by general readers and scholars. A good short essay on James Thurber is Robert Secor's "Walter Mitty and Lord Jim" (*ELN* 25:74–77). Secor examines Conrad's influence on Thurber and Thurber's frequent allusions to *Lord Jim*. Thurber so identified with Conrad's heroes that E. B. White portrayed him as a Conrad character in an introduction to a collection of Thurber's criticism. Growing out of his own identification with Lord Jim are Thurber's fictional references to Conrad's character. Secor presents Walter Mitty and Jim as two characters who have dual (real and imagined) lives. The difference is that Mitty "shares none of the stature of Conrad's protagonist," says Secor, who believes that the concept of Lord Jim's "inner life" may have provided Thurber's framework for "The Secret Life of Walter Mitty."

b. John Steinbeck, John Dos Passos, and Others.

R. S. Hughes's *Beyond the Red Pony: A Reader's Companion to Steinbeck's Complete Short Stories* (Scarecrow) is the first complete study of Steinbeck's entire short-fiction canon and functions as a bibliography and a guide to the stories. The synopses and discussions of the hard-to-find stories are especially valuable. As Hughes points out, the rarely reprinted stories of Steinbeck's later period are biographically and stylistically important.

John Ditsky's "Some Second Thoughts About the Ending of *The Wayward Bus*: A Note" (*UWR* 20, i:85–88) is a revision of Ditsky's earlier position—a revision prompted by "Louis Owens's eminently reasonable" *John Steinbeck's Re-Vision of America* (see *ALS 1985*, p. 255). In his article "The Wayward Bus" Ditsky suggested that significant changes in the lives of the passengers were promised by the novel's ending. However, after reading Owens's comments on his essay, Ditsky writes that "it seems clear enough that any changes have not been all that sweeping." Ditsky maintains that the novel is blatantly allegorical and gives an excellent reading based on Revelation, but he now admits the possibility of *ironical* allegory on Steinbeck's part. His use of Revelation allows him to respond to several of Owens's questions about the novel. Not only is Steinbeck's novel an allegory, but his characters "have lived life as though it were allegory," concludes Ditsky. Thomas G. Evans provides an excellent study of *The Grapes of Wrath* as a political novel that is at once popular and modernist. Evans's article, "Impersonal Dilemmas: The Collision of Modernist and Popular Traditions in Two Political Novels, *The Grapes of Wrath* and *Ragtime*" (*SoAR* 52, i:71–85), suggests that political novelists like Steinbeck and E. L. Doctorow were interested in reconciling popular and modernist aims, or what Evans calls "a collision of the aesthetic values of literary modernism . . . with those of the popular political novel." Steinbeck achieves this reconciliation by establishing genre situations and then undercutting the reader's expectations for the genre. Evans also points out Steinbeck's ambivalence and "impersonal style" as elements of the "balancing act." The impersonal style serves both reading formations by being characteristically modernist while allowing the close identification with the characters essential to a popular audience. Evans's reading of *The Grapes of Wrath* in the context of his thesis is fine work. Evans also makes the important point that political novels are not, of necessity, artistic failures: "The political novel is thus a genre that is inherently mixed, and to approach it only as a manifestation of mass culture or to judge it strictly by the standards of modernist criticism is to prejudge its success or failure as a work of art and to underrate its potential."

David Sanders's *John Dos Passos, A Comprehensive Bibliography* (Garland) will be indispensable to Dos Passos scholars. Sanders explains his indebtedness to previous bibliographies, but his work is the most exhaustive to date. Sanders's extensive primary bibliography of Dos Passos's works provides a detailed publication history and physical descriptions of first editions.

Michael Clark, author of *Dos Passos's Early Fiction, 1912–1938* (Susquehanna), believes that American traditions can illuminate the basic aesthetic principles and issues in Dos Passos's early writings.

While recognizing Linda Wagner's earlier *Dos Passos: Artist as American* (see *ALS 1979*, pp. 224–25), Clark maintains that Wagner's study was most successful when examining Dos Passos's later, more consciously historical works. In Clark's opinion, Walt Whitman and William James influenced the world vision of Dos Passos. From Whitman, Dos Passos acquired a respect for nature and "man's vibrant interior life," even though, in Dos Passos's early fiction, this inner life is often thwarted in its attempt to respond to the blighted landscape surrounding it. Dos Passos's firm belief in pragmatism was rooted in the writings of William James.

In *Shifting Gears* (No. Car.) Cecelia Tichi traces the development of modern, industrial sensibilities and demonstrates how this post-industrial perspective influenced 20th-century literature, most notably the works of William Carlos Williams, Ernest Hemingway, and Dos Passos. The technology of "girders and gears," Tichi argues, is the technology of "interconnected component parts," and the same "design awareness" exhibited by the engineers of this technology, she continues, forms the basis for the writing styles of these three authors. The core of Tichi's thesis is her belief that modern writing styles arose from the then new emphasis on engineering "structures and machines able to function with maximal efficiency and minimal waste." The advent of the computer age enables Tichi to view the "machine world of the gear-and-girder technology" from an objective and analytical perspective, and she correctly cites gear-and-girder sensibilities as merely "formulations of reality and not as reality itself." New formulations of reality or not, however, there is little doubt that many American writers recognized the need for reinvigorating imaginative literature "in accordance with the terms of a new world," overturning, in the course of their writing, the earlier Romantic notions of a holistic, spiritual world. Tichi's challenging and compelling study expertly supports her view that the "American industrial-age passion for component-part design" influenced not only the social but the literary sphere of American life as well.

Ray Lewis White provides a fascinating look at John Dos Passos's relations with the U.S. Government in his article, "John Dos Passos and the Federal Bureau of Investigation" (*JML* 14:97–110). An inquiry was prompted by Dos Passos's alleged association in 1933 with the Communist International in Shanghai, and he was interviewed by the FBI at his Richmond, Virginia, home in 1952. After introducing the situation, White presents the entire FBI summary of the interview, filling in the gaps with helpful documentation. As White points out, the interview summary shows a newly conservative Dos Passos disillusioned with his earlier affiliations. Dos Passos scholars will appreciate White's having made the interview summary accessible since, as he writes, "the record of such agreeable collaboration may reveal clearly Dos Passos's extreme reactionary political movement and expression of fierce anti-Communism—movement and mood more rightward than previously documented."

Sybil Weir contributes much-needed attention to Ann Petry's often overlooked novel in her essay, "*The Narrows*: A Black New England Novel" (*SAF* 15:81–93). Weir convincingly links *The Narrows* to the traditions of New England literature, suggesting that "Petry is indebted to Nathaniel Hawthorne as well as to Richard Wright" and that "*The Narrows* belongs to the tradition of domestic feminism and realism created primarily by New England women writers as well as to the experience Petry had in Harlem in the 1940's." Abbie Crunch is very much the New England matron, and she "adheres rigidly to genteel standards of ladylike conduct because she believes only those standards offer her a way to control her destiny in a chaotic, threatening world." Most important to Petry's New England perspective is her acceptance of Hawthorne's "chain of 'dark necessity.'"

Marion Meade's *Dorothy Parker: What Fresh Hell Is This?* (Villard) is a poignant biography of a talented yet self-destructive artist. Since virtually none of Parker's papers survive, Meade was forced to rely on the memories and resources of the writer's friends. In spite of this potentially limiting circumstance, the book is richly detailed. Meade addresses Parker's literary output with a sharp focus on the circumstances surrounding composition, and her work may inspire further critical analysis.

Running against critical consensus is George Montiero's "All in the Family: John O'Hara's Story of a Doctor's Life" (*SSF* 24:305–08). Montiero sides with Robert Emmet Long in asserting that "A Family Party" is not simply a sentimental tribute to O'Hara's father; rather, it is a biting parody of small-town smugness achieved through an ingenious narrative structure. Montiero writes that "A Family Party" is "the story of the town of Lyons, which, in turn, is the story of the American small town that invariably 'uses' its benefactors, scraping up its thankfulness at the last in one showy gesture."

ii. Southerners

a. **General.** *Conversations with Peter Taylor* (Miss.), published in the Literary Conversations Series and edited by Hubert H. McAlexander, compiles in one volume 14 interviews given between 1960 and 1987. In his interviews Taylor discusses not only his own life and writings, but also the lives and works of the many noted authors who were acquaintances of his, including Robert Lowell, Jean Stafford, Allen Tate, and John Crowe Ransom. One does, as McAlexander claims in his introduction, see in the chronological progression of the interviews the maturation of Taylor as an artist, a maturity most visible in two lengthy interviews, one by J. William Broadway in 1985 and the other by Barbara Thompson in 1987 for *The Paris Review.* Throughout *Conversations with Peter Taylor,* the reader discovers influences on Taylor and his artistic methods that may not have before been apparent. Also noteworthy for Taylor scholars is Lamar York's "Peter Taylor's Version of Initiation" (*MissQ* 40:309–22), which cogently examines the rites of passage in Taylor's stories.

b. **Robert Penn Warren, the Agrarians, and Others.** Although there was relatively little scholarship on Warren published in 1987, his own "Portrait of a Father," published by *SoR* (23:33–67), is of particular interest. This warm and moving essay about R. F. Warren exhibits Warren's flair for history, especially personal history filtered through time and recollection. He refers to his father as "a man of mystery" because he had little to say about his past or his ancestors. Warren has made no concerted effort to probe into factual records, mentioning only those bits of family history that have come to him almost by chance. But the author's memories are vivid, the incidents he shares, telling. This tissue of remembrance is an intimate portrait of Warren's father and the people in his life.

The Lytle-Tate Letters, ed. Thomas Daniel Young and Elizabeth Sarcone (Mississippi), presents the correspondence of two of the most important figures in southern letters, Andrew Lytle and Allen Tate. This correspondence demonstrates the great concern that each man had for the techniques and aesthetics underlying his art, yet, more than this, it documents their friendship. Indeed, as the editors maintain in their introduction, rarely in literary history have two such writers existed "who confided so completely in each other." Although

The Lytle-Tate Letters is important for the insight it provides into each of these writers' works, for the two discussed in detail the merits and faults of various of their works in progress, it also illustrates the sensibilities of the Nashville writers.

Close Connections: Caroline Gordon and the Southern Renaissance (Putnam's) by Ann Waldron is certain to fuel the recently kindled fire of interest in Gordon's life and work. Waldron's lively and readable book effectively utilizes correspondence, interviews, and other sources to present an intimate picture of the artist. The focus on Gordon's place within a vast literary and social context illuminates the influences on her artistic and personal development. *Close Connections* also contains valuable accounts of the genesis and aims of Gordon's works. Veronica Makowsky's "Caroline Gordon: Amateur to Professional Writer" (*SoR* 23:778–93) contains three excerpts from her Gordon biography. The focus of Makowsky's book is Gordon's struggle to establish herself as a writer while maintaining her roles as a wife to Allen Tate, a mother, and the lady of a house normally filled with guests. Gordon found the act of writing a "torment," and it was this aversion to the agony of the creative process coupled with existing distractions that pulled Gordon away from her work and made her a less prolific writer than she might have been. As Makowsky points out, Gordon has been overlooked and undervalued, and she is often identified solely in terms of her role as Allen Tate's wife. Jerry Herndon's refreshing reexamination of *Aleck Maury, Sportsman* in his article "Aleck Maury's Tragic Sense of Life" (*UMSE* 5[1984–87]: 203–14) is an important contribution to Gordon studies. Herndon states that although critics have generally been in accord about the novel's carpe diem theme, there is disagreement about "the ultimate meaning of Maury's life." After a brief review of past critical comment on this issue, Herndon questions Andrew Lytle's reference to Maury's "feckless manhood" and his contention that Maury is a product of diminished antebellum values and structure. Herndon is successful both at refuting critics who see Maury as an irresponsible man whose life is a tragic waste and at defending the view that Maury succeeds to some extent in the battle against time simply because he lives for the experiences of each day.

Rosemary M. Canfield-Reisman, editor of *The Collected Stories of William March* (Alabama), believes that her subject is one of the most underrated of 20th-century southern writers. Since the majority of his works are out of print and he is seldom anthologized, the publication of this comprehensive collection of his short fiction is something of an event in the world of southern letters. March's stories, which analyze human nature in a masterly fashion, are, as Canfield-Reisman maintains, imbued with a "peculiarly Southern sensibility, a sensibility which infuses all of his work, whatever the setting." As Canfield-Reisman insists, March's themes are universal. His fiction deals with disillusionment and entrapment and has an energy that precedes from his anger at the South's "cruelty, hypocrisy, and repressiveness." March's anger, however, was not derived from a hatred of the South; perhaps he loved the South too well, and his anger was aroused when people failed "to live up to its loveliness."

c. **Flannery O'Connor, Eudora Welty, and Others.** Given the wide range of publications in which O'Connor's interviews originally appeared, many of which are little known or are now out of print, *Conversations with Flannery O'Connor* (Mississippi) is an especially valuable addition to the literature of O'Connor scholarship. Editor Rosemary M. Magee provides many fresh insights into both O'Connor's life and her writing, placing her "within a literary and historical and social framework."

Underlying O'Connor's fiction, John F. Desmond asserts in *Risen Sons, Flannery O'Connor's Vision of History* (Georgia), is a "Christian vision of history conveyed analogically through the literal action." Desmond begins his study with a brief overview of biblical metaphysics, then examines how the doctrine of the analogy of being illustrates O'Connor's embedding of the biblical analogue of the Christ event "in an authentically creative way within the literal level" of her stories. Desmond's is an intriguing thesis that contradicts the many earlier Manichean analyses of O'Connor's fiction, yet his study convincingly demonstrates that O'Connor's self-described "incarnational art" is based upon the existence of the historical act of redemption, not as a static theme within her work, but as a history "generated dramatically from within the action itself."

The Fall 1987 issue of *Studies in the Literary Imagination* (20, ii) is entirely devoted to O'Connor. This "Flannery O'Connor and the South" volume is edited and introduced by Ted R. Spivey, who contributes one of the 11 articles. In "Flannery O'Connor's 'Intellectual Vaudeville': Masks of Mother and Daughter" Loxley F. Nichols presents a superlative study of O'Connor's comic genius as revealed through her letters. In reference to O'Connor and her mother, Nichols mentions "a balance in their intellect and personality that manifested itself clearly in O'Connor's comic voice and produced a 'comedy team,' so to speak, with Regina playing the indispensable 'straight man,' and O'Connor providing either the punch line or the wry perspective that jogs the anecdote into comic distortion." An excellent examination of O'Connor's reception and influence in other countries is provided by Waldemar Zacharasiewicz in "Flannery O'Connor Among Creative Readers Abroad: A Late Encounter with the Georgia Writer." Zacharasiewicz offers a brief overview of O'Connor scholarship in France, Germany, and Great Britain. He pays particular attention to Canada, since this country is not only responsible for much excellent criticism, but has also produced creative writers like Rudy Wiebe and Jack Hodgins, who were greatly influenced by O'Connor. In "Flannery O'Connor and Onnie Jay Holy and the Trouble with You Innerleckshuls," Marion Montgomery argues that O'Connor was not anti-intellectual, as is often suggested, but, rather, that she was dismayed by the "pride of intellect" she saw in modern Gnosticism. Montgomery refers to Gnosticism as "a movement of mind against existence" and describes Julian and Haze Motes as O'Connor characters "who attempt to elevate and enlarge the self over creation, at the expense of insistent reality." This essay does a particularly good job of emphasizing the universality of O'Connor's themes. Montgomery quite correctly asserts that O'Connor characters have often been explained away as "backwoods psychopaths" by readers fleeing "self-recognition." In "Flannery O'Connor, James Joyce, and the City," Ted R. Spivey discusses Joyce's influence on O'Connor as a modernist and the shared concerns of the two writers. Spivey writes that what "Joyce did was to confirm her belief in her most significant subject—the religious individual who is trying to flee God but, as she said of Joyce's Catholicism, 'can't get rid of it no matter what he does.'" "Naming in the Neighborhood of Being: O'Connor and Percy on Language" by Emily Archer addresses O'Connor's and Percy's shared belief in the importance of accurate naming. Both writers were disturbed by the modern tendency toward abstraction and separation of spirit and matter. Archer writes that the "exorcism of the spirit of abstraction in this age will thus depend upon those who practice straight seeing and truthful naming."

Alice Hall Petry's "Julian and O'Connor's 'Everything That Rises Must Converge'" (*SAF* 15:101–08) is an exceptional essay that picks up where Josephine Hendin left off after suggesting a link between the Julian in O'Connor's story and Julian the Apostate of Rome. Both Julian and the Apostate are from aristocratic backgrounds of dubious value, but each longs for a return to the past. The two are withdrawn, intellectual, snobbish "misanthropes" who display "an impulse towards self-destruction" and seem to have little contact with reality. Petry also mentions a "fundamental duplicity" common to both Julians that shows up "in their ostensible support for social minorities." Furthermore, despite rejections of Christianity by Julian and the Apostate, the ends of their stories (fictional and factual, respectively) indicate a victory for Christianity. Petry concludes, "In her creation of Rayber, Haze Motes, Joy-Hulga, and a host of others who use intellectualism, reason, and formal learning in their doomed attempts to deny Christ, Flannery O'Connor evidently found confirmation—if not direct inspiration—in the remarkable story of Julian the Apostate." Another example of entertaining, solid scholarship by Petry is a short piece entitled "O'Connor's 'Everything That Rises Must Converge'" (*Expl* 45, iii:51–54). Based on the frequent references to the YWCA in the story, Petry believes that "the Y serves as a gauge of the degeneration of the mother's Old South family, and, concomitantly, of the breakdown of old, church-related values in the United States of the mid-twentieth century." By the 1960s when Julian's mother is involved with the YWCA, what had been a thriving, socially vital organization has lost its focus. Petry argues that this decline "parallels the decline of the Old South—and the old America—embodied in Julian's mother."

Maris G. Fiondella's "Augustine, The 'Letter,' and the Failure of Love in Flannery O'Connor's 'The Artificial Nigger'" (*SSF* 24:119–29) is as ambitiously complex as its title suggests. Fiondella uses Augustine's writings coupled with Freudian theory to reexamine the story "as a study of narcissism." According to Fiondella, the reader's ability to detect inherent irony in the presentation and rhetoric of Mr. Head's discourse and to distance himself from Mr. Head's point of view is essential to understanding the story. In his impressive essay "Positive Destruction in the Fiction of Flannery O'Connor" (*SLJ* 20, i:45–60) Richard Kane writes, "The fiction of Flannery O'Connor suggests that destruction can be positive, that violence can instruct, and that evil may be the agent of good." Kane finds examples of this positive destruction in "The Displaced Person," "A Circle in the Fire," and "The Comforts of Home." Characters in each of these stories are forced to enlarge their visions after being confronted with "irrational forces" in the form of other characters or phenomena. In "Exhortation in *Wise Blood*: Rhetorical Theory as an Approach to Flannery O'Connor" (*SCRev* 4, i:92–105) L. B. Kennelly makes use of Edwin Black's theory of rhetorical exhortation to examine O'Connor's technique and purpose in *Wise Blood*. O'Connor's work was driven by a genuine desire to save the "wingless chickens," her term for the spiritually blind. As Kennelly convincingly argues, *Wise Blood*, which is informed by this desire, clearly exhibits the characteristics of "exhortative discourse."

"Flannery O'Connor, the New Criticism, and Deconstruction" (*SoR* 23:271–80) by Ted R. Spivey suggests that the tenets of deconstruction and a sense of intertextuality must be brought to bear on O'Connor's work for the most complete edification. O'Connor herself leaned toward deconstruction in her "opposition to logocentrism" and her integration of a variety of texts. Speaking of future O'Connor criticism, Spivey asserts that "surely her work is important enough to receive the careful attention of those who still work in the New Critical tradition as well as those who are now firmly entrenched in deconstruction." Two short pieces that make interesting side-by-side reading are A. R. Coulthard's "Flannery O'Connor's 'A View of the Woods': A View of the Worst" (*NConL* 17, i:7–9) and Tony Magistrale's "An Explication of Flannery O'Connor's Short Story 'A View of the Woods'" (*NConL* 17, i:6–7). Coulthard finds fault with "muddled symbolism," weak characterization, and an absence of humor, and concludes that "'A View of the Woods' is O'Connor's most atypical—and weakest—story." Tony Magistrale, on the other hand, speaks of "A View of the Woods" as "a subtle and seldom cited O'Connor tale" and expresses admiration for the story's symbolism in particular.

In "Doodlebug, Doodlebug: The Misfit in 'A Good Man is Hard to Find'" (*NConL* 17, iv:8–9) Terry Thompson contends that Flannery O'Connor subtly but intentionally connects the Misfit with the doodlebug or ant lion of the South. Like this unusual insect, the Misfit catches his prey in a hole in the ground. Thompson also points out references to the Misfit playing in the dirt and the fact that he has a "buggish appearance." Thompson concludes: "In an oblique yet meaningful way, the author alludes to her main character's similarity to the patient and efficient ant lion, serving thereby to further emphasize that the South of the story is a bleak land of Snopesian-style scavengers who demonstrate the Darwinian concept of survival of the fittest." In "Flannery O'Connor's 'Parker's Back': the Key to the End" (*NConL* 17, ii:11–12) Dan G. Burns looks to the words of Elihu in Job to explain the ambiguous ending of "Parker's Back." Burns believes that Parker's tears are tears "of ecstasy, signaling redemption."

Welty, A Life in Literature, ed. Albert J. Devlin (Mississippi), is a collection of ten essays dealing with Welty's works and a 1986 interview with the author. Harriet Pollack, in an excellent essay entitled "On Welty, Her Style, and Her Audience," argues that Welty, using what she calls "obstruction" as a means of "connection" with the reader, possesses a style demonstrating "the primacy of the text in the reading process." "The House as Container: Architecture and Myth in *Delta Wedding*" by Dorothy G. Griffin is a fine mythic examination of the image of the house in *Delta Wedding*, and Danièle Pitavy-Souques's "The Modernity of Eudora Welty" demonstrates the modernist tendencies of Welty's narrative technique. Perhaps most fascinating, however, is Patricia S. Yeager's analysis of Welty's *The Golden Apples* in "Eudora Welty and the Dialogic Imagination." In this essay Yeager borrows from the critical vocabulary of Mikhail Bakhtin to illustrate the "emphasis on sexuality and intertextuality" in *The Golden Apples*. Yeager's feminist perspective and contemporary background lead her to discover Welty's use of Yeats's poetry as masculinely biased "tropes of the imagination that must be redefined to include women as well as men."

Eudora Welty (TUSAS 15) by Ruth M. Vande Kieft, one of the earliest and most highly regarded volumes in Twayne's United States Authors Series, was significantly revised in 1987. This seminal work in Welty criticism now includes chapters on *Losing Battles* and *The Optimist's Daughter* and a chapter devoted to "Where Is the Voice Coming From?" and "The Demonstrators." In the final chapter Vande Kieft tries "to show a few of the patterns relating her [Welty's] life to her fiction." She is assisted in this aim by Welty's *One Writer's Beginnings*. These important additions and revisions are in keeping with the excellence of Vande Kieft's original study and will insure her continued standing as a leading critic of Welty's work.

Welty scholars will once again be well served by the *Eudora Welty Newsletter*. Michael A. Benzel's "Textual Variants in 'Powerhouse'" (11, i:1–6) and Pearl A. McHaney's "Textual Variants in 'At the Landing'" (11, i:6–11) are as valuable as they are expertly written. W. U. McDonald, Jr., ed. of the newsletter, is to be congratulated

on his fine collection of Welty materials exhibited recently at the
University of Toledo's Ward M. Canaday Center. Richard W. Oram
and his staff produced a handsome exhibit catalog.

"Vision and Revision in Eudora Welty's 'Death of a Traveling
Salesman'" (*SAF* 15:145–59) by Lawrence Jay Dessner is a fascinating glimpse into the creative process. Dessner presents several
examples of the extensive changes in Welty's revised version of "Death
of a Traveling Salesman" and explains the wisdom behind the alterations. He particularly details Welty's shifting of narrative focus from
omniscience to Bowman's point of view. Barbara Harrell Carson's
"Eudora Welty's Heart of Darkness, Heart of Light" (*SCRev* 4, i:
106–22) is a superior analysis of *The Optimist's Daughter* and of
Laurel's struggle with the loss of her family. Carson writes of Welty's
belief in opposites that "converge in a non-dualistic reality." Furthermore, these are "opposites existing simultaneously and, by their
existence, giving rise to the other." For Laurel, death gives rise to
life, despair becomes hope. Gail L. Mortimer's "'The Way to Get
There': Journeys and Destinations in the Stories of Eudora Welty"
(*SLJ* 19, ii:61–69) examines journey and destination motifs in "Death
of a Traveling Salesman" and "The Key." Mortimer explains Welty's
belief that man's obsession with destinations and final goals in life
prevents him from experiencing day-to-day existence. Mortimer's
insightful analysis of "The Key" is based on an understanding of the
conflicting aims and desires of Albert and Ellie. His discussion of the
symbolism of the key is excellent.

In *"Delta Wedding* and the Kore Complex" (*SoQ* 25, ii:120–30)
Madelon Sprengnether presents a reading that is informed by Nancy
Chodorow's theory of female development. As a counterpart to
Freud's Oedipal model, Chodorow offers the myth of Demeter and
Kore (Persephone). The mother/daughter relationship as expressed
in this myth, Sprengnether suggests, "may offer a point of departure
for understanding the thematic and narrative configurations of a
mother-centered novel such as *Delta Wedding.*" Sprengnether demonstrates a particular sensitivity to Welty's intricate narrative structure, which she describes as a "rhythmic alternation, an almost
imperceptible movement in and out of the consciousness of several
characters, all significantly female." Nancy D. Hargrove's "Portrait of
an Assassin: Eudora Welty's 'Where Is the Voice Coming From?'"
(*SLJ* 20, i:74–88) is a fitting tribute to Welty's descriptive powers and
uncanny insight into human nature. Hargrove uses background de-

tails and numerous pertinent quotes by Welty to establish the historical and creative milieu of the story's development. In addition, she
discusses Welty's style as it relates to the characterization of the assassin: "Using the technique of internal dramatic monologue and
various devices such as colloquial diction, repetition, and symbolic
imagery, Welty lets her character reveal his own traits."

Richard N. Albert addresses the amazing accuracy of Welty's
portrait of Fats Waller in his delightful essay, "Eudora Welty's Fats
Waller: 'Powerhouse'" (*NMW* 19:63–71). Albert suggests that Welty's characterization of Waller, written after seeing him perform in
Jackson, must have been based either on a wider knowledge of the
artist's life or on a remarkable "improvisation" of her own, inspired
by the musician's performance. An unusual and engaging short piece
on Welty is David Robinson's "A Nickel and Dime Matter: Teaching
Eudora Welty's 'A Worn Path'" (*NMW* 19:23–27). Robinson explains how he uses the nickel passage from "A Worn Path" in his writing classes to test the students' "ability to see how facts can be fitted
into different interpretive patterns." He also includes his students'
insightful interpretations of the puzzling incident involving Phoenix,
the hunter, and the stolen nickel.

Scholars paid scant attention to Carson McCullers in 1987, but
enthusiasts may be interested in my "Carson McCullers: Novelist
Turned Playwright" (*SoQ* 25, iii:36–51), a look at McCullers's involvement with the theater that includes histories of her successful
play version of *The Member of the Wedding* and the disappointing
run of *The Square Root of Wonderful*.

Zora Neale Hurston's Their Eyes Were Watching God (Chelsea)
collects what, in editor Harold Bloom's opinion, is the best criticism
available on Zora Neale Hurston's novel. Bloom is correct in his assertion that all of the critical works chosen for inclusion are excellent.
Robert B. Stepto's essay describes Hurston's novel as "a truly coherent
narrative of both ascent and immersion," a theme similar to that examined by Missy Dehn Kubitschek, who views the novel's heroine as
both a quest figure and a participant in a "group ascent narrative,"
enriching Eatonville by communicating the understanding she gained
through her self-discovery and self-definition. Lorraine Bethel's essay,
which Bloom describes as "a manifesto for black feminist criticism,"
suggests that the novel depicts "Black women seeking their own
identity and defining themselves through bonding on various levels."
Barbara Johnson's essay deconstructively examines the great power

of Hurston's rhetorical skill, and Houston A. Baker analyzes the work for subtextual dimensions based upon the "economics of slavery."

Katherine Anne Porter: Conversations, ed. Joan Givner (Mississippi), is an important volume that supplies the most complete selection of autobiographical information concerning the author currently available. George Cheatham finds evidence for a more positive interpretation of the ending in *Pale Horse, Pale Rider* than is usually offered. In his essay "Fall and Redemption in *Pale Horse, Pale Rider*" (*Renascence* 39:396–405) he suggests that "underpinning *Pale Horse, Pale Rider* is the symbolic structure of the fall of mankind, mankind's consequent suffering and death, and mankind's subsequent redemption." Cheatham sees Adam Barclay as a composite Adam/Christ figure whose sacrificial death to save Miranda suggests both the fall of man and the redemption of man through Christ. Cheatham's evidence for a more optimistic reading of the conclusion is based on Porter's numerous references to the Gospel and the association of Adam and Christ. Miranda has been saved by Adam's selfless love and now "chooses to live." Robert H. Brinkmeyer, Jr., offers a superior study of the role of memory in Porter's life and work in "Endless Remembering: The Artistic Vision of Katherine Anne Porter" (*MissQ* 40:5–19). During the 1920s, after becoming disillusioned with "the pure pursuit of art" and distressed about the world situation, Porter returned to her southern heritage and searched "deep within the realm of memory" as source and substance for her writing. For Porter, true contact with memory required a "dialogue" with an inner self. Brinkmeyer examines Porter's theory in the context of "The Jilting of Granny Weatherall," "Portrait: Old South," and "The Old Order."

d. Thomas Wolfe and Erskine Caldwell. John Lane Idol's fine volume, *A Thomas Wolfe Companion* (Greenwood), is designed for the inexperienced reader of Wolfe's fiction. Even those already familiar with Wolfe's writing will find it a handy discussion of Wolfe's characters, themes, and publication history. In *The Complete Short Stories of Thomas Wolfe* (Scribner's) Francis E. Skipp presents all of Wolfe's short stories "for better or for worse pretty much as he intended them to be read." In addition to the 58 previously published stories, *The Complete Short Stories of Thomas Wolfe* includes for the first time in print "The Spanish Letter," important for its display of Wolfe's passionate detestation of fascism and the evil of the Third Reich. This publication may help reduce the damaging and persistent perception of Wolfe as a racially prejudiced and socially unaware author. Skipp describes in his preface his methods for restoring the stories to the form in which Wolfe intended them to be published. The foreword to this volume is an enlightening discussion of Wolfe's fiction by the poet James Dickey. Dickey provides a powerful argument as to the great value of Wolfe's artistic vision.

David Herbert Donald claims in his preface to *Look Homeward, A Life of Thomas Wolfe* (Little, Brown) that having access to all of Wolfe's papers and not having to spare the feelings of Wolfe's surviving siblings enabled him to "trace his [Wolfe's] career more fully than any previous biographer." Although Donald characterizes Wolfe's novels as "remarkably uneven," his respect for the author's writings is obvious. Firm in his conviction that Wolfe possessed enormous self-conscious artistry, Donald devotes considerable attention to the relationship between Wolfe and Maxwell Perkins.

Another contribution by Donald is his article "Look Homeward: Thomas Wolfe and the South" (*SoR* 23:241–55) in which he describes Wolfe's complex and often problematical relationship with the South. Donald suggests three reasons why Wolfe insisted on his southern identity: first, Wolfe had grown up in the South and felt most comfortable around southerners; he was as happy, or happier, in the South than he was anywhere else; and finally, "Wolfe considered himself a Southern writer because the South provided him his truest and best themes as an author."

Frank C. Wilson's fascinating piece on Wolfe's death, "In Search of the Tubercle Bacillus: The Death of Thomas Wolfe" (*Mosaic* 20, iii:57–63), reexamines the circumstances of the author's demise in light of hospitalization records that have been missing until recently. These records allow Wilson to question the theory put forth in 1974 by James Meehan that Wolfe was killed by the fungus Coccidioides immitis, which he supposedly picked up on a trip to the Southwest. Wilson convincingly argues that it is unquestionably more likely that Wolfe died of tuberculosis of the brain.

An entertaining look at the nature of autobiography and fictional autobiography and their similarities is provided by O. Alan Weltzien's "*Look Homeward, Angel* and Wolfe's Autobiographical Imperative" (*CEA* 49, ii–iv:89–101). Weltzien contends that *Look Homeward, Angel* demonstrates the autobiographical method at work. He says of Wolfe as autobiographer that "from an omniscient present he surveys and interprets his past." Interpretation is an important concept in fictional autobiography, for the author's corpus of recollections is altered and arranged for present purposes. Weltzien has a firm grasp of autobiography as a genre and uses this basis to draw out the essence and focus of Wolfe's novel. Carol Johnston's *Thomas Wolfe, A Descriptive Bibliography* (Pittsburgh) will be a valuable research tool.

Erskine Caldwell's autobiography, *With All My Might* (Peachtree), never fails to be entertaining. Caldwell explains that he attempted, in his fiction, to reveal "with all . . . [his] might the inner spirit of men and women as they responded to the joys of life and reacted to the sorrows of existence."

iii. Expatriates and Émigrés—Nabokov, Miller, Nin, and Rand

Yet another excellent volume in the Understanding Contemporary American Literature series is Stephen Jan Parker's *Understanding Vladimir Nabokov* (So. Car.). Before presenting a clear and effective analysis of each of Nabokov's major works, Parker supplies a brief biographical sketch and a short overview of characteristic aspects of Nabokov's fiction. Whereas Parker admits that each of Nabokov's novels is "invested with a discrete individuality," he believes that certain generalities may be discovered within them. Each of Nabokov's protagonists, for example, is a "consciousness liberated from the everyday affairs of social man." More specifically, he asserts, Nabokov's major concern in his fiction is to demonstrate how an individual's consciousness actively shapes the reality it perceives.

Charles Nicol examines Nabokov's connections with the science fiction genre in "Nabokov and Science Fiction: 'Lance'" (*SFS* 14, i:9–20). Although he claimed to "loathe science fiction," Nabokov had great respect for H. G. Wells, and Nicol points out that Nabokov's works can often be read as science fiction. In Nabokov's short story "Lance," Nicol identifies "two running metaphors [mountain climbing and medieval romance] that profoundly alter the surface plot"—a surface plot which has the characteristics of a science fiction work. Nicol concludes that since Nabokov believed that successful fiction creates "an alternate universe," then "every work of art is in one triumphant sense a work of SF." Peggy Ward Corn provides a thorough examination of the interplay between Shade's poem and Kinbote's notes in her essay " 'Combinational Delight': The Uses of the

Story Within a Story in *Pale Fire*" (*JNT* 17:83–90). Couching *Pale Fire* within the tradition of Russian doll fiction (stories within stories "characterized by interruption"), Corn describes the complex intertwining that causes Kinbote's commentary on the poem to be commented on by the poem in turn. Carol M. Dole's "Innocent Trifles, or 'Signs and Symbols'" (*SSF* 24:303–05) is an imaginative speculation on the role of the fruit jellies in "Signs and Symbols." Dole, who wryly discovers an anagram in the names of the jellies spelling "theme," sees them as "a signpost, directing us to the part of the story in which the theme is most evident: the paragraph describing referential mania."

S. E. Sweeney's "Nabokov's Amphiphorical Gestures" (*StTCL* 2: 189–211) is an ambitious study of the writer's complex use of metaphor. Sweeney's term for this type of metaphor is taken from a passage in *Bend Sinister* in which Nabokov describes the "extreme simplicity of heaven in the acrobat's amphiphorical gesture." Sweeney suggests that this coinage of Nabokov's "implies not only a two-sided sign—a gesture made with both arms—but also a metaphor with two possible interpretations." The article examines examples of such metaphors in *Bend Sinister* and *Speak, Memory*. These metaphors are "characterized by extended analogies; baroque, seemingly uncontrolled imagery and rhetoric; and inherent ambiguity" and are uniquely Nabokov. In his article "Practicing Nostalgia: Time and Memory in Nabokov's Early Russian Fiction" (*StTCL* 2:253–70) Philip Sicker addresses Nabokov's artistic preoccupation with memory as evidenced by his early Russian works. Sicker points out that "these short works reveal not only a complex theory of time but also the remarkable strategies that he had already devised for retrieving and safeguarding its treasures." This strategy involves seeing present events as future memories. Sicker describes the role of memory and especially this type of memory in several of Nabokov's Russian stories. Nabokov's interest in time and memory is akin to Proust's, but unlike the fleeting Proustian glimpses of the past, the memories of Nabokov's characters can be prolonged. Sicker writes: "For Nabokov, the key to invigorating memory is, paradoxically, to compound the act of recollection—to project oneself into a hypothetical future and, thus, view the composed but fleeting present image with the 'distinctness and relief' of an object recovered from the past."

Of certain interest to Anaïs Nin and Henry Miller scholars is the fifth volume of *Anaïs: An International Journal*, ed. Gunther Stuhlmann. Especially important are an excerpt from E. James Liberman's new biography of Otto Rank, a never-before-published interview with Nin, and Stuhlmann's contribution to the journal, "The Genesis of 'Alraune'—Some notes on the making of *House of Incest*." This volume also contains Nin's letters to Lawrence Durrell from 1937–39 and an intriguing essay by Valerie Harms entitled "The Dream is the Key—the drafts that became *House of Incest*." Several other notable pieces include Alfred Perles's portrait of Nin, an entertaining sampling of Wambly Bald's "La Vie de Bohème" column, and Beatrice Commengé's " 'The Street Where I Lived'—On the trail of Henry Miller." The appearance of *A Literate Passion* (Harcourt), the correspondence of Nin and Miller, along with the publication of *Henry and June* (Harcourt, 1986), selections from Nin's diary, represents the complete record of the passionate relationship between Miller and Nin. *A Literate Passion,* ed. Gunther Stuhlmann, presents an account of the Miller-Nin relationship that had heretofore remained unpublished. Although Miller's *Letters to Anaïs Nin* appeared in 1965, all references to their intimate involvement were omitted; thus this new volume is the definitive text, not only for observing both authors' development as serious writers, but for examining the personal aspects of their correspondence as well.

James T. Baker in his preface to *Ayn Rand* (TUSAS 501) makes the claim that, at long last, Rand will be given "a fair and objective assessment by someone who . . . neither hates nor loves her," but who, he hopes, "sees her as she is." Baker's study begins with a presentation of Rand's "life and times" and then proceeds to examine her creative writing, her philosophical essays, and the major themes and theories that Rand espoused. In his discussion of *Anthem* he observes: "A reader who is unwilling to suspend disbelief on a grand scale will find *Anthem* ridiculous." Similarly, he maintains that an "outsider looking at her career" must judge *Atlas Shrugged* as merely "a huge burst of ideological wind." However, Baker does present several arguments for the ultimate value of Rand's philosophy and writings.

Frank O'Connor's work receives welcome attention in Michael Liberman's "Unforeseen Duty in Frank O'Connor's 'Guests of the Nation' " (*SSF* 24:438–41). Liberman convincingly argues the thematic importance of the words "duty" and "unforeseen," both of which appear more often in the 1954 revised version of the story.

Carl Herzig's "Roots of Night: Emerging Style and Vision in the Early Journalism of Djuna Barnes" (*CentR* 31:255–69) is a superlative examination of Barnes's journalistic career. According to Herzig, the balance that Barnes sought between objective journalistic distance and subjective involvement created a tension that electrified her later writing. Herzig describes several of Barnes's articles and the characteristic style and concerns that were already taking root. For example, Barnes's interest in the "dichotomies between the animal and the human, and between nature and civilization" can be traced to the 1915 article "Djuna Barnes Probes the Souls of the Jungle Folk at the Hippodrome Circus." Herzig astutely links Barnes's fascination with fading figures like Lillian Russell and Diamond Jim Brady with Barnes's characters who are also "caught between the contrasting images of public cosmetics and private paunches and are reminded daily of their mortality by the pervading odors of the flesh."

iv. Westerners

Maureen Ryan states at the outset that her study *Innocence and Estrangement in the Fiction of Jean Stafford* (LSU) concentrates on Stafford's "presentation of the experience of women in modern American society." First, Ryan insists, the "complexities and horrors of the modern human condition" dictated for Stafford the "distanced, objective stance of the ironist." Also, she continues, Stafford's ironic vision was reinforced by the characteristic "antithetical impulses" of the American literary tradition, and it is Stafford's "manipulation of the paradoxically varied yet similar strains in American literature" that lends her work its "diversity and vivacity." More important to Ryan's thesis, however, and incorporating the two previous assertions, is Ryan's belief that "Stafford the ironist and Stafford the American are tempered always by Stafford the woman." The value of Stafford's fiction lies in its examination of "the female role in society and women's reactions . . . to their situations," an inversion of the traditional theme of male development that demonstrates the young female struggling to reach maturity in the face of adverse circumstances.

Claire Mattern's "Rebels, Aliens, Outsiders, and the Nonconformist in the Writing of Mari Sandoz" (*CEA* 49, ii–iv:102–13) offers an interesting look at Sandoz's background as well as pertinent discussions of the rebel/outcast characters in her fiction.

Mary Jean DeMarr's "Ruth Suckow's Iowa 'Nice Girls'" (*Midamerica* 13[1986]:69–83) is a comprehensive look at the women in four of Suckow's novels. Because of the relative unfamiliarity of these novels, DeMarr must summarize as well as interpret and does an admirable job of presenting sufficiently complete plot synopses while bringing out that which is related to her thesis. Suckow is interested in the themes of "woman's centrality in family and home and the yearnings of some women for achievement on a broader stage," but her characters are not merely thematic devices, as each is fully developed and well rounded.

In "Edwin Corle and the White Man's Indian" (*ArQ* 42:68–76) Carl R. Shirley investigates the extent to which Corle—who was praised for his realistic portrayal of Indians in *Fig Tree John*—achieves the same objective in *People on Earth*. Shirley contends that although the novel's ending is regrettably sentimental, the character portrayals are objective. Corle achieves this aim by avoiding narratorial intrusion and comment and by making the reader "draw his own conclusions."

An original and important work on Ross Lockridge's *Raintree County* is Park Dixon Goist's "Habits of the Heart in *Raintree County*" (*Midamerica* 13[1986]:94–106). Goist uses *Habits of the Heart: Individualism and Commitment in American Life* (a 1985 work by Robert Bellah and other social scientists on community versus isolation in 20th-century America) as a jumping-off point for discussing the same theme in *Raintree County*. Goist explains that the "tension between individualism and commitment to community forms a major conflict at the very heart of the book." *Raintree County's* John Shawnessy wrestles with this conflict all his life and unlike many other heroes of American fiction elects to remain in his community. "The resolution of that tension in the novel is an uneasy one," explains Goist, "for while Mr. Shawnessy is outwardly a respected member of the community, the lower case mr. shawnessy continues to live in a vivid imagination which struggles against all social restrictions."

Elaine Neil Orr presents in *Tillie Olsen and a Feminist Spiritual Vision* (Miss.) an in-depth "religious interpretation" of Tillie Olsen's literature. "Olsen's writing requires a religious comprehension," Orr maintains, "not only because of the life affirming vision it discloses but because it is based in hope." Although she recognizes the sexist, racist, and class-conscious world depicted by Olsen in her writing, Orr sees "image clusters," metaphors of wholeness and coherence, within Olsen's texts. These metaphors provide an interpretive base leading ultimately to a transcendent vision that does not ignore "the realities of suffering." Olsen's revelation of the spiritual truths underlying the traditional female experience of motherhood, Orr continues, encourages a transformative vision free from the patriarchal emphasis of traditional religious thought.

William Saroyan, The Man and the Writer Remembered, ed. Leo Hamalian (Fairleigh Dickinson), is self-billed as the first volume "honoring Saroyan for his achievement." As such, it contains an overview of Saroyan's life and work by Brian Darwent, several excellent critical essays, personal recollections of Saroyan by his children and others, and a small sampling of his correspondence. Hamalian expertly arranged this volume so that each of the entries chosen for inclusion builds upon the others to present a full and admiring view of the artist. The Armenian Saroyan, Hamalian insists, understood the experience of immigrants in America, "the modern tragedy of deracination and exile," as few other writers have.

v. Bellow, Malamud, and the Jewish-American Experience

In the Mainstream, The Jewish Presence in Twentieth-Century American Literature, 1950's–1980's (Greenwood), by social historian Louis Harap, offers an examination of "Jewish development as refracted in the nation's literature." As well as a chapter on critics such as Trilling and Kazan, Harap presents chapters devoted to Bellow and Malamud and their ideological and artistic developments as Jewish writers. Although Bellow is not essentially religious, Harap writes that he "clung to the basic Jewish affirmation of the value of life." Malamud, who sees himself as an American writer rather than as a Jewish-American writer, nevertheless shares Bellow's rejection of nihilism and "dehumanizing tendencies"—a rejection which, Harap maintains, separates them from their non-Jewish contemporaries.

The second edition of *Saul Bellow, An Annotated Bibliography* (Garland) by Gloria L. Cronin and Blaine H. Hall focuses on the annotation of significant contributions to Bellow scholarship. It is "designed as a simple index and not as an exhaustive concordance." Since there is no published biography of Bellow, the listing of biographical sources is especially valuable.

"Bellow's Shawmut: Rationalizations and Redemption" (*SSF* 24: 375–80) by Karl F. Knight offers a thoughtful analysis of the "constructed rhetorical appeal" that Harry Shawmut makes to Miss Rose in Bellow's "Him with His Foot in His Mouth." As Knight points out,

Shawmut is not an entirely reliable narrator since his letter to Miss Rose is calculated for effect. Shawmut's rhetoric accentuates the actual suffering caused by "his age, poor health, and isolation." However, in his description of those sufferings that will elicit sympathy and in his clever explanation of past improprieties, Shawmut appears something of a manipulator of human response. Knight writes that "Harry Shawmut serves up a comic and pathetic mixture of heartfelt confession and self-justification." Knight also contributes another brief look at a Bellow work in "Sexual Irony in Bellow's 'What Kind of Day Did You Have?' " (NConL 17,ii:10–11). Knight suggests that Katrina merely exchanges father figures when she leaves the home ruled by her chauvinistic bourgeois father to serve the equally patronizing and vile Victor Wulpy.

Another important work on Bellow is David D. Anderson's look at the author's views of Chicago entitled " 'That Somber City' Since Midcentury" (MMisc 14[1986]:58–69). Chicago as seen by the still innocent and idealistic Augie March in The Adventures of Augie March and Chicago as seen through the jaded eyes of Albert Corde in The Dean's December are two very different towns. Augie's Chicago is big and brassy and corrupt, but it is also a very personal town where human beings still exist as individuals. Conversely, Anderson writes, "Corde's Chicago is that of a city and a corruption grown impersonal, inhuman, unmanageable." Anderson provides sound analyses of Chicago's role in the two novels and a useful discussion of Bellow's own complex feelings about the city. Another Bellow article worthy of note is Steven Marcus's "Reading the Illegible: Modern Representations of Urban Experience" (SoR 22[1986]:443–64). Marcus is concerned with the ways Bellow and Thomas Pynchon follow or depart from "the classical modern conception of the city." Most of Marcus's study is devoted to Bellow's evolving fictional representations of the city. In his early works Chicago is a "preternatural force, preverbal and primordial in its ancient sources of power, nature, and culture compounded in a mystery that is unfathomable and inexhaustible." But Bellow's position gradually changes, and New York and Chicago both come to represent "the contemporary Inferno" where communications have completely broken down.

Critical Essays on Bernard Malamud, ed. Joel Salzberg (Hall), collects in one volume not only a fine selection of previously published essays and reviews but also four new essays composed for this

volume. Salzberg, in his substantial and excellently annotated introduction, examines the critical response to Malamud's works from the
1950s to the present and demonstrates the development of Malamud
scholarship from the mythical and archetypal preoccupations of the
1960s to the psychological, oneiric, and contemporary approaches of
recent times. Salzberg also makes the astute observation that criticism
of Malamud's short stories "remains sketchy" and calls not only for
continued studies of the short stories, but also for a much-needed
critical biography of the author. Two hitherto ignored links between
Malamud's *The Natural* and *A New Life* are the subjects of James J.
Beyer's "Underpaid and Bumped Off: Two Unnoticed Malamudian
Repetitions" (*NConL* 17,i:10–12). Beyer notes that Roy Hobbs and
Sy Levin both receive precisely the same salary and that both replace
their predecessors at their jobs and in the arms of their women.
Beyer also brings out Malamud's pun in *A New Life* that alludes to
The Natural. Levin is told that Leo Duffy, who previously held the
position Levin now has, "had bumped himself off." Beyer sees this
as an obvious reference to Bump Bailey, Roy Hobbs's predecessor.

S. J. Perelman, in an early letter to his friend I. J. Kapstein, en-
treated him to read Vincent Van Gogh's letters, which he described
as presenting a "Slice Out of Life." In the same letter Perelman related how he "came as near to bawling as . . . [he had] in years
reading Gauguin's letters to Bernard." It is fitting that Perelman
should have valued so highly the correspondence of other artists, for
his letters, too, provide a slice out of life, and *Don't Tread on Me:
The Selected Letters of S. J. Perelman* (Viking) is a remarkably full
portrait of this complex master of wit. Editor Prudence Crowther
explains her motivation for undertaking the arduous task: "This book
was a search for a man I did not know well but was certain I wanted
to know better." Her delightful recounting of her own friendship
with Perelman in the last year of his life provides a personal glimpse
of the author's life that expertly guides the reader into the letters
themselves.

Steven H. Gale, who composed the S. J. Perelman entry for the
DLB (1982), considers Perelman "one of the major prose stylists
of American literature in the twentieth century." His current work,
S. J. Perelman, A Critical Study (Greenwood), is an expansion of
his earlier article and represents more than a quadrupling of its material. Gale's volume, well annotated and indexed, demonstrates the
ultimate value of Perelman's work in the genres of prose, movie

scripts, and drama. Examining both stylistic elements and thematic
concerns, Gale identifies three elements of Perelman's style: his innovative use of clichés, his inclusion of a "wide range of allusions that
flow through his writing like a vein of rich ore," and a "solid underpinning" derived from American-Jewish culture, or, more specifically,
the Yiddish theater.

vi. Iconoclasts and Innovators

Jan Gorak, who examines the fiction of Nathanael West, John Hawkes,
and John Barth in *God the Artist*, maintains that two principal views
of the artist have emerged in much modern criticism: the artist as
symbolist "omnipotent in mind" and the artist as naturalist "crushed
by power structures and language systems." Gorak, however, supports the view of the artist as "godly maker" and, tracing the development of the concept of the *deus artifex*, argues that it is a superior
model for the artist's activity, encompassing "both the symbolic and
naturalist poles of the artist's imagination." Gorak also forwards a
plea for realism, a "remobilization of the traditional mimetic energy
of the *topos*." The intriguing discussion of West's works that occupies
two chapters in *God the Artist* examines West's use of the *deus artifex
topos* to illustrate the relationships of artist, audience, and reality in
America of the 1920s and 1930s and demonstrates how West's fiction
shows a "*topos* being dissolved into its social context," the godly
artist in decline. An unusual work on West and Miller is Kingsley
Widmer's "Twisting American Comedy: Henry Miller and Nathanael
West, Among Others" (*ArQ* 43:218–30). Lively and opinionated, the
article discusses Miller's and West's use of that type of humor that
has traditionally been labeled "intellectual, mocking, pessimistic" and
"radical." Widmer suggests that the comedy of Miller, and especially
of West, is based on a parodic and deforming treatment of traditional
American humor like that of Mark Twain.

Robin Lyndenberg's *Word Cultures*, subtitled *Radical Theory
and Practice in William S. Burroughs' Fiction* (Illinois), demonstrates
that in Burroughs's experimental fiction the author was developing
ideas that, in light of contemporary theory, are recognizable as characteristic of post-structuralism and deconstruction. As Lyndenberg
observes, while *Naked Lunch* has received a fair amount of critical
attention, Burroughs's more experimental trilogy, *The Soft Machine,
Nova Express*, and *The Ticket That Exploded*, remains largely ig-

nored. Lydenberg maintains that whereas Burroughs's later and more accessible writings are often viewed as "an abnegation of his earlier experimental works," it is in the earlier novels that any real study of his theories and techniques must be based. Acting upon this premise, Lyndenberg concentrates upon Burroughs's four most experimental novels in *Word Cultures*. Burroughs challenged, just as the contemporary theorists do, "our conventional notions about the status of the author in the text, about the referentiality of language, and about the dualism of Western thought." In *Naked Lunch*, Lyndenberg's argument proceeds, Burroughs attempted to replace "moral and metaphorical rhetoric" with "the independence of truly literal language." All language, however, is recognized by Burroughs to be inherently linked with the symbolic systems of mortality and culture.

Regina Weinreich's *The Spontaneous Poetics of Jack Kerouac* (So. Ill.) is, the publisher asserts, the first study "to explore Kerouac's place in American literature by establishing the total design of his work." Weinreich analyzes Kerouac's technique as displayed in his autobiographical fiction. Kerouac intended his books, which he referred to collectively as the Legend of Duluoz, to be seen as "one vast book." Until now most critics have dismissed this claim by citing the lack of linear unity throughout his works, yet Weinreich sees throughout them a poetic unity that she explores through the use of jazz as a controlling metaphor. Kerouac's life, the subject of his narratives, provides the "riff" that he elaborates upon and magnifies through cyclical repetition. Similarly, just as jazz musicians of the bop era did, Kerouac attempted to "perfect a deliberate style that produces the illusion of spontaneity." Weinreich's observations about Kerouac's prose provide her with a perspective ideally suited to an effective, in-depth analysis of the author's fiction.

A World Outside (Texas), a new book-length study of the fiction of Paul Bowles, is important in light of what its author, Richard F. Patteson, terms the "surprisingly little critical treatment of Bowles's work" to have appeared to date. Patteson describes Bowles as "the most resolutely expatriate American writer since Henry James," and he argues that the "fact of expatriation itself" has been the most influential factor in the shaping of Bowles's work. Indeed, Patteson continues, "the question of security, along with the related issues of shelter and exposure, interiority and exteriority, is a concept that animates Bowles's fiction and gives it distinctive form." The most frequently recurring plot structure in the work of Bowles is movement "away from the apparently safe and domestic, toward the dangerous and alien." Most of Bowles's characters confront a crisis "in which the human need for security is overwhelmed by the hard metaphysical truth that there is no interior, no safe place, no humanly made structure that endures." Also, A World Outside is replete with references not only to other critical studies but also to autobiography and interviews as well, for, as Patteson states: "My approach does presuppose a connection between the human being and the stories he tells through his writings." In "The Affirming Silence: Paul Bowles's 'Pastor Dowe at Tacaté'" (SSF 24:381–86), Ralph St. Louis addresses the issue of language versus myth. St. Louis explains that Dowe is forced to confront the inadequacies of his rhetoric. After a brief conversion to the mythology of the Indians, the Pastor leaves the village and the story ends in silence. St. Louis speculates that the Indians "had no need for a teller who confused, as we all seem to do from time to time, language with power."

"Imagination, Control and Betrayal in Jane Bowles's 'A Stick of Green Candy'" (SSF 24:25–29) by Mark T. Bassett is an important contribution to studies of Jane Bowles's short fiction. According to Bassett, "A Stick of Green Candy" revolves around "the belief that a young girl can choose her role in society, or re-order society entirely, through the power of the imagination" and the loss of this belief that accompanies adulthood. Bassett suggests that the story of Mary, the little girl who betrays and then abandons her created world for the boy who invades it, is connected in an autobiographical sense to Bowles's own fear of losing artistic control.

Andrew Delbanco's "Holden Caulfield Goes to Law School" (New Republic 9 Mar.:27–30) offers an interesting account of J. D. Salinger's lawsuit against his would-be biographer Ian Hamilton, but the real value of the article lies in Delbanco's perceptive analysis of Salinger's career—a career that Delbanco believes "is closed, in both senses of the word." Delbanco doubts, despite rumors to the contrary, that there is another masterpiece waiting to be discovered among Salinger's manuscripts. Salinger is described as "a masterful, but a small-scale artist" who stopped writing for the public when "he knew he had lost his audience."

At the beginning of Robert A. Heinlein (TUSAS 522) Leon Stover states his hope that "fanship" will "suffice for criticism." He continues: "all the same, I hope my partisan treatment will invite readers unfamiliar with Heinlein to discover him and make their own judgments." Examining Heinlein within the literary tradition of Twain, Whitman, and even Stevenson, Stover finds certain themes that seem to be universals in Heinlein's works. These include Heinlein's strong sense of Calvinist determinism and his fervent belief in American values and the need to defend them. The traditional values espoused by Heinlein may offend some contemporary critics, but Heinlein's praise of "hard common sense" and "unsullied human dignity" have struck a responsive chord in his readers.

Georgia State University

15. Fiction: The 1960s to the Present

Jerome Klinkowitz

The ever-fluid nature of the term "contemporary" defies distinguishing labels that prove so helpful (if canonistically limiting) for earlier periods in American fiction. Rare is the scholar who can claim that his or her characterization of the present bears broader authority. The most familiar response among this year's critics is to claim neutrality amid the battles of interpretive systems, yet in nearly every case a determining factor can be found within these acts of perception—usually an unadmitted constraint that influences the choice of authors to be studied and interpretations of their work. Nostalgia for a style of humanism today's critics can only suppose informed previous literary eras is the most obvious constraint, but naive beliefs in more current systems also have a most distressing effect on our understanding of the present. As usual, the year's best scholarship and criticism forces itself to look squarely at the contemporary scene with neither false perceptions (seeing only what one wants, or feels psychologically necessary, to see) nor the negative hallucinations (not seeing something that is really there, because the terms of one's perception refuse to measure it) that make so much current work virtually worthless to sincere students of recent American fiction.

i. General Studies

Five substantial books written by scholars from around the world make 1987 a promising year, but the first three turn out to be disappointments because their authors fail to admit (and incorporate in their approaches) obvious prejudices about what they expect from contemporary fiction. Jan Gorak, writing from South Africa, argues in *God the Artist* that only a stable relationship with reality allows the fiction writer any moral stature. By this rubric he finds John Barth's *LETTERS* to be a much better work than *The Sot-Weed Factor* without considering the aesthetic substance of either work. While

Gorak's high moralistic approach sheds light on John Hawkes (who "focuses on the victimizer, the man who insists on his right to make his illusions our illusions"), it reduces our general understanding of the period to the truism that writer figures in these works "move from a desire for death to a reengagement with life"—a truism because this statement is allowed to stand unexamined as an endorsement of what fiction is supposed to be about. From Tel Aviv, Brian McHale submits *Postmodernist Fiction* (Methuen), a more useful study because it admits that resisting reality need not be the ticket to hell Gorak presumes it to be. This broader view lets him make more considered judgments of Barth and Hawkes, and also to understand the more fundamentally innovative work accomplished by Clarence Major, Ishmael Reed, Walter Abish, Raymond Federman, and Ronald Sukenick. But because of an unexamined allegiance to the reductive narratological formulations of Benjamin Hrushovski, McHale paints himself into the corner of proclaiming generic science fiction as the logical consequence of their aesthetics, while accepting the Eurocentric beliefs of Vladimir Nabokov as axiomatic to postmodern fiction (a fiction that in fact stands most of these axioms on their heads). But most regrettable is Alan Wilde's report filed from an Ivy League America only now, a decade and a half after the action began elsewhere, venturing into the area with his *Middle Grounds* (Pennsylvania). This inaugural volume in editor Emory Elliott's "Studies in Contemporary American Fiction" replicates the series' own announced intention of discrediting the field's polar organization of contending realist and antirealist camps by finding a compromise position in the middle where writers can write and critics can theorize in the style of happy harmony one finds, a century or two after the fact, in the individual periods characterizing the great cycle of American literature. But like Gorak's attempt to reinstate a Leavisite "Great Tradition" for current American letters, Wilde's reading of Donald Barthelme as an ironist, Thomas Pynchon as a Conradian deplorer of bestial extremes, Thomas Berger as an unsettling moralist, and Max Apple as a friendly manipulator of aesthetic and psychological orders tells us little about the reasons for and the effects of their ambivalent relationship to reality and the consequences of that relationship for their fiction's form. Wilde understands Grace Paley's use of fictive invention "as a function not of the free-floating, unanchored imagination . . . but of imagination inextricably entangled with a world that, at the very least, provides the foundation for whatever it is that invention intends and accomplishes," but his preference for a contemporary who presumes to dig deep (Raymond Carver) over one who sticks resolutely to the photorealistic surface (Ann Beattie) reveals Wilde's predisposition toward fiction that boasts an obviously humanistic message.

What hope, then, is there for a valid interpretation of the present? Edmund Wilson, Malcolm Cowley, and Alfred Kazin, after all, wrote accurately and convincingly about F. Scott Fitzgerald, William Faulkner, and Saul Bellow when those writers were their immediate contemporaries. Their own spirit of working close to the bone, yet with a steady touch unhampered by predispositions brought along as encumbering impediments, can be found in two unlikely places: Richard Kostelanetz's collected essays, *The Old Fictions and the New* (McFarland), and Larry McCaffery and Sinda Gregory's *Alive and Writing: Interviews with American Authors of the 1980s* (Illinois). Kostelanetz's sympathies are amazingly broad yet never uncritically sloppy: he can argue polemically for the avant-garde, yet also appreciate the commercial success of Donald Barthelme while deploring what he feels is the self-deceived uniformity of Ronald Sukenick and the Fiction Collective. Part of his duty is in noting how the conditions of production influence the product, a business-world concern far beyond the ken of Gorak, McHale, and Wilde, yet subtlely determinant nevertheless. It is the spirit captured by McCaffery and Gregory in their talks with Walter Abish, Max Apple, Ann Beattie, Raymond Carver, Samuel Delany, Barry Hannah, William Kennedy, Ursula Le Guin, Thomas McGuane, Tom Robbins, and Edmund White. Gorak's moral world denies the existence of phenomenologists such as Abish, semiotic comedians like Apple, and metaphorical acrobats like Robbins (not to speak of gay fiction by White). McHale reads Delany for his modernist poetics only, while Wilde cannot tolerate Beattie's dedication to making what she can at the level of surface. In *Alive and Writing* these authors are queried precisely as a well-thought-out essay interrogates a literary work, highlighting certain concerns and approaches but never operating within naive constraints that obliterate a major portion of the artwork at hand. The book's approach neither excludes nor simplfies, but instead employs two of the finest critical intelligences of our era to explore the range and specific process of each writer's craft. As such, *Alive and Well* becomes the single most important volume on contemporary American fiction published this year.

Gorak's, McHale's, and Wilde's appraisals are severely limited
by their secret agendas; more candor is shown by other critics who
approach contemporary fiction with specific conclusions in mind,
and if the reader is careful to understand those purposes some genuinely helpful insights can be gained. Modern versus postmodern is
a familiar opposition, though with an interesting twist in 1987 as
David Hayman's *Re-Forming the Narrative: Toward a Mechanics of
Modernist Fiction* (Cornell) praises what is in fact postmodern fiction while William V. Spanos's *Repetitions: The Postmodern Occasion
in Literature and Culture* (LSU) disparages it as destructive because
it is not modernist. Hayman sees John Barth dedicated to working
out the logic of an admittedly minimal situation ("Night-Sea Journey"), Robert Coover exploring the thematics of impossibility ("The
Brother") and the explosiveness of an unhierarchal verbal landscape
(*Gerald's Party*), Raymond Federman offering concrete combinations
of both vertical and horizontal parataxis, William H. Gass taking a
patently impossible sense of objectivity and making it both malleable
and oblique (*Willie Masters' Lonesome Wife*, which demonstrates
the "dynamic philosophical potential of textual impossibility"), and
Harry Mathews appreciating disorder and irreverence as qualities
productive of an unsettling, irrational, unexpected, and disturbing
style of narrative. The situation of an "impossible object" is for Hayman an invitation to reject the traditional mediation distance provides
and thereby to manifest one's artistic liberation from the need to
create verisimilitude. Spanos regrets such circumstances, seeing in
Barth the decenteredness of a fallen world, in Barthelme merely a
satiric critique of cultural and philosophical models, and in Pynchon
and Coover a reaction against sociopolitical systems with nothing offered in their stead. Their "freefloating neither/nor of infinite negativity" manages only to "destroy the archival teleological forms of
traditional narrative discourse and the structural expectations these
forms have inscribed on the reader's consciousness and thus recall his
ontological sociopolitical being-in-the-world as the human *case*," a
situation that seems bleak indeed and light years away from the fruit-
fully creative narrative universe Hayman has described. How postmodern fiction becomes virtually unreadable to someone unwilling to
consider narratological issues is all too apparent in Eugene Good-
heart's *Pieces of Resistance* (Cambridge), in which William Styron,
Donald Barthelme, Norman Mailer, and Raymond Carver are read
strictly in terms of their subject matter—a subject matter both Hay-

man and Spanos would agree does not even exist in the terms Good-heart continues to use. That Carver, who employs representational figures, and Barthelme, who often doesn't, are equally perplexing to Goodheart says something for Hayman and Spanos's common approach, for Pearl K. Bell's "Fiction Chronicle" in *PR* 54:99–114 displays a similar mystification with the fiction of Beattie, Carver, Mary Robison, and Renata Adler, preferring instead the more traditionally message-oriented works of Tama Janowitz and Deborah Eisenberg.

Four collections of essays by various hands make their own contributions. Guest editor Nicholas Delbanco presents the first of two special issues on "Contemporary American Fiction" with *Michigan Quarterly Review* 28:597–806. The most valuable of the "Symposium" contributions are by Steve Katz (pp. 756–58) who attacks the cowardly conformity that promotes minimalism and by Charles Johnson (pp. 753–56) who calls for a tradition of "writing excellence," because "Minimalist stories and supermarket fiction that sidestep the adventurous possibilities of metaphor, skim the surface of life, and hold back the explosion of many forms of diction on the page produce . . . stories that are thin and *detotalized* and lacking in the rich, interpretative possibilities of language and literary form." Especially noteworthy is Jefferson Humphries's "People Made Out of Words: New Ways of Looking at New American Fiction" (pp. 788–802) for its indictment of critical practice in failing to appreciate Katz's and Johnson's demands, and for Humphries's specific appreciations of fictionist/theorist Ronald Sukenick's more promising approach. Editors Loren Logsdon and Charles W. Mayer's *Since Flannery O'Connor: Essays on the Contemporary American Short Story* (West. Ill.) present a broad selection of commentary on the polar styles rejected by Alan Wilde, concluding that "only one kind of story truly counts," and that is the kind that is both realistic in terms of its approximation of the world and experimental in its approach to literary technique— by this axiom Kurt Vonnegut, John Cheever, and Joyce Carol Oates succeed, while Ann Beattie and Tobias Wolff fail (the single minimalist held up for praise is Raymond Carver, and he because his supposedly realistic fiction employs as much innovation in its narrative as do the works of Donald Barthelme). *Contemporary American Fiction*, ed. Malcolm Bradbury and Sigmund Ro (Arnold), is distinguished by Ihab Hassan's "Quest: Forms of Adventure in Contemporary American Literature" (pp. 122–37). Like the volume's editors, Hassan wonders what traditionally American literary traits will survive postmodernism, and it is his suggestion that a combination of autobiographical witness, adventure, and quest creates a uniquely productive "wound," a divided consciousness that generates such narratives as Norman Mailer's *Why Are We in Vietnam?*, James Dickey's *Deliverance*, John McPhee's *Coming Into the Country*, and Peter Matthiessen's *The Snow Leopard*, texts which are "extreme enactments of our fate in the universe," gathering virtually everything within them. My own "The Extra-Literary in Contemporary American Fiction" (pp. 18–37) in Bradbury and Ro's collection complements my "The New Fiction" (pp. 353–67), the essay discussing recent fiction in *The New History of Literature*; in the former piece innovative literary essays by Sukenick, Gilbert Sorrentino, Steve Katz, and Walter Abish are used to shed light on their own and others' fiction; in the latter, the quasirepresentational fiction of Stephen Dixon, Grace Paley, and Thomas McGuane is shown to extend the innovators' aesthetic breakthroughs to a reexamination of the generative sources for realistic narrative itself.

How current innovations in fiction grow out of a special milieu in cultural history occupies Ronald Sukenick's *Down and In: Life in the Underground* (Morrow). Ostensibly a social and literary history of the bohemian life in Greenwich Village and the East Village of the early 1960s, *Down and In* in fact chronicles Sukenick's own "conversion experience, that epiphany of self-recognition that is a discovery of a real self beyond the claims of official existence, and at the same time a ticket . . . to participation as a singular individual in a shared public life that subverts the claims of our homogenized mass-market culture." Partaking of Ihab Hassan's post-postmodern quest myth, Sukenick's journey through the underworld of America's bohemian tradition prepares us for his own emergence as a fiction writer and literary theorist demanding his place in the canon. In the 1950s and before, the underground remained outside of society. "Maybe it doesn't have to anymore," Sukenick concludes, underscoring the arguments of Katz and Johnson in *MQR*'s symposium. "Maybe instead of its romance with the outsider and the subversive, the underground is strong enough to make a stand for its point of view within the mainstream of the culture. Maybe subterraneans are moving once again from mere resistance to outright attack," surely a strategy that explains his own work in *In Form* (see *ALS 1985*, pp. 277–78). The rediscovery of Chandler Brossard, both in his works and as a spokesman, lends force to Sukenick's argument. The special Brossard issue of *Review of Contemporary Fiction* is valuable for the range of essays on his work but mostly for his own "Tentative Visits to the Cemetery: Reflections on *My* Beat Generation" (7, i:7–37), a memoir describing the nascent form of what would be known as 1960s innovation.

ii. Cynthia Ozick, Isaac Bashevis Singer, Philip Roth, and Norman Mailer

A quantum leap beyond the reductively thematic studies that too often characterize treatments of Jewish-American writers is made by Victoria Aarons's "The Outsider Within: Women in Contemporary Jewish-American Fiction" (*ConL* 28:378–93). Although the Jewish voice may well have become one of the norms for American fiction in recent years, "What we find in the writing of many contemporary Jewish women, such as Grace Paley, Tillie Olsen, Cynthia Ozick, and Hortense Calisher, is a self-conscious recognition of an outsider position in both American culture and Judaism." Instead of oversimplifying the "outsider voice" as a stereotype, these authors express their alienation through structural devices of language and sexual relationships. Whereas traditionally Jewish-American male characters could be "always a step out of line with the rest of America," these women writers and their female protagonists present the image of outsiders "paradoxically alienated from and drawn to a heritage from which they are excluded, and yet in which they play an important function—the silent foil of a male-dominated tradition."

Ozick herself receives the greater part of this year's attention. Sanford Pinsker's *The Uncompromising Fiction of Cynthia Ozick* (Missouri) stresses her strong cultural moralism and sees a progression in her work from Jamesian stylistics to a moral spokesmanship reminiscent of Emily Dickinson, Joseph Conrad, and Walt Whitman; unfortunately, this thesis is unsupported by any analysis beyond plot summaries and the cursory referral to the names listed above. More helpful is Janet Handler Burstein, whose "Cynthia Ozick and the Transgressions of Art" (*AL* 59:85–101) considers the literary implications of Ozick's belief that art is idolatrous and her justified accomplishments in risking such idolatry. Her didacticism is an inward-turning affair for Joseph Lowin; his "Cynthia Ozick, Rewriting Herself: The Road from 'The Shawl' to 'Rosa'" (*Since Flannery O'Connor*, pp. 101–12) finds that Ozick defines and resolves her anxiety of influence by rewriting not just classic texts but earlier work of her own. Such fiction writers make articulate subjects for interviews, and the best is drawn from her by Tom Teicholz in "The Art of Fiction XCV: Cynthia Ozick" (*ParisR* 102:154–90), where she speaks candidly about her habit of drawing on other texts as she fashions her own fiction.

Other Jewish-American writers fare more predictably this year. Long on meditation of purpose but short on how his effects are achieved is Grace Farrell Lee's *From Exile to Redemption: The Fiction of Isaac Bashevis Singer* (So. Ill.). Singer uses biblical images for his meaning and a sense of waiting for his answer, thereby balancing the holy and the secular. Love breeds human community, a microcosm of divine creation; sex itself becomes an "ecstasy of cosmic redemption," but again Lee's emphasis is on message rather than on the artistic manner employed in bringing about this state of affairs. Mark Schechner finds a key to the work of Norman Mailer and Philip Roth in a style of alienation grounded not in Jewishness but in a post-Marxian inner radicalism; in *After the Revolution: Studies in the Contemporary Jewish Imagination* (Indiana) he ponders the "fortunate fall" question of whether it is worth it to be Kafka, and answers that, after the Holocaust, the answer is "no." Therefore, *Advertisements for Myself* breaks the traditional mold to create a revolutionary new hipster mode, while Roth courts deliberate excess as a way of exploiting the volatility of invention. Specific comedic techniques are explored in editor Sarah Blacher Cohen's *Jewish Wry: Essays on Jewish Humor* (Illinois); "The Jewish Sit-Down Comedy of Philip Roth" (pp. 158–77) by Alan Cooper shows the root of Roth's humor in the situation of "rationalism being explored minutely while being grossly ignored," a style which gives a nasty edge to the otherwise plaintive voice and concludes not with a shrug for lovable losers but with an indictment of a "tribal defect." Maurice Charney's "Stanley Elkin and Jewish Black Humor" (pp. 178–95) begins from the same premise of comically ironic self-consciousness in an alienated observer, but sees this style of detachment and indulgence as leading to vaudeville in Elkin's work.

Norman Mailer's *The Executioner's Song* provides excellent material for Stephen Greenblatt, whose "Capitalist Culture and the Circulatory System" (pp. 257–73) distinguishes editor Murray Kreiger's *The Aims of Representation: Subject/Text/History* (Columbia). Mailer's novel is composed of media events, including intimate letters that have been purchased in order to be sold as a television mini-series that in turn sells other products. This combination of recreation/ entertainment, aesthetics, public activity, and private property creates a state of affairs beyond allusion and other critical terms; a new language is needed to articulate these new generative factors of narrative. Pugilistics as a sport is examined by Christian K. Messenger in "Norman Mailer: Boxing and the Art of His Narrative" (*MFS* 33: 85–104), where the writer is faulted for not fully engaging the sense of murder and of the body's dissolution he employs as part of male aggression within the compulsive agon. Less valuable than either of these essays is the latest full-length book, *Mailer's America* (Connecticut) by Joseph Wenke, which simply rehearses the familiar theme that our greatest literary artists succeed by retelling America's promise in the face of its debased millenial ideals. Totalitarianism threatens the democratic dream, just as the hipster implicitly defends it in his role as the American Adam; individuality leads to a parajournalistic role in following heroes and heroic events. All this has been assumed about Mailer for over a decade, but Wenke validly extends the thesis to *Ancient Evenings* as a codification of mythic imagination in the American grain.

iii. William Styron, Walker Percy, and Bobby Ann Mason

An avalanche of good, substantial work on Styron and Percy almost overwhelms scholarship on writers of the American South, but welcome attention to Bobbie Ann Mason indicates the canon may be expanding.

Judith Ruderman's *William Styron* (Ungar) is helpful for its study of very early manuscript sources for *Sophie's Choice*, especially within initial drafts of Styron's first novels; otherwise this study emphasizes historical roots, southern culture, and thematic summaries to the exclusion of detailed literary analysis. The year's best Styron work appears in the special issue of *Papers on Language and Literature* 23, guest-edited by Jackson R. Bryer and Melvin J. Friedman. The publication of Styron's 1953 manuscript, "Blankenship," together with an historical preface by James L. W. West III, is a major contribution, but also noteworthy are Bernhard Reitz's " 'Fearful ambiguities of time and history': *The Confessions of Nat Turner* and the Delineation of the Past in Postmodern Historical Narrative" (pp. 465–79) and Dawn Trouard's "Styron's Historical Pre-Text: Nat

Turner, Sophie, and the Beginnings of a Post-Modern Career" (pp. 489–97) for their abilities to read Styron's work in the light of current theory. A more traditional yet valuable close reading is provided by Gwen L. Nagel in "Illusion and Identity in *Sophie's Choice*: (pp. 498–513), in which Stingo's survival is linked to the novel's relative judgments on role-playing and madness.

Two books, a special issue, and several independent studies keep Walker Percy at the forefront of scholarship. In *The Fiction of Walker Percy* (Illinois) John Edward Hardy smashes two previously unbreakable icons by supplying personally self-contained readings of Percy's fiction apart from its supposedly informing philosophical theory. Yet the Percy family history is shown to offer shaping traditions and attitudes, Percy himself is recognized as an amateur of language and language theory (to the extent that he sees language as central to the human condition), and the "false humanists of the left" are dealt with as vexing factors within his fiction. Hardy's readings do help us see the weak characterization and point of view in *The Moviegoer* and recognize how the protagonist's poorly dramatized conversion demonstrates the difficulties of expressing such vision. There can be a critical debate with Percy's interpretation of God's mercy in *The Last Gentleman*, and *Love in the Ruins* can be appreciated for having divine love expressed in its more limiting forms. There are interpretive problems in *Lancelot* and *The Second Coming* as well, which Hardy's steadfastly critical approach reveals. The value of his work is shown by considering Mary K. Sweeny's profoundly uncritical *Walker Percy and the Postmodern World* (Loyola), a familiar reading of the fiction in terms of Percy's existentialist philosophy which deplores fragmentation and yearns for "a more honest world where words will mean what they connote." Her study is important, however, for its explanation of the complementary services provided by the theologians Romano Guardini (historical overviewing) and Pierre Teilhard de Chardin (evolving the universe) in suggesting that the Redemption, as part of the Fortunate Fall, will supply an answer to Percy's "why?" That Christian values are central to Percy's writing is demonstrated by editor Joseph Schwartz's work in assembling the special issue of *Renascence* 40. For both Schwartz and Percy, postmodernism's Gnosticism is seen to be the enemy, for its "insatiable desire for dominion over being" prompts seekers to "reject the created world in favor of their own creations." Although the issue's five other essays apply this concern to the broad range of Percy's work, Schwartz's own "Life and Death in *The Last Gentleman*" (pp. 112–28) presents the most compelling argument for this interpretation, based as it is on a reading of Guardini's *The End of the Modern World*, the centrality of which Sweeny has established at length, resolving matters in terms of Percy's fiction being totally acceptable if Guardini's theology is taken as a truth. Looking to M. M. Bakhtin yields a slightly different version, as Robert H. Brinkmeyer, Jr., shows in an earlier issue of the same journal with "Walker Percy's *Lancelot*: Discovering through Dialogue" (*Renascence* 40:30–42); meaning and understanding develop from the interaction of one consciousness with another, making the human condition a dialogic one, which is what Lance and Percival experience in this novel about the dream of self-sufficiency. The limitations of language do shape Percy's fiction, as shown by Michael Pearson in "Language and Love in Walker Percy's *The Second Coming*" (*SLJ* 20, i:89–100). But so does his awareness of family history, as Michael Kreyling explains in "The Percys: The Hero as Extraneous Man" (pp. 154–82) from his *Figures of the Hero in Southern Narrative* (LSU). Percy's heroes feel extraneous to their civilization and so seek to perform some act worthy of their name, even when their footing has been undermined—meaning that such protagonists cannot be one with life but can be men of the moment, creatures of pure action in a world where the world necessary to support a hero's stoicism has vanished.

Three substantial essays recognize Bobbie Ann Mason as a virtuoso of southern themes and techniques yet also a full-fledged participant in postmodern style. Rites of passage have, within our own day, become the signs of a determinedly phenomenological culture, and how Mason constructs a narrative of depth from these surface actions occupies Albert E. Wilhelm in his critically important "Private Rituals: Coping with Change in the Fiction of Bobbie Ann Mason" (*MQ* 28:271–82), which only needs to make reference to the technique of Gail Sheehy's pop classic, *Passages*, to be complete. Robert H. Brinkmeyer, Jr., fast distinguishing himself as one of the more astute commentators on southern fiction, places Mason both within and ahead of the tradition in "Finding One's History: Bobbie Ann Mason and Contemporary Southern Literature" (*SLJ* 19, ii:20–33); her "new direction" comprises a shared history Lewis A. Lawson fears does not exist and predicts a growing sense of control as characters become aware of the southern sign systems at play. Linda

Adams Barnes takes a more traditional approach in "The Freak Endures: The Southern Grotesque from Flannery O'Connor to Bobbie Ann Mason" (*Since Flannery O'Connor*, pp. 133–41); Mason shares a sense of redemption, internal degradation, and comedy with O'Connor, but uses these feelings to update the southern situation, although Barnes sees Mason as more the handmaid of contemporary confusion than as a savior from it.

iv. John Updike and John Cheever

While Updike's reputation rests on his established classics, Cheever scholarship continues to grow as both his major and minor works are subjected to new readings in light of developing theories and thematics. Steven M. Chanley covers familiar ground in "Quest for Order in John Updike's 'Pigeon Feathers': Updike's Use of Christian Mythology" (*ArQ* 45:251–63), reminding readers how this story codifies the cathartic process central to *Olinger Stories* and so important for the early years of Updike's career. How Cheever's texts seem richer with each succeeding year (and with each succeeding wave of critical developments) is apparent from the broad range of studies published this year. The man's compelling life story is an obvious attraction, specifically his recovery from alcoholism and how it relates to his work. Thomas B. Gilmore makes a convincing case for this approach in *Equivocal Spirits*. Cheever's interest in the topic is societal, not in the physiology of alcoholism itself but in its effects on marriages, families, and social groups; this interest fits Cheever's general concern with society as a structuring force, as demonstrated in "Goodbye, My Brother" and "The Swimmer." Wayne Stengel reads Susan Cheever's biography of her father as a document increasing his reputation beyond that of a chatty *New Yorker* mannerist; his "John Cheever's Surreal Vision and the Bridge of Language" (*TCL* 33:223–33) praises Cheever's work for its brooding sense of the displacement between appearance and reality that only language, here in the hands of a master fictionist, can bridge (by creating narrators who "use their imaginations and speech as mediation between senseless reality and an ironically coherent dreamworld"). Robert A. Morace's "John Cheever" (*CDLB* 5, pp. 140–53) shows how the "hardwon affirmations" achieved in *Falconer* allowed Cheever to be both conventional in form but contemporary in theme when writing *Oh What a Paradise It Seems*; Morace appreciates the solidity of the man's work, learning that 150 pages of notes were needed to produce the 15 pages of "The Swimmer." Especially ambitious is E. P. Walkiewicz's "Cheever's 'Metamorphoses' " Myth and Postmodern Short Fiction" (*Since Flannery O'Connor*, pp. 32–44), which considers how, in his short stories published after 1950, Cheever used self-conscious and reflexive narration in order to question both a Jamesian sense of realism and a Joycean sense of the artist-hero as an Odysseus or Daedalus returning to restablish an order—two questionings that distinguish postmodernism from the modern. That Cheever had a clear moral vision is established by Kenneth C. Mason in "Tradition and Desecration: The Wapshot Novels of John Cheever" (*ArQ* 43: 231–50); as "a harsh critique of modern American materialism," these two novels take a one-two punch at their subject, with *The Wapshot Scandal* being "excoriating" about what *The Wapshot Chronicle* only implies, in the process moving out from this specific community to encompass "all of middle America." How Cheever himself grew in this increasingly public role is clear from editor Scott Donaldson's excellently researched and meticuously indexed *Conversations with John Cheever* (Mississippi); always a hard subject to interview, Cheever remained reticent, perhaps evasive, and certainly reserved during his ordeals with alcoholism, but after drying out for good in 1975 his commentary became not only more open but intellectually much sharper, and therefore it is not surprising that of 28 major interviews conducted between 1940 and 1985, most are from after 1969 and the very best follow his recovery in the mid-1970s.

v. Realists Old and New

Now that literary theory has thrown the conventions of mimesis into question, taxonomies become blurred as to who is an unquestioning as opposed to experimental realist, just as for succeeding categories it is debatable which writers are experimental realists and which are real experimentalists. Even the nature of Truman Capote's work is thrown into question—not the old one of whether some of it is journalism as opposed to fiction, but whether his "authorial silence" makes him strong enough to endure the most rigorously deconstructive reading. Chris Anderson brings both Wayne Booth and Wolfgang Iser to debate how "the reading experience depends upon 'gaps' or 'blanks' " by which "what *is* said only appears to take on significance as a reference to what is not said; it is the implications and not

the statements themselves that give shape and weight to the meaning," an interpretation that illuminates the full range of Capote's
writing as surveyed in "Fiction, Nonfiction, and the Rhetoric of
Silence" (*MQ* 27:340–53). A more straightforward but justifiably in-
triquing approach using autobiographical keys is found in Blake
Allmendinger's "The Room Was Locked, With the Key on the Inside:
Female Influence in Truman Capote's 'My Side of the Matter'" (*SSF*
24:279–88). Capote's own anxiety at this influence led him to emulate
Eudora Welty in writing himself out of it.

Joyce Carol Oates is served less well by her critics. Eileen Teper
Bender's *Joyce Carol Oates: Artist in Residence* (Indiana) is one of
those unfortunate works that feels it must inflate its subject by deflating supposed adversaries. Bender's inaccurate and (for Oates's
purposes) unnecessary bad-mouthing of Barth, Barthelme, Gass,
Vonnegut, and Pynchon as "superficial fabulators" tells us little about
Oates's strengths, which are indeed drawn from the "personality
theory" of Jung, Laing, Lifton, and Maslow that Bender describes.
How Oates takes their protean "third force" of personality and turns
it to communal interests via a "fabulator's intertext" demands more
than a knee-jerk rejection of the work of Oates's academic contemporaries. Her testing of outworn myths in formats that resist reductive
readings is a topic deserving of more analysis than a quick comparison to the way Saul Bellow explores similar issues on the moral level.
More responsible is Greg Johnson's *Understanding Joyce Carol Oates*
(So. Car.), which takes the simple postulate that "Her particular
genius is her ability to convey psychological states with unerring
fidelity, and to relate the intense private experiences of her characters to the larger realities of American life" and tests it against the
polarities of Barth/Gass (possibilities of language and aesthetics)
and Dickens/George Eliot (profoundly social and philosophical
themes); again, one asks exactly how are her novels of ideas "increasingly bold and resourceful experiments with fiction," especially since
the doings of Barth and Gass do not sum up everything Oates isn't.

History remains central to critics' readings of E. L. Doctorow,
even though the decade's rush of essays on *Ragtime* seems to have
abated. In "From the Lion's Den: Survivors in E. L. Doctorow's *The
Book of Daniel*" (*Crit* 29:3–15) Michelle M. Tokarczyk concludes
that the author's intent is to show that "While minimal personal
resolution might be possible, political resolution appears not to be"
because there seems to be no way "for the American populace to

learn the lessons of history." In the most impressive piece of Doctorow work to appear in several years, "Doctorow's *Lives of the Poets* and the Problem of Witness" (*Since Flannery O'Connor*, pp. 83–92), Arthur M. Saltzman draws upon Ihab Hassan's seminal theory of "lower case authority" that sanctions the pre-disclaimed observations of *The Book of Daniel's* narrator; this puts Doctorow's explorations of "the inevitability and the necessity of imaginative imposition" within *Lives of the Poets* in the tradition exploited by William H. Gass and Gilbert Sorrentino.

Ann Beattie and Raymond Carver, in the past often linked together as key practitioners of fictive minimalism, are now more often distinguished in terms of their work's intentionality. Alan Wilde's *Middle Grounds*, reviewed in section *i.*, finds Carver the deeper moralist, an opinion shared by Kathleen Westfall Shute in "Finding the Words: The Struggle for Salvation in the Fiction of Raymond Carver" (*HC* 24, v:1–9); the initial minimalism in which "Carver's folk were bankrupted, pink-slipped, often left to stumble alone through a detritus that was at core artificial and peculiarly American" has in his later work moderated into a vision that allows his characters some hope and freedom (like many other Carver advocates, Shute attributes this change to his recovery from alcoholism). Michael Vander Weele does a better job of relating this change to textual matters in "Raymond Carver and the Language of Desire" (*DQ* 22, i: 108–22), although with Barbara C. Lonnquist's "Narrative Displacement and Literary Faith: Raymond Carver's Inheritance from Flannery O'Connor" (*Since Flannery O'Connor*, pp. 142–50) we are asked to credit Carver's profundity of epiphanic moments and self-consciously humanistic themes for producing what Lonnquist feels (but does not show) is "a narrative strategy in *Cathedral* that works within the traditional short story form, but allows him to exploit that form and go beyond the very tradition he supports." To her credit, Ann Beattie does not allow such easy admiration of supposedly uplifting themes. Her narrative is riveted to the page, just as the action it describes is limited to what can be described on the surface. The richness possible in such work is appreciated by Stacey Olster in "Photographs and Fantasies in the Stories of Ann Beattie" (*Since Flannery O'Connor*, pp. 113–23); like Diane Arbus, Beattie finds that "the photograph provides a harsh exposure of experience, which as a narrative model prevents the narrative impositions her materials self-consciously resist (thereby forcing themselves to be taken at face

value). Susan Jaret McKinstry joins Olster in making Beattie's stories
work on their own terms instead of by using them as occasions for
humanistic gesturing; her "The Speaking Silence of Ann Beattie's
Voice" (*SSF* 24:111–17) reminds us that no narrative can be completely value-free, and that Beattie's posture in the story is often expressed in silence rather than by words, juxtaposing closed and open
narratives rather than forcing a choice between them.

Who are the emerging neorealists? This year's scholarship targets
three names: Nicholas Delbanco, Lee K. Abbott, and T. Coraghessan
Boyle. The interplay between author as writer and author as character
serves as Gregory L. Morris's interpretation in "Nicholas Delbanco
in the Middle Distance" (*Crit* 29:30–45). Earl Ingersoll and Stan
Sanvel Rubin conduct " 'The Whole Reach and Tug of Passion': A
Conversation with Lee K. Abbott" (*InR* 11, i:1–10) that highlights
Abbott's feelings about being a southwestern writer but not a regionalist, a writer charmed more by "old words" than by specific landscapes. An introduction to "T. Coraghessan Boyle" by Michael Adams
distinguishes editor J. M. Brook's *DLB Yearbook: 1986* (Gale), pp.
281–86; Boyle's stories are eminently satirical of their subjects, to the
extent that they sometimes suffer from self-serving cleverness—a
tendency momentarily corrected in the Barthian metahistory of *Water
Music*, and then allowed to reappear in the satiric hipness of *Budding
Prospects*.

vi. Experimental Realists

A growing number of contemporaries—from Thomas McGuane to
Grace Paley—have developed along lines complementary to but not
completely consistent with the standards of mimetic realism. Jon
Wallace gets a good grip on this phenomenon in "Speaking Against
the Dark: Style as Theme in Thomas McGuane's *Nobody's Angel*"
(*MSF* 33:289–98). "Absence is everywhere in this book," Wallace
notes, "haunting the present like a presence" that is established both
in the narrative's action and in the language's syntax. McGuane's
novel questions itself, "because the speaker is not the omniscient or
limited-omniscient narrator he seems to be but another fictional character who has created a protagonist, and several other characters, in
order to discover himself. In a crucial sense, he *is* just talking to hear
himself talk, and the paragraph *is* supposed to be just sound—the
sound of a voice in search of an appropriate tone." A similar emphasis

of voice distinguishes Victoria Aarons's understanding of Grace Paley's art in "The Outsider Within: Women in Contemporary Jewish-American Fiction" (*ConL* 28:378–93), where narrative voice is "characteristically ironic—often tentatively humorous" as it draws on the pathos of characters and situations caught between identities.

A writer deserving of far more critical attention than he gets occupies the final chapter of *Balzac's Dolls*, an important collection of literary essays by Greg Boyd (Europa). In "The Story's Stories: A Letter to Stephen Dixon" (pp. 131–38) Boyd praises the conversational intimacy of Dixon's stories; their action is expressed by means of an exaggerated verbal insistence, and just as such gesturing can profitably disturb the conventions of speech, "so can the conventions of plot be disrupted within the confines of a given story," making their employment once again an innovative affair. The special number of *Review of Contemporary Fiction* (7, iii) devoted to Harry Mathews features interviews with Mathews conducted by John Ash (pp. 21–32) and by John Ashbury (pp. 36–48), but the issue's best contributions are those that explain the author's specific theories of composition: Warren F. Motte, Jr.'s "Permutational Matters" (pp. 91–99) and Welch D. Everman's "Harry Mathews's *Selected Declarations of Dependence*: Proverbs and the Forms of Authority" (pp. 146–53), each of which shows the immense amount of narrative that can be generated by "constrictive forms," a talent shared by Stephen Dixon as well.

vii. Joseph Heller, Kurt Vonnegut, Richard Brautigan, Jerzy Kosinski

Joseph Heller has, especially in his recent novels, become a literary figure who outstrips previous identifications. The special value of Robert Merrill's comprehensive and intelligent *Joseph Heller* (TUSAS 512) is that *Good as Gold* and *God Knows* can be interpreted as setting Heller apart from the Pynchon-Kosinski-Gaddis-Baldwin-Burroughs tradition of apocalypse in which leading critics have placed Heller, but without sacrificing the experimental elements of *Catch-22* and *Something Happened*. *Catch-22* itself demands an understanding beyond the easy labels of genre and literary stereotype; far beyond being a surrender to "the craziness of war," this novel satirizes the World War II tradition of popularization only to draw on models from the First World War, while its language moves beyond satire toward analogue and fable. Equal care with both language and action creates an environment in which readers can accept the protagonist of *Something Happened* "as an adequate representative of our own drastically limited possibilities, again without surrendering to a facile absurdism." Heller's two recent "Jewish" novels in fact make most sense when interpreted for their broadly humanistic rather than sectarian themes; as for their techniques, they grow more directly from the earlier works than serve as borrowings from Bellow, Malamud, or Roth.

A pause in Vonnegut studies (echoed by a perhaps fateful silence from Ken Kesey's critics) has allowed Asa B. Pieratt, Jr., Julie Huffman-klinkowitz, and myself to assemble and organize *Kurt Vonnegut: A Comprehensive Bibliography* (Shoe String), which counts and abstracts 265 critical analyses (beyond reviews) and 114 literary interviews, to which can be added Hank Nuwer's "A Skull Session with Kurt Vonnegut" (*SCR* 19, ii:2–23), in which Vonnegut describes how he fragments his plots to sustain narrative interest, part of the challenge he faced in writing *Galápagos* (the action of which lasts one million years), and also covers most areas of his autobiography with fresh, revealing material. An important biographical contribution is made by Vonnegut's first wife, Jane Vonnegut Yarmolinsky, whose *Angels Without Wings: A Courageous Family's Triumph over Tragedy* (Houghton Mifflin) tells how she and her husband adopted their three nephews when, within a few days in 1958, Kurt's brother-in-law died in a railway accident and his sister died of cancer. Although Yarmolinsky changes Kurt's and the children's given names, her retention of the Vonnegut surname invites scholars to attend to the specific characterization she provides of her husband's working habits and the style of their family life in the 1950s, 1960s, and 1970s. The values they shared and family goals to which they dedicated themselves provided a helpful commentary on what the author's life was like, especially during his earliest years as a professional writer. There is, moreover, an interesting coincidence in Yarmolinsky's choice for her central metaphor—a secret hidden in the family's barn—since the same image appears in Kurt Vonnegut's novel *Bluebeard*, which was written and published concurrently with Yarmolinsky's memoir, although there is no evidence that they were aware of the specific nature of each other's texts.

Richard Brautigan and Jerzy Kosinski's lives belie their styles of writing, the supposedly gentle hippie who loved charming metaphors dying most gruesomely by his own hand, while the self-professed master of macabre violence sparkles as a personal entertainer of jet-set lovelies and as an amusing talk show guest. Jay Boyer's *Richard Brautigan* (BSWWS 79) portrays a careful writer who knew exactly where his offbeat themes and "wacky" techniques were going, to the extent that his work can now be explored profitably by scholars of the Western American mythos and by French post-structuralists and other aficionados of postmodernism. Kosinski's success in establishing "a high degree of identification between the implied reader and the child protagonist" of *The Painted Bird* interests Terry Heller, whose *Delights of Terror* appreciates the way empathy is thus sustained much farther than most readers would wish or be able to go. "The construction of the boy's inner self is the central function of the implied reader" at the start, followed by the boy's own acquisition of empathy for moral codes around him; the novel's conclusion, however, exposes this view to a destablization and eventual deconstruction by the narrative operations of terror.

viii. John Barth and Thomas Pynchon

Last year's vacuum of work on Barth has for 1987 shifted to John Hawkes, while current studies of *The End of the Road,* "Echo," *LET-TERS, Sabbatical,* and the exhaustion/replenishment essays abound. Barth's career itself is helpful to Roger B. Salomon in *Desperate Storytelling: Post-Romantic Elaborations of the Mock-Heroic Mode* (Georgia), because the novelist's change from interest in debating morality to an obsession with the artifice of the artificial "destroys the vital dualism on which the mock-heroic is based" (removing the distinction between reality and dreams, effacing the past as memory, and denying a meaningful identity in a world of shifting masks and roles). "A more complex sense of what Barth's darkly comic universe is like" is what Joyce Dyer promises to explain in "Barth's Use of the Bust of Laocoön in *The End of the Road*" (*SLJ* 19, ii:54–60); her key is Jacob Horner's prize possession, a bust of the Trojan priest whose anguish admits "the hard fact that acting has destructive consequences" (Salomon's reading of "Echo" makes the complementary point that Barth allows Tiresias and Narcissus to be similarly subsumed). How Barth presses the limits of form, even to the risk of his own status as an artist, is considered by Marjorie Godlin Roemer in "The Paradigmatic Mind: John Barth's *LETTERS*" (*TCL*

33:38–50); his often-commented-upon "movement toward ultimacy" in fiction is here both the strength and the problem, for *LETTERS* is devoted to not only his work's fullest complexity, but also its "recursiveness." An extremely insightful treatment of the strategy behind such tactics is provided by Elaine B. Safer's "The Essay as Aesthetic Mirror: John Barth's 'Exhaustion' and 'Replenishment'" (*SAF* 15:109–17); Safer finds that Barth's reading of Borges in the former essay illuminates his own practice in *The Sot-Weed Factor*, sending the reader through a labyrinth, while the "Replenishment" piece's praise of Calvino and García Márquez reflects his own commitment to "the synthesis of straightforwardness and artifice." *Sabbatical* is the author's most accessible novel in two decades, a fact appreciated by Emory Elliott in "History and Will in *Dog Soldiers, Sabbatical,* and *The Color Purple*" (*ArQ* 43:197–217); there is "a new imperialism of the self" in contemporary fiction that Elliott defines as "deconstruction" (surely a questionable definition), which in Barth's novel empowers his characters to avoid naturalistic closure and instead write their own circular, self-renewing narrative as a cycle of eternal existence. A critic more knowledgeable about both contemporary fiction and the theory behind it is Gordon E. Slethaug, whose "Floating Signifiers in John Barth's *Sabbatical*" (*MFS* 33:647–55) shows how a Derridean sense of "floating narration" prevents any fixed or ascertainable content and meaning from establishing themselves in Barth's novel.

With *PNotes* postponing its double issue until next year, students of Thomas Pynchon need be satisfied with two interesting essays on *The Crying of Lot 49* and two book-length studies of *Gravity's Rainbow*. Peter L. Hays finds language to be a major element in the apparently simplest of Pynchon's three novels; in "Pynchon's Cunning Lingual Novel: Communication in *Lot 49*" (*UMSE* 5 [1984–87]:23–38) Hays examines the systems of communication that keep Oedipa Maas and Pierce Inverarity from getting together, with Pynchon using wordplay and allusive metaphors to "describe what appear to be closed and separate systems and then to puncture their hermetic state." Critical disagreement about Oedipa's relation to Oedipus attracts the attention of Debra A. Moddelmog, who in "The Oedipus Myth and Reader Response in Pynchon's *The Crying of Lot 49*" (*PLL* 23:240–49) shows that "the Oedipus myth does not function mechanically or simplistically, but instead requires the willing participation of the novel's readers" both on the level of theme and of technique.

A major reordering of our way of understanding Pynchon's major work is undertaken by Kathryn Hume in *Pynchon's Mythography: An Approach to* Gravity's Rainbow (So. Ill.) and in her complementary chapter, *"Gravity's Rainbow*: Science Fiction, Fantasy, and Mythology," from editors George Slusser and Eric Rabkin's *Intersections: Fantasy and Science Fiction* (So. Ill.). Pynchon's approach broadens our definition of science fiction by encouraging the interplay of one kind of SF (science as metaphor) with both fantasy and technical SF, adding non-Newtonian science for philosophical principles along the way. His mythology tends toward the most traditional functions, warning us about paranoia and technological control of the human. There is a mythological sequence to *Gravity's Rainbow*, Hume believes, and she charts its movement from Paradise to Apocalypse in a manner that makes the author much more conventional and even humanistic than other critics have assumed. His hero-myths are Faustian, Wagnerian, Orphic, and especially juvenile—traditional structures that are asked to struggle with especially fragmentary environments. Thomas Moore's *The Style of Connectedness*: Gravity's Rainbow *and Thomas Pynchon* (Missouri) is helpful for confirming and deepening what we already know about Pynchon's rich employment of a wide range of technological, scientific, and philosophical sources. Moore finds *Gravity's Rainbow* to be an explosion of modern culture's binary systematics of either/or; the novel offers instead a Jungian fluidity that underlines all frames, and a Borgesian metaphysics of dream that draws on structures existing only within the mind. Pynchon's lesson here is that nothing can be judged fairly from within a closed system, and so by drawing on diverse sources he strives to open his novel's form.

ix. Robert Coover, William H. Gass, William Gaddis, John Irving, and Don DeLillo

With Donald Barthelme's critics for the time having written themselves out, Robert Coover has taken the lion's share of attention within the first wave of 1960s innovators now forming the postmodern mainstream. The plasticity of Coover's work allows it to be read as conventional modernism, an argument advanced by Morton P. Le-

vitt in *Modernist Survivors: The Contemporary Novel in England,
the United States, France, and Latin America* (Ohio State). Unlike
Allen Thiher's immensely superior *Words in Reflection* (see *ALS
1984*, pp. 293–94), which surveys the same material, Levitt's study
posits that "there is no meaningful movement in the novel which
follows Modernism and takes its place." Granted, there is a new
sensibility in the air, but the modernist novel remains alive, having
suffered no break from what Levitt believes is a still operative
humanist heritage. Coover's technical reliance upon mythological
structures and themes provides Levitt with a chance to moralize:
his characters try to create their own mythologies and yet are destined
to fail, because nature has become too distant and society too in-
distinct for them to understand how myth works. Seeing Coover and
also Pynchon, Doctorow, and Barth in such negative terms does affirm an outdated humanism, but Levitt's attempt is seriously un-
balanced by his disclination to consider the positive effects of the influences studied so ably by Thiher. More appropriate readings are
found in "Robert Coover's Dirty Stories: Allegories of Reading in
'Seven Exemplary Fictions'" (*IowaR* 17, ii:100–121) where Louis
Mackey shows how these "self-polluting narratives" reverse Cer-
vantes's technique and "illustrate the impossibility of reading and
the difficulty of writing" precisely because the old humanistic axioms
are no longer operative. Two strong contributions to *Modern Fiction
Studies* 33 (a special issue on sports), Richard Alan Schwartz's "Postmodernist Baseball" (pp. 135–49) and Roy C. Caldwell, Jr.'s "Of
Hobby-Horses, Baseball, and Narrative: Coover's *The Universal
Baseball Association*" (pp. 161–71), praise the author for his em-
phatically postmodernist approach by which an artificial society is
able to self-consciously consider what myth offers it and by which
the ludic aspects of baseball itself can be examined while still generating a convincing narrative. In a similar manner two critics trace
source material to show how the author understands both the psychological richness of character even within the artifice of metafiction
(John Z. Guzlowski, "Coover's *The Public Burning*: Richard Nixon
and the Politics of Experience" [*Crit* 29:57–71]) and the metafictional
questions about closure that folk narratives traditionally ask (David
C. Estes, "American Folk Laughter in Robert Coover's *The Public
Burning* [*ConL* 28:239–56]).

William H. Gass is of great interest to Tony Tanner in *Scenes of
Nature* because of his compelling drive to penetrate the inwardness

of the other without getting involved in that otherness himself, a philosophical problem that in Gass's work yields interesting fictive results, not the least of which is a specifically postmodern style that exploits both the limitations and possibilities of language ("William Gass' Barns and Bees," pp. 248–73).

The immense range of the meganovel impresses Dominick La-Capra in *History, Politics, and the Novel* (Cornell); LaCapra's chapter, "Signed Phoenix and the Gift of Tongues: William Gaddis, *The Recognitions*" (pp. 175–202), recognizes it as an American work that engages larger European and world traditions; its satire of modern culture and society is accomplished by combining a limited amount of narrative experiment with a great deal of gripping pathos, a method LaCapra compares to Bakhtin's polyphonic orchestration of a carnival's contending voices, "the multi-discourses of our time." Zoltán Abádi-Nagy snares a rare interview in "The Art of Fiction CI: William Gaddis" (*ParisR* 105:54–89); on a visit to Budapest, Gaddis disavows the "experimental" nature of his fiction and explains how what the interviewer calls his "floated-dialogues" are introduced as a way of enlisting the reader as a collaborator; his characters proliferate originally for comic effect but eventually as a commentary on our entropic culture.

A thorough but reductive reading of John Irving's novel in terms of Robert Scholes's general theory is undertaken by William Cosgrove in "*The World According to Garp* as Fabulation" (*SCR* 19, ii: 52–58). Cosgrove would have us believe that Irving single-handedly refutes the experimental fiction of the 1960s; a better case for someone else doing just this is made by Paula Bryant, whose "Discussing the Untellable: Don DeLillo's *The Names*" (*Crit* 29:16–29) demonstrates how this novel's portrayal of how reality can be rewritten reinstates a faith in language. This author's absence from the period's major literary histories and the mistaken analysis of his work as "midfiction" by Alan Wilde distresses Tom LeClair, whose *In the Loop: Don DeLillo and the Systems Novel* (Illinois) and "Deconstructing the Logos: Don DeLillo's *End Zone*" (*MFS* 33:105–23) make a convincing case for DeLillo as the deconstructive novelist par excellence. LeClair believes that systems planning is the most typical American art form, especially those dynamic processes that combine energy to create nonmechanistic (as opposed to atomistic) wholes. DeLillo's contribution is to deconstruct deconstructionism, revealing not a system of differences but an ecosystem beyond experiment—the

product of "a larger reconstructive impulse" that also characterizes
the great expansive works of Gaddis, Coover, Pynchon, and Barth—
authors LeClair has praised for writing "the novel of excess." Language is indeed DeLillo's subject, but his fictions "create a plurality
of orientations—inward to the processes of language and fiction, outward to psychological, social, and ecological relations, and outward
as well to the readers solicited and confuted by DeLillo's rhetoric,"
the motive of which is often to overwhelm. LeClair's analysis is
especially valuable for its refutation of Wilde's and Leavitt's attempts
to recast this style of fiction as humanism; unlike their insistence upon
isolating specific absences as an implied critique of present trends,
LeClair reads the "novel of excess" for what it most positively is,
tracking an advance in innovative fiction rather than a reactionary
expression of past forms and values.

x. Ronald Sukenick, Raymond Federman, Walter Abish, Gilbert Sorrentino, and Kathy Acker

The style of innovative fiction developed by Sukenick, Federman, and
Abish is central to Ihab Hassan's *The Postmodern Turn* (Ohio State),
an integrated collection of this visionary critic's investigations of
literary postmodernism spanning 20 years. One value of such a work
is seeing Hassan's appraisals of contemporary fictionists brought together. Disinclined to write another *Radical Innocence* (1961), Hassan has nevertheless resisted the temptations into subgenres and
literary theories that have distracted others and has remained attentive and responsive to the fiction of generations succeeding his
own. Although his readings of Barth and Barthelme confirm accepted
understandings of their work, Hassan's analysis of Sukenick as a de-
votee not just of play but as one whose fatuousness prompts construc-
tive fantasy is particularly enlightening, given the critical establishment's belief that Sukenick's work is offensively undisciplined. His
"bossa nova" evaluation of plot, story, character, chronology, verisimilitude, imitation, allegory, symbolism, subject matter, and even
meaning itself troubles those who object that "that's not *Finnegans
Wake*. . . . Yet it is an ablation of the Wake," Hassan explains; "it is
the *Wake* without work, the surface as grimace, comedy as absurd
and precise play. Whether or not he meant it to be so, when God
became the Dreamer, everything became possible." Sukenick and

Federman's typographical experiments call into question the nature of the book itself, while Federman's play with plagiarism (as "playgiarism") shows that the replica "may be as valid as its model," another confirmation of how fiction need not represent anything beyond itself. Walter Abish's breaking up of the sentence (by means of obsessive alphabetization) and his ability to generate full narratives from the phenomenological surface are techniques to which Hassan is especially responsive, as evidenced in his own textual autobiography, *Out of Egypt* (So. Ill., 1986).

The interplay of theory and practice between Sukenick's own critical commentary and his fiction is examined by Julian Cowley in "Ronald Sukenick's New Departures from the Terminal of Language" (*Crit* 27:87–99). Language should allow readers to form connections "without intruding in a way that fortifies our sense of separation from the world"; but since in practice it doesn't, Sukenick devises formal strategies that liberate readers from conceptions of order that might precede his own act of composition, an approach outlined by the various essays of *In Form* (see *ALS 1985*, pp. 277). Louis Mackey considers a similar problem in "Representation and Reflection: Philosophy and Literature in *Crystal Vision* by Gilbert Sorrentino" (*ConL* 28:206–22); there are internal rules in fiction which prepare readers for what may come, but "Sorrentino's novel fouls this nest of assumptions" by deconstructing the difference between fact and fiction "in terms of which fiction is possible and intelligible." As a result, "*philosophy becomes what literature is*: an activity of language that, capable of neither totalization or termination, inaugurates the endless closure of representation in reflection." Black American authors such as Clarence Major and Ishmael Reed have undertaken the same experiments as Sukenick and Sorrentino, Bernard W. Bell reminds us in *The Afro-American Novel and Its Tradition* (Mass.), but believes that their apparent rebellion against conventions is in fact an incorporation of techniques from black folklore (which are reactions against imprisonment by white society); yet in a work such as *Emergency Exit* Major comes closest to full participation in Sukenick's revolution on purely aesthetic grounds, which is ironic considering that novel's rich employment of folk materials.

Walter Abish's winning of the first PEN/Faulkner prize for fiction has drawn him immense critical attention, the best of which is reflected in Alain Arias-Misson's "The 'New Novel' and TV Culture:

Reflections on Walter Abish's *How German Is It?*" (*FicInt* 17, i:152–64); composed of ingenious "text-traps," the novel cancels out conventional means of reading fiction until all that is left are flashes of pure image such as are available on television. How Abish uses these techniques to rethink the nature of subjectivity is covered by Robert Siegle in "On the Subject of Walter Abish and Kathy Acker" (*L&P* 33, iii–iv:38–58) where fiction is recast as "an ideal site" in which Abish arranges encounters between history, systems, and subjectivity in a way that contrasts with Acker's "freer hand" in using the "larger socio-political structures which effect the subject," especially "the problematic nexus of desire, love, and woman almost as a microcosm of the trace effects of 'the system' upon 'the individual.'"

xi. Women

The strongest work on women writers this year allies their interests with subgenres. In *Alien to Femininity: Speculative Fiction and Feminist Theory* (Greenwood) Marleen S. Barr identifies the male sex as a social problem fiction writers are wont to solve by extreme solutions, usually marriage or war. In the fiction of James Tiptree, Jr., the vision encompasses a biological change and reintegration within a third style of community; Marge Piercy uses time travel to other communities, while others experiment with warrior heroes, fantastic sexuality, and the reproductive aspects of mothering, all of which thematic approaches exert an influence on fictive form. Ursula Le Guin remains the leader of these efforts, and in "*The Left Hand of Darkness*: Feminism for Men" (*Mosiac* 20, i:83–96) Craig and Diana Barrow defend the author for ending love relations with marriage; Le Guin "posits typically biased heterosexual males as her main audience," and therefore creates in Genly Ai "a conventional male with whom masculine readers can identify, and who is also recovering suppressed female qualities."

Carol Thursten's *The Romance Revolution: Erotic Novels for Women and the Quest for a New Sexual Identity* (Illinois) is a sociologically based study by a scholar with a doctorate in mass communications who has worked as a market research consultant. It argues that the sociopolitical milieu shapes the content of mass media; as that shape changes, romances take new forms, especially as their readers function as critics and not merely consumers. Noteworthy is the neofeminist romance that places severe qualifications on the traditional notion that love conquers all. Both the sweet romance and the erotic romance increasingly portray their heroines as whole persons; as this New Heroine emerges, the need for the Other Woman as a plot device disappears, a paradigm Thurston derives from Ilya Prigogine's sense of "order through fluctuations." Similar patterns are observable in minority and native American fiction, according to Roberta Rubenstein's *Boundaries of the Self: Gender, Culture, Fiction* (Illinois), in which Maxine Hong Kingston's heroines, who cannot be heard because of their gender and ethnic origins, are marginalized even as the reader is made aware of their implicit challenge to narrative possibilities, while Leslie Silko's characters in *Ceremony* are able to reverse patriarchal premises and recover meaning and selfhood within female traditions. Especially valuable is Joseph Allen Boon's *Tradition and Counter Tradition: Love and the Form of Fiction* (Chicago) for its demonstration of how myths of romantic marriage and ideologies of gender influence the novel's form. A countertradition of new structures can upset the formal rules of sexual hierarchy (which demand happy endings, stable marriages, and contexts for male quests); the romance itself encourages a new style of quest in which an author can exploit open forms and unrestricted heroism, breaking down conventional sexual categories and limitations.

xii. Native American Fiction and the West

Once again, coverage of contemporary Native American fiction is restricted to the predictable figures: N. Scott Momaday, Leslie Marmon Silko, and James Welch. In "Native American Novels: Homing In" (pp. 580–620 of editors Brian Swann and Arnold Krupat's *Recovering the World: Essays on Native American Literature* [California]) William Bevis finds the three using materials and techniques drenched in tribalism beyond the ken of white people; as opposed to the mainstream novel's eccentric range, their novels demand a convergence and contraction toward the home tribe, where knowledge is formed and validated tribally with "home" being the operative society. Bevis's reading of *Winter in the Blood* reveals nature not as a symbol but as an integral part of the novel's contextual life.

Among commentaries on the American West, especially valuable are two contributions to editor Vera Norwood and Janice Monk's *The Desert is No Lady: Southwestern Landscapes in Women's Writing and Art* (Yale): Tey Diana Rebolledo's "Tradition and Mythology: Signatures of Landscape in Chicana Literature" (pp. 96–124) and Patricia Clark Smith and Paula Gunn Allen's "Earthy Relations, Carnal Knowledge: Southwestern American Indian Women Writers and Landscape" (pp. 174–96). Surveying the Chicano Renaissance of the 1960s, Rebolledo finds new value systems in which writers begin portraying working women of the middle and lower middle classes (instead of just the privileged upper classes), and seeing these characters beyond the status of "marginalization"; instead of simply Spanish interests, Indian and Hispanic are combined, with the signature of identity being the landscape (whether urban or integrated with nature). Smith and Allen's work discusses the usual ritual and ceremony, but in Luci Tapahonso they find a fresh vision of the wilderness as experienced from within a boarding school, and in the work of Joy Harjo they discover a living spirit in dialogue with her people who have moved beyond the traditional circumstances of southwestern life into cities across the full United States.

Experiments with fictive form and ventures into academic criticism draw Gerald Locklin's attention in *Gerald Haslam* (*BSWWS* 77), but a reluctance to engage the nature of postmodern innovations within the subgenre detracts from too many of the contributions to *A Literary History of the West*. Mark Siegel provides little more than a checklist confirming redundant developments in "Contemporary Trends in Western American Fiction" (pp. 1182–96), while treatments of minority writing are for the most part discussions of thematic concerns rather than of structural modifications of and challenges to the literary tradition (for that readers will have to seek out Ishmael Reed's anthological introductions to the multicultural and pluralistic American West). Understanding the present means more than listing MFA programs and small press catalogs, for there is an entirely new world of fiction existing beyond these academic confines, which Taylor's *History* unfortunately misses. When the field's vision is defined by a popular culture stereotype (such as the one advanced by Michael T. Marsden and Jack Nachbar in their survey, "Film and Print," pp. 1263–82), one's critical perspective becomes far too limited to appreciate the writers Reed introduced in *19 Necromancers From Now* (Doubleday, 1970) and *Yardbird Lives!* (Grove, 1978). The cover photo gracing this latter anthology—featuring such diverse yet patently Western talents as Reed, James Welch, Frank Chin, Lawson Inana, Victor Cruz, and Joe Bruchac—would have provided a better road map to the human territory than many of Taylor's contributors used. There *is* a West beyond Marsden's Marlboro Man.

University of Northern Iowa

16. Poetry: 1900 to the 1940s

Melody M. Zajdel

Three books attempting to broaden or reassess the modernist canon will interest readers of this chapter: David Perkins, *A History of Modern Poetry*, William Drake, *The First Wave: Women Poets in America 1915–1945* (Macmillan), and Sandra M. Gilbert and Susan Gubar, *No Man's Land*.

The most traditional is Perkins. In this second volume of his literary history he looks at poets since the 1920s to document their adherence to or modification of the high Modernist style identified with Eliot. He presents over 160 poets to show the "number and variety of poets worth serious attention" and to explore the contexts which shaped them. Although chapters like "The Impact of William Carlos Williams" and "The Later Poetry of Wallace Stevens" offer little new information, Perkins uses them (and a chapter on Pound) to show how modernism influences later poets. Perkins skirts making "a revaluation that would displace some poets for the sake of others," but his very choice of influential figures does just that. Although he mentions women poets (such as H.D., Moore, Bogan, Teasdale, and Millay) and black poets (such as Cullen, Hughes, and Dunbar), they remain minor figures. His decision to discuss their works only in regard to traditional criteria is precisely the point that Drake and Gilbert and Gubar will contest.

Drake's work is a good collective literary biography of women writers between the two world wars. Claiming to eschew assessing importance, Drake considers the lives of poets such as Teasdale, Millay, Wylie, Marjorie Seiffert, and Grace Hazard Conkling within the matrix of relationships which fostered their creativity. Drake finds that nurturing mother-daughter relationships and female cooperation are "an essential element in women's creativity," while traditional gender roles are overwhelmingly detrimental. Besides filling in a number of little-known biographies (on Eunice Tietjens, Conkling, Seiffert, and Anne Spencer), Drake's best work is his description of the supportive networks that women set up for themselves. Harriet Monroe at *Poetry* became a locus of one such network: Marianne Moore at *The Dial* was another. Particularly in Monroe's maintenance of a democratic aesthetic and audience, Drake acknowledges that "The clash between male conservatism and burgeoning female power [is] essential for understanding the modernist period." His conclusion is the starting point for Gilbert and Gubar.

No Man's Land is the first in a three-volume series extending the feminist literary history begun in *The Madwoman in the Attic* (Yale, 1979). Its main flaw is that as an overview it lacks the close readings that make for cogent and compelling argumentation. Gilbert and Gubar assert that modernism "is differently inflected for male and female writers." The result is precisely what their subtitle proclaims: the battle of the sexes becomes a War of the Words. The final three chapters are must reading. Chapter 3, "Tradition and the Female Talent: Modernism and Masculinism," argues that the "rise of literary women became not just a theme in modernist writing but a motive for modernism." It makes for powerful reading opposite Perkins's "The Poetry of Critical Intelligence," which shows the development of New Criticism. Chapter 4, " 'Forward into the Past': The Female Affiliation Complex," argues that gender differences invalidate Bloom's anxiety of influence theory for women and stresses the role of choice and continuity in establishing a matrilinear literary tradition. Read in conjunction with Drake, these arguments are strengthened, for Drake's book provides some of the concrete examples missing in *No Man's Land*. Finally, Chapter 5 ("Sexual Linguistics: Women's Sentence, Men's Sentencing") is a strong, direct attack on contemporary post-structuralist criticism of women modernists. Looking at poets like Stein and H.D., Gilbert and Gubar argue that women stand in a different relationship to "power, language and meaning" than their male counterparts. As always, Gilbert and Gubar are provocative. Their work, while the most controversial of the three, will assuredly be the most influential.

Two other books look at writers of this period. Lisa M. Steinman's *Made in America: Science, Technology, and American Modernist Poets* (Yale) is an important book, showing the relationship of science and technology to poetry in Williams, Moore, and Stevens. Steinman carefully explores why these poets use science and technology to defend their poetry in American culture. The first three chapters examine the cultural and aesthetic milieu that led poets to relate art to science in order to "authorize" poetry with reality. The final three chapters individually examine Williams, Moore, and Stevens. Williams's search for an American language led him to search for democratic and pragmatic analogues in technology and physics to bolster his theories. Moore's optimism in defending American creativity led her to view both natural science and poetry as parallel ways to explain the world, since neither allows us "to ignore facts nor to ignore the effects of human observation and evaluation." Finally, Stevens draws on Whitehead and Planck to show "the world celebrated by poetry was the same world arrived at by physics," an indeterminate world only understood by an act of imagination. Steinman's book is excellent both in its cultural overview and its individual readings.

Mutlu K. Blasing's *American Poetry* is a typography of rhetorics used in American poetry. She identifies four tropes in American poetry (metaphor, metonony, synecdoche, and irony), associates a poetic strategy with each (allegory, analogy, anagogy, and literalism), then proceeds to identify 19th- and 20th-century models for each. Blasing contends that 20th-century poets don't rely on a single historical origin, but use rhetoric to self-authorize their works. She places Stevens in the metonomy/analogy strain and sees his poetry as "an analogy between nature and imagination," while Hart Crane, in the irony/literalism vein, writes poetry which by its rhetoric "precludes certainties and unequivocal readings." Blasing does a good job of looking at how these poets (and their predecessors and successors) authorize themselves in Derrida's "play of language."

A final book is Harold Bloom's collection of 24 essays, *American Poetry 1915 to 1945* (Chelsea). All but one are reprints, and, as always, the essays are somewhat uneven in quality. Particularly noteworthy essays include Poirer on Frost, Bloom and Boroff on Stevens, Mariani on Williams, Lindberg on Pound, Slatin on Moore, and Gubar on H.D.

i. Moore

Marianne Moore's centenary has inspired a bumper crop of criticism: two strong books, one collection of essays, a special edition of *Field*, an exhibition catalog with essay, and at least one major article. An excellent analysis of the changes in Moore's poetry from 1915 to 1936 is John M. Slatin's *The Savage's Romance* (Penn. State). Slatin's detailed explications trace three phases in Moore's career, showing in each changes in form (including rhetorical strategies), themes, and Moore's relation to her male predecessors and colleagues. From 1921 to 1925 is a period of "resistance" and isolation, signaled by syllabic verse; 1921 to 1925 is a period of "accommodation" and increasing community, signaled by free verse; and, 1932 to 1936 is a period of "community" and "reconstruction" during which Moore returns to syllabic verse. Extremely interesting are the influences on Moore. The impact of Eliot's criticism is very well argued, as are the effects of Emerson, Hawthorne, Poe, Wordsworth, and James. Slatin's careful exegeses of individual works like "New York," "The Old Dominion," and "Part of a Novel, Part of a Poem, Part of a Play" are insightful and complete.

Slatin makes the point that Moore's best work was done in the 1930s. Several shorter articles support this idea in their collective condemnation of Moore's revisions. Both Stanley Plumly, "Absent Things" (*Field* 37:31–34), and Sven Birkerts, "She Disliked It, She Did" (*IowaR* 17, iii:154–63), look at Moore's final, three-line revision of "Poetry." While Plumly suggests it shows Moore's "understanding of and commitment to the uses of silence," Birkerts indicts it as Moore's "worst poem," an example of taking her concept of excising the superfluous too far. Similarly, David Walkers, "Imperial Happiness" (*Field* 37:18–23), and David Young, "Clipped Wings" (*Field* 37:43–49), see other Moore revisions as "sadly truncated," less interesting, and "appallingly 'safe' versions of her best early work."

The Poetry of Marianne Moore (Cambridge) by Margaret Holley is a clearly developed exploration of the relationship between Moore's voice and her sense of moral values. Moore's poetry moves in theme and form from "subjective judgement to objective embodiment to shared advocacy." Her changing narrative pronoun and her uses of quotation and catalog are examined to show Moore's development. After her experimentations in the 1920s and 1930s, Moore reaffirms that the individual self, a "vessel of indeterminacy," can still see and champion "determinate values."

Three varying biographical accounts look at (1) the relationship between Moore's paintings and poetry and her friendship with Nancy Davis (Marianne Boruch, "Thirst and Patience," *IowaR* 17, iii:141–53), (2) how Moore's notebooks and archives represent a resource for exploring both her poetry—how she transformed "visual images into poetic images"—and her working method (Patricia C. Willis, *Marianne Moore: Vision into Verse*, The Rosenbach Museum and

Library), and (3) the similarities Moore might have seen between baseball and her poetry (Nancy Knutson, "Baseball and Writing," *IowaR* 17, iii:164–66).

Feminist critic Susan Schweik has written an excellent article on Moore's "In Distrust of Merits" as a paradigm for the feminine war poem; she investigates the problems, based on gender roles, that critics like Randall Jarrell have with a woman author as the subject/ writer of war poetry ("Writing War Poetry Like a Woman," *CritI* 13:532–56). She warns that continuing to prefer war poetry rooted in real "experience" over the abstract works by women who deal with inner conflicts will codify sexual differences and render women "silent and invisible and static."

Finally, Harold Bloom's *Marianne Moore* (Chelsea) collects eight previously published essays and an introduction. The choices, published between 1965 and 1984, represent the diversity of Moore criticism: biographical (Vendler and Costello), literary historical (Kenner and Slatin), textual exegesis (Bloom and Hadas), contextual (Boroff and Bromwich), and feminist (Costello). All are significant critical essays, making this volume in the Modern Critical Views series particularly noteworthy.

ii. Jeffers

Robinson Jeffers was celebrated in a special issue of *American Poetry*, a new biography by James Karman, and a continuing series of articles and notes in the *Robinson Jeffers Newsletter*. Although there are some good essays—particularly those which suggest areas for future research—this centenary outpouring of criticism does not compare qualitatively with Moore's.

As editor of the special *American Poetry* issue (5, i), Tim Hunt includes more than critical essays. He prints comments from poets and fiction writers like William Stafford and Betty Adcock on the impact of "reading" Jeffers, an interview with John Hollander on placing Jeffers within the literary tradition, several transcripts of Jeffers's manuscripts at the Beinecke Library, and his own excellent bibliographic review, "Jeffers Studies 1987" (pp. 94–96). Three essays included in this volume are among the best on Jeffers this year. Pointing out that Jeffers "defied the critical formalism of his age," Terry Beers in "Robinson Jeffers" (pp. 4–16) suggests ways current feminist and deconstructionist critics might find Jeffers fruitful to examine. In a similar vein, Eva Hesse in "Poetry as a Means of Discovery: A Critico-Theoretical Approach to Robinson Jeffers" (pp. 17–34) links Jeffers to Lévi-Strauss, Derrida, and Kristeva via his Inhumanism, which she sees as anticipating "the new ecological ethics and the poststructuralist critique of . . . the subject/author. . . ."

Harold Schweizer in "Robinson Jeffers' Excellent Action" (*AmerP* 5, i:35–58) and Robert Zeller in "Robinson Jeffers: Literary Influences" (*RJN* 69:7–11), both look for Jeffers's literary predecessors. Schweizer locates the forerunner for Jeffers's Inhumanistic tragedies in Matthew Arnold's lyrics and "Empedocles on Etna," while Zeller notes that Wordsworth, Hardy, and E. A. Robinson all share Jeffers's "preoccupation" with cultural decline.

Biographical criticism remains central in Jeffers criticism. James Karman's *Robinson Jeffers, Poet of California* (Chronicle) is a general portrait of Jeffers for a nonacademic audience. Karman's primary intent is to locate Jeffers as a California poet whose life and works were shaped by the landscape in which he lived. I found most interesting his sections on Jeffers's relationships with other Carmel artists, such as George Sterling and Jack London. In the *Robinson Jeffers Newsletter*, previously unpublished correspondence and reminiscences continue to outnumber strong critical essays.

Finally, Jeffers's long poems are shown to be "modern verse novels" in which philosophical debates remain unresolved and the emphasis is on dialogic discourse, according to Patrick D. Murphy, in "Reclaiming the Power: Robinson Jeffers' Verse Novels" (*WAL* 22:125–48). In these verse novels the narrative voice is not "a sovereign master," hence the reader is empowered to construct the text's meaning. Murphy uses "Tamar," "Roan Stallion," and *The Women at Point Sur* to illustrate his point.

iii. H.D., Bogan, and Millay

H.D. criticism continues to thrive. Rachel Blau DuPlessis edited a special H.D. issue for *Sagetrieb* (6, ii), which included seven critical essays as well as H.D.'s "Borderline Pamphlet," a critical commentary on MacPherson's movie of the same name. Four of these essays show H.D. revising patriarchal literary conventions and forms. H.D. transforms Romantic conventions regarding landscapes and the Hyacinth myth into a "politics of female desire," in Cassandra Laity's "H.D.'s Romantic Landscapes: The Sexual Politics of the Garden" (pp. 57–

75). The Hyacinth story is her format for exploring homoerotic attachments, particularly her relationship with Richard Aldington. In "Scarlet Experience: H.D.'s *Hymen*" (pp. 77–100) Eileen Gregory sees H.D. using a traditional vehicle, "marriage poems." But in *Hymen* H.D. atypically focuses on the experience of the bride, or female subject. Marriage becomes the ritualization of "the coming of eros" to a maiden. Linking the erotic to the visionary, H.D. extends the ritual to parallel a woman's act of becoming a poet. Burton Hatlen uses a comparison and contrast to Dante's *Vita Nuova* and *Divina Commedia* in his essay "Recovering The Human Equation: H.D.'s 'Hermetic Definition'" (pp. 141–69) to measure H.D.'s revision of traditional love poetry. Hatlen evolves a "visionary/feminist" reading of "Hermetic Definition" that reveals how writing "is the true locus of creative power," not being the loved object. Finally, Michael Boughn looks at H.D.'s prosodic innovations and contrasts her deployment of rhyme, her speech-based metrics, and her "syntactic variations" with those of Eliot and Williams in "Elements of the Sounding: H.D. and the Origins of Modernist Prosodies" (pp. 101–22).

One of the most interesting essays in the *Sagetrieb* volume is S. Travis's "A Crack in the Ice: Subjectivity and the Mirror in H.D.'s *HERmione*" (pp. 123–40), which uses the writings of Luce Irigaray and Julia Kristeva to read the climax of H.D.'s novel. Travis applies Irigaray's "unity in pairs" and its resulting feminine subjectivity to Fayne and Her's relationship. Unlike other critics, Travis reads the final scene as an *un*ambivalent identification with other women by Her.

Also included in this special issue of *Sagetrieb* are two very useful reference articles. Susan Friedman's "H.D.'s Chronology: Composition and Publication of Volumes" (pp. 51–55) helps to untangle the complex dating of H.D.'s works, many of which appear in print years after they're written, or not at all. Michael Boughn's "The Bibliographic Record of H.D.'s Contributions to Periodicals" (pp. 171–94), the third section of his ongoing descriptive bibliography of H.D., likewise helps future scholars by organizing H.D.'s periodical appearances chronologically and noting each appearance of a work, not just its first appearance. The 220 entries span H.D.'s publishing career from 1905 to 1986.

San Jose Studies devoted its Fall issue (13, iii) to H.D. and Emily Dickinson. Although solid works, the five H.D. essays here are less developed than those in *Sagetrieb*. The strongest is Rebecca Blevins

Faery's " 'Love is Writing': Eros in *HERmione*" (pp. 56–65), which explores the idea that an "encounter with the body" is the first step on a woman's path to becoming a poet. Faery traces images of the erotic and the "body as pencil" in both *HERmione* and *Nights* to link the sexual woman with the visionary poet. Jeanne Larsen continues to look at love and gender in "Myth and Glyph in *Helen in Egypt*" (pp. 88–101). Larsen's reading of Helen changes woman from the object to the "true reader and creator of language." To do this, she deconstructs some Freudian myths of early Oedipal sexuality, the naturalness of gender, and the nature of war. Cynthia J. Goheen, "By Impression Recalled" (pp. 47–55), reevaluates *Tribute to Freud* and shows it is H.D.'s record of a reflexive self-quest rather than a true memoir of Freud.

Susan Friedman also investigates the Freud-H.D. relationship in the excellent "Against Discipleship: Collaboration and Intimacy in the Relationship of H.D. and Freud" (*L&P* 33, iii:89–108). Making extensive use of correspondence, Friedman shows how their relationship was "non-hierarchial," allowing Freud and H.D. to read the text of H.D.'s life as partners, not patron and passive receiver. Friedman suggests their collaborative mode might serve as a model of interaction for feminist-psychoanalytic critics reading Freud.

A final article by Fred D. Crawford, "Misleading Accounts of Aldington and H.D." (*ELT* 30, i:49–67), is part of the continuing biographical work on H.D. Crawford compares and contrasts seven fictional representations of the breakdown of H.D.'s and Richard Aldington's marriage. Crawford shows that stories by the two protagonists, and "friends" such as D.H. Lawrence, John Cournos, Brigit Patmore, and Louis Wilkinson, are all distorted. Each is self-justifying, leaving the reader aware that the truth of a relationship may not be discernible in either art or biography and is certainly not available in fiction purporting to be biography.

Recent feminist works on two seemingly opposite writers, Louise Bogan and Edna St. Vincent Millay, stress the achievement of women modernists in negotiating between the male and female poetic traditions. Gloria Bowles's *Louise Bogan's Aesthetic of Limitation* (Indiana) is an in-depth discussion of this point. A product of her time, Bogan internalized "male ideas of the woman poet" which led her to self-censor her topics and forms and to ruthlessly edit and suppress her work. Her perfectionism led to silence. Still, she successfully mastered formal, modernist theories and forms while retaining a gendered, personal emotion in her poems. Bowles wisely splits her book between an examination of the traditions and contexts which shaped Bogan's sense of herself and her art and an examination of her poems.

Two articles on Millay take slightly different approaches to the problem of being a modernist woman poet. Jan Montefiore's chapter on Millay, "Romantic Transcendence: Edna St. Vincent Millay," in her *Feminism and Poetry* (Pandora), pp. 115–25, focuses on Millay's place in the tradition of love sonneteers, but shows that while Millay's form is traditional, her subject (the woman as subject, not object of the sonnet form) is a radical departure for feminine heroines of texts. But the more probing work on Millay is Suzanne Clark's "The Unwarranted Discourse: Sentimental Community, Modernist Woman, and the Case of Millay" (*Genre* 20:133–52), which effectively argues that what modernism has historically deemed "sentimental" may be the very heart of a female tradition in literature. Millay practices the "poetry of inclusion" with her female readers versus modernist elitism which requires a "more academic priesthood" of readers. Millay's personal voice reinserts the female in the poetic text. Clark examines the polarity created between "the female or the literary," which is precisely the problem in Montefiore's and Bowles's books and a critical point in Drake and in Gilbert and Gubar. Dissertations on Bogan and Millay (one each) continue the emphasis on examining the poets' relationships to female experience in their works.

iv. Sandburg, Robinson, Crane, MacLeish, Masters, Ransom, and Cummings

Two works on Carl Sandburg trace the impact of politics on his life and poetry. *The Poet and The Dream Girl*, ed. Margaret Sandburg (Illinois), prints for the first time 95 of Lilian Steichen Sandburg's letters, 39 of Sandburg's, and 12 early poems, exchanged during their 1908 courtship. Central to the letters is the couple's mutual commitment to socialism and labor organizing and their determination that Sandburg's poems and their life together would reflect their political credo of equality. Adrian Oktenberg's "From the Bottom Up: Three Radicals of the Thirties," in *A Gift of Tongues: Critical Challenges in Contemporary American Poetry*, ed. Marie Harris et al., (Georgia), pp. 83–111, is a Marxist reexamination of Sandburg's

critical reputation, along with those of other professed proletarian
poets, Langston Hughes and Meridel LeSueur. Oktenberg notes that
it is the "activist view of their art" which has caused these writers to
be ignored. Rejecting the notion of "universal poetry," Oktenberg
argues that the particularity of time, place, and social restraints is
necessary to appreciate these writers.

Gerald B. Kinneavy's "Time, Space and Vision in E. A. Robinson's
Tristram" (*LangQ* 25, iii–iv:35–39) shows the acquisition of self- and
world-knowledge as the thematic center of Robinson's long poem.
Love, frequently cited as the theme, is the catalyst to a larger vision
of the world, a vision best embodied in the "resigned endurance" of
Isolt of Brittany. Jeanetta Boswell's *Edwin Arlington Robinson and
the Critics: A Bibliography of Secondary Sources with Selective Annotations* (Scarecrow) lists approximately 1,400 sources, alphabeti-
cally by author. The included subject index should be helpful to
users.

Dissertations continue on Crane's *The Bridge*. This year saw two
new ones as well as the publication of Maria F. Bennett's unrevised
dissertation, *Unfractioned Idiom: Hart Crane and Modernism* (Peter
Lang). Bennett compares Crane's images and theories of "fragmentation and transubstantiation" to Rimbaud and Baudelaire, as well as
situating Crane in the context of jazz, cubism, vorticism, and cinema.

Revision study is the key to MacLeish criticism this year. How
MacLeish revises the three published versions of Part Three of *The
Hamlet of A. MacLeish* to sharpen the contrasts between the Grail
Knight's quest and that of MacLeish/Hamlet is the topic of Lauriat
Lane, Jr.'s "MacLeish at Work: Visions of 'Bleheris'" (*ESC* 13, i:79–
90). Janis P. Stout's "Re-Visions of Job: *J.B.* and 'A Masque of Rea-
son'" (*ELWIU* 14:225–39) contrasts *J.B.* as a revision of the Book
of Job to Frost's closet drama from the same source.

In "Spoon River: Politics and Poetry" (*PLL* 23:347–63) Charles
E. Burgess chronicles how Masters's family experiences in local politics found their way into *Spoon River Anthology*, while Marcia Noe
in "The Johari Window: A Perspective on the *Spoon River Anthology*" (*Midamerica* 8:49–60) offers a psychological model by which
to examine characters in *Spoon River Anthology* without using biographical or social contexts. The Johari Window model analyzes the
role of communication (particularly self-disclosure and feedback) as
a theme.

Two essays on John Crowe Ransom look at how his form and

myths mediate between an objective reality and his desire to create subjective poetry. That Ransom's poetics defend "the independent status of the objective" from possible usurpation by the poet is the premise of Henry W. Russell in "John Crowe Ransom: The Measure of Civil Man (*SoR* 23:256–70). Louise Cowan in "Innocent Doves: Ransom's Feminine Myth of the South," *American Letters*, pp. 191–215, expands this idea by showing that Ransom's choice of the feminine to represent the mythic or ideal in his works necessitates that the gentlemen personas and poet approach her in all her manifestations "with love and respect." Assault and violation as an archetypal reality are balanced by restraint in his poetry.

Looking at E. E. Cummings's paintings and poetry from 1916 to 1927, Milton A. Cohen in *Poet and Painter: The Aesthetic of E. E. Cummings' Early Work* (Wayne State) traces how both are derived from his evolving aesthetics. Using Cummings's notebooks to reconstruct his aesthetic theories on wholeness, perception, form, and motion, Cohen examines how Cummings integrates his interest in poetry, painting, and aesthetics. This is an excellent overview of Cummings's aesthetic theories. Cohen convincingly argues that Cummings deserves his title of poet *and* painter.

v. Frost

Only one book was published on Frost this year, Johannes Kjørven's *Robert Frost's Emergent Design* (Humanities). Kjørven uses Frost's masques and later poems to show that the impetus for his writing is the quest to find the "significance of belief." Frost's search is not for self-discovery nor is it to know God. Rather, it is to choose to believe that "the origin of the questing spirit is . . . divine." Kjørven's major strength is his systematic reading of Frost's two masques. His weakness: at times his jargon seems dated and so do his sources, few of which are post-1980.

The South Carolina Review had a special issue (19, ii) on Frost, the first of what the editorial staff hopes will be yearly publications in cooperation with the Frost Society. Lesley Lee Francis examines the correspondence between Harriet Monroe and Frost from 1914 to 1936 in "Between Poets: Robert Frost and Harriet Monroe" (pp. 2–15). Frost and Monroe shared a mutual respect for each other's role in defending poetry to the public, even though they disagreed on poetic techniques. Patricia B. Wallace, "Robert Frost and the Poetry of Survival" (pp. 29–38), looks at a trait she sees as central to Frost's imagination: his negative capability. Frost engages less in a struggle for resolution of conflicts than to balance tensions. Wallace praises Frost in poems like "The Need of Being Versed in Country Things" and "In a Disused Graveyard" by noting that "Faced with impossible choices, Frost's imagination chooses both." In "Robert Frost's Strategies of Syntax in Selected Letters, 'The Silken Tent,' and 'The Gift Outright'" (pp. 19–28) Craig Challender explains how Frost's convoluted and inverted syntax serves to both capture our attention as readers and to thwart our grammatical and thematic expectations. R. F. Fleissner in "Enveloped in That Old Cloak: Edward Thomas, Wordsworth, and Frost's Untaken Road" (pp. 39–45) proves Frost's debt to Wordsworth's "She Dwelt Among the Untrodden Ways" by showing how Frost and Thomas consciously set out to adapt the poem. Fleissner charts the verbal parallels, word for word, between Wordsworth and his successors.

Another essay to detail Frost's affinity to Wordsworth is Annabel Patterson's "Hard Pastoral: Frost, Wordsworth, and Modernist Poetics" (Criticism 29:67–88). Patterson interprets "Build Soils: A Political Pastoral" as a political critique of the New Deal in the tradition of Virgil's First Ecologue and Wordsworth's "Prelude." Richard Moore, in "Of Form, Closed and Open: With Glances at Frost and Williams" (IowaR 17, iii:86–103), and Michael G. Cooke, in "Frost and Toomer: The Threshold of the Modern" (SWR 72, i:42–61), show Frost's affinities to and differences from his contemporaries. Moore suggests that Frost's themes so profoundly question existing values that his conservative form was almost necessary as an antidote, while the reverse was true for Williams. Cooke compares how Toomer and Frost remain uninterested in new forms, choosing instead to focus on the concept of the image in their poems.

Guy Rotella in "Comparing Conceptions: Frost and Eddington, Heisenberg, and Bohr" (AL:167–89) shows why Frost, as many modernists, was attracted to science. Both particle physics and the Heisenberg uncertainty principle changed the certitude science could claim for itself. The new ideas allowed room for free will and multiplicity. Eddington's The Nature of the Physical World was a source for Frost's appreciation of the similarities between poetry and science. Rotella's paper is enlightening.

Two biographical pieces are worth noting: The Life of the Hired Man, ed. Thomas H. Wetmore (Wright State), and "Frost Verbatim," ed. Devon Jersild (*NER* 10, i:8–20). Wetmore's edition of Wade Van Dore's autobiography recounts the 40-year friendship between Frost and his sometimes hired man, sometimes poet/friend, Van Dore. The two men shared common interests in farming and Thoreau, and Van Dore may have represented the underivative, nonacademic poet that Frost preferred. "Frost Verbatim" provides excerpts from transcribed notes Reginald Cook made of conversations with Frost from 1931 to 1952. The excerpts included here take teaching as their common topic.

Katherine Kearns's "'The Place Is the Asylum': Women and Nature in Robert Frost's Poetry" (*AL* 59:190–210) looks at Frost's view of the feminine. Nature and women resist control and as such are dangerous and potentially deadly to Frost's male characters. In his woods imagery particularly, Kearns sees Frost linking the earth, sexuality, women, and death. His final vision is one of "sexual anarchy."

vi. Williams

The image of women and the Feminine Principle also interest Williams critics. Two books and two articles look at Williams's poetic portrayals of women and the effects of his mother and wife on his poetics. The more tightly argued book is Kerry Driscoll's *William Carlos Williams and the Maternal Muse* (UMI), which traces the effect of Elena Hoheb Williams on her son's poetics. Williams identified physically, spiritually, and psychologically with his mother, making her his feminine creative double. As a result, his 30-year struggle to write a memoir of her, *Yes, Mrs. Williams*, became an autobiographical text of his own life and the subtext for his major works, *In the American Grain* and *Paterson*. Driscoll uses unpublished manuscripts and letters to show the evolution of Williams's textualization of his mother. His technique of "conversation as design" in *Yes, Mrs. Williams* allows for a syntactical as well as philosophical convergence with his mother/muse. Driscoll makes a good case that Williams's fascination with his mother's colorful and idiosyncratic language led to his interest in finding a distinctly American idiom.

Audrey T. Rodgers's *Virgin and Whore: The Images of Women in the Poetry of William Carlos Williams* (McFarland) analyzes the recurring image of the virgin and whore "as it emerged from Williams' complex vision of women accrued over a lifetime." Inclined to see experience in sexual terms, Williams came to equate women, the imagination, and the poem as the desirous Other to his male persona. Rodgers presents the sources for the virgin/whore dichotomy, tracing it back to Williams's favorite myths of Kore/Demeter and the unicorn and the maiden, as well as to his personal experiences as a doctor. The virgin/whore comes to represent the tension Williams sees poetically between imagination and experience. Over half the book details the thread of his virgin/whore imagery in his poems. These readings seem more useful than the source studies of the book's first half. Neither Driscoll nor Rodgers addresses the criticism of feminist critics, like Sandra M. Gilbert, that Williams's treatment of women is at best ambivalent, and more often, hostile.

Theodora R. Graham also applies biographical criticism to show the unique function of Florence Williams and their marriage in Williams's poetry, in "Williams, Flossie and the Others: The Aesthetics of Sexuality" (*CL* 28:163–86). Williams uses his marriage as a theme in his poems, for it allows him "a testing ground for his theories about sexuality, freedom and art." In his works Flossie moves from shadowy adjunct and repressive force, to a symbol of stability and nurturing love, to a "separate being" in Book III of *Asphodel*, which Graham claims is the proper end of both the poem and Williams's aesthetics of sexuality. Kathleen N. Monahan's "Williams' 'For Eleanor and Bill Monahan'" (*WCWR*, 13, iii:4–23) again uses biographical data to show how in this poem Williams accepts the previously external Feminine Principle as a part of himself.

Critics also explore the effects of locale and politics on Williams's poetics. David Frail in *The Early Politics and Poetics of William Carlos Williams* (UMI) and "Citizen Williams: Thirty New Items from the Rutherford Newspapers" (*WCWR* 13, ii:1–8) shows that Williams retained a politics of "nostalgia," which focused on "individuals and concrete human relations," much as his poems do. Both citizen and poet are active participants in their world. Williams's individualism becomes a part of his poetics in his belief that "poetry restored not only the individual's autonomy but also his power." Frail carefully reads *The Great American Novel* and *In the American Grain* within the framework of his discussions of politics and poetry. For the early Williams, as Frail points out in both pieces, art was "another form of local civil service."

In two essays, "Paterson Forty Years After *Paterson*" (*Sagetrieb* 6, i:95–108) and "Permanence and Change in the Paterson, New Jersey, of William Carlos Williams" (*JAmS* 21:422–26), William

Klink looks at the "transtextuality" of Paterson, the city and poem. Klink defines transtextuality as "meaning-effects that transfer from the text to its ensuing context and back again to the text." Hence, a reexamination of the poem's locale is an ongoing part of a deconstruction and reading of *Paterson*. Looking at the symbols of the river, city, and mountain, Klink shows that changes to the locale have changed the poem. Another deconstructive essay concerned with the reading of *Paterson*, although not its locale, is Margaret Dickie's essay, "Williams Reading Paterson" (*ELH* 53:653–71). A poet reading his own long poem as he continues to write and revise it presents a new element in the intertextuality of the work and may block later readers' "access to the text." Dickie points up the irony this generates for the reader of Williams: "this text which makes such a display of its openness is closed off."

The influence of the visual arts on Williams remains another active research area. An overlooked book by Christopher J. MacGowan, *William Carlos Williams' Early Poetry: The Visual Arts Background* (UMI, 1984), is the most extensive study of the influence of modern art and artists on Williams through his writing of *Spring and All* in 1923. MacGowan shows that Williams's awareness of modernist art predates the Armory show. MacGowan explores the aesthetic collaboration between Williams, Pound, Duchamp, Kandinsky, Demuth, Hartley, and Gris and makes a good point that Williams's later uses of visual arts frequently lack "the dynamics of the conflicting, overlapping, internally generated patterns" found in his earlier work. Other essays narrow their scope to individual artists' or movements' affinities with Williams. Williams uses Cézanne's method of concentrating on the details to gain insight into the real world, according to Christopher J. Knight's "William Carlos Williams, Paul Cézanne and the 'Techniques of Originality' " (*Mosaic* 20, ii:83–96). Patrick Moore shows how, moving to free verse, Williams used Cubist principles to enhance the visual dimension of his poetry on a page in "Cubist Prosody: William Carlos Williams and the Conventions of Verse Lineation" (*PQ* 65:515–36), while William Marling compares and contrasts notions of vision in Sheeler and Williams in "The Dynamics of Vision in William Carlos Williams and Charles Sheeler" (*BuR* 30, ii:130–43).

Several other essays are particularly interesting this year, for they engage in ongoing debates about Williams's use of science and his notions of history and origin. John Hildebidle's "Take Off Your

Clothes: William Carlos Williams, Science, and the Diagnostic Encounter" (*MLS* 17, iii:10–30) could profitably be read with Steinman's chapter on Williams. Hildebidle shows Williams's medical
training led to his incorporating diagnosis as a method and theme
in his work. For Williams, diagnosis is interactive observation which
becomes a dialogue between observer and object, a "dynamic inter-
change" which comes to validate the process of understanding above
the discovery of "truth." Hildebidle examines the short stories "Jean
Beicke" and "Old Doc Rivers," as well as poetry, to support his thesis.
Augustus M. Kolich also looks at the process of knowing in *Paterson*,
using not diagnosis, but the philosophical idea of "uncertainty," in his
essay "W. C. Williams' *Paterson* and the Poetry of Uncertainty"
(*Sagetrieb* 6, i:53–72). Similarly, he sees the tension between assertion and doubt as both the theme and method of the poem. Donald
Markos's "Embodying the Universal: Williams' 'Choral: The Pink
Church'" (*WCWR* 13, ii:21–32) goes against both Kolich and
Hildebidle, asserting that Williams retains a Platonic belief in "transcendent universals" and sees universals in the only place they can
be seen: in the particular. What is most interesting in Markos is his
discussion of recent changes he sees in standard critics like J. Hillis
Miller, James Breslin, Denise Levertov, and Carl Rapp, suggesting
they are leaning toward agreeing with him. His call for criticism to
sort out the "different strands of idealism" in Williams seems appropriate given the opposition suggested by these essays.

Two very good essays on Williams's notions of history and origin
came out this year. James F. Knapp's "Not Wholeness but Multiplicity: The Primitivism of William Carlos Williams" (*Mosaic* 20, i:71–
82) examines *In the American Grain* to show that primitivism for
Williams is not an escape back to a prelapsarian pure origin. Rather,
history and the writing of it are "a process of multiplicity narrowed
and closed." This is a major difference between Eliot and Williams.
John Pizer, "Involution in *The Great American Novel*: Reflections
on Williams and Walter Benjamin" (*WCWR* 13, ii:9–20), continues
to show the difficulty in "elucidating the notion of origin" in Williams. Using the German critic Walter Benjamin's idea of involution,
he suggests that Williams abandons the ideas of progress and evolution for the philosophical and technical notion of synchronicity. Thus
the primal is always present, never past and never reducible to a
single origin.

The work on Williams this year has varied in approach, with

biography and deconstructive readings being the most interesting. Surprisingly, although essays and books proliferate, there were no dissertations.

vii. Stevens

Over a third (five out of 13) of the dissertations done on American poets of this period this year were on Stevens, and three book-length critical studies were published, attesting to his current critical favor. Yet the single work most likely to receive attention is Frank Lentricchia's "Patriarchy against Itself: The Young Manhood of Wallace Stevens" (*CritI* 13:742–86). Not only are his comments on Stevens original, but the last third of his essay enumerates the flaws he perceives in current feminist literary theory, particularly as that theory is manifested in *The Madwoman in the Attic* (1979). Lentricchia calls for a return to literary historicity. Using biographical information, he looks at why Stevens was hesitant to become a poet. Primary among Stevens's concerns was the association of poetry with women (readers and writers) and its unsuitability as a vocation for a middle-class man who needed to earn a living. Lentricchia persuasively argues that Stevens's fears about his sexual identity as a writer are in fact "the canonical modernist issue of poetic authority." Lentricchia shows his point by locating disruptions in the text of "Sunday Morning." One such rupture occurs around an allusion to Keats, who as a male Romantic poet represents both what Stevens desires to become and what he most fears becoming. The part of Lentricchia's work likely to raise critical hackles is not his paper on Stevens, but his subessay "Reflections on Essential Feminism." Having earlier differentiated gender from biology or nature, Lentricchia critiques current feminist criticism which fails to do likewise. He accuses feminist critics of substituting matriarchy for patriarchy, without changing the core of definitions.

Michael Beehler in *T. S. Eliot, Wallace Stevens, and the Discourses of Difference* (LSU) uses primarily a semiotic approach to explore difference in Eliot and Stevens, not just as a theme but as the very form of their discourses. Alternating chapters between the two poets makes it possible to look at the process and problems of each separately. While both may overtly pursue a transcendent unity, their language, metaphors, and creative processes all point to indeterminacy as the basic truth of their worlds. There is not immanence around them or within them, only the dynamic self-generated cycle of thought and writing. Beehler's language is occasionally jargon-laden, but his linguistic analysis of discourse is fine.

A directly opposed premise is the basis for Joseph Carroll's *Wallace Stevens' Supreme Fiction: A New Romanticism* (LSU). Carroll looks at Stevens's development as "a struggle to overcome the metaphysical limitations of a simple dualism and to achieve a poetic absolute." Carroll sees Stevens as moving toward synthesis, what he calls either a supreme fiction or "a new romanticism." This book is a traditional developmental study, culminating with the assertion of a comprehensive Stevens mythology, the form and expression of which is in the longer poems of 1947–48: "The Owl in the Sarcophagus," "The Auroras of Autumn," and "A Primitive Like an Orb." Carroll draws lines of influence between Stevens and his Romantic literary forefathers: Keats, Shelley, Wordsworth, Tennyson, Emerson, and Whitman. Ultimately, Carroll confesses that Stevens cannot sustain his moments of unity, but he praises him for creating "a mode of poetic experience in which religious awe and Romantic wonder are still possible." Carroll's discussions of "The Owl and the Sarcophagus" and "The Auroras of Autumn" are especially good.

In *Wallace Stevens and Poetic Theory: Conceiving the Supreme Fiction* (No. Car.) B. J. Leggett identifies four influences on Stevens's poetic theory: I. A. Richards, Giambattista Vico, Charles Mauron, and Henri Focillon. Leggett does not chart references so much as tries to show how Stevens's poetics were enhanced by his reading of these theorists. The first three help shape Stevens's ideas leading up to the writing of "Notes Toward a Supreme Fiction." Leggett sees this poem as the apex of Stevens's belief that reality is created by an act of imagination. Focillon becomes the major influence after 1942, as Stevens moves back to a belief in a reality outside the mind, a position made clear in both "The Auroras of Autumn" and *The Rock*.

Several essays establish other philosophical influences on Stevens. James Lindroth in "Simone Weil and Wallace Stevens: The Notion of Decreation as Subtext in 'An Ordinary Evening in New Haven'" (*R&L* 19, i:43–62) shows how major themes in Weil "resonate" in Stevens's poem. David Bromwich shows how Stevens's definition of hero is shaped by the antithetical pulls of Nietzsche and William James in "Stevens and the Idea of the Hero" (*Raritan* 7, i:1–27).

A number of the essays look for sources for Stevens's poems. Four representative examples are Glen MacLeod's "Stevens and Surrealism: The Genesis of 'The Man with the Blue Guitar'" (*AL* 59:359–77), which shows the effects of Breton, the Surrealism exhibit at MOMA in 1936, and Picasso on Stevens's poem; Jacqueline V. Brogan's "Stevens and Stevenson: The Guitarist's Guitarist" (*AL* 59:228–41), which shows the influence of Robert Louis Stevenson's short story, "Providence and the Guitar," on Stevens's ideas of representation; D. L. Macdonald's "Wallace Stevens and Victor Serge" (*DR* 66:174–80), which shows how an excerpt from Victor Serge's memoirs of revolutionary Russia stimulated Stevens's defense on intellectual freedom in canto XIV of *Esthetique du Mal*; and John Kwan-Terry's "Of Pines, Beards and Several Chinamen: One Way of Looking at Wallace Stevens," in *Discharging the Canon: Cross-Cultural Readings in Literature*, ed. Peter Hyland (Singapore), pp. 54–72, which shows the elements and traditional symbols in Chinese art and poetry which attracted Stevens as a collector and a writer.

A final category of Stevens criticism that is well represented this year are readings of individual poems. Essays in this category again are varied in how they approach the works. Some are genre studies, like Ashby B. Crowder and Charles Chappel's "The Dramatic Form of 'The Idea of Order at Key West' and 'Peter Quince at the Clavier'" (*CollL* 14, i:38–48), which shows that the poems are actually dramatic monologues, not lyrics. Some are line-by-line glosses of themes, like Nancy W. Prothro's "'A New Text of the World': Wallace Stevens' 'Things of August'" (*NMAL* 10:Item 6), which looks at the meaning death gives to life in "Things in August." Some are playful, yet insightful, examinations of how themes and methodology work in both Stevens's poetry and criticism, like Richard D. Hathaway's "Wallace in Wonderland: Thirteen Ways of Looking at a Bantam" (*SoR* 23:557–68), which parodies Stevens's form to show how a poem can function like abstract art to help delay closure.

Montana State University

17. Poetry: The 1940s to the Present

Richard J. Calhoun

i. Overview

In 1987 there were exceptional books on two important poets, a biography and several articles on Sylvia Plath, a reexamination of the place of Elizabeth Bishop among American poets, serious questions raised about an "establishment" and "fringe" dichotomy in American poetry, and the arrival of volume two of what is the only standard history of modern poetry.

The place to start this year reviewing criticism on American poets whose primary thrust in poetry came since 1940 is with the second volume of the standard history of modern poetry, David Perkins, *A History of Modern Poetry: Modernism and After* (Harvard). Pertinent here is "Part Three: Postmodernism," pp. 331–660, the "after Modernism" section. Perkins's approach to recent American poetry is nonpartisan in rhetoric, although not in selection, a thoroughly orthodox establishment view, with few surprises, and no eccentricities. He provides a good introduction for anyone interested in finding out what is included under the designation postmodernism. He identifies as major precursors—Robert Penn Warren, Theodore Roethke, and Elizabeth Bishop; and he discusses the major figures after modernism—Robert Lowell, John Ashbery, A. R. Ammons, and James Merrill. He also acknowledges two events that signaled a change from modernism: a breakthrough, led by Richard Wilbur, Randall Jarrell, John Berryman, against the New Criticism; the confessional vogue that followed in the wake of Robert Lowell's *Life Studies*. Assigned a much lesser role is the movement toward "Open Form," emanating from Pound and Williams and guided by guru Charles Olson. Dispersed as a significant movement in Perkins's configuration is the "Beat Movement," with Gary Snyder listed under "Against Civilization," and Allen Ginsberg, under "Poetry in New York and San Francisco." Ferlinghetti earns very minor treatment, and Gregory Corso receives only mention.

Perkins explores postmodernism as an Hegelian "period style." The characteristics of this period style include a poetry that "seems spontaneous, personal, naturalistic, open in form and antagonistic to the idea of form, intellectually skeptical yet morally concerned and sometimes even righteous, and imbued with feelings of vulnerability, yet with the humor of resignation, acknowledging helplessness." He also acknowledges, but says little about, the tradition of "spontaneous speech," derived from Whitman and Williams, and the convention that "the poet is speaking," which he gauges as a counteraction to Eliot's stress on good poetry as always impersonal and as a response to New Critical explications of "autonomous" poems. A major difference between British and American postmodernism is that poetry in America reacted both to Modernist practice and to New Critical theory. He is exhaustive in his discussion of the forms used in contemporary poetry—"traditional and free verse in narrative, dramatic monologue, long meditation, list, catalogue, and lyric, including sonnet, song, chant, litany spell, and mantra," to which he adds collage, used in early poems by John Ashbery and in a few by Robert Duncan, and concrete poetry. . . ." I found Perkins's book serviceable as expressive of establishment norms, and I had hoped to cite his assessments of individual poets, but space has limited my comments to the poets who receive full-essay treatment—Ashbery, Ammons, Merrill.

Mutlu Konuk Blasing's *American Poetry* is an ambitious attempt to redefine poetic tradition in American poetry by redirecting attention from a single tradition, usually the Emersonian, to four lines of poetic succession—from Poe, Emerson, Whitman, and Dickinson. The critic identifying one Orphic beginning in Emerson whom Blasing takes on is Harold Bloom. Among contemporary poets, she pursues facets of Poe in the poetry of Sylvia Plath, of Emerson in Elizabeth Bishop, of Whitman in Frank O'Hara, and Dickinson in the poetry of John Ashbery. Blasing is concerned with poetic strategies, not with stylistic influences. Her critical approach combines the medieval critical practice of four levels of textual interpretation with Northrop Frye's archetypal phases to make a case for four "master tropes" or "types" of American poetry—allegory in Poe, anagogy in Whitman, and irony in Emily Dickinson. Her approach generates short but informative essays on Plath, Bishop, Ashbery, and O'Hara. The chapter on Plath is especially recommended.

In *A Gift of Tongues: Critical Challenges in Contemporary American Poetry* (Georgia) Marie Harris and Kathleen Aguero attempt to focus on poets whose work is not generally available because of their ethnic, regional, or social classifications. Included are overviews of Native American, Chicano, Appalachian, Puerto Rican, Japanese-American, black and gay poets, prison writers, and proletarian poets of the 1930s—Carl Sandburg, Langston Hughes—as well as unassorted essays on feminist criticism, Harold Bloom, and a few uncategorized poets. This is a useful collection of essays reporting diversity in American poetry; but it is far from being a unified book. The question as to whether this book is intended as a study of literature or of popular culture is not addressed.

Distinguished poets and critics met at the University of Alabama in October 1984 for a symposium on the eternal question—"What is a poet?" Their answers are now available in *What Is a Poet?*, ed. Hank Lazer (Alabama). What is of interest is the controversy that arose on the issue of the relationship between poetry and society. It begins with Louis Simpson's opening address, "The Character of the Poet" (pp. 13–30), in which he expresses a concern that placing lyric poetry on a pedestal permitting outer reality to be ignored has been accompanied by a decline of interest in poetry. He is especially troubled by the separation of lyric from narrative and discursive writing, resulting in poetry that is "as far from meaning as one can get without lapsing into nonsense, and it frequently crosses the line." Simpson champions "a poetry of human situations," which permits political poetry, "if it is the life we live," and if it preserves the distinctions between verse and prose.

Charles Altieri ("What Modernism Offers the Contemporary Poet," pp. 31–65) sees the clash as between those writers who seek to continue "the experimental spirit fostered by Modernism" and those who want poetry to return to "the social roles it once served." Much of his point is made through comments on two poems, Richard Kenney's "Speed of Light," and Donald Revell's "Motel View." He makes his case for the continuing relevance of modernism by asserting the superiority of Revell's "Ashbery-inspired" poem and by refuting the case for postmodernism made in Jonathan Holden's "Postmodern Poetic Form" (see *ALS 1983*, p. 358). He counters Holden's case for postmodernism with four strategies that modernist impersonality made possible for poetry—strategies against narcissism, strategies for seeing the mind's duplicities, strategies for making possible presentational antidramatic strategies for irony, and strategies for making it possible for poets to participate in a philosophical project on the nature of thinking begun in the early work of Wittgenstein. Altieri assigns himself only a modest position in the rear guard of any Modernist and Postmodernist debate; actually he is a major player.

Hank Lazer in "Critical Theory and Contemporary American Poetry" (pp. 247–69) responds to Altieri's "dangerous devaluation of lyric and religious poetry" in order to privilege "the full ironic and self-reflexive play of mind" in poetry. He advocates throwing out all misconceptions about poetry, including the two extremes of viewing poetry as "exotic intuition" or as "systematic presentations of abstract propositions." The talk was lively at this meeting, as the transcriptions of the panel that followed disclose, with some participants even walking out on papers. In the later 1980s the question of which way is best for poetry can become a subject for zealous controversy.

Last year I found that the *New York Quarterly*'s essays on "The Present State of Poetry" often provide helpful overviews. This year Burton Hatlen ("Present State of American Poetry, no. 7," *NYQ* 33: 106–15) gives his version of two kinds of poetry: a poetry which is part of the cultural mainstream and a poetry which is "culturally marginal." He provides a brief historical sketch. In the 1930s [actually well into the 1940s] a new Academic poetry emerged—at Vanderbilt with Ransom and disciples; at Princeton with R. P. Blackmur; at Yale with Warren and Brooks; at Michigan with Austin Warren; and at Minnesota with Allen Tate. The textbooks for this poetry were provided by Brooks and Warren. The generation of poets they influenced is identified by inclusion in Donald Hall, Richard Pack, and Louis Simpson, *The New Poets of England and America*. The other and rival tradition in American poetry was soon specified by inclusion in another anthology, Donald Allen's *The New American Poetry*, published to challenge the establishment with new poets, none of whom had appeared in Hall, Pack, and Simpson. Many of these looked to Williams and Pound, and some were instructed by a new guru, Charles Olson. Another entry in this war of American poetry was made in 1985 with Helen Vendler's *Harvard Book of Contemporary Poetry*, which included mostly poets from the old Hall, Pack, Simpson school, with a few token additions in order to give the appearance of a merger of traditions. Making it clear that any dialogue between traditions is now over and that a new nonestablishment group of poets is emerging is the *Morrow Anthology of Younger Poets*, ed. David Smith and David Bottoms. All this about anthology "wars" is a bit superficial.

The second contribution, no. 8 in the series, is made by Stephen Stepanchev (*NYQ* 34:105–21). He identifies four extraordinary talents in American poetry since 1945: Lowell, Berryman, Bishop, Plath, all of whom are dead. Fortunately, he finds exceptional poets among the living: Merrill, Snyder, Creeley, Bly, Ashbery, Ammons, Wilbur, Merwin, Baraka. Among the merely promising are Frank Bidart, Carolyn Forché, Lorenzo Thomas, Dave Smith, and Gary Soto. The poetry Stepanchev values is "a poetry of presence," which has taken to free verse to reflect speech rhythms, but is also given to experimenting with traditional measures. He categorizes the poets of the last 40 years as projectivists, whose poems are energized by the poet's breath: Olson, Duncan, Creeley; as Beat poets and subjectivists, who seek out "deep images" from the unconscious that are charged with the reality of sensory data: Ginsberg, Snyder, Ferlinghetti; as Confessional poets, who seek the particular over the universal, the personal over the archetype: Lowell, Plath, Sexton; as the New York School, urbane, ironic, with spontaneous descriptions of city life: O'Hara, Ashbery, Koch, Schuyler; and as feminists: Plath, Sexton, Piercy, Herschberger, Jong. I suppose such inventories suggest the variety of American poetry. What I find distressing in such listings is the "disappearance" of poets as various as Dickey and Nemerov, who are either of a persuasion not favored by the critic or who do not fit any of his categorizations. There is a certain lack of critical generosity among critics today.

If you saw the television film "Voices and Visions," you will love the book; well, almost. The companion volume is out, *Voices and Visions: The Poet in America*, ed. Helen Vendler (Random House), with a general introduction by the editor and separate introductions to Elizabeth Bishop and Sylvia Plath, by Helen McNeil and to Robert Lowell, by Vereen Bell. In her introduction Vendler tilts toward the Bloom version of an Emerson-generated Orphic vision in American poetry. She believes that what readers in our century have cared about is "to understand art as process." The contemporary poets she values are Lowell, Plath, Ammons, Bishop, Merrill.

Another book of consequence is Lynn Keller's *Remaking It New: Contemporary American Poetry and the Modernist Tradition* (Cambridge). Keller identifies a continuity between modernism and later poetry evidenced in a relationship between the great modernists and certain contemporary poets. Keller pairs Wallace Stevens and John Ashbery, Marianne Moore and Elizabeth Bishop, William Carlos

Williams and Robert Creeley, W. H. Auden and James Merrill, in a
focus on "the historical transmission and modification of modernist
poetic techniques." Each of these contemporary poets is shown to
be representative: Creeley, of the Black Mountain poets; Bishop, of
an interest in combining strict form and informal language and rhetoric shared by Lowell, Berryman, Jarrell, and more recent poets;
Ashbery, of the New York School and their tie to art; James Merrill,
of formalists like Anthony Hecht, John Hollander, May Sarton, and
Richard Howard. Keller is actually best on divergences. I especially
like what she spells out between Stevens and Ashbery: Ashbery's
more colloquial poetic diction; his greater determination to tie poetry
to immediate, ordinary living; the value placed on language that
actually communicates present feeling; a lesser faith in the modernist
belief in exactitude of words or metaphors; and a freedom from a
modernist anxious desire for coherence. Almost as deft is the handling
of Williams (viewed here as a more personal, less ironic modernist)
and Creeley, who, in the 60s, became more aware of language as an
arbitrary system. If Keller finds a major shared divergence on the
part of the postmodernists, it is their moving away from the modernist
desire for coherence and closure to seeing poetry as more of a random
and indeterminate process. This is an informative and sensible study
of modernist preoccupations still of concern to poets who have deviated significantly from some of the basic doctrines.

Paul Breslin's *The Psycho-Political Muse: American Poetry since
the Fifties* (Chicago) is a competent but unsympathetic study of
what has been recently neglected, the culturally radical poetry in
America in the 50s and 60s. Breslin looks afresh at the confessional
poetry of Lowell, Plath, and Berryman; the deep-image surrealism of
Merwin, Wright, and Bly; the projectivism of Charles Olson, practiced in their own individual ways by Levertov and Duncan. His
thesis is the sociopsychological effect of guilt from too much egoism
and from the wealth and power of postwar America. This guilt is
reflected in the poetry of the late 50s and reached a climax with the
protest movement against the Vietnam War in the 60s. Many of these
poets were Whitmanesque in a new way, desiring to cleanse themselves and their poetry of the corruptions of an America gone too far
down the path of materialism. Some saw the self as a microcosm of
the sufferings of the nation; others tried to escape the self entirely,
either through the Jungian unconscious, or through Olsonian process.

Their poetry encouraged careless writing under the excuse of spontaneity and a self-exhibitionism that the modernist doctrine of impersonality had sought to prevent. Breslin is well-read in the intellectual milieu of this period, and he mentions a great many poets. But he explores only a few, Lowell, Plath, Merwin, Wright, leaving out more recent manifestations, for example, Levertov and Rich, as if to suggest unsuitability for the present. It is indicative, perhaps, that he begins with Allen Ginsberg as the "representative man" and ends with John Ashbery "as the main candidate for major American poet in the 1980s."

There are far too many brief comments to report in the symposium, "Is There, Currently, an American Poetry?" (*AmerP* 4, ii:2–41), but one thing I find new is Marjorie Perloff's finding that there is not a consensus "mainstream," but rather sundry regional evaluations. James Merrill is the "penultimate poet" on the East Coast, but he is missing from many reading lists in the Midwest. Robert Duncan was venerated in Buffalo, but he was left out of Helen Vendler's *Harvard Anthology of Contemporary Poetry*. Perloff is also concerned that too much contemporary poetry has lost its traditional contact with "the changing language of common intercourse." She anticipates that literary historians in the next century will detect a trend in the 80s toward "a revival . . . of artifice, a renewed conviction that poetry is language made strange, discourse inherently unlike that of ordinary speech." Instead of a speech-based poetics, what is now admired is what is strange, different, and "indeed unnatural." She suggests that the pivotal figure in a return to poetic diction and in the aftermath of post-structuralism in the direction of a contemporary poetry of defamiliarized language and syntax is John Ashbery. Poetry may be viewed only as "a set of material signifiers that generate their own multivalent references."

Two regional studies deserve passing mention. From the mammoth *A Literary History of the West* I received only copies of essays on Robert Bly by Douglas Smith, on "Indian Poetry" by Patricia Clark Smith, and on "Present Trends in Western Poetry" by William Lockwood. Lockwood includes Edward Dorn, Richard Hugo, William Everson, and Josephine Miles. I can only report that there is also brief treatment of William Stafford by Gerald W. Haslam, of Jack Kerouac, Gary Snyder, and San Francisco, all by Dennis McNally.

Fifty Southern Writers after 1900 includes my essay on James

Dickey, George Lensing's on Randall Jarrell, James Justus on Robert
Penn Warren, and William Harmon on A. R. Ammons. All will receive brief attention later.

Sandra M. Gilbert and Susan Gubar's *No Man's Land* begins what
is planned as a three-volume study of the place of the woman writer
in the 20th century. In this admittedly revisionist and reductivist approach to literary history, the war between two views of poetry becomes a verbal battle of the sexes expressed in literature. Modernism
is perceived as a defensive masculine response to fears of growing
female potency in the later 19th- and early 20th-century society and
literature. Male writers and critics sought to define and control the
very nature of language in literature. This is potent feminist theoretical criticism, which allows individual writers only passing treatment.
Plath, Lowell, Berryman, and Rich are discussed, but only as passages
in their works reveal the social-psychological meaning of a sexual
conflict.

Concern about the fate of American poetry is also evident in the
previously cited symposium (*AmerP* 4, ii:2–41). Two points are made
which are worth repeating. Paul Christensen and Clayton Eshleman
also go on record as believing that there is an "official" American
poetry, with all the benefits and privileges, and a near orphan "far
fringe," left for the small publishers and little magazines that few
read. "Official poetry" promotes a belief that language is sufficient as
a defense against madness and chaos and to control emotions. The
"fringe" poets "have shown us that a disorderly language is as compelling as and perhaps more expressive than the ordered kind." We
are once again evoking poetry wars. Thom Gunn singles out a frequent target, Helen Vendler's "disastrous [Harvard] anthology," as
based on a belief that American poetry is like English poetry. David
Ignatow also fears for the health of American poetry, but finds a
strength in the personal voice, still evident in "multitudinous
voices . . . coming from every part of the country." The threat is that
an attempt on the part of academicians to form "small but effective
circles of admiration around specific poets to the exclusion of others"
will "destroy American poetry at its roots."

I append here, only because it does not fit anywhere else, an article for which the illustrations of paintings are essential, Fred Mora-
marco's "Speculations: Contemporary Poetry and Painting" (*Mosaic*
20, iii:23–36). This is an attempt to show how many contemporary
poets have evolved a kind of poetry that refers its readers, "directly

and indirectly," to the "visual inspiration that is its source." Three
poems and paintings are compared, Adrienne Rich's "Mourning Picture" and a folk painting by Edwin Romanzo Elmer; John Ashbery's
"Self-Portrait in a Convex Mirror" and the Italian Parmigiano's Renaissance painting; John Updike's "Gradations of Black" and abstract
expressionist paintings by Ad Reinhardt, Mark Rothko, Frank Stella,
and Franz Kline. The words of the poets, he concludes (quoting art
critic and poet Ashbery) are only "speculations," but they lift impressions of paintings that mean a great deal to the poets and convey
their impressions to readers in a language that "enhances, renews,
and sometimes even transforms the work of art that is their source."
Such preoccupations by poets will not soothe the concerns expressed
this year about recent poetry.

ii. The Middle Generation: Roethke, Lowell, Jarrell, Nemerov

Last year's group portrait of the Middle Generation poets, Bruce
Brawer's *The Middle Generation* (Archon), is surpassed in narrative
interest by Jeffrey Meyers's *Manic Power: Robert Lowell and His
Circle* (Arbor). Robert Lowell and his closest friends, Randall Jarrell, John Berryman, and Theodore Roethke, died in late middle age,
through suicide or from stressful living. Jeffrey Meyers, as he demonstrated in his biography of Ernest Hemingway, can expertly narrate
the inevitability of such finales in writers who were, in varying degrees, emotionally retarded since youth. He documents how they as
poets "felt they should seek suffering rather than happiness," and he
narrates adeptly how all "four poets obsessively pursued their private
myths, and persuaded each other and the public to believe them."
All this makes for fascinating reading: accounts of lives lived consistently in misery.

Meyers is better with similarities than with differences. Among
their similarities were loss of father, problems with mother, fighting
with colleagues and wives, and a shared turn toward the confessional
in poetry. Meyers's thesis is that their intensity led to a failure to be
content with what they had done. They had to be the best. Exemplary
is Lowell's observation that he and his friends "go at it with such
single-minded intensity that we are always on the point of drown-
ing." Yet there were differences, which deserve a hearing as well.
Berryman is the only certain suicide; Jarrell, only a probable. Roethke

and Lowell simply drove themselves on intensely to their heart attacks, as many troubled and obsessed people do. This study and Brawer's contribute to the legend about poets fatally predestined. However sensational and sad were the events of their lives, what is more germane is the quality of their poetry. My own interest would be in reading more about how Roethke and Lowell struggled to become better poets than Berryman and Jarrell ever did. Neither Brawer last year nor Meyers this year makes that comprehensible.

Peter Balakian's "Theodore Roethke, William Carlos Williams, and the American Grain" (*MLS* 17, i:28–38) is a reexamination of the "personal and artistic growth which marked the birth of a major poet [Roethke]" between the publication of *Open House* (1941) and 1946, when most of the poems were finished that were to be included in *The Lost Son and Other Poems* (1948). To Balakian this kind of "birth" is one of the most interesting things to study about the growth of a major writer; and he mentions similar moments for Whitman, Melville, and Faulkner. For Roethke self-discovery of his "existential core" "involved finding a literary voice and gaining the psychological self-awareness and emotional courage to wrestle with the primal realities of his past and the often painful traumas of his present." Self-knowledge was made accessible by "a corresponding change in his understanding of poetics" through discovery of a new working method of creating voluminous notebooks for the poetry he would write. Examination of these notebooks, especially those for 1943 and 1944, shows that he discovered the origins of self and the source of his poetry "in the fertile slime of nature," remembered from his father's greenhouse. By repossessing that world Roethke gained a symbol for "the world of fragile life" and "a glimpse into the subhuman." Roethke also records his terrible need for God, which led to an absorption in reading Evelyn Underhill on mysticism and the lives of mystics and saints to reinforce a belief that, when roaming the woods one night in November 1935, he had a mystical experience. God became an inscrutable presence that Roethke had to seek once again through his poetry. The final force was his friendship with William Carlos Williams, which led to a reorientation of his views of poetic language. Balakian documents Williams's influence, both from poems (I wish he had done even more) and from letters (he may give too much). There has been so much on Stevens and Ashbery, it is good to see something substantial on Williams and Roethke.

There is also a good little book out this year on Roethke, the best study so far in the series on "understanding" contemporary poets. This is Walter B. Kalaidjian's *Understanding Theodore Roethke* (So. Car.). Roethke is understood as an autobiographical poet, affected by the death of his father, with a sequential ambivalence toward literary fathers, and with a constant anxiety about identity. As a poet he paid careful attention to the physical world as part of his aim of establishing personal identity through direct participation in the natural process. Kalaidjian contends that, as a teaching poet, Roethke developed an interest in the performing dimension of poetry, in music and sound sense as important as visual imagery. He is credited with pioneering new directions in poetic form, style, and themes.

William Doreski's "Vision, Landscape, and the Ineffable in Robert Lowell's *History*" (*ELWIU* 14:251–67) is evidence, that, whatever the views of the man in the aftermath of Ian Hamilton's biography, respect for the poet remains. Doreski focuses on three broad concerns he finds in the sonnets in *History*: "poems about imaginative vision and physical seeing; poems about vision and landscape; and poems about the attractions and difficulties of abstractions, absolutes, and the ineffable." The common factor in these is "Lowell's passion to reconcile the terms of life and art." Even the formal difficulties of the poems, "their cramped and military beat," came from his intention "to balance perceptions of the transitory and fragmentary particulars of life with the desires for permanence and visionary wholeness in art." Doreski's evidence comes from a close reading of the fifth "1930's" sonnet, "History," "Man and Woman," "Bird," "Genesis," and, "Fears of Going Blind." Finally, he focuses on "End of a Year" as a lament for "the impossibility of fully resolving infinite problems in finite language wielded by semi-crazed poets." I agree with Doreski on the importance of these poems, even if Lowell eventually had to admit his failure as a poet to deal with contemporary problems and materials. Lowell demonstrated "his faith in poetry as a source of personal engagement and societal values," and he wrote some of the best poetry of his era.

I should make brief mention of Robert Giroux's edition of Lowell's prose, *Collected Prose* (Farrar Straus Giroux), which presents evidence of Lowell's importance as a commentator on his own poetry (selections from his abandoned autobiography) and as critic/reviewer, with worthy selections on his friend, Randall Jarrell, and on his student, Sylvia Plath.

Sue Mitchell Crowley in "Mr. Blackmur's Lowell: How Does

Morality Get into Literature" (*R&L* 19, iii:27–47) begins with what
was an embarrassment for the friendship of a great critic and a great
poet, R. P. Blackmur's negative review of Lowell's first book, *Land of
Unlikeness*. The two were friends, and Blackmur's associates in the
New Criticism were Lowell's critical fathers. Crowley adds another
unfavorable review, Blackmur's final assessment in a reference volume, *Religion in American Life*, which Lowell probably never saw.
She then proposes to read Lowell as Blackmur saw him. To Blackmur,
in expressing his rage at a fallen world, Lowell failed to find for his
poetry, "a tension of necessity . . . conflict accepted, not hated." Lowell
was one of those Jacob figures who wrestled with God, conscience,
and with our human behavior. Crowley then applies Blackmur's
theory to a poem that should have pleased Blackmur as a satisfactory artistic expression of Lowell's overtly religious impulses, "Beyond
the Alps."

Jeffrey Meyers's "Robert Lowell: The Paintings in the Poems"
(*PLL* 23:218–39) demonstrates that Lowell's use of the old masters
of painting (Breughel, Holbein, Titian, Cranach, Rembrandt, Vermeer, and Van Eyck) in his poems was for political purposes. For his
poems Lowell is able to find in paintings correlatives to express "his
deepest values, his most personal preoccupations, and his ideas about
religion, history, pacifism, and the spiritual element in love, marriage,
and pregnancy." Meyers shows Lowell does as well in appropriating
paintings as poets better known for this—Williams, Jarrell, Auden.

I should mention that Laurence Lerner (*CritQ* 29, ii:46–66) in
answer to the question "What is Confessional Poetry?" turns to
Lowell's "St. Mark's 1933." He observes in this poem "factual accuracy
of remembering, self-centeredness, self-abasement expressed in cli-
ches." Lerner associates confessional poetry more with the romantic
emphasis on personal immediacy than with "modern horrors."

This year was not the year for a continuing of the renewed interest in Randall Jarrell's poetry that was in such evidence last year.
George S. Lensing's "Randall Jarrell" (*Fifty Southern Writers*, pp.
270–79) surveys adequately Jarrell as man of letters—critic, novelist,
author of children's stories, translator, editor, as well as poet. Lensing emphasizes "the problem of human mortality and pain" in Jarrell's poetry, presented through use of fairy tales and folk legends,
evidenced in his war poetry; but he slights the poems that characterize
women. He properly identifies Jarrell's greatest strength as evidenced
"in his creation of human characters who may metamorphose." He

had a partiality for ordinary lives, more interest in "mythos," in "childlike fantasies or dream states in which characters act out dramas of human success and failure than in narrative plot." All of this is intelligent criticism and fair assessment.

Mark I. Goldman in "The Politics of Poetry: Randall Jarrell's War" (*SAQ* 86:123–34) defends Jarrell's war poems against the charge of impersonality by finding them not concerned with individual soldiers but with the impersonal nature of war. Reality in these poems is modified by the desire to escape either to a prewar paradisiacal world or to the primal world of childhood. He concludes that the most famous of these poems, "The Death of the Ball Turret Gunner," should be read in the context of the other war poems with the state characterized as the false mother.

An interesting item to note is Nelson Hathcock's "The Art of War: A Source for Jarrell's '1914'" (*AmerP* 4, ii:51–56), because it recalls a poem almost forgotten by critics, "1914," and documents that this prose poem is a commentary on Laurence Stallings's *The First World War: A Photographic History.*

An article on Howard Nemerov is especially appropriate now that he has come, as our third Library of Congress Poetry Consultant, to be regarded as our Poet Laureate. Gloria L. Young in "Finding Again the World" (*CP* 20:75–85) stresses Nemerov's concern with the epistemological problem of what we can know and how we can know it. Young finds affinities with Ortega y Gasset, Albert Camus, Roland Barthes, and Melville's Ahab. To Nemerov, the poet may be the means of uniting mind and world, the self and the other, and the world provides the voice of the eternal other. The focus in this essay is on "The Four Ages" and on Nemerov's intentions in *New and Selected Essays* (1985), where he demonstrates a new understanding of the possibilities of language in this search for reconciliation, Nemerov now views language as "an abstract and utterly arbitrary but totally articulated system of relations." His concern has shifted from "asking the meaning of a poem to questioning the meaning of meaning." Nemerov is viewed here as fashionable and current, a part of the "mainstream."

Nemerov, the man and the teacher, is remembered in Richard Hollinger's "Impressions of Nemerov" (*SR* 23:5–25). This is a good, old-fashioned character sketch of Nemerov's classroom role of "scholar-poet appearing the bum," with ample quotes/paraphrases of his in-class comments on poetry and insights into his own poems.

"Art's purpose is to show everything fits, even in a world of sordidness, the inevitability of a poem fitting together as if it had to. . . . It's the relationship of poetry with nature. Nature is in chaos if you look with an untutored eye. Yet poetry makes sense and order out of nature." Nemerov as teacher seems very much in touch with the formalism of his formative years as poet and teacher.

John Berryman's *Dream Songs* are also revisited by Luke Spencer (*CritQ* 29, i:71–80), and the occasion is the failure of critics "to detect some overall narrative, thematic, or chronological unity" other than the unfolding of Henry's life. Spencer believes that going to pieces was "the definitive collective experience of Berryman's poetic generation," and that we should not look for unity. The reader/critic should "trace the jaggedness of edges that do not fit and the broken contours of a design that could not fashion wholeness" out of the alienated private life and tormented areas of contemporary experience that this poem communicates. Spencer's view seems to be that a proper understanding is to realize that Berryman's sequence was written not out of a rage for order but a rage for chaos.

John Ciardi is remembered the year after his death in 1986 in "At Home at Words: An Interview with John Ciardi" (*New Letters* 54, i:47–63), in which Jeff Lovill reminds us that Ciardi was a man of letters of some consequence in the 50s and 60s. Ciardi was often a good critic, and it is to be noted that, though he had his doubts about *Dream Songs*, he still regarded *Homage to Mistress Anne Bradstreet* as "a powerful poem" and regarded James Dickey as "a very powerful writer." Dickey has "written some poems I do not imagine anybody would want to do without." He views both Roethke and Lowell as poets who came back to order by writing poetry. There are 42 short tributes, some new, some reprints in Vince Clemente's *John Ciardi: Measure of a Man* (Arkansas). These may not renew the reputation of the poet; but they do remind one of Ciardi as anthologizer, as teacher, at Bread Loaf, and at *The Saturday Review*. This is agreeable reading for all of us, who in one way or other, had some contact with Ciardi in his role as a widely read spokesman for poetry.

iii. The Poetry of Women: Bishop, Plath, Sexton, Rich, Levertov

No Man's Land has already been discussed as the opening theoretical volume in a revisionist feminist history of American literature. This year again there are a number of studies of contemporary women poets. Margaret Dickie's "The Alien in Contemporary Women's Poetry" (*ConL* 28:301–16) acknowledges the influence on feminist criticism of the claims of cultural anthropologists Shirley and Edwin Ardener that women constitute a "muted" group, whose culture is not contained by the dominant male group. She employs a term from Mikhail Bakhtin, "double-voiced discourse," to describe the conflict that has resulted as this "muted group" finds its cultural voice. To Bakhtin the dominant culture is always under attack by another voice from a popular and subversive culture. Dickie believes this is the circumstance of contemporary women's poetry: the voices are becoming more subversive than "muted," and literary strategies are more focused on attack than on meditation. Dickie then examines how women poets have been drawn to words that represent the "other" as alien. Examples supplied include Sylvia Plath's Dachau, Auschwitz, Belsen, Luftwaffe, Aryan, Panzer-man, swastika, Fascist, Meinkampf in "Daddy"; Holocaust, the Klan, Yankee Puritans, Quebec Catholics, Six-Day War, Ashkenazi, Zionism in Adrienne Rich's *Sources 5*, a work clearly more political than Plath's. She finds that younger women poets, instructed by Rich's politicizing of language and Plath's toying with historical terrors, have mined events of modern history to help express their "deepest sense of violation."

A major critic, Helen Vendler, writes on an important poet, Elizabeth Bishop, in "The Poems of Elizabeth Bishop" (*CritI* 13:825–38). She finds in three prose poems Bishop wrote in her fifties monologues attributed to a giant toad, a strayed crab, and a giant snail, significant reflections on her self and on her art. These creatures represent, respectively, the poet's sense of deformity, her "cold capacity for detachment," her sense of "foreignness in human society," and her repugnance toward anything, political, social, religious. Vendler chooses these animal parables to make the point that Bishop's objectivity has been praised by many critics, but her self-criticism has been overlooked. Vendler repeats much that has already been said: Bishop had relatively few subjects; her best poems are about the two places where she felt "best rooted," both "fully at home" and "fully estranged from"—Brazil and Nova Scotia; but "Bishop could taste for herself, each time she found another environment, her own chilling difference from it." "Into no territory could she subside gratefully and grip down into native soil." She resisted being classified with any group, even with women poets, happier to be in the company of her favorite English poets, Herbert or Keats. Still, Vendler concludes, Elizabeth

Bishop belongs to her own century, and she aspired to write a poetry neither dependent on religious or nationalistic feeling nor drawing on mythological resources. Her partiality for mapping and abstraction led her to landscape poetry about sky and ocean and away from historical, social, religious poetry. Vendler identifies a distinctive "Bishop style"—including an avoidance of closure (except for closure of questioning), a clarity of expression, a simplicity of effect and a naiveté of tone. Now that the epitaphs have been written, Vendler takes an objective view of Bishop's poetry and comes away with renewed respect for her distinctive style.

Priscilla M. Paton ("The Strangeness of This Undertaking: The Art of Elizabeth Bishop" AQ 43:5–18) also finds something startling about Elizabeth Bishop's present high standing with critics. After all, she is reticent and avoids "truth-revealing" confrontations, providing few clues inside and outside her poetry. Her range of both subjects and emotions seems limited, and her advocates often strain to unearth a great deal of feeling in her cool landscapes and conversational narratives. Paton detects a subtle art and an enigmatic clarity in her apparent narrative directness. If her poems are considered over the course of her career, a concern with such post-Romantic issues as "alienation and finding a home, loss and discovery, imagination and identity, love and separation" becomes apparent. Travel is essential: "through real and metaphoric journeys, the traveler-poet seeks the distinctions, meanings, limits and affections that form her self and bind her to the world." Bishop explores correspondences between physical terrain and the human life that dwells there. She plays with boundaries between what is external and what the mind perceives. Like Wallace Stevens she believes the mind can invent scenes, but she never strays too far from objective details. She takes pleasure in the physical world, but her emotional air is most often one "of muted sadness." Finally, Paton reminds us that Elizabeth Bishop earned the great respect of other writers, Lowell, Jarrell, Paz, Merrill for making ordinary seeing become poetic vision. This is one of the best cases made since her death for Bishop's importance.

James E. B. Breslin's "Elizabeth Bishop's *Geography III*" (*AmerP* 4, iii:34–39) concedes Bishop's remoteness, but considers *Geography III* as the book in which she "sternly confronts terrifying forces" that most powerfully subvert our attempts to order and to humanize experience. As she tries to latch on to details to "locate" herself, *Geography III* becomes a sustained meditation on the necessity of "identifying, and mapping the world." Maps are of value in identity crises because they offer stable knowledge from a vantage point outside time. This is obviously the time for reevaluations of Elizabeth Bishop, and the caliber this year is high.

Natalie Harris in "New Life in American Poetry: "The Child as Mother of the Poet," (*CR* 31:240–54) includes Sylvia Plath along with Ellen Bryant Voigt, Lisel Mueller, Judith Mintz, and Sharon Olds as poets who have written poems in which "the child is seen as a potentially integrative and redemptive force in life." In some of their poems the poet-mother embraces this force; in others, she rejects it. Harris examines three poems by Plath which reveal conflicting attitudes toward children. In "Nick and the Candlestick" a mother nursing a child finds in him a beauty that redeems her share of the world's ill. The poem suggests the "relatedness of all living and growing things on earth" and evokes "a redemptive image of the Christ child." In "Tulips" Plath dramatizes a mother's fear of the "wholeness, change, and participation in life" she associates with the image of the tulips and with her child. This same fear of life, evoked by the child, appears in one of her last poems, "Edge." Here, death is chosen over life as represented by the death of the children and of the mother. In all three poems the child represents change and participation in life. What is different in the last poem is that the attitude of the mother changes from positive to a negative image with Jungian overtones.

William Freedman ("Sylvia Plath's 'Mirror' of Mirrors" *PLL* 23: 56–69) starts with something which seems unpromising, the prominence of mirror imagery in Sylvia Plath's poetry, and does something fairly significant with it by importing psychoanalytic theory on the presence of mirrors into convincing readings of a number of poems. I was particularly impressed by his comments on the "generative, distortive, often menacing" function of the mirror imagery. His conclusion is that Plath finds mirrors demarcate our world but are radically less stable and reliable than we had imagined.

James E. Young's "I May Be a Bit of a Jew: The Holocaust Confessions of Sylvia Plath" (*PQ* 66:127–47) seems to promise much but delivers much less: Plath is not a Holocaust poet because she doesn't actually write about the Holocaust but instead "about herself figured as a Holocaust Jew, among other contemporary images of suffering." She was stirred by stories of persecution and of the Holocaust, in particular following the Eichmann trial. What she does in the poems in

Ariel with Holocaust and Nazi imagery is to freight her own personal torment with historical significance.

Linda Wagner-Martin's *Sylvia Plath: A Biography* (Simon and Schuster) is advertised as having the advantage of being the first book to draw on unpublished journals and on letters only recently made available, but it has the disadvantage that quotations at length from her poetry were not permitted. It was consequently impossible to do a literary biography, and what was written instead is a study of Plath's life through her roles as woman, wife, poet in the context of the mores of the 50s and early 60s. Revealed is a creative but adolescent female, trying to be both the ideal woman of that time and a creative poet. It all disintegrated under the combined pressures of financial worries, infant care, and her husband's infidelities. This biography is never sensational in its psychological revelations about Plath's relationship to her father, to her mother, to Ted Hughes. As literary biography it is more enlightening on *The Bell Jar* than on the poetry. If the design was to present a feminist view of what happened to a woman trying to be creative and to conform to roles expected of her, Wagner-Martin constructs a convincing case. The book includes a brief bibliography, useful as a guide to her correspondence, but otherwise supplanted by *Sylvia Plath: An Annotated Bibliography*, ed. Stephen Tabor (Meckler), and less useful than Steven Axelrod's "Plath's Literary Relations: An Essay and an Index to the Journals and Letters Home" (*RALS* 14[1984]:59–84).

Two other items merit mention. Hather Cam ("'Daddy': Sylvia Plath's Debt to Anne Sexton," *AL* 59:429–32) contends that in "Daddy" Plath is indebted to Sexton's "My Friend, My Friend," a poem she may have seen in one of Robert Lowell's workshops or in the discussions that followed in the Ritz bar. The main value of this comparison is to establish that Plath's is the better poem because she creates a situation where release from a parent requires ritualistic expiation.

Of less value is Ellin Sarot's "Becoming More and More Historical: Sylvia Plath's 'The Swarm'" (*CP* 20:41–56), which begins with Plath's answer when asked by an interviewer in October 1962 whether she had a keen sense of history: she was not a historian but found herself more and more fascinated by history. In poems like "Lady Lazarus" and "Daddy" evidence in her references to history suggests that she was working toward "public patterns to accommodate personal dread."

Finally, I call attention to "Sylvia Plath's Black Car of Lethe" in Blasing's *American Poetry*, pp. 50–63. The intention is to show how Plath's expressionist conception of language "traps her in a divided world, reducing the subject to the language of its expression, and the outside world to characters and props on the stage of the subject's expressionist drama." Blasing usefully diverts attention from the subject matter to the drama of the poem. In 1987 the interest in Sylvia Plath continues unabated.

Anne Sexton is a poet whose life needs sympathetic treatment and whose poetic reputation needs repairs. Diana Hume George in (*Oedipus Anne: The Poetry of Anne Sexton* (Illinois) tries to do something about this through a "psychic biography of gender." She sees Sexton in the tradition of Oedipus, a searcher for the truth: a female hero who sought self-knowledge and who suffered a tragic fate, becoming a victim of a society dominated by father figures. She assigned for herself as a poet an exploration of the family, of the myths and archetypes on the relationships of child and parent, woman and man, Christ and man/woman. Freudian studies are not in vogue, but George has the expertise and an appropriate subject for a convincing study. There is just a bit too much theory and too little attention to poems.

Though this was not the full year last year was for critical comment on Denise Levertov and Adrienne Rich, I cannot leave commentary on women poets without a status report on their reputations, as seen by Perkins in *A History of Modern Poetry*. Rich is clearly the more important poet in Perkins's judgment. She is assigned her own brief section (pp. 597–99), and her importance comes from abandoning her early formalism and creating a new "Richean emotional dialectic," portraying women "in order to rouse feminist consciousness in women readers." Levertov changed her poetry also, to one of political consciousness in the 1960s and to notebook genre personal poetry in the 1970s. But for Perkins's taste she has "the dubious merit of being a completely representative poet" (pp. 507–09). There should be more to report next year.

iv. The Older Generation: Warren, Rexroth, Oppen

James H. Justus ("Robert Penn Warren," in *Fifty Southern Writers after 1900*), esteems *Brother to Dragons* as one of Warren's greatest works and regards *Promises: Poems, 1954–1956* as being to Warren's lyric impulse what *Brother to Dragons* is to his dramatic impulse. The next volume, *You, Emperors, and Others,* confirms poetry as his "most congenial genre" and distinguishes the looser lines and the open forms as "his chosen poetic style." These volumes and those that followed in the 1960s, *Selected Poems, Incarnations,* and *Audubon: A Vision,* earned Warren the right to be "frequently spoken of as America's greatest living poet." Justus also reviews the paradox in recent Warren criticism: in the 1960s as admiration for his poetry grew, the critical reception of his fiction became more hostile. He makes a case that in the poems of the 60s Warren found his true style and at last became a major figure in American poetry.

Michael Heller's "A Mimetics of Humanity: Oppen's *Of Being Numerous*" (*AmerP* 4, iii:19–33) offers the most detailed analysis yet of George Oppen's *Of Being Numerous,* viewing it as an attempt "to establish the reality of something by recourse to imagistic procedures," but also "departing radically from the Imagism of Pound and from Eliot's 'objective correlative.'" In Oppen's poems the images are not intended to represent the poet's state of mind but to "validate a particular meaning or concept"; the image is not expressive but investigative. Heller concludes that it is this curiosity of the human mind to be drawn to other things that is "the source of our choice of being numerous" and which can earn humanity a definition.

v. Contemporaries

a. **Ginsberg, Ferlinghetti, Corso, Snyder, Everson.**   There is even a good word for an unfashionable book about which there were never many good words, Allen Ginsberg's *Mind Breaths.* Jay Doughtery in "From Society to Self: Ginsberg's Inward Turn in *Mind Breaths*" (*Sagetrieb* 6, i:81–94) points out that this book contains most of Ginsberg's poetry of the 70s and, with 36 poems, is his third largest collection. He believes that there are poems in *Mind Breaths* which signal an important thematic shift from the themes of the earlier poetry, which most critics have failed to see. He admits that there are negative judgments to be made, especially on Ginsberg's sacrifice of many qualities of his earlier poetry for the rhyming-couplet conventions of songs, for his dogmatic statements, and for personal details that appear irrelevant or even detrimental to the overall effect. Doughtery is actually better at analyzing reasons for Ginsberg's failures than at asserting the importance of this volume of poetry. He singles out the title poem, "Mind Breaths," to make his point: there is an inner calmness which allows the individual to take in the outer world without becoming emotionally disturbed, marking perhaps a significant change from the anger of *Howl* and *Kaddish.*

Ginsberg is interviewed by Robert Stewart and Rebekah Presson in "Sacred Speech: A Conversation with Allen Ginsberg" (*New Letters* 54, i:73–96). He agrees that there may be a renewed interest in Beat poetry on "a superficial level," because the political duplicity evidenced in Washington leads to a respect for a "poetics founded on straight heart and straightforward speaking in idiom and vernacular," something different from the "manipulating with craft speech writers have." Also, the poems of the movement have been kept alive in textbooks. He recalls personal problems he had with censorship and identifies the influence of Buddhist monk Chogyam Trungpa as augmenting Kerouac's injunction to write spontaneously. What is of interest here in much of his talk is on his early poetry.

Michael Skau in "The Poet as Poem: Ferlinghetti's Songs of Myself" (*CP* 20:57–76) regards the movement away from the universal "I" to the personal in Ferlinghetti's poetry as intended to reveal the poet to the reader rather than to illuminate his reader. What is new about Skau's approach is his observation that Ferlinghetti often expresses a point of view antithetical to his own, as in the character of "the pretended fool" in "One Thousand Fearful Words for Fidel Castro." Furthermore, Ferlinghetti's subjective poems are most successful when the speaker "is a self-effacing, comfortable presence generating wit and warmth," concentrating more "on the objects of observation rather than on the speaker's act of observing." His better poems are those which illustrate the trivialities of day-to-day existence rather than protest with a "howl."

Catharine F. Seigel in "Corso, Kinnell, and the Bomb" (*UDR* 18, iii:95–103) reports that there are surprisingly few poems in contemporary American literature with direct references to the bomb. Gregory Corso's 1958 poem "The Bomb" was one of the first to confront the nuclear bomb. Though it was dismissed by Hayden Carruth as "rant and shapeless anger," Seigel finds the "onomatopoetic ranting and raging" to be its strength. Another poem Seigel identifies is Galway Kinnell's poem from *Body Rags* (1968), "Vapor Trail Reflected in the Frog Pond." The vapor trail is from a SAC bomber. Kinnell is politically committed to this issue, having organized the 26

May 1982 forum, "Poets Against the End of the World." A second example is "In the Dead Shall Be Raised Incorruptible," where he refers to "the absolute night of radiation and silence." Kinnell's most specifically antinuclear poem is the most recent, "The Fundamental Project of Technology," from *The Past* (1985). For more on Kinnell, see *c* below.

Julia Martin in "The Pattern Which Connects: Metaphor in Gary Snyder's Later Poetry" (*WAL* 22:99–123) examines his use of metaphoric "structures" in three works—*Regarding Wave, Turtle Island,* and *Axe Handles.* She believes that earlier critics have tended to slight Snyder's later poems and to disregard his use of metaphor. To focus on metaphor, she employs Roman Jakobson's definition of metaphoric discourse and utilizes the influence of Zen Buddhism on Snyder, assigning particular importance to metaphors associated with the Goddess, including Vak, "Mother Earth," and Gaia, in Snyder's later works.

Jody Norton in "The Importance of Nothing: Absence and Its Origins in the Poetry of Gary Snyder" (*ConL* 28, i:41–66) examines the influence of the Chinese *shih* and the Japanese *haiku* upon the structure of the early poetry. As evidence of the effects of these influences, she notes the absence of a speaker's "I"; the frequent omission of articles, adjectives, and verbs; the practice of syntactical ellipses; "ellipses in the articulation of imagery"; and disjunctions. She concludes that Snyder's lyrics "depend as much on what they omit as what they include."

David A. Carpenter's *The Rages of Excess: The Life and Poetry of William Everson* (Wynham Hall) praises Everson for the religious poetry he wrote during the San Francisco Renaissance in the 1950s under the name Brother Antoninus. He attempts close readings of poems, and, unfortunately, he makes them seem now in the 1980s drier and more religious than they seemed in the context of the 1950s. He does not further Everson's poetic reputation. Lee Bartlett's *William Everson: The Life of Brother Antoninus* (New Directions, 1988), which will be reviewed next year, is *the* book on this poet.

b. **Olson, Creeley, Wright, Merwin, Stafford, Wagoner, Hugo.** For those interested in more primary materials, *Charles Olson & Robert Creeley: The Complete Correspondence,* vols. 7, 8 (Black Sparrow Press), ably edited by George Butterick, appeared this year. There is another account of Black Mountain and Olson and those he had influence on in Francine DuPlessix Gray's "Charles Olson and an American Place" (*YR* 76:341–52). Gray finds Black Mountain and Olson gripped by a 19th-century Romantic vision of the artist as pristine prophet and a unique and redemptive Americanism.

John Wilson's *Robert Creeley's Life and Work* (Michigan) is another volume of mainly reprints of criticism in the series "Under Discussion," with Donald Hall as the general editor. There is an introduction by Wilson, and, if you look carefully, a few unpublished short essays. Wilson finds criticism of Creeley divided into two camps marked by very divergent views: Hugh Kenner's judgment that Creeley is "one of the very few contemporaries with whom it is necessary to keep current"; John Simon's caustic statement: "There are two things to be said about Creeley's poems: they are short; they are not short enough." Wilson finds Creeley to be a poet who used traditional forms; but his association with the new art movements of the 50s and 60s, especially with Charles Olson and Projective Verse, led to what became an experimental side to his poetry. Creeley's earliest attention came from his linking of the Black Mountain School to the Beat movement, but he was soon directed toward abstractions through the influence of Abstract Expressionism in painting. His poems became "arguably minimal." In his most recent poems he has moved toward lengthening and making them less jagged and fragmentary, even eliminating the sharp irony of the early poems. The chief value of this study is the introduction; but it is useful to have a collection of essays, covering three decades of criticism, from the 50s, 60s, and 70s.

Kevin Stein in "The Rhetoric of Containment: Vulnerability, and Integration in the Work of James Wright" (*CP* 20:117–29) focuses on what he believes has been overlooked, Wright's rhetorical relationship with his reader. Indebted to Jonathan Holden's *Rhetoric of Contemporary Lyric*, Wright concentrates on the creation of a persona that assures the reader that he is in control of the disorder inside and outside himself. Beginning with *The Branch Will Not Break*, the persona becomes immersed in the outer world of experience and, consequently, more vulnerable. But he also begins to see order where he had assumed chaos and to become aware of the possibility of transcendence. He shares his awareness with the reader but still distances himself through not using personal pronouns. By the time of "To a Blossoming Pear Tree" (1977) Wright had shown a new concern for his reader and made a move toward story-telling, toward "the narrative of the prose form."

Robert Blakely in "Form and Meaning in the Poetry of James Wright" (*SDR* 25, ii:20–30) focuses on Wright's change from his early manner, "metric, often rhymed, often elegant" to the "demotic diction and free form" of his later works. The two styles represent, respectively, his training at Kenyon and at the University of Washington, and his natural vernacular style from his blue-collar background in Martin's Ferry, Ohio. They also serve as a reminder that there is more than "a single way to poems," and all ways were difficult.

Sanford Pinsker has produced a variation on TUSAS volumes, a three-in-one introduction, *Three Pacific Northwest Poets: William Stafford, Richard Hugo, and David Wagoner* (Twayne). He begins with a consideration of a fourth poet as the common influence on all three, Theodore Roethke. Pinsker admits that his three subjects vary widely in their thematic and technical interests but contends that they had a common home and relationship to "the general development of contemporary American poetry." The usual biographical sketches are provided, chief volumes glimpsed, and theme and characteristic techniques briefly assessed. Pinsker makes the strongest case for the importance of Stafford; but all three are shortchanged to some extent, especially since Pinsker quotes rather copiously.

c. Kinnell, Dickey, Merwin. At long last there is a good year for Galway Kinnell, with an engaging article and two books. The article is Susan B. Weston's "To Take Hold of the Song: The Poetics of Galway Kinnell" (*LitR* 31, i:73–84). Weston begins with a quote that helped ward off the effects of hearing a structuralist, a phenomenologist, a feminist, and a deconstructivist exchange ideas about poetry with no particular text before them. The passage from Kinnell's "Under Maud Moon" is a description of an infant who "puts/her hand/into her father's mouth, to take hold of/his song." She thought of this passage because of a feeling that we no longer take childlike pleasure in the text since the "song" is now regarded as an intellectual formulation. To Weston, Galway Kinnell is a poet in the post-Romantic tradition, "obsessed with death and metamorphosis," to whom knowledge comes through the senses, and thereby different from those poets who absorb intellectually and only by abstraction. He would have "little patience with the linguistic notion that every word is an abstraction removed from the thing it represents." She observes that he has also become a more positive poet: the birth of his two children changed the sense of isolation and "vacancy" in the nightmare vision of his earlier poems. His confrontation with death is different from the "gorgeous solipsism" Harold Bloom finds in most American poets, with an emphasis now on life and death, not just on death. By the end of *The Book of Nightmares* Kinnell has come to see poetry, like the music of a Bach concert, as the resolution of "individually felt pain." This is a well-constructed essay which uses Kinnell's poetry as an antidote for what she feels poisons much contemporary poetry.

Howard Nelson has brought together a collection of reviews and articles on Galway Kinnell: *On the Poetry of Galway Kinnell: The Wages of Dying* (Michigan). It is valuable as a first collection, and it reprints an important essay: "The Rank Flavor of Blood: The Poetry of Galway Kinnell," by Charles Molesworth (pp. 45–64), as well as reviews by James Dickey, Louise Bogan, M. L. Rosenthal, and Christopher Ricks. Nelson's introduction is new; and, if the reader looks closely, he will find a few short pieces published here for the first time. In his introduction," The Weight of Words, the Road between Here and There" (pp. 1–18), Nelson comments on the "distinctive weight in his words," in the imagery, in the concrete nouns, in the adjectives, in the "pungent verbs," contributing "to the poem's sensual life" and to a less formal beauty that makes it possible to "discover the glory of the ordinary." There is in Kinnell's poetry an "aural, almost tactile attentiveness to language," intended to bring "the poem down to a level of essential saying—as if he had found the true specific gravity of the subject . . . the elemental behind the particular." Kinnell belongs to a distinguished tradition in modern poetry, what to make of a diminished thing. His version leaves open the possibility of an ongoing meditation on time and mortality. For textbook examples of what can be done with the complexity of a Kinnell poem, I would recommend two short, previously unpublished pieces, Paul Mariani's "Kinnell's Legacy on 'The Avenue Bearing the Initial of Christ into the New World' " (pp. 191–202) and Joseph Bruchac's "I Have Come to Myself Empty: Galway Kinnell's 'Bear and Porcupine' " (pp. 203–09).

Even more welcome is Lee Zimmerman's *Intricate and Simple Things: The Poetry of Galway Kinnell* (Illinois), the first book-length study of this difficult and important poet, who, like a poet he has been compared to, James Dickey, can be categorized too rigidly and simply. Zimmerman begins with a statement from Kinnell on the moment when poetry begins: "When in the presence of the wind, or the night sky, or the sea . . . we are reminded both of the kinship and separation between ourselves and what is beyond us." He then proceeds to identify two different feelings about this reminder, a "feeling of strangeness and then of terrible kinship." Zimmerman attempts to show how Kinnell's "poetic enterprise derives from these two feelings." In his poetry this is represented as an "unreconciled conflict between pairs—separation and kinship, multeity and unity, particular flesh and communal spirit." In the greatest moments of Kinnell's poetry these opposites are "incorporated in a surpassing whole." Galway Kinnell belongs to a "Romantic" tradition that tries to find "the self in the world, the world in the self." As a 20th-century poet he has an overt connection to Williams, to that poet's immediacy and passion and glorification of the local"; but covertly he has a relationship to Eliot, a striving of the consciousness for the sacred, for Kinnell, Immanence, not Eliot's Incarnation. Zimmerman does well with the most obvious influence, the link to Whitman in subject, death, and in form, a poetry not contained in regular forms. The significant difference is that for Whitman there is optimism, for "there is really no death," and for Kinnell there are nightmares. Interesting, but less convincing, are the parallels drawn with Emily Dickinson. The greatest value of this important study comes from the close readings of Kinnell's major poetry. It is time we had a book on Kinnell, and this one begins very well.

James Dickey's poetry is still regarded as live and well in the *James Dickey Newsletter*. Gordon Van Ness in " 'When memory stands without sleep': James Dickey's War Years" (4, i:2–13) begins with a strong statement by Dickey in *Self-Interviews* that Eliot's theory of autotelic art is "absolute rubbish" and then goes on to comment on what Dickey's war years came to mean to him after he began to form a mythological interpretation of things from reading the Cambridge anthropologists (Francis Cornford, Jane Harrison, Bronislaw Malinowski, Franz Boas, and others) as a student at Vanderbilt. He came to see his years in the army air force as a personal rite de passage. To contrast his later view with the early, Van Ness turns to Dickey's accounts in his war letters. The point is well made that Dickey also came to believe that World War II "had exposed the split between modern man and his technological world." His interest in anthropology revealed that primitive man had lived in a world in which "he felt himself an integral part." As a poet Dickey had to reexplore the war and try to recapture the view of primitive man.

The best item on Dickey, "James Dickey as a Southern Visionary" (*VQR* 63:110–23), is by his favorite teacher at Vanderbilt and his patron at *The Sewanee Review*, Monroe K. Spears. Spears finds Dickey to be no regional chauvinist or Vanderbilt Agrarian, but a southerner who shares with Warren and other writers a deep concern with man's relationship to nature. His geography is often different from his mentors', a suburban world, but not far from a nature that remains wild. To Spears, Dickey is a visionary poet (Poe is his only southern predecessor) with a religious sense of "how wild, inexplicable, marvelous, and endless creation is." His poems are often sermons, prayers, invocations. Visionary poets do not age well, but the vision remains, changing in *Puella* from the cosmic vision he had reached in *The Zodiac* to the domestic. What is important about this essay is that Spears sees Dickey in the tradition of visionary poets, and as a "Southern visionary."

My account of Dickey in *Fifty Southern Writers after 1900* (pp. 136–46) finds most of his best poetry to have been written from 1957–67, chiefly affirmative poems seeking transcendence of the ordinary self and the literal, and occasionally achieving a vision. As a craftsman, Dickey carefully maintains formal control over each poem. In his poetry he imagines an escape from the ordinary by using devices such as empathetic exchange of identity, establishing a narrative setting, often with a touch of "country surrealism." At his best there is a distinctive voice, persona, and Dickey style. His transcendence is only a temporary escape but with the potential of giving life renewed meaning. I regard Dickey as an important postmodernist as a poet, reviewer, and critic, certainly not as a writer who can be readily dismissed too simply as an advocate of something called "the more life school." I admit that when Dickey moved on to a loose associational structure, he, too often, substituted rhetoric for the lyric and dramatic quality of his best poems.

I have found Harold Bloom's edited books on contemporary poets hard to come by. I was glad to see the one on James Dickey (Chelsea House), since Dickey provides a congenial subject for Bloom. The essays included are reprinted, but Bloom's introduction is mostly new and it represents a statement by an important and expansive critic on an important and neglected expansive poetic imagination. To Bloom, Dickey is "a throwback to those mythic hypotheses out of which strong poetry broke forth the bands of individuation whose heroic vitalism demanded a literal immortality for themselves as poets." What Bloom limits himself to praising is Dickey's "countersong to otherness." He likes a Yeatsian quality in Dickey's poetry that came to him "through the seduction of Roethke." Dickey's natural religion is "Mithraism." He is not a Christian poet but more of an Emersonian, an American Orphic and Gnostic. Bloom extols the Dickey of "The Other" and "The May Day Sermon" and ignores any other Dickey. He does little for the poetry Dickey has written since the 1970s, but he touches a major chord for the Dickey of the poems which meet the Bloomsian prescription.

Another first is a collection of essays on W. S. Merwin: *W. S. Merwin: Essays on the Poetry*, ed. Cary Nelson and Ed Folsom (Illinois), with an informative introductory essay by the editors, the usual reprints, and a few new essays. In their introduction Nelson and Folsom begin with comparisons between Merwin and Pound, both students of the Romance languages, interested in importing from these languages into English poetry, who became more (Pound) or less (Merwin) expatriates. Merwin is also compared with William Carlos Williams, with whom he has not often been compared, and with Wallace Stevens, with whom he has been often compared. The essay concludes by focusing on Merwin's changes in his poetic language from formal to the fragmented and, finally, to the conversational. William H. Rueckert contributes notes on "Rereading: *The Lice: A Journal*" (pp. 45–64) that are useful to any one who wants to reread this work. In other new essays Edward Brunner, "The Variable Caesura and the Family Poems" (pp. 276–95), concentrates on Merwin's use of the caesura, especially in the family poems. Ed Folsom, " 'I Have Been a Long Time in a Strange Country': W. S. Merwin and America" (pp. 224–49), discusses his change in style, beginning with *The Compass Flower*, as part of his pattern of return to America. Thomas B. Byers, "The Present Voices: W. S. Merwin since 1970" (pp. 250–73), begins with the poetry in the 6os that made Merwin a major postmodernist poet and discusses the need for him to change again in the 1970s by forming a dialectical relation to his great transcendental precursors, Emerson and Whitman.

The *Paris Review* interviews finally reached Merwin with Edward Hirsch's "W. S. Merwin, The Art of Poetry: XXXVII" (101:57–81). The interview reveals strong environmental concerns, originating with a childhood fascination with Indians and with nightmares that the whole world had become cities. The influences of John Berryman, and especially critic and teacher R. P. Blackmur, are discussed. Pound is identified as a means to medieval poetry and as a revelation of the importance of the ear in poetry. In his visits to Pound, Merwin was advised to take translating seriously. He notes that his own political activities began against the chemical warfare base at Fort Dietrich and continued with the antinuclear movement. With *The Moving Target* he came to distrust language, to believe that experience is something that we cannot articulate. There are still no interviews as comprehensive as those in the *Paris Review*.

d. **Ashbery, Ammons, Merrill.** Explicators can make John Ashbery's poetry seem significant but never uncomplicated, and I would be suspicious if anyone did. Mary Kinzie in a two-part article, "The Poetic Diction of John Ashbery" (*MP* 84:267-82, 382-400), passes my test perfectly; what she says is worth saying, but it is not easy to summarize. Part I is subtitled "Styles of Avoidance" and uses Ashbery's poem "Houseboat Days" as exemplary of a new kind of contemporary poem that takes its grammar more seriously than it does the organization of experience grammar traditionally serves. Ashbery fills his poems with concrete details, but deceptively so. They are used so as to be referable, not to experience, but to literary attitudes on such categories of concern as "travel, pain, longing, social tension, parting." Things in Ashbery's poetic world are objects of thought, not connected by "the rank, sequence, and domain in which they might ordinarily occur in nature but by the easy likelihood for their occurrence to Ashbery." For a sensibility analogous to Ashbery's Kinzie turns, not unreasonably, to Henry James. Part II focuses on the "stylistic contours of his resistance to the devices of literary meaning allied with realism, plot, and verisimilitude." She explains how Ashbery avoids prosodic media "that combine measure, interval, and euphony to reinforce semantic and rhetorical emphases" and abstains from number and formal alternation of stressed and unstressed syllables as part of his "styles of avoidance." He achieves the impression that "while moving towards the prosaic in his manners, he is moving towards prose in his rhythms."

Edward Haworth Hoeppner's "Visual Gestalt and John Ashbery's 'Europe'" (*CP* 20:87-97) turns to a book, *The Tennis Court Oath*, which has received little critical attention ever since "Harold Bloom dismissed it as 'a fearful disaster.'" Hoeppner seeks to redeem some of the poems from this judgment by using the poem "Europe" to suggest affinities with "the practice of erasure" in purely visual art. The artistic question is "how much could be erased and still have the sense of the original left?" For an analogy he turns to Merleau-Ponty's description of the disruption of the normal perceptual gestalt that a sick person might experience when contemplating wallpaper in his room if the figure becomes ground and what is ordinarily ground becomes the figure. This is the brand of dislocation evidenced in Jastrow's rabbit illustration and in poems in this volume, as evidenced by "Europe." He then attempts to prove the value of this not fully appreciated book by a detailed analysis of the poem showing that the poem has in the principle of erasure a "noteworthy modus operandi."

Patricia Altenbernd Johnson's "The Speculative Character of Poetry" (*CEA* 49, ii–iv:18–23) raises the question: How is poetry philosophical? She determines that when we use "philosophical" to characterize poetry we are recognizing its speculative nature. Her prime example of the speculative nature of poetry turns out to be Ashbery's much-examined poem, "Self-Portrait in Convex Mirror." The speculations are on "mirroring as the human movement of constant seeking and constant inability to find." Ashbery's poems pose a series of challenges to the human tendency to be narcissistic or solipsistic in this seeking, focusing on the self reflected in the mirror and placing everything else in the background. Ashbery shows how daily and familiar things intrude into this world and stresses the constant need for successive views. His poem illustrates the characteristics of how poetry is philosophical by being speculative through calling distinctions into question, through describing the process of "undermining the movement of its subject matter," and through stimulating the speculative nature of his readers. Ashbery's poem passes all three tests.

John Gery's "En route to Annihilation: John Ashbery's 'Shadow Train'" (*CP* 20, 99–116) describes the combination of frustration and enthusiasm that comes from reading a poet whose poems seem to have no real subject other than themselves. He discusses representative views of Ashbery: those who see endless linguistic operation with no creation; those who see a poetry of brilliant surfaces and verbal gestures with more stylistic fun than purposive meaning or coherent whole; those who regard him as a marvelous minor poet, but an "uncomfortable major one," because one can never remember ideas from an Ashbery poem; those who see in his work a new affirmation of freedom for the poet, by undermining each type of meaning found by C. K. Ogden and I. A. Richards in *The Meaning of Meaning*, an influential work on the New Critics' generation. Gery questions why a poet's "tolerance for negativity" and "dogged talent" for being both "engaging and perplexing" should gain him such attention and regard. He attempts to answer by examining "Shadow Train" as a significant attempt to waken us from the psychic numbness of business as usual with "the idea of meaninglessness, of absence, of futurelessness, of approaching annihilation . . . coupled with a notion of renewal." He sees in Ashbery's image of the shadow the familiar images of nuclear war and examines his treatment of time in relation to his strong expression of futurelessness. All there is in time is "the time it takes for nothing to happen."

David Perkins (*History of Modern Poetry*, pp. 614–32) regards Ashbery, along with Ammons, as "our most important contemporary poets in the meditative mode," which signifies that they do not "render actions or characters" or write overtly about their own experiences. Their poems are trains of thought, "interior ruminations addressed to no audience." The characteristic train of Ashbery's thought is an enactment of the mind's always baffled pursuit of reality. In *The Double Dream of Spring* (1970) Ashbery "first mastered the apparently discursive yet still disorienting style that has generally characterized his work since." Perkins is especially concerned with what it is that motivates the reader into second and later readings of poems that on their first reading seem hopelessly obscure. He believes that with these additional readings "the texts gradually clarify themselves" and that there is pleasure in the surprises that come from following where Ashbery's mind leads us." Perkins compares Ashbery to Wallace Stevens, arguing that he has "certain ideas" and "a recognizable tone of feeling," though he recognizes that he could have argued just the opposite: "that no ideas or feelings can be attributed to him at all." The ideas come from Ashbery's attempt to resolve a dilemma in modernism from the start: "If reality is either incoherent or entirely unknowable, any form—so far as it is form—must be inauthentic." He is a "postnihilist, post-Existentialist writer whose position can be described only in paradoxes." Perkins goes on to discuss form in Ashbery, focusing on parody, irony, paradox, all used so that his texts can deny what they predicate. What he values in Ashbery's style, far above that of other discontinuous poets, is that "he leads one to expect continuous sense." Perkins concludes by demonstrating through analysis of a few passages how Ashbery should be read. He seems to believe that Ashbery needs only a study of his poetry that would be the equivalent of what *Modern Poetry and the Tradition* was for the great modernists.

On A. R. Ammons I need to mention a 1986 item, a special issue on Ammons in *Pembroke Magazine* (18), with an "Interview with A. R. Ammons" (pp. 77–85) by Jim Stahl, and "An Interview with A. R. Ammons" by Shelby Stephenson (pp. 196–202), and more than a dozen short articles. I would recommend Gerald H. Bullis's "In the Open: A. R. Ammons' Longer Poems" (pp. 28–53).

It is also good to acknowledge a significant essay on a contemporary poet in *American Literature* (58:513–28), Stephen B. Cushman's "Stanzas, Organic Myth, and the Metaformalism of A. R. Ammons." Cushman is interested in Ammons's continuing meditation on poetic form. He soon renounced the "completed, external form" of his early poetry and became a self-proclaimed "free-versite," who, nevertheless, writes an occasional iambic string and who remakes form in order to break it again. Cushman insists that Ammons can neither be considered a formalist in the usual sense nor dismissed as an anti-formalist, since his need for some form is too acute. Through poetic form Ammons's struggles for reattachment, first "to the large capabilities of the human mind," second to the natural world "which preceded and remains separate from him," and third, "to whatever else, beyond these is available."

William Harmon (*Fifty Southern Writers after 1900*, pp. 21–32) contributes an interesting, but somewhat quirky, survey of Ammons's life and career as well as a review of criticism on his work. He reviews Ammons's three modes: "the short poem, the sustained sequence, . . . a middle-length poem of perception." In a literary milieu of modernist irony Ammons began writing poems with a theme of "continuity and harmony," and he progressed from delivering that theme in an "answerable style" into serious wordplay on the "capacity of language for ranges of meaning." To Harmon, Ammons is a refreshing reminder that "America has a poet who is still capable of genuine novelty, originality, and purity of vision."

Stephen Yenser's *The Consuming Myth: The Work of James Merrill* (Harvard) is the most comprehensive study of this poet yet. It covers everything Merrill has written from the privately printed *Jim's Book*, at the age of 15, to his verse play *The Image Maker*, first produced in Los Angeles in 1986. Yenser sees *Water Street* as the water-

shed volume, where Merrill first views a poem not as object but as
process. He confirms Merrill's relationships with the great modernists,
Yeats and Stevens, and with their predecessors, Mallarmé and Proust,
firmly connecting him to modernism. His thesis on Merrill's dualisms
would apply to most poets, but he makes it work convincingly with
Merrill's poems: whatever Merrill sees yields also to its contrarieties.
He explores these oppositions meaningfully in the poems, in the puns,
paradoxes, counterpointing; but he also suggests that Merrill sees
identity as well as difference, finding an interconnectedness in things
as well as their contrarieties. Yenser obviously knows his subject, and
he speculates meaningfully on the relationship of the man and the
poet. He clearly believes he is dealing with a major poet. Perhaps
Yenser should expose flaws as well as acclaim strengths. But that is
only a quibble. This is a good study and a handsome book, beautifully illustrated.

Merrill is the major living contemporary poet to David Perkins.
Adrienne Rich shares a chapter with Anne Sexton; John Ashbery
shares a chapter with A. R. Ammons. Merrill not only has a separate
chapter but is granted the climactic chapter (*History of Modern
Poetry*, pp. 638–50). To Perkins, he is "one of the most moving,
imaginative, and ambitious of living poets." He is "a virtuoso in
meters and stanzas, writing sonnet sequences, double sestinas, terza
rima, blank verse, syllabic verse, ballad stanzas, odes, and other patterns." He also writes free verse but "has never accepted open form."
Though he writes "accomplished" impersonal poems, "the ones in his
autobiographical mode appeal more powerfully." Perkins admires
both the shorter poems and the longer poems and believes that in
The Changing Light at Sandover Merrill successfully synthesizes the
modernist academic style of the 40s and 50s and the new conventions
of "Beat, Projectivist, Confessional, and Surrealist poetry." It is for
this reason that Merrill is assigned the final chapter in Perkins's
History.

vi. Final Comments

"Poets on the Line" (*OhR* 38) is an issue devoted to a string of comments by contemporary poets on the poetic line in poetry. Involved
are Louis Simpson, William Stafford, Diane Wakoski, Charles Wright,
David Ignatow, Wayne Dodd, Edward Hirsch, Mary Olive, William
Matthews, Robert Bly. There are many opinions expressed and prac-

tices described. The consensus is that free verse is alive, but so is the conviction that there is a need to balance it off with form. I want also to cite Lee Bartlett's interviews with poets, *Talking Poetry: Conversations in the Workshops with Contemporary Poets* (New Mexico). These are not "mainstream" poets; only Diane Wakoski, William Everson, and Thom Gunn receive mention in Perkins's *History of Modern Poetry*; but the interviews cover a wide variety of styles, with a special interest in language poets. They are actually conversations between working poets and apprentice writers in the creative writing program at New Mexico. Some of what is said is gossip; but a significant amount suggests resistance to an establishment view of contemporary poetry, which, once again, Helen Vendler's *Harvard Anthology* is cited as attempting.

Let me report final regrets: that there are books and articles that will have to wait for review because requests, letters, phone calls did not supply them in time for the deadline. Harold Bloom's books on modern poets, collections of what in his view are the best of previously published essays, with his own enlightening introductions, have been the hardest to obtain. This year only the Dickey arrived. I can only recognize the overview volume, *American Poetry 1946–65*, and the collections of essays on Lowell, Ammons, and Roethke. Nonetheless, there is no shortage of criticism: it continues to grow, by geometric progression, or so it seems.

Clemson University

18. Drama

Walter J. Meserve

In February 1987 a group of people—Jackson Bryer, Joyce Flynn, Bruce McConachie, Walter Meserve, Vera Mowry Roberts, Paul Voelker, and Albert Wertheim—met in Bloomington, Indiana, to formalize the creation of the American Drama Society. Officers were appointed subject to endorsement by a constituency meeting at a later date—president, Paul Voelker; vice-president, Bruce McConachie; secretary-treasurer, Joyce Flynn—and the organization's purpose was defined as promoting the "study of American drama as an aesthetic form of literary, theatrical and cultural communication which embraces the pluralism of the American experience." It was a definite if inauspicious beginning for a growing number of scholars whose associational needs have been met in the past at meetings of the Modern Language Association, the American Studies Association, and the more recent Association for Theatre in Higher Education. Long may it flourish! A future event of importance, following the several conferences in 1988 scattered across the world to celebrate the birth of America's only dramatist to win the Nobel Prize for Literature, will be the appearance in 1989 of the *Journal of American Drama and Theatre (JADT)*. Coedited by Vera Mowry Roberts and Walter J. Meserve and sponsored by the Ph.D. Program in Theatre and the Center for Advanced Study of Theatre Arts at the Graduate School of CUNY, this refereed journal will promote research on American playwrights, American plays, and American theater. Interested in historical assessments, theoretical commentaries, critical evaluations, and performance studies, the editors of *JADT* hope to encourage that thoughtful contemplation that will lead to a more enlightened understanding and appreciation of our literary and theatrical heritage and of America's continuing contribution to world literature and the performing arts.

i. Reference Works, Historical and Critical Studies

The *Reference Guide to American Literature*, 2nd edition, ed. D. L. Kirkpatrick (St. James), contains essays on a dozen plays as it ex-

plores American literature from Henry Adams, who did not write
plays, and George Ade, who wrote 24, to Lewis Zukofsky who tried
his hand only once. Introduced by Lewis Leary and Warren French,
the volume boasts high-quality essays and a well-devised chronology.
A *Literary History of the West* is an extensive undertaking which attempts to consider American drama but does so in a very unsatisfactory manner. James H. Maguire in "Western American Drama to
1960" (pp. 204–20) chose a topic which he was obviously not prepared to discuss. He begins his essay: "During the formative stage of
American drama, which lasted until about 1890, most American plays
consisted of slapstick and sentimentalism. . . ." Having firmly established his limited knowledge and his inadequate understanding,
Maguire provides little more than a quick survey of certain aspects
of pre-World War I drama. His first serious statements relate to
Sidney Howard's *They Knew What They Wanted* and the plays of
Lynn Riggs. Plays by Maxwell Anderson, Robert Sherwood, William
Saroyan, John Steinbeck, and William Inge are simply listed with
slight commentary. Gerald W. Haslam's "William Saroyan" (pp. 472–
80) gives a general appreciation of the author, without showing much
interest in his plays, and clearly credits Saroyan's son with more honest insight into his father's life and work than the younger Saroyan's
recent book warrants. A final essay in this large volume considers
"Contemporary Western Drama" (pp. 1232–44). "Western drama
since 1960 is thriving," writes Mark Busby, who then proceeds to
substantiate the contributions of Preston Jones, Sam Shepard, Mark
Medoff, and Lanford Wilson as well as a number of theater companies and their work with Hispanics, Indians, Chinese-Americans,
and blacks. Looking beyond reference books on American literature
and America's West to the teaching of American culture around the
world, I note that the editors of the October 1987 issue of *American
Studies International* published essays on American Studies Programs
in China, France, India, the Netherlands, Pakistan, and Spain. Of all
of these programs only the one in India showed any interest in American drama. Obviously, some educators still need to be educated.

One of the more interesting approaches to the study of American
drama this year appears in Brenda Murphy's *American Realism and
American Drama, 1880–1940* (Cambridge). Not a history of American drama nor an analysis of plays or theory, this book is a "study of
literary realism as it evolved in American drama." Professor Murphy

wants to know if a literary definition of dramatic realism exists and whether the theoretical ideas of late 19th-century realists influenced the work of American dramatists writing between the two world wars. One must remember the author's stated objectives and allow for her limited understanding of the American theatrical scene in the 1880s (chapter 1). Murphy's presentation of "Realistic Dramatic Theory," however, is particularly revealing as she analyzes works in terms of stagecraft, acting, dialogue, thought, character, and structure, and proceeds to outline the general realistic notions that will dominate 40 years later. For the plays of Mark Twain, William Dean Howells, Bret Harte, Henry James, Hamlin Garland, and James Herne her commentary is no more than adequate for her purposes. Her treatment of the 1890–1915 period is even more limited, but Murphy makes her point and proceeds quickly to the major substantiation of her thesis in the plays of Eugene O'Neill and the realists of the 1916–1940 era. Essentially, Professor Murphy's conclusions are not surprising, but her straightforward and carefully argued theory, though limited in depth and scope, provides an approach to scholarship in American drama that may develop into a contribution of substance.

Arguing against the treatment of "American drama as the ugly stepchild of American literature," Thomas P. Adler provides a critical reading and interpretation of the plays that won the Pultzer Prize. His book is entitled *Mirror on the Stage: The Pulitzer Plays As An Approach to American Drama* (Purdue). His division of the 57 plays from 1917 to 1985 into ten categories determined by the thesis idea of each play allows Adler to show audiences an image of themselves which he describes in term of personal issues, social topics, and cosmic concerns. Chapters have such titles as "Nora's American Cousins" and "The Ethic of Happiness." Although no striking conclusions are made—or could be expected—Adler's commentary and his organizational concept, as artificial as it appears, suggest a good deal about the interests of audiences and playwrights during a major part of the 20th century. *Dramatic Encounters: The Jewish Presence in Twentieth Century American Drama, Poetry, and Humor and the Black-Jewish Literary Relationship* (Greenwood) is Louis Harap's third volume on "Jewish Presence." The pertinent section is entitled "The Jew in Drama" (pp. 71–141), but Harap is not a student of American drama. His *Dramatic Encounters*, filled with simplistic statements and well-known information, treats the usual Jewish playwrights, provides an interesting approach to the work of John Howard Lawson, is grossly unfair to Paddy Chayevsky, whom Harap considers too commercial, and is generally limited in its value to scholars. M. Elizabeth Osborn suggests a broader view of American drama with a collection entitled *On New Ground: Contemporary Hispanic-American Plays* (TCG). Determined to "rectify our culture's neglect of this great body of work," she includes plays by Lynne Alvarez, Maria Irene Fornes, John Jesurun, Eduardo Machado, Jose Rivera, and Milcha Sanchez-Scott—each play prefaced by a stage history, biographical information, a photograph, and a comment by the dramatist.

Four new reference books should be noted and at least the first two added to the serious scholar's bookshelves. *Directory of Historic American Theatres* (Greenwood), ed. John W. Frick and Carlton Ward with a foreword by Brooks McNamara, lists about 900 theaters from 49 states (excluding Alaska) and the District of Columbia. And these are theaters which still exist; you can check them out—15 from the state of Maine, for example. With the distinguishing vital data for each theater and 80 illustrations, this is a work of interest to theater historians. Weldon B. Durham's second of three volumes, *American Theatre Companies, 1988–1930* (Greenwood), aspiring to present the "salient facts about resident acting companies in America," includes information on 35 art theater groups along with 70 stock companies. The basic organization—narrative essay, company personnel, repertory, and bibliography—remains the same as volume 1, as does the uneven quality of the entries. Many of the essays in this second volume are provided by the editor; a good number are written in a journeyman fashion—such as those on the Washington Square Players and the Yiddish Art Theater—and remain undistinguished. Others are excellent; some outstanding entries were created by Mari Kathleen Fielder. Particularly rewarding are the efforts of recent dissertation writers in such entries as the Salem Theatre Company and the Salt Lake Theatre Stock Company, and the general value of the volume should not be questioned. Always worthy of a note, volume 4 of *Contemporary Theatre, Film and Television,* ed. Monica M. O'Donnell (Gale), adds nearly 700 names to bring to 3,200 its limited but basic information on performers, directors, writers, producers, designers, managers, choreographers, composers, executives, dancers, and critics from the United States and Britain. James M. Salem's fourth edition of *Drury's Guide to Best Plays* (Scarecrow) updates its information to the 1984–85 season and now includes some 1,500 entries.

Introducing a collection of his "Dramatic Opinions" written between 1980 and 1986, Robert Brustein asks *Who Needs Theatre* (Atlantic Monthly). In spite of negative references to costs, personal hassle, and even physical danger, however, Brustein is still impressed with the immediacy of theater as a "communal act" that represents social history. Supporting his beliefs in an address delivered before the National Educational Theatre Conference, August 1986, Richard Moody—"The American Theatre, 1936–1961" (*ThS* 7:84–98)—charmingly reminisces to imagine what we would have missed had the American theater closed in 1936. Another believer, Oscar G. Brockett in his companion address, "The American Theatre, 1961–1986" (*ThS* 7:99–116), emphasizes the organizational and artistic types of development and change, the agencies interested in supporting theater, and the groups willing to assist playwrights—all part of the challenge of modernism that the theater must meet!

Three books treat various aspects of 19th-century American drama and theater. David L. Rinear's *The Temple of Momus: Mitchell's Olympic Theatre* (Scarecrow) underscores an important chapter in the history of American theater, for Mitchell's Olympic was the only New York theater consistently making money during the 1840s. It also produced in 1848 one of the greatest hits of all times in America: *A Glance at New York*. In spite of somewhat pedestrian prose, which suggests less excitement than Mitchell's work at the Olympic deserves, *The Temple at Momus* is authoritatively researched and provides considerable insight into the theater and culture of New York during the 1840s. Rinear is also particularly concerned with Mitchell's stable of playwrights: Henry Horncastle, William Knight Northall, and Charles Walcott. In another volume, evidently part of a new series, William L. Slout has edited Charles Durang's *The Theatrical Rambles of Mr. and Mrs. John Greene* (Borgo). Durang's essay on the activities of the Greenes during the 1820s first appeared in the New York *Clipper* in 1865, and to this essay Slout adds substantial editorial commentary. Charles H. Shattuck's second volume, *Shakespeare on the American Stage from Booth and Barrett to Sothern and Marlowe* (Folger), is surely a model of its kind. Not only a handsome volume, beautifully illustrated, the book contains masses of carefully researched information, admirably balanced by Shattuck's shrewdly intelligent approach, his fine sense of humor and pleasantly readable narrative. He does not care much for Augustin Daly, the "absolute master" of his theater whose cleaned-up versions of Shakespeare satisfied 19th-century audiences, but his chapter on "Augustin Daly and the Shakespearean Comedies" is excellent. Nor did Shattuck find much pleasure in Percy Mackaye's *Caliban by the Yellow Sands*, by which America celebrated Shakespeare's Tercentenary in 1916, but I would thank him for his sharp recognition of the vast growth of theater criticism in America and for his interest in the "massive study" that "needs to be made of theatrical criticism" toward the end of the 19th-century. My sentiments exactly!

ii. Comments on Theater and Musical Theater

Fred Bloodgood is a man of the past, a pitchman from the medicine show days who "made it my practice never to use one word where four will do," and "Talking" (*TDR* 31:39–56) is the perfect title for Brooks McNamara's presentation of Fred's art, told in the elegant, well-flavored language of the pitchman. Stephen Nelson traces the life and career of one of America's cockiest theater impressarios in *"Only A Paper Moon": The Theatre of Billy Rose* (UMI). A moody and mercurial showman and Barnumesque architect of spectacles, Billy Rose held theories of mass entertainment that stimulated two generations of theatergoers. From 1924 to 1962, from *Corned Beef and Roses* and *Sweet and Low* to the *Acquacade* in Cleveland (1937), Sally Rand's dance in *Let's Play Fair* (1938), and a variety of plays such as Hemingway's *The Fifth Column* and Ben Hecht's *We Will Never Die*, Billy Rose held a magic wand. Nelson's narrative, interesting and well documented, suggests a man of ideas whose contribution to American popular entertainment deserves more serious attention.

Julian Mates's *America's Musical Stage: Two Hundred Years of Musical Theatre* (Praeger) has been reprinted in paperback, a good buy for money-conscious students. With references to *The Shop Girl*, John A. Degen looks at George Edwards's 1894 play as a step in the growth of the English and American musical comedy: "The Evaluation of *The Shop Girl* and the Birth of Musical Comedy" (*ThS* 7:40–50). As usual, Degen's work is carefully researched and clearly presented.

iii. Approaching the Eugene O'Neill Centennial Celebration

Among those interested in American drama there are a significant number, no doubt influenced by William Archer's casual observation about the shores of Cape Cod in 1915, who determine its beginnings with the efforts of Eugene O'Neill. The slightest education on the subject should disabuse them of their elitest assumption, but bliss can be a comfortable condition. One should, however, make an effort to distinguish fact from opinion which is always subject to the changing currents of a contemporary criticism. A widely recognized opportunity to draw attention to the work of an American dramatist, however, should not be taken lightly. Scholarly machinery, always ready to take advantage of the populace's eagerness to celebrate, whether motivated by patriotism or love of spectacle—if there is a difference—geared up for the 1988 event. The publication in paperback of Virginia Floyd's *The Plays of Eugene O'Neill, A New Assessment* (Ungar) is a good illustration. Scholars, too, must remember the philosophy of the heroine's father in Royall Tyler's *The Contrast*.

The most interesting book on Eugene O'Neill to appear this year is *"As Ever, Gene": The Letters of Eugene O'Neill to George Jean Nathan*, ed. Nancy L. and Arthur W. Roberts (Associated University Presses). Dividing the letters into four parts—The Protégé and the Mentor, Colleagues, The Nabob, and The Masterworks—the Robertses introduce this collection of letters most efficiently, provide abundant illustrations, and, occasionally, prefatory remarks for letters. If anything, the letters are overedited. Nevertheless, insights into a man not celebrated for his sense of humor or personal enthusiasm are especially revealing. Essentially, this volume of letters provides scholars with a better understanding of O'Neill. What more could one ask?

Harold Bloom, an intelligent, well-read, and recognized scholar in fields other than American drama, edited three volumes of essays this year concerned with Eugene O'Neill. In each instance the essays, selected one is led to believe with the help of several research assistants, are well chosen and reprinted in the chronological order of their original publication dates. In his introduction to Eugene O'Neill's *The Iceman Cometh* (Chelsea House), part of a Modern Critical Interpretation Series, Bloom identifies O'Neill as "the most American of our handful of dramatists who matter much: Williams, Miller, Wilder, Albee, perhaps Mamet and Shepard." Part I of

Bloom's introduction to *Eugene O'Neill's* Long Day's Journey Into Night (Chelsea House) is repeated from the volume on *The Iceman Cometh*. In part II Bloom concentrates on the language in *Long Day's Journey*, utilizing long quotations from the play and so many comparisons with the work of other writers that he does not appear to have much to say about O'Neill's efforts. Bloom's third volume, *Eugene O'Neill* (Chelsea House) fails to introduce adequately any reader to the work of America's laureate dramatist. Beyond this general observation, I would note that of the three parts of Bloom's introduction to *Eugene O'Neill*, the first appears in every volume, the second comes largely from his introduction to *The Iceman Cometh*, and the third simply repeats parts of the essay introducing *Long Day's Journey*. Although the essays collected in these volumes are quite well chosen, the introductions smack more of commerce and its machinery than of critical acumen, and the series adds little to scholarship.

It is always difficult to provide an assessment of any value of the numerous short essays that appear in *The Eugene O'Neill Newsletter*. The best approach has seemed to be to list all essays and comment only when the title is not revealing or the observations seem particularly good. The Winter issue of *EON* includes the following: Lowell Swortzell, "O'Neill and the Marionette: Uber and Otherwise" (11:3–7); Tom Reed, "O'Neill's Nausikaa Episode" (11:8–9) concerned with *Anna Christie*; Paul D. Voelker, "Conspicuous By His Absence: Eugene O'Neill and a 1987 Provincetown Conference" (11:10–12); Romanian critic Petra Comarnescu's contribution of "Four Letters by Eugene O'Neill" (11:12–18); and David W. Bury, "Albee and the Iceman: O'Neill's Influence upon *Who's Afraid of Virginia Woolf?*" (11:18–21). The Spring issue reprinted three speeches from a 1986 conference on O'Neill and added comments by Gary Vena and Louis Shaeffer on Barbara Gelb's new play, *My Gene*. The Summer-Fall number included R. Viswanathan, "The Jungle Books and O'Neill" (11:3–7); Donald P. Duclos, "A Plank in Faulkner's 'Lumber Room': *The Emperor Jones* and *Light in August*" (11:8–13); Paul D. Voelker, "O'Neill's First Families: Warnings Through the Personal Equation" (11:13–18); Bette Mandl, "Family Ties: Landscape and Gender in *Desire Under the Elms*" (11:19–23); Marc Maufort, "The Legacy of Melville's *Pierre*: Family Relationships in *Mourning Becomes Electra*" (11:23–28); and Stephen A. Black, "The War Among the Tyrones" (11:29–31). As suggested ideas, lightly sketched to draw attention, these notes collected in the *Newsletter* are mainly valuable to O'Neill scholars for future reference—to be noted, perhaps discussed, enjoyed, or rejected.

As usual, comparativists looked at the plays of Eugene O'Neill this year but with less effect than one would imagine. Joseph L. Maleski and John H. Stroupe develop a rather elaborate but not very convincing argument in "Jean Anouilh and Eugene O'Neill: Repetition As Negativity" (*CompD* 20:315–26). Concerned with the obsession of each writer for tracing repetitions in life, the authors conclude that despite differences in approach—i.e., Anouilh's people reject life while O'Neill's people accept life and try to exist—the dramatists agree that man cannot live outside established society. Thomas P. Adler shows relationships between O'Neill's plays and Bergman's film in " 'Daddy Spoke to Me!': God's Lost and Found in *Long Day's Journey Into Night* and *Through a Glass Darkly*" (*CompD* 20:341–48). Adler's attempt to coordinate four characters—Edward/Minus and Ella/Karin—however, is not successful in illuminating anyone's understanding of either work. The purpose of Gary Vena's essay is also unclear: "Congruency and Coincidence in O'Casey's *Juno* and O'Neill's *Journey*" (ES 68:249–63). Although the number of comparisons between these two plays is startling, Vena finds no hard evidence to indicate that O'Neill attended the New York productions of O'Casey's plays.

In one of the better essays on Eugene O'Neill, Stephen A. Black emphasizes the rhythms, recurrent themes, and musical qualities in "O'Neill's Dramatic Process" (*AL* 59:58–70). After praising these qualities generally as they appear in *The Iceman Cometh*, Black provides a detailed discussion of the first scene of Act I of *Long Day's Journey Into Night* to illustrate the "shifting allusions" and a rhythmic structure, which he calls a "symphonic process," a dramatic process of character interaction for evoking pity and fear. Professor Black is less successful in arguing that *Beyond the Horizon* is "America's First Tragedy" (*ESC* 13:195–203). The assumption in his title crosses the grain of those who see no tragedy in American drama and also irritates scholars who claim earlier examples of tragedy. Furthermore, Black loads his argument with a self-serving and limiting definition of tragedy and immediately places O'Neill in the company of Sophocles and Euripides. It is, Black admits, a "large claim." In "Convergence and Divergence: Father and Son in *A Touch of the Poet* and *The Iceman Cometh* (*AL* 59:323–40) James A. Robinson details the influences of the father figure and the characteristics of melodrama in each play before suggesting, without pushing his argument too far, that the autobiographical unmasking in these plays indicates a development in O'Neill as man and as dramatist that allowed him to face eventually the issue in *Long Day's Journey into Night*. Michael C. O'Neill traces "Confession As Artifice in the Plays of Eugene O'Neill" (*Renascence* 39:430–41) from *Days Without End* through *The Iceman Cometh* to *A Moon for the Misbegotten*. He sees the artifice change from a dramatized confession to the creation of a god, within or outside the human psyche, and eventually to a concern for the power people have over one another. Looking at O'Neill's work from another perspective, Ronald H. Wainscott writes "Exploring the Religion of the Dead: Philip Moeller Directs O'Neill's *Mourning Becomes Electra* (*ThS* 7:28–39). In this carefully researched and impressive study Wainscott analyzes the work of designer and director to produce the play for the "ear" as well as the "eye and brain."

iv. Between the Two World Wars

Stage Left: The Development of the American Social Drama in the Thirties (Whitston, 1986) by R. C. Reynolds promotes the 1930s as a decade in which the American playwright changed from technician to artist. As sound as the idea may be, however, it should be made by someone far more conversant with the plays and playwrights of the period. Although Reynolds has read books by John Gassner, Arthur Hobson Quinn, and Joseph Wood Krutch, he does not show a firm understanding of American drama either before or during the 1930s, adequate knowledge of the plays of the period, or awareness of the writings of more than a handful of critics. It is interesting to me to find someone who attaches as much importance as Reynolds does to the plays of Philip Barry, particularly *Holiday* and *Philadelphia Story* which become boundary makers for Reynolds's theories of change, but the supporting evidence in Reynolds's five main chapters is far from convincing.

Few scholars have been interested in John Steinbeck's plays, and John Ditsky feels that Steinbeck's notion of drama deserves some attention. In "Steinbeck's European Play-Novella: *The Moon is Down*" (*StQ* 20, i–ii:9–18) Ditsky concludes from Steinbeck's use of scene, dialogue, and character that the author imagines the European world of 1942 as a stage. These observations, however, are not suggested as important to Steinbeck's dramatic or literary vision but appear built upon Ditsky's previous essay on "Steinbeck As Dramatist" (pp. 13–23) in *John Steinbeck: From Salinas to the World*, ed. Yamo Shigehara (Gaku, 1986). Raymond Conlon—"*The Fifth Column:* A Political Morality Play" (*HemR* 6, ii:11–16)—discusses the single full-length play of another fiction writer whose reputation in the theater is usually limited to the ring or the arena. Viewing *The Fifth Column* as Hemingway's "only truly ideological work . . . in which the action of the play and the behavior of the characters must be judged from a political point of view," Conlon discusses the effect upon the hero, Phillip, of Dorothy, the evil sociopolitical agent, and Max, the good political angel. Clifford Odets is a more familiar dramatist of this period, and Gerald Weales presents some ideas about Odets, yet with a certain discomfort that he manages to push aside to accomplish his objective with all of the daring wit and smug humor of a successful finesse. His essay is entitled "Clifford Odets's Children: or It Is a Wise Playwright Who Knows His Own Father" (*SAD* 2:3–18). Readily acknowledging the danger involved in "the charting of influences," especially "when theatrical giants are used to smother infant playwrights in their cradles," Weales proceeds to list characteristics of Odets's work worth imitating—settings, language, ideology—and then to suggest tenuous comparisons with plays by Miller, Williams, McCullers, Hansberry, Albee, and Mamet.

v. Women Playwrights

In the developing history of the American theater the real contribution of women playwrights has yet to be fully assessed, in detail or in spirit. Critical excursions to that end have been made into that dusky pre-1915 period of American drama, but the prejudice against drama in general combined with past attitudes toward women writers has proved to be a substantial barrier to scholarship. Perhaps the time has come for serious investigation as scholars become more aware of the neglect and begin to show a concern for women's work on the stage. The revised and expanded edition of *Women in American Theater*, ed. Helen Kritch Chinoy and Linda Walsh Jenkins (TCG), is a good sign. Each section has been updated and a new chapter has been added on "theatre artists working today." "New Problems, Practices and Perspectives" is an "eclectic gathering" of information on actresses, playwrights, and women in every part of the theater. The appended 50-page sourcebook of information relevant to women—awards, organizations, dissertations, feminist theater, lists of plays by women—is another valuable service provided by this volume, the kind of resource information that is available for playwrights, either men or women, in *The Dramatists Sourcebook* (TCG) and *The Playwright's Companion* (Feedback Theatrebooks), both annual publications.

Among women dramatists whose contributions to the development of modern American drama has been seriously underestimated, the name of Susan Glaspell should be at the top of everyone's list. Peripherally, her work has been considered with the activities of the Provincetown and the career of Eugene O'Neill; limited studies have also been made of her life and letters. Now C. W. E. Bigsby has edited *Plays by Susan Glaspell* (Cambridge)—*Trifles, The Outside, The Verge, Inheritors*—and provided an introduction which places Glaspell in a proper historical and literary milieu and briefly traces her life and work as a dramatist. On another front Bettina Friedl has edited *On to Victory: Propaganda Plays of the Woman Suffrage Movement* (Northeastern). The 20 plays and sketches collected are printed chronologically from *Woman's Rights*, 1856, by William B. Fowle, to *Unauthorized Interviews*, 1917, by Alice Duer Miller. It is a carefully prepared volume, an effective argument for the suffrage issue. Each play is well introduced; there are also 18 pages of illustrations plus a list of the best plays on suffrage written before 1920. The general introduction provides a good historical perspective on the subject in addition to a pertinent and interesting discussion of parlor theatricals, which during the last part of the 19th century were a major arena for suffrage plays.

The editors of the *Southern Quarterly* (25) devoted the entire Spring issue to a discussion of southern women playwrights. Milly S. Barranger was responsible for organizing the issue and led the discussion with "Introducing Southern Playwrights: A Perspective on Women Writers" (pp. 5–9), in which she laments the neglect of southern women playwrights over the past four decades and summarizes their development with particular emphasis upon a rising interest occurring during the 1950s. The generally familiar names of the playwrights treated in the following eight essays—Lillian Hellman, Carson McCullers, Alice Childress, Marsha Norman, Beth Henley, Sandra Deer—do not, however, support Barranger's strong

assertion of neglect, nor do the essays focus upon the significant contributions of these women as southern playwrights. Rather the writers
of these essays concentrate on idiosyncratic issues or approaches. W.
Kenneth Holditch, for example, attempts to show that Lillian Hellman's work is indelibly marked by the conditions of her upbringing.
In "Another Part of the Country: Lillian Hellman as Southern Playwright" (pp. 11–35) Holditch refers particularly to *The Little Foxes*,
Another Part of the Forest, and *The Autumn Garden* and suggests
that *Toys in the Attic*, though set in New Orleans, is not very southern.
The result of his efforts is, however, scarcely noteworthy.

Virginia Spencer Carr tells the interesting story of Tennessee
Williams's encouragement for Carson McCullers in "Carson Mc-
Cullers: Novelist Turned Playwright" (pp. 37–51), with some emphasis on *The Member of the Wedding*, but Carr has difficulty relating McCullers's work to the South. Gayle Austin's "Alice Childress:
Black Woman Playwright to Feminist Critic" (pp. 53–62) is a strong,
carefully organized essay in which *Trouble in the Mind* (1955) and
Wine in the Wilderness (1969) are discussed in terms of feminist
literary criticism. Understanding Childress as a critic of society, in
particular the portraiture of black women by male writers, Austin
outlines three stages of treatment: equality of male and female,
women's advantage, and a clear uncertainty in the male interpretation. It is a new and interesting approach to a playwright whose
career has truly been neglected. "I Remember Alice Childress" (pp.
63–65) by Polly Holliday, who acted in *Wedding Band*, is unhappily
brief but memorable for the insight it provides.

The last four essays in this Spring issue of *SoQ* treat currently
popular playwrights from the South. In "Doing Time: Hunger for
Power in Marsha Norman's Plays" (pp. 67–79) Lynda Hart analyzes
Norman's plays in terms of the imagery that shows woman's "elemental struggle for autonomy" as she confronts the unjust order in the
"social-sexual hierarchy." Billy J. Harbin chooses a thesis which
would appear to be more appropriate to the concept Professor Barranger had in mind for his essay on *Crimes in the Heart*—"Familial
Bonds in the Plays of Beth Henley" (pp. 81–94). Stressing the disintegration of traditional ideals as opposed to a thesis involving a quest
for fullfillment in social comedy, Harbin claims that Henley writes
about victims and their acceptance of the southern world in which
they live. Lisa J. McDonald compares Beth Henley and Marsha
Norman (pp. 95–104) as they "spearhead the invasion of women into

the mainstream theatre." She feels that they share a sensitivity toward their characters and an ability to tell a story and that they both use the "family framework" in their plays. They differ, however, in their sense of theatricality, their narrative techniques, and their sense of humor. Such a comparison may be interesting in ways not immediately apparent, but if it is significant in their work, McDonald provides no supporting argument. Sandra Deer is one of the South's promising new playwrights, just as Linda J. Herbert would appear to be a promising critic, at least as suggested by her essay on "Humor and Heritage in Sandra Deer's *So Long on Lonely Street*" (pp. 105–15). In a convincing presentation Herbert explains how Deer uses southern traditions, collects clichés and conversation of the South, and, in general, inspires people to reconsider their attitudes toward the southern heritage of social and literary conversation. In my opinion the essays in this issue of *SoQ* are sadly uneven, not so much in writing style as in originality of thought and substantive comment. Perhaps it is seldom otherwise in such an undertaking, but the stimulus resulting from the endeavor is surely healthy.

Three other essays dealing with women in the theater are worth noting. Philip C. Kolin's "An Interview With Jane Reid-Petty of New Stage Theatre" (*SoQ* 25, iv:39–46) identifies the founding director of Mississippi's New Stage Theatre in Jackson, provides a history of the NST and some information on its goals and policies. Jenny S. Spencer—"Norman's *'night Mother*: Psycho-drama of Female Identity" (*MD* 30:364–75)—explains why Norman's play is potentially more terrifying for female viewers who must identify with both characters on stage than for males who may remain detached. A good point which Spencer makes very effectively! In "Keep Tightly Closed in a Cool Dry Place: Megan Terry's Transformational Drama and the Possibilities of Self" (*SAD* 2:59–69), June Schlueter explains Terry's play as a response to Joseph Chaikin's Open Theatre. Because transformational drama, according to Schleuter, acknowledges the "shifting self," the developmental style of Terry's work offers unlimited opportunities for the actor and the audience. Alas, it seems that the playwright must take a backseat to everyone!

vi. Modern American Drama: Williams, Miller, Albee, Shepard, etc.

One must be rather careful how one uses the words *modern* and *contemporary*. Perhaps the concept of *currency* needs to be considered, but even that term suggests problems. *Essays on Modern American Drama: Williams, Miller, Albee and Shepard,* ed. Dorothy Parker (Toronto), does not alleviate the problem at all. As a collection of essays, five on Albee and four on each of the others, the volume provides some insights, unfocused as a group, on those American dramatists since World War II who have stimulated the greatest amount of discussion among critics and scholars. The only clear raison d'être for the collection, however, is the original publication of the essays— all appeared first in *Modern Drama.* Since *MD* accepts essays dealing with drama from the early work of Ibsen in 1850 to the present, the adjective in the title of Parker's volume is appropriate in one sense, but the problem remains.

a. **Tennessee Williams.** Books on the life and works of Tennessee Williams are now appearing with a frequency that rivals articles in journals. Roger Boxill's *Tennessee Williams* (St. Martin's), part of a Modern Dramatists Series, is an adequate presentation and a "comprehensive study," as advertised, only in the sense that Boxill presumably mentions every play that Williams wrote. After a chapter on Williams's early one-act plays, there are analyses of *The Glass Menagerie, A Streetcar Named Desire, Summer and Smoke,* and *Cat on a Hot Tin Roof.* A final 20-page discussion of "late plays" includes comments on 22 additional plays. Obviously, the limited space and the requirements of the series format encourages scholars to oversimplify, but many will agree with Boxill's observation that Williams is the "only genuine writer in the history of the American theatre." Irene Shaland's *Tennessee Williams on the Soviet Stage* (Univ. Press) suggests another view of this distinguished dramatist. After a succinct view of theater in the Soviet Union since 1939, Shaland describes the production and reception of Williams's plays produced there after 1960. Both *Streetcar Named Desire* and *Glass Menagerie* were appreciated, as one might expect, but the Russians had short shrift for *Orpheus Descending* and *Sweet Bird of Youth. Kingdom of Earth,* however, Shaland explains, is "closest to Russian self-consciousness." There is always a fascination in knowing how people from other lands respond to American art and literature, and the Soviet interpretation of Williams's plays will stimulate the imaginations of critics and historians, political and literary.

Hary Rasky was a friend of Tennessee Williams, and *Tennessee Williams, A Portrait of Laughter and Lamentation* (Dodd, Mead,

1986) is Rasky's story as he began to understand and like Williams
in the process of the many hours they spent together preparing a
film. Rasky's journalistic style is a little heavy, too elegant, self-
conscious, and frequently overwritten, but the volume contains an
abundance of detail and some new insights into one of America's
truly outstanding dramatists. And what a great title: "Tennessee said
that laughing was his way of lamenting." Harold Bloom's collection
of essays on *Tennessee Williams* (Chelsea House) is a simple journeyman's venture. From his introduction it is clear that Bloom knows
very, very little about American drama, and in volumes that promise
to introduce readers to a dramatist his approach serves no good
purpose.

In "The Making of Tennessee Williams: Imaging a Life of Imagination" (*CompD* 21:117–31) Marlon B. Ross argues that Williams
treated art as the supreme reality and life as the ultimate illusion. To
support his thesis Ross discusses two recent biographies: Dotson
Rader's *Tennessee's Cry of the Heart* (1985) and Donald Spoto's *The
Kindness of Strangers: The Life of Tennessee Williams* (1985). He
finds both books disappointing. Thomas P. Adler looks beneath the
Zelda and Scott Fitzgerald relationship and discovers Tom and Laura
in "When Ghosts Supplant Memories: Tennessee Williams' *Clothes
for a Summer Hotel*" (*SLJ* 19, ii:5–19). For Adler, the play is a confessional, a work that shows the depth of Williams's love for his
sister.

b. **Arthur Miller.** Harold Bloom, editor of *Arthur Miller* (Chelsea),
has few positive thoughts either about Miller or American drama in
general in his six-page introduction. The omnipresent and sweeping
character of his remarks, however, may impress some of his readers.
Should you wish to have another approach to the life and work of
Arthur Miller, read the dramatist's own story in *Time Bends* (Grove).

It might appear that the latest form of publication in aid of scholarship is the interview. Although this resource has long been an
accepted journalistic technique, published interviews and now collections of published interviews have become a popular entrée into
print for a growing number of professors. Clearly, there is an art to
conducting a revealing and successful interview, and just as clearly a
number of people who conduct and publish interviews of literary
people and theater artists have not mastered that art. I suspect that
Edward Albee might, if he cared, write a devastating essay on the

subject; he seems to have endured more ego-centered interviewers than most dramatists. Matthew C. Roudane, however, knows very well how to conduct a successful interview and in *Conversations with Arthur Miller* (Mississippi) has collected four decades of talk—39 interviews. Not all of these, however, can be considered models of what may be building into a new literary genre. Although the approach of June Schlueter and James K. Flanagan in yet another introduction to the works of *Arthur Miller* (Ungar) is obviously limited, it does bring Miller's activity up to date—to mid-1987. Writing in a straightforward manner, the authors are basically concerned with theme and thought in Miller's ten major plays—from *All my Sons* to *The Archbishop's Ceiling*—and pay little attention to structure or language. In their volume they tell the plot of each play and provide a brief commentary, placing a strong emphasis upon Miller's own feelings about his work. In an essay on Miller June Schlueter writes about the "complexities of truth and fiction" as revealed in Adrian Wallack's representation of the power struggle between life and art—"Power Play: Arthur Miller's *The Archbishop's Ceiling*" (CEA 49:134–38).

c. **Edward Albee.** Albee's popularity among scholars shows little sign of diminishing, and, as the years pass, more and more books appear that reprint the best essays on Albee, keep his plays in print, and continue to update and reevaluate his contributions to the drama. Matthew C. Roudane's *Understanding Edward Albee* (So. Car.) is a fair example of the first category. Harold Bloom, viewing Albee as "the crucial American dramatist of his generation" and padding his introduction with long quotations from *Zoo Story* and *Virginia Woolf*, provides a reasonable selection of Albee scholarship in a collection entitled *Edward Albee* (Chelsea). The *Selected Plays of Edward Albee* (Doubleday) reprints eight of Albee's 24 plays: *Zoo Story, The American Dream, Who's Afraid of Virginia Woolf?, A Delicate Balance, Box and Quotations from Chairman Mao, All Over, Seascape,* and *The Man Who Had Three Arms.* The brief introduction to this collection by the dramatist himself is slight, self-conscious, and self-indulgent. But why not?

Part of a "Modern Dramatists" series, the brief study of *Edward Albee* (St. Martin's) by Gerry McCarthy is of much higher quality than such series volumes usually attain. Although McCarthy reveals his sympathy for Albee's work and eagerly comments on the dramatist's increased control of his writing and of his commitment, he has also studied Albee's plays with the utmost care and arrives at some enlightening conclusions. His chapter entitled "Enigmatic Images" in which he analyzes *Tiny Alice* and *Chairman Mao* is one of his best discussions. The chapter on *Virginia Woolf, Delicate Balance, All Over*, and *Seascape* is excellent. His commentary on *Listening*, Albee's "most hermetic piece," is also well worth reading. In an essay which he calls "Cars and Traveling in *The Death of Bessie Smith*" (*CLAJ* 30:472–82) Philip C. Kolin chooses an insignificant detail and produces an insignificant argument suggesting that Albee, consciously or unconsciously, underscores his thoughts in a variety of ways. Henry I. Schvey feels that a careful study of Edvard Munch's painting "Death in the Sickroom" can stimulate one to a greater understanding of Albee's *All Over*, which he calls a "dramatic equivalent" of the painting. Although Schvey provides that necessary close analysis in "At the Deathbed: Edward Albee's *All Over*" (*MD* 30:352–63), the understanding it reveals concerning Albee's play is open to question.

d. **Sam Shepard.** Except for acts of God—the birth of O'Neill and the death of Williams—which make us pause to consider past contributions to American drama, the leading fascinator of the scholarly mind presently interested in American drama is Sam Shepard. In a hundred years or so readers may have cause to wonder, but today there is little mystery about his popularity. For our particular purposes the man's imagination, his original approach to life and language, and his theatricality surely provide almost endless opportunity for our own imaginings which, given the conditions of academe, we have a tendency to turn into essays and books.

Lynda Hart's *Sam Shepard's Metaphorical Stages* (Greenwood) places Shepard in the "context of modern theatre and modern psychology." In an analysis of Shepard's plays organized to show the dramatist as a writer of the 20th century ever aware of the theater and its relationship to man's needs, Hart attempts to dispel the "notion that Shepard's theatre is rootless." Always present in the distinct or vague background of his plays, she argues, are the themes and practices of Brecht, Pirandello, Ionesco, Artaud, and Beckett, as well as the experimental efforts of the Living Theatre and the Open Theatre. In support of these ideas throughout her book Hart outlines Shepard's metaphorical stages—from experimental expressionism through modified realism to epic domestic drama. It is obviously an approach

which gives Shepard considerable stature as part of a developing drama, but the presentation is strong and the argument well ordered.
. Other critics of Shepard's work may be equally ambitious to show a dramatist of substance and modernity but have chosen lesser and more selective approaches. William W. Demastes is interested in "Understanding Sam Shepard's Realism" (*CompD* 21:229–48). Unfortunately, Demastes does not appear to understand the critical terms he uses and vaguely writes of "reality" that "has literally become internalized" and of a "naturalist brand of realism." His essay does not help one understand anything about Shepard's work. Leonand Wilcox's "Modernism vs. Postmodernism: Shepard's *The Tooth of the Crime* and the Discourses of Popular Culture" (*MD* 30:560–73) contains a rewarding discussion of "the jubilant energy of Shepard's language," as the writer explores the division between modernism and postmodernism in Shepard's plays. Sheila Rabillard is concerned with the power of Shepard's theatricality over audiences in "Sam Shepard: Theatrical Power and American Dreams" (*MD* 30:58–71). Emphasizing Shepard's use of semiotics and the "phatic function" of his theatrical language, Rabillard feels that audiences are subjected to a violent theatricality which virtually demands that people pay attention to his themes. In another essay concerned with audience response—"Fool of Desire: The Spectator to the Plays of Sam Shepard" (*MD* 30:46–57)—Ann Wilson tries to complicate the obvious in an ingenuous discussion of "meaning in the theatre" and concludes that Shepard tries to please the spectator.

A number of critics this year expressed rather strong ideas about Shepard's presentation of men and women. In "Women and Other Men in Sam Shepard's Plays" (*SAD* 2:29–41) Rudolf Erben provides a strong masculine point of view. Arguing that the "modern, independent and socially active" women in Shepard's plays are not a satisfactory answer for Shepard's searching heroes, Erben declares that Shepard sees women as destructive forces in his America and, therefore, rejects them. Interpreting Shepard's plays in a different manner, Felicia Hardison Londré sees Shepard's masculinization of America as "an enlightened recognition of the feminine component at its full value" wherever it exists in American society. In her essay entitled "Sam Shepard Works Out: The Masculinization of America" (*SAD* 2:19–27) Londré concludes that a "true masculinization of America is a process of eliminating female marginalization." James D. Riemer selects a single Shepard play to discuss contradictory views of American manhood—"Integrating the Psyche of the American Male: Conflicting Ideals of Manhood in Sam Shepard's *True West*" (*UDR* 18, ii:41–47). Focusing on the different ideals of masculinity held by the two brothers in the play, Riemer shows the unsatisfying and disheartening conclusion in which the brothers' shifting views emphasize the true limitations of both ideals.

Two final articles, missed in my previous essay, require only a quick note. Rodney Simard—"American Gothic: Sam Shepard's Family Trilogy" (*TA* 4[1986]:21–35)—explains briefly that the roots of Shepard's subsequent accomplishments existed in his earlier plays. To this hoary idea he adds the observation that man must look inside himself for resolution, satisfaction, and harmony. Thomas P. Adler's "Ghosts of Ibsen in Shepard's *Buried Child*" (*NMAL* 10[1986]: Item 3) is brief and of little consequence. Adler elaborates on Ibsen's *sun* in *Ghosts* and Shepard's use of the same sound, words that audiences for both plays may hear as *sun* or *son*. Yet Shepard has said that he did not know Ibsen's play, and perhaps he can be credited with his own pun.

vii. Contemporary American Drama

Understanding Contemporary American Drama (So. Car.) by William Herman is part of a series, "Understanding Contemporary American Literature," ed. Matthew J. Bruccoli. Each volume is suggested as a guide for "students as well as good nonacademic readers." If it were necessary to explain this goal in detail, I do not think that many people would find it satisfactory. Herman's contribution to the series may serve that questionable purpose because it is a journeyman work providing functional information without intruding upon it a sense of style or the machinery of scholarship. After a brief preface establishing New York as the center of theatrical activity in America and 1964–84 as the period of his observations, Herman considers that score of years mainly in terms of theaters and dramatists who create experimental, avant-garde theater. The major part of his book consists of chapters on five dramatists—Sam Shepard, David Rabe, David Mamet, Ed Bullins, Lanford Wilson—with the greatest emphasis placed upon Shepard (57 pp.). In a sixth chapter of 20 pages Herman notes the work of Jack Gelber, Amiri Baraka, Arthur Kopit, Adrienne Kennedy, Jean Claude Van Itallie, and Marsha Norman. If this is a discussion of "contemporary American drama"—presumably the drama that one could see on the stage in America between 1964 and 1984—the bias shows. Why are Neil Simon, Tennessee Williams, Arthur Miller, and Edward Albee, to name a few obvious dramatists of this period, not considered *contemporary?* The writing of a book of this nature obviously presents a great many problems. Selections must be made, but the period should be covered adequately, and there should be critical assessments, not just plot summaries and biographical information. Herman also depends to a recognizable degree on the work of others—C. W. E. Bigsby, for example, in his first chapter.

Another way to try to understand contemporary drama is to interview the dramatists. Don B. Wilmeth does this with exemplary skill in "An Interview with Romulus Linney" (*SAD* 2:71–84). Instructive and revealing, the interview elicits excellent commentary on Linney's working habits, his interest in Japan, and his concern for directors, plus his observations on his historical plays and his autobiographical writing. John Louis Digaetani's "An interview with Albert Innaurato" (*SAD* 2:87–95) is less successful. The subject is seldom allowed to speak his mind, although Innaurato does admit that he has little hope for the theater which he considers "dead" and often does not even like his own plays. Another resource item for understanding contemporary drama is "Ronald Ribner: A Classified Bibliography" (*SAD* 2:97–117) by Philip J. Egan. It includes works, interviews (25 of them), criticism (23 items), reviews, and biographical information. Mainly, the author lists reviews—a pretentious and premature undertaking for both the compiler and the editor of the journal.

Among contemporary dramatists, Lanford Wilson was the subject of two book-length studies this year. Mark Busby, the author of *Lanford Wilson* (BSWWS 81), has the obligation of making Wilson a western writer. Born in Missouri, Wilson has some western credentials, and Busby emphasizes the theme in his plays of the civilized but destructive East vs. the free but anarchic West. The settings of Wilson's plays are also important to Busby, who must manipulate this concept a bit in his treatment of *The Hot l Baltimore*. Gene A. Barnett's *Lanford Wilson* (*TUSAS* 490) transcends the limitations of this series and produces an excellent book. Finding his subject always "interesting and challenging," whose work is "that of a committed artist," Barnett does as thorough a job as possible on a dramatist still reaching toward the apex of his career. The bibliography is excellent—all of Wilson's works plus ten unpublished plays owned by the author and

28 essays annotated by Barnett. The 19 short chapters in a 152-page book are a bit overwhelming and suggest an extended outline, but the structure fits Barnett's plan. One is impressed with the thoroughness of this writer who has read everything that Wilson has written and, in spite of an excessive show of admiration for his subject, produces a perceptive and thoughtful assessment. Examining each play in terms of plot, character, and dramatic techniques, he embellishes his very readable text with numerous quotations from Wilson: "I always start with a character who has a beef or a goal" (p. 89). This is a good first study of a dramatist whom Barnett describes as a straightforward realistic writer whose plays attract the general population.

"Working Worlds in David Mamet's Drama" by Dorothy H. Jacobs (*MMisc* 14[1986]:47–56) features a good thesis idea that is not well developed. Mamet's unique contribution to American theater, she writes, is the "dramatization of men at work." This is a valid point, which Jacobs discusses with reference to Mamet's use of *place* in his plays, but she stops short of explaining her insights in a more meaningful context. James P. Stout wants to know why people continue to treat the story of Job: "Re-Visions of Job: *J.B.* and 'A Masque of Reason'" (*ELWIU* 14:225–37). In his discussion of these two revisionary responses to *Job*, Stout concludes that Archibald MacLeish, a man of hope who sees no final truths, is concerned with the Book of Job, while Robert Frost, detached, intellectual, and without a stake in the outcome, writes about Job himself. It is a well-conceived study, and it is good to find scholars writing about poetic drama and men of letters who write for the stage. "Frank Rich in Conversation with Terrence McNally" (*DGQ* 24, 3:225–37) I note here only for those who want to read what a major newspaper reviewer has to say about the requirements and expectations the *New York Times* has for its critics.

Rather few items appeared this year on black dramatists. In "Charles Fuller and *A Soldier's Play*: Attacking Prejudice, Challenging Form" (*SAD* 2:43–56), William W. Demastes explains Fuller's work as "translating his black experiences" into "American experiences." Essentially, Demastes reveals Fuller as manipulating a theatrical formula by using a mystery plot to break the black character stereotype. In this manner Fuller contradicts the earlier approach of Amiri Baraka, who was interviewed by Sandra G. Shannon on the topic of his work as a director of his own plays and as Director of

African Studies, SUNY Stony Brook: "Amiri Baraka on Directing" (*BALF* 21:425–35). Shannon's questions elicit some good comments by Baraka on his own plays—on the use of music and color, for example, in *Black Mass*. His objective in his new position, Baraka explains, is to help actors understand his plays; a good director "always wants to know what the playwright thinks." Ever a defender of black people, still trying to tell people what to do, he wants plays which kick "white folks' asses" and also reveal the "complex reality" in which we live. It is a good interview. Floyd Gaffney's "Black Drama and Revolutionary Consciousness: What a Difference a Difference Makes" (*TA* 4[1986]:1–19) explores the changes in Afro-American drama since the Black Consciousness Movement of the 1960s, particularly in the plays of Baraka and Wole Soyinka and in the changing feelings of playwrights. Essentially, Gaffney writes a polemic of sorts, as he urges a linkage between the philosophical and the practical elements of theater, which he envisions as purely "functional" and related to the needs and desires of the community it serves. Looking at this statement from a detached point of view, one can see the limiting and even dangerous concept it espouses.

viii. Finally

For a number of years I have ended my essay with reference to Gerald Weales's annual assessment. This year Weales devotes most of his space to the new vaudeville, performance art, movement theater, or "whatever this recent eruption of theatricality" is called—"American Theater Watch, 1986–1987" (*GaR* 41:573–84). At first glance Weales's chosen subject seems far removed from American drama, as he discusses the "art as experience" of Bill Irwin and the current appeal of clowns and clowning on the American stage, the one-man or one-woman show, and Robert Woodruff's direction of *The Comedy of Errors*. This is American theater, however, the logical presentational medium for American drama, and from this version of Shakespeare Weales moves to the performance activity of Martha Clarke—*The Garden of Earthly Delight, Vienna: Lusthaus, The Hungry Artist*—and Robert Wilson's *CIVIL warS*. Never having felt comfortable with any of Wilson's experiments, it was heartening and even satisfying to me to have Weales say that the proper approach to Wilson's operas is for the viewer or auditor to "sink" into the "bath of sounds and images" provided and absorb "whatever is most valuable to him artistically or . . . emotionally." Further, Weales heightened my sense of self-respect by saying that "the reverberations Wilson sets off in me are likely to carry me into muddy water that obscures any potential deep significance." Another contributor to this nontraditional theater—Ping Chong, whose *The Angels of Swedenborg* was first produced in Chicago in 1985—Weales treats with a high sense of humor and takes seriously only on his own terms.

The point Weales is making, however, is very important. These performers are all "storytellers in a special sense," traditional storytellers and yet new storytellers participating in a performance in which they "are their own subject." It is clearly theater outside the mainstream theater, purposely removed from any literary record and therefore from any critical evaluation other than the review of the performance. Such theater eliminates the playwright, who is replaced by one who calls himself or herself the creator, whose effect or spectacle created may also involve speech. Even Martha Clarke has now progressed to this point. This situation in the theater, of course, has nearly always been so—as a shield for the theater artist's ego or as a ploy by that person to maintain control in a building (the theater) where the playwright may not be available, is not always welcome, may not want to go, and perhaps does not even belong and yet must fight there for recognition and the need to exist. Except for certain periods in theater history—which are always the most memorable because the playwright was accepted—the performing artists tend to usurp authority in a cooperative venture. The theater impressario— whether Barnum or Belasco or Brustein—will take control of the storyteller as well as the theater, that medium with which the dramatist and the critic must always contend.

With the unconventional there is usually the conventional. The time-honored realistic theater still exists in America along with the experiments of dramatists such as Sam Shepard and performing artists such as Robert Wilson. New plays appear each year, and Weales mentions A. R. Gurney, Jr.'s *Sweet Sue*, Romulus Linny's *Heathen Valley*, Constance Congdon's adaptation of *The Gilded Age*, and Arthur Miller's *Danger: Memory!*, to name a few. Such works are conveniently structured for scholarly evaluation, but theater, it must be remembered, is still an art of the moment, and the satisfaction that moment provides—in modern times, in all times—is achieved by literary and performing artists, each jealous of the other's contribution, each subject to a critic's standards. Who is to say how, or whether, one shows or says it? If the critic's lot is not a happy one, he or she still has the obligation to insist that the playwright is necessary for a healthy theater.

CUNY, Graduate School

19. Themes, Topics, Critcism

Michael J. Hoffman

Last year I began by saying that I had read more books for this chapter than ever before. I must again repeat that statement, with the proviso that I had better stop being surprised. There seems to be a geometric increase of books every year, and one wonders where it will end now that desktop publishing has become so easy. Carefully selecting books for this chapter becomes more necessary and more difficult. One does not wish to review merely the best-known critics or restrict oneself only to a few well-known presses, for, as we all know, the big presses often publish second-rate books and the smaller ones are often willing to risk publishing something offbeat and interesting that the more conservative houses will not touch.

Because of the need to control the length of this chapter, I am again forced to do a great deal of summarizing, and with only relatively few books have I been able to engage in an extended dialogue. With all that, I have still been able to write about fewer than half the books that were sent me for review. Five of the categories are the same as last year's, but I have added a sixth, "The Profession Examines Itself," the explanation for which will appear in the beginning of that section. As usual, I have tried (with a few exceptions) to discuss the books in each section in alphabetical order by the author's last name.

i. American Literature

The first book in this section is the largest and most attractive book I have been sent this year, Martha Banta's *Imaging American Women: Idea and Ideals in Cultural History* (Columbia), which surveys the images created of American women by the various media between 1870 and the First World War. According to Banta, in "a distinction familiar to art historians and philosophers, images of American women were *created* as ideas, not *found* as facts . . . image makers acted to impose their ideas upon the culture." With "astonishing frequency," she goes on, "those images were female in form. However masculine the political and commercial activities that controlled 'the main world,' the images dominating the turn-of-the-century imagination were variations on the figure of the young American woman and permutations of the type of the American Girl" (p. xxxi). With more than 500 black-and-white illustrations, most of them photographs, Banta documents this imposition on the culture. The larger categories into which she divides her study are "Images of Identity," "Images of Desire," "Counterimages," "Portraits in Private," "Between the Private and the Public," "Public Statements," and "Images for Sale." The great analysts of the period, for Banta, were Henry James and, surprisingly, Charles Dana Gibson, whose "Girls" say a great deal about the nature of that era. The book also contains interesting chapters on such writers as Wharton and Stein. While it has much to say about American culture of that period, and perhaps by extension our own, this is more a descriptive than a theoretical work. It is great fun to dip into, even if one does not read it all the way through.

William Boelhower's *Through a Glass Darkly: Ethnic Semiosis in American Literature* (Oxford), first published in Italy in 1984 but only now released in this country, defines a structuralist semiotic scheme for interpreting the ethnic content of American literature. The highly schematic organization is exemplified by the following passage in which Boelhower claims that "ethnic semiosis is ultimately organized on the basis of a topological system that generates an open series of such binary isotopies as old world/new world, emigrant/immigrant, ethnic/non-ethnic, presence/absence, origins/traces, dwelling/nomadism, house/road, orientation/disorientation. This spatiotemporal perspectivism provides not only a way of seeing but also a way of thinking that has its own type of ethnic *savoir-faire*. Ethnicity, therefore, is the major filter for evaluating and criticizing American cultural flight" (p. 13). Boelhower sees a central ethnic trope in the contrast of the Indian's empirical 'I am where my body is' with the colonist's need to set boundaries and use maps (p. 56). Developing this argument, Boelhower then claims that "ethnic semiosis can now be defined as nothing more nor less than the interpretative gaze of the subject whose strategy of seeing is determined by the very ethnosymbolic space of the possible world he inhabits. . . . Through the processing system of Memory and Project, the subject puts himself in contact with the foundational world of his ancestors, reproduces himself as member of an ethnic community, and is able to produce ethnic discourse" (pp. 86–87). An introduction by Werner Sollers reminds us of that writer's more considerable study of American ethnicity, reviewed here last year. Boelhower's book is not in Sollers's class, but as a theoretical essay it proposes some useful structural principles for scholars and teachers.

Another small book deserves brief mention for its study of the tall tale as a performance that enacts a responsive interplay between teller and audience, Carolyn Brown's *The Tall Tale*. Brown focuses on the ways that 19th-century authors transmute the materials of the tall tale into their more belletristic work. In the early chapters Brown establishes the theory, before she proceeds with readings of Augustus Longstreet, *Sut Lovingood*, and Mark Twain. Particularly interesting is her reading of the latter's *Autobiography*. While based to some extent on original fieldwork—e.g., Brown's attendance at actual tall-tale contests—the book does not seem to constitute a large advance over the most classic works in the field, except for its more specific approach to the performative aspects of the subject.

Brief mention also goes to another book that is an absolute delight to read: *Jewish Wry: Essays on Jewish Humor*, ed. Sarah Blacher Cohen (Indiana). Among contributors are a number of well-known scholars, including Irving Howe, Robert Alter, Sanford Pinsker, and Mark Schechner, and the topics range from more general considerations such as "The Nature of Jewish Laughter" and "Jewish Humor and the Domestication of Myth" to discussions of individual humorists such as Sholom Aleichem, Lenny Bruce, Sophie Tucker, and Woody Allen, with many of the essays being both wise and funny. As you might expect, some of the jokes that are quoted themselves make the book worth reading. Especially funny is a parody in Yiddish of "The Love Song of J. Alfred Prufrock," written by Saul Bellow and Isaac Rosenfeld, with a following translation into English (pp. 149–50). It is a masterpiece of "comic domestication." I wish, however, that someone at the press had persuaded the editor to prepare an index.

A book that could have been more interesting than it turned out to be is Robert B. Downs, *Images of America: Travelers from Abroad in the New World* (Illinois). A summary (in about 220 pages) of the travel writings of 40 visitors to the New World from the mid-18th century to the middle of the current one, it includes just about all the people you might expect. It is useful as a reference work because the individual essays are primarily summaries of each author's work, but except for a brief attempt in the introduction, there is little that deals with the broader dimensions of a fascinating subject.

A very engaging book is Michael Fried's *Realism, Writing, Disfiguration: On Thomas Eakins and Stephen Crane* (Chicago), a study by an art historian of the issue of representation and how it affects the works of two artists, a painter and writer, who were contemporaries. "What ultimately is at stake in both essays," Fried says, "is not a thematics of writing in general but more particularly a problematic of the *materiality* of writing as that materiality enters into Eakins's paintings and Crane's prose . . . the essay on Eakins is largely concerned with what it means for writing, as part of a historically specific network of cultural practices, to be something that can be painted, while the essay on Crane grapples with the more tortuous question of what it means for writing *in writing* to be an object that can be seen and hence represented" (pp. xiii–xiv). Fried claims, for instance, that in *The Gross Clinic* Eakins organized his famous painting not simply as a "realistic" painting but as to how it reflects other models in other paintings. Dr. Gross as surgeon thus becomes a self-representation of Eakins as painter. Similarly, Fried's discussions of Crane center on how the major figural trope in his work is that of the artist writing. Typical of the "representations school," Fried does not engage in historical generalization, and so we can only suppose the specific ways in which he means us to take Eakins and Crane as representing their time and place.

Brief mention goes to two thematic studies. The first, by Robert A. Gates, is *The New York Vision: Interpretations of New York City in the American Novel* (Univ. Press). The chapters are divided periodically, and each contains a brief outline of the social history of the period followed by an analysis of one or two writers such as Cooper, Melville, Wharton, Wolfe, Bellow, and Cheever. There is not much here that is original. In *Equivocal Spirits* Thomas B. Gilmore traces alcoholism and drinking in 20th-century literature. Many authors he includes are American, and some of the works (e.g., *The Victim*) contain a character (rather than an author) who is alcoholic. This is a well-written book, but I find that its focus on a limited theme encourages us to read complex works too much from a single point of view.

In *The Puritan and the Cynic: The Literary Moralist in America and France* (Oxford) Jefferson Humphries explores the question as to why, in so professedly moral a country as the United States, American authors have written "so little in the traditionally moralistic literary genres of maxim and fable" (p. vii). The result is a witty book on the subject of aphorisms and maxims and on the differing national styles for each. Humphries develops the aphoristic model from the French, beginning with La Rochefoucauld and continuing with Pascal, La Fontaine, and Maurice Blanchot. The Americans he chooses are Benjamin Franklin, Cotton Mather, Jonathan Edwards, and Joel Chandler Harris. Humphries compares the French and American aphoristic styles: "the French maxim depends on an acute tension between particularity and universality, a tension which must always install a distance within the maxim between observation of detail and pretention to truth, a distance which is always a potential source of irony . . . . This ironic distancing is not inscribed within Franklin's aphorisms, but rather between them and their author, and between them and their readers" (p. 21). Humphries does, however, find some parallels between Mather and Pascal, with a common source in Puritanism. He believes that the distinctions between current American and French styles of criticism and theory have developed out of similar roots. There is no one in American criticism quite like either Blanchot or Roland Barthes, for instance, in their use of the quotable aphorism. It is in modern poetry, however, that Humphries does find a closer connection, citing Marianne Moore and Wallace Stevens among others. The book is wise and amusing throughout.

Jefferson Hunter's *Image and Word: The Interaction of Twentieth-Century Photographs and Text* (Harvard) discusses books that contain both photographs and prose commentary, usually by different individuals. The author is less interested in books in which the prose serves as merely captions for pictures than in those books that have a thematic coherence. He has in mind such collaborations as those of James Agee and Walker Evans (*Let Us Now Praise Famous Men*) and Jean-Paul Sartre and Henri Cartier-Bresson (*D'une Chine à l'autre*), although he does include a few single-authored texts such as those by Wright Morris. Most of the authors and photographers are American, and Hunter focuses primarily on documentary texts produced during the 1920s, 1930s, and 1940s. This is more a descriptive than a theoretical account, but it is well versed in the language and materials of photography, and it contains a number of very good black-and-white reproductions.

Brief mention goes to Karol L. Kelley, *Models for the Multitudes: Social Values in the American Popular Novel, 1850–1920* (Greenwood), a historical/sociological study of books that were best-sellers. The focus here is on reading audiences, their composition, and the types of books particular social sectors were most likely to buy or borrow. Kelley studies gender differences, regional characteristics, economic and educational backgrounds. Her book provides useful background information for courses in the American novel of that period.

Michael Kreyling's *Figures of the Hero in Southern Narrative* (LSU) brings narrative theory to bear on some of the prime works of southern fiction. Rather than focus on the South as a region, Kreyling wants to discover the characteristics indigenous to southern narrative fiction; the aspect he claims as central is the southern view of the hero. Kreyling chooses the word "figure" deliberately, in the formal sense by which Erich Auerbach states that it is a "presence inscribed upon a culture's awareness, rooted in one historical event and auguring another" (p. 3). The doubleness of this usage is echoed by Kreyling's decision to write about figures that are impressed upon the cultural imagination of the South and therefore figure in the fictional narratives written by its best authors. Robert E. Lee is, for instance, such a figure, and it is against that figure that Kreyling measures the "heroes" of novels by William Gilmore Simms, Ellen Glasgow, William Faulkner, and Walker Percy—with a sidelong glance at southern figures that appear in Henry James and Henry Adams.

Another good book is by James L. Machor: *Pastoral Cities: Urban Ideals and the Symbolic Landscape of America* (Wisconsin). What the author finds special in his topic is the theme of "urban pastoralism," "a vision of environment in which city and country are equally valuable components in an evolving landscape best served when those components operate in harmony" (p. 14). He calls this "moral geography" (p. 15) a millenial vision that saw the American landscape as a "promised land . . . in which the garden and the city would be harmonized" (p. 46). Machor traces this theme from its beginnings in 16th- and 17th-century travel writings to its development in the Puritan moral vision. Some of his most persuasive chapters deal with the further development of this phenomenon in the writings of Jefferson and Emerson and culminating in the visions of Hawthorne and Whitman. For those writers, Machor claims, "the unmitigated power of urban pastoralism can be located in its seeming ability to reconcile conflicting ideologies: a belief in the necessity of urban expansion and a trust in the myth of the garden; a faith in progressive development and a commitment to an unchanging order" (p. 174). Such a vision is pervasive in all our most compelling writers (p. 176). I think this learned, well-written book is worthy of a place on the shelf beside such classic studies as Leo Marx's *The Machine in the Garden.*

A more perplexing but nonetheless engaging work is *Gold Standard* by Walter Benn Michaels. Because much of it will be discussed elsewhere in this volume, I shall limit myself to a few general remarks about its methodology. As a work of the "representations school," this book contributes to literary history by avoiding a statement of an overall theory about the nature of naturalism and its relationship to the history of the period. Its method is to trace the parallel representations of certain topics and images from economics, literature, and painting in a series of analyses that form an implied overview of what is going on in American letters at the turn of this century. Money, property, and representation are the major themes; Dreiser, Norris, Wharton, and Charlotte Perkins Gilman are some of the authors discussed. Not surprisingly, the overall avoidance of theory is pervasive, but the underlying assumptions behind Michaels's forms of representations are themselves quite theoretical. This is a well-written, brilliantly argued, and frustrating book.

Brief mention goes to a more traditional kind of literary history, as exemplified in a collection of essays by Roy Harvey Pearce, *Gesta Humanorum: Studies in the Historicist Mode* (Missouri). Pearce's foreword contains a spirited defense of the kind of contextualization that used to be called literary history. Like most polemics, it does not resolve anything, but it does put into clear context the kinds of issues that divide scholars like Pearce and Michaels. Most essays in this collection have been published previously. There are two on general topics and another seven that deal with specific authors and works, ranging from Thomas Paine, to Hawthorne, Whitman, Twain, and Stevens, and concluding with an essay on recent American poetry.

Mark Schechner's *After the Revolution: Studies in the Contemporary Jewish-American Imagination* (Indiana) establishes itself as one of the better books on this topic. This collection of essays includes as its subjects Lionel Trilling, Isaac Rosenfeld, Saul Bellow, Norman Mailer, Allen Ginsberg, and Philip Roth, focusing primarily on the 1940s and 1950s, with the exception of the chapter on Roth. Schechner also includes chapters on Wilhelm Reich and Freud, beginning his book with a discussion of the intellectual milieu of socialist radicalism that led to the foundation of the *Partisan Review*. Politics becomes mixed with analytic psychology, and the brew gives rise to a distinctive form of American fiction that we have come to call the "Jewish novel." The chapters are well-written and persuasive, and the various essays combine to make a coherent book.

Carol Shloss's *In Visible Light* is, like Hunter's *Image and Word*, a study of how writing and photography interact. It "is a book about how artists negotiate approaches to their subjects . . . a meditation about what surrounds a work of art" (p. 4). The American writers who serve as Shloss's subjects range from the mid-19th century to the present, from Nathaniel Hawthorne and Henry James to John Steinbeck and Norman Mailer. On Hawthorne, she writes, "Photography never suggested itself to Hawthorne as a formal model to be emulated; he was not interested in the novel of concretized experience. What distinguished Hawthorne was his insight into photography as a human activity . . . photography as well as writing involved a human dynamic—the photographer's interest in the scene and the subject's response to that attention" (pp. 49–50). Some of the best chapters are about the specific interactions of writers and photographers, such as the relationship of the aging Henry James preparing his New York Edition and the young Alvin Langdon Coburn taking the photographs that accompany its text; as well as the great collaboration of James Agee and Walker Evans on *Let Us Now Praise Famous Men*. It is fascinating to watch the developing self-awareness of the writers and photographers as each becomes more knowledgeable about the nature of the other medium and how the two can interact.

Another collection of essays by a senior scholar is Monroe K. Spears's *American Ambitions*, which brings together a number of pieces that Spears wrote during his long career as scholar and editor. Although he claims not to have begun as a specialist in American literature (he has edited Matthew Prior), most of these essays are on American topics, and most are on 20th-century poetry and criticism. All demonstrate a broad cultural underpinning and graceful prose. Among the most interesting are those on James Dickey, Robert Penn Warren, Cleanth Brooks, and "The Function of Literary Qualities." Spears, unlike Pearce, represents not so much a coherent vision of how to approach literature as an erudite eclecticism. As a result, one should probably dip into these essays rather than read them straight through.

One of my favorite books this year is Cecelia Tichi's *Shifting Gears*, a study of the deep effect that gear-and-girder technology had on the development of American culture, particularly from the 1890s to about 1930. This is a culture dominated by ideas of efficiency and utility, in which the engineer becomes the new culture hero and the efficiency expert the embodiment of the best principles of management, an age spanned by Frederick Taylor and Herbert Hoover. Tichi organizes her study by categories, exploring the relationship of the natural to the mechanical, the development of new sets of values, and the founding of a new architecture and new design. There are many wonderful photographs and black-and-white reproductions of paintings and advertisements. What *ALS* readers will find fascinating is the application Tichi makes to the major writers of our high modernist period, for she establishes the new culture as a prime metaphor of stylistic and formal innovation. Of fiction, she writes, "John Dos Passos invigorated the novel with engineering design, but his contemporary, Ernest Hemingway, . . . brought engineering values into prose style . . . . In the era of the antiwaste Efficiency Movement Hemingway's terse, economical lines brought engineering values into the very sentence itself . . . . The famous Hemingway style was essentially the achievement, in novels and stories, of the engineers' aesthetic of functionalism and formal efficiency" (p. 216). And of poetry: "William Carlos Williams spoke literally when he called the poem a machine made of words . . . . In the age of ubiquitous structural and machine technology Williams understood that writers in search of new forms could benefit from the conception of art as a structure with a framework and various fixed and moving parts intended to transmit energy. He understood that the poem was a design or arrangement of prefabricated component parts" (p. 268). These are not arbitrary formulations but come convincingly out of the rich context established earlier, and the metaphor of high modernism as a development out of the advanced levels of machine age culture is one that seems particularly useful.

One more book on New York intellectuals complements two that I reviewed last year. This one, Alan M. Wald's *The New York Intellectuals: The Rise and Decline of the Anti-Stalinist Left from the 1930s to the 1980s* (No. Car.), localizes its scope to those members of

the political left that turned increasingly against Stalin in the 1930s
and 1940s and established such journals as *Partisan Review, Dissent,*
and *Commentary.* Most, though not all, of the writers were Jewish,
and a number are now prominent in the neoconservative movement.
This historical study, based on a great deal of primary research that
includes more than 100 interviews, brings back vividly the ferment
of that period and the centrality of Trotsky in the passionate disagree-
ments among the stalwarts. The coverage of its topic appears to be
definitive.

Brief mention goes to the final book in this section, *Van Winkle's
Return: Change in American English, 1966–1986* (New England), by
Kenneth G. Wilson. The metaphor of Van Winkle's return relates to
the fact that Wilson spent 16 years as a major campus administrator
at the University of Connecticut and another four after that brushing
up on his scholarship before writing this book. His observations about
changes in our language are both trenchant and witty, telling us a
number of things we may not have noticed, such as the words that
are now admitted into dictionaries and those that are no longer in
common usage. He examines dictionaries, the influence on our language of various public figures such as William Buckley, and the ways
in which language choices reenact the never-ending conflict among
the generations. Wilson is not a professional linguist but rather a
student of language and its cultural and social uses. The book is a
lot of fun to read.

ii. Gender Studies

The continued production of books on feminism and other gender-
related issues gives clear evidence of the emergence of a major area
of literary study. Because of space limitations, most of these books
will receive brief rather than detailed mention. *The Ideology of Conduct: Essays in Literature and the History of Sexuality,* ed. Nancy
Armstrong and Leonard Tennenhouse (Methuen), explores that
literature which instructs women about how to behave in ways appropriate to their established social roles. The collection ranges from
"Medieval Courtesy Literature and Dramatic Mirrors of Female
Conduct" to the contemporary version of "The Beauty System," and
it covers literal instruction manuals as well as works of imagination
that are also designed to instruct and mirror the pattern of instruction.

The overall thesis is that literature not only records the process of establishing gender boundaries, it helps to create and reinforce them. As scholarly collections go, this one is more unified than most and the essays are of high quality. Authors include Ann Rosalind Jones, Thomas M. Kavanagh, Cora Kaplan, and Dean and Juliet Flower MacCannell.

Shari Benstock has edited *Feminist Issues in Literary Scholarship* (Indiana), a collection that focuses primarily on 19th- and 20th-century women writers. Ten of the essays appeared in volume 3 of *Tulsa Studies in Women's Literature* (1984–85), and the authors include a great many prominent names: Catharine R. Stimpson, Elaine Showalter, Nina Baym, Jane Marcus, Lillian S. Robinson, and Nina Auerbach. The book explores the aesthetic and political issues behind feminist approaches to literature, and it is of interest primarily because of the strength of individual essays. These include, in particular, "Women's Time, Women's Space: Writing the History of Feminist Criticism" (Showalter), "The Madwoman and Her Languages: Why I Don't Do Feminist Literary Theory" (Baym), and "Modernism of the 'Scattered Remnant': Race and Politics in H.D.'s Development" (Susan Stanford Friedman).

Nicholas Davidson's *The Failure of Feminism* (Prometheus) is basically a rearguard polemic against feminism which attacks some of the extreme positions expressed in feminist criticism. It is, however, a book not easy to dismiss because it is apparently thoroughgoing and scholarly and touches on a broad range of issues. What it attempts to do is plead for a balanced approach to issues of gender— not for a dismissal of feminism, but for more stress on appropriate ways to view both the masculine and the feminine. While acknowledging that the terms are themselves conventional, Davidson also believes that they are biologically inescapable and that we are therefore obliged for the health of our society to develop meaningful functional definitions of each. Davidson's rhetoric makes it difficult for us to take seriously his plea for balance because his prose is so caustic and his tone so partisan.

A book that deals well with the issue of antifeminism is *Nostalgia and Sexual Difference: The Resistance to Contemporay Feminism* (Methuen), coauthored by Janice Doane and Devon Hodges. The authors claim that post-structuralist analytic techniques can enable feminists to deal with the issue of representation in such a way as to help them counter a major antifeminist impulse which they term nostalgic. This nostalgia is a tendency to look longingly back at a time before feminism became a "threat," but the nature of the threat is not the same for all critics. Some wish to return to a time when there was supposedly no oppressive gender differentiation, some to a time before the establishment of patriarchy, some simply to the "good old days." Some of these critics are within the feminist movement, some outside it. The authors examine the rhetoric behind attempts at a nostalgic backward look in order to get beyond the surface statements, and they would probably have a wonderful time analyzing Nicholas Davidson. Their targets are many, and they range from Ivan Illich to *The World According to Garp*.

In *The Impact of Feminist Research in the Academy* (Indiana) Christie Farnham has edited a set of essays that assess the previous decade's feminist research. The collection, which is sponsored by the Indiana University Women's Studies Program, consists of a number of pieces by leading figures, most of which are not directly concerned with literature. The fields covered include history, religious studies, psychology, sociology, economics, science, politics, and Afro-American culture. I am impressed with the overall quality of the contributions and with the collective impression of a matured set of disciplines. I particularly recommend Louise Lamphere, "Feminism and Anthropology: The Struggle to Reshape Our Thinking about Gender"; Ruth Bleier, "Science and Belief: A Polemic on Sex Differences Research"; and Nellie McKay, "Reflections on Black Women Writers: Revising the Literary Canon."

Margaret Hallissy's *Venomous Woman* is a solid thematic study of the female who is poisonous either through her own agency or through that of a plant or animal. It traces this theme from the Middle Ages through the 19th century in both England and the United States. This complex of misogynistic ideas is seen as embodying the masculine fear of the feminine, its most well-known example in American literature being "Rappaccini's Daughter," a work to which this book devotes an entire chapter.

Sandra Harding is the editor of *Feminism and Methodology: Social Science Issues*, published jointly by Indiana University Press and the Open University Press of Great Britain. In the opening essay Harding asks, "Is There a Feminist Method?," a question that is explored and exemplified in the essays that follow. The answer seems to be that feminism has a point of view more than a method, and that its methodology is derived from the various disciplines that make use of that point of view. The disciplines represented in this book include philosophy, economics, psychology, sociology, and anthropology; but not literature. Most of the essays have been around for a while.

A very interesting collection is *Behind the Lines: Gender and the Two World Wars* (Yale), ed. Margaret Randolph Higonnet and three others. Most of the essays were presented at a Workshop on Women and War that was held at the Center for European Studies at Harvard in January 1984. The basic theme of *Behind the Lines* has to do with how the two world wars affected relationships between men and women. The various sections include considerations of the challenge to sexual identities of women active in the war effort, the ways wartime politics caused the concept of gender to be reconstructed, and the remnants of those experiences that continue to affect our lives. A number of the essays deal with literary figures, and some of the most interesting ones analyze the effect of propaganda on gender definitions. The book contains a number of wonderful reproductions of posters designed to warn us about the threat to our women of enemy soldiers and the threat to our soldiers of enemy women.

A major issue in gender studies is the appropriate role for men in feminist scholarship. This topic is explored in *Men in Feminism*, ed. Alice Jardine and Paul Smith (Methuen). The essayists discuss the overall benefits and liabilities of men's participation in feminist writing. The question appears to be vexing, and the essays show a lot of disagreement on the subject, not all of it merely polemical. The list of distinguished contributors includes Naomi Schor, Jane Gallop, Elaine Showalter, Terry Eagleton, Dennis Donoghue, Jacques Derrida, Richard Ohmann, and Robert Scholes. This is a lively book.

Naomi Schor's *Reading in Detail: Aesthetics and the Feminine* (Methuen) studies the use of detail in art and literature and the interest in it expressed by readers and observers. Schor claims that the interest in such detail is not accidental but political, and that the fact that we tend to associate women with an interest in detail demonstrates how such an interest has become gender-specific. Schor studies the pattern of this interest over the past 200 years in order to uncover the politics behind the "pervasive valorization of the minute, the partial, and the marginal" (p. 3). Schor's analysis (in "Archaeology") and her "Readings" are thoughtful, subtle, and lucid. Some of

her subjects include Freud, Barthes, Hegel, and the sculptor Duane
Hanson; all of her writing is informed by a rich theoretical sophistication.

iii. Modernism

The proliferation of books on modernism continues as the end of the
current century approaches. I shall begin this section with brief
mention of Hugh Ford's *Four Lives in Paris* (North Point), a book
that presents the lives of four American expatriates in the manner of
Lytton Strachey's dissection of lives that were characteristic of an
earlier age. Ford chooses a number of "minor" expatriates rather than
some more obvious ones in order to illuminate a corner of modernism:
critic Harold Stearns, George Antheil the composer, novelist and
short story writer Kay Boyle, and Margaret Anderson, editor of the
Little Review. These are pocket biographies concerned less with detailing the entire lives of their subjects than with making a point
about each one of them. While they are interesting to read, they lack
the bite of their model, and in each case the subjects left autobiographical writings that are more instructive about the period.

One of the major publications on modernism is the first volume of
Sandra M. Gilbert and Susan Gubar's *No Man's Land*. This three-
volume series (they are to appear at one-year intervals) continues
the study begun by the authors' important *Madwoman in the Attic*,
a study of the 19th century. The current work is concerned with both
male and female writers and traces the interconnected anxiety caused
by the rising power of women in the political and literary arena, the
corresponding male feelings of impotence, and the discovery by wom-
en of a female literary community complete with precursors who
themselves cause anxiety in women writers.

Gilbert and Gubar claim that "the rise of the female imagination
was a central problem for the twentieth-century male imagination. . . .
it is a modernism constructed not just against the grain of Victorian
male precursors, not just in the shadow of a shattered God, but as an
integral part of a complex response to *female* precursors and contemporaries. Indeed, it is possible to hypothesize that a reaction-
formation against the rise of literary women became not just a theme
in modernist writing but a motive for modernism" (p. 156). One
result of modernist women writers having female precursors has been
that "instead of the female author functioning, if at all, in women's

narratives as a repressed or maddened figure who is eclipsed by the docile heroine, she now appears in the work, though often ambiguously, as the representative of a power alternative to the plot which she nevertheless still fashions" (pp. 192–93). The book contains a myriad of quotations reflecting the struggle over this gendered anxiety. The free-ranging topical discussion covers about 100 years of literature, but because it is organized thematically it does not try to weave a historical account of how this strain developed in modernism.

The authors' erudition and range is extraordinary, from Tennyson's *The Princess* through classic modernist figures to recent writers such as Adrienne Rich and Joanna Russ. The argument and the writing are always lively, and the text moves much more quickly than that of *The Madwoman* because it is not so heavily involved in extended close readings. That job will be carried out by the two subsequent volumes, to which the current one is an extended thematic introduction.

Brief mention goes to Ihab Hassan, *The Postmodern Turn: Essays in Postmodern Theory and Culture* (Ohio State), a series of essays all of which have been previously published in periodicals or as chapters in books. This volume is designed to put all of Hassan's thoughts about postmodernism into one volume that has a sense of coherence as well as exemplifies the author's growth and development in style and thought over the last 20 years. Most of the essays are written in Hassan's apocalyptic style. A useful concluding chapter, "Prospects in Retrospect," places the discussion about postmodernism in a historical context and tries to extract what is useful from the term and the discussion that has surrounded it.

In *After the Great Divide: Modernism, Mass Culture, Postmodernism* (Indiana) Andreas Huyssen has written an important study that advances our ability to distinguish between modernism and postmodernism. The "Great Divide" to which Huyssen refers "is the kind of discourse which insists on the categorical distinction between high art and mass culture" (p. viii). Modernism has frequently been characterized as a reaction against popular bourgeois culture. Postmodern art incorporates mass culture and its forms within the guise of the avant-garde. It therefore challenges the modernist dichotomy between "high" and "low" forms of art and culture. Many of these ideas stem from the work of Theodor Adorno, but Huyssen is also critical of Adorno. He draws many, but not all, of his examples from German art and literature, and he ranges over many artistic forms, from opera to cinema, as befits the study of a movement that refuses to respect any rigid definition of form or genre. This is a stimulating and provocative piece of work.

Morton P. Levitt in *Modernist Survivors: The Contemporary Novel in England, the United States, France, and Latin America* (Ohio State) warns against easy generalizations about the death of modernism. He believes that "Modernism, in its fiction in particular, is still very much alive, still continuing to change and to grow . . . . I am convinced as well that we are wrong to insist that Modernism represents a break from our humanist heritage" (p. 5). He sees James Joyce as central to any tradition of humanistic modernism. This wide-ranging, erudite book convincingly demonstrates that many so-called postmodernist novelists are really continuing and developing further a modernist tradition. The American writers most used to exemplify this thesis are Thomas Pynchon, Robert Coover, E. L. Doctorow, and John Barth.

Two books that will be discussed elsewhere in *ALS 1987*, and one that will not, also make contributions to our understanding of modernism and deserve brief mention. In James Longenbach's *Modernist Poetics* Pound and Eliot are situated in relation to 19th-century theories of history in order to explain the use of the past in their poetry and criticism. Aside from strong readings of the poetry (Pound through 1917 and Eliot through 1922), the author relates well such historians as Wilhelm Dilthey, Benedetto Croce, Jacob Burckhardt, and Friedrich Nietzsche to the context of modernist poetry. In *Discovering Modernism* Louis Menand relates Eliot to the modernist movement through a discussion of his poetic and critical ideas and attitudes. Rather than focusing on historians, Menand relates Eliot to a context of writers and ideas that includes Lord Tennyson, Charles Darwin, Walter Pater, Joseph Conrad, and the Imagists. The early theoretical chapters are probably stronger than those that discuss Eliot's writings. Perry Meisel's *The Myth of the Modern: A Study in British Literature and Criticism after 1850* (Yale), although exclusively about British literature, has many good things to contribute to a theory of modernism. For Meisel, a sense of historical belatedness is key to the anxieties of modernist writers. In this he is similar to Longenbach, but Meisel engages more consciously in deconstructive readings. For him the modernist credo to "make it new" is a defensive stance rather than a creative rallying cry, in part because the modernists suffered from a sense that the great works of literature had already been written.

Marjorie Perloff's stimulating book, *The Futurist Moment: Avant-Garde, Avant Guerre, and the Language of Rupture* (Chicago), studies the implications of Futurism as a movement that occurred simultaneously across national boundaries. For Perloff, the "futurist moment" included cubism and vorticism; France, Italy, and the Soviet Union. The book looks at the implications of Futurism on postmodernism, and it studies manifestoes, poetry, painting, technology, and architecture. The rupture to which Perloff refers in her title is the one that exists between word and text, referent and meaning. This rupture is brought about by the "straining of the artwork to assimilate and respond to that which is not art . . . . It [the Futurist moment] represents the brief phase when the avant-garde defined itself by its relation to the mass audience" (p. 38). The prose and the argument are lucid, and the text is accompanied by a number of interesting reproductions. There is also an excellent chapter on Ezra Pound.

William V. Spanos's *Repetitions: The Postmodern Occasion in Literature and Culture* (LSU) is concerned with both a theory of modernism and with literary theory itself. It reads texts and cultural situations through the use of Martin Heidegger's "destructive hermeneutics." The topics include the relation of detective fiction to postmodernism, the occasion of postmodernism, "A Polemical Meditation on Marginal Discourse," as well as readings of Jean-Paul Sartre's *La Nausée*, Charles Olson's poetry and theory, and Percy Lubbock's criticism. The chapters are essays rather than pieces of a tightly argued book, but the overall text is unified by the author's method. Spanos is interested in re-creating the historical specificity of texts, a process antithetical to what he claims to be the usual practice of deconstructive critics.

I conclude this section with brief mention of Julian Symons, *Makers of the New: The Revolution in Literature, 1912–1939* (Random House), a lively journalistic treatment of the high modernist period and four key authors: T. S. Eliot, James Joyce, Wyndham Lewis, and Ezra Pound. This breezy work attempts to create a coherent narrative out of this material, and it has the failings of such an attempt, including forced connections and factual errors. It has only a modicum of useful textual analysis, but it is nonetheless an excellent review of the period, mixing literary history and biography with cranky personal judgments and a familiarity with the times and some of the major figures.

iv. The Profession Examines Itself

The past year saw the publication of a number of books that take a self-conscious look at humanistic education, the most well-known among them the two conservative best-sellers, Alan Bloom's *The Closing of the American Mind* (Simon & Schuster) and *Cultural Literacy* (Houghton Mifflin), by E. D. Hirsch. But although these were the best-known, they were not necessarily the most interesting for *ALS* readers. I have included a few such works because of their intrinsic interest and because they reflect the kind of critical self-consciousness that has been the best by-product of post-structuralist criticism.

James A. Berlin's *Rhetoric and Reality: Writing Instruction in American Colleges, 1900–1985* (So. Ill.) is the second volume of that writer's history of writing in American higher education. Not only an excellent history, the book contains a good overview of the various schools of writing instruction that have been and are regnant over the composition curriculum. It is probably not surprising to discover that almost all the current concerns about writing instruction have been expressed at some other period. Writing has always been part of the university curriculum, and it has always been subject to controversy. The conflict, for instance, between the notion of utilitarian writing and the opposed notion that writing should only be taught in relation to works of literature was a major controversy during the first decade of this century as embodied, respectively, in the Harvard and Yale schools of writing instruction. Such knowledge should give us an appropriate sense of irony about our contemporary absolutes.

Gerald Graff's *Professing Literature: An Institutional History* (Chicago) brings a sophisticated sense of theory to bear on the history of literary study in this country, assuming as it does that a literature department in itself states an implicit theory about how literature should be studied. Graff's irony opposes the belief that in a pastoral past we had truly humane studies, and he underscores "the delusion that academic literary studies at some point underwent a falling-away from genuine Arnoldian humanism" (p. 5). Graff's bête noire is the principle of field study, for by establishing the curriculum around purely chronological concerns "the field-coverage principle enabled administrative organization to take the place of principled thought and discussion" (p. 8). This historicization of literary study occurred during a time when the primary function of literature shifted away from "socialization" in a polite society into a subject that could be categorized and thus trivialized.

Graff has an unerring eye for the role of ideological presupposition in various periods of literary study and for those justifications written about the centrality of philology or, later, close reading. One's professional or cultural presupposition always assumes the role of a given when we justify our activities theoretically. Graff's definition of theory as "the self-consciousness generated when consensus breaks down" (p. 253) is better than many I have seen. The book is a good guide as to how to read current critical controversies, and Graff believes that in training graduate students we should above all educate them in precisely those issues that divide us. I should like to make this book required reading for anyone serving on a curriculum committee.

In *The Culture of Criticism and the Criticism of Culture* (Oxford) Giles Gunn claims that the current crisis in our culture stems from "disbelief," or the fact that religious and ethical concerns "have been culturally institutionalized in forms that strike many Western intellectuals as but subterfuges for the expression of various kinds of social, cultural, political, and even religious privilege" (p. x). Modern critical movements are attempts to develop a theory of culture that will replace those that are now the victims of our disbelief. Gunn harks back to thinkers like Emerson and, more recently, Lionel Trilling and Edmund Wilson, who saw the imagination as the ultimate root of moral consciousness, and he laments the ways in which the moral imagination has been called into question in recent cultural theory, a condition influenced by Nietzschean thought.

The book contains an interesting discussion of deconstruction as well as a cogent critique of American Studies. Gunn's heroes in theory are Kenneth Burke, Clifford Geertz, and Mikhail Bakhtin. He has a two-part definition of the humanities: (1) "those traditions of investigation and reflection . . . in which any given civilization has conducted its own self-scrutiny and, where necessary, has attempted to revise itself in behalf of a more capacious present and future . . ."; (2) they "simultaneously entail an exploration of the differences such forms have made to the societies, and the people living within them, whose imaginations they have helped shape and whose lives they have helped control" (p. 127). Aside from a tendency to wordiness, this erudite book is one of the better recent discussions of cultural theory and the humanities.

Russell Jacoby's *The Last Intellectuals: American Culture in the Age of Academe* (Basic Books) is not about the university but about intellectual life outside the academy, which he claims is shrinking. The decline of public intellectual life has occurred because of the expanding hegemony of academic professionalism. Jacoby laments the loss to our intellectual discourse of thinkers like Edmund Wilson and Lewis Mumford, along with such academic mavericks as John Kenneth Galbraith and C. Wright Mills, all of whom wrote for a large public on issues of broad general concern. Academics write primarily for other academics, and with no younger generation of public intellectuals emerging of sufficient stature, intellectual discourse in the United States will continue to suffer. This book is written in a lively polemical style that is nonetheless intellectually sinewy, setting itself up as the kind of discourse in and of itself for which Jacoby is nostalgic and whose lack makes him indignant.

In *Shapes of Culture* (Iowa) Thomas McFarland criticizes academic professionalization from within the academy. The shapes of culture to which he refers in these published lectures are those small areas of scholarly interest to which most of us are confined without sufficient reference to the larger issues (forms of culture) from which the smaller draw meaning. We know subfields but not the larger disciplines. A pithy quotation will serve as example: "Philosophy as part of culture, culture as part of life, life as perspective on being, constitute a series of presences stretched out between two absences. The first is indicated by the memory of past meaning; the second, by the hope of reclaiming that meaning. Between these two absences, across the texture of life, the winds of culture blow" (pp. 110–11). These general points are instructive, but McFarland finally does not take a strong enough position of his own, and so his work seems too much like yet another nostalgic lamentation.

Richard Ohmann's collection of essays, *Politics of Letters* (Wesleyan), takes a Marxist perspective on the study of letters in the United States. He makes here the kind of claims he made in his earlier book, *English in America*, that those of us who teach and do literary scholarship represent the class interests of monopoly capital and that we represent a professional elite that opposes a disenfranchised proletariat. These 20 essays are not, however, merely the ritualistic recitation of cant but are full of careful observation and terse, telling judgments. The four sections into which the book is divided give some sense of the range of discourse: "The Profession of Humanist," "Thinking and Teaching About American Literature," "Thinking and Teaching About Mass Culture," and "Literacy and Power."

v. Theory of Narrative

Again, I resist using the word "narratology," but by narrative I mean more than "fiction." The theory of narrative has become an especially lively branch of literary theory, as evidenced by many new publications in that field. In *Freud, Proust and Lacan: Theory as Fiction* (Cambridge) Malcolm Bowie uses those writers to develop a thesis that the construction of theory is like the construction of fiction—and vice versa. His book, he claims, is "about theory and about desire; about theories of desire and the desires of theorists; about theories held to be fictions and about a work of fiction thus classified by libraries and bookshops . . . that has as a main theme the pains and pleasures of the theorising mind" (p. 2). Bowie does an excellent job of relating Freud and Proust, and his exposition of Lacan and his usefulness for reading works of literature is one of the best I have read.

One of the most interesting works in this section is Lennard J. Davis, *Resisting Novels: Ideology and Fiction* (Methuen). "My argument throughout this book," says Davis, "will be that novels are not life, their situation of telling their stories is alienated from lived experience, their subject matter is heavily oriented towards the ideological, and their function is to help humans adapt to the fragmentation and isolation of the modern world. However, . . . I am not advocating burning books, I am advocating resisting them" (p. 12). Davis uses the word "resistance" in two major ways: first, "as the way politically oppressed groups fight back against the powers that oppress them" (p. 12); second, following the psychoanalytic meaning of "opposition," or the patient's unconscious interference against allowing associations to arise that will disturb a deeply rooted neurosis. We resist novels and they resist us. This persuasive book demonstrates the pervasiveness of ideology throughout all aspects of the novel, not just in its thematic content but in setting, dialogue, character, and plot. Well-informed about the latest developments in literary theory and theory of narrative, Davis also ranges over a grand spectrum of works of fiction. There are particularly good

chapters on the nature of ideology and on the relation of setting to
ideology. On a pettier note, my only complaint about this well-written
and argued book is the pervasive sloppiness of the proofreading.
    Brief mention goes to Dennis A. Foster, *Confession and Compli-
city in Narrative* (Cambridge), a study that describes the interrelationship between the writer of a text and the reader. Foster postu-
lates a more active reader than many reader-response critics who
tend to see the reader as a passive receptor manipulated by texts.
Foster believes that readers enter into a kind of compact with writers,
taking on their mastery of the material to become equivalent in authority to the authors themselves. He effectively analyzes a number
of major texts that lend themselves to this kind of reading, and the
book contains good chapters on *The Scarlet Letter* and *Absalom,
Absalom!*
    Alexander Gelley's *Narrative Crossings: Theory and Pragmatics
of Prose Fiction* (Johns Hopkins) brings deep philosophical learning
to bear on the problem of representation. The crossings referred to
in the title are those between what is fictional and what is not; Gelley
contends that fictional representation is grounded in such crossings.
We therefore need to develop a new aesthetics of fiction, "to discern
a method of indirection, of deviancy, that has been designated by
such terms as 'the figural,' 'the dialogic,' 'the parasitic' " (p. x). Gelley
probes the "negating or shadow side" of such conventional terms as
description, character, dialogue, setting, and scene to reveal the
"porous fabric" of fiction (p. xii). He makes use of almost all the well-
known post-structuralist critics in this effort, and his fictional subjects
incorporate novels from three centuries, including *The Confidence-
Man* and Hawthorne's "Wakefield." *Narrative Crossings* is not for the
beginning student of this kind of discourse.
    David Hayman's *Re-Forming the Narrative: Toward a Mechanics
of Modernist Fiction* (Cornell) could as easily have been placed in
the modernism section of this chapter, for its contribution to studies
in that area are as strong as its study of narrative. It is an exploration of the typology of narrative strategies in distinctively modernist
works of fiction. Hayman lists five types of narrative strategy: (1)
double-distancing; (2) impossible objectivity; (3) nodality; (4) the
self-generating novel; and (5) paratactics. Space will not permit an
exposition of each of these types, and so I shall focus on just "nodality" in hopes of giving the reader a sense of the richness of Hayman's ideas. The concept of nodality is to be applied to those modern-

ist works that "refuse to tell tales," whose plots "are attenuated and/or sublimated . . . . Such texts are frequently informed by systems of interrelated passages (scenes, images, visions, treatments of topics, and so forth) that do not contribute to a coherent and generalized narrative development but rather break the narrative surface, standing out against or being readily isolable before blending into the verbal context. The passages in question can best be regarded as nodes or clusters of signifiers in 'open works'" (p. 73). I find this an extremely useful distinction, one with any number of practical applications. This well-informed, sinewy book covers a large range of modernist works in a number of languages (Hayman is a well-known Joyce scholar).

Brief mention goes to an interesting book by James M. Mellard, *Doing Tropology: Analysis of Narrative Discourse* (Illinois), which develops and applies the tropological theories of Hayden White to Joseph Heller's *Something Happened, The Education of Henry Adams,* William Faulkner's *Absalom, Absalom!,* and John Updike's *The Centaur.* This work is intended as "an introduction to . . . the theory and application of tropes—for the scholar of literature who is interested in such disciplines as rhetoric, narratology, psychoanalysis, philosophy, and philosophy of language" (p. vii). Jacques Lacan, Kenneth Burke, and Giambattista Vico play large roles here in addition to White.

Gerald Prince's *Dictionary of Narratology* (Nebraska) is a very useful compilation of definitions of the terms used in narrative theory. Although the book contains an occasional fuzzy description, most of the definitions are quite clear and distinctly helpful. Prince is eclectic and uses the elements of many schools of theory. The book is well cross-referenced and it contains a carefully selected bibliography of the essential works in the field.

Peter J. Rabinowitz's *Before Reading: Narrative Conventions and the Politics of Interpretation* (Cornell) "is intended as a contribution to the continuing project of developing a coherent theory of how people read narrative" (p. 1). It focuses, however, on those "readers' starting points" which the author claims "can help us understand *how* interpretation comes about and what its implications are—not the implications of the particular texts at hand, but the implications of the very means we use as we go about making sense of them" (p. 3). This instructive book is an important contribution to reader-response theory and is one of the best works of that school to focus on fiction and on the interpretive assumptions we bring to the process of reading. The range of reference is impressive, and the writing is clear.

I conclude this section with brief mention of Hayden White's latest collection, *The Content of the Form: Narrative Discourse and Historical Representation* (Johns Hopkins), which contains eight previously published essays that extend the author's theory of tropology and refine his thought. Primarily on historical narrative, these essays raise basic issues about the adequacy of narrative discourse for history that have implications for all narrative. White deals with questions of authority, representation, context, and production, and he presents valuable analyses of Michel Foucault, Fredric Jameson, and Paul Ricoeur, as well as more general essays on the politics of historical interpretation and on "Method and Ideology in Intellectual History." As always, White is a provocative thinker and raconteur.

vi. Literary Theory

Because of the numbers of books being published in all areas of theory, it is in this section that I shall be forced to omit the greatest number of books that I might otherwise have included. I have tried to discuss those books that I thought have the best chance of retaining their interest a few years from now, but I am probably no better at predicting the future than anyone else, and so I give my apologies in advance to any authors I may have slighted. I am writing about fewer than half the books in theory that I was sent to review.

I start with a genealogical study of the roots of modern theory by Jonathan Arac: *Critical Genealogies: Historical Situations for Postmodern Literary Studies* (Columbia). Genealogy, Arac says, "aims to excavate the past that is necessary to account for how we got here and the past that is useful for conceiving alternatives to our present condition" (p. 2), a definition he supplements by reference to the theories of Nietzsche and Foucault. The three interrelated "geological strata" necessary to read contemporary criticism are "Coleridge's romantic metaphysics of symbol and imagination; Arnold's Victorian stance of disinterested, yet worldly, discrimination; and modernist, technical specifications of professional critical tasks," all of which working "together form the ground that current literary study has begun to shift" (p. 3). The book is divided into three sections according to the above criteria, with most chapters discussing the work of an important theorist. Arac writes well, and he is good at establishing the historic roots of contemporary critical positions.

David Carroll has coined a neologism in *Paraesthetics: Foucault, Lyotard, Derrida* (Methuen), a book written in reaction against what has come to be called the "anti-theory" movement. Paraesthetics approaches "art in terms of its relations with the *extra*-aesthetic in general. . . . [It] indicates something like an aesthetics turned against itself or pushed beyond or beside itself, a faulty, irregular, disordered, improper aesthetics—one not content to remain within the area defined by the aesthetic. Paraesthetics describes a critical approach to aesthetics for which art is a question not a given, an aesthetics in which art does not have a determined place or a fixed definition" (p. xiv). These questioners of art and literature do not form a school. Rather, the three authors mentioned in the title share a linkage in expectations and methodology instead of a consistency of doctrine. The book begins with Nietzsche as the archetypal critical questioner; then six chapters follow, with each of the three authors being central to two of them. The chapter titles give a good sense of the book's major concerns: "Aesthetic Antagonism/Lyotard," "Self-Reflexivity and Critical Theory/Foucault," "Deconstruction and the Question of Literature/Derrida," "Disruptive Discourse and Critical Power/Foucault," "Borderline Aesthetics/Derrida," "The Aesthetic and the Political/Lyotard." This wise book demonstrates well the fact that the major post-structuralist thinkers have been neither ahistorical nor apolitical, but that their insights have in fact allowed us to reformulate both history and politics.

The translation into English of all of Jacques Derrida's works continues this year with the appearance of three new books, along with a closely related work of secondary commentary. *Glas* and *Glas*- of Cézanne's to Emile Bernard. Derrida meditates on the four possi- work of Derrida's translated by John P. Leavey, Jr., and Richard Rand, and the second one written by Leavey with a foreword by Derrida. Describing *Glas* is not easy. It is written in two side-by-side columns (with an occasional third one narrowly placed on one side). In appearance the text looks a lot like the Talmud. The columns contain either quotations from J. W. F. Hegel and Jean Genet juxtaposed against one another or commentary by Derrida intermixed with these quotations. The selections from Hegel and Genet are intended to shed the light of implicit mutual commentary and to disrupt the

normal process of reading and interpretation. The role of the reader
is called into question as well, along with our belief in the continuity
of discourse. Everything seems fractured, all conventional categories
subverted, all expectations broken down. One should come to *Glas*
only after acquiring some familiarity with Derrida through other less
demanding works. The translation is, by the way, quite impressive.
Leavey's *Glassary* is intended as a gloss on *Glas*. It contains a brief
clever essay by Derrida on punning, followed by two lengthy introductory essays by Leavey and Gregory L. Ulmer ("Sounding the Unconscious"), the latter two being mingled in facing columns much as
in *Glas*. These juxtaposed essays, intended to comment on one another
through proximity as well as content, are followed by extensive notes
on the translation of *Glas*, and then by both a glossary and an index
to *Glas*. The mere production of these two books is a fine feat of
publishing by the University of Nebraska Press.

Brief mention will go to two more books by Derrida: First, *The
Post Card: From Socrates to Freud and Beyond* (Chicago), trans.
Alan Bass, a meditation in the form of a set of epistles on historical
continuities and discontinuities. Derrida questions the whole notion
of historical precedence, of the earlier preceding the latter, by questioning what would happen if we subverted that order and saw, for
instance, Socrates writing and Plato not. Derrida describes his own
procedure on the book jacket: "You situate the subject of the book:
between the posts and the analytic movement, the pleasure principle
and the history of telecommunications, the post card and the purloined letter, in a word the transference from Socrates to Freud, and
beyond." This book contains, by the way, some of Derrida's most interesting comments on Freud. *The Truth in Painting* (Chicago),
trans. Geoff Bennington and Ian McLeod, takes its title from a letter
of Cézanne's to Emile Bernard. Derrida meditates on the four possible interpretations of what Cézanne might have meant by his phrase:
"1. That which pertains to . . . *the thing itself* [that is, the painting
itself] . . . . 2. That which pertains, therefore, to adequate *representation*, in the order of fiction or in the *relief* of its effigy. . . . 3. That
which pertains to the *picturality*, in the 'proper' sense, of the presentation or of the representation. . . . 4. That which pertains to truth
in the order of painting, then, and *on the subject of* painting, not
only as regards the pictorial presentation or representation of truth"
(pp. 5, 6, 7). Four essays follow that deal with these questions and
take their source from not only paintings but meditations on art by

Plato, Kant, Hegel, Heidegger, and Meyer Schapiro. The book is difficult, discursive, personally idiosyncratic, repetitious, and brilliant. Shoshana Felman's *Jacques Lacan and the Adventure of Insight: Psychoanalysis in Contemporary Culture* (Harvard) is the best discussion yet of the importance of Lacan's work for the study of literature. Felman explains how Lacan's reformulation of Freud works as an overall system of interpretation, or way of reading. "Lacan embodies in my view, above all else, a revolutionized interpretive stance and (though he never formulates it systematically) a revolutionary theory of reading: a theory of reading that opens up into a rereading of the world as well as into a rereading of psychoanalysis itself" (p. 9). The relationship, for instance, between analyst and analysand recapitulates the structure of narrative and acts as a model for reading, interpretation, and teaching. Felman claims that the lesson of Lacan lies in "the fact that there is no psychoanalytic understanding that can dispense with narrative or truly go beyond it" (p. 14). Throughout this very personal book Felman uses the details of psychoanalytic knowledge and technique as models for the reading and interpretive process, and her readings of Lacan are perforce readings of Freud as well. The book is clearly written, aphoristic, sensitively argued, and full of the best kinds of surprises.

Brief mention goes to another new work by René Girard: *Job: The Victim of His People* (Stanford), part of his series on violence, the sacred, and the scapegoat. The Job of Girard's interpretation is not the heroic figure who questions and faces a hostile fate, but is instead a victim, a scapegoat of a community that is bent on nothing less than his destruction. Not really a book of biblical criticism, this sophisticated analytic study of a major text in Western literature uses the techniques of modern interpretation, and it is written with an aphoristic eloquence. Those who were moved by *The Scapegoat* will want to read this book.

One major contemporary French thinker who is at last being translated into English is Algirdas Julien Greimas, whose *On Meaning: Selected Writings in Semiotic Theory* has been published by the University of Minnesota Press four years after his major work, *Structural Semantics*, first appeared in English. Greimas is interested in how the theory of discourse relates to the production of meaning. His deep grounding in linguistics also informs his theories of communication. These essays are technical studies, with an austere rigor that comes across—perhaps because of the translation—as somewhat dry. Fredric Jameson's lively introduction makes a strong case for Greimas's importance as a thinker. We need such clarification of Greimas's work, and we get one in Ronald Schleifer's *A. J. Greimas and the Nature of Meaning: Linguistics, Semiotics and Discourse Theory* (Nebraska). This excellent introduction makes comprehensible much that is difficult and unclear. Schleifer examines Greimas's theories in the context of contemporaries such as Lacan, Derrida, Claude Lévi-Strauss, and Paul de Man, and this contextualization is helpful in judging the relevance of Greimas's work to students of letters. Reading these two books together is probably the best way to start on Greimas, to be followed then by a reading of *Structural Semantics*.

In *A World of Difference* (Johns Hopkins) Barbara Johnson continues the work she began in *The Critical Difference*. She claims that she begins "from two very different starting points at once: (1) a reading strategy designed to uncover the workings of 'differences within' and (2) a subject matter that asks the question of difference *as if* 'difference between' had referential validity" (p. 2). She divides the collection of essays into four sections: "The Fate of Deconstruction," "Significant Gaps," "Poetic Differences," and "Other Inflections of Difference," and she analyzes the work of a wide range of authors, from Molière to Zora Neale Hurston. Johnson is interested not only in problems of interpretation but also of pedagogy, and her writing has the clarity and persuasiveness of a good teacher.

Brief mention goes to Jeffrey Kittay and Wlad Godzich, *The Emergence of Prose: An Essay in Prosaics* (Minnesota), a theory of prose. The authors discuss the historical priority of verse in language, and they speculate on what differences in worldview emerged when prose increasingly became the dominant mode of discourse. They examine some of this change during the medieval period, and, going beyond periodicity, they speculate on the nature of prose in simple literacy, in the writing of history, and in the telling of fictional stories. It is not quite accurate to claim that this is the first attempt to develop a theory of prose as distinguished from other forms of language, but it may well be the first systematic attempt to discuss this particular critical difference, and the authors have produced a stimulating book that suggests a number of possibilities for further work in this area.

Julia Kristeva's *Tales of Love* (Columbia) is a sequel to *Powers of Horror* (1982) in its examination of the roots of human emotion. Kristeva studies love from the perspective of two traditions, a philosophical one that flows from Plato and a theological one flowing from Saint Paul, and in the course of each examination she covers the human history of love throughout most of the intervening centuries to the present. The points of view she brings to this powerful work of creative scholarship stem from her background in linguistics and her work as a practicing psychoanalyst. This is a very personal work into which Kristeva weaves events from her own life, including her own experience of childbirth in a chapter entitled "Stabat Mater," which is about the Virgin Mary.

Jim Merod's *The Political Responsibility of the Critic* (Cornell) begins from the assumption that we have recently witnessed a diminution of critical authority. In exploring the roots of this situation, the author finds that "all readers today stand between two cognitive worlds. The mostly visual, truly anticommunal world of advertising and commercial *entertainment*, controlled by giant corporate interests, opposes but also surrounds the world of literacy, the world of books and critical *thinking*. The outcome of that interaction is the world we live in, to some extent split between professional competence and cultural banality, to some extent integrated by the uneasy accommodation between corporate power (and state and military power) and intellectual work" (p. 13). The critic's task is to find the appropriate place to intervene in such a world. The basis of the book's polemic lies in the belief that criticism is a political act, and that pedagogical and critical concerns are also political. The critic must clarify our "social reality" (p. 33) and get beyond the " 'substitute world' . . . that is situated squarely in the reproductive heart of Western economic life (the university) but that locates its force elsewhere, in the transcendental realm of professional competence" (p. 51). Merod's idea of consciousness stems from writers like Foucault, Jameson, and perhaps especially Noam Chomsky. The book represents a solid challenge for us to integrate this critical consciousness into our work as teachers and scholars in order to make our institutions more critically aware and democratic.

J. Hillis Miller's contribution to the year's work in theory is *The Ethics of Reading*, originally given as the Wellek Library Lectures. This brief, provocative book asks what the reader's responsibility is in the act of interpreting any narrative. "I propose to argue," says Miller, ". . . that there is a necessary ethical moment in that act of reading as such, a moment neither cognitive, nor political, nor social,

nor interpersonal, but properly and independently ethical" (p. 1).
He goes on to clarify his assumption. "In what I call 'the ethical moment' there is a claim made on the author writing the work, on the
narrator telling the story within the fiction of the novel, on the characters within the story at decisive moments of their lives, and on the
reader, teacher, or critic responding to the work" (p. 8). Miller explores his thesis in "those places where we can see an author reading
himself or herself. Writers . . . are in one way or another exemplary
readers, perhaps even of themselves" (p. 102). James's prefaces are,
for example, major texts of rereading. Miller begins with the deconstructionist assumption that language is inadequate to meet our own
or its own expectations. Each text contains, in fact, the clues as to
how it should be read and where it breaks down. The examples Miller
gives of the ethics of authors reading themselves are cogent and convincing; but for a work that seems to promise a more definitive answer to the questions it raises, this one is finally a bit disappointing
because we seem to be told that there is an ethics of reading without
being made aware of what exactly it is. Perhaps, since reading is
doomed to ambiguity by the uncertainty of language, there is only
an ethical moment or impulse but not really an ethics.

The final work in this section is something of a letdown, all the
more so because it comes from such a well-known critic and theorist.
I refer to Tzvetan Todorov's *Literature and Its Theorists: A Personal
View of Twentieth-Century Criticism* (Cornell), trans. Catherine
Porter, a "personal" work that finally seems more quirky than stimulating because of its neoconservative critical bias. The third in a
series that includes the more successful *Theories of the Symbol* and
Symbolism and Interpretation, Literature and Its Theorists tries to
find a middle ground between what the author thinks of as dogmatic
criticism and the recent criticism (mainly post-structuralist) that he
sees as being nihilistic. "To put it rather succinctly," he writes, "this
book will deal both with the meaning of some twentieth-century critical works and with the possibility of opposing nihilism without ceas-
ing to be an atheist" (p. 2). The book contains adequate summaries
of critics that meet with Todorov's approval, such as Northrop Frye,
Bakhtin, Ian Watt, and Roland Barthes, but there is scarcely a mention of Foucault, and no mention at all of Derrida, Wolfgang Iser, or
Lyotard, to name but a few. It is one thing to argue against the enemy,
but to ignore it altogether seems unproductive and unworthy of a fine
critic.

vii. Conclusion

This was another relatively undistinguished year for theory and criticism, with the exception of a few interesting works here and there. We still await a more definitive work of the new literary history, although the first volume of Gilbert and Gubar's *No Man's Land* shows much promise, as does Walter Benn Michaels's book on American Naturalism. A careful reading of *The Columbia Literary History of the United States* (1988), ed. Emory Elliott, may well be illuminating in this regard. The attack on deconstruction continues with renewed vigor following the revelations of Paul de Man's early publications in the fascist *Le Soir* (Brussels) and the anti-Semitism of at least a few of his articles. Those essays are now being published along with reassessments of his work. This situation, along with the seemingly definitive revelation of Martin Heidegger's Nazism, may unfortunately discredit a movement that has had a lot of positive influence on literary study. What will arise in its place is not yet apparent, at least to this reader. But simply to return to the old philology, the New Criticism, or the old literary history are clearly not options.

University of California, Davis

20. Foreign Scholarship

i. East European Contributions

F. Lyra

a. **Pre-Twentieth-Century Studies.** The few publications—all of them Soviet—I was able to get hold of are hardly original within American literary scholarship at large, but they are mostly new in the Soviet context. This is, for example, the case with T. D. Venediktova's article on Ralph Waldo Emerson and his art of poetry: "R. U. Emerson i iskustvo poezii" (*Filologicheskie Nauki* 1:66–69). Her opening statement that Emerson's poetry was not studied either in Russia or in the Soviet Union is indeed corroborated by Valentina Libman's bibliography, *American Literature in Russian Translation and Criticism* (see *ALS* 1977, pp. 463–64). Small wonder, up to 1975 only four of his poems were translated into Russian ("Brahma," "Forbearance," "The Snow-Storm," and "Two Rivers"). In the essay Venediktova traces Emerson's changing image of the poet from that of a "bard," "a crystal soul," "sphered and cementic with the whole" to "a cripple of God, half true, half formed," "a dull uncertain brain." She follows the evolution of his weltanschauung as reflected in the poetry and his aesthetics. In consonance with other literary historians Venediktova states that Emerson was both "romantic and beyond it"; he was "a catalyst" in the evolution of poetic art in America. Most probably space restrictions prevented her from developing her thoughts and analyses of poems; yet her essay contains the ingredients of a valuable larger contribution to the study of Emerson in the Soviet Union.

A. M. Karinskii's article "Amerikanskaya romanticheskaya utopiya" [The American Romantic Utopia] (*Problemy amerikanistiki* 4[1986]:276–94) also may be considered as a preliminary study to a larger work. The author himself suggests as much when he writes that "it would be premature to make generalizations about the specific character of the American romantic utopia"—and for that matter the anti-utopia. But his article is hardly rife with substance. Taking Alfred de Vigny's distinction between "the truth of fact" and "the truth of fiction" as a point of departure, Karinskii briefly comments on Cooper, Melville, Emerson, and Thoreau. Most of the piece is a meditation on utopianism as a characteristic component of romantic consciousness. Noting the heterogeneity and contradictions of American romanticism, he sees them as sources of tendentious misrepresentations of the movement. He briefly discusses William Barrett's *Irrational Man* as an example of such distortion.

In the third volume of *Zarubezhnaya memuarnaya i epistolyarnaya literatura* [Foreign Memoirist and Epistolary Literature], a Leningrad University serial publication issued irregularly, we find an article by A. P. Apenko ". . . Gde vstrechayetsa deistvitel'nost' i vymysl. . ." [". . . where the Actual and the Imaginary . . . meet . . ."] (pp. 26–34). The Hawthorne specialist will easily recognize the quotation as coming from "The Custom-House" of *The Scarlet Letter*. This passage echoes Hawthorne's famous entry of 13 October 1848 in his *American Notebooks*. Apenko has selected various fragments from them to demonstrate their transformation in Hawthorne's fiction, mostly his tales, and to show how the correspondences between the diary entries and the fiction elucidate Hawthorne's "creative process," "esthetic concepts," and his understanding of "truth and reality." Perspicacious though his article is, for the sake of the Soviet reader and in line with the character of a noteworthy publication devoted to autobiographical writings in world literature, Apenko might have done better by presenting a comprehensive introduction to all of Hawthorne's *Notebooks* rather than belabor a subject well served by American Hawthorne specialists.

b. The Twentieth Century. The Moscow Vysshaya Shkola press brought out a second edition of Roman Mikhailovich Samarin's retrospective collection of criticism *Zarubezhnaya Literatura* [Foreign Literature] (the first edition appeared in 1978), which contains three contributions on American letters first published in the early 1960s: "Problema naturalizma v literature SSHA i razvitie amerikanskogo romana na rubezhe XIX–XX vekov" [The Problem of Naturalism in U.S. Literature and the Development of the American Novel at the Turn of the Nineteenth and Twentieth Centuries] (pp. 307–26); "O knige V. L. Parringtona *Osnovnye techeniya amerikanskoi mysli*" [On V. L. Parrington's *Main Currents in American Thought*] (pp. 326–44); "Ernest Kheminguei i ego *Starik i more*" [Ernest Hemingway's *The Old Man and the Sea*] (pp. 344–55). The republication of the work of a rigidly dogmatic Marxist, who as late as the end of the 1950s censured Soviet critics' interest in Faulkner, demonstrates that ortho-

dox thinking habits about American literature die hard. More important, as publications of Vysshaya Shkola are addressed to university
students of literature, books like Samarin's are meant to keep up those
habits. At least Samarin's ossified Marxism did not prevent him from
viewing American naturalism as a complex movement, and its representative works with discrimination, especially Jack London's. Ideological dogma required him to judge naturalism as a whole negatively,
particularly features derived from Spencer and Nietzsche. Only works
rooted in American working-class reality receive recognition, as
Samarin's basic aesthetic criterion is socialist realism. He extends
qualified approval of naturalism only to the degree that it contributed
to the groundworks of socialist realism.

Samarin's piece on *Main Currents* is a reprint of his "Introduction"
to its Russian translation, which appeared in 1962. By normal critical
standards an introduction is supposed to recommend, even if critically, but Samarin condemns. Just about the only thing he finds valuable in the work is the "great factual material" Parrington managed
to include. It was his bourgeois liberalism, of course, that prevented
him from producing a good literary history.

The essay on Hemingway is less about the masterpiece than a
commemorative survey article about the writer's entire output, which,
conventionalist that Samarin was (he died in 1974), he viewed in
evolutionary fashion: each successive major work marks a new stage
in the writer's development leading toward a perfection of his social
realist art. Never mind, for instance, the contradictions in *For Whom
the Bell Tolls*; unlike some other Soviet critics, Samarin at least had
enough tact not to accuse Hemingway of ideological deficiencies.
Thus *The Old Man and the Sea*—a few minor misgivings notwithstanding—emerges as a "testimony of inexhaustible richness of new
themes and new artistic means hidden in the realistic art of our
century."

In contrast to Samarin's stale essay on Hemingway, V. L. Makhlin's "O kul'turno-istoricheskom kontekste tvorchestva Khemingueya"
[On the Cultural-Historical Context of Hemingway's Work] (*Vest-
nik Moskovskogo Universiteta* 9:33–40) provides a thoughtful albeit
diffuse examination of Hemingway's poetics whose core Makhlin has
found in the writer's concepts of myth and hero as presented in his
letter to Malcolm Cowley occasioned by the publication of *The Old
Man and the Sea*. Makhlin's intrinsic approach constitutes a welcome
departure from the critical standards of socialist realism by which

the worth of a work of art, for example, *For Whom the Bell Tolls,*
is adjudged ideologically deficient. To do proper justice to the Soviet
scholar's contribution, one would have to compare his interpretation
with that of, say, Ivan Kashkin or Samarin. Such a comparison, however, would require a separate paper.

In "Novelistika v tvorchestve U. Folknera" [The Story in W.
Faulkner's Work] O. Yu. Tangyan writes on the theme that has been
thoroughly explored by Faulkner scholarship. Tangyan, however,
introduces a note that in the context of Soviet criticism sounds re-
freshingly new: he calls attention to the Old Testament as an important source of Faulkner's art and backs up the observation with the
writer's statement made during "Colloquies at Nagano Seminar"
(*Faulkner at Nagano,* p. 45). The Soviet scholar seems to be unaware
of the controversy over the question whether Faulkner should be regarded as a failed novelist or a successful short story writer. Predictably, for Tangyan he is the latter.

A. Mulyarchik's "Khudozhestvennaya literatura SSHA sevondnya:
Svet i teni" [American Literature Today: Light and Shadows] (*SSHA*
[1986]) reached me in German translation through *Kunst und Literatur* (6:731–38). Mulyarchik appears to be the Soviet Union's most
fastidious chronicler of and commentator on American fiction. In
the present article he concentrates on what he deems the most significant novels from 1983 through 1985. He critically synopsizes
John Updike's *Beck Is Back,* then reviews Philip Roth's *The Anatomy
Lesson,* deploring Roth's departure from realism, the "elimination"
of important social contents so characteristic of his early work. Norman Mailer's *Ancient Evenings* and *Tough Guys Don't Dance* get the
most extensive commentary. Both works are failures as they reveal a
cleft between idea and artistic realization. The former lacks "important spiritual problems," the latter contains neither social context nor
philosophical questions. Joyce Carol Oates's *Mysteries of Winter-
thurn* is also dismissed as a flop. The idea underlying it is interesting,
but its transformation into fiction causes her tremendous difficulties.
Mulyarchik passes a similar verdict on Joan Didion's *Democracy.* He
blames her for not having drawn a parallel with Henry Adams's
Democracy! Despite some reservations about Gore Vidal's liberal
democratic views, Mulyarchik acclaims his *Lincoln;* though Vidal
"fails to subject his hero to a consistent class interpretation," at least
"he tries to protect his spiritual legacy from the continued abuses of

conservative ideologues." Finally, he gives fair but short shrift to Helen H. Santmeyer's *And Ladies of the Club.*

In another article, "Realizm 'sub'ektivnoi prozy' v poslevoennoi literature SSHA (konets 40kh—nachalo 60kh godov)" [The Realism of "Subjective Prose" in Postwar American Literature] (*Problemy amerikanistiki* 4[1986]:294–314), Mulyarchik demonstrates basically a positive attitude toward subjective fiction as it contains components of realism so highly regarded by Soviet Marxist criticism. Having thrashed out some terms with which various critics and historians have described postwar American prose, Mulyarchik proceeds to analyze a number of subjective novels which he treats as "stages" in the evolution of "centripetal poetics." The subjective novels deserve to be admitted to the realm of realist literature on account of their protagonists' opposition to or victimization by American bourgeois society. From such a critical angle he is able to connect *On the Road; The Grass Harp; The Catcher in the Rye; Go Tell It on the Mountain; Lie Down in Darkness; The Assistant; Herzog; The Poorhouse Fair; Rabbit, Run*, but he views them with highly disproportionate attention. Whereas Salinger, Bellow, and Updike get several pages, Kerouac, Capote, Baldwin, Styron, and Malamud receive only a few paragraphs each. Whether Mulyarchik's recognition of the authors' works will invigorate their reception in the Soviet Union remains an open question. All the discussed writers are in various degrees represented in Russian translation presently, but a check with Valentina Libman's bibliography reveals that in 1975, the last year the bibliography covers, when all the authors had long been well established in their country, only *The Catcher in the Rye* and *The Grass Harp* were available in Russian.

The same issue of *Problemy amerikanistiki* contains a contribution by T. D. Venediktova, "Intellektual'nyi geroi v sovremenoi amerikanskoi proze" [The Intellectual Hero in Contemporary American Prose] (pp. 261–75). The author recognizes a link between Emerson's "The American Scholar" and the intellectual academic protagonists of many postwar American novels, but she does not explore the recognition at length, confining her analysis to the main characters of just four novels: Robert Penn Warren's *A Place To Come To*, Saul Bellow's *Herzog*, Norman Mailer's *An American Dream*, and John Gardner's *Mickelsson's Ghosts.* According to Venediktova, the fate of the intellectual hero in the contemporary American novel suggests that the traditional mental individualism of the American intellectual is now widely considered destructive for the hero's personality. It is a pity that she terminates her perceptive article on a flat note: "It is difficult to predict the subsequent fate of the intellectual protagonist in the American novel. To a large extent it will be shaped by the degree of social maturity of the American intelligentsia as a whole."

With the serial publication of Vladimir Nabokov's third novel, *Zashchita Luzhina* [The Luzhin Defence, 1929]—which was translated into English in 1964 as *The Defence*—in the periodical *Moskva* (1986), and a handful of poems in a couple of other periodicals, Nabokov ceased to be taboo among the Soviet literary establishment. To be sure, a few critics had discussed him earlier on various occasions, but their comments left little doubt as to his value. Thus, in his book *Spor idet o cheloveka* [The Dispute Is About Man] A. Mulyarchik connected the author of *Ada* with the black humorists John Barth and Thomas Pynchon, whose works generate negative associations in the Soviet Union, and considered *Lolita* a product of "the hollow period of postwar American history." Now N. Anastas'ev in an extensive article "Fenomen Vladimira Nabokova" [The Vladimir Nabokov Phenomenon] (*Inostrannaya Literatura* 5:210–23) announces his "return home." But Anastas'ev refuses to grant him either a Russian or an American identity. Drawing on both biographical and literary sources, he maintains that since childhood Nabokov had been repeatedly overcome with a "feeling of homelessness." Nabokov's identity, says Anastas'ev, is that of "a cosmopolitan." Traditionally, this term is charged with negative implications in Soviet thought, but Anastas'ev insists on its positive meaning. As a cosmopolitan, Nabokov should be regarded in the same class of writers as Joyce, Kafka, and Virginia Woolf, and he treats Nabokov's literary legacy with censorious discrimination risking the prediction that as "the author of *Ada* and *Look at the Harlequins* he will not live for long . . . but as the author of *The Defence, The Gift* and *Lolita* . . . he has a chance to stay on."

The Polish publication of John Hawkes's *The Lime Twig* and *The Blood Oranges* as well as Philip Roth's *Portnoy's Complaint* in 1986 induced Marcin Cienski to argue in "Hawkes i Roth: Metafora i model" [Hawkes and Roth: Metaphor and Model] (*Literatura na swiecie* 5–6:547–65) that both authors, who appear uncomparable, can be related by identifying their universal and American features.

The same issue of the periodical is almost entirely filled with material of and on American literature. Most of the space is given to Henry Miller; apart from translations of "Via Dieppe-Newhaven" and extracts from *Sexus* and *Tropic of Cancer*, there are several articles by both Polish and foreign critics about Miller, among them extensive fragments of George Orwell's "Inside the Whale," George Wickes's interview with the writer, and a chronicle. Miller is not a newcomer in Poland. As far back as 1964 there appeared in Polish translation *The Smile at the Foot of the Ladder*, later *The Colossus of Maroussi* and *A Devil in Paradise*. In addition, the volume contains an article by Elzbieta Oleksy on Walker Percy, "Alienacja Walkera Percy" [Walker Percy's Alienations] (pp. 422–29); her interview with the writer—a remarkable feat, as for many years Percy has shunned interviews; and a translation from his *Lancelot*. There are also translations of poems by Ezra Pound, Robinson Jeffers, and W. S. Merwin. Dorota Glowacka presents John Kennedy Toole and his *A Confederacy of Dunces* in "Gargantuiczna tragikomedia" [A Gargantuan Tragicomedy] (pp. 488–98) with translated fragments of the work. This part of the volume appropriately concludes with an essay by Anna Zniewierowska, "Poludnie czy Niepoludnie" [Is There a South?] (pp. 495–504), on the question whether there still is a southern literature. Her answer is ambiguous.

The wealth of the American material in the issue of *Literatura na swiecie*, whose editor and contributors (scholars as well as critics) have in the past repeatedly shown an abiding interest in American literature, seems to disprove the basic argument of my article "Watpliwa gościnność: O stanie recepcji literatury amerykańskiej w Polsce" [Questionable Hospitality: On the Reception of American Literature in Poland] (*Przeglad Humanistyczny* 7–8:187–97). In it I criticize the self-complacency widespread among the Polish literary establishment concerning its "hospitality" toward foreign national literatures, American included. The article exemplifies glaring gaps in the knowledge of American letters, the slowness in the reception of various American writers: e.g., *The Scarlet Letter*, which unabridged and well translated came out only in 1987—an extreme case to be sure. Still, the pace at which publishers bring out a translation nowadays never runs shorter than three years from the time of the original work's appearance, which has happened only with very few books; most of them appear after a lapse of many more years. For

balance, I point out past and present achievements, e.g., six editions
of *Moby-Dick* since 1954, marked improvement in the quality of
translations over the last 30 years, a qualitative increase in scholarship and criticism, partly documented in Jack R. Cohn's and Alina
Nowacka's *A Guide to the Study of American Literature in Poland*
(see *ALS* 1982, pp. 462–63).

Janusz Semrau's significant *American Self-Conscious Fiction of
the 1960s and 1970s: Donald Barthelme, Robert Coover, Ronald
Sukenick* (Poznan:Uniwersytet Adama Mickiewicza, 1986) became
available only in 1987. He presents the topic with lucid sophistication, although the structure of his study is schematic. After the introductory chapter (pp. 9–25), which deals with the cluster of concepts
characterizing (or attempting to characterize) contemporary fiction
(he seems to be most comfortable with the term "metafiction"),
Semrau develops the subject matter in three chapters, each devoted
to one of the writers. They receive nearly the same degree of attention: Barthelme (pp. 26–63), Coover (64–98), Sukenick (pp. 99–133).
The absence of spacious discrimination correlates with Semrau's
evasion of value judgments. But the various aspects and forms of
artistic self-consciousness peculiar to each writer are well presented.
Put in a nutshell, Barthelme's self-consciousness relies on "verbal
surfaces and linguistic terseness," Coover's on "structural and stylistic
elaboration," Sukenick's on "formal self-reflectivity." Consulted by a
reader uninitiated into their work, Semrau's study would in all likelihood prompt him to perceive Coover's type of self-consciousness
least prone to charges of narcissism, solipsism, or sterile avant-
gardism.

The title of Andrzej Weselinski's "Henry James, Graham Greene
and the International Theme: Two Modes of Writing" (*Acta Philologica* 14:148–66) tantalizes, but the text delivers less than it promises, if only because Weselinski limits his analysis to three works:
The Portrait of a Lady, The Golden Bowl, and *The Quiet American.*
The gist of the article is best revealed by the author himself: "The
three novels reveal . . . the movement of the pendulum of literary
fashion: from the pole which can be designated as modernist, symbolist, writerly, and metaphoric, towards the pole which is characteristically antimodernist, readerly, and metonymic, with a marked
tendency to express analogy through simile rather than metaphor,
and, last but not least, which is oriented towards the wider area of
social and political reality."

c. **Miscellaneous.** Aleksandr Nikolaevich Nikolyukin's *Vzaimosvy-azi literatur Rosii i SSHA: Turgenev, Tolstoy, Dostoevsky i Amerika* [Interrelations of Russian and American Literatures: Turgenev, Tolstoy, Dostoyevsky and America] (Moscow: Nauka) is a follow-up of his *Literary Relations Between Russia and the USA* (see *ALS* 1982, pp. 460–61). The present study deals more extensively with subject matter closer to the literary scholar's home turf than the earlier volume. Nikolyukin's task has been backed up by numerous scholars who have already explored various fragments and phases of Russian-American literary relations. He acknowledges his debts to them in numerous footnotes, but his book lacks a bibliography—a serious drawback, if not a deficiency.

Nikolyukin opens the study with remarks on the concepts of romanticism and realism—yet another manifestation of the spell-like power these concepts hold on Soviet critics. This is also true of "typology," which he considers a key procedure in the investigation of interrelations. Though his typology does not elicit deep insights into either nation's 19th-century literature, at least it may stimulate close rereading of the works of N. A. Polevoy, A. A. Bestuzhev-Marlinsky, A. Pogorelsky, V. F. Odoevsky, N. V. Gogol on the one side of the divide and Irving, Hawthorne, Melville, Poe on the other. Nikolyukin handles them in a highly selective way so that much of his discussion is incidental rather than comprehensive, and complementary to other scholars' earlier research, including his own. But his general opinions on the similarities of and differences between American and Russian romanticism seem appropriate as are the marginal observations on the absence of a truly epic picture of Russia in the country's romantic literature comparable to that of Cooper's or Scott's, though from the beginning Russian critics kept commenting on the similarities between Cooper's and M. N. Zagorkin's as well as I. I. Lazhechnikov's romances. Lermontov's dream of creating a historical trilogy on Russia after the manner of Cooper's first four Leatherstocking Tales never materialized because of his untimely death.

Turning to the main topic, Nikolyukin examines it in three lengthy monographic chapters devoted to "Turgenev and American Writers" (pp. 77–131), "Leo Tolstoy and America (The Russian Writer and American Literature)" (pp. 132–237), "Dostoevsky's Heritage and the Literature of the USA" (pp. 238–84). He is chiefly concerned with external histories of the mutual relationships and with the mediators, both critics and translators, at least with some of them, such as Nathan H. Dole, Isabel Florence Hapgood, Jeremiah Curtin, Constance Garnett, and Eugene Schuyler, the last of whom occupies a special place in American-Russian literary relations as the one who introduced all three Russian classics to the English-speaking world. One wishes Nikolyukin had also told us more about the other translators. Overall, the American side of the relationship interests Nikolyukin more than the Russian, which corresponds to the historical literary situation: none of the Russian writers found American literature as congenial to their needs, except Tolstoy with regard to the transcendentalists, as W. D. Howells or Henry James found the Russian novelists to theirs. However, Nikolyukin blames James mildly for having only partially understood Turgenev whose "poetic realism developed and strengthened the realistic current in American literature at the end of the nineteenth century and decisively blunted the impact of French naturalism" (p. 123). Nikolyukin perhaps overrates Turgenev's role in post-Civil War American letters, but there is no question that thanks to Howells and James, Turgenev became the first Russian writer to be so widely accepted in America. He was soon followed by Tolstoy. The Soviet scholar is particularly intrigued by the question "why have Americans discovered Tolstoy's artistic world earlier than writers and readers of western Europe" (p. 132)—a rather irrelevant issue which Nikolyukin, fortunately, examines by probing the circumstances which account for the Americans' "discovery" of Tolstoy. Another question Nikolyukin is interested in concerns the reasons for Tolstoy's intense preoccupation with and enthusiasm for the transcendentalists, and his attitude toward Whitman and vice versa. But the bulk of the chapter deals with the Americans' reception of Tolstoy. American contemporary writers saw to it that he remained in touch with American letters. They kept sending him their works which Nikolyukin gleaned from V. F. Bulgakov's manuscript deposited in the writer's museum at Yasna Polyana, describing Tolstoy's library. Besides works of Poe, Hawthorne, Longfellow, Harriet Beecher Stowe, Emerson, and Thoreau, the manuscript lists books of Bellamy, Garland, Bret Harte, Sinclair, Twain, Traubel, Hearn, Howells, and Whitman. Nikolyukin asserts that about each of them and Tolstoy one could devote a study.

The chapter on Dostoevsky is entirely devoted to the American side of the relationship. Nikolyukin accounts for his late arrival in America, and Eugene Schuyler's and Randolph Bourne's as well as Constance Garnett's roles in his presence there; and he gives 20 pages (pp. 264–84) to "Dostoevsky and Faulkner: Typology of Confluence and Differences." It is the only literary relationship examined by Nikolyukin in depth.

Throughout Nikolyukin's work the American writers' interest in and appreciation of the Russians appear most often in the form of testimonials which occasionally read like a roll call in American literary history from the middle of the 19th century to our day, including Mailer, Styron, Heller, Joyce Carol Oates, and Mary McCarthy.

In the concluding chapter 5, "The American Writers of the Second Half of the XIX Century in Russia," Nikolyukin deals with the Russians' critical reception of Bret Harte (pp. 285–97), Twain (pp. 297–301), Henry James, Howells, Harriet Beecher Stowe (pp. 302–7), Bellamy (pp. 307–18), and Whitman (pp. 318–27). The chapter provides flesh and blood to Valentina Libman's bibliography, although he refers to her work only once. Nikolyukin closes the study with a chronological listing of Russian writers' works in American editions between 1867–1900 (pp. 328–37). A full bibliographical description of them would have been more useful to literary scholarship than the sheer enumeration of the authors, titles of their works in English, and the translators' names with most of which only the first and middle initials are given—an irritating practice in Soviet publications.

University of Warsaw

ii. French Contributions

Marc Chénetier

There is one item for review that looms large and sadly luminous on the French scene this year, given the untimely death of its author in the Spring of 1988. In effect, this foremost of French Americanists, Claude Richard, the editor of *Delta* (Montpellier), published in 1987 a volume of essays of exceptional quality entitled *Lettres Américaines* (Alinéa). His book reads the word "letters" in many ways, in its reference to literature as a whole, of course, but also in its epistolary and typographic meanings. Two essays on Edgar Allan Poe's Dupin and the motif of the "telltale heart" frame the collection, which includes studies of Hawthorne's *The Scarlet Letter*, Melville's *Moby-Dick* (this essay being an admiring reaction to Philippe Jaworski's

Le désert et l'empire reviewed here last year [see *ALS 1986*, p. 419]),
Thoreau's *Walden*, and Pynchon's *The Crying of Lot 49*. The collection constitutes an astonishing meditation on the role played by signs
and letters in American literature, be they Hester Prynne's *A*, Melville's hieroglyphic whale, or Poe's purloined document. Nourished
by contemporary philosophy and epistemology, admirably written, it
stands as a remarkable illustration of the most original and interesting
contributions French criticism can offer. Starting from the transcendentalist interrogations on the function of the letter, its remaining
powers as a sacred glyph, the problems posed by the act of naming,
Richard converses with Jacques Lacan, Jacques Derrida, Michel
Serres, and others in a highly personal voice and in ways that make
their influence totally unobtrusive. Gradually, an American poetics
of the letter emerges, illuminating both the interrogations of 19th-
century writers and the inheritance they bequeathed to their 20th-
century followers. Fittingly enough, this book is authored by a man
who spent over 20 years of his life exploring the thought of Edgar
Allan Poe, whose complete works he finished editing for Laffont
shortly before he left the French community of American literary
scholars cruelly and irreplaceably bereft. The collected works of
Edgar Allan Poe will thus be published in French in one single volume
next year, accompanied by his enlightening notes. There is some hope
that Claude Richard's book will come out in the United States some
time in the near future; it constitutes his last gift to a literary and
academic community for whom he was a constant fountainhead of
energy, the subject of its admiration and pride.

a. **Bibliography.**   Five items are to be mentioned in this general
section this year. Of great use to researchers is *A Descriptive Catalogue of French Periodicals of English and American Studies* (no. 1),
published by the University of Montpellier. This brochure will be
revised every year and lists over 50 journals dedicated to research in
the field of Anglophone studies. It can be ordered from Publications
de la recherche, Université de Montpellier, BP 5043, 34032, Montpellier Cedex. Jean-Marie Bonnet's "American Studies in France,"
published in *ASInt* (25, ii:20–40), includes a literary section (pp. 21–
27) and a selected bibliography of French research in the field of the
literature of the United States (pp. 34–36). The issue of *JSSE* (no. 9)
dedicated to Peter Taylor contains a bibliographical checklist that
covers the years 1934–86, and the issue of *Delta* (24) dealing with

André Dubus includes a selected bibliography. Finally, Michel Fabre's *AFRAM Newsletter* (no. 25) contains its usual wealth of information on Afro-American studies in France.

b. **Colonial Literature.** In collaboration with Professor Gay Wilson Allen, an old Whitman accomplice, Roger Asselineau coauthored *St John de Crèvecoeur: The Life of an American Farmer* (Viking), a biography of the "cultivateur américain," for which Professor Asselineau was able to investigate new biographical sources in the Normandy area. In "De la révolution à la contre-révolution? Gouverneur Morris, ambassadeur subversif" (*Les Etats-Unis: Conformismes et Dissidences*, Actes du GRENA, pp. 103–15), Serge Ricard explores the ambiguities of the stands taken by Gouverneur Morris and wonders whether he was not, to take up the words of Robespierre, among those who wanted "a revolution without revolution."

c. **19th Century.** The one salient article in this research area is Yves Carlet's "Epiphanie, Jérémiade, Prophétie: le Transcendantalisme et l'Histoire." It was published in a special issue of *RFEA* dedicated to the relationships entertained by history and fiction, which I edited with Pierre-Yves Pétillon (31:65–78) and for which André Bleikasten provided a most interesting theoretical framing piece: "Roman vrai, vrai roman, ou l'indestructible récit" (pp. 7–17) where the questioning of narrative and its impact on historical writing is assessed. In his article Carlet claims that revisionist and postrevisionist criticism in the United States has striven to re-Americanize the Transcendentalists by describing them both as the heirs of Puritanism and as the founders of the American Renaissance. He offers to revise this vision in his turn by claiming that Emerson's view of history is a form of "romantic paramnesia" and that the romantic opposition of myth versus history enabled the Transcendentalists to develop a strategy of disengagement not so much in line with Puritan orthodoxy but rather with the antinomian and separatist traditions.

Also in *RFEA* (31), Marianne Debouzy discusses Norris's *Mc-Teague* from the standpoint of history and ideology (pp. 31–40). The novel's relationship to its period is from this double angle a complex and contradictory one. On the one hand, Norris is heavily influenced by biological determinism, social Darwinism, and the cult of true womanhood. On the other, the story of McTeague and Trina shows the values of the time to be traps: the virtues of thrift and industry turn into perversions, the quest for money glorified by the Gospel of Wealth drives people to brutality and crime. Debouzy wonders whether the novel is not to be read as an indirect indictment of the greed and violence that prevailed in American society at that time. The only other article on this period that deserves a mention here is Roger Asselineau's "Innocence et expérience dans l'oeuvre de Henry James," a general piece published in *Le sud et autres points cardinaux*, ed. Jeanne-Marie Santraud (Sorbonne), pp. 65–74.

d. **Early 20th-Century Fiction.** The works of Willa Cather go on being translated into French (Editions Ramsay), and four novels are now out in new translations: *Death Comes for the Archbishop, My Mortal Enemy, O Pioneers*, and *A Lost Lady*. It is mostly with the first of these novels that Jean-Loup Bourget's article, "La théologie mêlée de Willa Cather" (*Caliban* 24:97–108) deals. It concludes that Cather's Catholicism in *Death Comes for the Archbishop* is both aesthetic and moral, that "the Catholic theme," to take up Edith Lewis's expression, is used to give voice to the nostalgia of a preindustrial age, and that the past is far from being totally idealized.

Moving on to the 30s, an article on Dashiell Hammett, whose *The Glass Key* was on the syllabus of Agrégation in 1986, appeared in *RFEA* (34), an issue otherwise given to "American Philosophy." Catherine Vieilledent's "Le *tough guy* et le déni des profondeurs" (pp. 553–64) argues that "hard-boiled fiction" deals with the becoming of "interior man" inherited from the 19th century. Comparing Hammett's and Hemingway's "objective" technique, Vieilledent proposes that its obscuring of psychological motivation subverts the hermeneutic code central to detective fiction. The "tough guy" dismisses those depths which foster explanatory commentary and thus questions the paradigmatic function of analytical discourse. A series of other articles on Hammett appeared in *Dashiell Hammett–Walker Percy* (vide infra for the latter), ed. Jeanne-Marie Santraud and Jean Rouberol (Sorbonne). Santraud introduces the volume with "Du Sang à la Une" (pp. 11–14), an investigation into the reasons for which police novels are read; the world of the detective story is then thematically explored by Marc Saporta's "Dashiell Hammett: Condamnation en appel" (pp. 25–50), Marcelle Vincent's "L'Univers de Dashiell Hammett" (pp. 51–58), and A. Sanford Wolf and Michèle Wolf's "Gangsters, politicians, prohibition and the 20s" (pp. 59–79). There is, as usual under these skies, a wealth of Faulkner research.

Ever-active Michel Gresset edited two volumes of international proceedings: one in 1986, which I could not discuss last year, and another in 1987. The first, *Faulkner and History*, ed. Javier Coy and
Gresset (Salamanca), contains 14 papers delivered at the Third International Faulkner Colloquium, four being French contributions.
Gresset's keynote address bore on "Faulkner's War with Wars" (pp.
13–28) and dealt with Faulkner's writings on various wars and his
fear that war was indeed not only bad in itself but bad for writing too.
François Pitavy's "William Faulkner: Fiction as Historiography" (pp.
39–50) asserts that "although Faulkner does not attempt to write history or even historical fiction . . . some of the contributions of the
Annales school derive from considerations which appear quite close
to problems Faulkner specifically addresses in his fiction." In " 'A
furious beating of hollow drums toward nowhere': Faulkner, Time
and History" (pp. 77–96), André Bleikasten examines the importance
that the narrative function has for Faulkner. History and myth in this
perspective fulfill complementary necessities, even though in places
the meditation on myth "ends in a total denial of history." "All we
can know about history," according to Bleikasten's reading of Faulkner, "is its turbulence and its impetus, the headlong rush, the frantic
race." Hence the title of his article. "History and Family Stories in
Faulkner from *Absalom, Absalom!* to *The Mansion*" is Jacques
Pothier's theme. He argues that even if [Faulkner] claimed that "we
aren't specifically concerned with [history]," history was, first, a reason why fiction writing was so important to people like him, and,
second, one of the important devices he used to turn his stories into
myth, concluding that "the mythical treatment of simple stories
through the contrapuntal use of history may be one of the most vivid
parts of Faulkner's heritage today."

The other collection, published in 1987, is *Faulkner: ATNP*, papers
from an International Faulkner Symposium held at Izu, Japan, in
April 1985. Outside of Gresset's presentation of his "French view"
(pp. 13–27), it contains three French contributions: Gresset's own
self-explanatory "A Public Man's Private Voice: Faulkner's Letters
to Else Jonsson" (pp. 61–73), an answer, no doubt, to André Bleikasten's "A Private Man's Public Voice" (pp. 45–60), which explores the
world of Faulkner's public pronouncements, and François Pitavy's
"William Faulkner and the American Dream: A Furious Affirmation"
(pp. 74–90), an attempt to follow the evolution of Faulkner's political
views.

440 Foreign Scholarship

In this very productive period Gresset also published two separate articles: "La mise en (s)cène du fantasme dans *As I Lay Dying*" (*Tropisme* 3:169–79) and "Faulkner's Self-Portraits" (*FJ* 2:2–13), while Bleikasten contributed "The Closed Society and Its Subjects" to *New Essays on Light in August*, ed. Michael Millgate (Cambridge). To remain with the South while moving on toward the contemporary period, I note two interesting pieces on Eudora Welty. Jean Rouberol's "Aspects du mythe dans 'The Wide Net' de Eudora Welty" (*Le Sud et autres points cardinaux*), pp. 51–55, and Danièle Pitavy-Souques's "A Blazing Butterfly: The Modernity of Eudora Welty" in *Welty: A Life in Literature*, ed. Albert J. Devlin (Mississippi).

e. **Contemporary Fiction.** The South (albeit less "deep") looms large, of course, in the work of Peter Taylor, to which *JSSE* devoted its entire ninth issue. Unfortunately, however, this issue contains only one article by a French Americanist: Simone Vauthier's "Trying to Ride the Tiger," a reading of "First Heat."

The other contemporary southern writer to appear in this year's critical readings is Walker Percy, whose presence on the syllabus of Agrégation in 1986 triggered a series of articles published in *Dashiell Hammett-Walker Percy*. Introduced by Jean Rouberol (pp. 83–84), the Percy portion includes four articles by French scholars: Peggy Castex's "Medicine and Malady as Metaphor in Walker Percy's Fiction" (pp. 85–102), Daniel Charbonnier's "La catastrophe et ses signes dans *The Moviegoer* de Walker Percy" (pp. 103–14), Colette Gerbaud's "*The Moviegoer* ou l'Homo Americanus et le 'Sombre Pélerinage Terrestre'" (pp. 123–44), and Rouberol's own "Espace et mouvement dans *The Moviegoer*" (pp. 145–51).

Offshoots of Anne Foata's dissertation on Andrew Lytle continued to appear this year with two articles: one was "American History and the Edenic Myth: Andrew Lytle's Images of the Garden of the World" (*Cahiers de l'Université d'Avignon* 5:213–42); the other, very much on the same theme, was "Les Etats-Unis dans l'oeuvre de Andrew Lytle: la vision historique" (*RFEA* 33:391–403); in it Foata examines the output of this other Tennessee writer as "literature of memory."

André Dubus was born in the South, even though, as he might put it, "We don't live here anymore." His work is at the center of what may be one of the last issues of *DeltaES* (24), once the remainder of the program planned by Claude Richard comes to an end. Edited by Patrick Samway, it contains an unpublished piece by

Dubus, "Blessings" (pp. 1–20), and two articles by French researchers. Annie Escuret gives her reading of "The Doctor" ("Une nouvelle
d'André Dubus: "The Doctor" ou le pont, le flot et l'enfant," pp. 109–
26), while Simone Vauthier reads "Sorrowful Mysteries," a story she
places "beyond realism" (pp. 127–49), Dubus being in her eyes a
writer who simultaneously transcends naturalism and modernism
without being "experimental."

Being far more "experimental" is the reputation of writers such as
John Barth and Donald Barthelme. Of the latter, Claude Massu has
read "At the Tolstoy Museum" in order to demonstrate that there lies
in this story a speculation on the architecture of text itself ("Les
architectures du texte," *Fabula* 9:21–30). Of the former, Françoise
Sammarcelli has been for years closely examining the mammoth
LETTERS. She reported twice on her findings this year. In *RFEA*
(31:93–104) her essay, " 'Cliothérapie,' historiographie, discours ro-
manesque: pour une aporie de l'interprétation," attempts to show
how the novel in question radically reorients the classical relationship
between history and fiction. She argues that "shifting from the uncertain representation of the real inside the fiction to the notion of the
real as fiction," the novel uses historical discourse as a metaphor of
fiction. In *RFEA* (32:171–82) Sammarcelli tries to demonstrate that
"the discomposure of the reader" is achieved in *LETTERS* through
the external and internal functioning of intertextuality ("Mise en
scène d'une manipulation"). In the same issue of *RFEA* Nicole Bensoussan ("Gore Vidal ou la pensée visuelle," pp. 163–70) analyzes the
impact on Vidal's prose of the visual arts. Influenced by the movies
and movie scripts, and therefore favorable to an explosion of the
structures of traditional fiction, Vidal remains attached to literary
values that seem to gainsay that position, promoting the novel as "the
purest form of art." One will have recognized here the "moral" stand
for which John Gardner became (in)famous. This "ghost of the ideal"
seems to haunt Mickelsson in his novel *Mickelsson's Ghosts* (1982),
and Catherine Chauche ("Mickelsson et le spectre de l'idéal," *RFEA*
33:377–90) explores the psychological and philosophical facets of
such a position, concluding that the balance Mickelsson achieves is a
most precarious one.

Other analyses and presentations of contemporary prose writers
include Hélène Christol's "Dissidences noires et guerre du Vietnam:
Bloods de Wallace Terry" (*Les Etats-Unis*, pp. 131–44); Marie-Claude
Profit's study of James Purdy's "Mrs. Benson," in *Visions Critiques*

(No. 3 bis); and Michel Turpin's "Bernard Malamud" ("Universalia 87," *Encyclopaedia Universalis*, Paris). It is also to be noted that two previously unpublished pieces by American Jewish writers were used to illustrate a new series of travel books (*Amérique des Villes*), published by Autrement in Paris. Boston gives Mark Mirsky an opportunity to explain how each of its streets has its own accent ("A chaque rue son accent," *Boston*, pp. 5–17), while the volume on New York features a delightfully fantastic piece by Jerome Charyn ("Les mésaventures de Fantômas," pp. 5–17). Another previously unpublished piece, by Robert Coover this time, graces *RFEA* 31:119–20; "in answer to the question 'Why do you write?'" Coover lists in poetic form the reasons he feels he can give for practicing his art.

Finally, let me mention the fact that a writer much too neglected in the United States, William Spackman, has just been honored in France: the translation of his *A Presence with Secrets* (*L'Ombre d'une Présence*) by Bernard Turle received the Prix Maurice-Edgar Coindreau for 1987.

f. **Poetry.** The *Revue Française d'Etudes Américaines* welcomed more than its usual share of articles on American poets this year. Pierre Deflaux in a piece on E. E. Cummings's *The Enormous Room* ("*The Enormous Room* de e. e. cummings: écriture d'une aventure ou aventure d'une écriture," *RFEA* 32:151–62), taking his cue from Jean Ricardou, describes the book at a "specific product of the Lost Generation," seeing in it a genuine autobiographical document as well as a stylistic experiment, escaping all definition. Also thematic in scope is Jean-Michel Rabaté's "Pound populiste?" (*RFEA* 31:41–52); there are, he says, "very few traces of real Populism" in Pound's forebears' historical views; Pound indeed sees his own delirium triggered by a return to the European origins of the movement; his "populism is underpinned by a mixture of totalitarianism and popular themes," and one should be careful to "draw the line between popular paranoia and authentic populism." Taffy Moore, who published a book on Marianne Moore in 1986, now returns to the subject in "Marianne Moore: The Raw Material of Poetry" (*RFEA*, 32:197–204), in which she posits that her poetry anticipates the stylistic and thematic concerns of postmodern literature. Also Pierre Lagayette, who defended his long dissertation on the work of Robinson Jeffers last year, now has published "Mort et création poétique chez Robinson Jeffers: l'exemple de Tamar" (*EA* 40:400–12); and *RFEA* (33:436–45) published, in an essay by Lagayette, the answers he had received from a host of contemporary poets (among whom are Cid Corman, Allen Ginsberg, Galway Kinnell, Denise Levertov, Czeslaw Milosz, Lawrance Clark Powell, Gary Snyder, Diane Wakoski, and Kenneth White) on their current assessment of the recluse of Carmel ("Robinson Jeffers: la redécouverte").

In *Multilinguisme et multiculturalisme: Diversité régionale*, ed. Jean Béranger (*Annales du CRAA*) Yves-Charles Grandjeat wrote on "Langages et images dans la poésie nuyoricaine" (pp. 199–214), while the themes of "Nuyorican" poetry were his subject in "De l'aliénation à la dissidence: les poètes nuyoricains" (*Les Etats-Unis*, pp. 59–76). Finally, in an article featured in *RFEA* (32:205–14), "Le rudimentaire et le primitif dans l'oeuvre poétique de George Oppen," Alain Suberchicot contends that "Oppen is no mere rhetorician." "His command of language," Suberchicot writes, "transcends technicalities, and dismisses psychology of the self as a prime mover of poetic creation." Distrusting imagination, Oppen wishes to explore "unsophisticated aspects of American and Mexican life."

g. **Theater.** The relative dearth of theatrical commentaries traditionally bewailed here is illustrated this year by the presence of only two, but these are most interesting, articles. Liliane Kerjan in "La comédie musicale: sources et limites du théâtre américain" (*RFEA* 32:227–34) may have an answer to the shortage in her subtitle. She describes musical comedy as the projection, even the tangible fulfillment of the American dream. Originally scanty, she says, musical comedy has now become an elaborate hybrid transposition of secular tragic choices and is increasingly regarded by the profession as the great indigenous American art form. Philippe Rouyer sees "A new kind of American writing" in David Mamet's plays (*RFEA* 32:215–26) because of Mamet's poetic use of marginal and everyday language. Mamet's theater thus becomes both vehicle and theme. Mamet, Rouyer argues, "avoids behaviorist psychology; by resorting to the theater-within-the-theater, the writing-within-the-writing techniques, he gives its concise, patterned and carefully-wrought language, which calls upon crude vocabulary, a truly creative dimension."

h. **Ethnic Literature.** The report on French contributions to the study of ethnic literature this year must fall under two headings, corresponding, first, to a list of individual analyses of black literary production, second, to the description of a volume of essays on multiculturalism.

Michel Fabre, as usual, leads the field in the first category with two articles. One deals with Ralph Ellison: "From *Native Son* to *Invisible Man*: Some notes on Ralph Ellison's Evolution in the 1950s," in *Speaking for You*, ed. Kimberly A. Benston (Howard); the other deals with "Langston Hughes's Reputation in France" (*LHRev*: 20–29). Also, several of his former students have written on major figures of black fiction. Jean-Michel Bizet authored an analysis of "Really Doesn't Crime Pay?" by Alice Walker ("Les Mémoires d'une Jeune Fille Rangée," *RFEA* 32:183–92), in which he proposes to prevent the reader from being led astray in the game of hide-and-seek in the story and to help him/her find the right path to the hidden truth in which the heroine learns how to master language and use it as a weapon. Claude Julien, who studies the burlesque in black American fiction ("Un rire à l'odeur de soufre: le burlesque dans la fiction noire américaine," *Burlesque et formes parodiques*, ed. Isabelle Landy-Houillon and Maurice Menard, *Biblio* 17:39–58), mainly focuses on the works of Ralph Ellison, while in "The Example of Chester Himes's *The Third Generation*" (*Sociocriticism* 4–5:143–57) he deals with "Space and Civil Rights Ideology." Finally, Françoise Salamand, in "To Be or Not to Be a part of the United States" (*Les Etats-Unis*, pp. 33–57) traces the itinerary of the black writer in John A. Williams's *The Man Who Cried I Am*.

Besides the article mentioned above, *Multilinguisme et multiculturalisme* offers an interesting variety of studies of ethnic texts. Represented in the collection are the worlds of the Russian émigré (Ginette Castro's "Logos et regard dans *The Odyssey of Katinou Kalokovitch*," a feminist reading of Natalie Petesch's novel, pp. 21–41), several works by Italian-Americans ranging from editor Jean Béranger's study of Pietro di Donato ("La référence à l'italien dans les romans de Pietro di Donato," pp. 81–98) and Robert Rougé's "Des Siciliens à Rochester, N.Y.: *Mount Allegro*, de J. Mangione," pp. 99–110, to Nicole Bensoussan's article on Mario Puzo ("L'italianisme dans *The Fortunate Pilgrim* de Mario Puzo," pp. 111–23, and Native American literature, as illustrated by James Welch's work (Bernadette Rigal-Cellard's "Le langage des lieux dans *The Death of Jim Loney*," pp. 61–77). There is also in the volume a sizable representation of Hispanic literature. Serge Ricard, who published an interview with

Rolando Hinojosa in *RFEA* (32:193–96), presents him here as the "bilingual chronicler of Belken County" ("Rolando Hinojosa, chroniqueur bilingue de Belken County," pp. 165–82); Jean Cazemajou focuses his attention on Villareal and Anaya ("Oralité et changement de code dans deux romans chicanos, *Pocho* (1959) de José Antonio Villareal et *Heart of Aztlan* (1976) de Rudolfo Anaya," pp. 127–46), while Christian Lerat presents one of Ron Arias's novels: "*The Road to Tamazunchale* ou la mort revisitée," pp. 147–64). This Hispanic panorama is completed by Yves-Charles Grandjeat's study of nuyorican poetry mentioned above, by Elyette Andouard-Labarthe's presentation of Alurista's prose and poetry ("Le sarape d'Alurista, pp. 215–27) and by Suzanne Durruty's "*Down These Mean Streets* de Piri Thomas," pp. 183–98. Altogether an enlightening volume, the value of which lies principally in its presentation of little-known ethnic talents to the French public.

This completes my report for 1987. Since this may well be the last I have the pleasure to write, I would like to take this opportunity to thank the editors, contributors, and readers of *American Literary Scholarship* for the many years of vicarious companionship I enjoyed with them through this task and these pages. I hope my reports have been of some use to an American public often unaware of the critical material produced abroad, and I remain at my colleagues' disposal should they believe I am in a position to furnish this or that piece of particular information on the work done on the literature of the United States by French Americanists.

Université d'Orléans

iii. German Contributions

Rolf Meyn

In contrast to the 1986 harvest, which was dominated by festschriften and publications on postmodern literature, the turnout of 1987 was more evenly distributed on 19th- and 20th-century literature and on literary history, criticism, and theory.

a. **Literary Criticism and Theory: Comparative Studies.** Theory and method of American Studies have always interested German scholars. A good example is Franz-Peter Spaunhorst's dissertation *Literarische Kulturkritik als Dekodierung von Macht und Werten am Beispiel ausgewählter Romane von Upton Sinclair, Frank Norris, John Dos Passos und Sinclair Lewis: Ein Beitrag zur Theorie und Methode der Amerika-studien als Kulturwissenschaft* (Lang). Spaunhorst's book is evenly divided between an attempt to formulate a theory of American Studies as cultural studies and the application of this theory to novels created by the writers mentioned in the title. The author begins with a history of the American Studies movement. He then examines the literature-minded approaches of the myth-symbol school, of functionalism, structuralism, semiotics, and deconstructionism (which he expects to be of major interest for this field) and their usefulness for the American Studies movement. Spaunhorst holds that the dichotomy between empiricism and hermeneutics prevents the rise of interdisciplinary theory. The author is in favor of a fusion of American cultural studies and American Studies, which are a product of American culture and at the same time an intellectual sanctuary for an authentic cultural experience. With the help of anthropological research done by Wolfgang Rudolph and Peter Tschohl, Spaunhorst constructs a model that conceives of culture as an organized and value-oriented system, with altruism, social responsibility, and egotism as invariables. Applied to the novels of Sinclair, Norris, Dos Passos, and Lewis, the model makes clear that these texts share a cultural criticism and the assumption that between 1905–06 and 1910–11 American culture changed into a "culture of simulacra." This means that self and cultural experience could only be realized in search of authentic self-knowledge, flight, or suicide. Walter Hölbling's *habilitationsschrift, Fiktionen vom Krieg im neueren amerikanischen Roman* (Narr), is doubtlessly one of the most remarkable 1987 publications. Hölbling traces the typical American war novel back to the Indian wars and the captivity narratives of Puritan times and the early 19th-century historical romances. The main part, however, is devoted to the modern war novel. In his chapter "Fiction as History" Hölbling deals with war novels such as Shaw's *The Young Lions*, Del Vecchio's *The 13th Valley*, Mailer's *The Naked and the Dead*, and Moore's *The Green Berets*, that is, novels which are still strongly indebted to naturalism, as it found its first expression in Stephen Crane's *The Red Badge of Courage*. An even greater part of the book, titled "History as Discourse," deals with John Hawkes's *The Cannibal*, Mailer's *Why Are We in Vietnam?*, Joseph Heller's

Catch-22, and Tim O'Brien's *Going After Cacciato*. These are by no means the only books scrutinized. Hölbling draws parallels to many other war novels and thus, using the authors mentioned above as focal points, creates a panoramic view that surpasses both in scope and in depth most of the recent studies having appeared on this theme. Hölbling astutely shows that Dos Passos, Cummings, and Hemingway, besides ridiculing the "crusade for democracy," were in search of a language which was able to express the discrepancy between nationalistic rhetoric and their individual experience of the senseless carnage of World War I. The novels of World War II continued this tradition, though without the extremes of an idealistic patriotism and disillusioned protest. The necessity to fight fascism in Europe and imperialistic Japan in Asia was never questioned, and, with the exception of Mailer and Burns, the novelists retained their beliefs in a democracy which would lead the world to a more peaceful period, though the danger of fascist tendencies in the United States was often mentioned. Hölbling emphasizes that even some important Vietnam novels belong to "Fiction as History." In Del Vecchio's *The 13th Valley* and John Briley's *The Traitors* social, ethical, and political goals are voiced; the possibility of rendering an "objective reality" is never questioned. War is understood as a social state of emergency, the abuses of which are criticized, yet ultimately seen as temporary. In the "History as Discourse" novels, that is, in novels like *The Cannibal, Catch-22, Going After Cacciato*, and *Slaughterhouse-Five*, traditional separation between war and peace is suspended, and chronological narrative structures, causal plot progression, and spiritualization are abandoned. Instead, the emphasis is put on language as "the most powerful kind of actuality" (Hawkes), on self-reflexiveness, on refusal to establish models open to interpretation, and on a concept of reality which can only be grasped subjectively. Yet these works still explore the possibility of human existence in a world in which violence and moral indifference have become legitimate means of power politics. Hölbling's *Fiktionen vom Krieg*, I am told, is being translated into English. I am sure it will be recognized as a major contribution to the discussion of modern and postmodern war novels on both sides of the Atlantic.

Another truly comparative study is Horst Immel's dissertation *Literarische Gestaltungsvarianten des Einwandererromans in der amerikanischen und anglo-kanadischen Literatur: Grove, Cahan, Rölvaag, Henry Roth* (Lang). Immel begins with a short discussion

of nonfictional immigrant literature, which he subdivides into pro-
motion literature, letters, autobiographies, and historical descriptions
such as William Bradford's *Of Plimouth Plantation*. Then follows a
chapter on the figure of the 19th-century American immigrant in mainstream literature, including Whitman, Emerson, Irving, Norris,
Howells, Garland, and Cather. Immel claims that the immigrant
novel is a term in its own right and as such not part of ethnic literature.
The immigrant novel at first sight seems to be rather schematic. Those
novels depicting the pioneer experience focus on the struggle between
man and nature and the taming of the wilderness. City novels have
Americanization as their centers. The loneliness in nature corresponds
to the isolation in the urban jungle. Similarly, the economic rise to
the status of independent farmer is analogous to the economic success in the production society of the metropolis. In each of the four
novels under consideration Immel discovers realistic details from the
author's own autobiography, yet they are always incorporated differently. Grove in *A Search For America* creates a fictional autobiography in order to cover some dark spots in his own past and to impose
himself as a mentor on Canada. Cahan's protagonist in *The Rise of
David Levinsky* is in many ways a reflection of the author himself,
who ironizes overzealous adaption and the lament over the loss of
identity. Rölvaag in *Giants in the Earth* researched the pioneering of
his Norwegian father and grandfather in the Dakotas of the 1870s
and wrote a novel about the immigrant on the frontier. Henry Roth
went back to his ghetto childhood in pre-World War I New York and
compressed the contradictions, conflicts, and dualities of his early
childhood into a complicated imagery in *Call It Sleep*. Immel shows
that in all four novels the arrival scene and a scene denoting a kind
of rebirth function as crucial elements. Grove's *A Search For America*
and Cahan's *The Rise of David Levinsky* are, furthermore, confessional novels with two protagonists who are intellectually superior
to their fellow beings. All four novels, Immel thinks, complain about
the extreme worldliness in America. Immel's study is without question
an important contribution to the exploration of this genre, which in
the United States too often has been discussed under the label
"ethnic literature."

Utopian literature, often in close connection with science fiction,
has met considerable scholarly interest over the last years. Three dissertations by female authors which I didn't have time to read last
year added important feminist perspectives to the criticism of utopian

literature. In her *Utopien von Frauen in der zeitgenössischen Literatur der USA* (Lang, 1985), Annette Keinhorst tackles an impressive variety of utopian novels by woman writers, from Joanna Russ and Dorothy Bryant to Ursula Le Guin and Marge Piercy, many of which are only rarely noticed by critics. Her thesis is that from the 1970s on, "critical utopian novels" prepared the ground for a renewal of utopian thinking which leaves more room for risk and change, in contrast to earlier, more static and harmonious utopian writing. Many of the feminist authors, Keinhorst holds, envision female societies which are anarchistic, decentralized, and deurbanized. There are no classes and no crimes. Community life is pervaded by family-like structures, yet group relations replace family ties. Ecological thinking and solidarity characterize the approach to nature. Utopia is the place which demonstrates how women could be, were they not alienated from themselves, objectified, devalued, separated from essential parts of their possible identity. At the same time, however, Keinhorst is well aware of divergent tendencies. "Sword and sorcery" plots with Amazon heroines occur in novels such as Jessica Amanda Salmonson's *The Swordswoman* (1982). Other untypical heroines briefly touched upon are women as saviors and healers who mostly perform their deeds for a utopian society without violence. According to Keinhorst, feminist dystopian novels also exist, though only to a small degree. The main trend in feminist writing, however, is the "critical utopian novel" as a medium of emancipating concepts. The starting point is a present that is marked by male suppression and a society dominated by male power and patriarchal values. Keinhorst's dissertation suffers a bit from the sheer mass of material that is covered. On the other hand, it provides the reader with an excellent overview of an important chapter of feminist literature.

Compared with Keinhorst's ambitious project, Dagmar Barnouw's *Die versuchte Realität oder von der Möglichkeit, glücklichere Welten zu denken: Utopischer Diskurs von Thomas Morus zur feministischen Science Fiction* (Corian: Meitingen 1985) consists of loosely connected essays on the utopian discourse, with an emphasis on the utopian novels of the 1970s and a special chapter on feminist works. The dissertation is in many ways a substantial addition to Keinhorst's undertaking. In contrast to both authors, Barbara Puschmann-Nalenz in her *Science Fiction und ihre Grenzbereiche: Ein Beitrag zur Gattungsproblematik zeitgenössischer angloamerikanischer Erzählliteratur* (Corian: Meitingen 1986) is bent on working out the character and the limits of science fiction by comparing it to postmodern novels by Burroughs, Pynchon, and Vonnegut. Her thesis is that science fiction, in spite of all its innovations and variations, is not a definite genre per se. In the light of the author's findings, this is plausible.

Among the 1987 scholarly production, a collection of essays, *Jewish Life and Suffering as Mirrored in English and American Literature/Jüdisches Leben und Leiden im Spiegel der englischen und amerikanischen Literatur*, ed. Franz H. Link (Schöningh), is a comparative study that ought to be discussed at some length. The bilingual title is misleading, since all the essays are written in German, though followed by a substantial summary in English. Of the contributions on American literature, Kurt Müller's "Das antisemitische Stereotyp in Hemingways *The Sun Also Rises*" (pp. 47–69) sees Robert Cohn first as an autobiographical figure, since he was modeled after a traveling companion, Harold Loeb, who was deeply offended when the novel was published. But Hemingway was also greatly influenced by current anti-Semitic clichés, which drove him into creating a figure embodying everything he hated most: an other-directed and parasitic mode of existence. Yet, Müller argues, Robert Cohn's function is far more complex because he is also a "mirror figure" for the other characters of the group, and those who maltreat him as a scapegoat have more in common with him than they realize. Ultimately, Robert Cohn as the author's creation is also a proof of Hemingway's lack of moral awareness. Waldemar Zacharasiewicz's panoramic overview "Innen- und Aussenperspektive des jüdischen Einzelschicksals im nordamerikanischen Schrifttum im ersten Drittel des 20. Jahrhunderts" (pp. 71–89) is concerned with the conflict between Orthodox religious heritage and acculturation, the dominant theme in so many Jewish-American autobiographies until 1930. The author believes that Cahan's *The Rise of David Levinsky* helped to create a negative stereotype—that of the avaricious, materialistic Jew, as he appeared in the works of the early Faulkner, Willa Cather, and Edith Wharton. The sordidness of urban life inspired quite a few Jewish "insiders" to describe their attempts to come to terms with it. This, the author claims, was the beginning of a distinctive Jewish-American literary tradition. Sepp L. Tiefenthaler in "Amerikabild und Amerika-Erfahrung in Isaac Bashevis Singers autobiographischen und erzählenden Schriften" (pp. 91–104) assesses one of the main representatives of this tradition. He defines Singer's Yiddish as an "existential metaphor," since the author's novels and stories, which have the shtetls of Eastern Europe as their background, are not historical fiction but parables of human greatness and baseness. Many of Singer's characters in his fiction dealing with America are Holocaust survivors or refugees who came to the United States shortly before World War II, haunted by the nightmares of Nazi persecutions. But America does not become a haven for them. Instead, Singer constantly depicts it as a place of rootlessness, disorientation, alienation, and materialism; in other words, for Singer America is not a promised land, but a "kingdom of the dead." Singer is also mentioned in Franz Link's essay "Jiddische und jüdisch-amerikanische Erzählkunst" (pp. 105–19). Link considers the Yiddish fiction in Eastern Europe and in the United States as a unity, since it always takes place in the shtetls of Eastern Europe and its culture with its religious traditions. For Link, Yiddish as well as Jewish-American fiction reached its climax at that moment when the cultural identity they were rooted in either dissolved by assimilation or began to change fundamentally. Link's thesis is that Jewish-American fiction writers like Bellow, Malamud, or Philip Roth are related to an earlier generation of writers (Michael Gold, Henry Roth, Daniel Fuchs) as Singer is to the classical writers of Yiddish fiction in Eastern Europe (Mendele Sforim, Sholom Aleichem, and Isaak Peretz). Hubert Hagenmeyer follows suit with his essay "Die Kontroverse über Philip Roths *Portnoy's Complaint*" (pp. 121–31). The author discusses the opposition Roth met after the publication of his novel, mainly from Jewish critics. Hagenmeyer claims that they were unable to see the justification of Portnoy's provocative analysis of Jewish-American middle-class reality. The controversy over *Portnoy's Complaint* left its marks on Roth's later writings, in which he more than once tried to explain to his readers the basic intention of his fiction. Franz Link then takes the floor again with his "Auschwitz and the Literary Imagination: William Styron's *Sophie's Choice*" (pp. 133–43). Link thinks that Styron overemphasized sexual fulfillment by exalting it into the religious sphere, just as he heightened evil into the tragic and heroic. In doing this, he cheapened and trivialized the Holocaust. Paul Goetsch concludes the collection with his "Der Holocaust in der englischen und amerikanischen Lyrik" (pp. 167–89). Goetsch finds four different kinds of Holocaust poems. In the first group either facts speak for themselves or Nazi officials are chosen as speakers, voicing their inhuman, bureaucratic attitudes. Other poems express the perspective of the victims and their psycho-

logical reactions to crucial experiences. In the largest group of poems
the choice of Holocaust themes is initiated by later events, e.g., the
Eichmann trial or the poet's visit to a former concentration camp.
Here, historical reality makes way for reflection and meditation.
Finally, some poets use the Holocaust theme to elaborate or even
dramatize private experiences, to Goetsch "a highly questionable matter." He thinks it remarkable that most Holocaust poets prefer traditional poetic techniques to surrealistic or other modernist approaches. All in all, *Jewish Life and Suffering* is an informative and
wide-ranging collection that with its surveys and studies of individual
writers should attract many readers.

An interesting contribution to a theme that now and then catches
the attention of scholars on both sides of the Atlantic is Cathy Waegner's "Der Teufel im American Dream" (*LiLi* 17:61–84). Waegner's
essay is not an exploration of Satan, as he entered literature through
John Milton, but an examination of the Faust tradition, which in
Waegner's opinion "interrelates with the 'American Dream' of democracy, progress, and the attainment of material wealth in the New
Eden." After outlining the American reception of the Faust myth,
Waegner turns to the Faust motif in folktales and popular literature,
where often a victorious Faust appears, whose trust in American
values helps him to outwit Satan. A concomitant tradition, shaped by
Puritanism, presents a Faust who is damned, as in some of Hawthorne's and Melville's romances. Finally, Waegner focuses on Fitzgerald's *The Great Gatsby*, Faulkner's *Absalom, Absalom!* and *The
Hamlet*, and on Jack Kerouac's *Doctor Sax*.

Some important comparative studies are also to be found in *Religion and Philosophy*, a record of the proceedings of a German-
American conference at Paderborn, 29 July–1 August 1986. Manfred
Pütz in his paper "Emerson and Kant Once Again: Is Emerson's
Thought a Philosophy Before, After, Beside, or Beyond Kant?" (vol.
2, pp. 621–40) claims that Emerson drew a lot of support from Kant,
since the latter for him had demonstrated that an intuitive grasp was
possible and that the moral law was the divine center of every human being, needing no empirical proof. Emerson's philosophy of in-
tuitionism, however, was unable to move beyond Kant. Also concerned with Emerson is Herwig Friedl's "Emerson and Nietzsche:
1862–1874 (vol. 1, pp. 267–87). Friedl convincingly shows how
strongly Nietzsche was influenced by Emerson and his metaphor of

the circle, although he hardly ever quoted him directly. Emerson's contemporary Emily Dickinson becomes the focus of another comparative paper. John E. Martin's "The Religious Spirit in the Poetry of Emily Dickinson and Theodore Roethke" (Vol. 2, pp. 497–518) is devoted to two poets of the 19th and 20th century who were not affiliated with formal religion, but who penetrated the surface reality to find a transcendent and mysterious meaning behind the world of externals.

b. **Literary History.** Long overdue is a brief mention of a literary history that appeared in 1985, *Die amerikanische Literatur bis zum Ende des 19. Jahrhunderts,* ed. Helmbrecht Breinig and Ulrich Halfmann (Francke). The book begins with a concise introduction by Breinig in which the national, philosophical, historical, and political characteristics of American literature are seen in all their contradictions. Different kinds of literature, e.g., "high" literature, ethnic literature, historiography, are touched upon, as well as copyright laws, book markets, distribution, and the reading public. Astrid Schmidt-von Mühlenfels follows with her chapter "Amerikanische Literatur vor 1800" (pp. 47–77), ranging from John Smith's travel report and the Puritans' writings on state and society to 18th-century autobiographies and the lyrics of Bradstreet, Taylor, and Freneau. Dieter Schulz's chapter "Frühe amerikanische Erzählliteratur" (pp. 78–99) treats early American prose literature from Royall Tyler and William Hill Brown to James Fenimore Cooper and John Neal. Helmbrecht Breinig assesses the two main representatives of the American Renaissance in his "Amerikanische Erzählliteratur um die Mitte des 19. Jahrhunderts—Hawthorne und Melville" (pp. 100–135). Melville to him has become a "model for the literature of the 20th century," an innovative author because of his self-reflexive and philosophical inclinations, a skeptical thinker bordering on nihilism, but also a nihilistic moralist. Hans-Wolfgang Schaller in his essay "Amerikanische Erzählliteratur 1865–1900" (pp. 136–73) concentrates on regionalism, Mark Twain, William Dean Howells, Hamlin Garland, Frank Norris, Stephen Crane, and Henry James. Nineteenth-century poetry is dealt with in Ludwig Deringer's and Roland Hagenbüchle's chapter, "Amerikanische Lyrik des 19. Jahrhunderts" (pp. 174–224). The authors begin with William Cullen Bryant and the fireside poets Longfellow, Holmes, Lowell, and Whittier, the last of whom they set apart from the first three because of his rural and Quaker origins. Emerson as the chief representative of Transcendentalism is discussed together with Thoreau and Jones Very, whereas Dickinson and Whitman and Poe and Lanier are tackled as two unequal pairs. Frederick Goddard Tuckerman, Herman Melville, Stephen Crane, and Edwin Arlington Robinson are subsumed under the rubric "Die Desillusionierung der Jahrhundertwende" (pp. 213–24). Ulrich Halfmann's chapter, "Amerikanisches Theater und Drama bis 1900" (pp. 225–59), ranges from the traveling stock company and the star system, that is, the hiring of British actors and sending them across the country, from the crude beginnings of American drama in colonial and revolutionary times (the pamphlet plays) to melodrama and the realistic playwright James A. Herne. Horst Dippel's "Historisches und politisches Schrifttum" (pp. 260–81) concludes the book. Dippel differentiates between three historical phases. The first one reaches from the Constitution to the Jacksonian era. The second comprises the antebellum period, followed by the Reconstruction Era. Of the historical and political writers Dippel discusses, John Taylor of Caroline, Cooper, Bancroft, Emerson, Thoreau, Prescott, Parkman, Brownson, Draper, Turner, Mahan, Brooks Adams, Tyler, Gronlund, Bellamy, and Veblen take most of the room. A thorough bibliography and a carefully arranged chronology of dates—the biographies of writers paralleled by important historical events—concludes this literary history, which in my opinion is a much-needed endeavor in German scholarship.

Literary history, though restricted to poetry, is also contained in *Amerikanische Lyrik: Perspektiven und Interpretationen*, ed. Rudolf Haas (Schmidt), a collection of surveys and interpretations of poems typical of their creators by various German scholars. Haas's introduction, covering examples from the Puritans to the moderns, is an ecclectic survey of American poetry, though the postmodern development is largely left out. This deficit is partly made up by Claus Clüver's chapter "From Imagism to Concrete Poetry: Breakthrough or Blind Alley?" (pp. 113–30). Clüver leaves no doubt that Concrete Poetry originated in Europe and Brazil; there existed no manifesto in the United States. Clüver's definition of Concrete Poetry is that it "employs a minimal amount of material from which it extracts a maximum amount of information," achieved by the creation of spatio-temporal visual and phonetic structures. Clüver believes that some points of the Imagist program were taken over directly by the Concrete Poets—both schools preferred small forms and relied on phonic dimensions of the verbal material. The concept of the ideogram, as developed in Pound's poetry, was also adopted by Concrete Poetry. Pound and his contemporaries of the "Poetic Renaissance," the decade from 1912 to 1922, also come under scrutiny in Volker Bischoff's essay "Tradition und Experiment in der amerikanischen Lyrik der 'Poetic Renaissance'" (pp. 63–76). According to Bischoff, these ten years were a crucial period because 19th-century traditions lived on, while a modern lyrical poetry developed. Pound and others put a strong emphasis on poetic techniques and saw art as a kind of discovery, a departure from fixed positions and a neglect of the audience. In contrast to them, Harriet Monroe stressed the community between poet and audience, which, as Robert Frost put it, should always recognize what the poet means. Bischoff sees the debate between "tradition" and "experiment" centered in the many discussions of the term "free verse."

In some respects Marion Soceanu's dissertation, *Das Federal Theatre Project und seine Dramen über amerikanische Geschichte* (Lang), is a pioneer work. She begins with an overview of the research done so far and then comes up with a thorough analysis of the Project as part of Franklin Delano Roosevelt's WPA. Her findings surpass many of the publications in this field. Of special interest is her description of the ideological skirmishes within the "German Unit" of the Project. Soceanu's interest, however, is, as the title says, directed toward the historical drama. Her thesis is that the concept of the historical drama as developed by the administrators of the Project shared a lot with the biographical plays of the 1930s dealing with famous historical persons, e.g., Maxwell Anderson's *Winterset* and Robert Sherwood's *Abe Lincoln in Illinois*, but also contained new elements. In the first place, the Federal Theatre Project saw its task as developing a theater which should reflect the nation, "its history, its present problems, its diverse regions and population." She then singles out 17 historical plays and analyzes them in the light of her findings. Synopses of all the plays and photocopies of important documents of the Project conclude this fine dissertation. Its only flaw, in my opinion, is that Soceanu fails to see how much the Project was a child of the second half of the decade, when the "rediscovery of America" pervaded the media world as a whole exactly along the lines which the author works out so well.

c. **Colonial Literature.** An essay I failed to read earlier is Hans Galinsky's "The German Contribution to the Discovery, Exploration, and Early Settlement of the Americas," in *A Heritage Fulfilled: German Americans,* ed. Clarence A. Glasrud (Moorhead, Minn.: Concordia, 1985), pp. 22–35. Galinsky calls our attention to a broad scope of German involvement with early America, ranging from name-giving, mapmaking, financing South American expeditions, to travel accounts. The rest of the essays dealing with colonial literature are to be found in Haas's *Amerikanische Lyrik* and Freese's *Religion and Philosophy.* In the latter collection Ursula Brumm assesses a rarely explored segment in her paper "Faith and Imagery in Puritan Meditation Literature" (vol. 1, pp. 61–75). To her, it is surprising that Puritan theologians who were highly suspicious of all concrete visual images in their efforts to preach meditation had a real hankering for verbal images. Self-examination, the necessary prerequisite for conversion, was achieved by simultaneously opening one's heart to the world and to experience. The turning to the heart is for Brumm a sure sign of a keen self-awareness and a new sensibility that also found its way into 18th-century literature. Winfried Herget in "The Role of the Community in the Puritan *Ordo Salutis*" (vol. 1, pp. 387–400) assumes that Puritans as followers of the Pauline principle believed that individual identity could only develop out of social relationships. Hence, inside and outside the family Puritans were expected to converse with others on the state of their souls. Yet in the course of history the Puritans realized that they could no longer hope for a common expectation of grace holding the community together because society and covenant community drifted apart. The "half-way covenant" was created to bring those denied full communion under the control of the covenant community. They in turn were expected to provide communal support for all who longed for salvation.

Puritan poetry is dealt with in Rudolf Haas's *Amerikanische Lyrik.* K. Dietrich Pfisterer selects Anne Bradstreet's poem "Autumn" in order to demonstrate that the seasonal world of objects is only a metaphor of the universal human existence in her poetry (pp. 131–42). Ursula Brumm's "Edward Taylor: 'Meditation I, 34'" (pp. 143–54) is an excellent introduction to Taylor's poetic style in general. It is also an astute analysis of Taylor's religious belief. For him, the fate of the soul was a drama acted out between the two poles of human nature. He depicts the incompleteness of man in crass images of sickness, stench, and decay and contrasts it with divine purity and glory, which he praises in images of light, radiance, and jewels.

d. 19th-Century Literature. The title of Elisabeth Hermann's dissertation, *Opfer der Geschichte: Die Darstellung der nordamerikanischen Indianer im Werk James Fenimore Coopers und seiner Zeitgenossen* (Lang, 1986), is slightly misleading since the author focuses on Cooper and treats his contemporaries William Cullen Bryant, Washington Irving, and others only very marginally. On the whole, however, Hermann's study is a successful attempt to show that Cooper and his generation were influenced by the French philosopher Condorcet and his concept of man's progress toward an enlightened stage of civilization. In this scheme the Indian appears as a member of a low-stage, static civilization, unable to change, whereas the whites represent civilization's irresistible progress. The disappearance of the Indians, tragic as it was, was nevertheless accepted as a logical step in the course of history, as the works of Cooper amply prove. Neither he nor his contemporaries could see how removal policies or coexistence of the red and the white race were to function. Hence, a dominant motif is the Indian who, in the America of Manifest Destiny, can only retain his true identity in a heroic death.

Cooper, the Indians, and Manifest Destiny are also frequently referred to in *Westward Expansion in America (1803–1860)*, ed. Wolfgang Binder (Palm), a collection of papers presented at a Franco-German colloquium held at the University of Erlangen. Of the German contributions, Heinz Ickstadt's "Painting, Fiction and the Rhetoric of Westward Expansion" (pp. 3–30) is the most panoramic. Ickstadt points to the fact that the image of the West implied not only a myth of nature, but also of agrarian and, eventually, even industrial civilization. The most sensitive artists understood that the transformation of savage nature into a garden was a painful process of exploitation and destruction, though they fervently hoped that a perfect civilization, the final result of progress, would justify the destruction of the American landscape and its original inhabitants. Painters like George Caleb Bingham, Emanuel Leutze, John Gast, and Thomas Cole depicted a West that was not only populated by heroic Americans enacting Manifest Destiny, but one that was turned into a garden by the pioneer's ax and the railroad. Fiction, however, revealed the inner contradictions of the rhetoric of westward expansion more openly. In his biography of Daniel Boone, Timothy Flint presented a pioneer who was the agent and the victim of civilization. Cooper, against all historical evidence, created a utopian image of agrarian harmony through a series of forced reconciliations between nature and technology in *Oak Openings* (1848). Of all concomitant writers, Melville in *Pierre* went furthest by bluntly denying the possibility that cultural regeneration was possible. In contrast to Ickstadt, Helmbrecht Breinig in his paper "'Turn your mind on the ways of the inner country': Cooper and the Question of Westward Expansion" (pp. 47–64) devotes his interest solely to Cooper. Breinig is opposed to the attempts of numerous scholars who see in Cooper predominantly an advocate of historical progress and Manifest Destiny. Cooper, Breinig intelligently argues, often used the word Providence in order to escape the responsibility to deal with history realistically. Furthermore, he never envisioned a future America which extended from sea to shining sea but one that ended at "the ocean of prairies." Manfred Pütz in his "Inward Versus Outward Expansion: Thoreau's Critique of Expansionist Ideology" (pp. 79–98) maintains that Thoreau's ideas of the West and westward expansion stood in close interrelationship with his view on reformism and reformers. Thoreau despised the expansionist ideology of his time, though he used its metaphoric language. But for him it served to describe an inward movement, that is, the constant need of the individual for self-reform, since he was well aware that expansionism and reform spirit entered an unholy alliance that even before 1860 had imperialist dimensions.

Hans-Joachim Lang turns to another writer who during Andrew Jackson's administration embarked on his career as a writer—Nathaniel Hawthorne. Lang's paper, "Biographical and Historical Parallels: Napoleon, Jackson, and Hawthorne's Robin Molineux" (pp. 99–125), deals with only one story, however. In his customary approach Lang first views the major critical interpretations of "My Kinsman, Major Molineux," then ponders the question whether the story is only a historical tale—with a national moral, of course—set at the eve of the American Revolution, or a disguised and allegorical presentation of the 1828 presidential campaign. Though the evidence is a bit scanty, Lang, albeit carefully, points to the possibility that the mob leader in the story could be Andrew Jackson himself. The European authority on Charles Sealsfield, Walter Grünzweig, follows with "American Birds of Passage: Westward Expansion in Charles Sealsfield's Fiction" (pp. 126–39). Grünzweig, after throwing substantial light on Sealsfield's position as a bicultural mind and stressing the fact that his novels are "textbooks of expansionist ideology," shows that when the author had completed his novels on the American West, he became very critical of this ideology. Nevertheless, Sealsfield was a staunch Jacksonian except for his strong antislavery attitude. Somewhat related to Grünzweig's paper is Wolfgang Binder's panoramic "Romances of the War With Mexico: Variations of and Responses to Expansionist Discourse" (pp. 237–66). Binder analyzes seven romances of the Mexican War, a field that hitherto has only rarely been dealt with. In all of the romances, Americans appear as heroes and saviors in Mexico, and in most cases bring home a bride who is white, of Hispanic background, and a member of the aristocracy. Enemies of the American expansion are the villains and frequently appear in the role of Catholic priests.

Two of the essays are only marginally connected with the theme of westward expansion in American literature. Gudrun Birnbaum's "Slavery and the White Protestant Churches" (pp. 151–79) is a substantial attempt to delineate the Protestant churches' attitude toward slavery from colonial times to the Civil War. Dieter Meindl's "Winning the West: The American and the Canadian Experience" (pp. 267–81) is, as the title says, a brief but thorough comparative study to point out the differences between the description of the westward movement both in the United States and in Canadian literature. Meindl is correct in emphasizing that there is "no myth of the West to speak of in Canada," although there was also a frontier and popular western character types like the "coureur de bois" and the Mounties. Canadian literature also reflected the dichotomy between western vigor and eastern culture. Yet the myth of the garden never exerted much influence in the face of the extreme climate and the immensity of the Canadian prairies. Thus it comes as no surprise that in the mid-1920s a group of writers—among them Frederick Philip Grove, Sinclair Ross, and Robert Kroetsch—created regionalistic novels, which had more in common with the products of European naturalism than with the midwestern farm novels created across the border. There is no Canadian formula western, Meindl holds, but a regional Canadian western novel.

After some preliminary essays, Walter Grünzweig had his dissertation on Charles Sealsfield published in 1987. His book, *Das demokratische Kanaan: Charles Sealsfields Amerika im Kontext amerikanischer Literatur und Ideologie* (Fink), is doubtlessly the most

comprehensive study on this Austro-American writer to come out so
far. Grünzweig begins with a thorough survey of the Sealsfield criticism from the beginning to the present. He then compares the writer's
work to that of contemporary American authors, notably those whom
Sealsfield had read—Timothy Flint, James Fenimore Cooper, James
Kirke Paulding, and William Gilmore Simms, all of whom had considerable influence on him. The next three chapters are devoted to
Sealsfield's "plantation novels," his portraits of Indians and his attitude toward nativism and anti-Catholicism. Grünzweig demonstrates that Sealsfield's Indians are on the one hand nature's noble-
men, the products of the romantic cult of primitivism. On the other,
they are obstacles to the march of civilization and are either to be
destroyed or removed, as was Jackson's declared policy. Consequently, Sealsfield was not interested in creating another tragic
Natty Bumppo figure, trailblazer and victim of civilization at the
same time. His hero was the sturdy pioneer, who as leader of a group
of settlers played a decisive role in transforming the wilderness
into an agrarian civilization. Sealsfield's anticlericalism and anti-
Catholicism should, as Grünzweig convincingly argues, only to a
small degree be attributed to the conditions in the Austrian empire
the author fled from, but more to his deep identification with a Jacksonian America which felt threatened by an imagined sinister alliance
formed by Mexico, Catholic settlers along the Mississippi valley, and
European monarchies. Grünzweig ends his dissertation with valuable
suggestions for further research and with reprints of reviews written
immediately after the first publications of Sealsfield's works. I hope
with the author that his excellent dissertation will encourage further
research on this writer whose novels and stories have been sadly
neglected.

Mark Twain has rarely been assessed in monographs during the
last decade in Germany, though important aspects of his works have
frequently been treated in books dealing with periods, genres, or
histories of ideas in American literature. This situation was changed
with the publications of two books, Helmbrecht Breinig's *Mark Twain*
(Artemis, 1985) and Karl-Otto Strohmidel's dissertation *"Tranquil
Ecstasy": Mark Twains pastorale Neigung und ihre literarische Ges-
taltung* (Gruner, 1986). Breinig's little book is part of a series of introductions to important American writers and themes I have commented on regularly over the last few years. Breinig certainly keeps

up with the high standard of these introductions, which in spite of their brevity offer concise and profound insights into the writers under consideration. Breinig begins with an introductory chapter on the historical context, on journalism, realism, and the different styles Mark Twain employed. He then turns to Twain's short fiction and travel books. Subsequent chapters are devoted to *The Gilded Age, The American Claimant,* the *Tom Sawyer* novels, *The Adventures of Huckleberry Finn, A Connecticut Yankee in King Arthur's Court, Pudd'nhead Wilson,* and "Those Extraordinary Twins," the *Mysterious Stranger* versions and other later attempts marked by the flight into imagination. A binational bibliography, including the most important criticism, closes this fine book. Strohmidel's dissertation is concerned with Mark Twain's inclination to pastoralism and its expression in his work. The author clearly shows that Twain always liked to satirize pastoralism and its way of looking at the world, but was himself too prone to this romantic tradition to avoid it. Strohmidel claims that for Twain there existed "characteristic points of reference," notably his recollections of Hannibal, the Sandwich Islands, the Mississippi, Lake Tahoe, California, Heidelberg, the Alps, and the Black Forest. They not only functioned as imaginative foils for the creation of individual passages but were important for Twain's creative process in general. In his later works, pastoralism, as part of the author's increasing retrospection, tended to become a yardstick for an unfinished reality. Strohmidel's dissertation is based on the findings of many Twain critics, but contains a lot of original insights, which make it a valuable contribution to recent Twain research.

Bret Harte has never ceased to enjoy scholarly interest over the last decades in Germany. In " 'The Luck of Roaring Camp': Bret Harte's Epyllion of an American New Beginning" (*Amst* 32:125–33) Armin Paul Frank and Helga Essmann with the help of German translations come to the conclusion that the many epic and mythic allusions woven into the texture of this story justify its interpretation as an epyllion "evoking a mythical new beginning in the Far West." Klaus Martens, in his subsequent paper, " 'Black Robe Chief' and 'Ci-Devant Blacksmith': Two Instances of Literary Translation as Transcultural History" (ibid., pp. 134–42), employs the same approach. He argues very convincingly that Longfellow's *Evangeline* possesses more cultural criticism than most critics have been willing to concede so far, since it contains two passages, one dealing with the

theme of immigration, the other with Catholicism. The German translations of *Evangeline* clearly indicate historical changes that took
place at the time of the various translations.

Nineteenth-century poetry is the chief subject of Rudolf Haas's
Amerikanische Lyrik. In "Die 'Fireside Poets' Bryant, Whittier, Longfellow, Holmes and Lowell" (pp. 39–62) Bettina and Herwig Friedl
turn to poets that for the last decades rarely aroused any interest
among German scholars. The Friedls do not satirize or minimize the
significance of these poets who toward the end of the century had
risen to the status of "praeceptores Americae," that is, personified
cultural institutions buttressing the family, the Protestant churches,
and the American republic. The Friedls explain the poets' weltanschauung by scrutinizing their use of a popular symbol of cosmic
totality, the sea, which all five of them employed quite often and differently from Whitman, because to them it was part of a divine plan,
being normally invisible in the everyday world. Another common
denominator was the Fireside Poets' relationship to their revered
Scottish colleague Robert Burns, whom even the Beacon Hill aristo-
crat Holmes praised as a singer of the common man. Yet, as the Friedls
remind us, there are essential differences between the Fireside Poets.
Bryant's landscapes were to him reflections of a universal nature, the
order of which unfolded remorselessly and regardless of individual
happiness. Whittier, on the other hand, was an egalitarian democrat
who tried to bridge the gap between rural people and the urban
middle class.

Also included in Haas's collection are interpretations of single
poems by 19th-century Americans. Martin Christadler's "Philip Freneau: 'On the Anniversary of Storming the Bastille . . .' " (pp. 155–77)
is a good example of how a single poem can serve as a starting point
for a substantial evaluation of a poet's achievement. Freneau, Christadler points out, created republican lyrics, but they rarely contained
allusions to the people, the core of any republican historical myth.
Instead, abstract concepts appeared as acting powers. If Freneau
created scenes and types of everyday life, he did so for humorous and
satirical reasons. Besides, he had increasing difficulties in seeing a
teleological principle at work in history. Franz H. Link's "Edgar Allan
Poe: 'The Raven' " (pp. 186–97) is restricted to this poem, which for
Link is a paradigm of the crisis and simultaneous triumph of romantic
imagination.

e. 20th-Century Literature. Helga Oppermann's dissertation, *Das Engelsmuster: Zur Theorie und Geschichte, Analyse und Interpretation eines kulturellen Deutungsmusters des Weiblichen: Exemplifiziert an ausgewählten Stücken aus der amerikanischen Theaterliteratur der Zwanziger Jahre* (Olms, 1986), is a remarkable study, not only because of the theme—she examines the "Angel in the House" pattern in plays of the 1920s, an undertaking that to my knowledge has never been done—but also because of the base she starts from. The first part of her study is concerned with the theory and history of the "Angel in the House" pattern, which, as Oppermann succinctly outlines, is a "defensive construct," the reflection of the male's desire for safety, but also the projection of his mistrust. The author presents the situation from both a male and a feminist point of view. She lucidly illustrates that the "Roaring Twenties" with all its talk about emancipated women and feminism was largely a myth. The flapper achieved some freedom only in a kind of private playground. Male playwrights, however, recognized that a new kind of woman was necessary, as plays such as Eugene O'Neill's *Before Breakfast* (1916), James Forbes's *The Famous Mrs. Fair* (1919), George Kelly's *Craig's Wife* (1925), and Sidney Howard's *Lucky Sam McCarver* (1926) amply prove. Oppermann discovers in the prescribed selflessness presented in the plays by female playwrights also a latent self-destruction. "The Angel in the House" ultimately learns that the death of her husband corresponds with potential freedom and a chance of self-awareness. All the plays of the 1920s demonstrate that the male's role had lost much of its self-complacency. At the same time the "Angel in the House" pattern no longer could provide two different spheres, one for the man, the other for the woman. According to Oppermann, this was due to the clash of Freudian theories with this pattern, after which the precarious balance between the two spheres was irrevocably lost.

American theater in the 20th century enjoyed quite a vogue in 1987, since a special issue of *Amerikastudien* was called *Theater in den USA.* Of the German contributions, Herbert Grabes focuses on "Myth and Myth Deconstruction in American Plays of the 60s and early 70s" (*Amst* 32:39–48). Based on myth theories posited by George Sorel, Eugen Böhler, and Roland Barthes, Grabes investigates Jean-Claude van Itallie's trilogy, *American Hurrah,* and Jack Gelber's *Sleep* and discovers three ways of myth destruction, namely, a partial

destruction by satirical exaggeration or parody, implicit diffusion of
contemporary myths through rational and analytical procedures, and
the creation of artificial myths. A fourth aspect is added with Klaus
Schwank's "Drama as Functional Art: The Political Use of Myth in
Amiri Baraka's *A Black Mass*" (*Amst* 32:81–86). Schwank shows how
in Baraka's play the myth of white supremacy is destroyed and replaced by a myth of black supremacy. Thus the black revolutionary
play becomes what Schwank calls "a new kind of social play," aiming
at the creation of a new consciousness and a new sense of collective
identity. The classical theater tradition in America also continues to
attract German scholars, as with Bernd Engler's "Thornton Wilder
and Lukrez' *De Rerum Natura*: Anmerkungen zur Rezeption epikure-
ischer Philosophie in *The Ides of March* and *The Eighth Day*" (*Arcadia* 22: 270–83). Engler claims that in addition to Kierkegaard and
Sartre, it was the Roman poet and Epicurean philosopher Lucretius
who influenced Wilder at a time when he doubted a secured Christian worldview.

American literature between the two world wars was explored
in some other articles. Hans-Jürgen Grabbe in "The Ideal Type of
the Small Town: Main Street in a Social Science Context" (*Amst* 32:
181–90) looks at Sinclair Lewis's *Main Street* from a sociological point
of view and concludes that the novel is equal, if not superior to, the
social science study of a midwestern town in the 1920s. The Midwest
is also the theme of Kurt Dittmar's "Carl Sandburg: 'Chicago,'"
(*Amerikanische Lyrik*, pp. 223–39). Dittmar not only comes up with
a concise analysis of Sandburg's poetic techniques, but with a brief
but excellent description of the poet's position within the Chicago
Renaissance and the role of Chicago in American art and poetry in
general. In this book two other modernist contemporaries are dealt
with in Hans-Joachim Zimmermann's "Ezra in der Unterwelt, Oder
Homer Wird Noch Gebraucht: Beobachtungen zum Canto I von
Ezra Pound" (pp. 261–84) and my "Edward Estlin Cumming: 'I
Sing of Olaf Great and Big'" (pp. 285–94). Zimmermann's painstaking analysis of Pound's Canto 1, the history of its genesis and changes
until its final version in 1925, makes this essay a valuable addition
to the Pound criticism that has been published on this canto so far.
My brief chapter on Cummings's antiwar poem touches poetic technique as well as his position as an uncompromising individualist at
a time when most of his colleagues turned to ideology for support.

Most of the 20th-century scholarship was again directed toward the period after World War II. Our survey will start with three dissertations. Hans-Joachim Stute's *Der amerikanische Existenzialismus Norman Mailers* (Lang) does not begin with another interpretation of *The Naked and the Dead,* as one would expect, but with *Barbary Shore,* which Stute thinks to be profoundly influenced by Hannah Arendt's *The Origins of Totalitarianism* (1951). In contrast to Arendt, however, Mailer depicted the individual's victimization by the totalitarian state as a psychic and emotional drama. This theme was continued in *The Deer Park,* with what Stute calls "the categorical imperative adaptation" becoming paramount. The center of the dissertation is Stute's delineation of the concept of Mailer's existentialism from *The White Negro* on, with its ingredients of violence as existential self-realization. Stute discovers a philosophical dichotomy between "existentiality" and romanticism permeating Mailer's work. This explains the neoprimitivist stance which is visible in most of Mailer's novels and puts them in a national tradition, together with Faulkner and Hemingway. Stute holds that Mailer does not believe in collective existentialism because his existentialist hero is often the charismatic leader. In his later works mysticism becomes a strong component of existentialism and the opposite pole of totalitarian reality. To the aging Mailer, mysticism, instincts, and emotionality are superior to the rationality of our technical civilization. Stute's dissertation, stimulating as it is, has one flaw: the author draws many parallels to other writers which too often are not illustrated by specific texts.

The preoccupation of many German scholars with postmodernism, which I attempted to illustrate over the last few years, is finally filtering down to the level of dissertations. Michael Winkemann's *Wirklichkeitsbezug und metaliterarische Reflexion in der Kurzprosa Donald Barthelmes* (Lang, 1986) examines Barthelme's short fiction only. The author thinks that Barthelme, like Barth, Coover, and other postmoderns, turns away from mimetic-realistic writing and resorts to fantasy, fairy tales, classic and contemporary myths, the playful-reflexive thematization of the narrative act, and the emphasis on textual autonomy. Yet in spite of his language experiments and metaliterary games, Barthelme's short fiction always contains "topical references" to real events in American public life and sociological observations. Winkemann maintains that Barthelme projects the picture of a highly differentiated, technical society in which there exists an unbridgable gulf between the cold rationality of the social system and the emotionality of the individual. Society exerts psychological pressure like a superfather. Probably the first monograph on Richard Brautigan in Germany is Claudia Grossmann's dissertation, *Richard Brautigan Pounding at the Gates of American Literature: Untersuchungen zu seiner Lyrik und Prosa* (Winter, 1986). Grossmann sees Brautigan's early career as poet and novelist in close affinity with the Beat Generation but also influenced by the French Symbolists. The early novels, *Trout Fishing in America, In Watermelon Sugar,* and *The Arbortion: A Historical Romance,* search for a dynamic life free from the restrictions of society. Yet throughout his career Brautigan maintained a considerable distance from his work. Death as a leitmotif extends through Brautigan's poetry and prose and is at the core of his last novel, *So the Wind Won't Blow It All Away* (1982). Grossmann claims that the source of inspiration in Brautigan's poetry has to be looked for in Far Eastern philosophy and aesthetics, a thesis which is cogently illustrated by a very good analysis of some of his most important poems. This well-written dissertation with its fine balance between close textual analysis and excursions into the historical and philosophical background of his writing is a major contribution to Brautigan scholarship.

Brautigan's postmodernist colleagues Vonnegut and Pynchon were by no means neglected in Germany. Peter Freese in "Inverted Religions as Sense-Making Systems in Kurt Vonnegut's Novels" (*Religion and Philosophy,* vol. 1, pp. 213–40) is puzzled by the fact that Vonnegut is a confirmed atheist who holds in disdain all organized religion, but at the same time in novel after novel devises new religious systems and even argues that mankind needs a new religion. After going through most of his novels, Freese surmises that for Vonnegut God as a supreme mover either does not exist or cannot be understood by man. Therefore, religions cannot be divine laws but can only be judged by the degree to which they provide their adherents with a "protective sense of community." Modern man is in danger of destroying himself because he has made his belief in the infallibility of science and technology into a quasi-religion, which in reality only leads mankind into apocalypse. To avoid this catastrophe and to avoid lapsing into fatalism, man has the right, if not the duty, to construct religions which preach love and responsibility in a godless world of cruelty and injustice.

Gabriele Schwab's "Die Ökologie des Textes: Zu Thomas Pynchons *Gravity's Rainbow*" (*Amst* 32: 345–56) is a highly theoretical attempt to contemplate "one of the important novels of this century" in a field of tensions that is based on various forms of "closeness" and on multidimensionality, which to Schwab seems to point to a four-dimensional world of the space-time continuum. *Gravity's Rainbow* is, as the author claims, not an entropical text. The interplay of figural representation and narrative perspective suggests a new form of text, the "cyborgs," cybernetic organisms whose images of the world are the children of technological imagination and shaped by transindividual semiotic systems and power structures.

My overview will end with three proponents of the realistic tradition in modern American literature. Hanspeter Dörfel reminds us how strongly John Updike's *Rabbit* trilogy is dominated by the protagonist's desperate attempts to come to terms with the idea of death (which is also a search for God) in his "God in John Updike's Trilogy" (*Religion and Philosophy*, vol. 1, pp. 177–96). Carin Freywald, investigating Faulkner's novels *Light in August* and *A Fable* in "The Metamorphosis of the Christ Image in Selected Novels by William Faulkner" (ibid., pp. 241–66), shows that in *The Fable*, in contrast to the earlier novel, the Christ figure is no longer an individual character but an abstraction or a type, a "conceptionalized figure." William Faulkner is also the theme in Bernd Engler's outline of the critical reception of *Absalom, Absalom!* in "William Faulkner's *Absalom, Absalom!*: Five Decades of Critical Reception" (*REAL* 5:221–70). It is not only useful in regard to this one novel, but also to tendencies in Faulkner criticism in general. Furthermore, it demonstrates that in spite of new critical theories any "interpretive progress . . . will also depend on a more thorough 'assimilation' of the insight of past generations of critics."

Universität Hamburg

iv. Italian Contributions

Massimo Bacigalupo

This was a rather lean year, with only a handful of critical volumes and scholarly editions, and a scattering of articles in different places. Some of the year's major efforts seemed open to considerable objections in terms of method and execution. So my task is brief but not easy.

a. **General and Comparative Works.** Ugo Rubeo collected in *Mal d'America: da mito a realtà* (Rome: Editori Riuniti) 15 lively interviews with Italian writers, critics, and directors (among them Michelangelo Antonioni, Dante Della Terza, Mario Soldati, Italo Calvino) on their attitudes to America, and added excerpts from previous observers (Emilio Cecchi, Antonio Gramsci, Cesare Pavese, Mario Praz, Elio Vittorini). The stages of the "America-sickness" illustrated by the interviews are familiar: in the late 1930s Vittorini and his associates took to the freedom and directness of American writers (Fernanda Pivano interview); in the 1950s scholars and artists turned to the American Renaissance and to Eliot, striking a balance between Marxism and New Criticism (Agostino Lombardo and Luigi Squarzina interviews); the 1960s brought in a new bunch of angry young men who were attracted by the "counterculture," but mostly became professors and deconstructionists (interviews with Luigi Ballerini, poet Antonio Porta, Alessandro Portelli, Paolo Valesio). Novelist Alberto Moravia (b. 1907) has seen it all happen and has some personal observations to make on the American conjunction of "Puritanism," by which he means repressed sexuality, "and folly," and on the "Alexandrian" nature of American literature: Poe and James are to him typical decadent writers, Hemingway is "not really a novelist, rather a narrator of himself, almost a poet" (p. 173).

A technical, linguistic discussion of Vittorini's debt to Hemingway and Saroyan is offered by Carmela Nocera's "Vittorini e la lezione americana" in *Lingua letteraria e lingua dei media nell'italiano contemporaneo: atti del convegno internazionale* (Florence: Le Monnier), pp. 335–58. But in the Italy of 1987 admirers of William Saroyan are more scarce than acolytes of Harold Bloom and Paul de Man: an anthology of Yale critics on the sublime appeared as *La via al sublime*, ed. Marshall Brown, Vita Fortunati, and Giovanna Franci (Florence: Alinea).

The mythical and exotic elements in the work of an earlier critic are discussed by Caterina Ricciardi in "Anatomia di un mandala: il modello critico di Northrop Frye," *L'esotismo nelle letterature moderne*, ed. Elémire Zolla (Naples: Liguori), pp. 187–208. This is a comparatist volume with three more articles on American subjects, to be mentioned subsequently. That criticism inevitably ages but in some cases maintains its uses is the burden of my discussion of John Livingston Lowes's *The Road to Xanadu*, in the afterword to my edi-

tion of S. T. Coleridge, *La rima del vecchio marinaio, Kubla Khan,*
trans. Giovanni Giudici (Milan: S.E. Studio Editoriale).

In my article " 'Life Is an Ecstasy': A Transcendentalist Theme in
Whitman, Pound, and Other American Poets" (*Interspace* [Univ. de
Nice] 3:107–20), I claim that "the nature of consciousness . . . con-
sidered and celebrated per se, without reference to any particular ob-
ject of knowledge or world" was a peculiar theme of Emerson and
Thoreau and was forcefully presented by major 19th- and 20th-
century poets, from Walt Whitman and Emily Dickinson to Wallace
Stevens and Ezra Pound.

b. 19th Century.　In her book *Frammenti di un sogno: Hawthorne,
Melville e il romanzo americano* (Milan: Feltrinelli) Barbara Lanati
gives a rambling account of her subjects' lives, writings, and contexts,
freely moving back to the Marquis de Sade and the birth of the novel,
and forward to the Civil War, Ambrose Bierce, Henry James, and the
development of American art and photography—material not for one
but for many books, that does not wholly hang together. Lanati takes
as her focal point the Agatha letters and suggests that Hawthorne's
and Melville's inability to write up this material signals a crisis in
their careers, both men moving into their later phases and eventually
lapsing into silence, while also becoming estranged from each other.
Agatha in this view would be the crucial absence or missing link in
the two writers' story, and of course in the development of the (American) novel. Lanati's writing, however, is too vague to be more than
suggestive; indeed, it is not clear how literally she means us to take
her own metaphors. For a more detailed review the reader may consult Claudio Gorlier, "Tra Melville e Hawthorne il mistero di una
donna," *La Stampa*, 23 January 1988.

The second volume of Ruggero Bianchi's new Italian edition of
Melville, *Mardi* (Milan: Mursia), has a detailed and reliable introduction (pp. ix–lxxx) and a somewhat less reliable translation, by
the editor, of this puzzling novel. For example, I am not sure that
"Skyeman" is well rendered as "Uomo del Cielo," without so much as
a note explaining the reasoning behind this, and a whole sentence
added in the body of the text to give it a spurious authority (p. 16).
"Uomo del cielo" had also been Emilio Tadini's choice in his lively
translation of 1965 (Florence: Vallecchi), but this edition had no
scholarly ambition and in fact opened with an ingenious interview

with the author of *Mardi*. Also, Bianchi has chosen to translate the
Mardi poems in rhyme, which is very strange and leads to much
padding, and he devotes several pages of his introduction (pp. lii–lvi)
to discussing the metrics—of his translations. So what is to become
the first complete edition of Melville in Italian is beginning to look
less than satisfactory, though nonetheless meritorious (everything
has been diligently annotated, including Hero and Leander and
"Eleusinian mysteries" in chapters 38 and 41, which again raises a
question of audience). The editor should have the next volumes
checked for possible inaccuracies and perhaps reconsider his policy
of metrical translation.

Another Melville problem novel is the subject, possibly for the
first time anywhere, of a book-length study, Giuseppe Nori's *La scrit-
tura sconfitta: saggio sul Pierre di Melville* (Rome: Bulzoni, 1986).
This is a philosophical reading that does not address *Pierre*'s status
as literature (which has been challenged since the book's appearance), but takes the novel as the record of a tortuous speculative
struggle. Nori claims, and convincingly proves, that the issues debated in *Pierre* have astonishingly close parallels in such works as
G. W. F. Hegel's *Aesthetik*, Friedrich Nietzsche's *Jenseits von Gut
und Böse*, Martin Heidegger's *Einführung in die Metaphysik*, and
recent writings by Hans-Georg Gadamer and others. In so doing he
contributes considerably to the appreciation of a much-maligned
novel. His book is eloquent (for he is clearly thrilled by his subject)
but controlled, wide in reference but mostly pertinent and accurate.
The approach is intentionally limited, but in this case I believe productive.

Edgar Allan Poe's 1835 review of Alessandro Manzoni's *I promessi
sposi*, which attracted attention a while ago (see *ALS 1986*, p. 456),
is reprinted and annotated in Fredi Chiappelli's pamphlet *Poe legge
Manzoni* (Milan: Coliseum). In his 40-page introduction, Chiappelli,
a Manzoni specialist, compares the plague scenes of the Italian novel
with "King Pest" (1835) and suggests that some elements of Manzoni's style are visible in other stories, e.g., "The Assignation." Ro-
berto Cagliero has a brief subtle account of *Eureka* and "Never Bet
the Devil Your Head" in "La critica dell'ornamento nei saggi e nella
narrativa di Poe" (*Quaderni di lingue et letterature* [Univ. di Verona]
12:21–37).

Alessandra Contenti has been doing work on a popular writer who
spent most of his life in Italy, Francis Marion Crawford. She edited

and translated *Uomo a mare!* e *La cuccetta superiore* (Marina di Patti: Pungitopo, 1986) and wrote the ample introduction to *La strega di Praga*, trans. Daniela Daniele (Pordenone: Studio Tesi). To *L'esotismo nelle letterature moderne* she contributed a good discussion of *The Witch of Prague* and *Mr. Isaacs*, "Praga, Simla e Francis Marion Crawford" (pp. 51–66).

Henry James was born 11 years before his friend Crawford, so I think that from this year he should go into my 19th-century section. He was suitably paid homage to by the 19 contributors to *Henry James e Venezia*, ed. Sergio Perosa (Florence: Olschki), which collects the proceedings of a conference held in 1985 at the Giorgio Cini Foundation of Venice. I will not discuss the seven non-Italian contributions (Michel Butor, Leon Edel, Tony Tanner, James W. Tuttleton, Barbara Arnett Melchiori, Jeanne Clegg, Aladàr Sarbu), nearly all of them devoted to aspects of James in Venice. Of the Italian papers, seven also have Venetian themes. Alide Cagidemetrio ("Scelta di città: Venezia, Black Balloons and White Doves," pp. 53–64) uses the diary of James's friend Constance F. Woolson to illuminate some symbols. Rosella Mamoli Zorzi's excellently researched paper, "Henry James in un diario 'veneziano' " (pp. 135–58), describes another, unpublished, diary, written mostly by Ariana and Daniel Curtis and preserved in the Biblioteca Nazionale Marciana, and gives us glimpses of "poor Henry James" (as he was to Ralph Curtis) and his life at the Palazzo Barbaro and on a heretofore unknown country outing. Giorgio Melchiori (whose paper, like Glauco Cambon's "The Mazes of Venice," pp. 95–108, is in English) makes some acute observations on "the complex and peculiar identity of Venice as an essential place in James's moral universe"—an identity fully realized with *The Wings of the Dove* ("Henry James: Burbank or Bleistein," pp. 117–26). Marilla Battilana, author of *Venezia sfondo e simbolo nella narrativa di Henry James*, recently reprinted (Milan: Laboratorio delle Arti), returns to her subject in a comparative context ("Venezia elemento letterario: strategie di assimilazione in James, Mann, Proust," pp. 171–88). Alberta Fabris Grube illuminatingly compares "Howells e James a Venezia: due scrittori e due modi di interpretare la città" (pp. 189–202); Venice, we remember, is not necessarily romantic to Howells, just as James came to find in 1904 that "Venice, to tell the truth, has been simply blighted and made a proper little hell (I mean what I say!) by 'people'!" (p. 156). However, scholars who are so fortunate as to meet at the Cini Foundation know otherwise. Sergio Perosa develops his previous books in an account of the International Theme and of James's metafiction ("Henry James: romanziere di due mondi e fra due secoli," pp. 13–36). Francesca Bisutti addresses narrative point of view in "A Landscape Painter" and "The Friends of the Friends" ("Due racconti in forma di diario: una breve storia dell'Io jamesiano," pp. 203–18). Bianca Tarozzi draws a rich comparison with Goethe's *Die Wahlverwandtschaften* in "Le affinità elettive in *The Golden Bowl*" (pp. 233–46). Biancamaria Tedeschini Lalli discusses the linguistic implications of a forgotten article ("America ed Europa in 'The Speech and Manners of American Women,'" pp. 247–62). Agostino Lombardo's "Le Prefazioni come romanzo dell'artista" (pp. 263–75) closes this notable volume with the pithy observations which have been incorporated in his introduction to *Le prefazioni* (see *ALS 1986*, p. 465). Lombardo also discusses early James and American realism in his afterward to *Tutore e pupilla*, trans. Alessandra Cremonese (Rome: Editori Riuniti), with a good introduction by the translator. In his preface to *Henry James e Venezia* Sergio Perosa is perhaps just a little too certain that our small world's conference pilgrims are in no way "publishing scoundrels" (p. viii), yet this homage to the Master from Venice is on the whole a fine thing.

c. **20th Century.** Some papers given at a 1985 conference in Rome on the 1930s in the United States are gathered in *LAmer* 24–25 (1984), among them four Italian contributions on U.S. literature. In "Gli anni '30 e la crisi del Modernismo statunitense" (pp. 29–36) I show how high modernism was thought of as dead and buried by the new generation of the 1930s, only to return with a vengeance in subsequent decades, when Pound, Eliot, Williams, and Stevens proved themselves the central figures of the midcentury. Stefania Piccinato's "Da Langston Hughes a Richard Wright: percorso di una ideologia e di una poetica" (pp. 153–66) considers the literary politics of the Harlem Renaissance, while Maria Anita Stefanelli's "Aspetti sociolinguistici della poesia di William Carlos Williams" (pp. 223–41) compares Williams's linguistic convictions to the tenets of H. L. Mencken and provides a "sociolinguistic" reading of *Paterson* II, Part 2. Language is also used by Elèna Mortara as a key to enter the polyphonic world of *Call It Sleep*, in which for example literary English is used for Yiddish to suggest a language of origin, and all kinds of variant or mutant English coexist ("Da Babele al silenzio: il romanzo sinfonico di Henry Roth," p. 135–52).

A literary descendant of Henry Roth is treated with notable competence by Giordano De Biasio in "Il mondo kafkiano di Bernard Malamud" (*Lingua e stile* 6 [1986]:44–60), which is a good reading of "Take Pity," a wonderful story on the classic Malamud theme of the outsider seeking admission to a closed world. This De Biasio shows to have close parallels in Kafka, especially *The Castle*. In the field of ethnic literature other events were the publication of Jerre Mangione, *Ricerca nella notte*, trans. Giuseppe Massara (Palermo: Sellerio), and Fedora Giordano's compilation, "North American Indians in Italian (1950–1981): A Bibliography of Books," in *Indians and Europe*, ed. Christian F. Feest (Aachen: Herodot-Rader), pp. 489–503.

Fedora Giordano has also written with acumen about several once-popular novels of Frederic Prokosch, namely *The Asiatics, The Seven Who Fled, Storm and Echo* ("Esotismo e nostalgia delle origini nei romanzi di Frederic Prokosch," in *L'esotismo nelle letterature moderne*, pp. 165–86). Prokosch is chiefly known, in Italy as elsewhere, for his gossipy memoir of 1983, *Voices*. Another kind of popular literature, SF, in particular Kurt Vonnegut's *The Sirens of Titan* and Philip K. Dick's *Time Out of Joint*, is treated by Carlo Pagetti and Oriana Palusci in "SF e Post-moderno: due modelli narrativi" (*AION/Anglistica* 28, iii[1985]:131–56). The Genoa publisher Costa & Nolan gave us another volume of American plays (by Tina Howe, Albert Innaurato, Miguel Pinero, David Rabe), *Nuovo teatro d'America*, with a knowledgeable introduction by the editor, Mario Maffi. The 1986 anthology of short fiction by David Leavitt, Susan Minot, and others, *20 Under 30*, was translated with the title *Americani anni '80* (Parma: Guanda). Fernanda Pivano in the preface gives her benedictions to yet another generation of American writers.

More concentrated work was done on poetry. In "Roma nella letteratura americana del Novecento" (*Studi Romani* 35:172–91) Andrea Mariani finds that Baroque Rome often brings out the Puritan in such visiting poets as Anthony Hecht, Horace Gregory, James Merrill, John Ciardi, and Richard Wilbur. Mariani also contributed a lengthy and stringent discussion of Horace Gregory, "Esotismo e classicismo nella poesia di Horace Gregory," to the miscellany *L'esotismo nelle letterature moderne* (pp. 141–64).

Wallace Stevens did not visit Rome; nevertheless, Mariani reminds us that he wrote one of his major poems on the city. Interest in him in Italy continues steady. *Notes Toward a Supreme Fiction* had been translated long ago by the late Glauco Cambon (*Letteratura* 11–12 [1954]) and aptly commented on in his *Tematica e sviluppo della poesia americana* (Rome: Edizioni di Storia e Letteratura, 1956). Now Nadia Fusini has offered a new, distinctly creative version of Stevens's master poem, *Note verso la finzione suprema* (Venice: Arsenale) and added a dazzling 70-page apparatus (introduction, footnotes, endnotes) in the oneiric style I spoke of in *ALS 1986*, p. 464. Fusini treats *Notes* as a sort of sacred text and writes her own apocryphal variations on what she takes to be Stevens's metaphysics, wasting little time with questions of source, context, and style (she ignores Michel Benamou's and B. J. Leggett's essential groundwork on these prosaic matters), and somewhat obscuring the humor and sheer mischievousness of the poem, not to mention its epigrammatic quality.

Edgar Lee Masters, a discovery of the days of Vittorini, continues to attract publishers: a new translation, the fourth, by Antonio Porta, of *Antologia di Spoon River* has appeared (Milan: Mondadori). On the other hand, William Carlos Williams's *Immagini da Bruegel*, trans. Ariodante Marianni (Parma: Guanda), had its first Italian publication. A selection from the New Directions volume of the same title, it unfortunately omits all but the first section of "Asphodel."

Angelo Tonelli wrote a lonely article on Pound, "La maschera divisa" (*Paragone* 444:48–58), drawing a few conclusions from my edition of *Homage to Sextus Propertius* (see *ALS 1985*, pp. 552–53). Pound was also the victim of the year's major flop, perpetrated by a nonacademic, Maria Luisa Ardizzone, who edited *Ezra Pound e la scienza: scritti inediti o rari* (Milan: Scheiwiller). This handsome but misbegotten volume, on the frontispiece of which the editor appears as author, gathers 33 miscellaneous pieces by Pound in an attempt to document his interest in science. Some, like the "Postscript" to Gourmont, are easily available elsewhere, others are reprinted from periodicals, four letters (to Douglas Fox, Albert Einstein, Bertrand Russell), and six papers, among them the long essay "Machine Art" (1927), are printed here for the first time. This will make the book of interest to scholars, though the English text is unreliable and the translation very poor (for example, "man makes a song" is rendered as "l'uomo sogna" on p. 85). "European Paideuma," an important article of 1939 (not 1940) never printed in its entirety, is given in Douglas Fox's heavily edited and toned-down version rather than in Pound's racier original (excerpts of which appeared in Charles Norman, *Ezra Pound*, 1960). Ardizzone tones it down even further by removing (p. 230) several paragraphs on the "indispensable . . . function of Germany in the next forty years" (the article was intended for German readers) and on the "semitic microbes" in Christianity. This anxiousness to present Pound only in the supposedly best light is as damaging to the "Idaho kid" as it is to the scholarly pretensions of this volume. Oddly, there is no index of the titles of the documents collected, only of the Roman numerals supplied in brackets by the author-editor herself.

A better service to Pound's Italian readers was rendered by Loretta Innocenti, who translated *Antheil* (1924) as *Trattato d'armonia e altri scritti musicali* (Florence: Passigli), adding an introduction and notes. The booklet has a magisterial afterword by Marcello Pagnini; the translation, saving a few lapses, is accurate enough.

Annalisa Goldoni and Marina Morbiducci edited for their students the anthology *Black Mountain: poesia & poetica* (Rome: Euroma), adding two informative articles on Charles Olson and Robert Creeley and a bibliography. Also intended for a student audience, and very solid in its research and annotation, is Bonalda Stringher's *Introduzione alla poesia di Hart Crane* (Verona: Morelli), which includes a 60-page introduction and 19 poems.

Mary de Rachewiltz's selection of 100 E. E. Cummings poems of the more temperate sort was reprinted in an attractive volume, *Poesie* (Turin: Einaudi), and got a celebratory review from a shrewd nonspecialist Enzo Golino ("Cummings poeta verde," *La Repubblica*, 13 November); the translation is a feat of ingeniousness, with the occasional misunderstanding (e.g., pp. 57 and 233, lines 7–8). Five other poems, from *Is 5*, were offered by Marcello Pagnini in a small magazine devoted to the comic, *Téchne* 1 (1986):13–26. Marilla Battilana gave Kenneth Fearing what may be his first Italian hearing by translating and introducing four poems in *L'ozio* 2, iv:65–73. Finally, Bianca Tarozzi translated Elizabeth Bishop's "Roosters," "Sandpiper," and "House Guest," and added a good little essay, "Figurazione animale" (*In forma di parole* 8, i:87–120), while I did the translation for a special edition of Dana Gioia, *Two Poems/Due poesie* (Verona: Ampersand).

Università di Udine

476 Foreign Scholarship

v. Japanese Contributions

Keiko Beppu

Literary conferences have often been instrumental in the production
of books in this country; papers presented are likely to result in publication of books in one form or another. This is a well-established
practice among our scholars and is no new phenomenon. What is
new about such academic activities in recent years is the increasingly
international dimension those literary conferences have come to as-
sume, and also the changing role we play at such literary feasts, so
to speak, where a Japanese professor often figures as a host and *not*
as the reserved guest he used to be. It seems that American literary
study in Japan has finally been catching up with other foreign scholarships on American literature.

The most significant accomplishment for 1987 in this respect is
the publication of *Faulkner: ATNP*, a fruit of the International Faulkner Symposium held at Izu in April 1985, with the general theme
which has become the title of the book. Another example, though
much smaller in scope, has evolved out of the Specialists' Conference
at the Kyoto American Studies Summer Seminar held in the same
year: *The Gilded Age and American Writers*, ed. Tajiro Iwayama
(Yamaguchi). What all of this amounts to is the solidification of
Japanese scholarship on American literature; there is no better indication of our scholarly achievements than a turnout of more than 20
substantial book-length studies during 1987.

The distinctive feature of Japanese scholarship on American literature for the year is the preeminence of works done on general literary
themes and traditions rather than on individual American writers,
which was often the case in the past. Certainly, our all-time favorite
19th-century writers such as Poe, Hawthorne, Melville, and James
constitute the center of critical attention in those general studies.
Likewise, with two highly commendable books and a half-a-dozen
articles to boot, Faulkner is still the most important and controversial
20th-century American writer among scholars and students here. And
last but not least, American women writers and feminist issues continue to interest our scholars. Hiroko Sato's *America no Katei-
shosetsu: Jukyuseiki no Joseisakka-tachi* [The Domestic Novel in
America: 19th-Century Women Writers] (Kenkyusha) and Konomi
Ara's *Onna no America* [Women's America] (Kadensha) address
themselves to that critical concern.

These and other individual works for 1987 are classified for this review as follows: literary history; general studies; studies on individual novelists; studies on individual poets; and American studies. The articles here surveyed are restricted (with a few exceptions) to those published in our major academic journals: *EigoS*, *SELit*, and *SALit*.

Among numerous literary histories published each year, Kichinosuke Ohashi's *America Bungakushi Nyumon* [The Literary History of the United States: An Introduction] (Kenkyusha) is a convenient handbook to American literature compactly planned for college students. But it is meager, though understandably so, in the field of poetry; no contemporary poet receives mention. A more ambitious attempt is *America Bungaku o Manabu Hitono tameni* [An Invitation to American Literature] ed. Tajiro Iwayama (Sekai). *An Invitation* is a unique literary history; its editorial rationale is not so much the chronology of literary events and movements or listing of writers and poets in that order as it is a strategy for surfacing a surprisingly multifaceted reality of American literature in its historical perspective and simultaneously in its complex sociopolitical context, which bears a vital relationship to our contemporary society.

What makes *An Invitation* a unique literary history is the inclusion, along with discussions on "Popular Culture" (by Kohji Oi) and "Women and Literature" (by Keiko Beppu), of a chapter on "Young Japanese Novelists and Contemporary American Literature" (pp. 299–313) by Ichiro Hayashi. The chapter examines the intricate ways in which young Japanese writers respond to American literature. Conversely, the assumption is that Japanese culture and literature have become a part of contemporary American writings; there is a growing awareness on the part of Japanese scholars and the reading public as well of cross-cultural exchanges between the two countries. This question of cultural interdependence receives more extended exploration in Kenzaburo Ohashi's book examined first among the general studies on American literature.

Valuable scholarly achievements for 1987 in the field of general studies with an historical perspective on American literature are Kenzaburo Ohashi's *Atama to Kokoro: Nichibei no Bungaku to Kindai* [The Head and the Heart: Japanese and American Writers in the Modern Age] (Kenkyusha); Takuo Miyake's *Doh Yomuka America Bungaku: Hawthorne kara Pynchon made* [Reading American Literature: From Hawthorne to Pynchon] (Kyoto: Apollon-sha); *America no Shosetsu: Riron to Jissen* [The American Novel: Theories and Practices], ed. Iwao Iwamoto and Takeshi Morita (Liber); the aforementioned *Kinmekki-Jidai to America Bungaku* [The Gilded Age and American Writers]; Hiroko Sato's *The Domestic Novel in America: 19-Century Women Writers*; Masako Takahashi's *America Nambu no Sakka-tachi* [Southern American Writers] (Nan'undo); and *America Bungaku ni-okeru Kazoku* [The Family in American Literature] (Yamaguchi) by Yuko Eguchi et al.

The Head and the Heart by our distinguished Faulknerian is a collection of essays which previously appeared in various academic and literary journals. Indeed, the essays make an excellent comparative study of Japanese and American literatures. Ohashi's contention that the estrangement between the "head" and the "heart" is the "modern disease" that ails Japanese and American writers who work in similar social and cultural milieux rings a bell for many of our readers. Ohashi makes the most of his expertise on such writers as Poe, Hawthorne, Melville, and Faulkner, *and* on modern and contemporary Japanese novelists—Natsume Soseki, Junichiro Tanizaki, and Kenji Nakagami. Faulkner is an alleged "Muse" for the last-mentioned Japanese writer, whose contribution to *Faulkner: ATNP* is examined later.

Takuo Miyake's *Reading American Literature: From Hawthorne to Pynchon* is also a collection of essays written during the too-brief career of this dedicated Hawthorne scholar. The collection was edited and posthumously published with the collaboration of his friends. *Reading American Literature* well represents the range and diversity of Miyake's academic interest. The first part of the book includes nine of his essays on Hawthorne. Miyake's discussions of "The Gentle Boy," "My Kinsman, Major Molineux," and "Young Goodman Brown" (pp. 70–131) make an excellent study of the American writer, which reveals Miyake's aesthetics of the Barthesian "discourse" or "narration." In the second half of the book is one of the best discussions yet on Poe's "The Fall of the House of Usher" (pp. 191–202) along with essays on a few 20th-century American writers—Salinger, Pynchon, and Updike—dealing with the question of narratology in Pynchon's *V* (pp. 261–74) and in Updike's *Rabbit* trilogy (pp. 275–97). The last essay in the collection is an anomaly; yet "The Image of Home in Contemporary Japanese Fiction" (pp. 347–71) is a companion piece to Miyake's earlier essay on "The Three 'Houses' in American Renaissance Writings" (not included in the collection). Furthermore, as Ohashi and others will testify, the critic's approach to American literature via Japanese literature, either deliberately or unconsciously made, is something that comes natural to Japanese scholars of American literature.

As Miyake's discussion on narratology in Hawthorne's short stories shows, American novelists have been extremely self-conscious about their "art of fiction"; many have written their own apologia, not excepting Hawthorne's Preface to *The House of the Seven Gables*. The critics of American literature in turn engage themselves in a similar preoccupation—how theory applies to practice. Such is the focus of exploration in *The American Novel*, a collection of essays by our promising young scholars. The writers discussed are Hawthorne, Melville, Twain, James, Hemingway, Faulkner, Bellow, Erica Jong, Barth, Raymond Federman, and Coover. The discussions of individual writers are preceded by close examinations of fictional theories (sometimes replaced by translations); and Iwao Iwamoto's introduction, "The American Novel and Its Theories" (pp. 7–21), covers the ground well; it is a succinct survey of developments in American fiction.

The Gilded Age is likewise a collection of essays contributed by some of the participants in the 1985 Kyoto American Studies Summer Seminar. Each essay tries to clarify the meaning of "the Gilded Age" by examining American writers who represent the period: Henry Ward Beecher, J. W. DeForest, Twain, Whitman, Henry Adams, Howells, James, Crane, and Owen Wister. The list is what one might have expected—no women are represented. Just the same, the essays by our experts show insightful and penetrating readings.

Of special importance is Shunsuke Kamei's "Whitman and the Gilded Age" (pp. 55–71), which focuses on Whitman's *Specimen Days* and comes up with another face of the great American poet. Another interesting essay in the volume is Takashi Sasaki's reading of Wister's *The Virginian* and its hero, "The Cowboy on the Train" (pp. 157–75); Sasaki's title itself reveals the comic caricature of what he calls "the premodern" hero at the turn of the century. Taken as a whole, *The Gilded Age* is quite a successful scholarly venture, which incorporates diversified perspectives on that transitional period in American history and its impact on the creative imagination of American writers who lived through it. Alan Trachtenberg made a special contribution to the volume: "The City and Literature in the Gilded Age"; and there were two delegates from Korea and one from the Philippines at the conference.

Hiroko Sato's *The Domestic Novel in America* deals with some representative "scribbling women writers": Susanna Rowson, Catharine Maria Sedgwick, Susan Warner, Maria Cummins, Elizabeth Stuart Phelps, Fanny Fern, Harriet Beecher Stowe, Elizabeth Stoddard, and Louisa May Alcott. With elaborate biographical sketches of some of these lesser-known women writers together with synopses of some of their similarly lesser-known novels, *The Domestic Novel in America* provides a neat antithesis to the "American Idea" which dominated the sociocultural milieu of the American Renaissance.

Sato offers ready and insightful answers to the questions which led her to write the book: the emergence of women writers in the years between 1820–70; the popularity of the particular genre which became for them the sole and effective means of spiritual support as well as financial reward. The accounts of their lives are often as enthralling as the stories they wrote; these are indispensable to Sato's discussion because their life stories reveal complex socioeconomic factors which engendered these "scribbling women writers" at that particular time in American history. In this respect, like *The Gilded Age*, *The Domestic Novel in America* is a period study conducted from a woman's point of view and brings the body of their literature to our attention as a "countertext" of the period.

The author is no outspoken feminist, yet Sato offers a few feminist interpretations throughout her discussion. The observations are incisive, supported by solid scholarship, and often provocative. Sato argues that the morals by which Richardsonian novels taught young girls to be "good wives and mothers" ironically became for these women writers (and their enlightened readers) the practical means for self-identification and for self-realization. Observations like this, however, remain as such and are not elaborated. Even so, the very fact that these writers are made available to our critical investigation is noteworthy. *The Domestic Novel in America* is a memorable breakthrough in the androcentric Japanese scholarship on American literature. In this connection the following articles deserve mention here: Kazuko Watanabe's "The Mask of Louisa May Alcott the Writer— with Special Reference to *Work* and 'Behind a Mask'" (*KanAL* 24:22–36) and a special feature on black American women writers (*EigoS* 133:8–20).

Masao Takahashi's *American Southern Writers*, the culmination of some 30 years of research by one of our seasoned scholars, is the first book-length study dealing with southern literature as a whole from the 17th century to the present. As such, the book is a panoramic literary history of the American South. Despite its size (running close to 600 pages), however, it is best characterized as an excellent compendium on the subject.

The first part (pp. 13–112) examines the sociohistorical background of the American South as an entity, and a good introduction to the second part (pp. 115–246) takes up individual writers of the "New South" (1875–1905): George Washington Cable, Joel Chandler Harris, Mary Noailles Murfree, James Lane Allen, and Thomas Nelson Page. The rest of the book is devoted to five of the great southern writers: Ellen Glasgow, William Faulkner, Thomas Wolfe, Robert Penn Warren, and William Styron.

As in the case of *The Domestic Novel in America*, *American Southern Writers* provides compact biographies of the writers followed by discussions of their representative works. Since society in the American South and its mores are frequently compared to ours, and Japanese scholars and readers respond favorably to southern writers (our reception of Faulkner is an eloquent index), Takahashi's accomplishment is greatly appreciated.

The last book in this group of general studies on American literature is a unique collection of essays, *The Family in American Literature*. It is unique in that all the contributors are young, promising women scholars who are former students of Professor Eguchi, who has retired from Tokyo Women's Christian University. The collection is an illustration of what feminism has done to liberate male-dominated academe in this country.

The 13 essays plus the special contribution by Eguchi, "The Motif of the Double in Flannery O'Connor's Fiction," examine various images of the family portrayed by different American writers. The selection covers the spectrum of American literature fairly well: Poe, Hawthorne, James, Gilman, Cather, Porter, Nin, Welty, Styron, Bellow, Oates, and Morrison. The inclusion of such southern women writers as O'Connor, Porter, and Welty closes the gender gap in Takahashi's *American Southern Writers*. The following two essays in particular deserve brief comments: Michiko Shimokoube's Lacanian reading of Hawthorne's "The Birthmark" (pp. 15–27) is a valid application of a new critical theory; whereas Kiyomi Sasame gives a good introduction to Charlotte Perkins Gilman, one of the early feminist writers (pp. 51–64). Furthermore, *The Family in American Literature* is, in a way, a sequel to Sato's *The Domestic Novel in America* since the question of home or family is one of the central concerns in both studies.

In comparison with the phenomenal achievement registered in the general studies already surveyed, books on individual writers and poets were meager in 1987. Even so, there were a few invaluable studies done on 19th- and 20th-century writers: Hiroaki Dehara's *Henry James no Shosetsu: Sono Shinsoishiki to Giho* [The Novels of Henry James: The Sense of the Unconscious and the Technique] (New Current); Kiyohiko Murakami's *Theodore Dreiser Ron: America to Higeki* [The Tragic Vision in the Novels of Theodore Dreiser: Tragedy and American Society] (Nan'undo); the aforementioned *Faulkner: ATNP*; and Kenzaburo Ohashi's *Watashi-no-uchinaru Faulkner: Text no Shuhen Kara* [My Personal Faulkner: From Marginalia] (Nan'undo).

No American writer is, perhaps, more self-conscious about the art and act of writing than Henry James. Recent new theorists have conducted a thorough examination of James's magnum opus, which has yielded an overwhelming amount of new James scholarship. Attempts also have been made among Japanese Jamesians to apply new critical tools to the reading of the Master. One such example is Hideo Nakamura's article, "The Sanctum of *The Wings of the Dove*" (*SALit* 24: 17–31). Hiroaki Dehara's *Novels of Henry James* is a collection of essays previously published in different academic journals, with one exception, which Dehara claims is a deconstructionist approach to *The Wings of the Dove* written for this book. Other works of James examined are four novellas of the 1890s: "The Beast in the Jungle," "The Altar of the Dead," "The Jolly Corner," and "The Third Person." Dehara's discussion, in three parts, of *The Wings of the Dove* takes up about half the book. Despite the claim Dehara makes for the last chapter on *The Wings of the Dove*, his critical position is essentially conventional and only moderately deconstructionist.

Dehara is intrigued by the Jamesian "world of words" as opposed to "the extensional world"; he tries to riddle out how the intricate mechanism of words, signs, and symbols functions in James's fictional world. The writer's interest in psycholinguistics and Jungian psychology is best employed in his discussions of "The Beast in the Jungle" (pp. 7–19) and of *The Wings of the Dove* (pp. 147–83). Interestingly enough, "the beast" in "The Beast in the Jungle" has become a functional critical sign in Dehara's discussions of *The Wings of the Dove*. To show the range and variety of our James studies, two other essays deserve our attention: Jiroo Kai's "Early Novels of Henry James" (*EigoS* 133:158–62) and Mikiko Ikeda's "From Wilderness to the Picturesque—Poe, Hawthorne, James, and the Ideal Landscape" (ibid. 114–16). The first article examines the place of nature, civilization, and history in James's early novels *Roderick Hudson* and *The Portrait of a Lady*. The second is an interesting speculation on "the picturesque" in Poe, Hawthorne, and James.

Of the studies done on individual American writers for 1987, Kiyohiko Murakami's *The Tragic Vision in the Novels of Theodore Dreiser* is a paramount achievement. It is the first full-scale study of Dreiser, who has long been neglected by Japanese scholars as an old-fashioned naturalist. Murakami challenges such stereotypes of Dreiser; it is an ambitious attempt to present him as a writer of authentic American tragedy. Murakami is persistent and tenacious in his implementation of the Aristotelian concept of tragedy on all of Dreiser's eight novels. Understandably, the chapter on *An American Tragedy* (pp. 181–226) is charged with the critic's enthusiasm. At first sight, the tragic vision—not to say the Aristotelian tragic vision—and the naturalist's deterministic view of the world seem a great paradox. Yet Murakami is relentless in his scholarly pursuit, exploiting relevant scholarships (including Ellen Moers's pioneering work and others) and his readings in Nietzsche, and he succeeds in making his point that it is the tragic vision of the world that moves the characters in Dreiser's novels, and that they are no mere victims of external forces over which they have no control.

The concluding chapter (pp. 263–78) is a well-gleaned summary of the "critical battle" over Dreiser scholarship in the United States; the bibliography is well-prepared and up-to-date, especially in Japanese scholarship on this great 20th-century writer. Whether one agrees with Murakami's critical position or not, the discussion is first-rate scholarship, and *The Tragic Vision in the Novels of Theodore Dreiser* is a monumental achievement.

William Faulkner has always been one of the most-studied American writers in this country. There is Ohashi's three-volume *Faulkner Studies* (1977–82), and the translation of his complete works (25 vols.) is an indication of the novelist's popularity with our reading public as well as with Japanese scholars. Two books on Faulkner came out in 1987: *Faulkner:ATNP* and Kenzaburo Ohashi's *My Personal Faulkner*. As has been mentioned, *Faulkner: ATNP* is a memorable outcome of the International Faulkner Symposium held in 1985; an equal number of nine foreign and Japanese Faulknerians contribute essays, which reevaluate the late Faulkner, who has been slighted in Faulkner criticism.

In the book's first chapter Ohashi and three French Faulkner scholars discuss "Faulkner and the 1950's"; the second chapter includes studies on individual works—*A Fable*, the Snopes trilogy, and *The Reivers*—by five Japanese, one German, and two American Faulknerians; in the third chapter the importance of Faulkner's late career is discussed by a Norwegian, an English, and a Japanese expert; the last chapter includes special contributions by Cleanth Brooks and by the Japanese novelist Kenji Nakagami. The list of contributors is impressive; so is the objective of the book and its international scope.

A few sample essays are Fumiyo Hayashi's "The Critical Difference: Faulkner's Case in *A Fable*" (pp. 91–109); Ikuko Fujihira's "The Indestructible Voice of the British Battalion Runner in *A Fable*" (pp. 127–46); and Masao Shimura's "Pynchon and Faulkner" (pp. 282–303). As the title indicates, the first essay is an application of (Barbara) Johnsonian and reader-response theory to *A Fable*; Hayashi argues that "as in *Billy Budd*, the function of reading/misreading and the ambiguous relation between decidability and ambiguity dominates the story of *A Fable*." Fujihira's discussion focuses on the British battalion runner and points out the character's positive aspects denied by such critics as Keen Butterworth. Masao Shimura traces Faulknerian echoes in the postmodernist American writer Thomas Pynchon, which makes quite a readable essay. His contention is that the use of the same core myth (Orpheus-Christ) in Faulkner and Pynchon clarifies "the ultimate difference of the two novelists' styles and imaginations." Available in English, *Faulkner: ATNP* is indeed a valuable addition not only to Japanese scholarship on the novelist but also to Faulknerian scholarship worldwide.

Ohashi's *My Personal Faulkner: From Marginalia* is a collection of our noted scholar's miscellaneous essays, notes, and travel sketches previously published in various academic and literary journals. *My Personal Faulkner* gives glimpses into a scholar's life, professional and personal, and makes enjoyable reading for those similarly engaged in the study of American literature. The essays and sketches here collected are sometimes more revealing of Faulkner the writer and of his imaginary world than Ohashi's more formal essays on the novelist. "Faulkner and the Image of Family" (pp. 233–55) is best appreciated perhaps along with the chapters in *The Family in American Literature* previously mentioned.

As for the articles on Faulkner, here it suffices to list some representative ones: Yosuke Murakami's "Faulkner, History, and Genealogy" (*KanAL* 24:27–50); Takako Tanaka's "*Sanctury*: The Dead End of Seeing" (ibid. 24:51–65); Naoto Sugiyama's "Community and Individual in Faulkner's *The Hamlet*" (*SALit* 24:49–62); and Sanae Tokizane's Derrida monologue on reading Faulkner, "Writing—Literature, Letters, Theory" (*EigoS* 133:262–66). The first two are available in English.

There was no significant study published on contemporary American novelists in 1987. Other than those included in the general studies surveyed earlier, the following contemporary writers have received critical consideration: John Hawkes in Hitomi Nakatani's "Counseling Novels—An Approach to John Hawkes" in English (*SALit* 24:87–101); and Jerzy Kosinski in Hideo Kotake's "The Folkloristic World of Jerzy Kosinski's *The Painted Bird*" (ibid, pp. 103–17).

Important books published on individual American poets for 1987 are Toshihiko Ogata's *Shijin E. A. Poe* [Edgar Allan Poe: The Poet (Yamaguchi); Minoru Hirooka's *America Gendai-shi ni-okeru Whitman-zo* [Walt Whitman and Contemporary American Poets] (Yamaguchi); *Ezra Pound and Japan: Letters and Essays*, ed. Sanehide Kodama (Black Swan); and Akira Minami's *Shijin no Sugao: Sylvia Plath to Ted Hughes* [The Poet Unmasked: Sylvia Plath and Ted Hughes] (Kenkyusha).

In recent years significant works have been completed which deal with Poe's stories or with the Gothic tradition in Poe. Also, as we recall, there are chapters on Poe's fictional works in the general studies examined above. Toshihiko Ogata's foremost concern in *Edgar Allan Poe* is, however, with Poe's poetry as a whole, which is demonstrated in Ogata's beautiful translations of all the poetical works and poetical theories. As such, *Edgar Allan Poe: The Poet* is a work of art rather than a critical study of the poet, even though the first part of the volume (570 pages), called "Studies", includes a sympathetic critical biography.

Minoru Hirooka's *Walt Whitman* examines literary influences of

Whitman on modern and contemporary poets: Pound, Hart Crane, Stevens, William Carlos Williams, and Allen Ginsberg. The term "America Gendai-shi" (meaning contemporary American poetry) in the title is misleading since only Ginsberg, with a passing remark on Louis Simpson, is treated in the book. Hirooka uses the terms "modern" and "contemporary" either interchangeably or side by side, calling Whitman "the father of modern American poetry."

Hirooka's essay, "The Shore Ode Motif in Whitman and Williams," written in 1983, constitutes the core of the book. His expertise on Williams is evident in the two chapters on the doctor-poet, which occupy a little less than half the volume. Hirooka's discussions in these chapters stand out both in a positive and negative way. Positively, they are well informed and convincing; negatively, they throw the rest of the book off balance. There have been studies done on the impact of Whitman on later American poets, but no comprehensive study such as Hirooka's has been completed. In this sense, *Walt Whitman* is a welcome achievement for Japanese scholarship on American poetry. Certainly, it is no superficial influence study.

Ezra Pound and Japan is a valuable addition to Pound scholarship, even though readers may be limited to those whose particular interest lies in the poet's relation to this country. The letters written by Japanese artists to Pound, who was working with W. B. Yeats on the translation of Japanese Noh dramas, and essays by Pound contributed to Japanese newspapers and journals document the poet's lifelong (dating from 1911 to 1968) involvement with the art and culture of Japan. The letters are arranged roughly in chronological order, the editor, who is a famous Poundian, Sanehide Kodama, explains, to show "a historical overview of Pound's involvement with the art and culture of Japan."

Arika Minami's *The Poet Unmasked* is an attempt, among other similar speculations, to reveal "the real Sylvia Plath" and correct the self-created image of the poet as a suicidal romantic girl with "an Electra complex." Ironically, while unveiling the poet, Minami's monograph creates another persona of Sylvia Plath—that of a motherly poet who longed for love, not death.

With regards to articles on individual poets, let me refer to Masao Tsunematsu's chapter in *The Gilded Age*, which discusses the poems of Stephen Crane (pp. 135–55), and Hiroko Uno's article (in English), "Optical Instruments and 'Compound Vision' in Emily Dickinson's Poetry" (*SELit* 64:227–43).

Important accomplishments made in the last group of books for 1987 are Konomi Ara's *Women's America*; Shunsuke Kamei's *Puritan no Matsuei: America Bunka to Sei* [The Descendants of the Puritans: Sex and American Culture] (Kenkyusha); and the same author's *Kohya no America* [America the Wilderness] (Nan'undo).

Konomi Ara's *Women's America* is a collection of readable essays about American life from a feminist point of view. The first section contains journalistic reports and comments on various issues women in America face today—topical newspaper or magazine clippings which highlight feminism in America. The second half of the book traces a history (or better still evolution) of what Ara calls the "New Feminism of the 60's and 70's" with a valid assessment of the movement which has continually had an impact on the lives of Americans, both women and men.

Shunsuke Kamei's *The Descendants of the Puritans* is a well-informed historical exploration of how the Puritans of the 17th century and their descendants dealt with sex in life and in various forms of art. It is also a sociological study of the American temperament, which is best characterized as "Puritan." Kamei argues that Americans, idealistic and dead serious in their "pursuit of happiness," often find themselves in an awkward situation as to the question of "sex," which becomes synonymous with "life." (Coincidentally, these two words are homonyms in Japanese.) Due to their "Puritan" frame of mind, Americans fluctuate between the extremes of severity (expressed in enforcement of the Comstock Act and censorship of art and literary works) and laxity (free love and other utopian experiments). As usual, Kamei's prose flows smoothly, drawing upon often hilarious episodes from historical documents, literary works, and popular culture—cartoons, films, popular novels, and pornography.

America the Wilderness by the same author is, like many others surveyed here, a collection of essays and marginalia previously published in journals, periodicals, and encyclopedias. Yet the essays and marginalia thus collected in the first volume of *The Works of Shunsuke Kamei* make an insightful and readable analysis of American civilization, which provides a helpful guideline or side view to the study of American literature. Like Kamei's books on the similar subject, *America the Wilderness* is a valuable accompaniment to "criticism" written by our scholars of American literature. His critiques of the American people and their culture strike at the heart of the matter, surfacing the mysterious vitality of the country which he else-

where calls "The Sacred Land of Liberty" (see *ALS 1979*, p. 527).
This the author of *The Descendants of the Puritans* and *America the
Wilderness* achieves because he tells it "slant," a strategy in which
Dickinson believed "success lies." Indeed, American studies has be-
come an indispensable part of American literary studies in this
country.

Kobe College

vi. Scandinavian Contributions

Jan Nordby Gretlund, Elisabeth Herion Sarafidis, Hans Skei

The Scandinavian work in American literature during 1986 and 1987
reveals not only the expected interest in Robert Frost and Sylvia
Plath, but also attention paid to fairly unknown contemporary poets
William Stafford and Frederick Morgan. Some good work has been
done on Scandinavian immigrant literature, Stephen Crane and Henry
James received some attention, and Edward Albee is popular, but the
favorite topic among Scandinavian critics of American literature is as
always and without contest the social realism of writers like Charles
G. Norris, Claude McKay, and John Dos Passos; even Ernest Hemingway and Flannery O'Connor have been studied for their social awareness. The only new aspect is the increased emphasis on seeing the
realistic fiction from a feminist point of view. William Faulkner receives the attention he deserves, as could be expected, but it is perhaps pleasantly surprising that John Gardner and some postmodern
novelists have finally begun to be written about in Scandinavian
publications.

Johannes Kjørven's study *Robert Frost's Emergent Design: The
Truth of the Self In-Between Belief and Unbelief* (Solum) has difficulties in finding its place among the fields of literary scholarship,
religion studies, and theology. It must nonetheless be regarded as a
valuable contribution to Frost studies. Kjørven does not practice what
he calls "the formalist mode," which would probably mean to study
literature as literature (with emphasis on its "literariness," to speak
in formalist terms). Instead, his study is *personal*, because Frost's
voice was personal and invites readers to participate in a dialogue
and become aware of themselves as they read. The problem of belief

and unbelief may well be hard to discuss in a formal study, yet these problems are set forth, discussed, lived through, and perhaps even solved in *literary* texts, and the thematic discussions cannot and should not be pursued without due observation of "formal problems." A related problem is Kjørven's use of the writings of Bernard Lonergan as framework or scaffolding. The study may have profited from being closer to recent Frost scholarship, and from a stronger emphasis on the Henry James connection in Frost's religious poetry. But Kjørven studies Frost's poetry as a whole, and the book has numerous excellent and convincing readings of difficult texts, even though it contributes to our understanding of Frost more through sudden insight and valuable details than through its approach and structure.

Thomas Bredsdorff's *Den bratte forvandling* [The Sudden Change] (Gad) is a biographical and critical work on Sylvia Plath and her achievement. Bredsdorff argues that we will remember Plath for the final fourth of her about 200 poems from her mature years, through which she became "one of the most important poets of the 20th century." Integrated in Bredsdorff's text are 36 of Plath's poems in Danish for the first time and in a fine translation by Uffe Harder. Bredsdorff attempts to save Plath from her Marxist (Sol Zollman), feminist (Robin Morgan), Christian existentialist (David Holbrook), and psychologist (Judith Kroll) critics without fully rejecting any of these approaches. As a journalistic scoop, Bredsdorff includes some comments by Dr. John Horder, Plath's physician during her final years. Surprisingly, he has not been heard before, although he knew the poet well and tried to help her by talking to her daily during her final weeks. In spite of Bredsdorff's stated intentions, the book is really a literary biography; his study proves how difficult it is, even in an honest attempt to write on Plath's poetry and fiction, not to get lost in biographical speculations, rumors, hearsay, and wishful thinking. But Bredsdorff's book also maps Plath's development in her poems, and he shows their unique qualities and her vision of—"a sudden change."

Two contemporary American poets dealt with by Scandinavian scholars are William Stafford and Frederick Morgan. Lars Nordström's interview with Stafford: "Willingly Local: A Conversation with William Stafford about Regionalism and Northwest Poetry" (*SN* 59:41–57) is accompanied by a selected William Stafford bibliography. Stafford good-naturedly fends off attempts at labeling his work and grouping him with other poets, defending the uniqueness of his

voice and his art. His view of himself as a regionalist poet is best
summed up in this quote: "Yes, I feel alive by touching the earth
where I am, and this is said in various ways by various people. But I
do feel local, willingly local, in fact gloriously local. And it's just a
matter of liking the diet where you happen to live and that's both a
fact and an ideal." The essay on Frederick Morgan: "Poesin: mer än
en gång till underjorden" [The Poetry: More than a Pathway to the
Lower Regions] (*Artes* 6:7–17) is introductory in nature, liberally
sprinkled with translations of the poet's work, and in part based on
two interviews granted to Leif Sjöberg. It is an engaging piece, aiming at an overview of Morgan's poetry and identifying death and love
as his major themes.

Øyvind T. Gulliksen's "In Defense of a Norwegian-American
Culture: Waldemar Ager's *Sons of the Old Country*" (*AmerSS* 19:
39–52) presents Ager's position in Norwegian America in the beginning of this century and goes on to discuss his novel *Sons of the Old
Country*, which was not published in English in the United States
until 1983. Gulliksen's emphasis is on the thematic impact of the book,
but he also makes interesting observations on how Norwegian and
American history and the popular genres influenced the very structure of the novel. Swedish-American fiction, a largely uncharted territory awaiting the efforts of literary sociologists, is the topic of Lars
Furuland's "The Swedish-American Press as a Literary Institution of
the Immigrants" (*Uppsala Multiethnic Papers* 7[1986]:125–33). The
failure of literary scholars to deal with this fiction can be seen as an
effect of their almost exclusive interest in elite authors and elite
works; as the immigrant fiction generally showed little aesthetic creativity, it was disregarded by researchers. But with the resurging
interest in ethnic groups, both in the United States and Sweden, has
come the realization that "an attempt must be made to evaluate the
role which all Swedish-American literature played in a wider context
of communication." Furuland advocates studies less centered on
individual writers and stresses that emphasis should be placed instead on other forms of publication such as journals and newspapers,
brochures, hymnals, and songbooks.

Charles G. Norris's fate was to be much acclaimed in his day
only to be relegated to an insignificant place on the outskirts of literary history in our time. In a fair-minded essay, "The Undeserved Neglect of Charles G. Norris" (*SN* 59:25–39), Rolf Lundén attempts to
redress this injustice and rekindle interest in Norris. Lundén feels

Norris "should get credit for his commitment and his skillful crafts-manship." The social criticism of Norris can be put into five major categories: marriage, women's liberation, education, industrial strife, and the dream of success. Lundén points out that even though Norris saw his role as that of an educator, fired by a very strong social com-mitment, he always sought to present fairly the complexities of the issues he chose to fictionalize, and the charges against him of being tractarian are therefore not really justified. Lundén's analysis of *Pig Iron* shows Norris to be a competent writer, somewhat earnest and humorless, but adept both in portraying human relations and in bring-ing to life scenes of everyday struggle.

Carl Pedersen examines the concerns of black and white writers of the post World War I era in his "The Harlem Renaissance and the American Twenties" (*AmerSS* 19:1–12). A number of writers from the 1920s are referred to and their work considered in the context of the increasing urbanization of the decade. John Dos Passos's *Man-hattan Transfer* and Claude McKay's *Home to Harlem* are examined in some detail. Pedersen argues convincingly that white writers re-acted against the creation of the urban wasteland by clinging to old visions of a virgin past, whereas black writers through urbanization managed to recover a past that had been suppressed and to salvage a usable black history.

John Dos Passos is also the subject of Clara Juncker's " 'Somebody Loves Me, I Wonder Who . . .': Dos Passos' Working Girl" (*AmerSS* 19:27–37). In this essay Juncker makes it clear that although Dos Passos was far from blind to the social injustice around him, he did in his early career have some rather romantic notions of the working girl's life. And even though Anna Cohen in *Manhattan Transfer* may be seen as the victim of industrialization, Dos Passos finally credited only his male workers with a potential function in the revolutionary struggle. The women are frequently portrayed as the materialistic corrupters of male commitment. The working girls remain insignifi-cant as a group, and they are, it is argued, the forgotten victims of sex and class in Dos Passos's fiction.

Åsebrit Sundquist's *Pocahontas & Co.: The Fictional American Indian Woman in Nineteenth-Century Literature: A Study of Method* (Solum) would hardly qualify as a literary study for many readers since it both advocates and follows a *quantitative method.* If one does not go to the extreme, this may, of course, be done with good results. Here, the questionnaire-computer method is defended with a vigor that indicates great doubt on the author's part. Sundquist's aims are at least threefold: to analyze descriptions of female American Indian characters in 19th-century literature, to show how these portrayals conform to certain stereotypes (non-Indian), and to prove that a quantitative analysis can be useful in describing general trends and patterns in character descriptions. In addition, the book has an obvious feminist perspective, and it is a fresh, courageous, well-informed, and well-organized work. But it may be founded on assumptions about literature (e.g., fictional character) and interpretation of literature that modern literary theory (hermeneutics, to mention a useful approach) could have helped the author avoid. Still, *Pocahontas & Co.* is well worth a study.

Brita Lindberg-Seyersted's brief study of literary friendships and relationships in *Ford Madox Ford and His Relationship to Stephen Crane and Henry James* (Solum) may be seen in relation to her *Pound/Ford: The Story of a Literary Friendship* (New Directions: 1982) in the sense that both are studies in literary lives, using letters and memoirs in critical *biographical studies*. In the present volume Ford is the main character. In chapter 1 his contacts with Stephen Crane in England from 1887, when they both came there from work as war correspondents, are outlined and analyzed. Most interesting for the glimpses Ford gives us of the famous writer who would die so young, this chapter is (by necessity) very brief. The "Troubled Relationship" is a chapter on Ford and Henry James, the great master. It is extensive and includes much original material, some of which has not been published before. In this way the book also makes an interesting if minimal contribution to James studies, although Lindberg-Seyersted rightly holds that Ford is important not only for the information he gives about others, but for his own personality and work. She even contends that Ford in his tetralogy *Parade's End* "reached a mastery on a par with the Master's own achievement" (p. 92).

Bent Haugaard Jeppesen's *Hemingway i hamskifte* [Hemingway's Sloughing] (Sydjydsk, 1986) is a study of a transformation during the 1930s of Hemingway's political ideas from an early nihilism to an undisguised left-wing radicalism, which Haugaard Jeppesen traces in Hemingway's writings up to 1940. The argument is in two parts: first a general introduction to Hemingway's works from the 1920s, and second a detailed account of the postulated shift in his political views. Close readings of Hemingway's fiction up to the fall of 1940 are mixed with interpretations of his correspondence and journalism from that period, and the main emphasis is on his development during the Spanish Civil War. In spite of the thorough documentation of Haugaard Jeppesen's attempt at proving an ideological shift in Hemingway's politics in the 1930s, it is not totally convincing. Even if Hemingway in his letters from Spain did align himself with the Stalinists in the Republican Army, and if he did accept central doctrines in communist interpretations of the world situation, this would not mean that we have to see all of his fiction up to 1940 from this perspective. In general, there is an unsound and unconvincing mixture of fiction and biography in Haugaard Jeppesen's study, mostly because he often fails to distinguish between Hemingway's opinions and those of his fictional characters, but also because he so obviously reads the fiction solely in order to confirm his thesis.

Hans Skei is one of the contributors to the Japanese collection of essays on *Faulkner: ATNP*. In "William Faulkner's Late Career: Repetition, Variation, Renewal," Skei asserts that Faulkner basically remained within his imaginary kingdom even after the Nobel Prize and continued doing what he was best at. His late work is by no means only echoes and reminiscences of past great work, although Faulkner reused material to an unusual extent. Skei concludes that Faulkner's "late career" is an integrated part of his whole career and that this period of his life should not be set apart as something special.

Realist of Distances: Flannery O'Connor Revisited, eds. Karl-Heinz Westarp and Jan Nordby Gretlund (Aarhus) is a collection of essays by international scholars on the southern writer. It includes two Scandinavian contributions. In his "Flannery O'Connor's Development: An Analysis of the Judgement Day Material" (pp. 46–54), Karl-Heinz Westarp concentrates on O'Connor's lifelong revisions of her first story "The Geranium." The essay shows how the three published versions of this material reflect the phases of O'Connor's artistic development from its first promise over the realistic intermediate "An Exile in the East" from the 1950s to the final perfection of "Judgement Day," published posthumously. Jan Nordby Gretlund's "The Side of the Road: Flannery O'Connor's Social Sensibility" is an attempt to show the presence in her fiction of her social awareness, which is often ignored by her Catholic critics. Through an analysis of "The Displaced Person" and other stories, it is demonstrated that large social issues were often the subject of her fiction.

Love and death have significant roles in Janina Nordius's tightly structured and well argued "John Gardner's *Nickel Mountain*: A Modern Comedy" (*SN* 59:217–29). Seeking the coherent moral structure of the novel, Nordius enlists the aid of Dante's *The Divine Comedy*, exploring how Gardner gives his work another dimension, apart from the realistic one, through a network of allusions to the medieval poem. The journey to self-knowledge of Henry, the protagonist, parallels the journey described by Dante, and Nordius finds that Gardner's extensive use of the poem "is a way of expressing and emphasizing allegorically the ideas he is preoccupied with in the novel." The ideas are familiar to readers of Gardner's novels: man's search for the meaning of his existence and his struggle to accept the limitations of a free will.

American postmodern fiction has aroused only scant interest in Scandinavia. The postmodern fiction is relatively unknown primarily because only few of these novels and short stories have been published in translation, and little Scandinavian scholarly work has been done in this field. Therefore, Danuta Zadworna-Fjellestad's Alice's Adventures in Wonderland *and* Gravity's Rainbow: A Study in Duplex Fiction (Almquist & Wiksell, 1986) is all the more welcome. Chapter 1 is devoted to *Alice* and the modes of reading it provokes, chapter 2 deals with *Gravity's Rainbow*, and chapter 3 takes up Donald Barthelme's "Views of My Father Weeping" and Robert Coover's *The Universal Baseball Association, Inc.* The aim of the study has been to define the kind of metafiction Zadworna-Fjellestad terms "duplex": a fiction which explores the phenomenon of intertextuality and attempts to actively involve the reader and to disclose to him his interpretative methods. Because the kind of reading it provokes is of crucial importance to duplex fiction, Zadworna-Fjellestad focuses her analysis on the reader and reading response, stating: "It is my contention that duplex fiction subverts the differentiation between the naive and self-reflexive reading and instead asks for a critical reading which savors frictions and interplay between various—often incompatible—interpretations." Her method is investigative in that her definitions of what constitutes duplex fiction and the critical reader it demands do not precede but evolve from her analysis of the texts. Zadworna-Fjellestad has written a reader-oriented book, both in subject and method. The analyses are interesting on the whole, but the definitions are perhaps somewhat lacking in substance. She does, however, stress that duplex fiction and the categories of readers are "modes of investigation and not terms describing discrete literary species." In that sense her undertaking is open-ended, and her tools are waiting to be used, perhaps sharpened, by other literary scholars. Kjeld Enemark's *Talen og Overføringen* [Speech and Communication] is subtitled an analysis of the function of speech in *Who's Afraid of Virginia Woolf* (Aarhus, 1986). Enemark is a psychologist, and psychology is the subject of this book, but in his use of Edward Albee's play he has also written an impressive literary analysis. His argument is that in our speech we reveal our unconscious reality, which simply comes to life when we speak, and this is what makes conversation an instrument for treatment in psychological analysis. Three-fourths of the book is an analysis of the play, whereas the final fourth is about the use of speech and dialogue in psychological treatment. The study is focused on the microsocial exchange in dialogue, in argument, and in ironic comment at the heart of Albee's art. Enemark examines the relation between the individual and reality in the play through a detailed study of the use of language. It is, of course, a tribute to Albee that his play is judged to be so realistic in its intense psychological games that its characters can be made the subjects of professional psychological analyses, as if George and Martha really did exist. What happens in *Who's Afraid of Virginia Woolf* is only dramatic insofar as the dialogue is dramatic and moves to the limits of the possible, the accepted, and the real. Enemark demonstrates how Albee's drama conceptualizes the subconscious areas of the minds of George and Martha, which is what makes the play a subject for linguistic, literary, and psychoanalytic analysis. The psychoanalytic approach to the dialogue of the play produces discoveries and interpretational insight which a literary approach in itself would not be able to match. Enemark's study is a valuable contribution to our understanding of the relation between drama and psychoanalysis.

Odense, Uppsala, Oslo Universities

21. General Reference Works

J. Albert Robbins

First, a prefatory note. Reference works which are directly related to the subject of earlier chapters will be reviewed in those chapters. This leaves as my task noticing the more general reference works that do not belong exclusively elsewhere.

The most impressive new reference work is a 1,229-page, two-volume treatise called *Fifty Southern Writers Before 1900* and *Fifty Southern Writers After 1900: A Bio-Bibliographical Sourcebook*, ed. Robert Bain and Joseph M. Flora (Greenwood). The large panel of contributing authors follows the same structure: a biographical sketch, discussion of the author's major themes, assessment of the scholarship, chronological list of works, and bibliography of selected criticism. In the first volume one of the major writers is Edgar Allan Poe, whose section takes up 24 printed pages. Others run to proportionate lengths: John Pendleton Kennedy, 10 pages; William Gilmore Simms, 20 pages; Thomas Nelson Page, 11 pages; Thomas Holley Chivers, 13 pages.

The "after 1900" volume, of course, glitters with literary stars: Barth, Dickey, Faulkner, Glasgow, Hellman, Hurston, Mencken, Flannery O'Connor, Katherine Anne Porter, Styron, Robert Penn Warren, Welty, Tennessee Williams, Thomas Wolfe, Richard Wright, and 35 others. These volumes are a useful starting point for students faced with an unfamiliar writer as well as a useful refresher for mature scholars.

It might seem that the large *Reference Guide to American Literature* (St. Martin's) does much the same thing for all of our writers as the Bain-Flora volumes do for the South; and indeed the *Guide* provides short biographies, lists of publications, selective bibliographies, and critical essays. And there are brief, signed essays on major works. However, a closer look shows that the *Guide* is largely an updating and repackaging of two 1980 titles in the publisher's Great Writers Student Library series, with no acknowledgment of this except to call the new *Guide* the "2nd edition." With its new title and large, double-column format, the *Guide* invites comparison with the latest *Oxford Companion to American Literature*. But the *Guide*, it seems to me, speaks to a student—not a broader, professional— audience. I would much rather have the 5th edition *OCAL* on my shelf than the *Reference Guide*.

A standard reference work on first editions is *First Printings of American Authors: Contributions Toward Descriptive Checklists*, ed. Philip B. Eppard (4 vols., Gale, 1977–79), now enlarged by a fifth volume. (For scope and format of earlier volumes see *ALS 1977*, p. 512, and *ALS 1978*, pp. 490–91.) As in the earlier volumes, there is preponderant attention to the 20th century. In the fifth volume there is one 18th-century writer (Edward Taylor); four 19th-century authors of secondary importance and interest; and 49 from the 20th century—the most prominent being James Baldwin, Truman Capote, John Cheever, James T. Farrell, Norman Mailer, Bernard Malamud, Vladimir Nabokov (books in English only), Joyce Carol Oates, Upton Sinclair, and John Updike. There is a cumulative index to all five volumes.

The *DLB Yearbook 1986*, ed. J. M. Brook (Gale), has a dozen or so essays and documents of interest to specialists in American literature. John C. Broderick discusses the new poet laureateship and the older Library of Congress post of consultant in poetry (dating back to 1937) (pp. 30–38). The documents on Faulkner and the People-to-People Program are reproduced (pp. 39–58), and Thorne Compton reports on "The Randall Jarrell Symposium" (pp. 59–70). Matthew J. Bruccoli has a note on "Packaging Papa: *The Garden of Eden*" (pp. 79–82), followed by an interview with the Scribner editor of that posthumous book ("An Interview with Tom Jenks," pp. 82–87). There are summaries of the year in fiction, poetry, literary biography, and publishing; and there are updated entries on Joan Didion, by Mary Doll (pp. 247–52), and William Faulkner, by David Krause (pp. 252–68).

Volume 5 of *Contemporary Authors: Autobiography Series* (Gale) has autobiographical essays by 13 American writers, born mostly in the 20s and 30s. Six are poets (Elizabeth Jennings, Carolyn Kizer, James Koller, Carl Rakosi, Aram Saroyan, Keith Wilson), six are writers of fiction (Jonathan Baumbach, Daniel Fuchs, George Palmer Garrett, Jr., George V. Higgins, Susan Shreve, Kate Wilhelm), and one writes nonfiction (Wayne Booth). As usual, there is lavish use of illustrations.

Another form of personal writing is diaries, and this year a two-volume guide was completed and published. The joint title is *American Diaries, An Annotated Bibliography of Published American Diaries and Journals* (Gale). Annotations are brief, ranging from about 30 to 125 words. Volume 1 covers 1492 to 1844 (published 1983); volume 2, 1845 to 1980 (published 1987). There are name, subject, and geographic indexes. The primary editor is Laura Arksey.

Yet another variant is Joyce D. Goodfriend's *The Published Diaries and Letters of American Women: An Annotated Bibliography* (Hall). The arrangement is chronological by year, from 1669 to 1982. Materials are accessed by author and subject indexes. The subject index I find imperfect. There are no subject headings for plays, drama, poetry, short story, novel, fiction. These topics are buried somewhere in the 73 references to "writers."

Interviews—or as some prefer, conversations—continue to have wide appeal. The most venerable series are those published in the *Paris Review* and collected from time to time in book form. The newest of these is *Writers at Work: The* Paris Review *Interviews*, seventh series, ed. George Plimpton (Viking, 1986). The Americans in this volume are Malcolm Cowley, William Maxwell, May Sarton, Elizabeth Hardwick, John Ashbery, John Barth, Philip Roth, and Raymond Carver.

The University Press of Mississippi has three volumes of conversations: M. Thomas Inge's *Truman Capote: Conversation*, Rosemary M. Magee's *Conversations with Flannery O'Connor*, and Joan Givner's *Katherine Anne Porter Conversations*.

First cousin to the interview is the memoir, and there is a book on this literary form, *Inventing the Truth: The Art and Craft of Memoir*, ed. William Zinsser (Houghton Mifflin), given first as public talks in New York, 1986. The three persons relevant to American literature are Annie Dillard (Pulitzer Prize for nonfiction, 1974), Alfred Kazin, and Toni Morrison. Last year (1986) a similar volume came from a similar series of talks: *Extraordinary Lives: The Art and Craft of American Biography*, ed. Zinsser (Houghton Mifflin). The one talk relevant to American literary study is Richard B. Sewall's "In Search of Emily Dickinson," pp. 63–90.

The Dictionary of American Children's Fiction, 1859–1959 was noted in *ALS 1985*, p. 502. There is now a companion volume by the same editors, Aletha K. Helbig and Agnes Regan Perkins, with the same title except for the dates of coverage (1960–1984). Both are published by Greenwood. Gale has an expanding set of books on writing for children, two of which were noted in *ALS 1985*, p. 502. Two more (*DLB 52*, 1986; and *DLB 61*, 1987) are both edited by Glenn E. Estes. The former is titled *American Writers for Children Since 1960: Fiction* and the latter, *American Writers for Children Since 1960: Poets, Illustrators and Nonfiction Authors*. The *DLB* use of illustrations serves as essential supplement to text.

For its genre and years of coverage, H. W. Hall's *Science Fiction and Fantasy Reference Index, 1878–1985* (2 vols., Gale) should be a standard guide to materials in the field, including books and articles in English and in languages other than English. These are large-format, two-column pages associated with Gale volumes. The first volume alphabetizes authors; the second, subjects.

The most definitive and authoritative descriptive bibliographies are the Pittsburgh series in bibliography, issued by the University of Pittsburgh Press. Matthew J. Bruccoli has now done three Fitzgerald bibliographies in the series, the first noticed in *ALS 1972* (pp. 131–32) and the second in *ALS 1980* (pp. 173–74). The new, third volume—the revised edition of *F. Scott Fitzgerald, A Descriptive Bibliography*—the author says, "corrects and augments" the two earlier works. However, some sections in the earlier books have been dropped in the revised edition so the early works are not fully obsolete.

In 1986 Meckler initiated a new series of literary bibliography with two author bibliographies: Stuart Wright, *Walker Percy: A Bibliography, 1930–1984*; Michael Hargraves, *Harry Crews: A Bibliography*; and a general title by William McPheron, *The Bibliography of Contemporary Poetry, 1945–1985: An Annotated Checklist*. I have seen only McPheron's book, which divides the subject matter into general works (a mere eight pages) and single-author studies of 121 poets in 62 pages. The four titles published in 1987 are bibliographies of Alice Walker by L. H. Pratt and Darnell Pratt and of Robert Gover by Michael Hargraves; and two general volumes: *Bibliography of Contemporary American Fiction, 1945–1987: An Annotated Checklist*, by William McPheron and Jocelyn Sheppard; and *Bibliography of Personal Writings by Women to 1900*, by Gwenn Davis and Beverly A. Joyce.

Scarecrow has added two titles to its bibliographies. One is Robert B. Harmon's *Steinbeck Bibliographies, An Annotated Guide*; the other, treating five writers, is Jeanetta Boswell's *Spokesmen for the Minority . . . A Bibliography of Sidney Lanier, William Vaughn Moody, Henry Timrod, Frederick Goddard Tuckerman, and Jones*

Very, with Selective Annotations. Garland is publisher of Gloria L.
Cronin and Blaine H. Hall's *Saul Bellow: An Annotated Bibliography*
(2nd ed.). Robert Duncan now has a descriptive bibliography, compiled by Robert J. Bertholf (Black Sparrow, 1986).

The reliable guide through many matters of style has long been
the *Chicago Manual of Style*, but the intricacies of electronic data
processing have been only tangentially addressed until now. This
updating has now been accomplished in the new 143-page *Chicago
Guide to Preparing Electronic Manuscripts, for Authors and Publishers* (Chicago). The preface tells us that the University of Chicago
Press "since 1981 . . . has been accepting electronic manuscripts and
producing typeset proof directly from magnetic media supplied by
authors." This handbook sets down the principles by which novice
and sophisticate can be guided into and through the electronic wilderness. Many revisions and enlargements will inevitably ensue in so
volatile a field as "electronic manuscripts."

For some time the *MLA International Bibliography* has been
available for on-line searching of the DIALOG databank (see *ALS
1984*, p. 578). The coverage in the DIALOG file, I am told, goes back
to 1964. Now, using new technology, the H. W. Wilson Company has
made recent years (1981–87) of the *Bibliography* available on CD-
ROM (compact disk with read-only memory). There are plans to update this file quarterly and to issue on a second disk appreciable
earlier years of the *Bibliography*. The above dates of coverage are,
of course, likely to be obsolete once these words reach publication.

Publication of research and criticism is an integral part of professional life for graduate students and professors; yet many have
spotty familiarity with the intricacies of the publishing world. Many
advanced graduate students, for example, are unsure how to turn a
dissertation into a publishable book. How many are truly familiar
with a lexicon of terms—such terms as copyright, permissions, fair
use, contract, subvention, camera-ready copy, electronic copy, copy
editing, house style, proofreading, royalties, art work, textbooks and
trade books, vanity presses? How best to pick a scholarly journal for
a submission? Should one send a manuscript article to four or five
journals simultaneously? What is a referee? These and other relevant
matters are the subject of Beth Luey's splendid *Handbook for Academic Authors* (Cambridge).

Indiana University

Author Index

Subject Index

DATE DUE

GAYLORD

PRINTED IN U.S.A.